LOUIS BOUYER, of the Oratory
Dom JEAN LECLERCQ, monk of Clervaux
Dom FRANÇOIS VANDENBROUCKE, monk of Mont-César
and LOUIS COGNET, priest at Clermont-Ferrand

A HISTORY OF CHRISTIAN SPIRITUALITY

II

THE SPIRITUALITY OF THE MIDDLE AGES

Uniform with this Volume

*

A HISTORY OF CHRISTIAN SPIRITUALITY, Vol. I:
The Spirituality of the New Testament and the Fathers

A HISTORY OF CHRISTIAN SPIRITUALITY, Vol. III
Orthodox Spirituality and
Protestant and Anglican Spirituality

THE SPIRITUALITY OF THE MIDDLE AGES

DOM JEAN LECLERCQ
DOM FRANÇOIS VANDENBROUCKE
LOUIS BOUYER

THE SEABURY PRESS • NEW YORK

Second paperback printing

1982

The Seabury Press
815 Second Avenue
New York, N.Y. 10017

Originally published as *La Spiritualité du Moyen Age*

English translation by The Benedictines of Holme Eden Abbey, Carlisle

Library of Congress Catalog Card Number: 63-16487
ISBN: 0-8164-2373-3

Printed in the U.S.A.

TABLE OF CONTENTS

Appendix

BYZANTINE SPIRITUALITY

by Louis Bouyer

PREFACE

This second volume of *A History of Christian Spirituality* deals with what is customarily called the Middle Ages, as though it were merely an intermediate period between ancient and modern times. In fact it has its own importance, and includes two periods. The first is a continuation—not simply a repetition—of the age of the Fathers, in a different historical setting; it stretches from the time of St Gregory the Great to that of the disciples of St Bernard at the end of the first Cistercian century; from the sixth century to the beginning of the thirteenth. The second begins in the twelfth century and goes on till the dawn of the sixteenth century. Once again the evolution of spirituality takes place in a new historical setting. The medieval age, if there is one, is therefore the twelfth century during which the two periods coexist, so to speak, before one passes into another.

This in itself is sufficient to show that in the history of these changes a "century" is nothing but a convenient approximation, though it has been used, especially in the second part of the book, as a convenient term.

In a general way, and precisely because the development of spirituality runs parallel to the forms and structures of a temporal society, the authors have tried all through the book to show the writers and texts in the milieu in which they existed, and without which they cannot be fully understood.

It was clearly not possible to cover a thousand years in detail in a single volume: many of the facts referred to are given simply as examples, and the reader can add to the list. It has been thought useful, in a domain of whose history more and more is becoming known, to give a fairly large bibliography, so as to indicate lines of research on the many problems only too briefly touched on here.

The object of this present work is not to suggest definitive solutions of every problem—though inevitably on certain occasions a particular point of view has been adopted—but to stimulate an interest in the study of the loftiest manifestations of life in Christ Jesus.

The authors of this volume wish to express their gratitude to all those who have helped them by their criticism and advice; especially Dom O. Lottin and his collaborators for the second part, and His Grace Archbishop Basil Krivochéïne for the appendix.

TRANSLATORS' PREFACE

The translators acknowledge with much gratitude the encouragement and help they have received from Professor David Knowles, lately Regius Professor of Modern History in the University of Cambridge; Professor H. P. R. Finberg; the Reverend Dom Gerard Sitwell, O.S.B., and the Reverend Maurice Bévenot, S.J. They are also very grateful to Mr Rogers and Miss Burrows of the Bodleian Library; and to Miss Nan Cameron for her patience and skill in typing.

Quotations from Scripture are from the Douai version; the quotations from the Philokalia are from Père Bouyer's version.

Some minor changes in the text and notes have been made by the authors in order to bring the English edition up to date.

PART ONE

From St Gregory to St Bernard

FROM THE SIXTH TO THE TWELFTH CENTURY

by

DOM JEAN LECLERCQ

Benedictine of Clervaux

I

THE TEACHING OF ST GREGORY

1. The Spiritual Work of St Gregory

When St Gregory became Pope the Middle Ages had already begun: in the East in the sixth century the course of history developed on the same lines as it had in the world of antiquity, but in the West a new world had come into being with the barbarian invasions. St Gregory played a part in both the old and the new: his life and work have been touched on in the first volume of this trilogy* because they are part of the patristic age; his immediate influence was on a Christian society and a monasticism whose ideals and structure were inherited from the past; but his teaching, developed in the atmosphere of that tradition, became the chief source of medieval spirituality, and therefore the threshold of the new age is the place to describe it.

The richness of his personality and a spiritual life which reached sanctity bore fruit in writings which were among those most widely read; during the following centuries medieval spirituality found in them most of the elements which it needed, and it enriched them as it absorbed them. St Bernard, while keeping to the same lines of development, made his own contribution to St Gregory's thought: it consisted of a sensibility heightened by the six centuries of religious experience which had prepared the way for further progress in theological thought.

St Gregory's doctrine reflects his whole life: his work brought him into contact with very varied circles, and all his teaching is addressed to all men. He had as a layman been Prefect of the City; then, turning his home on the Coelian into a monastery, he spent five years there; he was appointed one of the regional deacons of Rome; from 570 to 586 he was apocrisarius in Constantinople; in 590, when he was about 50, he became Pope and died in 604. Thus his life varied during long periods between one of involvement in

* [pp. 616, 618, — Trans.]

the world, contemplation in a monastery, and the labours of a pastor of souls.[1]

He is an intellectual whose mind does not take its delight in purely speculative thought, but turns rather to the practical; and both because of his own constant ill health and his contact with the world of men, he has an acute sense of human weakness: all his teaching is instinct with moderation.

His written works are as varied as his life: there are a large number of his letters as pope, most of which he composed himself[2]; his own personal piety shows itself in the actual wording of the prayers and benedictions in them. His commentaries on the text of Scripture include the *Morals on Job*,[3] *Homilies on Ezechiel*[4] and on forty of the gospels read at Mass[5]; an exposition of the first book of Kings[6] and the Canticle of canticles[7] (he did not however write the whole of these two last). The *Morals* are conferences which he gave to his monks in Constantinople: it is his longest work and not all its parts are of equal excellence of style or content; the commentary on Ezechiel is shorter, but equally valuable. The Pastoral Rule[8] was dedicated to his brother bishops in the person of one of their number. The four books of the Dialogues[9] are more popular in character: the endings of the periods are sometimes rather lame, the style less careful. St Gregory certainly wrote some of the prayers of the Gregorian Sacramentary[10]; there is no actual proof that he took any part in the development of the Church's chant, but however that may be, public worship (it was at Mass that he preached his homilies on the Gospels) played a great part in his life, and a profound sense of the mysteries of the liturgy underlies all his spirituality.

He wrote therefore for all sorts and conditions of men—the working classes, monks, and the clergy—and his teaching is of an essentially pastoral character, whether he is speaking of the practice of moral virtue, or of contemplation. According to the circumstances he emphasizes one or other aspect of our life in Christ, but

[1] He has described his own career in *Epist.*, V, 53.

[2] Ed. *Mon. Germ. Hist. Epist.*, I–II, Berlin, 1891–9.

[3] Ed. P.L., 75, 509–1162; 76, 9–782.

[4] P.L., 76, 786–1072.

[5] P.L., 76, 1075–1312.

[6] P.L., 79, 17–468. On the question of its authenticity see P. Verbraken, "Le texte du commentaire sur les Rois, attribué à Saint Grégoire", in *Rev. bénéd.*, LXVI (1956), pp. 39–62, 159–217.

[7] P.L., 79, 471–92 A (On the question of its authenticity, see B. Capelle, "Les Homélies de Saint Grégoire sur la Cantique", in *Rev. bénéd.*, XL (1929), pp. 204–217.) The rest, col. 492–548, is by Robert of Tombelaine (†1090).

[8] P.L., 77, 13–128.

[9] Ed. U. Moricca, Rome, 1924.

[10] Cf. K. Gamber, "Hat Gregor der Grosse ein Sakramentar verfasst?" in *Ephemerides liturgicae*, LXXIII (1959), pp. 139–40; and A. Ashworth, "The Liturgical Prayers of St Gregory the Great", in *Traditio*, XV (1959), pp. 107–62.

never without recalling the duties which are common to all men: and he succeeds in adapting himself to all his hearers. His thought is that of the society in which he lived, which, in spite of the intellectual collapse of the age, was a highly cultured one. His inability to grasp the metaphysical bearing of certain truths is balanced by the clear simplicity of his mind. It comes naturally to him to express his thought in symbols, though the abstract has little attraction for him. In his use of imagery he has that poetic touch and lack of convention which is the mark of genius. His prose is now taken seriously, and gone are the days when because of its poetic style it was considered slightly childish; on the other hand St Gregory wrote for his own times, and there is a sort of humorous charm about his writing which can be misunderstood. Like that other great theologian, St Francis de Sales, he uses a great many illustrations and metaphors which are not to modern taste, but which enchanted his readers. His lengthiness and repetitions, the slowness with which he expresses his thought, take for granted an age of leisure which we no longer know; that is what makes it difficult to give a short account of his actual writings: the most one can hope to do is to point out a few of the lovely evocative phrases which occur over and over again, and the words which were specially dear to him.

As we shall see, the Holy Scriptures are high in the order of his literary sources; but while it is clear that St Gregory owes much to St Augustine and to Cassian,[11] it would be difficult in the present state of research to assess his debt to the Fathers or to early monasticism. What did the East contribute to his thought? He knew no Greek, but a good many of the Greek Fathers could be read in translation. He had read St Athanasius' life of St Anthony, and borrows from it in the *Dialogues*,[12] but his own experience of life was too full for him to be bookish; one finds few direct borrowings from Origen, and the similarity between their writings may derive from a common tradition, or from their personal reading; the spiritual relationship (particularly in their attitude to the Scriptures) discernible between the two great commentators need not necessarily mean that the earlier influenced the later. Compared with the other Latin Fathers Gregory has a slightly Eastern flavour which is hard to define: further study is needed to analyse it. On the other

[11] For an excellent discussion of the matter, see R. Gillet in the Introduction to the *Morales sur Job*, Paris, 1959 (coll. "Sources chrétiennes"), pp. 81–102. This chapter owes much to Dom Gillet, and I am most grateful to him. P. Courcelle, "Trois Récits de Conversion au VIe siècle dans la lignée des Confessions de Saint Augustin", in *Historisches Jahrbuch*, LXXVII (1958), pp. 456–8, points out borrowings from the *Confessions* in the *Moralia*.

[12] B. Steidle, in "Homo Dei Antonius", in *Antonius Magnus Eremita*, Rome (*Studia Anselmiana*, 38), 1956, pp. 148–94, points out parallels.

hand he is cautious in his attitude to the doctrine of the pseudo-Dionysius.[13] He does not quote profane authors, and in fact avoids their vocabulary, because it is pagan. He uses Cassian's terms, but not in a technical sense: he turns the specialized vocabulary of the monastic life into words appropriate to all Christians.

St Gregory's originality lies in his power to adapt and alter everything. He has been unfavourably compared with St Augustine: his thought is said to be on a much lower level, that there is as it were "a lowering of voltage": but in fact his is both a movement from the metaphysical to the moral plane, and a raising of intellectual activity to the level of mystical experience. The trend of St Gregory's thought is less intellectual and more consistently mystical than St Augustine's. He is a thinker but without the didactic approach of a professor; and though his processes of thought are not expressed in philosophical terms, he has an underlying philosophy of life: his conception of the relationship between man and God. His philosophy is that of the spiritual life, the search for God, and the formulas he makes use of often have a fuller meaning than would the terms of abstract philosophy, because they signify a doctrinal content which derives from his having lived for many years with the "problem of God". His is a true theology, not merely a theodicy.

It is not easy to give an account of his thought, because one cannot fit it into a purely speculative frame, nor is there perceptible in it a scientific working out of the relationship between man and God. His teaching is a synthesis of this idea, not a systematic building up of a body of doctrine: and it cannot be grasped by analysing in turn his biblical or other themes, the terms he uses, or the various classes of society he is addressing: because, irrespective of his audience or his subject, his every sentence reveals the same experience, and under different aspects the doctrine is always the same. Even if one knew exactly the order in which his works were written it would not help, because the same assumptions underlie them all; and his whole life is summed up in his teaching, even though the pontificate was the period when all his works were written. In the same way it is impossible to make a distinction in his works between what belongs to one discipline or to another: with Gregory, dogma and spirituality are one; faith and the life of faith are part of the same experience; he never separates the practice of virtue from contemplation, nor the latter from the mysteries which are its object. In this living synthesis, however, one question is fundamental to all the others: What are the various forms and

[13] Cf. E. Boissard, "La doctrine des anges chez Saint Bernard", in *Saint Bernard théologien*, Rome (*Analecta S. Ord. Cist.*, ix, III–IV), 1953, pp. 126–7.

the different states of life that the search for God takes? At the centre of the problem lies his teaching on the two modes of this quest: good works (*action vertueuse*) and contemplative prayer, though the latter holds the primacy, since Gregory is above all the doctor of contemplation.

St Gregory's ideas can best be summed up by bringing together the terms he uses and the biblical themes which moved him to write. What follows can all be found in his writings, but lack of space makes it impossible to refer to more than a few passages, which may serve as an introduction to the whole of his work.[14]

2. *The Three Orders*

To understand Gregory's teaching on the two states of life, one must look to his writings as a whole, not to a few isolated passages, even explicit ones. One must observe his method of dealing with every kind of Christian, note his behaviour towards them, before showing what were the ideals he set before them. He takes pains to adapt himself to each of the categories of people with whom he has to do or to whom he speaks. The third book of his *Pastoral Rule*, the longest one, is devoted to an illustration of "Sermons should be of many different kinds"; he immediately applies this principle to thirty-five sorts of hearers, each differing from the other in their virtues, their natural dispositions and their occupations: he then contrasts these with a similar number of Christians. This kind of distinction often recurs in a book: sometimes on the same page, Gregory comes back to it: "there are some . . . there are others . . . *sunt nonnulli*, or *plerique*." He sometimes divides his hearers into two, three, four or even more categories, his *ordines*, but in practice it is to three classes of men that he offers his spiritual doctrine.

The first are what we should call the laity: those living in the world, but not in the ranks of the clergy. St Gregory speaks of them in mass as the *plebs* and describes them as "children of the Church". Inevitably he corresponded chiefly with those among them who, like himself, were in high office, but he feels himself bound to them all, and his teaching on the exigencies of the moral law and on contemplative prayer in the *Homilies* on Ezechiel and the Gospels, sublime though it was, was given in the basilicas of Rome to all who came to hear him. He reminds the wealthy that they must be

14 There is a well-chosen anthology of passages from St Gregory in F. Bouchage, *Saint Grégoire le Grand, Méthode de vie spirituelle tirée de ses écrits*, Paris, 1930. Nor as a means of approach to St Gregory should the very full indices be neglected which the Maurists added to their edition of his works, and which are to be found in P.L., 76, 1313–514 and 77, 1467–594. There is a bibliography on St Gregory in R. Gillet, *op. cit.*, pp. 110–13, and in several later works which will be referred to further on.

detached; and to those who are married he recommends patience, and warns them not to let the pleasures of the flesh extinguish in them the desire for heaven.

But the chief shepherd speaks more often to the clergy, that "militia" which has charge of the churches, and to all to whom God has given the care of souls. He gives them various titles—"shepherds, preachers, teachers, rulers, prelates, *praesules* or *praepositi*"—but the duties of which he reminds them constantly in his letters and other writings (especially in the first two books of the *Pastoral Rule*) are always the same. They are essentially to know and practise "the art of ruling souls"—that *regimen* which (in a phrase which goes back to the philosophical tradition of antiquity, but which Gregory may well have borrowed from the ascetic phraseology of the monasticism of his time) is the "art of arts"[15]; they must be able to preach, and have a practical knowledge of how to fulfil their ecclesiastical functions; and he underlines the interior dispositions they must have: the three most important are zeal for right conduct, *disciplina*; charity which engenders patience and pity, a desire to adapt oneself and to condescend to all; and humility which is a guarantee of purity of intention, which avoids elation and preserves a man from the dangers of adulation, and which makes for rectitude and an absence of self-love. Chastity of heart and life will complete the work, and thus what Gregory calls "the priestly heart"[16] will attach itself to nothing but the search for God and its neighbour's good.

Finally St Gregory gives much thought to monks and nuns. The other two classes consist of people still involved in the cares of the world or the Church: monks, unlike married people, are "continent", and differ from all other Christians, laity or clergy, in that they are withdrawn, *remoti*.[17] The chief note of their state of life is stillness, *quies*,[18] an abstraction from the lawful occupations which absorb other members of the Church. They are *extra mundum* because they have renounced all bodily appetites and are free from all the ordinary cares of life.[19] Monks are called to contemplation even more than the rest of men, since their whole way of life is a means to it. A great part of their time ought to be given to the *lectio divina* and to manual labour; while they are not precluded

[15] "Ars est artium regimen animarum", Reg. Past. I, I. For the sources of this formula see I. Hausherr, *Direction spirituelle en Orient autrefois*, Rome, 1955, pp. 56–9.

[16] *Reg. Past.*, II, 2; *Epist.*, I, 25; VIII, 33, cf. G. Hocquard, "L'idéal de pasteur des âmes selon Saint Grégoire le Grand", in *La tradition sacerdotale*, Le Puy—Paris, 1959, pp. 143–67.

[17] *Ez.*, II, 5, 19; II, 6, 6; *Mor.*, V, 55.

[18] *Epist.*, I, 9, 30, 41, 67, etc.

[19] *Epist.*, I, 5; *Dial.*, II, 35.

from receiving Orders, there is a certain danger in their doing so, because ordinarily speaking the clergy is involved in work which is not easily compatible with monastic life; however, in the *Opus Dei*, that work of God which Gregory sees as a pastoral task,[20] they are engaged in "a service of the Church", which can be reconciled with the life of a monk. Moreover, by abstaining from evil they are able by their example and even by word to teach others the life of virtue. In practice St Gregory never hesitated to use monks for certain work in the Church.[21]

The ideals which St Gregory puts before monks were those common to the monasticism of his time. There is nothing in his writings to show that he knew of the Rule attributed to St Benedict of Monte Cassino.* There is only a tenuous connection[22] between passages in St Gregory's works on the monastic life and the Institutions described in the Rule, but there is complete agreement between the spiritual programme of St Benedict and that set forth by St Gregory in his works, more particularly in the second book of the Dialogues, in which he describes the life and miracles of the abbot of Monte Cassino.[23]

Thus it is that the only difference between the various categories of members of the Church is that of office—love makes of the Church a "diversity in concord", *concors diversitas*,[24] and in the service of this love there is only a distinction of function.

Among the biblical images of the Church which St Gregory uses so frequently in his writings, the Temple and the Tabernacle are his favourites: by comparing the Church with a spiritual building he shows both the diversity of her members and their unity. The

* [The view that the traditional Rule of St Benedict was the work of some unknown master, and that St Gregory was not familiar with it, has been put forward by some recent scholars; but it has by no means won general acceptance. Cf. D. Knowles, *Problems in Monastic History* (Birkbeck Lectures, 1962), London, 1963.—Trans.]

20 Cf. K. Hallinger, "Papst Gregor der Grosse und der Hl. Benedikt", in *Commentationes in Regulam S. Benedicti*, Rome (*Studia Anselmiana*, 42), 1957, p. 299.

21 Cf. R. Rudmann, *Mönchtum und Kirchlicher Dienst in den Schriften Gregors des Grossen*: place and date of publication unknown (1956). It is known that St Gregory sent monks to England to convert the inhabitants; cf. P. Meyvaert, "Les 'Responsiones' de St Grégoire le Grand à Saint Augustin de Cantorbéry", in *Rev. d'hist. eccl.*, LIV (1959), pp. 779–894, in favour of the authenticity of the answer of Gregory to the leader of the expedition. Cf. also R. Gillet, "Spiritualité et place du moine dans l'Église, selon St Grégoire le Grand", in *Théologie de la vie monastique*, Paris (Aubier), 1961.

22 A. Mundò, "L'authenticité de la Regula S. Benedicti", in *Commentationes . . ., loc. cit.*, pp. 105–58; K. Hallinger, *art. cit.*, pp. 231–319. [Also A. Mundò, *Rev. bénéd.*, LXXI, 3–4 (1961), and P. Meyvaert in *Scriptorium*, XVII, 1, 1963.—Trans.]

23 O. M. Porcel, "San Gregorio Magno y el Monacato", in *Monastica*, I, Montserrat, 1960, pp. 1–95.

24 *Mor.*, XXVIII, 21–4.

Church is the whole of the faithful, because they are one in Christ, in spite of the difference in their function and in the degree of their conformity to the Gospel. The good that is in them is the work of the Church, and it is she who remedies those deficiencies of theirs from which she suffers; she shows everyone the same path of return to God: that of the "two lives".

3. The Two Lives

St Gregory describes them very clearly: "the active life consists in giving bread to the hungry, in teaching wisdom to him who knows it not, in bringing the wanderer back to the right way, in recalling one's neighbour to the path of humility from that of pride, in giving to each what he needs, in providing for those who are committed to our care. In the contemplative life, however, while maintaining with his whole heart the love of God and his neighbour, a man is at rest (*quiescere*) from exterior works, cleaving by desire to his Maker alone, so that, having no wish for action and treading underfoot all preoccupations, his soul is on fire with longing to see the face of his Creator."[25] St Gregory goes on to develop these differences, illustrating them by two sets of figures from the Bible, traditional in this connection, which he often uses: Martha and Mary, and Lia and Rachel. The former, Jacob's first wife, was hard-working and fruitful, but blear-eyed, whereas Rachel, who was beautiful but barren, saw well. Gregory does not invariably compare the two lives: often he writes of the contemplative life only. The expression *vita contemplativa* occurs forty-four times in the *Homilies* on Ezechiel and twenty times in the *Morals*. In a general way the impression he gives is that the active life is ordered to the salvation of our neighbour by our labours, and the contemplative to our own salvation through the work of prayer.[26] The distinction, however, frequently has two different meanings which must not be confused, though Gregory sometimes mingles them. There is a limited sense in which the two lives are what we should now call two "states of life" in the Church, and in that sense they are distinct. In the course of time, especially from the end of the Middle Ages, the phrase came to have this meaning; but in a wider sense, the one St Gregory uses more often, the two lives are two kinds of activity —asceticism and prayer—and in this sense they are complementary, since both have their place in each state of life.

There are different shades of meaning in the relationship between the two lives: even in the limited sense of "states of life" they are

[25] *Ez.*, II, 2, 8; cf. *Mor.*, VI, 56–61. *Ez.* 1, 3, 9–12.
[26] Cf. C. Butler, *Western Mysticism*, 2nd ed., London, 1926, pp. 248–73.

not incompatible, and in fact in most people they should be combined. St Gregory sometimes speaks of the relationship between them, and sometimes examines them separately: he admits that for some, especially for monks and nuns, the contemplative life may gradually exclude all direct work for their neighbour. Nowhere does he theorize about it or define such a vocation precisely, but he often gives the impression that he has a very great esteem for this life as far as it can be lived on earth, since it is an anticipation of our life in heaven.

His advice to everyone is to follow the rule he has adopted himself: to prefer "stillness" and the life of prayer, and abstraction from the cares which distract the soul in its quest for God, but not to resist the signs by which God calls many of his children to labour for their neighbour and to serve the Church. In fact for many the ideal is what was later called "the mixed life": that which Christ our Lord led during his public life. This is especially the case of those who have the care of souls: they are not to be completely absorbed by their pastoral duties, but to keep alive the desire for contemplation, giving themselves up to it for as long as they are able, keeping all the time they can spare from their "office" for that purpose.

Most people, then, are to give themselves at one moment more to the service of God, and at another more to that of their neighbour, finding their equilibrium in this alternation: but these two lives are in reality only two forms of the same charity: both are our means of union with God. St Gregory comes back again and again to the conciliation of the two lives in one and the same love.

In a still wider sense they represent two necessary aspects of Christian activity—good works and prayer. In that sense there can of course be no question of putting one absolutely first; according to circumstances a man will tend at one time more to one than to the other, and again the necessary equilibrium may be found in an alternation of effort.

The contemplative life is not something specially reserved to monks; it is open to all men, including the laity, even if in fact only a few attain it. A soul which leads an active life well develops a desire to obtain "the grace of contemplation", to reach "mystical understanding", to penetrate into the "interior" mysteries,[27] and therefore a life especially ordered to the quest for moral perfection should lead more quickly than any other to contemplation. In this sense the two kinds of life are different ways of uniting action and

[27] *Mor.* V, 55–6; XXXI, 101–2, etc. Cf. A. Ménager, "Les divers sens du mot 'contemplatio' chez saint Grégoire le Grand", in *La Vie spirituelle*, Suppl., vol. LIX (1939), pp. [160].

contemplation. In them two different degrees of knowledge by faith are attained by two categories of the faithful: there are those who raise themselves to the heights where God is contemplated and reach peaks which others do not; they raise themselves to "secret places", to "sublime and hidden" realities. In this sense (which does not contradict what he has already said but qualifies it), Gregory teaches that "the active life is that of the many, the contemplative of the few".[28]

4. *God and Man*

St Gregory's whole aim is to point out to men the way of return to God. His writings are a synthesis in which the same truths recur, but there are certain leading ideas which enable the reader to summarize his thought in a provisional way, and to work out later the elements which compose it. The first expression which comes to mind is that by which Gregory so often describes God: "boundless light." Somehow the whole of St Gregory's teaching seems contained in embryo in this perception of the transcendence of God: a transcendence made up of simplicity, clearness and purity. He frequently describes the misery of the sinner, emphasizing thereby man's impotence in the presence of God; whence comes the necessity for men to take to themselves the means of salvation which he has given them in Christ. Man is drawn to him by contemplation, in a naked prayer full of light; for contemplative prayer is a contact with a splendour so far above man, that in order to reach it he must be free from everything that is not the divine light, and attain to a simplicity and poverty of spirit which reflects and participates in its infinite purity. In an act of adoration and humility, of love and self-forgetfulness, a man feels something of this purity: he knows it in not knowing it; for if he had not some knowledge of it he would not realize that it is utterly unknowable. His asceticism is governed by this theocentrism: contemplating God, the soul feels the nothingness and defilement of anything to which she still clings which is not him; she wishes to disengage herself, so as to remain in the presence of God with nothing in her which could be an obstacle to the light. She wishes to forget and, as it were, "to sleep to all other things". More and more, grace takes possession of her, and it perceives that gradually the power of grace breaks all her attachments to creatures. God and man are St Gregory's two contrasting poles, and they are brought together by salvation through Christ in the Holy Spirit. Man takes hold of this remedy for his own powerlessness by the labour of an asceticism whose fountain-head is con-

[28] *Mor.*, XXXII, 4.

templative prayer. The doctrine of the vision of God is particularly Gregory's own: he holds that all men must attain to it in some degree, and he shows them that it is God himself who is the object of their vision. Vision tends towards light, and this light is the very nature of God, and as such inaccessible to all that is not God. In a series of superlatives Gregory sets forth God's pre-eminence, and in negatives his transcendence. He is invisible, incomprehensible, ineffable, uncircumscribed, that is, without limits.[29] He is eternity. He is the one self-existent Being, the principle of all that is and in consequence he is immutable, and foreign to him is that change "which is an imitation of death".[30] He is immortal, impassible, incorruptible and unvarying. He is simple, "he is all that he has".[31] Life, strength, light, wisdom, truth in him are one with his being. He is eternal: not only unending, but ever wholly present to himself, altogether identical with himself, and with himself alone. He is unchangingly one and the same Being.

He is thus because he is spirit: in no sense is he material and therefore limited, circumscribed or enclosed. He is "incorporeal light". He is the sun, the fire, the source of the light that enlightens the soul of man. He is his own brightness, and the principle of all light. Creation is ruled by him, its maker, and his providence orders all things. He is the cause of all causality, the life of all that lives, the reason for the existence of all rational creatures.[32] He is over all things since they exist through him, but nevertheless is outside them, since he is above them all. All things are upheld by him, he fills all things and surpasses everything.[33] He is present to all things, not simply as coexisting with them but in them, and they in him. It is by his knowledge of them that he is present to all things, since by his omniscience they are created. Only by paradox can we describe this transcendental omnipresence of God. All things are enclosed in him, but he is not contained by them; there is nothing he does not penetrate, yet he remains distinct from everything. His presence in everything does not diminish his substance, nor does he become a part of what he has brought into being. All things are before him and he is ever the "observer" of a world which his very look protects. All existence is "before his face" and "beneath his eyes". He searches the hearts of men: in order to realize his presence it is enough to recall his omnipotence. God is ever-present, and waits for us to recognize him. He judges us from within ourselves,

[29] M. Frickel in *Deus totus ubique simul. Untersuchungen zur allgemeinen Gottesgegenwart im Rahmen der Gotteslehre Gregors des Grossen*, Freiburg in Breisgau, 1956, quotes passages, and has drawn up a list of the Gregorian use of terms quoted here.

[30] *Mor.*, XXV, 9.

[31] *Mor.*, XVI, 54

[32] *Mor.*, XXX, 17.

[33] *Mor.*, II, 20.

hidden but active in the depths of our hearts, a witness dwelling in the very centre of our souls, ever coming to the aid of his creatures. He protects them, arranges all things for their welfare, and gives them abundant grace; moreover, it is he who makes them present to each other: "We are one, we are close to each other in him who is everywhere."[34] So it is that the very idea of God determines man's attitude to him and to his neighbour; it is the beginning of all knowledge of God and of all charity.

What is man before this God who infinitely surpasses him and yet draws him to himself? The boundlessness of the Godhead is matched by the narrow limits which enclose man: a creature by nature he is ontologically transitory; like all things in time he comes to an end. At every moment, like all that is mutable, "he ceases to be what he was, and begins to be what he was not"[35] in him "the future is in perpetual flight into the past".[36] Moreover, he is naturally fleshy, opaque, incapable of apprehending God; yet because he is also a rational spirit he has an aptitude which he can never lose for knowing God in some degree. By raising him to the state of grace, God had developed man's natural capacity for drawing near to him; he had placed man, whom he had created in his own likeness, in paradise, willing that he should share eternally in his own happiness. This world, which has the appearance of reality, is transitory, ever in flight and subject to corruption, and it can never be man's ultimate aim. It can never satisfy his need for infinite light. Man was created for heaven, to see God, to be transformed into him by the flame of his love; he was made for an incorruptible dwelling-place, to enjoy a peace, a rest and a bliss which would never end, where his very body would partake of the divine light. For all eternity he was to be a companion of the angels.[37] This was his vocation which had raised him above his natural limitations, and which he lost by sin. Adam was made in the image and likeness of God, and wished to be equal to him; tempted by the devil, he followed his example, refusing to submit to the commandment of God, who therefore cast him forth. Being a rational soul, he could not lose his vocation to know God; he still had a trace of it, but he could no longer fulfil it: his understanding was blinded, his will weakened, and there was discord between the flesh and spirit. He had lost his original justice and was at war with himself; his whole life lay in the shadow of corruption and death.

[34] *Epist.*, V, 41. [35] *Ez.*, I, II, 20.
[36] M. Frickel, *op. cit.*, p. 98.
[37] L. Weber quotes relevant passages in *Hauptfragen der Moraltheologie Gregors des Grossen*, Lucerne, 1941, pp. 106–39. Cf. also M. Walther, *Pondus, Dispensatio, Dispositio: Werthistorische Untersuchungen zur Frömmigkeit Papst Gregors des Grossen*, Lucerne, 1941.

The sin of Adam weighs on all mankind, and this heritage is made more burdensome by each man's own sins. Henceforward man can prefer a fleeting pleasure to God himself, and temptation is his normal state. Thus, sin begetting sin, man moves ever further away from his true end. He has within him the root of every vice.[38]

St Gregory is always drawing this picture of human frailty for us: man will only be set free from his weakness when he realizes clearly his unceasing need of God, his own inability to satisfy that need, and so his absolute dependence on God. He must live in the consciousness that he is both a creature and a sinner: this profound self-knowledge is his first step towards the knowledge of God. By faith and contemplation he will come forth from himself into that paradise which God has never ceased to will for him, getting back something of that vision of the light for which he was created. The more he knows of his wretchedness, the greater will be his understanding of God's mercy towards him. "We are amazed at the mercy of God when we remember our wretchedness: recalling what we were, we understand to whom we owe what we are."[39] St Gregory often uses the two words "wretchedness" and "mercy", both to sum up the primordial contrast and to resolve the problem it presents.

5. *The Way of Salvation*

Between God and man lies the domain of what Gregory calls the divine economy (*dispositio, dispensatio*) of the ways of God: "the way of salvation" and "the way of the Redeemer" by which God draws near to man; and the journeyings of grace and human effort leading man to God. Between God and man there was need of a mediator,[40] and it is of this aspect of Christ and under this title that Gregory so often speaks of him. He shows the part he plays by a long litany of the Messiah's titles, and the biblical figures which typify him: he is the cure of our wretchedness, the physician who heals our sickness, the link between us and his Father, the door through which we go to him. In him the light of the Word was concealed as in an earthen vessel, that we might not be dazzled by it.[41] Here again Gregory uses light as a comparison: Christ shines like the figure of brass that Ezechiel saw,[42] solid and glowing. He is as that amber-like metal (*electrum*) which, when alloyed with silver, makes it shine more brightly, and when with gold subdues its splendour.[43] Like Job who typifies him, he willed to undergo our

[38] Cf. L. Weber, *Hauptfragen . . .*, pp. 224–44.
[39] *Ez.*, II, VI, 21. [40] *Mor.*, XXII, 42. [41] *In Ev.*, XXXIV, 6.
[42] *Ez.*, II, I, 9. [43] *Mor.*, XXVIII, 5.

weakness. He knew temptation, suffering and death, thus giving us a perfect example of patience and sacrifice.[44] St Gregory emphasizes the necessity of meditating on the Passion, for there we see our Lord most clearly as Mediator and Redeemer, since in his passage from the flesh to the glory of the spirit he accomplished what men aim at in contemplation: to go from the visible to the invisible, from what is without to what is within, from faith to understanding, from the humanity to the divinity. The further man progresses in faith and the mystical understanding of the Scriptures, the deeper he penetrates into the mystery of Christ. Some, the *parvuli*, cling above all to his humanity; others, the *perfecti*, reflect more on his divinity[45]; but whichever way the soul is drawn, its preference is only a question of emphasis; the two realities are inseparable, and since man must contemplate them both, he may well resolve this necessity by an alternation, at one moment considering Christ in his humiliation, at another in his glory. The grounds of our hope are above all the Resurrection and the Ascension: the humanity brought God near to us, but though it revealed him, it veiled him; his Ascension, though it took him from our sight, yet made it possible for him really to dwell among us and in a more spiritual way. Our Redeemer is in heaven,[46] concealed from us, as was the Ark of the Covenant, by the veil of the Temple. We meditate on the sacred humanity and conceive a longing to contemplate it in the light of the divinity; looking on our Mediator is already, *iam quidem*, a beginning of the beatific vision.

Man, if he would have a share in Christ's work of redemption, must meditate on him, and learn to imitate him: contemplation is both the condition and the result of any progress in virtue. St Gregory brings before us the Passion of Christ to stimulate our love for God; a love which flows from contemplation and proves itself by its imitation of Christ. In a touching passage on what to say to the sick, he dwells at greater length than elsewhere on the circumstances of the Lord's Passion, on his sufferings of mind and body.[47] His teaching is admirable, and in his own constant ill health he must have put it into practice. Still, even here, as in his works as a whole, his aim is not to arouse our compassion for Christ, now in glory, it is more a question of objective worship of the humiliation of the Passion by which God showed his love for us and wrought our salvation. St Gregory has not so much in mind the human sufferings of our Lord as the dignity of his person: he never loses sight of the transcendence of God by tending to emphasize the

[44] *Mor.*, XXXI, 104; *Ez.*, II, I, 16
[45] *Mor.*, XXXI, 104; *Ez.*, I, IX, 31.
[46] *Ez.*, II, X, 21.
[47] *Reg. Past.*, III, 12.

humanity of Christ. Our Redeemer was God, and without sin. Christ now suffers in his Church, as formerly he suffered in Job. By his spirit he is present in every member of the Church, those who preach and those who listen, and those who are weighed down by the burden of their miseries. Henceforward it is through Christ that the divine action takes place in men. He dwells in the souls of his elect, filling them, and penetrating them through and through; there he presides, and rules them as a king on his throne.[48] Gregory also compares our Lord, though less often, to the bridegroom both of the Church and the soul. He sees in him not so much our brother as our Lord and Creator, and, a title he often gives him, our Father.[49] It is for us to love him as our bridegroom and to revere him as our Father. He it is who will lead us to his Father, but his own attitude to us is one of paternal tenderness and strength. As our judge will require much of us, but yet be ever ready to forgive: *districtus*[50] and *pius*. Gregory sums up, in his aspect of our Lord which he so often shows us, the attitude of adoration and loving fear that we should have towards him.

Lastly, it was not enough that he should redeem us and set us the example we must follow: our Mediator intercedes for us, our Judge is our advocate with the Father; we must pray to him through whom all our prayer is made. St Gregory in his letters and elsewhere stresses the importance of this prayer: he does sometimes speak of the saints also as interceding for us, but gives little place to this compared with the importance he gives to prayer to Christ. For him the psalms speak of Christ, or more often express his prayer; in them the words *Deus* and *Dominus* refer to him; Gregory's letters and the doxologies of his homilies often contain prayers to Christ; he even sometimes speaks of the sacrifice of the Mass as being offered to him.[51] There is a certain lack of precision in his vocabulary which reflects a synthetic rather than a systematic conception of the divine mystery. Sometimes he preaches one omnipotent Lord, Father, Son and Holy Spirit: sometimes he prays to Christ and at other times to the Father through Christ; one feels that he is as conscious of his relationship with Christ as of that with the Father through Christ. He never separates, in fact at times he makes no explicit distinction, between the different ways in which God draws near to man: what matters is that in some way God does come; *venire* is one of his favourite words in connection with our salvation. The Word who came in the flesh, the Judge who will

[48] *Mor.*, XX, 11.
[49] *Mor.*, VIII, 1; XIX, 20; XVI, 65; VII, 13; IX, 62–3; *Ez.*, II, x, 15, 24.
[50] *Mor.*, XXX, 83; *Ez.*, I, xi, 5.
[51] *In Ev.*, XXXVII, 7; cf. *Dial.*, IV, 60; cf. M. Balsavich, *The Witness of St Gregory the Great to the place of Christ in Prayer*, Rome (Saint Anselmo), 1959.

come at the last day, in Our Lord and redeemer, by whom God comes to us and we go to him. He came at the Incarnation, he will come again in judgment, and he comes unceasingly to the soul which opens itself to receive him.

6. *The Gifts of God*

He comes by his Holy Spirit whom he sent to us after he had returned to the Father, and it is he who completes the work of our salvation. The Son is the Word, but the Holy Spirit is the tongue[52]; through him Christ speaks, and through him the word is brought to our minds. Man understands the mystery of Christ, the mystery of his divinity and incarnation, by the work of his Spirit.[53] At Pentecost he appeared as tongues of fire, because he enlightens us and at the same time inflames our desire and sets us on fire with love.[54] He also reveals himself like a breath of the hot wind from the South, bringing us the warmth of fervour.[55] By the gifts of the Spirit, God "touches" us as it were by "fingers".[56] His coming is both the last of the divine works in man, and the means by which they are affected. Man's salvation is brought about by God's revelation of himself: in the plan of the divine economy mankind learnt first of the transcendental omnipotence of God, then of the incarnation of the Son, and finally of the work of the Spirit. It is not otherwise with his work in the individual.

St Gregory does not, like St Augustine, put forward a psychological theory of the Trinity, in which the powers of the soul are the image of the divine Persons. We find the Trinity everywhere in his writings, because they all tell how the Lord has ever intervened in history to save mankind and every man, by the knowledge and love of the mystery that is himself. Each of the three Persons was revealed in succession as time went on, but the work was always that of the whole Godhead. In the same way, the three Persons are inseparable in their action in the soul, yet in the order in which they work in contemplation man perceives and adores them as distinct.

The Holy Spirit enlightens man by the several gifts in which he manifests himself, for his gifts are only other than himself as different effects of the one action in the soul. Indeed, Gregory sometimes describes the Holy Spirit as "the Gift" *par excellence,* though more often he speaks of the different aspects in which he is manifested, the various ways in which he unites man with God.

[52] *In Ev.*, XXX, 5. [53] *Mor.*, XV, 20. [54] *In Ev.*, XXX, 5.
[55] *Ez.*, II, I, 6; *Mor.*, I, 2.
[56] *Ez.*, I, x, 20. "Mox ut tetigerit mentem, docet, solumque tetigisse docuisse est", *In Ev.*, XXX, 8.

The three daughters and the seven sons of Job are an image of the virtues and gifts with which the Holy Spirit endows the soul—Faith, Hope, Charity, and the seven gifts named by Isaias as given in the Vulgate.[57] He uses, too, other figures for them, notably the building which Ezechiel saw in a vision.[58] All these realities, however, are united, since they are one and the same grace, the same participation in the divine life of the Father, through the Son, in the Holy Spirit, though in the Church this grace varies according to the office and progress of each individual Christian. Though St Gregory brings together many elements which are found in a much later theology of the Holy Spirit, he does not make a rigid system out of them: he uses the expressions he takes from the Bible to give an idea of the innumerable forms which grace takes in the divine economy.

In one passage he explicitly describes the soul's ascension, the return to God, under the figure of Isaiah's seven Gifts of the Spirit.[59] Fear, from being servile becomes filial, and united with love, is "chaste"[60]: making the soul less afraid of offending God and so incurring his judgments, than of displeasing him and so being separated from him. Piety is the attitude towards God induced by religion; a loving reverence which softens our hearts and makes us merciful to our neighbour who is the object of God's love. In order to please God and serve our neighbour, piety must be enlightened by knowledge; when we see our duty, fortitude enables us to do it, since it takes courage to conquer the flesh, to overcome temptation and to trust God in adversity; the gift of counsel will prevent the soul being too confident of her strength and so yielding to presumption: it will moderate her efforts, making her watchful, and will check undue haste; understanding will make her realize the evils which burden her, and how great is her need of God, and will enlighten her more and more on what God is and what she is in herself. Finally wisdom will teach her how to carry out what understanding has shown her. Wisdom is the highest of the many forms of the gift of the Spirit, that light which enlightens, *lumen illuminans*,[61] by which God raises man to himself in Christ. Through this gift of wisdom the soul acquires a profound stillness, a participation in the very peace of God; and is established in the truth, becoming capable of contemplation.

In the incarnate Word, God came to man; the Spirit of the Father and the Son comes to the soul by his Gifts, and the soul can now

[57] Cf. F. Westhoff, *Die Lehre Gregors des Grossen über die Gaben des Heiligen Geistes*, Hiltrup, 1940, pp. 4–9.

[58] *Ez.*, II, 8, 4.

[59] *Ez.*, II, 7, 7.

[60] *Mor.*, XXXIV, 40.

[61] *Mor.*, XVIII, 81.

go to God by contemplation. This ascent comes about to a greater or lesser degree in all the faithful, in every "man of God", but it is in the whole Church, of which the individual is but a part, that it comes about completely. The mystical body of Christ receives the fullness of the gift of the Spirit, each man taking to himself the part that God has willed for him. One can say of St Gregory's spirituality that it is "ecclesial" in the sense that it applies at one and the same time to the whole Church and to each soul. St Gregory often makes no distinction between the "Church" and "the just man" and "the Christian". It is the Church who undergoes God's action in each of her members; the whole Church goes through the same phases and alternations as does the Christian soul; she prays, she weeps, she is tempted, she is strengthened. Though she does not sin, yet she has compassion on the frailty of her children, and it is through her that Christ raises them again.

The heavenly city is made up of angels and men: the angels are first of all our models. In heaven they stand in the presence of God, and during his earthly life were present to Christ. Thus they show man his destiny: to see God and to love and praise him for ever; they teach him even now to give himself up to contemplation as far as he is able; and they are ready to lead him to God. They are filled with light and charity like the purest gold.[62] There were those among them who shut themselves up against the divine light, to enjoy as their own the brightness they had received. They rebelled against the light,[63] and now they try to drag men after them, but the rest help the elect of God to keep their gaze fixed on him. The angels, both because they are pure spirit and because they cleave to God, have already part in his immutability; their life of contemplation is not subject to change. Their vision of God is immediate, without intervening image or sensible perception, so that they themselves have become light. Man aspires to this wisdom and joy, the food of the angels, *angelorum cibus*.[64] Indeed, the angels, *ministrando* and *adjuvando*,[65] come to his aid and protect him against the solicitations of the devil who tries to draw him away from contemplation. Sometimes God even speaks to man through an angel, as when he appeared to Abraham.[66] In contemplation man unites himself with the angels who are his exemplars: he has so to speak already taken his place among their choirs and is with them in the light.[67]

[62] *Mor.*, XVIII, 71; XXXII, 48.
[63] *Mor.*, XIX, 4.
[64] *In Cant. cant.*, 2.
[65] *Mor.*, XXX, 64.
[66] *Mor.*, XXVIII, 1–3.
[67] *Mor.*, XXXI, 99–100. Cf. L. Kurtz, *Gregors des Grossen Lehre von den Engeln* Rome, 1938.

Another help for man in his journey towards God, indeed one of the chief instruments of his salvation, is Holy Scripture. It is by the words of God that man learns to know the "heart of God"[68]: through the Scriptures comes the knowledge of God; how to return to him, and the grace to do so. We wait eagerly for the day when we shall understand them; their obscurity urges us on to find out their meaning; by their light this longing is fed and grows. But we must go to Scripture to seek for wisdom, not to satisfy an idle curiosity; we must read *ad refectionem* not *ad quaestionem*[69]; we should see in the Scriptures a mirror reflecting the vices we must correct and the virtues we must develop.[70] This is especially the role of the great figures St Gregory speaks of so much. Adam underwent every human experience: profound contemplation and temptation, sin and punishment, then hope and forgiveness. Abraham, who was privileged to talk with God, is the example of faith and humility, obedience and contemplation. Jacob is the symbol of God's election, and of perseverance in desiring a blessing. Moses, the type of friendship with God, and an example of patience and submission. David one of prayer and repentance, and Elias of courage in suffering and waiting for the Lord. All the prophets had some understanding of the mystery of God and his plan of salvation for men and teach us to wait for him, and to long for his coming. We admire the penance of St John the Baptist and his self-effacement before the Lord when he came at last. St Peter excels in his burning devotion to Christ, in his repentance, and by the humility with which he used his authority. As for St Paul, he is all things to all men, a zealous shepherd, joyful in suffering and temptation, a contemplative on fire with charity.[71] The building of which the Scriptures speak, especially the temple of Ezechiel's vision, are made up of the lessons these saints teach us, symbolizing at the same time the building up both of man's interior dwelling-place and of the heavenly Jerusalem.

God speaks to us in Scripture, but also by the events of our lives; they are the signs of his action in the world and in our souls; the temptations which try our fidelity, the scourges by which he

[68] *Epist.*, IV, 31. On St Gregory and the Scriptures see some excellent passages by B. de Vrégille, art. "Écriture Sainte", in *Dict. de spiritualité*, fasc. XXV, Paris, 1958, col. 169–76.

[69] *Mor.*, XVIII, 21.

[70] *Mor.*, II, 1. Cf. J. Leclerq, "Use and Interpretation of Scripture from St Gregory to St Bernard", in *The History of the Bible in the Western World*, Cambridge, 1961.

[71] W. F. Bolton, in "The Suprahistorical Sense in the Dialogues of St Gregory, I", in *Aevum*, XXXIII (1959), pp. 206–13, has shown that St Gregory thus interprets biblical models, not only in his commentaries on Scripture, but also in his *Dialogues*.

punishes and converts us, the afflictions which purify our hearts: all these ways of God with men, these forms of his *dispensatio* towards them, are so many "judgments of God". This biblical phrase which Gregory often uses represents God's thoughts about a man, his decisions concerning him, which are hidden but effectual. We must adore them, revere—that is fear and love—them, and accomplish them as soon as they are manifested to us. At the last day will come the great final judgment, which man can anticipate by judging himself with severity now, by conforming himself ever more closely to God's will. In St Gregory's mind the day of judgment is near; he sees in the cataclysms and the extraordinary happenings of his time, the domination of the Lombards and the misery it brought with it, evident signs of that coming of Antichrist, which will precede the return of the Lord. But he sees in all this a reason for men to avoid the anger of God, by freeing themselves from this passing world, turning away from sin, and working to build up the city of God which is nearing completion. This eschatological point of view is behind all St Gregory's religious and missionary labours and even his political activity. It does not paralyse him with fear, but rather encourages him: the time has come to work, to prepare oneself, to do one's part in preparing the world for the great work the Lord is doing in it.[72]

So it is that the effect of grace is not confined to God's intimate action in man's heart: our circumstances, the vocation to which the Church calls some of her children, are all graces we must understand, and receive with gratitude. St Gregory always emphasizes the gratuitousness of all these means of salvation: it all comes about by God's free choice.

He expresses this view in his description of those who receive these graces. Sometimes they are "the righteous"—those who have the right attitude towards God, who realize that they owe everything to him; sometimes "the faithful"—those who keep grace intact; again "the upright"—those who do not deviate from this attitude towards God, nor swerve away from him towards themselves or the world as do "the perverse": the "saints"—meaning those who are abundantly simple, sincere and upright in their search for God, and to whom all twistings and duplicity are foreign. Yet more often he uses that Old Testament expression which was fulfilled in the New: *electi*. Election is the first grace and the prin-

[72] For the attitude of St Gregory towards eschatology see a collection of passages and some judicious observations on them by R. Manselli, "L'escatologismo di S. Gregorio Magno", in *Atti del primo congresso internazionale di studi Longobardi*, Spoleto, 1952, pp. 383–7, and *La "lectura super Apocalypsin" di Pietro di Giovanni Olivi, Ricerche sull'escatologismo medioevale*, Rome, 1955, pp. 5–16.

ciple of all grace: the "elect" are those who persevere in grace till they attain its fruition. Their attitude, as opposed to that of the "reprobate", is one of longing,[73] they reach out towards God and are determined not to lose his gifts, but to see them increase, and this till their probation ends with the last judgment. *Electi*: the word sums up the gratuitous nature of our life in Christ, and the perseverance it demands of the Christian.

7. The Service of God

In the sense of a personal ascesis all men are committed to the active life, no one is at liberty to reject it. It is a "servitude" that must be undergone in order to attain to contemplation.[74] Seen as devotion to one's neighbour, especially in the form of pastoral work, it consists in teaching others how to transcend this world, and helping them to do so. It is a moral question: the Christian must know how to practise virtue and to teach it to others. A history of spirituality is not the place to describe it; and in any case it has already been very well done.[75] In St Gregory's ascesis is seen as a work of purification in order to contemplation. So the practice of virtue, of good works, is referred to here because it is a condition of the interior life. St Gregory emphasizes the place of charity, which he identifies with the "Law of Christ". As one law has various forms, so charity expands and blossoms in all the other virtues.[76] On the other hand he speaks little about the practice of different virtues in the sense of the acts that proceed from them. He is only concerned with intention, since he is writing of the interior life in which the value of external acts is that of their intention—the root and condition of them all, the "*radix intentionis*".

In St Gregory's work there are often whole passages referring to the heart: with him it is less the affective power than the centre where the intention is formed and purified. Everything depends on this centre: in a biblical phrase dear to him, man must always *redire ad cor*: he must keep his heart pure from all that could blind or disturb it—the *custodia cordis*—from self-love and its results, anger and the other vices. The heart is as it were personified, able to perceive the judgments of God; it sees them (*oculus cordis*), hears them (*auris cordis*), tastes them and takes them in by the understanding (*in ore cordis*). Certain attitudes of mind develop as a result of this searching for absolute purity before God: they are reducible to three, humility, patience and repentance. Humility is

[73] Cf. J. Leclerq, "St Grégoire, docteur du désir", in *L'amour des lettres et le désir de Dieu*, Paris, 1957, pp. 30–9.

[74] *Ez.*, I, 4, 10–11 [75] L. Weber, *Hauptfragen. . . .* [76] *Mor.* X, 7.

the "guardian of the virtues", the "root of good works"; the whole soul is turned in the wrong direction by pride and elation, which also proceed from the heart: *elatio mentis, superbia cordis*. They vitiate the intention even if the action has the outward appearance of good, and Gregory is ever denouncing them, pursuing them into the recesses of the heart where they hide themselves. Always and from all he requires *humilitas cordis*, "discipline" in act, and humility in intention. He gives a wide meaning to humility, seeing it as a kind of generic virtue connected wth compunction, leading to contemplation, of which it is the fountain head. It is man's fundamental attitude towards God, and the other virtues are simply its various manifestations. Since humility is the condition and the safeguard of all virtue, God does everything possible to enable man to acquire it and preserve it: he sends him trials and every kind of affliction, allows temptation to attack him even at the risk of sin, so that he may avoid pride.[77] Humility cannot be separated from patience, the other "root and guardian" of virtue: by it we accept without murmuring the chastisements God sends us, bearing with them as he bears with us, loving him as he loves men. By patience we follow the example of Christ, by charity enduring all things. Patience and humility are two aspects of the same attitude before God: that of a beggar in his presence. They lead to a realization of our vital need of God: we long for him, and wait for everything from him.

If man wishes to be open to the grace of God, to prepare himself for God's work in his soul, he must do penance: accept the sufferings that God sends him, and inflict others on himself. St Gregory is above all concerned with purity of intention: he does not say much about fasting and abstinence, and other practices of mortification, his emphasis is rather on discretion and confession. The former is compounded of discernment and moderation[78]; by it we learn what we are to do, and how we are to respond to the voice of God in our heart. With regard to confession, it concerns not only actions but thoughts. One of the means of preserving humility is to confess to God and to his representative the secret and crooked ways which endanger the purity of our heart.[79] St Gregory speaks comparatively little about the affections of the heart, but on the other hand the question of conscience has a large place in his teaching, connected as it is with his view of compunction. He gives this latter word many shades of meaning, suggesting rather than stating the inner

[77] "Qui de virtute se extollit per vitium ad humilitatem redit." *Mor.*, XXXIII, 25; cf. *ibid.*, 26; Gillet, *op. cit.*, p. 59.

[78] Cf. A. Cabassut, art. "Discrétion", in *Dict. de spiritualité*, fasc. XXII–XXIII, Paris, 1956, col. 1322.

[79] *Mor.*, XXII, 31–4.

realities which, though they appear separate, are really united in one idea: compunction is in its etymological sense a "prick" of grace in the soul,[80] a sort of wound by which God makes us realize our wretchedness, "wakes" us from the sleep of false security, and keeps alive in us an abiding sorrow for sin. Compunction has four qualities, according to whether God reminds man of his past sins, of the judgment to come, of the evils of this present life, or of the joys of heaven which he should long for: *Ubi fuit, ubi erit, ubi est, ubi non est.*[81] Yet more often St Gregory shows us compunction typified by the land watered from above and below, in the Book of Josue,[82] or the two altars of the temple, one for the flesh of beasts and one for incense.[83] They are in fact two aspects of the same attitude: at one moment fear of sin and of the judge who will punish it is uppermost (the compunction of pain and sorrow) and at another love,[84] begetting a confidence based on contempt of self, and a burning desire for heaven. This compunction of love comes from the highest states of prayer; it is a joy, a *jubilus,* but it always brings with it a nostalgia for heaven. Here compunction is already contemplation; and at every level it unites the active to the contemplative life, is a part of both, and leads from one to the other. The treasures of contemplation, then, are already tasted as the fruits of the active life: inward peace, stillness of heart, and a calm which overcomes the irrational motions of the flesh as Axa the daughter of Caleb sat upon the ass[85]; detachment in prosperity from all that is transitory; a new realization of the difference between this life and that of heaven, between cleaving to man or to God, between self-love and charity; serenity in the midst of the alternate torments and joys which God sends to the soul, that she may learn that it is dangerous to slumber in the heavenly consolations which she needs. There must be alternations in the sphere of asceticism and purification as everywhere else, since on earth the soul only feebly shares in the divine immutability, only sees a ray of the uncircumscribed light.

8. *The Vision of God*

Man's end is to see God. St Gregory is for ever telling us this, and at the same time reminding us that while man is bounded by the flesh, weighed down by his condition as a sinner, he cannot see

80 Cf. P. Régamey, "La 'componction du coeur'", in *La Vie spirituelle,* Suppl., XLIV (1935), pp. [65]–[82].

81 *Mor.,* XXIII, 41. 82 *Dial.,* III, 34. 83 *Ez.,* II, 10, 19–20.

84 *In Ev.,* XVII, 10–11.

85 *Dial.,* III, 34. P. Régamey, *loc. cit.,* p. [69], suggests this passage is the origin of the comparison of the body to "Brother Ass".

the uncircumscribed light in its fulness.[86] In what way then is contemplation the object of all man's desires and efforts? St Gregory of course uses contemplation in more than one sense: five principal ones[87] have been recognized, but these could easily be added to,[88] since with him its meaning often depends upon its context. Usually, however, he means a prayer which unites us with God, and according to the person and the occasion is more or less affective or more or less intellectual. Contemplative prayer leads to a two-fold vision of God, or more precisely two degrees of that vision of God which man may hope for in this life: the vision of desire, and rapture. St Gregory in his writings does not invaribly draw a clear distinction between them, and in fact his doctrine of contemplation is the same in either case.

All men are called to look at God. A look, even if it does not attain its object, is a wish to see, and in this sense it sees what it tends to: *videre per appetitum*.[89] This look can only be one of faith, since its object is hidden. Gregory uses words like "mystery", "secret", "arcana" when he speaks of it. This vision of faith embraces its object obscurely like a man seeing at night or looking at something in a thick fog, *per caliginem*. The cloud is made by images between man and the light of the Godhead, for in this life God can only be known by images, though he is not contained by them.[90] This vision, however, imperfect though it be, is the beginning of the beatific vision: in heaven the object of contemplation will be the same, but our sinful flesh will no longer be an obstacle between man and God. Even now this vision of faith is a seeing and an apprehension by the spirit (*mens*), not an analysis and arrangement by the reason (*ratio*), which is only one of the functions of the spirit. The vision itself is a gift of God, but man can prepare himself for it and develop it by the labour of recollection and meditation; the purifications of the active life and the occupations of the contemplative life are its necessary condition; and it is nourished principally by reading the word of God and reflecting on the mysteries of Christ.

It is not in seeing, then, that the vision of faith consists, but in looking with love and a great longing to see. It is not merely a knowledge of God, an act of the understanding, but an act of love

86 *Mor.*, XVIII, 88; XXXI, 102.

87 Cf. A. Ménager, *op. cit.*, Suppl., LIX (1939), pp. [145]–[169]; LX (1939), pp. [39]–[56].

88 Cf. G. Farkas, *Typische Formen der Kontemplation bei Gregor dem Grossen*, typewritten thesis, Rome (Gregorian University), 1948.

89 *Mor.*, XXII, 6: "Quid hoc in loco videre dicitur nisi desideranter intueri?", *ibid.*

90 *Mor.*, V, 53.

by which we possess the divine truth though as yet only imperfectly and obscurely, whereas in heaven we shall lay hold of it fully and clearly. This foretaste only gives us a glimpse of the divine light, but the happiness this feeble glimmer brings is so great that it keeps alive in us a longing for the complete bliss of heaven.

With St Gregory contemplation is a "perception", and a "feeling" rather than an "experience"; but this perception is more than cognition or a merely intellectual apprehension, it is a wisdom, a knowledge which already savours its object though it is not yet fully satisfied—*sapor, non satietas*.[91] It is a knowledge through love, a perception exercised by a love which is in itself a knowledge. *Per amorem agnoscimus*[92]; *amor ipse notitia est*.[93]

All men must tend to this degree of contemplation. Some men of God however, at certain moments in their lives, are given the grace to go beyond this. We read in Holy Scripture that several of the patriarchs and prophets "saw God"[94]; St Paul was rapt into heaven and God showed him "the power of his Majesty"[95]; St Benedict saw the whole world in a ray of the sun because "for the soul that sees its Creator all creatures have shrunk; for truly to the extent to which she sees the light of the Creator things created are diminished in her eyes".[96]

Some contemplatives, then, see God. What exactly does that mean? St Gregory asserts firmly that man cannot in this life apprehend the divine essence: there can be no common measure between a creature limited by the flesh and the infinite light of the Godhead; between the fundamental impurity of a sinner, even redeemed, and the transcendent purity of God. Even those saints who are said to have seen God could therefore only have seen him in images, unless they were at times freed from the body by a mystical death and so were able to penetrate into the eternal light of the Godhead.[97]

St Gregory is not concerned with solving the question, for even if it were possible it could only happen in extreme cases. At a lower level, however, it can happen that a soul is "rapt out of itself, raised beyond itself"[98] in the act of contemplation, which never lasts for long. "Now the soul is raised beyond its function of giving life to the body, and the understanding, which is only one of its aspects, also transcends itself."[99] But this going forth from the world and

[91] *Mor.*, VIII, 49.
[92] *Mor.*, X, 13; cf. *In Ev.*, XIV, 4.
[93] *In Ev.*, XXVIII, 4.
[94] *Mor.*, XVIII, 88.
[95] *Mor.*, XX, 9; XXVIII, 13; VIII, 48; X, 17; *Epist.*, VII, 25.
[96] *Dial.*, II, 35.
[97] *Mor.*, XVIII, 89; cf. R. Gillet, *op. cit.*, pp. 27–36, and A. Schaut, "Die Vision des Heiligen Benedikt", in *Vir Dei Benedictus*, Münster, 1947, pp. 217–57.
[98] *Mor.*, XXIV, 11.
[99] R. Gillet, *op. cit.*, p. 37. Cf. C. Butler, *op. cit.*, p. 83.

oneself, this transcending, is always fleeting. "*raptim, per transitum*". It is given hurriedly and as it were secretly, *quasi furtim.* It is a *mora contemplationis,* a little space. "The soul cannot remain long in contemplation",[100] "it cannot cleave for long to the light",[101] "it cannot remain for long beyond itself."[102] Heaven has barely opened to it and through a crack it has only seen a pale reflection, almost nothing: *tenuiter, exiguum valde* "*vix parum aliquid*"[103]; but even this glimpse of eternity which it has seen "through a glass and in a dark manner" is too much for its weakness, and it falls back, borne down by the immensity of something so sublime.[104] The spirit is hurt by the brightness, blinded as though by a flash of lightning, as it were struck by a thunderbolt—the *reverberatio—et tamen repulsus amat,*[105] and yet its love is not checked. Amazed, man is thrust back, brought back again to his own weakness, until once again he is raised beyond it. The moment of delight in God is followed by suffering and temptation which purify him, proving his love and kindling his desire. The law of alternation which is found all through St Gregory's teaching holds good even in contemplative prayer.

He suggests rather than analyses contemplative prayer in his description of it. There is a certain lack of precision in all he says, which is inherent in the mystery he tries to explain, and one can only give an account of his thought on the subject by singling out the ideas which he puts together. Moreover, the two visions of God—by desire and by rapture—which have just been described are simply two moments of the same vision, two phases of one act. The mystical life finds its unity in the love which is common to all who contemplate.

It is still an imperfect love, and proportionate to the knowledge we have received: "where the measure of knowledge is less, there also the measure of love is less".[106] *Hic interim,* until we reach heaven, our love is no stronger than our knowledge, "we shall not be all on fire until we are where we wholly see him whom we love".[107] But though we are still far from him in knowledge, yet we draw near to him by love; even those who only see God from afar—*procul conspiciunt*—are close to him by love: *iam per amorem iuxta sunt.*[108]

The vision of God by rapture is fleeting and transitory, but the vision of desire and love is unfading and never ends until the soul,

[100] *Ez.*, I, 5, 12. [101] *Mor.*, VIII, 50. [102] *Dial.*, II, 35.
[103] Cf. A. Ménager, "La Contemplation d'après Saint Grégoire le Grand" in *La Vie spirituelle*, Suppl., IX (1924), pp. [273]-[275].
[104] *Ez.*, I, 5, 12. [105] *Mor.*, X, 13. [106] *Ez.*, II, 9, 10.
[107] *Ibid.* [108] *Mor.*, XXVII, 8.

taken from this world, is at last satisfied: "when it looks on him whom it loves, its love will burn even more strongly".[109]

9. *The Significance of St Gregory*

It has not been possible in this short sketch to do more than draw attention to certain essential aspects of St Gregory's doctrine: there is no room in one short chapter for explanations and additions; for them the reader must go to St Gregory's works themselves and to the many excellent studies on them. All that has been attempted here is to include the chief characteristics of his teaching.

His mysticism is one of "vision", the form of his spiritual teaching one of knowledge rather than union. Even in his commentary on the Canticle of Canticles, in spite of the themes it offers, he speaks more of the vision of light than the embraces of the bridegroom. In the same way, he does not say much about the sensible concomitants of contemplation, or of its extraordinary forms. He is always concerned with a naked faith and prayer, silent and pure, going straight to the sublime and hidden realities which are its object.

In his concern for absolute purity St Gregory pursues as an illusion any turning back to self, or even to the supernatural reactions which may accompany a knowledge of God, and warns the soul against anything which could arrest its flight to God: yet there is nothing lacking in his teaching; though it is not affective it has a considerable psychological content: that is why it has an affinity with medieval teaching. It sheds light on all the problems of the Christian soul in search of perfection and union with God. When explaining the mysteries, St Gregory does not touch so much on their dogmatic content as on their value for man's sanctification and their spiritual efficacy. He shows how the soul takes possession of them, and lives and is nourished by them.

All the streams of holiness and of doctrine by which the Church had lived of old flowed into Gregory: the riches of the Bible, the liturgy, the Latin and some of the Eastern Fathers. By his synthesis of them, these treasures were passed on and so to speak made easily digestible to those who came after him. His simplicity, his unspeculative outlook were suited to the needs of the world which grew up as the result of the barbarian invasions. He made a unity out of that inheritance from the past of which he was the reservoir;

[109] *Ez.*, II, 2, 9. Because it is by death that we pass into the light, we must love and desire it (cf. Gillet, *op. cit.*, pp. 48–50) in spite of the temptations and struggles with the devils which accompany it and which we must fear. Cf. A. Bush, "An Echo of Christian Antiquity in St Gregory the Great: Death a Struggle with the Devil", in *Traditio*, III (1945) pp. 369–80.

and from him flowed out streams which developed and differentiated themselves. He was to be the spiritual father of the Middle Ages in the West.[110]

[110] Evidence of the influence of St Gregory in the Middle Ages has been collected by H. de Lubac, *Exégèse médiévale*, Paris, 1959, pp. 538–48, *Le moyen âge gregorien.*

II

THE IRISH INVASION

WHILE Gregory was committing the traditional teaching of the Church to writing, the barbarians were settling in the West. Ireland and the West of Britain had been spared, and from there a kind of Christian invasion was being prepared, which from the beginning of the sixth century flowed over other parts of Britain, and reached the Continent. This celtic Christianity must be considered separately: in Ireland it long preserved its distinctive features, and in other places up to the ninth century it still had an influence. The chief stages in its history are summed up by the names of St Patrick and St Columbanus; the significance of the latter cannot be understood apart from the personality and work of the former, although St Patrick himself belongs to the patristic age.[1]

1. The Influence of St Patrick

Celtic Christianity was fashioned by the work of St Patrick and his disciples. Before his time there had been Christians in Ireland, but no organized Christian communities. He was a native of the North West province of Roman Britain, but it was the monastic centres of Gaul that prepared him for his task. Captured by Icelandic pirates at the beginning of the fifth century, he spent at least six years as a slave on their island before he succeeded in escaping to Gaul in a trading ship. He then returned to his family and later went back to Gaul, possibly to Lérins off the coast of Provence, where monasticism was flourishing, though all we know from his own writings and from other sources is that he spent some time at

[1] The fundamental work on the subject is still *The Sources for the Early History of Ireland*, by J. F. Kenney, vol. I, New York, 1929. One of the chief sources is the collection of hagiographical texts edited by C. Plummer, *Vitae sanctorum Hiberniae partim hactenus ineditae*, 2 vols, Oxford, 1910, and *Lives of the Saints from the Book of Lismore* by W. Stokes, Oxford, 1890. For thirty-five years Fr Grosjean, S.J., has published in *Analecta Bollandiana* and elsewhere learned studies under the title of *Notes d'hagiographie celtique*. This chapter owes much to his writings and to the information he has so generously provided. For a translation of St Patrick's writings see that of L. Bieler in *Ancient Christian Writers*, vol. 17, London, 1953.

Auxerre learning the beginnings of monastic and priestly life under the aegis of St Amâtre and St Germanus. The latter gathered a group of his clergy round him who, towards the end of his episcopate, formed themselves into a regular monastic community. It was as a bishop that Patrick went back to Ireland, but his training had been that of a monk, and left him with a great love for the monastic state. The Church he founded was governed by the bishops and clergy, but monasticism had a considerable place in it. Patrick organized the conversion of the country, sending out fervent converts as missionaries. These were monks and nuns, for he encouraged his clergy (without, however, compelling them) to live in communities which were also seminaries for future apostles, under an austere monastic discipline; these monk-missionaries were aided by consecrated virgins, some of whom continued to live in their own homes, while others went with the bishop on his apostolic journeys.

In many ways St Patrick followed the tradition of St Eusebius at Vercelli, St Augustine at Hippo, St Martin at Tours and especially St Victricius at Rouen, of whom he speaks, and whose example seems to have had a strong influence on him. The whole of St Patrick's work is marked by a missionary bent and severe asceticism.[2]

It would seem that the bishops who succeeded those whom St Patrick had established developed a less monastic outlook in matters ecclesiastical, particularly under the influence of priests and other clerics from Britain who from the middle of the fifth century onwards had settled in Ireland as a result of difficulties in their own country. As the numbers of Christians increased and there was nothing to prevent those who wished to from leading a monastic life freed from all pastoral cares, both men and women entered newly founded monasteries which in principle were no longer dependant on the bishops. These new monasteries tended towards an anachoretic form of life; they were grouped together in monastic "dioceses", *parochiae*, of a mother abbey with dependent daughters. Among the illustrious names connected with them are Finian of Clonard, Comgall of Bangor, and Kevin. At the same time the communities of consecrated virgins developed: St Brigid of Kildare played a considerable part in organizing them and binding them together, though this federation only lasted a short

[2] The writings of St Patrick have been edited by L. Bieler, *Libri epistolarum Sancti Patricii*, Dublin, 1952; for his life and work see P. Grosjean, S.J., *Analecta Bollandiana*, LXII (1944), pp. 42–73; and LXIII (1945), pp. 100–19, 243–56. On his piety see W. Kinsella, "The Spirituality of St Patrick's Confession", in *Irish Eccl. Record*, XCI (1959), pp. 161–73, and L. Bieler, "Glimpses of St Patrick's Spiritual Life", in *Doctrine and Life*, 1961, p. 126.

while. The abbesses, however, exercised a great authority, even over clerics. Light needs to be thrown on the question of interdependence of the Welsh and Irish monasteries; though their history is distinct, relations seem to have been kept up between them. In any case St Patrick (†461) lived long enough to settle his own work on a firm foundation and to give Irish Christianity a character it was to keep for a long time, with monasticism as the preponderating influence; many high positions in the Irish Church were filled by or became the prerogatives of abbots and monks.

2. *St Columbanus and his Disciples*

St Columbanus was born in Ireland about 563.[3] Although, unlike many of his contemporaries, he was brought up at home and not in a monastery, it was in an environment touched by the austere monasticism of the time. When he grew up he decided to abandon the world, and leaving his own part of the country, he entered the strict community of Bangor; he was professed there when he was about twenty, ordained priest a few years later, and became master of the monastic school. When he was about thirty he was seized with a desire to go even further away from his own home, and in 591 with some of his disciples he left Bangor for Gaul. Soon after his arrival there he preached at the court of Childebert, King of Austrasia, whose favour he gained, and was given permission to settle in the Vosges, at Luxeuil and other places. He gathered more disciples round him and they founded a monastery. It increased in numbers and divided and settled colonies in at least two different places. It was for this community that St Columbanus wrote his *Rule for Monks*, and the penal code called the *Rule of the Community* or *Domestic Rule* (*regula cenobialis*). He probably also wrote two Penitentials—chiefly for the clergy and laity but also for monks—bringing something of Irish severity into Gaul. In this, as in other matters, he came into conflict with the bishops and nobles, and after various wanderings through Gaul he was forced into exile. He journeyed through Germany and Switzerland with St Gall and a group of monks and finally settled at Bobbio in Lombardy, where he died in 615.[4] In his travels he set up monasteries, which in their

[3] St Columbanus must not be confused with St Columba, abbot of Iona, although in old sources their lives are often mingled, cf. J. Leclerq, "Un ancien recueil d'hagiographie columbanienne", in *Analecta Bollandiana*, LXXIII (1955), pp. 193–6. The latest work on the life of St Columbanus is that of G. S. M. Walker: *S. Columbani opera*, Dublin, 1957, pp. IX–XXXIV; on his work, *ibid.*, pp. XXXV–LXXII, bibliography, pp. LXXII–XCII. There is also a good account of his life in *Les vies des Saints et Bienheureux . . . par les Bénédictins de Paris*, vol. XI, Paris, 1954, pp. 713–22.

[4] There is a reproduction of a map of the journeys of St Columbanus in *Mélanges Colombaniens*, Paris, 1951, pp. 152–3.

turn founded others.[5] The example he set was one of great austerity, denouncing vice and reprimanding princes; yet he attracted men of every class, educating their children, and turning many of them towards the monastic state. Other Irishmen, following St Columbanus's example (though many of them, like St Fursey, had not come under his influence) went to Cornwall, to Wales and to Scotland, and others to Western Gaul and Spain. Some of these "Scots" as they were called settled in monasteries, some envangelized the countryside, others brought with them to Gaul and elsewhere what remains of classical and patristic literature their country had preserved; all added vigour to Western monasticism. Thus a group of Irishmen, probably from Kildare, established themselves at Liège; later on in the ninth century one of their countrymen (his very name "Erigena" shows him to have been a Scot) was to make a synthesis of faith and philosophy which would bear fruit in the twelfth century; and Sedulius Scotus and other learned Irishmen were to contribute much to the revival of learning, and spirituality under Charlemagne.[6] This Irish activity of the sixth, seventh and eighth centuries is known to us from sources which are not always easy to use. Many of the Lives were written, or re-written, or added to much later (sometimes as late as the twelfth-fourteenth centuries), with the result that side by side with facts that may be taken as probable or certain are stories which are quite fantastic. Of the other writings of the period, works on computation, the Holy Scriptures, the virtues, the monastic life, many still await further study and publication.[7] It is, however, possible from the sources already available to see what were the special characteristics of the light that spread from Ireland. It has been spoken of as a "mystical invasion": it is more properly described as a wave of austerity, a kind of flood of asceticism. It owed much to monastic tradition, but it added to it a note of missionary activity, together with a certain almost harsh gravity, a slightly Pelagian tendency; it was the spirituality of a poor country, a land where it was hard both to make a living and to live virtuously.

[5] There is the study of the origins and character of one of these foundations—the double community of Evoriac, afterwards called Faremoutiers, by J. O'Carroll, "A Columbanian Convent in Gaul", in *The Irish Theological Quarterly*, XXV, 1958, pp. 227–46.

[6] Cf. C. M. Cappuyns, *Jean Scot Erigène*, Louvain–Paris, 1933, pp. 32–3. J. Gross, "Sedulius Scottus ein verspäterer semipelagianer", in *Zeitschrift für Kirchengeschichte*, LXVIII (1957), pp. 322–32, has shown that Sedulius' commentaries on St Paul handed on, up till a late period, ideas which drew their inspiration from ancient Pelagian circles.

[7] Cf. P. Grosjean, S.J., in *Sacris Erudiri*, VII (1955), pp. 67–98 and B. Bischoff, "Il monachesimo Irlandese e suoi rapporti col continente", in *Il monachesimo nell'alto medioevo e la formazione dellà civiltà occidentale*, Spoleto, 1957, pp. 121–138.

Many parts of Britain and elsewhere are said to have been evangelized by these Scots, but what in fact they did was to found hermitages and monasteries. Their object in leaving their own country had not been to be missionaries but pilgrims, and it was chiefly by their life of asceticism and prayer that their influence was exerted.[8] During the sixth and seventh centuries their spirituality had so considerable an influence that its essential features must be considered.

3. The Teaching of St Columbanus

On the Continent one of the writings which had a great influence in spreading the purest Irish spirituality was the Life of St Columba by Adamnan. Soon after it was written it became widely known, and only ten years after Adamnan's death the monks of Reichenau owned a copy made by a monk who became abbot of Iona in Scotland; it then came into the possession of the monastery of Schaffhausen, where it still is. St Columbanus is therefore only one of the representative figures of Irish religious life, and perhaps not of its finest side, but because of his writings he is the one who is best known. He had had no education except in Latin; his gifts were those of a man of action, and he knew how to express his thought. Though Irish teaching was by word of mouth, Columbanus wrote various works which happen to have been preserved better than many others. In contrast with the great Irish monks of his day who were on the whole erudite men and grammarians, Columbanus's oratory was of a popular kind, and he had no hesitation in taking part in political activities.[9] In his own country many more learned men gave themselves up to an exegesis of Scripture which for the period reached a high level: Columbanus would only admit of that interpretation of a passage which after little study seemed clear to him. His writings are of a practical nature: two Rules can safely be attributed to him, though possibly the texts that we possess are not the primitive ones; there is some discussion as to the authorship of the penitentials, four poems and thirteen short sermons or instructions,[10] but the same fundamental ideas appear in them all, whether they were actually written by him or by one of his disciples.

The first is of the decrepitude of this world. In the verses *de mundi transitu* and elsewhere Columbanus repeats again and again

[8] This fact is now recognized by historians: e.g. N. Chadwick, *The Age of the Saints in the Early Celtic Church*, Oxford, 1961, pp. 79–81. "This is something quite different from missionary work, or even mission work."

[9] Cf. N. Chadwick, *ibid.*

[10] Cf. C. M. Cappuyns in *Bull. de théol. anc. et médiév.*, VIII (1959), p. 210 and note 639.

that all things pass away; this world "rolls on towards its end", "resting on the pillar of vanity"; it will fall away and disappear,[11] "it is already in its decline".[12] Man too is passing away; by definition he is a transitory being, *in via*[13]; he ought to live as though he were dying,[14] in a kind of "terror".[15] Columbanus describes man's wretchedness in harsh terms, with a strong and crude realism[16]: "Woe to thee, human misery ... wretched art thou, O man, unhappy creature who lovest things more than thine own self".[17] We stumble blindly in this dark uncertain life[18]; any security it gives us is illusory[19]; God alone is our refuge, man's whole dignity lies in his being made in the image of God,[20] free to love his Creator and Redeemer; "If you suppress that liberty, you suppress his dignity".[21] Man can find again this likeness to God by "humility of heart and spirit".[22] "Humility of heart is the soul's repose", by it we are made happy[23] and we give joy to others. "Let us be humble and gentle, amiable and agreeable to others (*communes*) so that the King who is humble and yet exalted may reign in us."[24] Columbanus has many warnings against intellectual conceit: "It is not in argument, *verborum disputatione*,[25] that you must seek for the supreme knowledge". Pride and argument teach one nothing about God,[26] it is always a question of the "interior man"[27] and of "purity of heart".[28] "Scrutinize your own conscience."[29]

The second great duty of the Christian is to be "unwearying in charity". The charity we have towards our brethren must be discerning, humbly going out to the lowly, *amator mediocrium*.[30] Columbanus loves to speak of the oneness of the Church, insisting that Christians must be one in spirit,[31] since he who loves unity has part in the Church's unity; he wishes "all men's wills to be in agreement, as also their way of life, so that they may have true peace, and unbroken charity".[32] He himself is of two minds: "he wishes to work for the salvation of many, and yet for himself he longs for the hidden life".[33] It is for us "ever to tend towards heaven, to press

[11] *S. Columbani Opera*—ed. G. S. M. Walker, *Scriptores latini hiberniae*, vol. II, Dublin, Inst. Adv. Studies, 1957. *Instr.*, III, p. 72. The references which follow are from this edition.

[12] *Epist.*, V, p. 40; *De mundi transitu*, p. 184.

[13] *Epist.*, IV, p. 36.

[14] *Instr.*, III, p. 76.

[15] *Epist.*, V, p. 42.

[16] *Instr.*, VII, pp. 90–2.

[17] *Instr.*, III, pp. 76–8.

[18] *Instr.*, VI, p. 88.

[19] *Epist.*, V, p. 44.

[20] *Instr.*, XI, p. 106.

[21] *Epist.*, IV, p. 34.

[22] *Epist.*, IV, pp. 31–4. *Instr.*, II, p. 70.

[23] *Reg. mon.*, IX, p. 140.

[24] *Inst.*, X, p. 104.

[25] *Inst.*, I, p. 64.

[26] *Inst.*, II, p. 66.

[27] *Inst.*, II, pp. 68–70.

[28] *Inst.*, II, p. 72.

[29] *Epist.*, IV, p. 36.

[30] *Epist.*, VI, p. 58.

[31] *Epist.*, II, p. 20.

[32] *Epist.*, II, p. 14.

[33] *Epist.*, IV, p. 28.

on to the prize, to long for what is above and to thirst after God".[34] It is by transcending them that we shall reconcile fear and security, fervour and hope, all that Christ asks of us, by which the soul is made at once joyful and sorrowful. "How sweet it is for a mother to hear of the coming of a son for whom she has waited long"[35]: that is how God wishes us to long for him. "To sigh impatiently for heaven is the way not to be attached to earth." "The bread of angels", the vision of God, awaits us in heaven; where our heavenly Father dwells is our native land.[36] To love the angels who love God is to lift up the eyes of our heart,[37] to long to see as they do "the radiant face of Christ, more lovable than anything else".[38] We are to imitate our Lord in his voluntary sufferings: "The true disciples of the crucified Christ follow him with a cross . . . in it are hidden all the mysteries of salvation."[39] Jesus, "like a true father", came down to us[40]; now he is in glory we must follow him there. "We are sorrowful because he is no longer with us, but we exult when we read that we shall see him as he is." So we must not be overcome by sorrow.[41] "Love knows no sadness: I speak of spiritual love",[42] that "love of God which renews his image in us".[43] When he sings of the love of Jesus only, which increases our thirst for God. Columbanus uses the language of the mystics: he speaks of our need to "know what we love", he quotes from the Canticle of Canticles, he recalls the action of the Holy Spirit in our souls, profound yet sweet, healing that wound of love which makes us desire grace more ardently as we stretch out our hands to it, by which our thirst for God increases as he quenches it. "Happy is that soul whom love thus wounds."[44]

Columbanus is addressing himself primarily to monks. The *Rule* he wrote for them consists almost entirely of a series of chapters on those virtues which make for spiritual progress. There is nothing new in what he says; he sets before them the example of Christ, and draws his inspiration from the old monastic writers, especially Cassian and St Basil. It is a question of attaining charity through purity of heart, the martyrdom of voluntary poverty, mortification and the obedience which humbles "a proud liberty".[45] In a short chapter he lays down the rules of the canonical office. Each of the Hours is to be followed by silent prayer, and Columbanus reminds

[34] *Epist.*, VI, p. 58; cf. *Epist.*, II, pp. 20–2.
[35] *Epist.*, V, p. 56.
[36] *Inst.*, VIII, p. 94.
[37] *De mundi transitu*, p. 184.
[38] *Ibid.*, p. 182.
[39] *Epist.*, IV, pp. 30–2.
[40] *Epist.*, V, p. 48.
[41] *Inst.*, IV, p. 82.
[42] *Inst.*, XI, p. 110.
[43] *Ibid.*, p. 106.
[44] *Inst.*, XII, p. 114; XIII, pp. 116–20.
[45] *Reg. Mon.*, IX, p. 138.

his monks that in accordance with true tradition this will be accomplished "without distaste—*sine fastidio*"—since each one will undertake it as best he can according to the capacity of his soul, his strength and abilities, his age and his health, his training and the time he can give to it: in short "according to each one's fervour", but "all share equally in an unceasing intention to be in heart and spirit with God".[46] Their rule of life is found only in the *Domestic Rule* where the punishments for infringements of regular discipline are laid down. These are often so severe that from the seventh century onwards additions from contemporary or older Rules were made to the original text to modify its harshness.[47] The observance seems to have been more austere than is suggested by the actual text of the *Rule for Monks*, which contains a chapter not found in other Rules (for example, that of St Benedict) entitled *On Discretion*. Discretion is defined as a "moderating science" which makes of every virtue a just mean between two extremes; it is a gift by which God gives to the soul the light of discernment; it avoids conceit and is a guarantee of humility.[48] In another place St Columbanus says explicitly: "the affliction of the body bears no fruit without moderation of soul"[49]; he is not therefore as extreme as he is sometimes made out to be; he requires due measure to be observed. In medieval teaching, however, words like "discretion", and ideas of a just mean, are often ambiguous: according to the high or low level of mortification that an author or a spiritual master wishes to see observed, the norm of discretion varies, and so by definition the term is a relative one. St Columbanus was well aware of this, and if one compares what he expects of his disciples with some of the eccentricities related of the ancient solitaries, he was not without discretion.

St Columbanus, unlike St Gregory, did not elaborate a great body of doctrine; the directions he gives are inspired by Cassian and St Jerome, and the observances he prescribes are drawn from those of his own country. Though they never met, these two masters of the spiritual life were contemporaries and knew of each other. There is not extant any answer from St Gregory to the letter Columbanus wrote to him putting forward with great vigour the Irish method of calculating Easter in opposition to the Roman one;

[46] *Reg. Mon.*, VII, p. 132.

[47] Cf. Walker, *op. cit.*, pp. L–LI. Writings wrongly attributed to Columbanus are published, *ibid.*, pp. 198–214. Further information about Irish monasticism may be found in the *Regula cujusdam patris*, P.L., 66, 987; the short treatise *De duodecim abusivis saeculi* (ed. CSEL, III, 3, 152) written in Ireland about 630–50, and owing much to Isidore, which was copied and commented on all through the Middle Ages; and the authors whose writings are listed in E. Dekkers–A. Gaar, "Clavis Patrum Latinorum", in *Sacris erudiri*, III (1951), pp. 190–7.

[48] *Reg. mon.*, VIII, pp. 134–8. [49] *Inst.*, II, p. 70.

we know however that St Columbanus had a great esteem for St Gregory: he says as much to him, telling him that he has read his *Pastoral Rule*, asking for his *Homilies on Ezechiel*, and begging him to elucidate the latter part of the Canticle of Canticles and the "obscure passages in Zacharias".[50] He drew his inspiration for the penitentials from St Gregory's teaching, though he lacks the latter's comprehension of human frailty, and during his lifetime writing to a synod held in Gaul, holds Gregory up as a saint, putting him on a level with St Jerome. What Columbanus says in more than one place on the transcendence of God,[51] and man's longing to see him, gives the impression that he owes much to this master he so much admires; and yet the two men were very different. A stray sentence here and there betrays a sensitive heart, even occasionally a shade of tenderness, but the Irishman's gravity is always harshly austere. He spends little time on the psychological aspect of problems of conscience; the interior man's disposition must be one of complete renunciation. It is as a man of action, impressive by his example, that he affected those about him: his disciples modelled themselves on their master, influenced not so much by his ideas as by his burning fervour. Gregory's gentler influence lasted longer, but Columbanus's harshness was effective at the time; possibly his violence was fruitful for the men of that rough and brutal age.

4. Ireland, the Land of Monasticism

St Columbanus, writing to the bishops of Gaul, might say that St Jerome, "there is one law for the clergy, and one for monks, for they are separated by a great gulf from each other",[52] but in fact in Ireland there was very little difference in their way of life. It has been said that there "monasticism attained a popularity without parallel in any other country or at any other time",[53] so that "the most striking characteristic of the period is an intense enthusiasm for the monastic idea"[54] and this inevitably had a considerable effect on the life of the Irish Church. The monasteries founded by Columbanus on the Continent were large communities ruled by an abbot, living the normal monastic life. In Ireland, however, they were under the authority of the bishop (who in the fifth and sixth centuries was an abbot, or a monk designated for the office by his abbot) and often consisted of a small community attached to one of the churches which were built wherever groups of Christians were to be found. These latter, laymen, *laici*, are not to be confused

[50] *Epist.*, I, p. 10.
[51] *Ibid.*, pp. 60–6, 74, 106.
[52] *Epist.*, II, p. 20.
[53] J. Ryan, *Irish Monasticism*, Dublin, 1931, p. 167.
[54] Ryan, *op. cit.*, p. 186.

with the *relaici* or *conversi*, men who in adult life had renounced the world and, leaving their own lands, had come to do penance by taking on themselves the yoke of the monastic life. Religious women too, deaconesses[55] and nuns, had a considerable influence. Normally the sons of nobles were brought up either at home or in a monastery, but in some cases boys not destined to become monks were educated by nuns, who if the need arose took the place of the maternal uncle whose duty it was in Irish tribal society to ensure the continuance of a family by protecting the male children. Monasteries were often built in secluded places, in some cases where a community of pagan worshippers had formerly made their home; indeed some saints founded them on islands which could easily be defended, or on spurs of land jutting out into the sea, which they fortified against invaders.

Cassian's teaching that the ascesis of the coenobium leads as a rule to a life of contemplation in solitude was accepted without qualification. From the end of the sixth century onwards[56] many monks adopted for a time, sometimes for long periods, the life of a hermit. Later on a sort of seasonal reclusion tended to become a regular institution: when summer began, a "perfect monk" would settle on an isolated rock off the coast, and give himself up to contemplation till the coming of winter made it impossible for him to stay there any longer; and some of the elders, who not being kin to the founder of the monastery could not become its abbot, but had been deans (that is, head of a monastic cell or village), would end their days as hermits.[57]

In each community only some of the monks were priests or clerics, enough to celebrate the liturgy. The monastic idea was that of an army in which man fights as a soldier of Christ; or of a martyrdom; for a monk, since he could not obtain the "red" martyrdom of blood, sought the "white" one by renouncing the world, and the "green" one of extreme austerities.[58] Irish monasticism thus resembled in many ways both in its ideals and practices that of the ancient East and that of Gaul under St Martin.

5. *Penance and Exile*

In medieval Ireland, as in the ancient world, the monastic life was a form of the life of penance, and it is only in that light that it

[55] Cf. P. Grosjean in *Analecta Bollandiana*, LXXIII (1955), pp. 298, 322.

[56] Text in L. Gougaud, *Christianity in Celtic Lands*, London, 1932, pp. 99–101; Ryan, *op. cit.*, pp. 219–20, 259–60.

[57] Cf. K. Jackson, *Studies in Early Celtic Nature Poetry*, Cambridge, 1935, pp. 93–109.

[58] Cf. L. Gougaud, "Les conceptions de martyre chez les Irlandais", in *Rev. bénéd.*, XXIV (1907), pp. 360–73.

can be fully understood. Everywhere a man did penance by entering the *ordo paenitentium*, whence he could pass to the *ordo monasticus* or even, when he had fulfilled the prescribed satisfaction, to the clerical state; but in Ireland penance as an expression of repentance and a means of reparation included a practice which assumed a greater importance there than elsewhere: confession. It formed of course part of a sacrament, but as an inheritance from the East it was a common ascetic practice in all Irish monasteries. Private confession had always existed side by side with public penance; still, it was usually only made on a deathbed, and its general adoption by those in good health in monasteries and elsewhere is due to Celtic Christianity. From this practice developed both the "confession of devotion" (particularly recommended before Mass)[59] and the tradition of the role of confessor or spiritual father—the "friend of the soul". There grew up too those extraordinary compilations, the medieval Irish Penitentials: a list of sins, with suitable punishments. Many of them soon disappeared, but those which survived helped to form the conscience of the West,[60] though they do not necessarily represent a general system of discipline. Their authors had in mind "to carry a system of legal compensations into men's relations with God": an evil is to be healed by its contrary, the glutton must fast and the chatterer keep silence. The scale of penalties does not often rise very high, and in the prologues confessors are admonished to show discrimination and to arouse contrition in their penitents. These penitentials, in spite of the opposition of various Councils provoked by their abuse, had a very considerable influence in Ireland, England and the Continent: they were frequently transcribed, and occasionally in use until a late period—for example in Iceland in the fourteenth, Spain in the fifteenth and Northern Italy in the sixteenth centuries.

The Irish system of private penance affected the whole growth of spirituality; "it accentuates a feeling in man that his relations with God can take the form of an effective dialogue"[61]: absolution is asked for in consideration of a conversion entailing sacrifices, and the Lord grants a pardon. It was this intimate communication of man with God that opened the way to indulgence, private Masses, and penance undertaken voluntarily for the redemption of souls. People began to realize that the punishment merited by one man

[59] E.g. St Columbanus, *Reg. Cenob.*, 30, ed. Walker, p. 180.

[60] The best work on this kind of literature is J. T. MacNeill and H. M. Gamer, *Mediaeval Handbooks of Penance, a translation of the principal libri poenitentiales and selections from related documents*, New York, 1938. See also L. Bieler, *The Irish Penitentials*, Dublin, 1968.

[61] G. le Bras, "Les pénitentiels Irlandais", in *Le miracle Irlandais, textes réunis sous la direction de Daniel-Rops*, Paris, 1956, p. 188.

could be undergone in his stead by another, and this commutation of penance gradually led to indulgences: from the eighth century onwards there are found what were later called plenary indulgences for the dead.[62] It was, moreover, from this motive that a later monasticism propagated the practice of taking the discipline[63]; so it may be said that the Irish method of penance "levelled out one of the highways of devotion".[64]

A rigorous penitential discipline kept up the monastic spirit of penance and spread it abroad. It demanded a high degree of austerity, almost of heroism: its safeguard and moderation lay in discretion, humility and obedience; St Columbanus himself insisted on the importance of the dispositions of the heart.[65]

Fasting as a form of asceticism was particularly strict during the three Lents, "that of Elias in the winter, of Jesus in the spring, and of Moses in the summer".[66] It seems that some, the *aquatici*, took nothing but water.[67] Manual labour was exacting, some monks actually drawing the plough themselves. The genuflections and prostrations were simply copied from the *metanoia* taught by the ancient monks in the East, but more specifically Irish were the long watchings with arms outstretched in the form of a cross[68] and the reciting of prayers while immersed in cold water.[69] The degree of mortification required was high, and yet it was humane enough to be practised by great numbers.

One of the forms that penance took in Ireland especially was "the service of God in penance, or the pilgrimage"[70]; in the lives of the Irish saints like a refrain comes "to go on a journey for the name of the Lord" or "for the love of Christ", "for the healing of the soul" or "to win the heavenly kingdom". The custom of journeying "had become second nature to the Irishman".[71] The explanation may lie in the fact that in a country where the network of family relationships was very close, to leave one's own people was one of the greatest of renunciations, so, in order to detach themselves,

[62] Cf. MacNeill and Gamer, *op. cit.*, pp. 142–7. An important part in this development was played by the treatise *De arreis*; cf. G. le Bras, art. "Pénitentiels", in *Dict. Théol. Cath.*, XII, II (1933), col. 1162, 1163.

[63] See p. 118.

[64] G. le Bras in *Le miracle Irlandais*.

[65] Cf. Ryan, *op. cit.*, pp. 222–3, 250–3 for texts which are an echo of St Columbanus.

[66] Ryan, *op. cit.*, p. 393. Gougaud, "Le jeûne en Irelande", in *Dévotions et pratiques ascétiques au moyen âge*, Paris, 1925, pp. 143–54.

[67] Cf. P. Grosjean in *Analecta Bollandiana*, LXXVI (1958), pp. 413–15.

[68] Gougaud, *Christianity in Celtic Lands*, pp. 93–5.

[69] Gougaud, "La mortification par les bains froids spécialement chez les ascètes celtiques", in *Bull. d'anc. litt. et d'archéol. chrét.*, IV (1914), pp. 96–108.

[70] These were considered equivalent; see a text edited in *The Ancient Laws of Ireland* (Rolls Series), III, Dublin–London, 1873, p. 31.

[71] Walafrid Strabo, *Vita S. Galli*, II, 47. P.L., 114, 1029.

Irishmen went as far away as possible. They were men particularly sensitive to homesickness, and therefore wanted to prove their generosity by exiling themselves; we hear of many Celtic saints tormented by anguish of soul at being separated from their native land. They went in search of solitude, and the long journeys involved perils and weariness which the pilgrims added to by watchings and fastings, thus accomplishing a prescribed or self-chosen penance[72]; it could also become an opportunity of bearing Christ to those who lay in ignorance: the missionary activity and monastic expansion of medieval Ireland had their origins in the asceticism of self-chosen exile.

6. *Prayer and Love*

Monastic life in Ireland was directed towards contemplation, but the question arises as to what form it took. Of what kind was the prayer of these huge communities and these innumerable hermits? One of their principal occupations was reading the Bible, as we know from their own statements and the manuscripts in which they copied and explained the Scriptures, many of which survived the destruction of the centuries and still await classification.[73] Pocket sacramentaries were known on the Continent, but only in Ireland did the traveller feel the need to carry about with him a small Gospel.[74]

First in the work of prayer was the Mass, which was always solemnly celebrated with ceremony and preparation. In the monasteries it was said on Sundays, feast days, and on the death of a brother. So great was the concourse of the faithful who came that the churches could not hold them. They merely passed through the church and, if the weather was not too bad, stood in the open round one of the great crosses which can still be seen, and there a sermon was addressed to both monks and laity. Frequent communion was encouraged, and the monks, though not obliged to, usually went to communion at every Mass, having first been to confession. The Mass is often spoken of as the offering of a sacri-

[72] G. B. Parks, *The English Traveller to Italy*, Stanford University Press, 1954, pp. 17–18. Ryan, *op. cit.*, pp. 213, 249, 261–3. On pilgrimage as a form of asceticism in Christian antiquity and in Celtic tradition, see H. von Campenhausen, *Die asketische Heimatlösigkeit in altchristlichen und frümitteralterlichen Mönchtum*, Tübingen, 1930, pp. 16–23; and B. Kötting, *Peregrinatio religiosa*, Münster, 1950, pp. 302–7.

[73] Cf. B. Bischoff, "Wendepunkt in der Geschichte der Lateinischen Exegese in Frümittelalter", in *Sacris erudiri*, VI (1954), pp. 189–281, and P. Grosjean, S.J., *ibid.*, VII (1955), pp. 67–98.

[74] Cf. P. MacGurk, "The Irish Pocket Gospel Book", in *Sacris erudiri*, VIII (1956), pp. 249–70.

fice.[75] Many carried a consecrated Host about with them in a chrism box resembling a reliquary; it was a custom among pilgrims, and for abbots when they worked in the fields with their monks.

Psalmody was held in great honour, as the essential part of the *cursus* of the liturgy.[76] Practically all knew the psalms by heart; Latin had been a foreign tongue to them and the psalter was their primer. The psalms were explained by means of glosses in Celtic, some of which have been preserved; and as soon as they understood they learnt them by heart, a real necessity in northern countries where during the long winter the hours of daylight are short. One of the oldest series of "Christian titles to the psalms"[77] was in use in Ireland from the sixth century onwards, and there was also a mnemonic version of the Martyrology. Many Rules order the private recital daily of the "three fifties", that is, a whole psalter.[78] There are very few references to any other specific practice of private prayer: Cassian's teaching was taken for granted and his method of praying prostrate was followed.[79] As far as we know, prayer on the whole was simple, though it did not exclude some use of the understanding and the imagination. St Columbanus recommended what he called *studium*, as a means of knowing and fulfilling the will of God: "But it must be undertaken devoutly and calmly. What helps man to persevere with it? The understanding."[80] Many of his short sermons with their elevations on the transcendence of God and their descriptions of the wretchedness of man are like meditations. His biographer gives a picture of him "carrying the Scriptures over his shoulder and arguing with himself"[81]; he would pull the book from his bag and commune with himself on the reflections he drew from it.

According to a tenth-century tradition at Bobbio, St Columbanus, probably during a vigil, "saw the heavens opened"[82]: the lives of various monks give other instances of raptures, ecstasies, angelic visions and conversation with angels.[83] Usually, however, prayer consisted of the chanting of long litanies, called *loricae* because they were thought of as breastplates ensuring heavenly protection[84]:

[75] Ryan, *op. cit.*, pp. 346–51.

[76] Gougaud, *Christianity in Celtic Lands*, pp. 329–34.

[77] See p. 63, note 71. *Série de St Colomba*, ed. P. Salmon, *Les "tituli psalmorum" des manuscrits latins*, Rome, 1959, pp. 48–74.

[78] Gougaud, *op. cit.*, p. 90.

[79] Ryan, *op. cit.*, p. 331.

[80] *Instr.*, III, p. 72.

[81] Jonas of Bobbio, *Vita Columbiani*, I, 8, ed. B. Krusch, in *Scrip. rer. Germ. in us. schol.*, 1905, p. 106.

[82] *Mirac. S. Columb.*, I, ed. Mabillon, *Acta SS O.S.B.*, II, Paris, 1669, p. 41.

[83] Texts in Ryan, *op. cit.*, pp. 332–3.

[84] Gougaud, "Étude sur les 'Loricae' celtiques et sur les prières qui s'en rapprochent", in *Bull. d'anc. litt. et d'archéol. chrét.*, I (1911), pp. 265–81; II

a great part of them was taken up with the Trinity and the mysteries of our Redeemer—his Birth, his Baptism, his Passion and his Glory—and parts of his Body were invoked in phrases which are thought by some to bear a resemblance to the *Anima Christi*.[85] The phases of our Lord's life were also invoked: "By thy contemplative life, we beseech thee hear us; by thine active life, we beseech thee hear us."[86] Possibly the titles given to our Lady in the *loricae* owe their inspiration to the writings of St Ildephonsus; and a place of honour is given to Irish saints, especially to pilgrim saints. The forces of nature, which played so great a part in Celtic mythology, are called upon to praise God, who is blessed for having created them; protection is implored against temptation, and against the perils of journeys. There are special litanies for the dying and to arouse contrition before confession. Little by little these tireless invocations, unending waves of supplication, pass into adoration[87]: both they and the Celtic hymns[88] show the fervour of true contemplation.[89]

(1912), pp. 33–41, 101–27. The texts themselves are edited by C. Plummer, *Irish Litanies*, London, 1925.

85 Gougaud, *ibid.*, II (1912), p. 40.

86 Ed. Plummer in *Irish Litanies*, p. 102.

87 On the form and content of Irish prayer, see W. Godel, "Irisches beten im frühem Mittelalter", in *Zeitschrift für Kath. Theol.*, LXXXV (1963), pp. 261–321 and 389–439.

88 Ed. J. H. Bernard and R. Atkinson, *The Irish Liber Hymnorum*, London, 1898.

89 Several of the components of ancient Celtic spirituality are found, much later, in the Irish tradition; for example in St Patrick of Dublin in the eleventh century. His works have been edited by A. Gwynn, S.J., *The Writings of Bp Patrick, 1074–1084*. On the fleetingness of life, see pp. 78–83 and 106–24, and on the longing for heaven, p. 114.

III

SPIRITUALITY IN THE BARBARIAN KINGDOMS

1. In the Wake of St Gregory

THE barbarian kingdoms which were founded on the ruins of the Roman Empire were finally converted to Christ during the pontificate of St Gregory and the middle of the eighth century; a conversion which bore fruit both in the spiritual life and for European civilization. The Angles, Saxons and Jutes in Great Britain, the Franks in Gaul and later in Germany, the Visigoths in Spain and the Lombards in Italy accepted Christianity (purifying it if they had already received it tainted with Arianism), learnt to live according to its requirements, and played their part in its propagation. Over vast territories Christians were brought face to face with the realities of the spiritual life, and as the history of the Church was linked with the particular political vicissitudes of each kingdom, the rhythm of spiritual evolution varied with the problems the Church faced. Despite its complexity, however, certain common factors give the period a unity. There survived a legacy of ancient Christianity strongly marked by two influences, the Roman Church and monasticism, the latter drawing its inspiration from the examples and the writings of the East; everywhere young nations with no traditional culture accepted the Gospel with fervour and simplicity; and the effect of the Celtic monks and missionaries was felt in many countries. Little by little, during centuries which were to leave considerable traces on later history, these streams mingled, and the period can therefore be considered briefly as a unity.

Another unifying element was the literature which nourished this great religious movement, and though it is not very varied or abundant it gives us some knowledge of the period. Certain of the writings describe the spiritual life of the times: this is particularly true of the *Lives* of the saints,[1] though they are not an easy source

[1] Edited in *Mon. Germ. Hist. Script. rerum Merov.*, 7 vols, Hanover, 1885–1920.

to use, because many of them were written long after the events they describe, and even those which are contemporary or nearly so are often written more on traditional lines than as an accurate account of observed facts: legend and miracles play a larger part than likelihood. They do, however, give a picture of the circles in which they were written and read. A particular importance attaches to the evidence recorded by St Gregory of Tours (†590), a contemporary of the pope St Gregory, in his works *On the Glory of the Martyrs* and *On the Glory of the Confessors*, because all later hagiography modelled itself on them and on three earlier ones: *The Life of St Anthony* by St Anastasius, *The Life of St Martin* by Sulpicius Severus and the *Dialogues* of St Gregory the Great. The significance of the medieval *Lives* lies not so much in the facts they relate as in the Christian ideal they typify. Other writings, some of them pastoral letters, more often decrees of Councils, point out the principles and the rules by which the saints attained to this ideal, and collections of prayers show how God and the saints were addressed.

Lastly there are works on asceticism and the life of prayer: all bear to a greater or lesser degree the stamp of St Gregory's teaching,[2] since very early on the great pope's writings had circulated widely. The *Moralia* were written for Leander, the future bishop of Seville, and St Braulion, bishop of Saragossa (†651), begs the monk Taion, who was to succeed him, to procure him the works of St Gregory.[3] The view that the monks whom Gregory sent from the monastery on the Coelian to England took with them or later received writings of his, is confirmed by the fact that some very ancient manuscripts are of English origin—St Columbanus, we noted, asked St Gregory for those of his works which he had not yet read.[4] Passages from St Gregory's writings were put together in the form of centos—like that of Taion of Saragossa[5]—or other compilations: many of them are found in the *Liber Scintillarum* of Defensor of Ligugé, an anthology of ascetical writings widely known throughout the Middle Ages.[6] St Martin of Braga and St Ildephonsus of Toledo and the other Spanish doctors borrowed exten-

[2] Cf. J. Leclerq, "Contemplation du VI au XII siècle", in *Dict. de spirit.*, II Paris, 1953, col. 1934–6.

[3] Edited by J. Madoz, *Epist. de S. Braulio de Zaragossa*, Madrid, 1941, pp. 184–185.

[4] See *supra*, p. 39.

[5] Ed. P.L., 80, 723–990.

[6] Ed. H. Rochais, in *Corpus christianorum*, 117, Turnhout, 1957, pp. I–XXXV, 1–308. In St Gregory's own lifetime one of his disciples had put together a commentary on Scripture from his writings. Cf. R. Etaix, the "Liber testimoniorum de Paterius", in *Rev. des Sciences Rel.*, XXXII (1958), pp. 66–78.

sively from him,[7] and the two most considerable writers of the period, St Isidore of Seville and the Venerable Bede, also made extensive use of him. The *Sentences* of St Isidore had a great influence. Bede, who admired St Augustine, was in some ways closer to St Gregory in his style and the psychological outlook revealed by his use of words.[8] He is probably the most original of the writers of the time. It was a period which took its ideas from the Fathers of an earlier age—particularly St Gregory, St Augustine, and St Jerome—and from the early monastic sources of St Basil and Cassian.[9] The question is how the ideas themselves were worked out.

2. *The States of Life*

A man's state of life determines the forms which his asceticism and prayer will take, but in this particular period it is not always easy to draw a hard and fast line between the different ways of Christian life: there is a reciprocal influence and mutual penetration in the different milieux. In the apparent confusion between them it is impossible to define the various categories of Christians, and this had been the case in the West since the fifth century. As a result of recent work on the sources for the period, several hypotheses have been put forward[10]; all that will be done here is to try to describe, relying on facts which appear to be established, a period whose very confusions had a decisive influence on later developments.

The role of the towns and cities, and above all the City *par excellence*, Rome, in the evangelization of the Continent after the barbarian invasion had no counterpart at first in Ireland. St Patrick and his successors had found no organized Christian communities; they had brought them into being in centres which subsequently became towns, and in scattered monasteries in waste lands. In Gaul and Italy it was as a rule the cities that had received the Faith and

[7] Cf. J. Fernández Alonso, *La cura pastoral en la España romanovisigoda*, Rome, 1955, pp. 112, 121–6 and *passim*.

[8] On Bede's sources, and his esteem for St Gregory, cf. M. L. W. Laistner, *The intellectual heritage of the early Middle Ages*, Ithaca, 1957, pp. 117–49: *The Library of the Venerable Bede*.

[9] For example, St Braulio in the letter cited above (see *supra* note 3, pp. 183–9) also asks for the *Conferences of Cassian*, and the *Lives* of St Honoratus ofLérins and St Germanus of Auxerre.

[10] Cf. B. Luyckx, "L'influence des moines sur l'office paroissiale", in *La Maison Dieu*, 51 (1957), pp. 55–81; E. Dekkers, "Les anciens moines cultivaient-ils la liturgie?", *ibid.*, pp. 31–54, and especially P. Salmon, "Aux origines du Bréviaire Romain", *ibid.*, 27 (1951), pp. 114–36. C. Dereine, art. "Chanoines", in *Dict. d'hist. et de géog. ecclés.*, XII, Paris, 1953, col. 362–4. S. J. P. van Dijk in *Sacris erudiri*, XII (1961), pp. 428–35. There is an excellent list of the monasteries of Rome from the fifth to the tenth centuries, showing which of them were basilical in G. Ferrari, O.S.B., *Early Roman Monasteries*, Rome, 1957.

kept it, and in many cases had become a refuge for monks driven from their solitude by the invaders. Some churches in the countryside—"presbyteries" or "oratories"—which were still in existence or had been restored, were served by individual clerics whose centre was an urban church—cathedral or basilica. To these churches were attached one or more communities: firstly the clergy proper, but in addition monks. The clergy, subject to the ecclesiastical canons, were sometimes called *canonici*, but neither in name nor in fact was there always a very clear distinction between the canonical and monastic community. Sometimes together they formed the basilical community, called the *monasterium*, and depending on the bishop. The bishop's representative or *vicarius* to whom was given the care of the Church and the clergy, was known as the *abbas*; so that the terms "monastery" and "abbot" now no longer meant exclusively the buildings or the superior of a monastic community. Even the word "monk" covered a great many categories of persons: it was used for the clergy or for monks serving a church in their place, and sometimes for one leading a devout life. *Monachus* was therefore synonymous according to circumstances with *clericus*, *vir ecclesiasticus* or *canonicus*; but it was also used for *pauper, frater, devouts, custos, serviens, conversus, penitens, oblatus, religiosus*. The same word could have very different meanings: in Spain, for example, *confessor* meant both the penitent who went to confession and the priest to whom he went; and since the monastic life is a life of penance it could also mean *monachus*.[11] It is, however, clear from the sources as a whole that often groups of fervent Christians formed themselves into one or more communities round a basilica. The members of these *monasteria*, containing both clerics and laymen, differed from the "eremitical" type of monk whose austere life was given to prayer in solitude: the chief mark of these basilican monks was their assiduous celebration of the public prayer of the Church. But as the rule of St Benedict, with its precise regulations of the monastic life, spread throughout Europe during the seventh and eighth centuries, there appears again a distinction between the different kinds of Christian ascetics, though as a result of the confusion of the earlier period the solemn celebration of the liturgy tended to become the chief work of the monks.

3. *The Penitents*

Though in practice it was not always clear, both in the writings of doctors like St Gregory and St Isidore and in the decrees of the

[11] Cf. J. Perez de Urbel, *Los Monjes españoles de la edad media*, Madrid, 1945, II, p. 175–6.

Councils, the distinction between the clergy, the monks and the laity existed in principle, and it could be seen that in spite of the ambiguity of the terms used there was a difference between the various states of life, each having a spirituality proper to itself. Among the laity themselves two classes of the faithful can be distinguished. The first consisted of Christians as a whole, the people, who lived what Bede calls the *vita popularis*[12]: they had been taught the duties of the Christian life as catechumens (the *de cognitione baptismi* of St Ildephonsus of Toledo shows what a high level this teaching could reach).[13] This training was kept up by the ordinary preaching which was enjoined on the clergy by the Councils, and at a betrothal or wedding definite teaching was given on the unity and indissolubility of marriage, the mutual duties and respective rights of husband and wife, and the obligation of fidelity on the part of the husband.[14] In spite of all this it would seem that the faith of the people as a whole was fairly unenlightened. Their simplicity and credulity inclined them towards the marvellous, and led them into superstition and magic, errors which the pastoral care of the bishops and their helpers tried to remedy. In addition to these "ordinary" Christians there was also a lay élite which gathered round the monasteries and churches, made up of fervent souls who had determined to do penance in the state of "conversion".[15] Some of them were fulfilling or prolonging a public penance imposed for grave sin, others were voluntary "penitents". Some of the men retired permanently into solitude, for a longer or shorter period, but the majority lived in the city either in a community or in their own home. This was usually the practice of the women who became penitents: widows who in order to lead a devout life would not marry again, and girls who wished to embrace the state of virginity could live *in domibus propriis*. Both men and women undertook to dress simply, to attend assiduously the offices of the Church, to give themselves to private prayer and an austere life, living in perfect chastity or, if married, in continence. This *ordo* or *status poenitentium* was under the care of the bishop or of an abbot of a community of monks or clerics. It was a particular state of life, different from that of the ordinary laity or the clergy, more like that of

[12] Letter to Egbert of York, n. 15, edited by C. Plummer, *Ven. Bedae opera historica*, Oxford, 1896, p. 418.

[13] P.L., 96, 111–92. Another example of catechesis is in the *de correctione rusticorum* of St Martin of Braga († about 579), ed. C. W. Barlow, *S. Martini episcopi Bracarensis opera*, New Haven, 1950, pp. 183–203.

[14] Cf. J. Fernández Alonso, *op. cit.*, pp. 415–34.

[15] Cf. C. Vogel, *La discipline pénitentielle en Gaule des origines à la fin du VIIe siècle*, Paris, 1952, pp. 102–203; J. Fernández Alonso, *op. cit.*, p. 542 and *passim*; G. Meersseman, O.P., and E. Adda, "Pénitents ruraux communautaires en Italie au XII siècle", in *Rev. d'hist. ecclés.*, XLIX (1954), pp. 344–5, note 5.

religious though not to be confused with it. It was a kind of third order or more precisely a secular institute, entry into which was by means of a promise described by words like *conversio, propositium, professio* or *religio*.[16]

The fact that these groups of fervent lay people came into existence was not without its effect on the subsequent history of spirituality. These penitents lived in fear of the Judgment; they kept up in themselves and around them a sense of sin, and they showed the demands of austerity to the uncouth society of their time. They found in confession and spiritual direction the consolation they needed. The rites of reconciliation, linked as they are with the paschal mystery, upheld them in Christian hope. These generous souls attended the liturgy and offices of the Church assiduously, but for the most part they were illiterate. Formulas of prayer easily learnt by heart were composed to help their private devotion, such as litanies or series of invocations to our Lady. A short penitential known as that of St Boniface makes a distinction between the prayer which consists of psalmody (*psallere*) and that made up of Paternosters (*patere*)[17]: this word, which is also found elsewhere,[18] is not limited to the Our Father but applies equally to the Hail Mary and the lesser prayers, with which both of these were surrounded in the "Little offices" which were an equivalent penance to a whole or a third of a psalter (150 or 50 psalms) or the same number of other prayers.[19] The rosary and many other later forms of piety are remotely foreshadowed in the prayers of the penitents.

4. *The Pastors*

As the spiritual life of the laity was nourished by the clergy, so they in their turn received from the bishops all that they needed for their ministry: authority, rules of conduct and ideals. The duties of a churchman had been laid down by St Gregory the Great, not only in the *Pastoral Rule*, written for bishops, but also in other writings, particularly in the *Commentary on the Book of Kings*, where he often draws a parallel between the role of the king in Israel and the bishop in the Church. His teaching was absorbed

[16] Cf. P. Galtier, "Pénitents et 'convertis'", in *Rev. d'hist. ecclés.*, XXXIII (1937), 1–26, 277–305; art. "Conversi", in *Dict. de spiritualité*, II (1953), col. 2218–24.

[17] "Si minus vult psallere et non vult patere", ed. J. Schneller, *Liturgia sacra*, Lucerne, 1840, vol. III, p. XIII. Cf. G. G. Meersseman, O.P., "Der Hymnos Akathistos", in *Abendland*, II, Fribourg, 1960, pp. 10–11.

[18] Cf. Du Cange on the word "patere".

[19] See *supra*, p. 44. G. Meersseman, O.P., in *Freiburger Zeitschrift für Philosophie und Theologie*, I (1954), pp. 145–6, has shown that from the eighth century onwards the praises of the names and attributes of Mary are more and more found in the form of litanies.

and put into practice. Indeed in those terrible times when the people often lacked leaders and examples, many bishops were the columns which supported the city spiritual and even temporal. After their death their lives were written down and read in the divine office as an ever-present example. The holiness of their life, the zeal and charity they had shown in their preaching and in the help they gave their neighbour in every need were thus brought to the attention of all men.

The bishops' own actions and those of the Councils in which they met together tended little by little to make of the clergy what they should never have ceased to be: an order. Too often they had lacked that organization which alone could uphold and preserve their moral life and safeguard their spirituality.[20] The pastoral ideal worked out by St Gregory had ceaselessly to be inculcated into them, and they had to be given the means of fulfilling it. St Gregory's programme formed a whole: it is only for the sake of clarity that its various points are described separately. The first was to recall to their obedience those of the clergy who had loosened the ties which bound them to the bishop: either wandering clerics, or priests in the service of great lords, living in their *villae* in the country districts. They were uneducated, and, free from all ecclesiastical control or stimulus, they were liable to every moral weakness. St Isidore speaks of them as "acephalous, that is headless, clerics" in contrast with "ecclesiastics, those who are ruled by the bishop".[21] To bind them again to authority meant bringing them back to a stable life, to living in a fixed place both on account of their pastoral duties and to preserve the purity of their morals; for in these times of confusion and brutality the notion of a celibate clergy became more and more general, and took the form of law for priests, deacons and subdeacons: those who exercise a ministry in the Church must be pure in body and soul. Men's weakness naturally failed in many cases to respond to such a demand, but the Councils and the doctors of the Church were never weary of calling it to mind. The common life was one of the methods advocated to help the clergy to live chastely. It existed in varying degrees in different places and at different times, but it prepared the way for what was to develop into the institution of canons regular.

The bond which united the clergy to the bishop was most clearly seen in the celebration of the Divine Office. The clergy of the city and country parishes were responsible as a whole under the direction of the bishop for preaching, administering the sacraments and

[20] Cf. R. Laprat, "Le sacerdoce chrétien du VI au IX siècle", in *Prêtres de hier et d'aujourd'hui*, Paris, 1954, pp. 63–111.
[21] *De eccles. off.*, II, III, 1; P.L., 83, 779.

celebrating public worship. The latter, however, did not take place in each church or oratory every day, or indeed every Sunday; if possible the clergy and laity gathered round the bishop and his cathedral clergy for the Eucharist and certain offices, notably Matins and some of those canonical Hours whose *cursus* was gradually being fixed.[22] As the clergy met successively in different churches, the whole office was not said in any one of them, nor were the clergy individually bound to its entire recitation.[23] The writings of the period dwell more on the communal aspect of piety, with participation in the public worship of the Church as its principal act, than on private devotion.

Finally, the pastoral duties of the clergy assumed different forms, according to time and place: it was sometimes a question of keeping up the Faith among nations who were already Christian, or evangelizing those who had not yet received it. There is very little indication of the methods of conversion to be employed, but on the other hand a ceaseless insistence on the necessary condition of all pastoral work—worthiness of life in the pastor—for how he lives is as important as how he preaches. In particular he must show himself disinterested over money or other payments which may be offered him in return for his services.

Bede's admirable letter, written to Egbert of York in 734, gives an idea how high a spiritual life could be set before a bishop and his clergy towards the end of this period.[24] It begins with a reminder of St Paul's instructions to Timothy and Titus, and of St Gregory's in the *Pastoral Rule* and the Homilies on the Gospels, and goes on to describe in detail the duties of a pastor towards the faithful of so many different kinds, whose faith he has to nurture. It is impossible to summarize, but it breathes that exquisite spirit of charity which is at pains to adapt itself to all men. The laity, or those among them who do not understand Latin, are to learn the Creed and the Lord's prayer in their own tongue; they are to be taught to say them daily and even to sing them, so that there may spring up in them a love of the truths they contain. They are to be told to bless themselves frequently, and it is to be pointed out to them "how salutary it is for every kind of Christian to receive each day the Body and Blood of the Lord". Even married people, provided they show a certain degree of continence, might often be able to "receive the heavenly mysteries". As for the ministers of the Church, purity of life and the absence of every kind of greed will help them to "feed their

[22] Cf. P. Salmon, *Le lectionnaire de Luxeuil,* II, Rome, 1953, pp. 57–64.

[23] Cf. P. Salmon, "Obligation de la célébration de l'office", in *L'office divin,* Paris, 1959, pp. 86–9.

[24] Ed. Plummer, *op. cit.,* pp. 405–23, and P.L., 94, 657–8.

flocks", aided by the grace of Jesus, the "supreme Shepherd" and the model of all pastors.

5. *The Influence of the Monasteries*

One of the dominant characteristics of the period, and important in a picture of the times, is the place given to monasticism.[25] In the Christian communities which were already in existence or which were coming into being, monks kept the ascetic ideal at a very high level and gave an example of prayer—lessons which the clergy, laity and bishops profited by; indeed in many cases the latter themselves were monks, and if they were not they are sometimes made to appear as such in the *Lives* which recount their virtues (one of the reasons for the popularity of the *Lives* of St Radegund was that she was a nun as well as a queen). The monasticism of the period is not easy to describe because, great as was its influence, it cannot be seen as a definite order. Only little by little (as with the clergy and the laity) did a definite organization appear, and this was due in part to the Benedictine Rule from which it took its form. During the seventh century the Rule is increasingly attributed to the abbot of Monte Cassino whose miracles had been recounted by St Gregory, and it gradually became the "Rule of Monks" to the exclusion of other rules which were less precise or poorer in wisdom and moderation.

Yet for two centuries monasticism continued to prosper under what has been called the *regula mixta*,[26] and the state of monastic law is reflected by its way of life. As has been seen, in the "monasteries" in the sense that the word often has at this time, the liturgy came to play a greater part, and to that extent the monks worked less with their hands. Monks were more often clerics; they served the altar and so had the right to live by the altar. Thus by their functions, and as property owners, there came to be points of similarity between the monastic and canonical orders. The majority of the monastic rules drawn up during this period do not so much lay down an observance as set forth a programme of asceticism; the *Rule of Monks* of St Columbanus is an example, and other writings whose dates and authors are not known exactly are of the same

[25] R. Oliger, "Le Monachisme mérovingien", in *La Vie spirituelle*, LXXIII (1945), pp. 56–69 has given a general account of it.

[26] Cf. K. Hallinger, "Papst Gregor der Grosse und der Hl. Benedikt", in *Commentationes in Regulam S. Benedicti*, Rome (*Studia Anselmiana*, 42), 1957, pp. 259–70; 318–19; G. Penco, "La prima diffusione della Regola di S. Benedetto", *ibid.*, pp. 335–9; G. Marié, "Ste Radegonde et le milieu monastique contemporain", in *Études mérovingiennes*, Paris, 1953, pp. 219–25. C. Dereine, *loc. cit.*, col. 358–62.

nature.[27] Sometimes one or the other of these rules was adopted, and sometimes borrowings were made from several of them; indeed in Spain there grew up little by little those compilations, the *codices regularum*, which became handbooks for the use of abbots.[28] In some places the usage followed that of the *Regula Patrum* or *Regula Macarii* which was later called *The Rule of the Master*. In other places a different rule, or a combination of several rules, was followed; and the many Celtic foundations meant that the *Rules* of St Columbanus predominated to some extent; until as time went on the Benedictine *Rule* asserted itself, little by little. Its advantage was that it laid down a precise and complete observance, making a distinction between clerical and monastic life, and so could take the place of other rules. Various historical circumstances, especially, it appears, the influence of the papacy,[29] contributed to its adoption; and from the second half of the eighth century onwards the "Benedictine centuries"[30] succeeded what has been called the Celtic age.

All the Rules, however, including that of St Benedict drew on ancient sources[31]: the teaching of St Basil and the Fathers of the Desert, and of St Augustine, too. They owed much to ideals common to the founders of monasticism both in the East and in the West, and the writings of Cassian and the ancient monks were also known. St Martin of Braga had caused a translation of the *Verba Seniorum* to be made and had himself made an anthology of the *Sententiae Patrum*. St Martin of Tours was considered the perfect type of holiness, because he had been at the same time a monk, a bishop, a missionary and a wonder-worker: he had proclaimed before men, before the great ones of this world, and before the devils, the absolute choice that man must make of God. In writing about him, Sulpicius Severus had illustrated all the essential activities of the Christian life, and his *Life* during the following centuries was copied, read, put into verse, summarized, imitated and enlarged upon in every way.[32] For hagiography, which is the faithful reflection of its period, the man of God was no longer the martyr but the confessor, whose witness lies in the asceticism of the monastic

[27] C. Gindele, "Die römische und monastische Uberlieferung im ordo officii der Regel St Benedikts", in *Commentationes*, pp. 172–4, gives a list of these Rules with their dates when these are known.

[28] A. Mundò, "Il Monachesimò nella penisola iberica fino al sec. VII", in *Il Monachesimo nell'alto medioevo e la formazione della civilità occidentale*, Spoleto, 1957, pp. 72–108, especially pp. 95–101.

[29] Cf. T. Leccisotti, "Aspetti e problemi del monachesimo in Italia", in *Il Monachesimo*, pp. 318–19; E. Franceschini, *ibid.*, pp. 501–6.

[30] Cf. J. O'Carroll, "Monastic Rules in Merovingian Gaul", in *Studies*, XLII (1953), p. 418.

[31] C. Butler, *S. Benedicti Regula Monachorum editionem critico-practicam*, Freiburg, 1912.

[32] Cf. C. A. Bernouilli, *Die Heiligen der Merovinger*, Tübingen, 1900, p. 33.

profession, which had become both the new form of martyrdom and the *militia Christi*.

A revealing example of the current conception of a monk and his place in the Church is preserved in a sermon by an anonymous Spanish bishop of the end of the sixth or beginning of the seventh century.[33] Preaching before clerics and laymen an encomium on what he calls "monks", its author distinguishes between those who live in solitude in the desert and those who live in cities: the latter, he says, are even more meritorious, since though they live near their fellow men, yet they do not allow themselves to be deceived by the mirage of fleshly desires; they live the common life according to a rule, and do works of mercy (the bishop does not say that they preach the Gospel); their prayer is in hymns and psalms and canticles of praise and in the Sacrifice of our salvation. They find in all this a prayer of the heart: *psalmis et canticis spiritualibus . . . corde orent, mente psallant*. They are cut off and separated from men, but they know themselves to be in communion with the whole Church. "With them are all the holy patriarchs, prophets, and martyrs; they know that the apostles and all the other priests, indeed the whole Church of Christ, is with them to strengthen them: and together they exult in Christ." The idea that the monks pray for the clergy and laity is not suggested; rather are they in need of the help of the Church in order to remain faithful to their calling. At all events they give themselves up to psalmody as to a privileged labour. For a monk, unlike a cleric, was personally bound to say the Divine Office (though this obligation was later laid on the clergy too); the Benedictine Rule prescribes that those who are absent from the prayer in common must make it up by saying it in private, if possible at the same time as the community is reciting that canonical Hour; since in all monastic churches all the Hours must be celebrated each day. Moreover, it presupposes the stability of the monk: and under the influence of the Benedictine rule monasticism had moved towards stability. There were still a great many hermits living in isolation, more or less attached to a community, but the number of wandering monks tended to diminish. In England especially, monasticism harmonized the various forms and aspirations of Christian asceticism. Bede, in the *Story of St Cuthbert*, shows the saint preaching the Gospel to the ignorant, living the common life with his brethren, and then, with their approval

[33] Ed. M. C. Diaz y Diaz, *Anecdota Wisigothica*, I, Salamanca, 1958, p. 82, on the question of date, see *ibid.*, pp. 74–9. On monasticism in the Iberian peninsula in the Visigothic period (sixth–seventh century), cf. C. Barant, art. "Éspagne", in *Dict. de spirit.*, IV (1961), col. 1099–103. On spiritual writers—St Martin of Braga, St Leander of Seville, St Isidore, SS Ildephonus and Julian of Toledo—cf. *ibid.*, col. 1103–7.

and the consent of his abbot, going away to find solitude on Farne Island, "leisure for divine reflection", and he holds that to pass from the active to the contemplative life is to mount upwards.[34]

In Spain and elsewhere there existed double monasteries, of two separate communities, one of monks and the other of nuns, living near each other under a common Rule.[35] The monastic life for women, whether in these double monasteries or where there was no like community of monks, developed along the same lines as that of the monks. The nuns lived under the same rule and led a similar life.[36] They manifested their conscience to their "abbess" who is their "spiritual mother".[37] They had the same longing to leave their country and as exiles to go on pilgrimage to Rome. St Boniface agrees that an abbess, who because of the cares of her position can no longer enjoy "the quiet of the life of contemplation" in her monastery, can find again "freedom to contemplate" by becoming a pilgrim.[38] During his career as a missionary he turned to St Lioba and other nuns, who came to his help by prayer and by copying out books he had need of. He was in correspondence with several among them, and their letters to each other, full of what he calls "a spiritual love" and "a friendship of the Spirit",[39] written with such tenderness and at times with such ardour, show what grace could do in these souls. Though the society of the period was violent and warlike, yet for some in the monastic life an exquisite sensibility could be joined to an ardent generosity.[40]

Two names, at the end of this period, symbolize two aspects of monasticism. St Bede at Jarrow is the type of the scholar monk, never leaving his cloister and dividing his time between prayer and study[41]; his life, like his writings and his teachings, is serene[42];

[34] *Vita Cuthberti*, ch. 9 and 16–17, ed. B. Colgrave, *Two Lives of St Cuthbert*, Cambridge, 1940, pp. 184 and 206–16.

[35] Cf. S. Hilpisch, *Die Doppelklöster*, Münster, 1929; Fernandez Alonso, *op. cit.*, pp. 492–7.

[36] Cf. J. Rambaud-Buhot, "Le statut des moniales chez les Pères de l'Église, dans les Règles Monastiques et les collections canoniques jusqu'au XII siècle", in *Ste Fare et Faremoutiers*, Faremoutiers, 1956, pp. 149–74; P. Schmitz, *Histoire de l'ordre de St Benoît*, VII, Maredsous, 1956, pp. 9–44.

[37] Text in Vogel, *op. cit.*, pp. 159–60; letter of Eangytha and Bugga to St Boniface, ed. M. Tangl, *S. Bonifatii et Lulli epist.*, in *Mon. Germ. Hist. script. rer, germanici nova series*, I, Berlin, 1955, ep. 14, p. 25. The expression "spiritual mother" is one going back to antiquity in the East. Cf. I. Hausherr, *Direction spirituelle en Orient autrefois*, Rome, 1955, p. 261.

[38] Letter of Eangytha and Bugga, *loc. cit.*, p. 26.

[39] *Epist.*, XCIV, p. 215. *Epist.*, XXVII, p. 48, ed. Tangl.

[40] See Montalembert, *Monks of the West*, vol. II, pp. 709–24, New York, 1905.

[41] See also J. H. Newman, "The Mission of St Benedict", in *Historical Sketches*, London, 1890, vol. II, pp. 428–40.

[42] His teaching has been studied by M. T. A. Carrol, *The Venerable Bede, his spiritual teaching*, Washington, 1946, especially on prayer, pp. 198–215; cf. also

St Boniface tells us of himself that he was tormented by two feelings, "*amor Christi et amor peregrinationis*".[43] The latter is that form of asceticism which Celtic monks so often practised—exile[44]: Boniface left his own country, like Abraham, and in 716 went from his English monastery of Nursling to the Continent.[45] There, various circumstances and the voice of God within him led him to evangelize Thuringia and Friesland and other neighbouring countries. He went back to ask the pope, Gregory II, to confirm him in his mission, and returned to preach and to found churches and monasteries; he became bishop of Germany, went thence to Gaul where he worked to reform the Frankish Church; and was martyred in 754 near Dokkum in Friesland.

Monks and nuns were his helpers in the work of evangelization, but they must not be seen in terms of modern missionaries, dispersed over the countryside, preaching and working. This was only true of some of them; on the whole it was not so much the monks as the monasteries which planted the Faith: they became centres of religious life and of culture in every sense of the word. In them learning was acquired, children who would afterwards become monks or priests were educated, and men were taught to cultivate the land.[46] As this network of civilization slowly spread as had the old Roman settlements, fresh churches were founded and new monasteries established. Yet these monks still lived in accordance with their true vocation of men vowed to prayer and penance in the cloister. Thus when St Rambert, who was not himself a recruit for the monastic life but for preaching the Gospel in Scandinavia, left the abbey of Corvey where he had been staying, he took with him only one monk of the monastery, with the consent of the abbot and community.[47] The monastery founded at Werden by St Liutger,

F. Vernet, art. "Bède le Vénérable", in *Dict. de spirit.*, I, Paris, 1937, col. 1322–9 See *infra.*, p. 66.

[43] *Epist.*, XCIV, ed. Tangl, p. 214.

[44] Cf. J. Leclerq, "Mönchtum und Peregrinatio in Frümittelalter", in *Römische Quartalschrift*, LV (1960), pp. 212–25; and "Le monachisme du haut moyen âge", in *Théologie de la vie monastique*, Paris (Aubier), 1961, pp. 437–45.

[45] That Boniface left his own country not only to preach the Gospel, but also to practise a more perfect detachment is made clear by his biographers. S. Willibald, *Vita Bonifacii*, 4, ed. W. Levison, *Vitae S. Bonifatii*, Hanover–Leipzig, 1905, pp. 15–16; the author of the *Vita altera*, ch. 7, who recalls Abraham (Gen. 24, 17; 12) and says that Boniface went into exile to find martyrdom, ch. 7, *ibid.*, p. 17; *Otloh of St Emmeran*, I, 5, *ibid.*, pp. 121–9; and finally St Liutger, *Vita S. Gregorii Traiectensis*, ch. 3, ed. W. Diekamp, Münster, 1881, p. 70.

[46] Cf. S. Hilpisch, "Bonifatius als Mönch und Missionar", in *Sankt Bonifatius*, Fulda, 1954, p. 21; and especially E. de Moreau, art. "Boniface (saint)", in *Dict. d'hist. et géog. ecclés.*, IX, Paris, 1937, col. 892–3.

[47] *Vita Rimberti*, ed. G. Waitz, in *Scrip. Rer. Germ.*, *vita Anskarii*, Hanover 1884, ch. 12, pp. 90–1, ch. 21, p. 97.

Bishop of Münster, was one of contemplatives.[48] There are plenty of similar examples[49] to show that though there were monk apostles, monasticism as an institution was not apostolic except in the old sense of the word. The monks lived a life of renunciation in common, working for the missionaries as much as the life of the cloister allowed; in particular copying manuscripts needed by a Boniface or an Ansgar.

The monks were therefore not a substitute for the clergy. St Boniface makes a clear distinction between their respective parts in the work of evangelization. Speaking of his helpers he writes: "they are almost all exiles, *peregrini*: some are priests stationed in various places to serve the Church and minister to the people; others are monks living in *cellae* and children who are being educated".[50] The biographer of St Lioba who had come from England into Germany to train the nuns there, says of Boniface that "he built monasteries so that the people should be enchanted with the Faith, not so much by the action of churchmen (*gratia ecclesiastica*) as by the communities of monks and consecrated virgins". He brought over clergy, but also and perhaps even to a greater extent he organized a regular monastic life.[51] It was said of St Ansgar that he remained completely a monk: *foris apostolus, intus monachus*,[52] and the same phrase could be applied to St Boniface. The latter advised Lietbert, archbishop of Canterbury, to preach with courage according to St Gregory's teaching in his *Pastoral Rule*,[53] and was himself an example of this zeal. Judging by his letters and the stories told by his biographers, his piety, exhortations and teaching were limited to the fundamental doctrines of a simple catechesis, those of the synoptic Gospels and St Paul's writings on Christian morality. He spent no time in explaining the theory of the demands that the kingdom of God makes on the Christian; but he emphasized the necessity of fleeing all sin, of a humble service of one's neighbour, of faith and confidence in God, and he taught the power of prayer and the happiness of the everlasting reward. His teaching

[48] Cf. J. Leclercq, "St Liutger dans la tradition monastique", in *La Vie spirituelle*, Feb., 1960, pp. 144–60. German translation in *Erbe und Auftrag*, XXXVII (1961), pp. 292–305.

[49] Cf. J. Leclercq, "St Anschaire", in *La Vie spirituelle*, XLI (1960). "A monk is not by his profession a missionary," wrote E. de Moreau in *Un Missionaire en Scandinavie au IX siècle, St Anschaire*, Louvain, 1932, p. 24, in accounting for the problems brought about by the slowness and retreats in the spread of the Gospel, in Germanic lands.

[50] *Epist.*, XCIII, ed. Tangl, p. 213.

[51] Rudolph of Fulda, *Vita Leobae*, 10, ed. *Mon. Germ. Hist. Scriptores*, XV p. 125.

[52] Adam of Bremen, *Gesta Pontif. Hammaburg.*, I, 35; *Mon. Germ. Hist. Scriptores*, VII, p. 297.

[53] *Epist.*, LXXVIII, ed. Tangl, p. 169.

has been sometimes called "monastic", but it was probably what was needed by the Germans, who were receiving the Gospel for the first time.[54] St Boniface neglected none of the missionary labours which had been entrusted to him, but it is the fact that his work was a monastic one that merited for it the name of apostolate. Following the first disciples of our Lord, he had given up his family and his native land to serve God in complete disinterestedness. This monk, by doing much for the reform of the clergy in Gaul and their establishment in the German lands, crowned the work of the Church in this long and stormy period; he was the precursor of the Carolingian renewal.

6. *The Christian Hero*

The foregoing is a panoramic sketch of the Christian life of the laity, the clergy and the monks. It remains to point out the elements common to the whole spirituality of the period, both in asceticism and prayer. In the field of asceticism the first thing to be noted is that while in St Gregory the largest place is taken by questions of intention and interior purification, From now onwards practices of exterior mortification rank first. During these centuries in which the new Christian nations were emerging from barbarism, an intense need was felt for outward penance, though even with regard to this an evolution took place.[55] At the beginning, the violence of men's nature and the unchecked prestige of the ascetic powers of certain Egyptian solitaries had had the effect of giving a marked preference to extreme forms of austerity. The Christian hero—*sacer heros, miles Christi* as he is often called in the *Lives* of the time—who wishes to fight against his passions, flees from the world, takes refuge in solitude, undertaking the severest fasts and sometimes eccentricities of which the authority of the Church disapproves. Thus the deacon Walfroy in the sixth century tries to imitate Simeon Stylites by spending the winter with bare feet on a pillar in the harsh climate of the country round Trier. "You are on the wrong road", say the bishops, "because you have not taken into consideration what kind of a country this is."[56] But little by little, as monasticism became organized, and life everywhere more stable, asceticism took on more moderate forms. It was not that men were

[54] On this see the penetrating pages of J. Lortz, "Untersuchungen zur missionsmethod und zur Frömmigkeit des Hl. Bonifatius nach seinen Briefen", in N. Götzinger, *Willibrordus*, Luxemburg, 1940 (re-printed 1958), pp. 247–83.

[55] Cf. K. Weber, "Kulturgeschichtliche Probleme der Merovingerzeit in Spiegel frühmittelaltlichen Heiligenleben", in *Studien und Mitteilungen zur Gesch. des Bened. Ordens*, XLVIII (1930), pp. 347–403.

[56] St Gregory of Tours, *Hist. Francorum*, VIII, 15, ed. *Mon. Germ. Hist. Script. rer. Merov.*, I, 333–6.

less generous, but that their generosity found expression in a charity directed more towards the common good. It was a time when wars, with the horrors they brought with them, were frequent; and the bishops and the monks canalized the zeal of the fervent for the social benefit of Christian civilization: the exercise of various crafts, agriculture, building and rebuilding, the care of deserted children and the poor and the sick, the redemption of captives and the relief of prisoners.[57]

There was a certain danger in these developments. There had been a risk of extravagance in the absolute and unchecked flight from the world: the fact that in the eighth century the Church was taking her place in the secular economy made for a certain attachment to the goods of this world. Some hermits had refused gifts of land as though the offer were a temptation[58]: but from the Carolingian period onwards monasteries produce forged charters or falsify the *Lives* of saints in order to assert their rights over huge territories.[59] Between these two opposing tendencies, it was the mark of true asceticism to choose the mean which suited the time and the place.

However different might be the form they took, the same feeling lay behind all these mortifications: men were vitally conscious of their condition as sinners. The scenes of cruelty and corruption which they witnessed and the vehemence of their own passions made clear to them how great was the gap between men and the ideals of the Gospel. They waited for the judgment of God not only, indeed not chiefly, on their own soul and life, but on this sinful world: their minds were filled with the last and universal judgment rather than with the particular judgment. As far as this latter was concerned it could in some sense be forestalled by confession of sins. St Isidore had said, "It is most true that the just man judges himself in this life that he may not be condemned by God to an eternal punishment. A man judges himself when he punishes his evil deeds by doing penance."[60] The saint's long treatise, *Synonyms on the lamentations of a sinful soul*,[61] elaborates the theme of contempt of self and of all that is of this world, and encourages in a soul a desire to find God by the path of renunciation and expiation. His fundamental idea is that of compunction, which he sums up on St Gregory's lines.

Absolute separation from the world took the forms of vowing

57 Text in Weber, *art. cit.*, pp. 372–403.

58 St Gregory of Tours, *Vitae patrum*, 5, *Mon. Germ. Hist. Script. rer. Merov.*, I, 667, quotes the example of St Lupicinus.

59 Cf. W. Levison, *Die Politik der Jenzeitsvisionen des frühen Mittelalters, Aus Rheinischer und Fränkischer Frühzeit*, Düsseldorf, 1948, pp. 230–46.

60 *Sent.*, II, 13, 2–3; P.L., 83, 614.

61 P.L., 83, 825–68.

virginity; becoming a monk or hermit; living in a foreign land, *peregre*, either permanently or for the duration of a particular journey, and exposing oneself to the dangers and fatigues inherent in a pilgrim existence, not excepting the perils that it might sometimes involve for virtue itself. These risks, however, were lessened by the control exercised by ecclesiastical authority over the pilgrims' itinerary, and by the hospices which charity had provided along their way.[62] The monasteries of women played their part also in keeping before men the ideal of a life entirely detached from the world and completely vowed to the search for God. St Aldhelm (†709) sings in prose and verse the praises of virginity, taking as his examples the Fathers of the desert, the monks of old, the saints, men and women, of Rome and of the Old Testament; and he reminds his hearers of St Gregory's teaching on the subject.[63] To the nuns, his disciples, he recommends, without giving them precise instructions, prayer and assiduous meditation on the Scriptures.[64] The *Method of living well* by St Martin of Braga, written to a king for the laymen who are his helpers, is more a treatise on morals than on spirituality, being an exposition of the four cardinal virtues, taken from Seneca without any reference to Revelation.[65] It was often copied—a proof that the natural virtues were also appreciated in those rough times. But to know to what heights of austerity the fervent Christian could attain one must go, though with the precautions needed by this kind of literature, to the *Lives* of those many saints who were putting into practice the precepts of the Gospel.

7. *Prayer*

An exact distinction cannot always be made between the writings meant for liturgical worship and those whose object is to nourish personal devotion, any more than it is always easy to see clearly the difference between the various states of life. To begin with, the piety of the age was communal, consisting in the first place of taking part in the eucharistic sacrifice. During the whole of this period Mass was celebrated more frequently, and gradually it became the rule for the Holy Sacrifice to be offered daily. The Divine Office—called *cursus horae, opus Dei, officium, ordo ecclesiasticus*—which was made up of the canonical Hours for different times of day and the *vigiliae* for the evening or night office, was at first proper to monks, but little by little became part of the duty of

[62] Cf. Vogel, *op. cit.*, 160–3; W. Levison, *England and the Continent in the Eighth Century*, Oxford, 1946, pp. 36–44. H. von Campenhausen, *op. cit.* Tübingen, 1930, pp. 24–9.

[63] Ed. *Mon. Germ. Hist. Auct. antiq.*, vol. XV.

[64] *Epist.*, VI, *ibid.*, p. 497; VII, p. 500.

[65] Ed. Barlow, pp. 231–50.

the clergy.[66] For everyone, clergy, monks and laymen, the pastoral importance of the liturgy was very great: it put before them the spiritual values of Christianity by means of readings from the Bible and the Fathers; and the sermons they heard at Mass spoke to them of Sunday which is always a renewal of Easter, and the other seasons and feasts which recall the mysteries of our salvation. The *laus perennis*, that is a psalmody uninterrupted by day or night, was carried out in different ways in some monasteries by relays of monks[67]; in the majority of the others the Office was sung in church when the clergy and faithful took part in it, and in an oratory when the monks were alone.[68]

The foundation of all these liturgical offices, the book which fashioned the piety of the Middle Ages, was the Psalter: it was by spelling it out that men learnt to read, as many of the *Lives* of the saints[69] and other documents[70] show. However—and this is important—the Church did not give the psalms to the faithful "in the raw", so to speak, without a commentary. In manuscript every psalm had titles which pointed out its meaning.[71] Since the psalms were considered difficult to comprehend, a key was given to them by short phrases explaining their prophetic meaning, so that by this means they might be understood and loved. It was in the christological rather than the allegorical or moral sense that they were prophetic, since every psalm was held to have been said by Christ, written in foreknowledge of his redemptive work, or meant to be recited in reference to the mysteries of his life. There are many series of these "Christian titles to the psalms", some dating from the fifth and sixth centuries, others older, and they were all in widespread use till the thirteenth century. They took their inspiration from the Latin and Greek Fathers, and especially from Origen; and they formed one of the essential elements of the piety of the times. "Collects" or prayers were said after each psalm for the particular Christian grace of which it was the occasion: there were also various series of these.[72] Finally there were epitomes containing only one

66 Cf. P. Salmon in *La Maison Dieu*, 27 (1951), pp. 128–31.

67 Cf. P. Cousin, "La psalmodie chorale dans la Règle de St Colomban", in *Mélanges colombaniens*, Paris, 1951, pp. 186–9, and G. Gindele, "Die Gallikanischen 'laus Perennis'—Klöster und ihr 'ordo officii'", in *Rev. bénéd.*, LXIX (1959), pp. 32–48.

68 Cf. P. F. Anson, "The Evolution of the Monastic Choir", in *Downside Review*, LXVII (1949), pp. 184–7.

69 Cf. P. Riché, "Le psautier livre de lecture élémentaire d'après les vies des saints mérovingiens", in *Études mérovingiennes*, pp. 253–6.

70 E.g. St Valeris, *Replicatio sermonum a prima conversione*, n. 6, ed. C. M. Aherne, *Valerio of Bierzo, an ascetic of the late Visigothic period*, Washington, 1949, p. 129.

71 Cf. P. Salmon, *op. cit., supra*, p. 44, note 75.

72 Ed. L. Brou, *The Psalter Collects*, London, 1949, Henry Bradshaw Society.

or two verses of each psalm which together made up a kind of synthesis which was sometimes divided into three long prayers, each corresponding to fifty of the psalms: their object was to sustain private prayer.[73] Other formulas—prayers, hymns, litanies—were in use either in public worship or to sustain the personal devotion of the clergy, monks or penitents. Several things that are later found in the Breviary go back to this period, and the *Visigothic Book of Prayers* dating from the beginning of the eighth century contains some prayers which were written for liturgical use.[74] Others which are found in the *Book of Cerne* and the Carolingian[75] *Libelli precum* also date from this time. Thus in the seventh and eighth centuries in different countries there existed an ancient and to some extent common fund of *preces*, which were called *privatae, peculiares, furtivae.*[76] These collections of prayers were compiled chiefly in Celtic and Anglo-Saxon circles (the one influencing the other), though this kind of devotion seems, to begin with, to have been practised chiefly among the Irish. As these prayers, inspired by the liturgy though used apart from it, answered the needs of many, they soon spread into England and the Continent. In the first half of the ninth century particularly, they were brought together in separate little books, or added to the backs of many of the beautiful psalters of the Carolingian age. They went on being copied until the coming into use first of manuscripts, then of printed books of Hours, in which moreover many of them found a place.[77]

At this time devotion turned especially towards the Cross of our Lord,[78] towards the relics and tombs of saints, and towards the Mother of God. Many of the compositions of the Visigothic collection are addressed to her,[79] and St Ildephonsus and his imita-

'Où en est la question des psalter collects?", in *Studia patristica*, Berlin, 1957, II, pp. 17–20.

[73] Cf. L. Brou, "Les psautiers manuscrits Esc. A III-5, Toulouse 144 et leur 'Psalterium abbreviatum' final", in *Hispania Sacra*, IX (1956), pp. 379–90; and V. Jomeras, in *Rev. d'hist eccl.*, LIII (1958), pp. 211–12.

[74] Ed. J. Vivès, *Oracional visigotico*, Barcelona, 1946; on the question of date see p. XIII.

[75] See *infra*, pp. 88f.

[76] For their names, especially the last, see the texts noted by A. Wilmart in *Rev. bénéd.*, XLVI (1936), p. 291, n. 1, and P.L., 101, 468 A. See also *infra*, p. 119.

[77] For the history of these devotions cf. H. Barré, "Les premières prières mariales de l'occident", in *Marianum*, XX (1959), pp. 139–75. I owe a great deal to the author of this learned study. Cf. also J. Leclercq, "Anciennes prières monastiques", in *Studia monastica*, I (1959), pp. 379–92.

[78] Cf. E. Delaruelle, "Ste Radegonde, son type de sainteté et la chrétienté de son temps", in *Études mérovingiennes*, Paris (1953), p. 73; M-M. Dubois, "Le culte de la Croix en Gde Bretagne aux VIIe et VIIIe siècles, et l'influence des hymnes de Fortunat sur quelques poèmes anglo-saxons", *ibid.*, pp. 75–83.

[79] Ed. Vivès, *op. cit.*, pp. 67–79.

tors wrote learned treatises and sermons in her praise which are full of fervour and poetry.[80]

Towards the end of the sixth century Venantius Fortunatus of Poitiers wrote the very fine *Pange Lingua* and *Vexilla Regis* in honour of the Cross and the *Quem terra pontus aethera* in honour of the Blessed Virgin: these three hymns ultimately found a place in the liturgy of the universal Church.

Solitary prayer is not specifically referred to in these writings. It is said of the saints that they devoted themselves to prayer, and all the doctors of the spirtual life speak of imitating their example, but only rarely explain how to do so: the vocabulary and the notions of Cassian and St Gregory are taken for granted, and it is not thought necessary to recall what they taught. "Meditation" and "prayer" are referred to in more than one place as being customary practices, and on occasion the time for them and their duration is laid down,[81] but what they consist in is not specified. The basis is reading, chiefly of Holy Scripture and the commentaries on it of the Fathers. St Isidore put many passages from Origen in his *Questions on the Old Testament*, of which an abridgement was made by Bede,[82] and thus handed them down to later centuries. Reading was normally *lectio aperta* or out loud, and St Isidore notes that if it is prolonged it is wearisome and leaves little impression on the mind; it must therefore be brief and followed by a moment's reflection: the voice ceases and rests so that the tongue can repeat in silence the words which have been heard: this is the *lectio tacita*: the book has been laid aside in order to reconsider, *rectractare in animo*, what was in it. In this way a man "can read without trouble and remember what he has read, never again to forget it".[83] The same saint speaks also of another form of reflection: to discuss together a passage which has just been read, and during the comparing of notes, the *collatio*, questions which have arisen in the hearers' minds are put to the abbot.[84] The first of these methods is exactly what is meant by the traditional term *meditatio*.[85] According to

[80] St Ildephonsus, *De virginitate perpetua beatae Mariae*, ed. Blanco García, Madrid, 1937; the fourteen sermons of the pseudo-Ildephonsus, P.L., 96, 239–84, have the Blessed Virgin as their theme. They were written at different times and in different places, but some of them go back to the seventh century. Cf. H. Barré, "Le Sermon 'exhortatur': est-il de St Ildephonse?", in *Rev. bénéd.*, LXVII (1957), pp. 10–33.

[81] E.g. St Ferréol (†581), *Regula ad Monachos*, 19, P.L., 66, 966; *Regula tarnatensis*, 6, P.L., 66, 980.

[82] Cf. J. Châtillon, "Bède et Origène", in *Mélanges bibliques André Robert*, Paris, 1957, pp. 537–47.

[83] *Sent.*, III, 14, 8–9; P.L., 83, 689.

[84] *Ibid.*, 1–2, P.L., 83, 688; *Reg. mon.*, 7–8, P.L., 83, 877.

[85] On the traditional meaning of *lectio* and *meditatio* cf. J. Leclercq, *L'amour des lettres et le désir de Dieu*, Paris, 1957, pp. 19–23; 71–73; E. von Severus, "Der Hl. Ignatius als lehrer des Betrachtenden Gebetes", in *Geist und Leben*,

St Fructuosus,[86] to Defender of Ligugé[87] and to Bede, the *meditatio* is an exercise of the memory, which carries on the *lectio*, and prepares the soul for the *oratio*; it is in this last, according to Bede, that the "consolation of the Scriptures" is tasted. This prayer, which is nourished by the word of God, is an attention to God, remaining simply before him—*intentio*. It maintains compunction in its twofold aspect: sorrow for sin and longing for heaven. This "prayer of the heart", this "pure prayer", should be frequent rather than long drawn out. But Bede goes on to say that if a man gives himself to it assiduously it will procure for him in repose of spirit, *otium spirituale*, that "familiarity with the Holy Scriptures" which is the source of the highest joys.[88] It is through the teaching of Isidore and Bede, and the other authors who echo them, that the doctrine of Cassian and St Gregory the Great was handed on to the barbarian peoples.

There must have been during this period true contemplatives for such passages on prayer[89] to have been written or appreciated: but very rarely does any writer refer to his own life of prayer. St Valerius in his autobiography relates his conversion, his struggles with devils, the difficulties which every kind of foe raised up against him, but he reveals none of the secrets of his interior life.[90] In another work he speaks of the visions of heaven and hell that the monks had told him of.[91] St Aldegund of Maubeuge in the second half of the seventh century wrote down, possibly in her native tongue, her visions and revelations[92]: they are of a highly imaginative character, like many similar phenomena in the *Lives* of the period, and one needs to be cautious in admitting their authenticity. But to know how the man of God contemplated the mysteries one must again go to Bede the peacemaker. He takes occasion in interpreting various passages from the Bible, especially from Exodus and the Canticle of Canticles, to speak as though from experience of the soul's ascent of the mountain of God, and its attainment to the repose of the Sabbath. He speaks of it often as something other than the active life and practice of virtues, and of a greater value:

XXIX (1956), pp. 273–83, has shown that the essence of this traditional method of prayer is found in the *Exercises* of St Ignatius, particularly in the "repetition" of a text from the Bible.

[86] *Reg. mon.*, 2–3, P.L., 87, 1000–1.

[87] *Liber Scintillarum*, ch. 81, ed. H. Rochais, pp. 230–4.

[88] *De templo Salomonis*, *Epist.*, P.L., 91, 736–8 and 94, 686.

[89] *Sent.*, III, 8, P.L., 83, 679–80.

[90] *Ordo quaerimoniae ...*, *Replicatio sermonum a prima conversione*, ed. Aherne, *op. cit.*, pp. 69–161.

[91] *Dicta ad Donadeum*, ed. Férnandez Pousa, pp. 110–14; *De Bonello*, pp. 115–118.

[92] *Vita S. Aldegundis*, n. 18, ed. Mabillon. *Acta SS O.S.B.*, II, Mâcon, 1936, p. 812. Cf. S. Axters, *La spiritualité des Pays-Bas*, Louvain–Paris, 1948, p. 13.

"There is only one theology, that is the contemplation of God. It surpasses every virtue and all merits."[93] The contemplative life, "the speculative life" is to "long to see with the choirs of angels the face of the Lord and to rejoice eternally with those blessed spirits in the vision of the glory of God".[94] Some few, even in this life, by meditating on our Saviour's humiliations, by holy reading, fasting and prayer, "are able to perceive all the light that shines forth in Christ's mysteries".[95] Contemplation is a gift from above depending not on the goodwill of the soul that gazes, but on the grace of God which comes when he wills. This "light of divine contemplation" is only given to "a small number of more perfect Christians", and even they are given it "for a time, through a glass in a dark manner" and "at the cost of enormous labour: that of faith by which the heart is purified".[96] Thus in the best of its representatives the period of the barbarian kingdoms held faithfully to the doctrine of St Gregory the Great; all who had a spiritual life, and who had occasion to speak of it, followed the pattern he had traced out once and for all. They did not go deeply into his teaching, only taking in what was essential and ignoring the delicate touches and different shades of meaning which made up the richness of the great pope's doctrine.

The Church's tradition of contemplation was preserved, if no more, in these barbarous times, and adapted to the needs of rough natures in a society as yet barely organized. In spite of what it lacked, the period was a truly formative and fruitful one for the Christian West, and left a definite mark on later centuries.

93 *In Lucam*, III, 11, C.C.L., 120, p. 226. "Una ergo et sola est theoria, id est contemplatio Dei . . ." Cf. Cassian, *Conf.*, 23, 3.
94 *Ibid.*, III, 11, 471; III, 9, 455.
95 *Ibid.* Cf. *In Cant.*, II, 2, P.L., 91, 1104.
96 *In Cant.*, II, 2, P.L., 91, 1108–9.

IV

THE CAROLINGIAN RENEWAL

THE Carolingian period, the hundred years beginning shortly after the middle of the eighth century, was one in which Western Christendom settled down under the dominant influence of the Franks. The dynasty of Charlemagne (whose reign from 768 to 814 is the centre of the period) reigned over the Franks in the time of his predecessor Pepin the Short, during his own reign as king and then as emperor of the West, and even after his death and the division of the empire. His aims are summed up by the two mottoes on the coins of his reign: on the one side *Religio Christiana* and on the other *Renovatio Romani Imperii*. His aim was to establish an empire, with all the organization and unity of government that implied: but the new order was to be a Christian one, dominated by the Church, and built up on a conscious return to the Roman Empire in its Christian days. The idea was not so much to "create" as to "renew", "reform", "repair".[1] It was, however, inevitable that what was inherited from an earlier period should be taken into account, and the result was a compromise between the new tendencies and things as they were. In the spiritual domain the influence of St Gregory and the Fathers of ancient monasticism remained paramount, but religious institutions began to take shape, and the different states of life became more distinct; a conscious wish for intellectual culture made for a more considerable literary production. The aim was to imitate, and in fact the outcome was the production little by little of a spirit which survived the political structure of the empire. What were its characteristics, and what forms did it take in different milieux?

1. The Training of the Laity

Among the laity the groups of penitents, oblates and fervent Christians, which had already come into existence in an earlier

[1] On these tendencies of the Carolingian period cf. P. Schramm, *Kaiser, Rom und Renovatio*, Berlin, 1929, I, pp. 41–3; H. Fichtenau, "Il concetto imperiale di Carlo magno", in *I problemi della civiltà carolingia*, Spoleto, 1954, pp. 251–98.

period, especially round the monasteries, became more numerous and more highly organized. According to Ambrosius Autpert there are three categories among the faithful: virgins, those who live in continence, and married people who fulfil the duties of their state.[2] It was in favour of the last-mentioned, the *boni conjugati*, and in fact of all those who make up the "family of Christ, the flock of the supreme Shepherd",[3] that the pastors of the time expended a zeal which showed itself in sermons, in a huge correspondence on matters religious[4] and in various treatises. A letter, probably written by Rhabanus Maurus for Queen Judith, the second wife of Louis the Fair, shows the programme of prayer and austerity which made up the "manner of doing penance", the *modus paenitentiae*, of a great lady in the world.[5] Unfortunately only the beginning of the letter has been preserved, but it gives a glimpse of the spiritual exercises of many of the fervent, of those less illustrious "penitents" who have left no traces in the literature of the time. Another revealing work is a treatise by Jonas of Orleans (†844) on the training of the laity: *de institutioni laicali*.[6] The bishop, formerly a monk of Micy, had been asked by Manfred Count of Orleans to show him, and all who like him were bound by marriage, how to live devoutly. Jonas begins by noting that there are indeed books on the "Institution" of canons or of monks, but up till now no one has brought forth from Scripture or the Fathers what could be of help to the laity. The first and third books of his work are for all the faithful, the second for those among them who are married. It is true that St Isidore had already given some guidance on the ascesis proper to Christian princes and to judges and lawyers[7]: but from now on there are further additions to this class of literature, sometimes to the address of the emperor and of kings, indeed sometimes written at their own request. Jonas of Orleans wrote his *De institutione regia*,[8] Smaragdus of Saint Mihiel († *c.* 830) his *Via regia*,[9] Agobard of Lyons (†840) a pamphlet *On the comparison between ecclesiastical and political governments*,[10] Adelard of Corbie (†826) one *De ordine palatii*,[11] and Hincmar of Rheims (†882) a book *On the person and ministry of a king*.[12] To

[2] Text in J. Winandy, *Ambroise Autpert, moine et théologien*, Paris, 1953, p. 57.
[3] Expressions used by Agobard, *Sermo exhortatorius ad plebem*, I, P.L., 104, 267.
[4] Ed. *Mon. Germ. Hist.*, *Epist. Karolini aevi*, 5 vols.
[5] Ed. A. Wilmart, "Lettres de l'époque carolingienne", in *Rev. bénéd.*, XXXIV (1922), pp. 238–42.
[6] P.L., 106, 121–78.
[7] *Sent.*, III, 49–56, P.L., 720–8.
[8] P.L., 106, 279–306.
[9] P.L., 102, 933–70.
[10] P.L., 104, 291–8.
[11] The actual text is lost, but was used by Hincmar; cf. M. Mähler, art. "Adalard", in *Dict. de spirit.*, I, Paris, 1937, col. 186.
[12] P.L., 125, 833–50.

the nobles at court or elsewhere Paulinus of Aquileia addressed his *Liber exhortationis*[13] and Sedulius Scotus his *De rectoribus christianis*.[14] In 843 Dhuoda, the wife of Count Bernard of Septimania, wrote her *Liber Manualis* for the benefit of her son at the court of Charles the Bald.[15]

All these writings which were for general use helped to form the conscience of many of the laity. They all insist on the responsibility of the prince. This is great, above all if he be the emperor, clothed with the sacred kingship, since he has at his disposal a power which is both temporal and spiritual, and is, as it were, charged by God with the maintenance of order in the whole of the West.[16] Moreover, all those who are charged with government share in the same ministerial function: they are the servants, the "ministers" of God, for the good of the people. Their power comes from God, and must therefore be exercised according to his will. The universe is so constituted that the common man is subject to his sovereign, and the latter to his Lord. David, Solomon and the other kings of Israel are the models for a Christian prince. His duties are summed up in being faithful to the teaching of the Gospel though surrounded by the honours and opportunities which power provides; "the Kingdom of Heaven must be dearer to him than an earthly kingdom",[17] "he must find greater happiness in the Christian faith and in humility of heart than in ostentation and sensual delight".[18] First of all he must not quarrel with the authority of the Church, and in particular he must carry out what the Pope directs. As ruler he must be just and merciful, and moderate in his coercion; presents and adulation should leave him unmoved, and he must maintain concord in his entourage, among his councillors, and indeed among all his people. He must put his trust in God in peace as in war.

Hincmar addressed himself to the task of justifying the right of the ruler and those who fight under his obedience to kill by waging war; and to setting a limit to this right. The king is a public individual: it behoves him to fulfil not only his own personal duties, but those inherent in the collective responsibility that is his. He must be taught not only the general duties of Christian morality, but those of a strenuous life of asceticism and prayer. He ought

[13] P.L., 99, 197–282. [14] P.L., 103, 291–332.

[15] P.L., 106, 109–11; amended text by A. Vernet, "Un nouveau manuscrit du 'Manuel' de Dhuoda", in *Bibliothèque de l'École des chartes*, CXIV (1956), pp. 18–44.

[16] Cf. R. Folz, *L'idée d'empire en Occident du V au XVI siècle*, Paris, 1953, pp. 26–35.

[17] Agobard, *De compar. regim.*, 7, P.L., 104, 298.

[18] Hincmar, *De instit. regia*, 9, P.L., 125, 989.

to endeavour with a pure and disinterested heart to think with the Church, to be upright in his intentions; reading the Holy Scriptures will maintain his love for Christ our Lord. He must enter into himself, examine himself, accept just rebukes, welcome "the inspiration of God".[19] Paulinus of Aquileia draws a parallel between "the spiritual knight and the earthly knight"; the labours of the latter, and the precautions with which he surrounds himself, aiming only at a transitory good, should be a lesson to the Christian prince, who must make every effort to obey Christ, and receive from him the virtues which will bring him to heaven.[20]

Jonas of Orleans demanded of princes and indeed of the laity in general a real "conversion". The monk spoke to the king as though to a monk. So that the inward man may grow in him, and he may remain united to "his creator, his eternal and immortal friend", he wishes the king, like all "who profess the Christian life", to confess his faults daily to God in prayer, to have ever before him the day of his death, and to fear the day of judgment. All this is reminiscent of the Rule of St Benedict.[21] Elsewhere he writes: "Thy sins are written in a book: erase them with thy tears, as with a sponge".[22] He advises the laity to go more often to Communion than on the three great feasts, even as a rule at every Mass: this not only through custom, but "out of devotion".[23] But they must prepare themselves,[24] especially by confession: this too was a monastic practice.[25] The acknowledgment of their faults must be a daily one, accompanied by "a cry from the heart".[26] Their interior life will be sustained not only by reading the Holy Scriptures, but by frequent prayer,[27] which for choice should be made in a consecrated church.[28] Dhuoda suggests to her son for his devotions prayers made up of extracts from the psalms, and invocations to the Cross.[29] Prudentius, Bishop of Troyes (†861), put together an abridgment, a *Breviary of the Psalter,* for a noble lady to use while travelling.[30] Many of the compositions in the Carolingian books of devotions were therefore meant for those of the laity who could read, as well as for the clergy, and the characteristics of the period left their mark on the spiritual

[19] Agobard, *De divisione imperii*, 5, P.L., 104, 291.
[20] *Liber exhortat.*, 20, P.L., 99, 212–14.
[21] *De instit. regia epist.*, P.L., 106, 284; cf. *Rule of St Benedict*, ch. IV.
[22] *De instit. laicali*, I, 15, P.L., 106, 152.
[23] *Ibid.*, II, 18, 202–4.
[24] *Ibid.*, 204; *De instit. regia*, 16, 304.
[25] See *supra*, ch. 2, p. 41.
[26] Paulins of Aquileia, *Liber exhortat.*, 28, P.L., 99, 223.
[27] *Ibid.*, 225.
[28] Jonas of Orleans, *De inst. laicali*, I, 11, P.L., 106, 143. Hincmar, *De cavendis vitiis*, 5–6, P.L., 125, 897–908.
[29] *Liber manualis*, 10–11, P.L., 106, 113–14.
[30] P.L., 115, 1451–6.

training of the laity. A more defined social organization was coming into being in which the various "orders" become distinct from one another, though more closely bound together. On the ascetic level the layman is bidden to care for the "common people",[31] particularly the poor; to reverence the clergy and respect their liberty; the great are not to consider the churches on their domains as private property or confer benefices on unworthy clerics; in all these matters they are to consider themselves bound in conscience by the emperor's decisions.[32] With regard to the life of prayer, its exponents were mostly monks, and it is as such that they spoke to the laity, trying to inculcate into them their own traditional practices and interior dispositions.

2. *Clerics and Canons*

In the one Church there are three "orders": laity, religious and clerics, and it was at this time that the differences between them were more clearly formulated,[33] with the appearance of the characteristics of the spiritual life proper to the *ordo clericalis*. Already in the first half of the ninth century in some countries there had been regular meetings of the clergy of a deanery: they usually took place once a month and consisted of a conference and prayers in common. In the towns there were groups of priests, "confraternities", who did not lead the common life but voluntarily bound themselves to come to each other's material and spiritual assistance.[34] In addition to this there can be seen an effort to organize and unify which for centuries was to affect profoundly the lives of a great part of the clergy. There were two stages in this work: the first is bound up with the name of St Chrodegang, bishop of Metz, who drew up about 754 a rule for the clergy of his episcopal city, to enable them to live according to the requirements of what he calls "the canonical order, the *ordo canonicus*". Chrodegang took his inspiration in great part from the Rule of St Benedict, and his own rule spread to some extent. In one of the recensions in which it has come down to us, all that was peculiar to the Church of Metz has

[31] The expression is used by Christian Druthmar *in Matt.*, prol., P.L., 106, 1263.

[32] Jonas of Orleans, *De inst. laicali*, II, 19, P.L., 106, 204–8.

[33] Rhabanus Maurus, *De cleric. instit.*, 2, P.L., 107, 297; *De sacris ordin.*, 2, P.L., 112, 1166.

[34] Cf. G. G. Meersseman, "Die Klerikervereine von Karl dem Grossen bis Innocenz III", in *Zeitschrift für schweizerische Kirchengesch.*, XLVI (1952), pp. 1–42, where can be found the rules of an association of this kind. Later the laity were admitted to these "confraternities"; cf. *ibid.*, pp. 81–112 where some twelfth-century rules are given.

been eliminated, making it of a general character.[35] Gradually this Rule became the first of the statutes of the order which in a new sense was to be the *ordo canonicus*, "the order of canons". Chrodegang's aim was the promotion of the liturgical life, and he arranged its details according to the usages of Rome. For those among the clergy who were prepared to adopt it, the Rule laid down a certain measure of community life: they might each own their own house and enjoy the usufruct of the *precaria* they held from the Church, but they were to have a common dormitory and refectory. St Chrodegang even expressed a hope that they would renounce all private property, and live the life of the apostles round our Lord, or the first Christians in Jerusalem, the *vita apostolica*. The clergy were not compelled to adopt the rule, but it set before them an ideal, and was an indication of the way in which their life would develop.

A second stage took place when the Council held at Aachen in 817 promulgated a rule for those who, bound to the *canonica professio*,[36] were obliged to live "according to the canons". This new code of law drew its inspiration from the earlier one, but it is more precise and fuller; Louis the Pious wished it to be applied everywhere. It recalls first of all the canons: that is, the decrees of the Councils and the writings of the Fathers concerning the life of the clergy. St Gregory is most frequently quoted, with St Isidore who took his teaching from him; then St Augustine and St Jerome and Julian Pomerius whose *De vita contemplativa* was attributed to St Prosper.[37] In the last chapter the differences between canons and monks are defined: the dignity of the first is greater, because the life of the clergy is immediately subject to the authority of the Church; the second lead a stricter life. Evangelical perfection is their common ideal, but their means differ. Monks are bound to a greater austerity, to a more complete dependence on their superiors, to absolute poverty, since, "wishing for nothing save heavenly realities", they have renounced all earthly things. Canons keep as much of their freedom and private property as is compatible with

35 Cf. C. Dereine, art., "Chanoines", in *Dict. d'hist. et de géog. ecclés.*, XII, Paris, 1953, col. 365. One version of the rule is in P.L., 89, 1097–120. Cf. M. E. Morhain, "Origine et histoire de la 'Regula Canonicorum' de St Chrodegang" in *Miscellanea Pio Paschini*, II, Rome, 1948, pp. 173–85.

36 Ed. *Mon. Germ. Hist. Concilia*, II, 1, 308–421. Some historians give the date of the Council as 816, others 817; in fact there was a "pre-council" in 816, and there were moreover additions to the body of statutes known as the Capitula of 817, which is the more important date. See J. Semmler in *Corpus consuetudinum monasticarum*, I, Siegburg, 1963, pp. 425–31.

37 On the considerable influence exercised by this treatise during the Middle Ages, cf. N. L. W. Laistner in *Miscellanea Giovanni Mercati*, Rome, 1946, II, 344–58.

the common life whose object is to ensure them a living, to safeguard chastity, to enable them worthily to celebrate the Divine Office. These are the aims of the rules which follow. The epilogue with which it closes is reminiscent of the Rule of St Benelict, and thus this document, whose object was to make a clear distinction between canons and monks, owes something to the monastic code. In fact, since henceforward the principal function of both was to celebrate the liturgy, monks and canons came to resemble each other, both in their manner of life and their work. At the same time the austerity of the monks in general gained for them a higher regard from the body of the faithful, popes and princes had more confidence in them, and their influence in the Church was greater.[38] Inevitably the Rule of Aachen was kept neither everywhere nor always, but it held up an ideal before the clergy, which the Church for long urged them to follow.

This conception of clerical spirituality is reflected in various writings: letters and capitularies, promulgated by Councils or by bishops, like those of Theodulph of Orleans (†821),[39] treatises like those of Amalarius,[40] Walafrid Strabo[41] and Rhabanus Maurus. The last mentioned wrote a sort of manual for the training of the clergy, *De clericorum institutione*.[42] In his treatise *On sacred orders*[43] and in the first book of his *Disciplina ecclesiastica* (the second is devoted to the manner of catechizing the ignorant[44]) he repeats the greater part of it.

Every author who writes of the life of the clergy was at pains to point out that he was only a compiler, handing on the teachings of the Gospel and of the Fathers, and this is perfectly true. The principal sources were the writings of St Isidore and either through him, or by a direct contact with the text itself, those of St Gregory the Great.[45] We have, however, no transcriptions in this period of what St Gregory says on the knowledge of God; for these first centuries of the Middle Ages, he is in some sense a master of novices rather than a mystical doctor. The part played by the extracts made from his works is analogous to that of Rodriguez' *Christian Perfection*

38 This is noted by Dereine, *art. cit.*, col. 370: on the influence of the Rule of Aix, see *ibid.*, 366–7. There was a parallel movement of reform among the canonesses, whose rule was promulgated at Aix in 817 under the title of *De institutione sanctimonialium*; cf. E. Amann, *L'époque carolingienne*, Paris, 1937, p. 264. P. Schmitz, *Histoire de l'ordre de S. Benoît*, VII, Maredsous, 1956, pp. 59–60.

39 P.L., 105, 191–224.

40 *Liber officialis*, ch. 4–14, ed. J. M. Hanssens, *Amalarii episcopi opera liturgica omnia*, vol. II, Vatican City, 1948, pp. 209–36.

41 *De ecclesiasticarum rerum exordiis et incrementis* P.L., 114, 919–66.

42 P.L., 107, 293–420.

43 P.L., 112, 1165–92.

44 On a new witness to the influence of St Gregory on the Carolingian period, cf. H. Rochais in *Rev. bénéd.*, LXVII (1957), pp. 141–50.

45 P.L., 112, 1191–262.

in modern times. St Gregory took medieval man by the hand; he was the paternal guide those generations felt the need of, and he was ultimately to lead them to the term of the spirituality of the Middle Ages, the heights reached by St Bernard.

During this middle phase, the Carolingian period, the spiritual doctrine put before the clergy was not of a very interior nature. On the ascetic level they were enjoined to avoid the seven deadly sins, to exercise their priestly ministry in a disinterested spirit, to be zealous shepherds of their flock. In the treatises on baptism there was more question of the rites accompanying the sacrament than of the method of preparing the neophyte for it.[46] A sermon which can be attributed to Paulinus of Aquileia shows that the preacher's aim was to be understood by an audience of very simple souls.[47] Rhabanus Maurus advises prayer both before preaching, to obtain light and the grace of efficacious words, and afterwards, in thanksgiving and to maintain humility.[48] However, nearly everything said on the subject of prayer referred to the Divine Office: the clergy were instructed about the cycle of the liturgy, about vestments and sacred ornaments, on each of the canonical Hours, on the chant, on the text and the music of the Antiphonal, on the various rites and what they signify, and the pomp with which they are accomplished in Rome, even on the computation of the calendar. They were reminded of the need of being trained in the liberal arts, especially in grammar, so that they might understand the prayers of the Church. Indeed the salient characteristic of the ecclesiastical life of the time is this uniting of cultural and spiritual values.[49]

3. *The Rise of Benedictinism*

The monasticism of the period is one in which the influence of the Benedictine Rule grows and becomes almost exclusive. In Bede[50] there are indications of this, but it is first explicitly referred to in the writings of Ambrose Autpert, a monk and then abbot of St Vincent on the Volturno, in Southern Italy, where he died about

[46] For example, Leidrad of Lyons (†816), *De sacrament baptismi*, P.L., 99 853–72; Amalarius, *De caeremoniis baptismi*, P.L., 99, 890–902; Theodulph of Orléans, *De ordine bapt.*, P.L., 99, 223–40.

[47] Ed. J. Leclercq in *Rev. bénéd.*, LIX (1949), pp. 156–60.

[48] *De cleric. inst.*, III, 39, P.L., 107, 418–19.

[49] Cf. J. Leclercq, *L'amour des lettres et le désir de Dieu*, Paris, 1957, pp. 40–52.

[50] M. T. A. Carroll, in *The Venerable Bede*, p. 226, Washington, 1946, notes an explicit mention of the Rule of St Benedict, ch. VII, in Bede, *In Esdram*, P.L., 91, 892 A. But there are other places where, without St Benedict being mentioned, reminiscences of his Rule can be recognized, e.g. *Hist. Abbatum*, I, ed. C. Plummer, Oxford, 1896, p. 365 (cf. *Rule of Saint Benedict Prol.*); *Epist. ad Ecgbertum*, n. 11, *ibid.*, p. 415 (cf. *Rule of Saint Benedict*, ch. 64).

784.[51] He wrote a long commentary on the Apocalypse and some minor works, notably *The Conflict of Vices and Virtues*,[52] some sermons,[53] and a prayer against the vices,[54] all of which had a considerable influence. They were generally attributed to other authors, and all through the Middle Ages were copied and interpolated. Their author has been called "a monk and a theologian", and the first representative of monastic theology.[55] He owes much to his predecessors, Bede and the authors of earlier ages, Isidore and above all Gregory and Augustine, yet there is a personal note in his teaching. His doctrine is set in a great vision of the mystery of the Church. Our Lady has a large place in it. Asceticism is shown as a struggle in which every Christian is engaged, and especially those who have chosen the straight path of the counsels which, he says, are quite distinct from the "ordinary commandments".[56] The monastic life is made to help them in this combat. Autpert reacts against the notion that it is necessary to abandon one's native land in order to achieve perfection; he holds that, given stability, a man can sanctify himself in his own country. A well-led monastic life makes for a spiritual leisure, which Autpert calls the "sabbath calm" which makes contemplation possible, By meditating on the mysteries of Christ with fervour and tears in the interior silence of the desert of the spirit, they become known in a higher way than by the intellect alone: *cum amaris, apprehenderis*.[57] In this there is an echo of St Gregory's teaching on knowledge through love.

Even before there was any question of imperial authority or the work of reformers, the search for God in a monastic life under the rule of St Benedict seemed to be the mode of life which the times needed. The first example of which the details are known is the monastery of St Riquier in northern France towards the end of the eighth century. It was a kind of "holy city", with a population of seven thousand, including three hundred monks, one hundred children in the monastery, a hundred and ten soldiers and many families, ruled over by the Abbot Angilbert (who was probably a

[51] Cf. J. Winandy, *Ambroise Autpert, moine et théologien*, Paris, 1953. On the works of Autpert see J. Winandy, "L'oeuvre littéraire d'Ambroise Autpert" in *Rev. bénéd.*, LX (1950), pp. 93–119.

[52] P.L., 40, 1091–106.

[53] These are identified and the references given in J. Winandy, *Ambroise Autpert* . . ., p. 11.

[54] Edited and translated, *ibid.*, pp. 103–45. On the influence of this work cf. J. Leclercq, "La prière au sujet des vices et des vertus", in *Analecta monastica*, II, Rome (*Studia Anselmiana*, 31) 1953, pp. 7–17.

[55] J. Winandy, "La contemplation à l'école des Pères: Ambroise Autpert", in *La Vie spirituelle*, LXXXII (1950), pp. 147–55.

[56] Text in J. Winandy, *Ambroise Autpert*, p. 58.

[57] Texts *ibid.*, passim, and J. Leclercq, art. "Contemplation", in *Dict. de spiritualité*, II, Paris, 1953, col. 1936.

layman). He added to the duties imposed by the Rule of St Benedict a whole collection of ritual prescriptions, litanies, processions from one of three great churches or five minor chapels to another.[58] It has been said that "all this was just a *mise en scène*; the actual play was the singing",[59] and this indeed was the chief occupation of the monks. They had no longer time to work—a whole crowd of merchants and servants did that for them—but had become experts in the solemn work of prayer according to the Roman rite.

One must bear these facts in mind when considering the part played in monastic history by St Benedict of Aniane. Supported by Charlemagne and Louis the Pious, he carried out his reforms first in the monastery of Aniane, then at Inden, introducing a manner of monastic life which appears paradoxical: the Rule of St Benedict was to be adopted everywhere,[60] yet at the same time he added to it extra liturgical practices of such length as to make its observance practically impossible.[61] The apparent contradiction must be looked at in the light of the tendencies of the Carolingian period, and the whole trend of monastic evolution, which was towards this sort of compromise. Benedict of Aniane's work was not entirely an innovation, but rather a making obligatory of practices which were already in existence, and which although widespread had up till then only the force of custom.[62] By now the occupations of the monks only differed from those of the clergy by their more elaborate "ritualism". Yet St Benedict of Aniane insisted very firmly on the importance of that other traditional essential element, the *lectio divina*. In the rules which he lays down for Garnier his disciple, he emphasises the part of knowledge in the path to wisdom: the study of the Holy Scriptures, of Origen, of St Augustine, of St Jerome and above all of St Gregory leads to an understanding of the faith which will blossom into love; prayer, reading, meditation and study help towards contemplation.[63] By "fixing the eye of the heart on God who is love and eternal truth" in whom

[58] Cf. J. Hubert, "St Riquier et le monachisme bénédictin en Gaulle à l'époque carolingienne", in *Il monachesimo nell'alto medioevo e la formazione della civilta occidentale*, Spoleto, 1957, pp. 293–309.

[59] E. Bishop, "Angilbert's Ritual order for St Riquier", in *Liturgica historica*, Oxford, 1918, p. 330.

[60] As has been pointed out by J. Winandy in "L'oeuvre monastique de saint Benoît d'Aniane", in *Mélanges bénédictins*, St Wandrille, 1947, pp. 231–41.

[61] This has been brought to light by P. Schmitz, "L'influence de St Benoît d'Aniane dans l'histoire de l'ordre de S. Benoît", in *Il monachesimo* . . ., Spoleto, 1957, pp. 401–15.

[62] P. Schmitz points this out, *ibid.*, p. 547; cf. also pp. 614–15. That the originality and influence of Benedict of Aniane has been exaggerated is pointed out by C. Molas, "A proposito del 'ordo diurnus' di san Benito de Aniane", in *Studia monastica*, II (1960), p. 205–22.

[63] Ed. J. Leclercq, "Les 'munimenta fidei' de Saint Benoît d'Aniane", in *Analecta monastica*, I, Rome (*Studia Anselmiana*, 20) 1948, pp. 61–74.

"nothing but the immutable is contemplated", a monk will prepare himself "to pass from faith to sight". Monastic life had already evolved along certain lines, but Benedict of Aniane kept a place in it as far as he could for the earlier ideals: the way in which he combined the spirit of the ancient monasticism with the developments which had come into being in the early Middle Ages laid the foundations of all subsequent monastic history, and was responsible both for the prosperity of the Benedictine Order and for the crises which it had to overcome. Finally, there were two commentaries on the Rule of St Benedict which gave Western monasticism its essential spiritual features. The first, which was written shortly after 845, and attributed variously to Paul the Deacon and to Hildemar, spread in several versions throughout the Frankish lands and southern Italy.* For centuries it exercised considerable influence[64]: it was copied, summarized and interpolated.[65] It is not without importance because it comments on an earlier text and earlier traditions to which its author frequently refers. It is moderate, and at times says little more than the text itself, but it enhances the spiritual teaching of the Rule by means of grammatical glosses, biblical comparisons and reminders of sources and observances. The author defines the place of the coenobitic life in the evolution of the life of perfection. The prophets in the Old Testament, St John Baptist, the apostles round our Lord and after his death, St Paul and St Anthony, are all examples of that life consecrated to God to which St Benedict was to give a coenobitic form: for one can live for God equally well in solitude as a hermit. Hildemar, in the text he is commenting on, is speaking of the organization of the common life, which however, is not necessary in order to safeguard the "spiritual brotherhood" which is enjoyed in it, for the latter is founded on the unity of the same baptism, the same spirit, the same hope and the same Church.[66] To Hildemar the common life is flexible: on three occasions he speaks of its relations with the solitary life. Writing on the beginning of the first chapter of the Rule, he agrees that though St Benedict recommends the hermit's life to those who have lived in community sufficiently long to be able to do without the common life, yet only the few would profit by this

* [On this question see also Dom Cuthbert Butler, O.S.B., *Saneti Benedict Regula Monachorum*, Freiburg im Breisgau, 1912, pp. XVI, XVII, and D. Knowles, *op. cit.*, ch. II, pp. 18 et seq.—Trans.]

64 Cf. W. Hafner, *Der Basiliuskommentar zur Regula St Benedicti*, Münster, 1959. The text was edited as that of Hildemar by R. Mittermüller, Ratisbon, 1880, and as that of Paul the Deacon in *Bibliotheca Casinensis*, IV, *Florilegium Casinense*, Monte Cassino, 1880, pp. 3–173.

65 Cf. J. Leclercq, "Le commentaire de Teuzon sur la Regle bénédictine", in *Stud. und Mitt. zur Gesch. des Benedikt Ordens*, LXIV (1952), pp. 5–12.

66 Ed. R. Mittermüller, Ratisbon, 1880, ch. 63, p. 574.

solution: for the majority of monks the common life is the better.[67] Over the eighth degree of humility* he reminds his readers that there is a controversy between those who hold that a monk may retire to the desert, and those who hold the contrary view: he himself favours the first opinion "if he goes in search of a greater good".[68] Finally, with regard to the last chapter of the Rule he holds that a man may go "either into solitude or to a stricter monastery", if it is to find "freedom of soul" and make his salvation more sure.[69] Hildemar, following St Benedict, encouraged in the coenobite a sense of the supernatural, an intense love of Jesus Christ, absolute renunciation, the sense of the presence of God and his angels, "chaste fear",[70] and that obedience and longsuffering which are truly a martyrdom.[71] He endeavours to understand what St Benedict has in mind; like him, he forms men's consciences; he stresses the value of a monk's confessing to his abbot or "to a spiritual brother" not only his deeds, as some held, but also his thoughts—since this is one of the ways to attain perfect humility.[72] The monk's time must be divided between the active and the contemplative life, that is between manual work and prayer. The one is a condition of the other: "When the time comes to read, the monk who has performed his manual labour well will receive the gift of contemplation or of tears; while he who has not worked with his hands according to the Rule will not be able profitably to give himself to reading."[73] Hildemar gives precise guidance on how to pray. He realizes, of course, that the common work of prayer includes offices over and above those which St Benedict had prescribed.[74] But in all this "psalmody" we are in the presence of God, for then more than ever "we believe that God beholds us".† We pray by speaking, but not in many words, so that by paying attention to them our spirit is rendered quiet and serene, enjoying the invisible light as much as is possible to human nature. As things are we cannot look at God all the time, because of our earthly occupations: they bring with them a sort of complexity to our soul or at least a twofold division: "the eyes of our heart no longer turns simply to God."[75] Yet during the

* [The eighth degree of humility is for a monk to do nothing except what is authorized by the common Rule of the Monastery, or the example of his seniors —Trans.]

† [Cf. *Rule of St Benedict*, ch. XIX.—Trans.]

67 *Ibid.*, ch. 1, p. 63.

68 *Ibid.*, ch. 7, p. 257.

69 *Ibid.*, ch. 73, p. 635.

70 *Ibid.*, ch. 7, p. 213.

71 *Ibid.*, ch. 7, p. 231.

72 *Ibid.*, ch. 7, p. 242. [St Benedict's fifth degree of humility is "to hide from one's Abbot none of the evil thoughts that beset one's heart, nor the sins committed in secret, but humbly to confess them".—Trans.]

73 *Ibid.*, ch. 48, p. 476.

74 *Ibid.*, ch. 52, p. 498.

75 *Ibid.*, ch. 19, p. 314.

psalmody it is easier to achieve this simplicity if the mind accords with the words we speak—*mens notra concordet voci nostrae*.[76]

To pray in silence, privately and without words, is difficult, and therefore such prayer must be short if it is to remain pure.

> The Greeks pray often but for a short time. We should remain prostrate in prayer as long as by the help of God we can disregard evil thoughts; but if we realize that they have the upper hand, and that we no longer find joy in prayer, we should rise up and take a book or go to some kind of work; for the psalmody is one thing, and to give oneself up to prayer another. If a monk fulfils his obedience St Benedict does not forbid him to use the gift of tears, provided that he continues in his obedience even when it has come upon him. When he comes to the oratory to perform the Office he may stay there after it is accomplished if under the inspiration of Divine grace he finds joy in doing so; but his abbot must know that he is doing so. The holy Benedict knew that the spirit of man, because of its weakness, cannot engage in the divine exercise of prayer without being troubled by evil thoughts; that is why he said that prayer must be short. We are disturbed by our thoughts at other times also, but particularly when we pray: and since prayer should be pure of all vain thoughts, it must, given human infirmity, be short. But rightly did blessed Benedict add "unless by the inspiration of divine grace it be prolonged". Thus he who remains prostrate in prayer when he has been overcome by vain thoughts acts against the Rule, and so does he who has received the divine gift of prayer enabling him to pray for long without being disturbed or interrupted by evil thoughts and yet lightly gets up and goes away.[77]

We learn from Hildemar that it was the custom to lie prostrate in private prayer[78]; except for those few short moments to which all were obliged there could be no rule for its duration, since it depended on grace, the *donum orationis*. Hildemar specifies that the abbot must be told of this gift some days before it can be indulged in: it is not a question therefore of a passing inspiration but of a lasting disposition, what we should call today a "state of prayer". In a life where the celebration of the liturgy had already come to occupy a great place, contemplation nevertheless held the primacy, and the esteem in which it was held is shown by the fact that it was for the abbot to discern and regulate it.

[76] *Ibid.*, ch. 19, p. 317.

[77] *Ibid.* ch. 20, p. 319. Hildemar's teaching on "short and pure" prayer goes back beyond St Benedict to St Augustine and Cassian. The texts are pointed out in P.L., 49, 818, note b. The same teaching, summing up that of Cassian, may be found in Rhabanus Maurus *In I Tim.*, II, P.L., 112, 589–90, and in *De cleric. instit.*, II, 10–13, P.L., 107, 329–31. Cf. *infra*, p. 88, note 127.

[78] The same doctrine is found later on, cf. *infra*, p. 139.

In another place Hildemar says: "If contemplation comes upon a monk while he is reading or working, he is not to be debarred from tears: he may leave his reading or work and go and give himself up to contemplation in the oratory. But few are in this state. . . . He who does not pray with tears and singleness of heart must not go into the oratory, or at least not delay there, for many deceive themselves, and since they do not lift up their heart with tears they waste the time they should spend in an obedience or in reading."[79] Prayer is not therefore to be the same for all. For everyone the Office is to be followed by private prayer which must be brief and pure; in addition, for the few there will be long periods of silent prayer.

Smaragdus had written another commentary on the Rule not much later than 817. It is more literary in form, less spontaneous: its author is at times more concerned with the theory than with the problems and observances of the monastic life. On the solitary life he merely says "it is better for the monk to live in a monastery".[80] On prayer he also points out that it must be brief and frequent.[81] His teaching on asceticism and the life of prayer is on a very high level,[82] and is taken from the ancient monastic writers and the Fathers of the Church, particularly St Gregory. His *Diadem for Monks*[83] is compiled of passages from their works, and thus completes his *Commentary on the Rule*. Both these writing had a great and lasting influence: the *Commentary* in particular helped on the reform of Benedict of Aniane and played a part in spreading the Benedictine Rule[84]; the *Diadem* was shorter and so more often copied; it completed the association of St Gregory's teaching with that of St Benedict and his Rule: henceforward the monastic tradition in the West was Benedictine. To train the clergy, the compilers of the age of Charlemagne had drawn on St Gregory's *Pastoral Rule*, but in the formation of the monks it was to the great pope's writings on contemplation that they gave the preference.

4. *The Christian Warfare*

As in the earlier period, asceticism and the life of prayer have certain characteristics which are common to every class and so

[79] *Ibid.*, ch. 52, p. 498.
[80] *Comment. in Reg. S. Bénéd.*, ch. 1, P.L., 102, 728.
[81] *Ibid.*, ch. 20, p. 840.
[82] Cf. J. Leclercq, *Smaragde et son œuvre*, introduction to *La voie royale. Le diadème des moines*, La Pierre-qui-vire, 1949, pp. 3–23; Art. "Contemplation", in *Dict. de spirit.*, II, Paris, 1953, col. 1937–8.
[83] P.L., 102, 593–690.
[84] C. J. Bishko, "Salvus of Albelda and Frontier Monasticism in tenth-century Navarre", in *Speculum*, XXIII (1948), pp. 559–90.

need distinguishing. With regard to asceticism there appeared more and more a tendency towards orderliness, a concern for moderation: the Christian was now not so much the hero of a personal combat as a soldier of an army in array, of an organized force. No longer were the extremes of bodily mortification sought after, the perils of exile, the hard fight against the elements: the soul itself was the battleground. To be sure, the Christian must fight, and Rhabanus Maurus takes the title of the third of the book of his *Ecclesiastical Dicipline* from St Augustine—*De agone Christiano*—but in it he sets forth the efforts of those "whose heart is the dwelling-place of Christ",[85] and this inner warfare is on the psychological plane. Ambrosius Autpert, before describing it as "a conflict between vices and virtues", notes that the times are no longer those of outward persecution: "there are some monks whom no evildoer would openly dare to resist."[86] But within men themselves are found opposing motives for doing what is right or yielding to what is wrong, and in the form of a debate they meet face to face; treatises and anthologies furnish arguments for a dispute in which the "virtues of the soul"[87] had to gain the victory. Uprightness of heart and purity of intention had become more important than prowess in fasting or the dangers of the *peregrinatio*. In the vocabulary of this asceticism the word "heart" recurs frequently, and the spirit of the age came near to that of St Gregory, taking its inspiration from him, and quoting him largely.

Penitentials were still being drawn up; but the best of them and the most widely known are concerned more with the moral aspect of the expiation of faults and with the dispositions of the soul than with particular sins.[88] It was no longer held to be sufficient to draw up a tariff for evil deeds. It was a question of judging motives and estimating responsibility.[89] Rhabanus' treatise *De modo paenitentiae*[90] shows an effort to interiorize penitential practices; it contained not only immediate penalties, but a theory, even a theology, of repentance and confidence in divine forgiveness, of a peaceful awaiting of the last judgment; for in this interior asceticism an important place was given to a consideration of man's end; he was to prepare himself not only for death and the judgment

85 P.L., 112, 1229.

86 Ch. I, P.L., 40, 1092.

87 Jonas of Orleans, *De instit. laicali*, 24, P.L., 106, 218.

88 Witness the titles of Halitgarius' penitential, *De vitiis et virtutibus et de ordine paenitentium*, P.L., 105, 651, and of that treatise of Rhabanus, *De vitiis et virtutibus et peccatorum satisfactione*, P.L., 112, 1335.

89 See, e.g., Book IV, *De judicio paenitentium laicorum* of Halitgarius' *De vitiis*, P.L., 105, 681.

90 P.L., 112, 1304.

which will follow it, but also for the end of the world[91]; and as a result he is not so much afraid as conscious of the gravity of the duties which are incumbent on him as a Christian. Rhabanus gives a long description of "the joy that is to come",[92] and Jonas in his treatise *On the training of the laity* (*De institutione laicali*) describes at length the happiness which will be the reward of the elect after the resurrection.[93] Emmo begins his work on the virtues by a whole book dedicated to "the love of our heavenly country".[94]

All these tendencies are mirrored in the hagiography of the time. Due attention is paid to asceticism and it has its place in the *Lives* of the saints. But less is said than in earlier days of their austerities; stress is laid on their prayers and good works, and they are praised for a hidden martyrdom which does not show itself in great outward sufferings.

There was a higher level of culture in the monasteries, but hagiography shows that there was less corporal austerity. The monks took greater care of the body, paid more attention to cleanliness, and in one historian's words "nobody was hungry unless he could not avoid it".[95] Probably the influence of lay abbots, even the Angilberts, made for an asceticism which was in a sense more humane, not to say more comfortable, and gradually opened the door to laxity and decadence. The spiritually minded, most of whom were monks, resisted this tendency towards easy-going, and both in their lives as these have come down to us and in their writings they show a remarkable equilibrium between the aspiration of men's hearts towards absolute purity and the advantages that prosperity brings. In Ireland, where the teaching was based on that of the ancient monastic writings, the influence of the monks had produced an almost monk-like asceticism among the clergy; in the Frankish empire also the monastic influence was preponderant and took its inspiration from the same sources, but the solemn celebration of the liturgy was henceforward to take up a great part of the monks' day and thereby modify the forms of their asceticism. Many monks led a life much like that of clerics; some of their abbots were not monks, nor even clerics. There was nothing to prevent a religious from sanctifying himself under these conditions, but at a later date an inevitable reaction took place in favour of an ideal which was nearer to that of the fathers of monasticism.

[91] E.g. Hincmar, *De cavendis vitiis*, preface and 4; P.L., 125, 860, 892; Rhabanus, *De modo paenitentiae*, 14, P.L., 112, 1319; Agobard, *De compar. regim.*, 6, P.L., 104, 297.

[92] *De modo paenitentiae*, 15, P.L., 112, 1321.

[93] P.L., 106, 275.

[94] P.L., 118, 875–88.

[95] Texts in L. Zoepf, *Das Heiligen Leben in X Jahrhundert*, Leipzig, 1908, pp. 125–31.

5. Sacred Literature

Carolingian piety was deeply influenced by two things: interest in the Bible and love of the liturgy. The latter took pride of place; indeed it was to some extent for the sake of public worship that men studied the Scriptures. In an encyclical in 789 Charlemagne made this aim clear: "Many desire to pray well, but because of faulty books they pray badly."[96] To find a remedy for this difficulty the text of the Bible was revised so as to have the pure text of St Jerome, and many exact copies were made. The work was done by Theodulph, bishop of Orleans, and by Alcuin (whose name is especially connected with it), and the text produced—the Vulgate—remains even to our own day the most widely read. Alcuin's Bible is only one of the witnesses to that renewal of love for the Scriptures which was the result of the religious and cultural revival undertaken by Pépin, continued by Charlemagne, and carried to its highest point of achievement by Louis the Pious.[97] Several copies of the Bible which are still in existence are linked with the names of princes of the house of Charlemagne—Bibles of Charlemagne, of Louis the Pious, of Charles the Bald; Book of the Gospels of Lothair—and monasteries and churches had copies of them. Often they were made into works of art—the fine parchment, the beauty of the gold and silver lettering, the splendid binding ornamented with precious stones and ivory and enamel, the richness of the illuminations illustrating sacred history and showing our Lord in majesty: all this was done with care "for the love of Christ", "for the honour of his name" as Alcuin says in dedicatory poems he wrote for some of the copies. These large and beautiful Carolingian Bibles (of which about thirty are still in existence), whose iconography made them so valuable, remain as magnificent witnesses to a powerful spiritual movement which drew its inspiration from the fundamental sources of Christianity.[98]

From this love of Scripture came the wish to understand it. Commentaries appeared for readers of every class—laymen, priests, monks and nuns. Rhabanus Maurus explained Paralipomenon for Louis the Pious so that by the manner in which he ruled he might learn to serve the true King; and also the books of the Maccabees[99]; to Lothair he dedicated commentaries on Ezechiel and Jeremias,[100]

[96] Ed. *Mon. Germ. Hist. Poetae aevi carol.*, I, 287, v. 19; 285, LXV, v, v. 18.

[97] Cf. S. Berger, *Histoire de la Vulgate*, Nancy, 1893, pp. 145–299; H. Quentin, *Mémoire sur l'établissement du texte de la Vulgate*, Rome–Paris, 1922, pp. 249–297.

[98] For a list of Alcuin's manuscripts see B. Fischer, *Die Alkuin-Bibel*, Freiburg-im-Breisgau, 1957, pp. 13–14; for Theodulph's manuscripts see T. Ayuso Marazuela, *Vetus latina Hispana*, I, *Prolegomenos*, Madrid, 1953, pp. 361 *et seq.*

[99] P.L., 109, 279, 1125.

[100] P.L., 110, 494; 111, 723.

to the Empress Judith those on Esther and Judith.[101] Angelomme of Luxeuil gave Lothair his *Ennarationes in Cantica Canticorum* to enlighten his "careful meditation" of the Scriptures.[102] To help the clergy in their pastoral labours Smaragdus commented on the epistles and gospels of the Mass.[103] To various bishops Rhabanus sent his writings on some of those early books of the Old Testament which are so full of teaching on the mysteries of Christian initiation,[104] a fact he never fails to point out in his prefaces and elsewhere. It was with the object of helping the nuns of Sainte Marie de Soissons in their life of contemplation that Paschasius Radbertus wrote for them a commentary on the forty-fourth psalm,[105] and his commentary on the Gospels for Gontaud de St Riquier was written to enable him to teach the children more easily.[106] Glosses on the canticles of the liturgy, on extracts from the Old Testament and St Paul, as well as on the epistles and gospels for Sundays and Feasts, were made in the monastery of St Germain at Auxerre by Haymon, Héric, Rémi and their anonymous disciples.[107] On the whole the authors of all these commentaries made no pretence at originality. They drew copiously from the writings of St Jerome, St Augustine, St Isidore, the Venerable Bede and many others, not least from Origen. Some admitted to borrowing from him—"with caution" according to Smaragdus[108] and Rhabanus Maurus.[109] Others, without admitting it, and possibly unconsciously, drew from him by way of Isidore and St Gregory. Some of Rhabanus's commentaries were lifted bodily from Origen.[110] In a copy of a commentary on the epistles of St Paul by Sedulius Scotus there are no less than two hundred and fifteen references to Origen noted in the margin.[111] It was his care in disengaging the spiritual sense from the literal meaning that endeared the great

[101] P.L., 109, 539, 635. [102] P.L., 115, 551.
[103] P.L., 102, 13. [104] P.L., 108.
[105] P.L., 120, 993. On the exegesis of Paschasius, cf. H. de Lubac, *Exégèse médiévale*, II, Paris (1961), p. 199–210.
[106] P.L., 120, 33.
[107] It is not yet quite certain which writings are to be attributed to what authors of the school of Auxerre in the second half of the ninth and the beginning of the tenth century (Rémi died in 909). It is generally agreed that Héric is the author of the homilies printed under his name in P.L., 95, 1169–566 *passim*, and also of those in the mss. Palat. lat. 431, and Rheims 1407, while the commentaries printed in P.L., 116, 695–1086 and 117, 11–295 are by Rémi. Those of Haymon are in P.L., 117, 362–815, 819–75. An *expositio missae*, P.L., 101, 1246–71, is also to be attributed to Rémi. Cf. H. Barré in "La lettre du pseudo-Jérôme sur l'Assomption, est-elle antérieur à Paschase Radbert?", in *Rev. bénéd.*, LXVIII (1958), pp. 213–25.
[108] P.L., 111, 1276. [109] P.L., 108, 247.
[110] Cf. J. Châtillon, "Isidore et Origène", in *Mélanges A. Robert*, Paris, 1957, pp. 544–546.
[111] Cf. A. Landgraf in *Zeitschrift für Kath. Theol.*, LXXIX (1957), p. 418.

Alexandrian to them all: they were on their guard against some of his views on specific points of doctrine, but it was to him that they went through the translations of Rufinus and St Jerome to learn the spiritual meaning of that Holy Scripture so many of whose books he had explained. Origen therefore, with St Jerome, appears foremost among the founders of medieval spirituality.[112] Rhabanus Maurus admits that the admirable commentary of Hesychius of Jerusalem was the source from which he drew much of his explanation of Leviticus.[113]

Carolingian exegesis is spiritual but very rarely personal. The taste of the period and the exigencies of Charlemagne's reforms in the cultural sphere sometimes introduced the elements of grammar and philosophy into these commentaries. Christian Druthmar, a monk of Corbie, in a commentary on St Matthew which he wrote for his brethren at Stavelot, invokes the liberal arts,[114] philology and the disciplines of the schools. His writings are more of an intellectual nature, and on the whole his style is cold, but at times, especially when he speaks of the Passion of Christ, his words flow more freely and he expresses his love in a cry: "Miserable wretches! you ought to have kissed his feet, and behold you bound his hands![115] Affections play an even greater part in the commentary on the Passion written by Candidus (†845), Rhabanus Maurus's successor at the head of the school of Fulda. He bursts into cries of admiration over the patience of our Saviour, and over the compassion which God put into the heart of the good thief.[116] Christ is the source and the model of all love.

The object, however, of all these commentaries is not to formulate the reactions of the reader to the mysteries revealed in the Scriptures but rather to point out the place these hold in the whole economy of our salvation, and to make clear their redemptive value and their universal bearing on the well-being of the Church. It is not the commentary itself which should turn reading into prayer, but meditation, "ruminating", on it. Smaragdus and the others handed on the traditional teaching on this point: for them as for their predecessors meditation was the effort of fixing the sacred words in the mind by constantly repeating them.[117] This unceasing attention to the words of Scripture is the remedy against temptations, particularly against those that creep into prayer itself: Hincmar taught, following St Gregory and Bede, that it is when

[112] On the influence of Origen in the Middle Ages see H. de Lubac, *Exégèse médiévale*, Paris, 1959, pp. 221–40 and *passim*.

[113] P.L., 108, 247.

[114] P.L., 106, 1266.

[115] P.L., 106, 1480.

[116] P.L., 106, 80, 94.

[117] Smaragdus *In Reg. S. Ben.*, P.L., 102, 784; *Diadema*, P.L., 3, 597. See *supra*, pp. 65–66.

one prays that temptations can be more violent than ever.[118] Meditation is the means "of transforming words into deeds"; it is the path towards the vision of God: "by reading the Holy Scriptures we have already begun to know a little of the bliss of Heaven."[119]

6. *Liturgical Devotion*

The same influences were responsible for the growing liturgical devotion of the time.[120] From the beginning of the eighth century Frankish churches had begun to use the so-called Gelasian Sacramentaries from Rome. Pepin favoured this tendency towards a single use, and Charlemagne authoritatively enforced unity, again chiefly by the help of Alcuin, who revised the sacramentary, missal and lectionary, giving to the liturgy of the West some of the essential characteristics which it still has. Indeed it has been said of Alcuin that he is "a partner of our own piety".[121]

The close connection between public worship and intellectual culture made possible a solemn performance of divine worship in a setting of great beauty: the ceremonies were lengthy and the adornments rich and skilful. It became common to introduce into this public prayer new literary compositions, particularly hymns. They were not part of the use of the Roman Church, nor at first of the Carolingian reform, but were admitted by other churches. Gradually however the Gallican Church made room for these poems in which the writers formed in the newly created schools expressed their fervent genius. These *carmina* (of which there are volumes)[122] were probably in many cases not intended for official liturgical prayer, but they were the expression of a personal devotion in line with it, breathing its air and setting forth its themes. The chant also underwent a rebirth: Amalarius, Agobard and others undertook the correction of the Antiphonal, with the object of restoring their original purity to the melodies as to all the other constituent parts of the "divine psalmody".[123]

[118] *De cavendis vitiis*, 6, P.L., 125, 906 C–D, gives the same teaching from *Bede Homil.*, I, 22, ed. *Corpus christianorum*, 122, pp. 160, 151–6.

[119] Rhabanus, *De eccles. discip.*, III, 1233–4.

[120] Cf. M. Andrieu in *Les "ordines romani"*, II, Louvain, 1948, pp. XVII–XLIX; P. de Puniet, "La liturgie sous les carolingiens", in C. Poulet, *Histoire du christianisme*, II, Paris, 1934, pp. 78–88; E. Bishop, "La réforme liturgique de Charlemagne", in *Ephem. Liturg.*, XLV (1931), pp. 186–207.

[121] G. Ellard, *Master Alcuin Liturgist, a partner of our piety*, Chicago, 1956. Cf. also H. B. Meyer, *Alkuin zwischen Antike und Mittelalter*, "Ein Kapitel frühmittelalterlischer Frömmigkeitsgeschichte", in *Zeitschrift fur Kath. Theol.*, LXXXI (1959), pp. 306–50.

[122] Ed. *Mon. Germ. Hist. Poetae latini aevi Karolini*, 4 vols, G. M. Dreves–C. Blume, *Analecta hymnica medii aevi*, Leipzig, 1886–1922, *passim*.

[123] Agobard, *De divina psalmodia*, P.L., 104, 325–30, *De correctione antiphonarii, ibid.*, 329–40. Amalarius, *Prologus antiphonarii*, ed. J. M. Hanssens, *op. cit.*, I, pp. 361–3; *De ordine antiph., inid.*, III, pp. 13–224. Charlemagne, in a capitu-

One of the results of the adoption by the Frankish churches of the Roman calendar was that solemn feasts became numerous. The life of the clergy itself was more and more organized around the Mass and the Canonical Office: they were now obliged to take part each day in the solemn celebration of all the Hours in their church, though in 817 the Council of Aix (contrary to the aims of St Chrodegang) did not insist that those of the clergy unable to be present at the solemn office should make it up in private.[124] The words of the public prayer were continued in devotional formulae which resembled the *Libelli precum*,[125] invocations alternating with "hymns" composed of verses from the psalms; and in the *Flores Psalmorum*, verses taken from the psalms in their numerical order gathered together in one prayer.[126] These prayers are a kind of "act" of contrition, adoration and supplication; in fact they express what Rhabanus Maurus calls every "legitimate" attitude of devotion, particularly those recommended by St Paul. As to how these "private prayers" (*peculiares orationes*) were to be said, the rule was that of the old monastic tradition: to say them often and without distractions—*pure frequenter*.[127] Through everything of this kind, whether poetry, prose, music, as well as in iconography, run certain major themes, above all that of our Redeemer's victory. In letters to the emperors and empresses of the period mention is made of Christ, the King of kings, whom princes and their ministers must serve, and at the beginning of many of the liturgical and biblical manuscripts is a full-page picture of the *Majestas Domini* in which our Lord is enthroned in glory surrounded by angels and the symbols of the evangelists, having as his sceptre the Cross by which he triumphed. Rhabanus Maurus composed a great treatise in praise of the Holy Cross: it was illustrated with twenty-eight figures, each rather intricately inscribed on a background of letters placed side by side which, taken together, made up a poem: the first one begins "King of kings and Lord".[128] The Blessed Virgin holds a

---

lary of 789, n. 80, prescribed the study of the Gregorian chant. *Mon. Germ. Hist. Capit.*, I, p. 61.

124 P. Salmon, "Obligation de la célébration de l'office", in *L'office divin*, Paris, 1959, pp. 30–1.

125 Ed. A. Wilmart, *Precum libelli quattuor aevi Karolini*, Rome, 1940; analysed by F. X. Haimerl, *Mittelalterlischer Frömmigkeit im spiegel der Gebetsbuch —Literatur Süddeutschlands*, Munich, 1952, pp. 5–19.

126 The *Collectio psalterii Bedae sive Psalterium parvum* which probably goes back to the time of Bede has been known since the time of Alcuin; ed. in *Corpus christianorum*, 122, Turnhout, 1955, pp. 452–70; *Flores psalmorum*, P.L., 40, 1135–8; *De psalmorum usu.*, P.L., 101, 465–508; *Officia per ferias, ibid.*, 509, 612.

127 Rhabanus Maurus, *De cleric. instit.*, II, 10–12, P.L., 107, 329–30. These chapters follow and are a necessary complement to the author's previous ones on liturgical prayer. See *supra*, p. 74.

128 P.L., 107, 141.

greater place in the piety of the period than might be thought,[129] and eastern tradition still influenced devotion to her.[130] Sermons on Mary by Ildephonsus and Bede were re-copied, and in addition new ones were composed by Ambrosius Autpert and many other anonymous writers. There is evidence too that it was from this time onwards that there grew up the custom of celebrating a votive Mass in honour of our Lady on Saturdays: the prayer *Singularis meriti* spread widely[131] and prayers to our Lady are found in other collections such as that of Nonantulus, of which the so-called *Book of prayers of St John Gualbert* was a replica.[132] In matters of doctrine theologians directed their attention to two questions which are not unconnected: Mary's virginity and her assumption. Ratramnus wrote a defence of Mary's virginity before the birth of our Saviour,[133] and Paschasius Radbertus explains in what sense this birth was virginal[134]; he also wrote a *Historia de ortu sanctae Mariae*[135] but his chief work on Mary is the homily on the Assumption long attributed to St Jerome, which was frequently copied and up to our time read in the Divine Office.[136] This work is not simply a theological statement; it has a great devotional content and in the mileux where it was read it encouraged an intense fervour. In treatises and sermons, doctrine and devotion went hand in hand: it was a spirituality where feeling was subordinated to an intelligent adherence of the spirit to the mysteries of faith.

In contemporary writings on the Holy Eucharist as in the *De vitiis cavendis* of Hincmar, and in other works of asceticism there is the same balanced outlook; the Mass and Holy Communion are

129 On this point I would not adopt a less cautious attitude than, following E. Sabbe, "Le culte marial et la genèse de la sculpture médiévale", in *Rev. Belge d'arch. et d'hist. de l'art*, XX (1951), pp. 101–25, I had done in "Grandeur et misère de la dévotion mariale au moyen âge", in *La maison Dieu*, 38 (1954), pp. 123–8. Cf. H. Barré, "La royauté de Marie au XIIe siècle en Occident", in *Maria et Ecclesia*, vol. V, Rome, 1959, pp. 93–4; L. Scheffczyk in *Das Mariengeheimnis in Frömmigkeit und Lehre der Karolingerzeit*, Leipzig, 1959, brings together considerable information, though there are a few gaps which H. Barré has pointed out in *Rev. d'hist. ecclés.*, LV (1960), pp. 551–3; the author shows that the reaction against adoptionism laid an emphasis on the theme of "Dei genitrix gloriosa"—the glorious motherhood; without however neglecting the "human" aspect. He also points out what importance was attributed to the perpetual virginity of Mary and to the parallel between Eve and Mary in the doctrine of the Redemption.

130 Cf. J. Ebersolt, *Orient et Occident*, Paris, 1954, pp. 41–8.

131 P.L., 101, 1400; cf. J. Leclercq, "Dévotion et théologie mariale dans le monachisme au moyen âge", in *Maria*, II, Paris, 1952, pp. 552.

132 P.L., 146, 971–80. Cf. A. Wilmart in *Rev. bénéd.*, XLVIII (1936), p. 259.

133 *De eo quod Christus ex virgine natus est*, P.L., 121, 81.

134 *De partu virginis*, P.L., 120, 1367.

135 P.L., 30, 308.

136 P.L., 30, 126; cf. H. Barré, "La lettre du pseudo-Jérôme sur l'Assomption est-elle antérieure à Paschase Radbert?", in *Rev. bénéd.*, LXVIII (1958), pp. 203–225.

the centre of all piety.[137] The necessity of a preparation of heart before receiving the Sacrament is stressed, but Holy Communion remains above all an act of faith in the victory of the risen Christ. "Eat of life, drink of life. . . . It is Christ that we eat, and yet he still lives though he has become our food: because though they killed him, he rose again." "The Good Shepherd gave his soul for us, so that his Body and Blood might become a sacrament for us: that his flesh might be the food of the sheep he had redeemed."[138]

The third theme is the Eucharist. It brings back to our mind the Passion, by which Christ has freed us from death; by it we may partake of the fruits of his victory, until we see him face to face and not as now under the appearances of the Sacrament.[139] As with our Lady, so with the Blessed Sacrament, the development of devotion and doctrine go together. Rhabanus Maurus in his treatise *On the formation of clerics* devotes a considerable space to Communion and its rites.[140] Paschasius Radbertus,[141] Ratramnus of Corbie[142] and Florus of Lyons[143] wrote on the dogma of the Eucharist, and though they disagreed on some aspects of its explanation their aim was the same: to increase the fervour with which the Christian partakes of "the feast where each day the King of all creation unites himself with his bride".[144] On the subject of the effects of the Eucharist on the soul Paschasius recalled the miracles told by St Gregory,[145] and Florus of Lyons applies to Holy Communion those passages from St Augustine on the intimacy of God and the soul and their mutual possession of one another. "Let the faithful soul love chastely, holding all that is temporal as vile so that it may possess the eternal good. Let the loving soul cleave to God, clinging to him in prayer, binding herself to him by a spiritual embrace, and desiring what he brings when he gives himself."[146]

7. *Erigena and the Knowledge of God*

The general recognition of the importance of liturgical worship did not prevent a doctrine of contemplation from taking shape, particularly in the monasteries. As in Cassian and St Gregory it is

[137] Ch. 6–8, P.L., 125, 904–15.
[138] *Ibid.*, ch. 10, 923 D; 924 A; 914 D.
[139] Ratramnus, *De corpore et sanguine Domini*, 100, ed. J. N. Backhuizen van den Brinck, Amsterdam, 1954, p. 60.
[140] Ch. 31–3, P.L., 107, 316–26.
[141] Paschasius Radbertus, *De corpore et sanguine Domini*, P.L., 120, 1267–350.
[142] Ratramnus, *De corpore et sanguine Domini*, ed. citée (note 138 *supra*).
[143] *De expositione missae*, P.L., 119, 15–72. On the theological aspect of the controversy cf. E. Amann, *L'époque carolingienne*, Paris, 1937, pp. 315–20.
[144] Paschasius Radbertus, *De corpore et sanguine Domini*, prol., P.L., 120, 1266.
[145] *Ibid.*, IX, 7–12, P.L., 120, 1298–1303.
[146] *De expositione missae*, 20, P.L., 119, 32.

linked with purity of heart: the two first books of a work of Rhabanus Maurus for Hatto Bonosus, Abbot of Fulda, have the significant titles *De videndo Deum* and *De puritate cordis*. The work is on a high level: the soul will only be satisfied when it sees God, but even in this life the desire for God which calls for asceticism and controls all our spiritual exercises will bring us to the heights of contemplation.[147]

Paschasius, at the end of his treatise *On Faith, Hope and Charity*, also speaks of that knowledge by love which unites us in desire to God, *per amorem intelligentiae*. This is that "chaste and devoted love" through which the soul to some degree takes hold of reality and loves what it has learnt to know, *apprehensa diligit*: by means of this love it will one day delight in the embrace of the Bridegroom.[148] Candidus of Fulda recurs to the same theme in a letter: the only way in which we can see God, in the measure possible in this world, is by purity of heart: "O my soul, purify thyself by faith, be master of thy body and make it the servant of virtue. Strive to enjoy God".[149] The object of all this teaching is to stimulate the practice of virtue and prayer: its whole tone is traditional, and though St Gregory and Cassian are not explicitly quoted or referred to, their thought and their expressions are easily recognizable. Candidus was expressing his opinion in a controversy which was to enable a very original mind to speculate on the knowledge of God, and to put forward quite new views. Certain texts in St Augustine had given rise to the question whether after the resurrection God could be seen with the eyes of the body.[150] Rhabanus Maurus, Gottschalk of Orbais, Hincmar and others propounded answers in which they endeavoured to reconcile apparent contradictions in the great bishop's writings. In 850, however, there arrived at the court of Charles the Bald an Irishman called John, surnamed Scotus or Erigena, probably a deacon or some kind of cleric. In his writings and translations he took a line of his own, turning for choice towards Greek thought. He translated into Latin the Pseudo-Dionysius, the *Ambigua* of Maximus the Confessor and the *Treatise on the creation of man* by St Gregory of Nyssa; wrote commentaries on the Pseudo-Dionysius, on the *De nuptiis philologiae et Mercurii* of Martianus Cappella,[151] and on the Gospel of St

147 P.L., 112, 1261–1303, especially 1282–97.
148 Ch. III, 14, P.L., 120, 1487–90.
149 *Num Christus corporeis oculis Deum videre potuerit*, 6, P.L., 106. On Candidus see *supra*, p. 86.
150 Cf. M. Cappuyns, "Note sur le problème de la vision béatifique au IXe siècle", in *Rech. de théol. anc. et médiév.*, I (1929), pp. 98–107.
* [See vol. I, pp. 517–20, 422–6.—Trans.]
151 Ed. C. E. Lutz, *Johannis Scotti annotationes in Marcianum*, Cambridge (Mass.), 1939. The other works of Scotus are in P.L., 122. On the question of

John, though of the last only extracts have survived. His most important work is a long and in some places obscure dialogue of a speculative character, *On the division of nature*. In the ninth century, though St Gregory was the chief source of all spiritual teaching, St Augustine remained unchallenged as the master of all philosophical and theological speculation. John Scotus's originality lay in his turning rather to the Greek Fathers and, through them, introducing Platonism into the Christian thought of the West.

This is not the place for a complete analysis of Erigena's teaching, it has already been excellently done[152]: but some notice must be taken of his particular conception of the knowledge of God, which was later to have some influence on spirituality. Before him, the search for truth had been seen above all as a means of combating error and reforming morality: for Erigena the truth is not so much a rule of life as an object of contemplation, something to be known for its own sake. He was, so to speak, eaten up with the desire to know God by means of Holy Scripture.[153] But this is difficult to understand; to do so requires great effort on the part of man, and a light from God which will enable the human spirit to go beyond that moral and allegorical sense of which sufficient has been said by the Fathers. Erigena's thought is, of course, a kind of religious intellectualism, an aspiration based on faith toward a "higher knowledge" which he called *altior theoria* or *contemplatio theologica*. To go from "simple faith" to wisdom, the soul must pass through knowledge by sense, beyond the words of Holy Scripture and all creatures. In these the *ratio*, which is the second degree of knowledge, discerns the hidden realities they signify. They are so many manifestations of God, "theophanies", that the reason when purified must interpret aright, ever going beyond what words and things say, carrying to infinity the limited perfections they reveal so as to apply them to God. Then the third degree, the *intellectus*, receives from the divine excellence "an absolutely simple and supernatural knowledge"[154] which is essentially inexpressible. This is the way of return to God, the *reversio*. There is a continuity between sensible and intellectual knowledge, between learning and wisdom, between faith and contemplation. All must pass through the first degree, though this is inadequate: the distance between

---

their authenticity and for a full account of their author see the excellent monograph by M. Cappuyns, *Jean Scot Erigène*, Louvain–Paris, 1933, on which I have relied for what follows. Cf. also A. Forest in Fliche-Martin, *Histoire de l'Église*, XIII, Paris, 1951, pp. 9–30.

[152] M. Cappuyns, *Jean Scot Erigène*, Louvain–Paris, 1933.

[153] *De div. nat.*, 3, 10, P.L., 122, 649–60; translated by M. Cappuyns, *op. cit.*, p. 273; 5, 8, 10, P.L., 122, 10, translated *ibid.*, 291.

[154] Cf. Cappuyns, *op. cit.*, pp. 291–302.

man the sinner, and the reality of God can only be bridged by the grace of illumination.

In order to describe this journey Erigena borrows a distinction from the Pseudo-Dionysius: there are two "theologies", two ways of speaking about God. Affirmation applies to the Creator all that is best in his works; negation denies to God every limitation inherent in creation, and in all that can be said or thought about creatures. God is beyond all things, he is "superessential" goodness and truth (*super* is a word Scotus uses often); to apprehend him fully is both the result of reflection and the effect of grace, and can only be done in Christ. God is the principle of all creation. One and triune, he comes down, so to speak, into the "primordial causes", and then through them into creatures. The primordial causes share according to a hierarchical order in the excellence of God: they are goodness, being, reason, truth, eternity and the other truths we can affirm of him. The Word is their principle, and in him they are united as rays coming forth from a centre. In the Incarnation the Word by the very fact of his *inhumatio* "came down as man into the effects of the primordial causes, for the sake of their salvation to whom as God they are eternally and unchangeably present; he reintegrated the effects in their causes in an ineffable union".[155] Thus God is at the same time the principle and the term of all things, and it is by the very close union of the Divine Being with human nature in the Word incarnate that this human nature can be rehabilitated, can carry out this *reversio*, the return to God which is the object of all the effort made to know him. Christ, perfect man, with a body and its senses, assumed a complete human nature, excepting sin alone and some of its effects, such as ignorance. As Redeemer he saved all things, sanctified them: he is the principle of salvation of all mankind, and through his merits man's nature at the resurrection will regain its primeval state. But there is more: then he will "deify" the elect: "every creature will appear changed into God alone, though it remains wholly itself." Thus in himself Christ sums up perfect humanity, that purity and light in which man tries to share by his knowledge of God.

Scotus, in explaining the vast and subtle doctrine of which this is but a short summary, used novel expressions translated from the Greek, occasionally somewhat clumsily; they were misunderstood and brought a condemnation upon him in the thirteenth century. There was of course a certain vagueness in his thought, but his effort to reflect on God and his mysteries was an original and vigorous one, and later on, in the twelfth century, William of St

[155] *De div. nat.*, 5, 24, P.L., 122, 912; cf. Cappuyns, *op. cit.*, pp. 361–2.

Thierry was to modify his intellectualism, integrating it into traditional spirituality. In fact however, Scotus had little influence[156] on his own times and the generations immediately following; he appears like a meteor at the end of the Carolingian period. His aim, which was to raise the spirit of men to a higher level of thought, was premature; the men of his time had no wish to change their habits and ways of thinking. The Carolingian was less the creation of something new than the gathering up and reorganization of the heritage of the past: indeed Isidore and Bede in an earlier age had to some extent shown greater originality than the compilers of the eighth and ninth centuries. But it was at least an age of fervour and order, and it handed down to the generations which succeeded it not only institutions, which bear in themselves germs of decay, but an accumulation of teaching which sooner or later—and the latter adverb is true for Erigena—would prove fruitful for Christian spirituality.

[156] Cf. P. Chevallier, art., "Denys l'aréopagite", in *Dict. de spirit.*, fasc. XVIII–XIX (1954), col. 319–21.

V

FERVOUR IN A TIME OF ANARCHY AND REFORM

IN the tenth and eleventh centuries more than at any other time in the history of the Church two contrary tendencies can be observed: a drift towards decadence and a movement of reform, one resulting from the other. The first came from the anarchy following the collapse of the Empire; with the disappearance of the centralized power which had organized Western Christianity on a basis that ultimately endured, the Church fell "into the power of the laity"[1] who on the whole did not concern themselves with her real interests; even Rome itself did not escape. Great abuses were the result: schisms and scandals in the Papacy, churches and monasteries seized by seculars, and among the clergy simony and incontinence. And yet throughout the whole of this troublous period the Church showed her vitality: in the monastic order there was a movement of protest showing itself first at Cluny and then elsewhere, and promoting reform in every country. With the re-establishment of the Empire in 962 under Otho I, ecclesiastical institutions and districts took shape again, churches and monasteries regained their freedom, and Christendom expanded to the east of Europe. Though the vicissitudes of the Holy See were not ended, the dynasty of Otho protected it, and shortly after the middle of the eleventh century (during the years when Hildebrand was the counsellor of the Papacy, and then from 1073 to 1085 Pope himself as Gregory VII) it took the lead in a religious revival. The "Gregorian reform" is the term of earlier efforts, and only took effect slowly. For two centuries more decadence and reform co-existed side by side, the latter gradually gaining the upper hand and giving the spirituality of the time its peculiarly fervent though reactionary character, with all its possible exaggerations.

Historically monasticism was the unifying factor in the development of reforms: they were started by abbots, and their success was

[1] Part of the title of vol. VII (E. Amann and A. Dubois) of *L'Hist. de l'Église*, ed. Fliche-Martin, Paris, 1940.

ensured by the monks who became popes or cardinals in the second half of the eleventh century.[2]

1. The Christian Knight

On the rare occasions when the laity as such were the object of the written teaching of the time, morality rather than spirituality was preached to them. Otloh of St Emmeran notes that it is Christians who persecute their fellow Christians, depriving the poor and the churches and monasteries of what they need[3]; it is to the natural virtues that they must be brought back, to the elements of virtue. Yet the Church did not limit herself to that: in an anarchical society she encouraged a mutual interdependence and a respect for the duties that sprang from it. To this end she made use of the network of feudal relationships which had already come into being, endeavouring to give them a religious value by insisting on the moral significance of fidelity: the fidelity of the nobles to the king, of vassals to their suzerain, of all men to their Lord; and equally the duties of princes and the powerful towards their subjects. Customs like the truce of God also contributed towards bringing charity into men's lives and maintaining it in their habits. Little by little there came into existence a feeling of solidarity among Christians, and feudalism tended towards Christian chivalry. Already by the end of the tenth century the Church blessed the knight's arms and prayed that he might bear them for the benefit of God's servants, and the defence of the weak.[4] In the second half of the eleventh century Bonizo of Sutri (†1086) in his *Book of the Christian Life*, dedicated to Gregory VII, could demand of *milites* that they should "keep faith with their lord, willingly giving their own life to protect him: and fight to the death to uphold the public weal". Theirs also is it to defend the widow and the orphan, to do battle against heretics and schismatics.[5] Addressing himself to princes, judges, and all classes of the laity, Bonizo reminds them of the integrity to which each man is bound, in accordance with his office or work[6]; there is even one kind of layman, the knight, who may have to lay down his life in the fulfilment of his duty.

[2] On the psychological background of the fundamental spiritual ideas touched on here, see the interesting and on the whole true remarks of P. Rousset, "Recherches sur l'émotivité à l'époque romane", in *Cahiers de civilization médiévale*, II (1959), pp. 53–67. On the historical and institutional framework of the period for one important region see B. Bligny, *L'Église et les ordres religieux dans le royaume de Bourgogne aux XI et XII siècles*, Grenoble, 1960.

[3] *Liber manualis*, I, P.L., 146, 246–7.

[4] Cf. E. Amman and A. Dubois, *op. cit.*, pp. 483–7, and A. Fliche, *ibid.*, vol VIII, Paris, 1940, pp. 462–78.

[5] *Liber de vita christiana*, ed. E. Perels, Berlin, 1930, pp. 248–9.

[6] *Ibid.*, pp. 242–3.

As far as the laity were concerned the Gregorian reform had two principal objects: to integrate them more into the ecclesiastical community, by a closer participation in the prayer and work of the Church, and to loosen their hold on the clergy and ecclesiastical institutions. The latter aim had as its corollary to detach the clergy from those secular affairs which were the province of the laity.[7] This double task is reflected both in the disciplinary decisions and in the spiritual literature of the time.

Spiritual writings to the address of the powerful, or of those living in the world, are rarer than in the preceding age. Some of Peter Damian's writings[8] are of this character, but on the whole he is more concerned with morality and the duties of a man's state of life than with prayer and asceticism. However, on one occasion, the saint urges Rainier, Margrave of Tuscany, not to delay in fulfilling the penance of going on pilgrimage to Jerusalem given him when he had confessed his sins.

> Those who live by a Rule, acknowledging the rights over them of the religious life, whether monastic or canonical, must not change their state; but we exhort those who live in the marshes of this world, or who, having enlisted in a spiritual militia, do not keep its laws, to take the road to exile, and by leaving their own country to make satisfaction to the Judge who is to be regarded with terror; thus by jouneying they will find rest, and in an alien land they will earn the right to live in their heavenly home.[9]

He advises the Duchess Beatrice to show her detachment from riches by helping the churches: "Give the earth in exchange for heaven!"[10] His wonderful correspondence with the Empress Agnes can hardly be considered as addressed to a person living in the world, since she had given up her throne and lived in Rome as a nun among nuns.[11] It was to her that John of Fécamp sent a little book on contemplative prayer and a very fine letter.[12] Anselm of Lucca (†1086) drew up some long and beautiful prayers for the Countess Mathilda of Tuscany who was so great a help to St Gregory VII.[13] It is clear then that some among the laity gave

[7] Light has been thrown on this whole question by G. Miccoli "Per la storia della pataria Milanese" in *Bolletina dell'Istituto storico Italiano per il medioevo*, LXX (1958), pp. 112–13.
[8] *Epist.*, VII–VIII, P.L., 144, 435–98.
[9] *Epist.*, VII, 17, P.L., 144, 456. [10] *Epist.*, VII, 14, P.L., 144, 453.
[11] Cf. A. Wilmart, "Une lettre de St Pierre Damien à l'impératrice Agnès", in *Rev. bénéd.*, XLIV (1932), pp. 125–46; J. Leclercq, *St Pierre Damien, ermite et homme d'Église*, Rome, 1960, pp. 127–31.
[12] Cf. A. Wilmart, "Deux préfaces spirituels de Jean de Fécamp", in *Rev. d'ascet. et de myst.*, XVIII (1937), pp. 3–44. J. Leclercq and J. P. Bonnes, *Un maitre de la vie spirituelle au XI siècle*, Paris, 1940, pp. 211–17.
[13] Ed. A. Wilmart, "Cinq textes spirituels composés par Anselme de Lucques pour la Comtesse Mathilde", in *Rev. d'ascet. et de myst.*, XIX (1938), pp. 23–72.

themselves up to prayer, to the *peculiaris oratio*; Peter Damian, when reminding Cinthius the Prefect of Rome that his first duty is to govern the City well, thought it necessary to add, "Take care that your zeal for the private prayer which perhaps you try to make does not lead you to neglect the duty of keeping good order among the people who have been entrusted to you".[14] During these iron centuries many among the laity had a spiritual life; the annals of the times and the Lives of the saints have kept the record of men like Otho III[15]; or the founder of Cluny,[16] William the Pious, duke of Aquitaine; and the father of St Odo,[17] who combined an ardent piety with great generosity. The monastic revival was a reaction against the greed of a great number among the laity, but it could never have taken place without the spirit of detachment in many of the others.

2. The Apostolic Life

The tenth and eleventh centuries saw, amidst grave irregularity, the dawn both of a renewal of fervour and of a reorganization of life among the clergy.[18] Pastoral teaching as far as can be seen from the canons was still in the tradition of the Fathers. Otloh of St Emmeran points out to the clergy the passages from the Bible which they should oppose to each of the vices,[19] for the Holy Scriptures were still their inspiration in the efforts needed to live in accordance with their state of life and fulfil their duties. The chief dangers which threatened them were ignorance, avarice and incontinence. As weapons, the councils, the bishops and the spiritual writers recommended the study of the word of God, and upheld the ideals of detachment and chastity. They emphasized the necessity of prayer. Peter Damian tells a bishop that he should pray without ceasing, "ruminating" (that is, meditating, in its traditional sense) passages from the Bible. "When you are going from one place to another, or on a journey, or about some necessary business, let your lips continually ruminate something from the Scriptures, grinding

[14] *Epist.*, VIII, 2, P.L., 144, 463.

[15] See, e.g., the praise given him by Bruno of Querfurt, *Vita quinque fratrum*, ed. R. Kade, in *Mon. Germ. Hist. Scriptores*, XV, p. 724, 30–4; cf. also V. Meysztowicz, *La vocation monastique d'Otton III*, *Antemurale*, IV, 1958 (Institutum historicum Polonicum Romae), pp. 27–76.

[16] On the piety of William and the other Dukes of Aquitaine in the tenth century, cf. A. Wilmart in *Rev. d'ascet. et myst.*, XVIII (1937), pp. 26–7, and E. Sackur, *Die Kluniacenser*, Halle, 1892–4, *passim*.

[17] John of Cluny, *Vita S. Odonis*, I, 5–9, P.L., 133, 45–7 gives St Odo's testimony to his father's sanctity.

[18] On the state of the life of the clergy see J. F. Lemarignier, "Le sacerdoce et la société chrétienne de la fin de IXe siècle au milieu du XIIe siècle", in *Prêtres d'hier et d'aujourd'hui*, Paris, 1954, pp. 113–52.

[19] *Liber de admonitione clericorum et laicorum*, ch. 4–5, P.L., 146, 252–5.

the psalms as in a mortar, so that they may ever give forth an odour as of aromatic plants".[20]

Once again the Church's remedy for the vices of the clergy was to insist on the advantages of the common life.[21] This had already been the object of the reforming canons of the Carolingian period, and particularly of the rule for the clergy promulgated at the Council of Aix in 817; and the way of life it recommended had spread widely and rapidly. In many places communities of priests, as well as providing for public worship, had kept schools for the training of future clerics. These "canons" did not undertake the care of parishes, but they did care for pilgrims, travellers and the poor. Many of these communities were fervent and made for a very high level of virtue: but the very way in which the "canonical institute" developed endangered its ideals. It became the custom for each canon to enjoy the revenues of a particular prebend, and these, together with a share in the chapter's possessions, excited the cupidity of laymen or of clerics who had no vocation to the common life. Inevitably a worldly spirit grew up, especially in the smaller communities, and the canons began to live without a rule, like people in the world, *saeculariter*, or like those "secular" clerics who were unfaithful to their moral obligations and their pastoral duties. Covetousness and a life entangled in worldly affairs led many priests to break the law of celibacy. They married, and provided for their children from the goods of the Church. Some among them went so far as to justify such a course and to defend "married priests", considering it quite legitimate that the faithful should pay for the upbringing of the "priest's sons".[22]

In order to remedy this state of things, the Church undertook what was the most energetic of her reformations before the great one of the sixteenth century, which as a matter of fact was in many points only the fulfilment of the earlier one. Towards the middle of the eleventh century there was a reaction on the part of the more zealous of the reformers against the rule of Aix, which was accused of having allowed private property and individual dwelling-places. Hildebrand, Peter Damian and others urged the clergy to tend towards apostolic perfection; to live as did the Twelve, "to imitate the primitive Church", to live together, having all things in common. Thus *saecularis* came to denote a cleric who owned private property whether he followed the rule of Aix or not, and the reformers set

[20] The text is among "Inédits de S. Pierre Damien", in *Rev bénéd.*, LXVII (1957), p. 158, by J. Leclercq.

[21] Cf. C. Dereine, art. "Chanoines", in *Dict. d'hist. et de géog. eccles.*, XII, Paris, 1953, cols. 367–82.

[22] Bibliography in M. L. Colker, "Fulcorii Belvacensis Epistolae", in *Traditio*, X (1954), pp. 234–5.

up as an ideal the *vita regularis* or *canonica*, that is, a strictly common life. But it never became obligatory: a council in Rome in 1059 recommended it, but was content to urge as a minimum the observation of the Rule of Aix. Nevertheless the "apostolic life" remained the ideal for the clergy, with the result that the clerics who conformed to it, and they were not few in number, tended to become regulars, religious living a monastic life. To encourage them in this state, St Peter Damian brought up a new argument[23] which had a lasting effect. He expatiated on the etymology of the word *clericus*, which denotes "the part and portion of God": if a man is part of God's heritage, he must renounce all earthly heritage and live on God's wealth in the Church; but if men propose to live by the Church they must do as in the first apostolic community, have all things in common; it is the primitive Church which must be their model, *primitivae ecclesiae forma*. In this way the regular canons were a kind of monastic order—a community made up of "those who live according to rule in a cloister under an abbot". As is every form of religious life, theirs too was to be "a school of Christ" where, taught by the Holy Ghost, they would learn detachment from the things of this world. Only by renouncing all private property can there be concord of mind and pure prayer. "How can a man give his mind to the psalmody in choir, if he is for ever thinking of the money in his coffers?"[24]

There was, however, one difference between the life of the regular canons and that of the monks: the former united the contemplative and active life, which was not the normal custom of monks, for the canons combined the liturgical life with the duties of the *cura animarum*: in every other respect their renunciation of the world was that required by monastic tradition. In one of the earliest complete rules drawn up for the regular canons, the spiritual teaching and many of the observances are borrowed from Rule of St Benedict, though without its being named; and the psychology of "conversion" is described in terms inspired by St Gregory's writings. Whether the question is that of detachment, purity of heart, fear and love, sense of sin and hope, or simply that of daily observances, the ideals of asceticism put before the clergy were, as in the time of St Chrodegang, those of monasticism, the only form of religious life known at this period. The needs of the Church were once more met, this time by a way of life which was a middle course between that of the monks and the later regular clerks: but it was

[23] On the novelty of this argument cf. C. Dereine, "Le problème de la vie commune chez les canonistes, d'Anselme de Lucques à Gratien", in *Studi Gregoriani*, III, Rome, 1948, p. 292, n. 44.

[24] *Opusc.*, 24, I, P.L., 145, 483–5. Cf. J. Leclercq, *St Pierre Damien . . .*, pp. 93–97.

also a step towards a further differentiation of "states of life", each of which was to have a spirituality adapted to its needs. As yet the teaching on prayer for the clergy was that handed down from the Fathers; and in the rules of the canonical institutions the ordering of the Divine Office took the largest place. There were passages from St Ambrose, St Augustine and St Gregory inculcating the necessity of prayer, but not specifying how it was to be made, and the interior life was normally nourished by reading and meditating on the Scriptures.[25]

3. The Monastic Revival

Monasticism differs from the clerical life, even that of the regular clergy, because it is ordered solely to asceticism and contemplation. As Abbo of Fleury (†1004) says, "the life of the clergy is a faithful mirror of the whole mystery of the Church, as the habit and profession of the monk is the example of all that is highest in penance".[26] Monks are, so to speak, specialists in the contemplative life, *contemplativae vitae sectatores*: theirs it is "with Mary to cover the feet of the Lord with their tears, and enclosed in their monastery to bring their conscience before the judgment seat; to expose and confess, and above all to weep for, their own sins and those of their neighbour".[27] Peter Damian, who exerted himself so greatly on behalf of the clergy, spoke to the same effect. It was generally recognised that if the life of the canons regular resembled that of the monks in some point of observance, there was still an essential difference in their way of life: the care of souls is a normal part of the calling of the clergy, but not of the monk. His vocation, because it is "disengaged", since it is directed towards God only, shares in a sense in God's mystery—and it is itself mysterious. As the author of the *Liber de unitate ecclesiae conservanda* writes, the monk's very habit, that long garment with its wide sleeves, is a symbol of the Cross and its mysteries: "as the word monk is in a sense the name of a mystery, so the cowl has as it were the virtue of a sacrament."[28] It was because of monasticism that the iron centuries were also contemplative centuries; possible never has there been so much prayer in the Church as then.

It by no means follows that all monks attained to an exceptional degree of virtue, or that there were no abuses in the monastic order

[25] Cf. J. Leclercq, "Un témoignage sur l'influence de Grégoire VII dans la réforme canoniale", in *Studi Gregoriani*, VI, Rome, 1959, pp. 173–228.

[26] *Apologeticus*, P.L., 136, 465 A.

[27] Abbo of Fleury, *Epist.*, VIII, P.L., 136, 430 C.

[28] Ed. *Mon. Germ. Hist. Libelli de Lite*, II, 278, 36–7. "Sicut enim monachus est vocabulum quoddam mysterii, sic et cuculla est quaedam virtus sacramenti."

itself.[29] The monks, as a means of combating abuses and freeing the monasteries from the lay stranglehold which prevented their playing their part in the life of the Church, were the first to set up an organization for mutual help and defence. Up to this time the abbeys had been completely independent of one another; now there grew up associations or federations whose juridical ties were very flexible, having often come into existence owing to the influence of one reformed monastery on others. These spiritual "filiations" made possible the spread of "customaries" which were both the means and the symbol of the revival.[30] The unions came into being round what has been called "key monasteries"[31] which had themselves drawn up collections of statutes, *consuetudines*, which laid down a particular application of the Rule. Little by little these unions were to give birth to the "congregations" and to the first of the religious orders, that of Cluny, the *ordo cluniacensis*. On the continent the reforming movement was dominated by three names, Cluny, Gorze, and in Italy, Monte Cassino. Cluny, which was founded in Burgundy in 910, spread throughout France, into Spain and Italy, to England* and even in the north and east of Europe and as far as Poland. Gorze was founded in Lorraine in 933, and its influence was chiefly felt in north-east Europe and throughout the Empire, though other great abbeys in these regions remained autonomous and themselves became centres of reforming activity. Gorze and Cluny, however, typify the two main streams of reform. There were certain differences between them. In Germany since the time of St Boniface, and in England, the abbeys had played a part in the evangelization of the country and were therefore more closely bound up with local churches and their needs; and there were also differences in habit, daily observances and liturgical usages in the areas under the respective influence of the two monasteries, but these were distinctions rather than oppositions.

In England many of the abbeys were cathedral monasteries, and

* [Cf. also E. Sackur, *Die Kluniacenser*, 2 vols, Halle, 1892, 1894, *passim* and D. Knowles, *The Monastic Order in England*, Cambridge, 1950, p. 29.—Trans.]

[29] On the circumstances in which a monk's life might be passed see, e.g., P. Cousin, *Abbon de Fleury-sur-Loire*, Paris, 1954. On the reform of St Gérard of Brogne see *Rev. bénéd.*, 1960, pp. 1–240.

[30] A list of customaries will be found in U. Berlière, *L'ascèse bénédictine des origines à la fin du XII siècle*, Paris–Maredsous, 1927, pp. 24–36. K. Hallinger, *Gorze-Kluny*, Rome, 1950, pp. 883–4; M. Alamo, art., "Coutumiers monastiques et religieux", in *Diction. de spiritualité*, II (1953), col. 2454–9. Some texts of customaries and a diagram showing the filiation of monasteries in B. Albers, *Consuetudines monasticae*, I–V, Monte Cassino, 1905–12; the filiations from Gorze are shown in K. Hallinger, *op. cit.*, *passim*.

[31] Cf. J. F. Lemarignier, "Structures monastiques et structures politiques dans la France de la fin du Xe et des débuts du XIe siècle", in *Il monachesimo nell'alto medioevo*, Spoleto, 1957, p. 364.

therefore the *cura animarum* had a certain place in their life. It has been said that between 800 and 940 monastic life had in fact disappeared in England,[32] but a powerful revival took place, chiefly under the aegis of St Dunstan and St Ethelwold, one of whose results was the drawing up between 957 and 965 of the *Regularis concordia*, an "agreement on a regular life", between the English abbots. The great upsurge of monasticism which they brought about owed its inspiration to the customs already in force on the continent.[33] At the beginning of the eleventh century one of St Ethelwold's disciples, Aelfric, translated the Old Testament and various monastic writings into Anglo-Saxon, and wrote various spiritual works in the same tongue. Italy was influenced by much that went on to the north of her frontiers, but her own contribution to the movement was an Eastern influence due to the many Italo-Greek monks on her soil.[35] Little is, however, known of it as yet, and it is therefore difficult to discern. Everywhere monasteries of women, too, profited by this general revival, and by the importance which the canonical collections attributed to their way of life.[36] All through Christendom there was a rebirth of abbeys great ánd small which, in spite of inevitable weaknesses, stored up reserves of fervour and a spirit of prayer from which the Church drew vital strength for her reforms.

During the eleventh century lay brothers appear in the *familia* of some of the Benedictine monasteries. This was an institution destined to develop among the Benedictines and to spread to the Carthusians and Cistercians and elsewhere. It opened a path of spirituality to countless souls, for these *famuli* were able to come to the religious life, to the *conversio perfecta*: their vocation was a specialized one to the lowly service of the monks, so that the latter could more freely give themselves to the duties of their state.[37] Heymon of Hirsau makes the special function of these lay brothers very clear, showing what in their turn they receive from the monks: "The monks use the services of the faithful lay brothers in the administration of external possessions, and these in return receive

[32] D. Knowles, *op. cit.*, pp. V, 31–6.

[33] Ed. T. Symons, *Regularis concordia*, London, 1953. Cf. E. S. Duckett, *St Dunstan of Canterbury, a Study of Monastic Reform in the Tenth Century*, London, 1955; H. Dauphin in *Rev. bénéd.*, 1960, p. 177.

[34] Cf. M. M. Dubois, art. "Elfric", in *Dict. de spiritual.*, IV (1961), col. 559–64.

[35] Cf. J. Leclercq, *St Pierre Damien*, p. 40.

[36] Cf. J. Rambaud-Buhot, "Le statut des moniales", in *St Fare et Faremoutiers*, Faremoutiers, 1956, pp. 163–74; P. Schmitz, *Hist. de l'ordre de S. Benoît*, VII, Maredsous, 1956, pp. 59–81.

[37] Much has been written on the origins of *conversi* or lay brothers: the only dependable work is that of K. Hallinger, "Woher kommen die Laienbrüder?" in *Analecta S. Ord. Cist.*, XIII (1957), pp. 1–104 [but cf. D. Knowles, *op. cit.*, pp. 419–20, appendix XXIII.—Trans.]

from the monks what is necessary for the care of their souls; and they imitate as far as is possible outside the cloister, the discipline of the monastery"[38] and Ulrich of Cluny writes to William of Hirsau :"You have deserved that free men and even nobles should humble themselves to serve you daily as servants, looking for no other life than the eternal one of heaven."[39] These *conversi* were of a new kind, differing from those of earlier centuries in that they were true religious, bound by vows. Through their Office, which like that of any unlettered layman consisted chiefly of *Paters* and *Glorias*, they often led a life of intense and simple prayer.

All over the Benedictine West there was as a whole the same conception of the monastic life, though its institutional framework was flexible enough to allow of certain monks leading a solitary life in the shadow of the abbeys.[40] Its chief occupation was that which takes up the largest part of the customaries, the work of prayer. In the life of the community the method of performing the liturgy was minutely laid down: to the Divine Office provided for in the Rule of St Benedict there had been added extra psalms and additional offices, processions and litanies, and various prayers and ceremonies; these in their turn gave rise to innumerable literary and musical works—a "religious art"—to which are due many of our masterpieces. This religious humanism is recalled by the names of Notker of St Gall (†1022) and his disciples Hartmann, Waldo, Solomon, Gerald and the two Eckharts.[41] The majority of these writers, some of whose admirable works are still in use, were anonymous; their work celebrates the glory of the cycle of the saints and the feasts of our Lord, but above all that of the Paschal mystery. With simple enthusiasm they composed, for the Resurrection, the Ascension and Pentecost, songs of triumph and splendid joyous hymns, whose poetry shines forth in their simplicity and clarity.[42] But in contrast, where prayer is spoken of, nothing very much is said about mental prayer. Not that there was any lack of this. The Carolingian

[38] *Life of William of Hirsau*, 23, P.L., 150, 914.

[39] *Consuet. Cluniac. Epist. Nuncupatoria*, P.L., 149, 637. B. Rudolph (†1080), the fourth prior of Camaldoli, speaks in the same sense in his *Constitutiones*, ch. 46 (ed. Mittarelli-Costadoni, *Annales Camaldulenses*, Venice, 1755, Vol. III, col. 537, and ed. Subiaco, 1944, p. 45) of the laymen who serve the monks being for them what the Gabaonites were for Israel, and he applies to them the verse of St Paul "alter alterius onera portate . . ." (Gal. VI, 2).

[40] Examples from Gorze are quoted in K. Hallinger, *Gorze-Kluny*, *passim* (cf. p. 988; Anachorese); for Cluny and the other centres of monastic influence, cf. J. Leclercq, "Pierre le Vénérable et l'érémitisme clunisien", in *Petrus Venerabilis*, Rome (*Studia Anselmiana*, 40), 1956, pp. 99–112 and "Nouveaux témoins sur l'érémitisme bénédictin" in *Rev. bénéd.*, LXVIII (1958), pp. 85–86.

[41] Cf. W. von den Steinen, *Notker der Dichter und seine geistige Welt*, Berne, 1948.

[42] Cf. J. Leclercq, *L'amour des lettres et le désir de Dieu*, Paris, 1957, pp. 219–35,

revival which was the origin of all this liturgical development made provision for "private prayer".[43] In the *Ordo Qualiter* towards the beginning of the ninth century it was laid down that after Compline "all shall keep the greatest silence of tongue and heart and shall pray in secret, remembering their sins not without tears, sighs and groans, but in such a way as not to disturb each other".[44] In later customaries there are allusions to similar practices: "let each one pray as God gives him to do."[45] In the *Regularis Concordia* it is laid down in several places that between the Offices the monks shall "remain seated in church, given up to prayer".[46] On rising in the morning, as they are dressing, "each one on his own, as God shall put it into his heart by a divine inspiration, in silence and with all the intention of his heart, shall sanctify what he does by prayers or the recitation of a canonical Hour or the seven penitential psalms.[47] Unceasing prayer is, then, the rule; and as a rule it expresses itself spontaneously in the words that are sung in choir. After Compline, "should it happen that a monk in his fervour wishes to continue his prayer, let him do so".[48] After the Matins of the last three days of Holy Week, "let those brethren who will go to their rest, but those who for the sake of their spiritual exercises prefer not to, shall in the most complete silence, do what the good of their soul requires".[49] For most of the customaries, the time after Compline, when the cares of the day have grown blurred, is considered especially favourable to "private" or "secret" prayer.[50] In community this is always to be short, but between the Offices each may and should give himself up to it according to his degree of "fervour", that is according to the grace of prayer that he has received. Prayer is one of the normal occupations of a monk; for everyone it is to be frequent and short, while for some there is nothing to prevent it being longer; but these are the exceptions, as Hildemar says in his Commentary.[51]

In this the Benedictine tradition of the Middle Ages shows a wonderful continuity: while public worship was regulated even in its most minute details, private prayer was not touched on save in passing; it is seen in the framework of the liturgy, it follows or precedes an Office, or is the continuation of one of the canonical Hours; the liturgy is its nourishment and its life. But by its very nature even its duration cannot be regulated, except when it is

43 "*Secrete orare*", Albers, *op. cit.*, III, 67.
44 *Ibid.*, III, 48.
45 *Consuetudines cluniacenses antiquiores* 7, ed. Albers, II, p. 6.
46 Ed. Symons, *op. cit.*, p. 14.
47 *Ibid.*, p. 15.
48 *Ibid.*, p. 42.
49 *Ibid.*, p. 36.
50 Various *Lives* bear witness to the practice, e.g. the *Passio S. Adalberti*, II, L., 137, 870.
51 See *supra*, pp. 80, 81.

necessary to recall that prayer in common must be brief. At the very moment when public prayer had reached its highest point of development and organization, private prayer was at its most spontaneous and simple.[52]

4. Cluny and Unceasing Prayer

In considering the monastic revival the historian is in a privileged position with regard to Cluny, for there can be seen at work more clearly than in many other cases that institution of prayer which the Benedictine life had become.[53] Our information comes from various sources; not merely codes of laws, or expositions of principles, but also hagiographical writings which to a great extent mirror the real life of a number of the great abbots whose fervour gave a new inspiration to their monasteries; from these writings too a great deal may be learnt about their monks.[54] It is true that Cluny was not, as some historians have held, the only great centre of reform, nor did it invariably take the lead in the evolution of institutions and ritual; but if it was not the originator of every change it had the greatest and most lasting effect on the whole revival. Where it did not take the place of other influences it introduced its own customs among them. Its close ties with the Apostolic See in the eleventh century made it one of the principal instruments of ecclesiastical reform, and St Peter Damian himself, whose own views led him in a different direction from that of Cluny, recognized that it was an "incomparable" monastery.[55] What was it in Cluny that called forth the admiration even of those whose ascetic ideals were very different? Simply the perfection of its organization of prayer. This organization was in itself only one element of a far larger programme in which monasticism looked back to what was essential in its origins, justifying itself by its traditional theology.

It was from its first abbot, Blessed Berno, that Cluny had received its specific character, in particular exemption by which it had secured

[52] On the life of prayer in the English monasteries see the valuable and balanced account by D. Knowles, *op. cit.*, pp. 470–1. His remarks are true of other places. On the monastic spiritual writers of the time see P. Schmitz, *Hist. de l'ordre de S. Benoît*, II, Maredsous, 1942, pp. 365–94. On "La spiritualité à S. Riquier", J. Hourlier in *Rev. Mabillon*, L (1960), pp. 1–20.

[53] If Cluny occupies a larger place here than other great monastic centres, it is only because, for reasons which will appear, there is more information available about this monastery than about many others. It does not seem that anything very different could be said of the life of prayer at Gorze or elsewhere, as far as can be judged in the present state of research into medieval monastic horaria: it is a region still open to exploration.

[54] Cf. *Les Saints abbés de Cluny—Textes choisis et presentés par R. Oursel*, Namur, 1960.

[55] *Epist.*, VI, 2, P.L., 144, 372.B.

complete independence of lay control through a close attachment to the Apostolic See.[56] The real founder of Cluniac spirituality, however, was Berno's successor, St Odo (924–42). His outlook can be learnt from his writings and his acts. Among the former were a long scriptural poem, *the Occupation*;[57] *Conferences*;[58] and a collection of extracts from the *Morals* of St Gregory,[59] to whom, as his style and ideas show, he owes much. He even took from Gregory his thoughts on the approaching end of the world—as with the great pope, the scourges and abuses in the world around him convinced him that the final doom was near.[60] The effect was to make his work even harder to find a remedy for every kind of evil wherever it might be found, starting with the abuses in monastic life itself. For this purpose the first thing to do was to convince the monks of the value of their state of life; St Odo reminds them that it consists in keeping before the world the mystery of Pentecost, in showing mankind what the Church essentially is: the holiness of God communicated to men. It is for monks to go out of this sinful world, to be strangers to it, as it were outside it, *extra mundum fieri*, and to become, as far as is possible to human frailty, dwellers in paradise. The silence and peace of eternity must begin for them here and now; they must live as the angels, joining with them in the eternal praise of God; each one by asceticism sharing in the depths of his heart in the mystery of Christ.[61]

In this atmosphere of spacious theology, this life whose centre was God, the whole point of the celebration of the liturgy could be understood. It was a worship and an asceticism. All that the monk had to do was to adhere to the inexhaustible marvels that the Church spread out before the eyes of his faith, throughout the Christian year. A ceremonial whose etiquette was regulated in its least details made it possible to carry out with, so to speak, a delicate technique, the service at the court of the King of kings. It called for sustained effort and perpetual self-abnegation from each one, always, and at all times. On the other hand, this complicated ritual could not be allowed to become an obstacle to the secret

56 Cf. J. F. Lemarignier, "L'exemption monastique et les origines de la réforme gregorienne", in *A Cluny*, Dijon, 1950, pp. 288–340.

57 Ed. A. Swobada, Leipzig, 1900.

58 P.L., 133, 517–38.

59 Cf. J. Laporte, "St Odon, disciple de St Grégoire le Grand", in *A Cluny*, Dijon, 1950, pp. 138–43.

60 Cf. R. Manselli, "La 'Lectura super Apocalypsin' di Pietro di Giovanni Olivi" in *Richerche sull'escatologismo medioevale*, Rome, 1955, pp. 32–6.

61 Cf. K. Hallinger, "Zur geistigen Welt des anfänge Klunys", in *Deutsches Archiv.*, X (1954), pp. 417–45, "Le climat spirituel des premier temps de Cluny", in *Rev. Mabillon*, XLVI (1956), pp. 117–40; and J. Leclercq, "L'idéal monastique de St Odon d'après ses œuvres", in *A Cluny*, pp. 227–32; and "Le monachisme clunisien", in *Théologie de la vie monastique*, Paris (Aubier), 1961, pp. 447–57.

prayer of the heart, and this danger was avoided by a familiarity with Cassian, St Gregory and even the Areopagite. St Odo's successor, St Majolus (954–994), had a great love for the writings of St Gregory,[62] and one morning he was found asleep, his head pillowed on a manuscript of Dionysius which he had been reading for several hours during the night.[63] St Odilo (1048), who succeeded him, wrote some devotional prayers called *The Spiritual Medicine*, homilies for the feasts of our Lord and our Lady, and hymns in her honour and in honour of St Majolus.[64] Although, as he himself said, tropes were less in favour at Cluny than "among the Teutons",[65] he put no check on the ritual and the development of the liturgy in the monastery, which, as the successive customaries show,[66] reached its culminating point during the long tenure of office of St Hugh (Abbot 1049–1109). In all these customaries, as in all similar ones, private prayer is only alluded to in the way in which St Benedict speaks of it. "If perchance a brother desires to pray by himself (*oratio peculiaris*) let him go out and do it speedily: *sub brevitae orationem faciat.*"[67] This milieu shaped by the solemn prayer of the Church did not, however, preclude private devotion: only, like the liturgy, the latter expressed itself in terms of the sacred Scriptures, particularly of the psalms. The celebration of the liturgy in common was a stimulus to the mind of the individual; during the times of silence, in the midst of every occupation, the words of the Office came back to his heart and lips. It was the custom in England to recite psalms while washing; at Cluny while working in the kitchen or sacristy. Prayer took hold of the monk's whole life—a prayer which was not simply a heedless mumble, but came from the depths of a soul sanctified by the mysteries of Christ. Through their veneration for the feasts of our Lord and the acts of his life, and contemplation of his Passion and Resurrection, they lifted up their hearts to what these accomplish for our salvation, and communicate and make ever present to us. It is at this time that Masses are found "in honour of our Saviour's humanity"; as a means by which men might unite themselves with the particular divine work which it had accomplished in them.[68] This overflowing liturgical life

[62] St Odilo, *Vita S. Maioli*, praef., P.L., 142, 943.

[63] Syrus, *Vita S. Maioli*, III, 17, P.L., 137, 775.

[64] P.L., 142, 939–1038. For a critical judgment on his works, and a life and sketch of St Odilo, see J. Hourlier in a work to be published, *St Odilon.*

[65] Ulric of Cluny, *Consuet, cluniac.* I, 24, P.L., 149, 672.

[66] Ed. Albers, *op. cit.*, II; Ulric of Cluny, *Consuet. cluniac.*, P.L., 149, 635–778. Cf. H. Philippeau, "Pour l'histoire de la coutume de Cluny", in *Rev. Mabillon*, XLIV (1954), pp. 141–51; J. Leclercq, *ibid.*, pp. 37–42; K. Hallinger in *Zeitschr. der Savigny stift. Kan. Abt.*, 1959, pp. 99–140.

[67] *Consuet. cluniac. antiq.*, II, ed. Albers, II, p. 3.

[68] Cf. J. Leclercq, "Sur la dévotion à l'humanité du Christ", in *Rev. bénéd.*, LXIII (1953), pp. 128–30.

gave birth to hymns and prayers and praises of every kind to the Mother of God, and to devotional practices like the servitude of Mary by which Odilo gave himself to our Lady as a vassal to his lord.[69] He shows us Mary as the model of what should be the occupations of the contemplative life: "*Orabat, legebat*"[70]; and in a burst of tender and confiding love he writes the invocations which St Bernard would one day turn into the famous *Respice stellam, voca Mariam*.[71]

Private Masses came to take an ever-growing place in the piety of the times: St Odilo on his death-bed had the number of Masses he had said since his ordination counted on an abacus.[72]

The individualism of which this was a beginning was a development along the lines of devotion fostered by the *libelli precum* since Merovingian times; it was not particularly affective, being contemplative rather than theological or speculative.[73] The medieval monk was not given to reflecting on his own sufferings, or analysing his interior trials; to him anything which hindered the flight of his soul to God was a temptation of the devil and he turned his eyes towards the Cross triumphant. All his asceticism, the network of observances which restrained him was in order to his liberation. He knew that purity of heart and the vow of virginity are the conditions of a truly contemplative life, so he willingly accepted the precautions of the customaries against his frailty; and always he turned to the Bible.[74] It is said of St Odilo that "this book of divine contemplation was ever in his hands, and he spoke always of the Holy Scriptures". The monks worked, read, wrote: what is known of the library at Cluny is sufficient to show that the liturgical offices did not take up the whole of their time or activity.[75] Their aim, however, was not to produce original work. Their essential asceticism lay perhaps less in the complex of fasts, abstinence, and vigils that the customaries describe, than in a continual self-abnegation for the benefit of common worship, with the truths it imprints on the heart

[69] Jotsaud, *Vita S. Odilonis*, XIII, 44. *Acta SS Bolland*, I, Antwerp, 1643 p. 70. Cf. O. Ringholtz. *S. Odilo der grosse Marienverherer*, Einsiedeln, 1922.

[70] *Serm.*, 12, P.L., 142, 1024.

[71] *Serm.*, IV *De incarn.*, P.L., 142, 1003–4. On the sources of this theme cf. H. Barré, "S. Bernard, docteur marial", in *S. Bernard théologien*, Rome (*Analecta S. Ord. Cist.*, IX, III–IV), p. 111.

[72] St Peter Damien, *Vita S. Odilonis*, P.L., 144, 928–9.

[73] Cf. G. de Valous, *Le monachisme clunisien*, Ligugé–Paris, 1935, I, p. 329; J. Leclercq, art. "Contemplation", in *Dict. de spirit.*, II, Paris, 1953, col. 1040–1.

[74] Jotsaud, *op. cit.*, I, 6, P.L., 142, 901.

[75] Cf. J. Leclercq, "Cluny fut-il ennemi de la culture?", in *Rev. Mabillon*, XLVII (1957), pp. 172–82; "Spiritualité et culture à Cluny", in *Spiritualità Cluniacense*, Todi, 1960, pp. 101–51; "Pour une histoire de la vie à Cluny", in *Rev. d'hist. ecclés.*, LVII, 1962. P. Lamma, *Momenti di storiografia Cluniacense*, Rome, 1961.

and the words it puts on the lips. Prayer held the monk of Cluny wherever he might be; and in the asceticism of a conventional life which St Odo described as a society of mutual supervision,[76] each had to efface himself. It was for each monk individually to widen his learning and to cultivate a personal love for our Lord and a devotion to our Lady; he might in the Scriptorium or workshop complete one of those anonymous masterpieces which the world still admires: but the great work of his life was to put himself completely at the disposal of a society whose chief task was to carry out exactly a service at court. Any time which was not given to solemn praise was filled by spiritual reading, private prayer, and unpretentious manual labour—the *fraterna servitia*—and all this had as its background the divine words learnt in choir or meditated on during times of silence. Probably what one may call the habit of prayer has never been carried to greater lengths. Cluny was the chosen home not so much of the *laus perennis* as of the *oratio continua*.[77]

5. *St Romuald and his Disciples*

Traditional Benedictine monasticism was cenobitic in character though in particular cases it had a place for the recluse. But in a period in which the flood of vice had penetrated even to the clergy, certain fervent Christians were driven by way of compensation towards extreme forms of austerity, first among which was the search for solitude. In the tenth century Grimlac, living as a hermit in some part of Lorraine or its neighbourhood (where precisely is not known), wrote the first rules for recluses known in the West.[78] He took his inspiration from St Chrodegang whose own teaching came from St Benedict, and the whole work is much influenced by St Gregory whom he quotes several times. What he says of compunction of heart[79] and assiduity in reading and prayer[80] is in line with St Gregory's teaching as it had been handed down by Isidore, Defensor, Hildemar and Smaragdus. Grimlac does not actually mention St Benedict, but reproduces the passage in which it is said that

[76] St Odo thus describes it in two verses of the *Occupatio* (Bk VII, vv. 145–6) which are reminiscent of Gen. 4. 9, "Am I my brother's keeper?"

"Mutua quo fratres melius praesentia servet
Alter ut alterius quasi sit custos vicissim."

[77] A. Wilmart, *Auteurs spirituels et textes dévots du moyen âge latin*, Paris, 1932, pp. 77–8, has given a very good description of the Cluniac school.

[78] Text in P.L., 103, 575–663. An analysis will be found in P. Doyère, art. "Érémitisme", in *Dict. de spirit.*, fasc. XXVIII–XXIX (1960). On the possible relations of Grimlac with Gorze, cf. J. Leclercq, "Reclus et recluses à Metz durant le moyen âge", in *Rev. eccl. du diocèse de Metz*, LIII (1953), pp. 23–4.

[79] Ch. XXIX–XXX, P.L., 103, 617–19.

[80] Ch. XXXVIII, P.L., 627–9.

prayer must be "short and pure unless by an instinct of divine grace it be prolonged".[81] St Benedict had said this of the prayer made by all after the Office was ended, but Grimlac was writing for recluses who made their prayer alone, except when they came to their window and, though staying in their cell, yet "recite the Scriptures together, giving themselves to holy prayers and encouraging one another in the service of God".[82] He thus applies to the solitary life the traditional teaching that prayer should be brief but so frequently renewed that it becomes continuous.[83] In fact he asks the question plainly: can a man, following St Paul's counsel, pray without ceasing? Some have said that it is done by observing the Canonical Hours, but this answer is inadequate. "For us there must never be a moment when we are not praying . . . when we cannot pray with our lips, we must do so in our heart."[84] Grimlac's rule was an attempt to adapt the Benedictine Rule and tradition to a way of life quite different from that which St Benedict himself had in mind, and it does not seem to have spread.

In Italy, however, within Benedictine monasticism itself, an eremetical tendency began to appear which resulted in a type of regular life different from that which tradition had built up on the Rule. In the second half of the tenth century it took shape around the powerful personality of St Romuald. He had reformed and even founded *cenobia*, but his preference was for hermitages, and it was in these that his posterity continued. His particular contribution to monasticism was to bring order and regularity into the lives of those isolated recluses who gave themselves up to prodigies of austerity. He enjoined a rule on them, and for that reason deserves to be called "the father of spiritual hermits, of those who live according to a rule".[85] The rule he imposed was that of St Benedict to the extent that it could be adapted to the eremetical life.[86] He had innumerable disciples, of most of whom nothing is known. Bruno of Querfurt, writing of the death of two brothers John and Benedict, expressed his own longing for martyrdom, at the time when St Adalbert had been put to death because he wished to evangelize the pagans of eastern Europe. Romuald and his disciples were urged not so much by apostolic zeal as by asceticism: for them, as for St Boniface and the ancient Celtic monks, the "love of exile" was a

[81] Ch. XXXI, P.L., 103, 620.

[82] Ch. XVI, P.L. 103, 595.

[83] Ch. XXXI, P.L. 103, 620.

[84] Ch. XXXII, P.L., 103, 621–2.

[85] Bruno of Querfurt, *Vita quinque fratrum*, ch. 2, *Mon. Germ. Hist. Scriptores*, XV, p. 718. On the sources for the meaning of this expression cf. G. Tabacco, "Privilegium amoris. Aspetti della spiritualità Romualdina—from *Il Sagiatore*, IV, 2–3, Turin, 1954, p. 19, note 120.

[86] Cf. J. Leclercq, "St Romuald et l'érémitisme missionaire", in *Rev. bénéd.*, LXXII (1962).

form of self-renunciation, an opportunity of leaving all things[87]; the world and its ease, the earthly country and, if God willed, life itself.

The teaching by which St Romuald prepared his disciples for this wholehearted sacrifice has come down to us. "Sit in thy cell as it were in paradise; cast far behind thee every memory of this world; watch over thy thoughts as a fisherman keeps an eye on the fish. There is a path in the psalms which thou must never leave. Since thou art still in the fervour of a novice and canst not accomplish everything, let thy spirit move hither and thither in psalmody, seeking to understand its meaning. When in reading thy mind wanders, leave not thy book but hasten to find a remedy by seeking to understand. Before all things, place thyself in the presence of God in fear and trembling like him who stands before the emperor. Go onwards to the total destruction of thine own self—*destrue te totum*—stay still as a chick, happy to receive the grace of God; for did his mother not feed him he would have nothing to eat."[88]

The perfect simplicity of this teaching led those who had the strength to put it into practice to the possession of God. "Solitude is like gold; it gives the living God to those who thirst for Him."[89] In St Romuald's thought, as in that of his two great Italo-Greek contemporaries, the theologians St Nilus of Grottoferrata (†1005) and St Simeon the New Theologian (†1002), tears of compunction are a cry to God and a sign of his presence. Burning with love, Romuald would sometimes cry out, "Beloved Jesus, beloved Jesus, thou art sweet to me as honey, thou art my ineffable desire",[90] and these outpourings would alternate with violent conflicts against the Devil who attacked him and beat him, and assailed him with every kind of temptation. St Romauld's great figure illustrates that phrase in the Rule of St Benedict, that the hermit is one who goes to the desert to "fight alone".[91]

Such a man could not fail to have an influence, and his teaching lived on in two congregations of eremitical Benedictine monks, that of Fonte Avellana and that of Camaldoli. The first was inspired by one of the most energetic spirits of the century, St Peter Damian (†1072). In his first book, *"A Life of St Romuald"*,[92] he sets out a programme of which his whole life was the fulfilment. In it he holds high the ideal of the solitary life, and makes much

[87] See *supra*, p. 58.
[88] Bruno of Querfurt, *Vita quinque fratrum*, ch. 32, *ed. cit.*, p. 738.
[89] *Ibid.*, ch. 2, p. 719.
[90] St Peter Damian, *Vita B. Romualdi*, 16 and 31, ed. G. Tabacco, Rome, 1957, pp. 40 and 68. Cf. also Tabacco, *Privilegium amoris, loc. cit.*, p. 9; and J. Leclercq, *S. Pierre Damien*, pp. 24–35.
[91] *Reg. S. Bened.*, ch. 1.
[92] Ed. Tabacco, *loc. cit.*

of St Romuald's part in the reformation of the clergy—the two objects to which he was to direct his own energies. As regards the first, as Prior of Fonte Avellana (he would never be called abbot) he wrote a small work called *On the eremitical order*, and a *Rule for hermits*[93] in which he makes it clear (as he does in his letters) that his own preference is for the solitary life. He did not, however, refuse to take *cenobia* under his care: he governed some and founded others, but his primary aim was to give shape to an anachoretical life lived in common, which should have the forms of prayer and asceticism proper to the common life. He worked out a profound and yet exact theology of the communion there is between the great collective prayer of the Church and the soul which prays alone.[94] During this time he was also engaged in a battle against simony, incontinence and ignorance among the clergy. Having become, against his own wish, bishop and cardinal of Ostia, he devoted himself with his customary ardour to the interests of the Church and of "his monks", particularly those hermits who had adopted his rule. He was soon free for a time from his curial work, though later he was given several other tasks, one of which was to take him to Cluny; and it was from Fonte Avellana during his latter years that he sent forth a series of spiritual writings which give shape and form to his two works, the reform of the Church and the organization of the eremitical life in common.

His teaching is on a grand and varied scale. He was the first to evolve the theory of *sancta simplicitas*, that complete detachment by which he who uses knowledge is never enslaved by it. He was one of the most learned men of his day, whose education and personal gifts gave him a high degree of culture; a poet, a writer of much talent, learned in Canon Law and theology, but he was above all a prophet crying out against everything within himself or around him that could hold him bound to this world. His only desire was for heaven, whose joys he sang in burning words. A true disciple of Origen and St Gregory, his aim was to transcend all created things: he saw in exegesis as much as in asceticism the means of raising himself above his own limitations to the purely spiritual, to God, "tasted", felt, known by love in that interior silence of the soul which is the beginning of paradise, of the sabbath of contemplation. And yet this contemplative could rage: he was one of the

[93] *Opusc.* 14 and 15, P.L., 145, 327–64, ed. R. Brezzi and B. Nardi, *De divina omnipotentia ed altri opuscoli*, Florence, 1943. Cf. G. Miccoli, "Théologie de la vie monastique selon St Pierre Damien", in *Théologie de la vie monastique*, Paris (Aubier) 1961, pp. 459–83.

[94] *Opusc.* 11: *Liber qui dicitur Dominus vobiscum*, P.L., 145, 231–52. For extracts see J. Leclercq, *S. Pierre Damien*, pp. 265–73, appendix; *Selected Writings on the Spiritual Life*, tr. P. McNulty, London, 1959.

violent who bear away the kingdom of heaven; he was a fighter whose teaching was of spiritual warfare. He was obsessed by the presence of the devils he resisted, and warned his disciple that the solitary "goes to his cell in order to make war on the devil",[95] "O desert", he cried out, "terrible art thou, O desert, the dwelling-place of evil spirits",[96] and he reminded him that during the forty days our Lord spent in the wilderness he was tempted by the devil, and lived among wild beasts.[97] Yet the desert is at the same time an abode of delight, a thalamum, a place where the soul is united to God,[98] for Christ dwells there; the conflict in which the soul itself is at stake can be resolved by a tender love towards the mysteries which he wrought as man. Words failed Peter Damian to express the graces of contemplation which were given to him in his solitude "concerning the humanity of our most holy Saviour, or the unspeakable sight of the glory of heaven".[99] He desires "to have on his lips that infinitely precious Blood" which flowed from Christ on his Cross.[100] "Often it seemed to me that there was really present to the eyes of my soul Jesus Christ hanging upon the Cross, pierced by the nails; and coming near, my thirsty lips received the Blood which fell drop by drop."[101] "Leaving to others, more favoured than ourselves, the majesty of his divinity, let us be content with his Cross alone."[102] A similar wave of tenderness bore him towards Mary, made him an onlooker as she feeds the Son of God: "Blessed are the breasts whose delicate milk drops between the lips of a child: they feed him who is the lord of angels and of men. This milk is a very slight thing and yet it gives strength to the Creator, and he who in his power rules the storms waits for a few drops from a virgin's breast."[103] It was a period marked by the decay of religion and by great brutality: yet tenderness such as this could be shown by as unwavering a reformer, as austere a disciple of St Romuald, as Peter Damian.

At Camaldoli, between 1080 and 1085, Blessed Rudolph wrote the *Constitutions* in which he is said to have collected together the traditions inherited from St Romuald: they differ on some points from those of Fonte Avellana, but like the latter are ordered to a

[95] *Opusc.* 15, ch. 4, P.L., 145, 338.
[96] *Opusc.* 11, ch. 19, P.L., 145, 250.
[97] *Ibid.*, quoting St Mark, 1, 13.
[98] *Opusc.* 11, ch. 19, P.L., 145, 248, 250.
[99] *Opusc.* 19, ch. 5, P.L., 145, 432. Cf. V. Vailati, "La devozione all'umanità di Cristo nelle opere di S. Pier Damiani", in *Divus Thomas* (Piacenza), 1943, pp. 78–93.
[100] *Carmina et preces*, 26, P.L., 145, 927.
[101] *Opusc.* 19, ch. 5, P.L., 145, 432.
[102] *Opusc.* 32, ch. 8, P.L., 145, 557.
[103] *Serm.* 45, P.L., 144, 743.

solitary life. They begin by praising it: "It purifies the soul, enlightens the mind, engenders knowledge, sharpens the intelligence; it is a union with God, a conversation with the angels, a desire for heaven, a meditation on eternity."[104] The hermit's occupations are to pray, to read, to scourge himself, to practise *metania* (repeated inclinations in which he touches the ground with his hands),[105] and he is to accompany these last, which had been handed down from the Fathers of the Desert, with prayers. A certain number of psalters as fixed by the *Constitutions* with additional prayers, *cum adjectionibus*, were to be recited daily, according to the time of the year. In the actual choice of practices of asceticism—scourging, *metanoia* and "other exercises"—the hermit had great liberty; "he will undertake them according to his strength and as they may seem useful to him, or as divine grace shall inspire him. In such matters there can be no constraint, only what the will freely suggests as an offering."[106] The life at Camaldoli was definitely contemplative; any exterior work was only to be an exception.[107] But contemplation there was more a matter of "silent meditation" than the performance of the Divine Office: in fact the recluses were dispensed from some parts of it,[108] and the chant which held so large a place at St Gall and at Cluny was reduced to a minimum: "for it behoves us rather to weep than to sing." In countries already under the influence of Gorze and Farfa, Grimlac and the disciples of Romuald bear witness to the fecundity of that Rule of St Benedict which could inspire such very different traditions.

6. *Austerity*

It may be asked whether circumstances did not tend to produce a common spirituality, monastic or otherwise. It was a period in which hagiographical and historical accounts abound, but there are few treatises on spirituality, and the writings as a whole are more ascetical than mystical. The Carolingian order had in a way lightened the Church's difficulties, but the battle began again when she and her saints reacted against the excesses, the abuses and the errors of the period which followed. The life of this world and its concupiscences tempt men to sin; and many found a remedy which they adopted with fervour and generosity: to leave all things and follow Christ. The ideal set before all Christians was the flight from the world, which is accomplished most fully by the martyr, the hermit or the recluse, and by others, according to their ability,

[104] Ch. I, ed. Mittarelli-Costadini, *Annales Camaldulenses*, Venice, 1755, III, p. 512.

[105] *Op cit.*, ch. XXXII, 527.

[106] *Op. cit.*, ch. XXXV, 528.

[107] *Op. cit.*, ch. XXXVIII, 530–1.

[108] *Ibid.*, p. 548.

by the practice of asceticism. Men, rough, violent and passionate, acutely conscious of their tendency to sin, and measuring daily the distance that separates them from the purity of God, turned themselves towards extreme forms of penance and absolute separation from the world: reclusion and rigorous bodily sufferings. Monasticism, owing to its prosperity during the Carolingian period and a certain compromise between its way of life and that of the canons, had to some extent lowered its level of ascetic practice, and this led to a reaction: at Cluny as at Gorze emphasis was again laid on austerity. In particular outside the traditional Benedictine monasticism, fasting and scourging took an ever larger place: in the *Lives* of the time sleeping on the ground, *metanoia* and other corporal penances are spoken of as the normal conditions of sanctity. The Christian was conscious of his impotence to resist the flood-tide of vice which he saw rising in himself and in the world, and so sought refuge in penance, demanding from a thorough asceticism the satisfaction of his need of interior peace and assurance of salvation. In every class of society men abandoned their ordinary way of life: peasants left the land and monks their abbeys to become hermits, bishops relinquished their dioceses, and knights parted from their wives to enter monasteries; the Emperor Otto III abdicated to live in extreme poverty.[109] As the depravity of morals increased, virginity or continence in marriage appeared to many as an ideal, and an unfailing means of union with Christ. It was said of the maiden Aldegund who longed to consecrate her whole existence to Christ that she was "hungry and thirsty for him".[110] This wave of asceticism showed itself in three ways: the eremitical life, the high value set on pilgrimages, and the fashion for scourging. The two first are not unconnected, because men separated themselves from society and journeyed afar to seek detachment and to be alone with God. Hermits and recluses are found everywhere: they are met with in the lives of John of Gorze,[111] of St Odo and all the abbots of Cluny.[112] The nun Hroswitha wrote six dramas in the style of Terence (though, as may be imagined, on quite other sub-

[109] Texts in L. Zoepf, *Das Heiligenleben im 10 Jahrhundert*, Leipzig, 1908, pp. 112–36. Cf. also E. Delaruelle, "Style de vie héroïque", in *Comitato internazionale di scienze storiche X Congresso . . . Relazioni*, III, Florence, 1955, pp. 322–31.

[110] Hucbald de St Amand, *Vita S. Aldegundis*, II, 7, P.L., 132, 863.

[111] Jean de St Arnoul, *Vita S. Joannis Gorsiensis*, III, 21, ed. *Acta SS Bolland*, Feb. III, 699; III, 25, 700; IV, 31, 701; VIII, 69, 708.

[112] Texts in J. Leclercq, "Pierre le Vénérable et l'érémetisme clunisien", in *Petrus Venerabilis*, pp. 107–8. On the recluses of Gorze and within its jurisdiction see J. Leclerc, "Reclus et recluses à Metz durant le moyen âge", in *Rév. eccl. du diocèse de Metz*, III (1952), pp. 356–61.

jects), of which two are concerned with the life of a recluse and the others with martyrdom.[113]

In times of prosperity the masters of the spiritual life often speak of the hidden martyrdom of the well-led monastic life, but now as a reaction against abuses there came to the fore both in souls and in the spiritual literature of the period the notion of the martyrdom of blood. To die for Christ was a chance offered to those who carried the Gospel to the heathen; and martyrdom was granted to some who set out for the boundaries of Christendom. The author of the *Passion* of St Adalbert makes it clear that the saint looked as much for exile and martyrdom as for the apostolate, when as a rich young man he decided "to go into exile—*peregrine proficisci*—so as to become old in poverty under a foreign sun; all hard and bitter things seemed sweet to him because of Jesus, his well-beloved".[114] Later on, repulsed by barbarians, he set forth in search of others, knowing that there he would find "martyrdom for himself or baptism for them".[115] Even if the Christian does not find death in exile it is a means of mortification: Bruno of Querfurt makes this point about one of the disciples of St Romuald: "He left his own land where he might have been of use to many, and crossing mountains and valleys and rivers, he came to a country whose tongue he could not speak."[116] It is in this that lies the burden of exile, the *peregrinationis labor*.[117]

Men of every rank, nobles and churls, clerics and prelates, monks and abbots, all took the road to Jerusalem or some distant sanctuary. Some died on the way on land or at sea, others when they reached their goal, by the tomb of the saint they had come so far to venerate. Some were made prisoner by the Saracens, and often not redeemed for many years.[118] For all, these long pilgrimages with their great and weary labours were a means of proving their love and generosity.[119]

The discipline was another way of supplementing martyrdom—to beat oneself till one was worn out, or to be beaten till the blood flowed, was martyrdom willed; it was to imitate our Lord and the apostles who had been tortured by the scourge; it was to persecute oneself. St Peter Damian wrote several treatises to justify this particular ascetic practice. "When with my own hands in the presence of God I strike myself, I prove my devotion to suffering and

[113] P.L., 137, 975–1062. [114] Ch. XIII, P.L., 137, 872.
[115] Ch. XXV, P.L., 137, 883.
[116] *Vita quinque fratrum, ed. cit.*, p. 727, 12–13.
[117] *Ibid.*, p. 724, 37.
[118] Cf. J. Ebersolt, *Orient et Occident*, Paris, 1954, pp. 49–56.
[119] Cf. E. R. Labande, "Recherches sur les pélerins dans l'Europe des XIe et XIIe siècles", in *Cahiers de civilization médiévale*, I (1958), pp. 159–71, 339–48.

what I wish and would will to suffer if the torturer were there. Since in spite of my longing I have not the opportunity of martyrdom, by riddling myself with blows I at least show how fervently I desire it. Were a persecutor to bind me, I should be my own executioner, since I should allow him to bind me. Thus Christ was delivered to the torturers as we read in Holy Scripture, not only by the hands of Judas, but by his Father and his own hand also."[120] Neither the penance nor the means of performing it were invented by the hermit of Fonte Avellana: he simply encouraged and defended a practice which had already been held in great esteem long before his time, and which was used with renewed fervour in the circles touched by the teaching of St Romuald. In fact St Peter Damian moderated the zeal of those hermits who deluded themselves by thinking the whip was sufficient for everything. He reminded them that its use was always to be accompanied by prayers, usually psalms which were said by heart. He emphasized the reparatory, or rather compensatory, value of sufferings endured out of love and in a spirit of prayer. Here was the last fruit of the Irish *Penitentials*, for a man could discharge the public penance deserved by his neighbour, by suffering in his stead.

To scourging other feats of valour could be added: the wearing of heavy breastplates, or iron rings which restricted the movements of the limbs and wearied their wearer in every way. The hermit cardinal went on his legations thus armed, and he recounts with delight the life of an athlete of Christ whose aims are made clear by his name: Dominic of the Breastplate.[121] Peter Damian, however, like St Romuald, called for "discretion",[122] which only confirms what was noted earlier[123] as to the ambiguous character of the word. Discretion in the sense of moderation still remained a characteristic of the asceticism in the Benedictine monasteries of the old tradition, where the labour of mortification lies chiefly in the exact and careful practice of monastic observances. St Hugh is the symbol of this equilibrium in the midst of the excesses of vice and virtue of the period: when Peter Damian wished to introduce extra disciplines and fastings at Cluny, the wise Hugh asked him to try living for a week as a Cluniac. "Eat with us first, and then say whether you think our food needs more seasoning"[124]—a proof that

[120] *Epist.*, VI, 27, P.L., 144, 416. Cf. J. Leclercq, *St Pierre Damien*, pp. 100–5, and E. Bertaud, art. "Discipline", in *Dict. de spiritualité*, fasc. 22–3, Paris, 1956, col. 1302–8.

[121] *Vita Rodulphi et Dominici Loricati*, ch. 5–13, P.L., 144, 1009–24.

[122] Texts in J. Leclercq, *St Pierre Damien*, pp. 49, 54, 147.

[123] See *supra*, p. 38.

[124] *Miracula S. Hugonis*, 15, *Acta SS Bolland*, April, III, 669.

spiritual men even in these rough and fervent days did not lack a sense of humour.

7. The Bible and the Liturgy

With the development of vocal prayer went a corresponding growth in the use made of Holy Scripture, which became the food of both public and private prayer. By an understanding of the words themselves, by a yielding to the word of God, vocal prayer becomes mental prayer, as St Benedict wished: *mens nostra concordet voci nostrae*. Everything with which the inspired texts are surrounded has but one object—to make them penetrate into the lives and practice of men. According to a saying of St Ambrose in an anthology of the period, "Blessed are they who read the divine Scriptures and turn them into deeds."[125] In the ejaculations which the soul breathes forth when freed from any precise occupation to which it is bound by rule, the Word of God re-echoes; for these *orationes furtivae*, as they are called, are an epitome of Scripture, a commentary on the words they use. Many references in the writings of the time show that the laity read the psalms, not in their liturgical order but in that of the Psalter, beginning afresh at the last psalm. This was sometimes a form of private prayer, but was more frequently employed in procession from church to church. It was also at this time that books of prayers for the laity became widespread, and in these the psalms which took up a large part of the volume were arranged more according to the order of the Canonical Hours.[126] The formulas of private prayer, therefore, consisted chiefly of verses of the psalms; St Rambert in his *Life* of St Ansgar (†865) describes their composition, and, so to speak, their use:

> He had made, out of those passages from the Bible which move to compunction of heart, for each psalm a little prayer of his own, *propriam oratiunculam*, which he called his relish, *pigmentum*, because by it the psalms became more agreeable. He did not heed the arrangement of the words, for he sought compunction of heart. In his *pigmenta*, in turn he praises God's omnipotence and justice, he reproaches himself, he congratulates the

[125] John the Man of God, *De ordine vitae*, ch. 2, P.L., 184, 566; see *infra*, note 129.

[126] Writings on these uses of the psalms are quoted by J. Stadlhuber, "Das Laienstunden Gebet vom Leiden Christi in seinen mittelalterlischen Formen", in *Zeitschrift für Katholische Theologie*, LXXII (1950), pp. 286–325, and G. Miccoli, "Per la storia della pataria Milanese", in *Bollettino dell'Istituto storico Italiano per il medio evo*, LXX (1958), pp. 109–10.

[127] *Vita S. Anscharii*, ch. 59, P.L., 118, 1002. On the word *pigmentum* and its medieval equivalents see Du Cange, *Glossar.*, *sub voce*.

saints because they are obedient to God, he weeps for the wretched and the sinful, saying that he was worth less than the least of these. When those who were singing with him had finished the psalm, he would silently turn over these short prayers in his mind.[127]

A hundred years later Otloh was to analyse his interior trial with a psychological acumen almost worthy of our own day. He finds a solution for them all in sacred Scripture; the Bible is for him, as it is for all, the school of every progress in asceticism and prayer. By reading it "the eyes of the inward man are opened, and understanding what heretofore he had not understood of Scripture and the rest, he is astonished at having been so heavy and so blind. Then he goes ever further in holy reading, and what at first he read from fear and a longing for forgiveness, now that he has begun to love he reads that he may also know the wonders of the wisdom and mercy of God. He tastes how sweet the Lord is, he meditates on his law day and night; he no longer stops at the historical meaning or superficial value of the words themselves; he searches out the secrets of the mysterious truths which are hidden, especially in the Old Testament."[128] St Romuald had already given the essence of the thought of the time on the ways of mental prayer: *una via est in psalmis*.[129]

The writings of William of Volpiano[130] (†1041), of Peter Damian,[131] of John the Man of God,[132] and of other anonymous authors,[133] the devotions, prayers and treatises, all the spiritual writings of the period, near the biblical stamp. The Scriptures were used as freely in them as in the liturgy: not so much as historical writings to teach men about past happenings, but as an inexhaustible source of contemplation and sacred poetry. Man comes to faith by living in the Church and sharing in her mysteries; and it is the task of Scripture not so much to instruct in that faith as to make it penetrate into the whole of man, and into every part of his life.

Not much was written about the liturgy—it goes without saying

128 *De cursu spirituali*, 3, P.L., 146, 146; trans., B. de Vrégille, *Dict. de spirit.*, XXV, 184; cf. H. Lubac, *Exégèse médiévale*, Paris, 1959, pp. 571–86: *Exégèse Monastique*.

129 See *supra*, p. 112.

130 *S. Willelmi Divionensis Abbatis et Fructuariae fundatoris opera*, Turin, 1797, ed. E. de Levis.

131 Cf. A. Wilmart, "Le recueil des poèmes et des prières de S. Pierre Damien", in *Rev. bénéd.*, XLI (1929), pp. 342–57, and "Les prières de S. Pierre Damien pour l'adoration de la Croix", in *Rev. des Sciences relig.*, IX (1929), pp. 513–523.

132 Ed. P.L., 147, 477–80; P.L., 184, 559–84. On the author himself see A. Wilmart in *Auteurs Spirituels*, pp. 64–100.

133 On all this literature the work of A. Wilmart cited above is a rich and inexhaustible storehouse of information.

that it was of prime importance—but a great deal was being written for it. A large number of the innumerable sequences, tropes, versicles, motets, the poetry in every kind of metre and the hymns of all sorts that filled volumes, were written during the tenth and eleventh centuries and sung with delight during the divine offices. In them religious thought overflows with a burst of triumph, expressing the wonder felt by all men and particularly by monks, at the thought of the majesty of God, at the recollection of the mysteries of Christ.[134]

These are also the golden centuries of sacred drama, those *ludi* in which the words of the liturgy were carried on to the stage. The plays were simple but redolent of the atmosphere of the sacred text, to which they kept closely.[135] The obligation for a cleric to make up in private the Office he had not celebrated in public was becoming general, by means of the canonical collections,[136] but the shortage of complete Office books modified the saying of the Office in private, and whether at Fonte Avellana or elsewhere it inevitably consisted chiefly of the psalms. The ordinary and usual prayer of the Church was public worship, made more comprehensible by new treatises on the music[137] and ceremonies[138] of its rites and formulae, as well as by the reproduction of earlier works. Communion, at least in the monasteries, was frequent or even daily, and only in case of sin was it necessarily preceded by confession.[139] The *Regularis Concordia* laid it down that the monks should go to confession every Sunday to their "spiritual father", the abbot, "or to his representative".[140] In some places the monks were recommended to go every day, in some cases to a priest of their choice.[141]

Rathier of Verona[142] and Anselm of Lucca[143] have left prayers

[134] Cf. J. Leclercq, *L'amour des lettres et le désir de Dieu*, pp. 222–7.

[135] Cf. K. Young, *The Drama of the Mediaeval Church*, Oxford, 1933; J. Leclercq, "Dévotion privée, piété populaire, et liturgie au moyen âge", in *Études de pastorale liturgique*, Paris, 1944, pp. 156–69; E. Franceschini, "Il teatro postcarolingio", in *I problemi communi dell'Europa postcarolingia*, Spoleto, 1955, pp. 307–11.

[136] Cf. P. Salmon, "Obligation de la célébration de l'office", in *L'office divin*, Paris, 1959, p. 38.

[137] Cf. J. Leclercq, *L'amour des lettres . . .*, pp. 228–9.

[138] *Berno of Reichenau, opuscula*, P.L., 142, 1015–58, and M. Gerbert, *Scriptores ecclesiastici de musica sacra*, II, St Blaise, 1784.

[139] Cf. K. Hallinger, *Gorze-Kluny*, pp. 975–6; D. Knowles, *The Monastic Order in England*, p. 469. *Regularis Concordia*, ed. Symons, p. 19.

[140] Ed. Symons, p. 18.

[141] "Accedit ad sacerdotem ad quem potissimum voluerit", Ulrich of Cluny, *Consuet.*, ch. II, P.L., 149, 707.

[142] P.L., 136, 443–50.

[143] Ed. A. Wilmart, "Cinq textes de prières", in *Rev. d'ascét. et de myst.*, XIX (1933), pp. 49–60, 69–72.

which are really "acts before Communion"[144]: it was unthinkable that private prayers should be unconnected with the liturgy or with the Scriptures. Among the most beautiful testimony to the fervent piety of these centuries are the prayers to our Lady; there was still much devotion to the saints, and in the monasteries prayer for the dead had a considerable place[145] (It was St Odilo in fact who propagated the celebration of the Office of All Souls on November 2nd),[146] but there was above all an increase in the number of holy places dedicated to Mary, to some of which came pilgrimages to venerate her statue.[147]

Cluny was in the forefront of this movement; the nuns of Marcigny, influenced by St Hugh, took Mary as their abbess[148]; the glories of the Mother of God were set forth in antiphons like the *Alma redemptoris Mater*, sermons like those of Fulbert of Chartres,[149] and the treatises of Alberic of Monte Cassino[150]; her feasts became more numerous, and the custom grew up of celebrating Mass on Saturday in her honour. In fact this period with its mixture of vice and fervour saw a blossoming of devotion to Mary hitherto unknown in the West.[151] From the Scriptures and tradition were brought forth new riches to be poured into the treasure-house of the liturgy, which, far from smothering such devotion, stimulated it and at the same time kept it healthy and well balanced.

8. John of Fécamp and Contemplative Prayer

At the end of the period lived a writer who was for a long while, as he had wished to be, forgotten. He had called himself "poor John—*misellus Johannes*" and was nicknamed "Jeannelin"—a diminutive which need not conceal the importance of John of Fécamp. His writings, attributed to some of the greatest authors—

144 As A. Wilmart puts it, *ibid.*, p. 41, note 42.

145 Cf. J. Leclercq, "Documents sur la mort des moines", in *Rev. Mabillon,* XLV (1955), pp. 165–80; XLVI (1956), pp. 65–81.

146 Cf. H. Philippeau, "Contribution à l'étude du culte collectif des trépassés, in *Rev. d'hist. eccl. suisse*, LI (1957), pp. 45–57.

147 Cf. J. Leclercq, "Dévotion et théologie mariales dans le monachisme bénédictin", in *Maria*, vol. II, Paris, 1952, pp. 553–6; P. Cousin, "La dévotion mariale chez les grands abbés de Cluny", in *A Cluny*, Dijon, 1950, pp. 210–18.

148 "Notre Dame Abbesse", in *Priez sans cesse: 300 ans de prière*, Paris, 1953, pp. 175–7.

149 P.L., 141, 319–25. On their authenticity cf. R. Laurentin in *Court traité de théologie mariale*, Paris, 1953, p. 144.

150 The actual text is lost; cf. R. Cellier, *Hist. gén. des auteurs sacrés*, Paris, 1757, vol. XXI, p. 94.

151 Cf. J. Leclercq, "Grandeurs et misères de la dévotion mariale au moyen âge", in *La Maison Dieu*, 38 (1954), pp. 123–8. H. Barré, "Prières mariales du X siècle", in *Ephem. Mariolog.*, X (1960), pp. 195–221; *Prières anciennes de l'Occident à la Mère du Sauveur. Des origines à St Anselme,* Paris, 1962.

St Ambrose, Cassian, Alcuin, St Anselm and St Bernard—had an immense influence: the number of manuscripts and old editions of them show that until the spread of the *Imitation of Christ*[152] at the end of the Middle Ages he was one of the most widely read of spiritual writers. He is a perfect representative of the medieval spirituality which preceded him, for in him blossom forth the traditions of the Fathers, of early monasticism, of St Gregory and the writers and reformers of the Carolingian and later centuries. In him are also found the currents of spirituality peculiar to various countries. He was born near Ravenna, and lived there as a hermit for some time. He followed his uncle, the great reformer St William of Volpiano, whose disciple he was, to Fruttuaria and the foundation of St Benignus at Dijon. In 1017 Jeannelin was sent to the monastery of the Holy Trinity at Fécamp and became its abbot in 1028. From 1052 for some years he ruled over his own abbey and St Benignus as well. In 1054 he was in England where Fécamp owned property. He was also in touch with the abbeys of Flanders and Lorraine, and kept up his connection with Italy, going there in 1050. He wrote twice to the Empress Agnes. He may also have made a pilgrimage to the Holy Land and on his journey been taken prisoner by the Saracens. He therefore had a personal knowledge of the prosperous monasticism of Richard of St Vanne in Lorraine, St Hugh in France, and St Peter Damian in Italy. He never lost his nostalgia for the early days of solitude, yet took up generously his work as abbot and reformer. In his writings can be seen his desire for both the austerity of the desert and the balanced life of the cenobite.

He has left writings of two kinds: firstly, various short works—poems, letters, prayers—in particular the prayer *Summe sacerdos* which under St Ambrose's name is still part of the prayers before Mass in the Missal. His fullest works, however, and those in which his style and what lay behind his influence are most clearly shown, are books of prayers, really successive drafts of the same long invocation to God. The first is a *Confessio theologica* in three parts, composed before 1018, which was rearranged and completed under the name of *Libellus de scripturis et verbis patrum.* About 1050 this work was turned into a *Confessio fidei* in which more space was given to dogma (though the first draft was re-copied and

[152] John of Fécamp has been revealed to us by A. Wilmart in various places in his writings, but particularly in *Auteurs Spirituels.* Cf. also J. Leclercq, "Écrits spirituels de l'école de Jean de Fécamp", in *Analecta monastica,* I, Rome (*Studia Anselmiana,* 20), pp. 91–114. An account of the life of John of Fécamp, with a study of his writings, is given in J. Leclercq–J. P. Bonnes, *Un maître de la vie spirituelle au XIe siècle: Jean de Fécamp,* Paris, 1946, in which some of his works are published. The following pages are a summary of this book.

abridged). Extracts were made from all these works, some of which found their way into the collection of meditations attributed to St Anselm. Others were diffused even more widely over a long period under the supposed authorship of St Augustine. In his writings John of Fécamp shows a deep culture and a remarkable style, but it was his experience of the life of prayer which gave the devotions he wrote the note of sincerity to which their success was due. He was so completely master of himself that he dwelt in profound peace. In the life of the spirit he experienced fervent longings, but violent contrasts were unknown to him; in him all takes place and is expressed with a gentleness and serenity due less to natural disposition than to the contemplation of God.

Like St Augustine, from whom he takes his inspiration directly, he "confesses God", he praises him, he glorifies him, he gives him thanks. All his prayer is a eucharist, a "theology" in the old meaning of the word, a hymn of wonder. He speaks under the inspiration of God, to Him about Himself. He tells of his gratitude for the mysteries of our redemption, of his poverty and need of God's grace. He finds the words he needs in Holy Scripture, in St Gregory, in the Carolingian *Libelli Precum*, in the liturgy. He can truly say, "My words are but those of the Fathers", and yet it is also true that he puts them together in his own way to form a harmonious whole.

He emphasizes the transcendence of God, who is infinitely beyond us, and yet is accessible to us through the mediator Jesus. He dwells on those aspects of the life of our Saviour which most clearly show his love for us, especially on his Passion. But he never forgets that the Son of God now reigns in a glory that can never change, to which he wishes to bring us and of which he has given us an earnest in the Blessed Sacrament. With tenderness, ardour and confidence he desires Christ: *te Christe . . . te volo*. He longs for him here below, as he gives himself to man by faith, in the sacraments, in the grace of prayer. He longs to enjoy him in that life of heaven which is barely tasted in contemplation. The sense of the sweetness of God penetrates his whole being, causing him to shed tears of repentance and longing. This aspiration towards what is beyond, this devotion to heaven which is one of the dominant characteristics of monastic spirituality, and to which St Gregory, St Peter Damian and so many others gave fervent and poetic expression, is also one of John of Fécamp's favourite themes. All this shows how profound a mystic he was, "blessed with the noblest charismata".[153]

[153] A. Wilmart, *Auteurs spirituels*, p. 137, which quotes this phrase from John of Fécamp himself.

There is no method which can give an experimental knowledge of God's sweetness, but John wished to prepare others and give them a desire for that which he could not communicate to them. To that end he was in the habit of sending the prayers he had composed, with letters explaining the use that should be made of them. He advised those who read them to unite themselves with the words, making them their own, repeating them to God as a form of words which gives expression to the feelings it elicits. For contemplative souls those prayers could become their own because they were traditional and the personality of their author vanished behind the sayings of Holy Scriptures, the Fathers and the liturgy.

John of Fécamp's teaching emphasizes (if this can be said to be peculiar to him) the importance of reading. He takes it for granted that it is difficult for most men, even for contemplatives, to pray for long spontaneously, and therefore they must fix the attention of their mind, the eyes of their heart, on a text which will, if reflected on and savoured, put the soul into a state in which, when God wills, it can rise above itself. He has left a description of pure prayer which is admirable in its precision and discretion: it comes at the end of that *Confesso theologica* which should end in contemplation:

> There are various kinds of contemplation, by whose aid the soul which has devoted itself to thee, O Christ, finds joy and advancement. Yet my spirit rejoices in none of them as in that wherein, putting aside all else, she raises the eyes of her heart purely and simply towards thy Godhead only. What peace and joy, what rest does the soul which tends to thee enjoy! When my soul longs for the divine vision, and as far as it is able sings of its glory, behold the burden of the flesh is less wearisome, the tumult of thought grows quiet, the weight of our mortality and our sorrows no longer deadens our faculties as they are wont to do; all is peace and quiet. The heart is aflame with love, the soul joyful, the memory strong, the understanding full of light: and my whole spirit, burning with the desire of beholding thy beauty, is borne away by the love of the unseen realities.

This was the most explicit writing on contemplative prayer since St Gregory, and the flights of soul of which it is an epitome make of John of Fécamp "the most remarkable medieval spiritual author before St Bernard". His is the most explicit conception of that prayer which exists in germ in the Rule of St Benedict, and was developed by Hildemar and others. The monk living in the atmosphere of the liturgy reads and meditates on the word of God,

[154] Latin text in *Un maître de la vie spirituelle*, p. 182.
[155] A. Wilmart, *Auteurs spirituels*, p. 127.

continuing thereby the Divine Office; his prayer is short and frequent, so often and so spontaneously renewed that it becomes continual. And sometimes, "by the inspiration of a divine instinct", it becomes contemplation, plunging the soul into a silence which anticipates that of heaven.

VI

THE NEW ORDERS

DURING the second half and particularly towards the end of the eleventh century new institutions came into being, whose object was to promote the life of perfection. They brought into the spiritual life the results of the canonical and political reforms of Gregory VII and had considerable repercussions on the history of spirituality. They were, moreover, a kind of reaction against the tendencies of the preceding period, and to realize their full significance it is necessary to look at the crisis which led to their development.

1. The Crisis of Monasticism

The state of things which reached its culmination, particularly in France,[1] between about 1095 and 1145 has justly been described as the crisis of monasticism, though its protagonists had had their precursors in the eleventh century, particularly in Italy. Benedictine monasticism was enjoying an era of prosperity: monasteries had multiplied, the number of monks had increased, the abbeys were becoming ever richer owing to the gifts they received and the wisdom of their abbots' administration; customaries and rituals were developing an extreme rigidity, and at the same time it was becoming evident that the traditional Benedictine form of monasticism no longer satisfied the ascetic aspirations of many generous souls. The reaction which was to take place outside the *ordo monasticus* began first of all within it: its two fundamental tendencies were a wish for a life more apart from the world, and for one in which the monks, above all the abbot, should not be the owners of vast domains. The crisis through which traditional monasticism was

[1] This expression was used for the first time by Dom G. Morin, "Rainaud l'Ermite et Yves de Chartres: un épisode de la crise du cénobitisme au XI–XII siècle", in *Rev. bénéd.*, XL (1928), p. 104. Cf. J. Leclercq, "La Crise du monachisme aux XI et XII siècles", in *Bolletino dell'Istituto storico Italiano* (1958), pp. 19–41.

passing was shown in precisely these two not unconnected ways: a return to solitude and a movement towards poverty. Considerable townships had often grown up round monasteries which had been founded originally in the depths of the country, and the personal aspirations of some of the monks towards long and solitary prayer and severe corporal mortification were often incompatible with the burden of a community life organized down to its last detail. It was of course true that in individual cases the eremitical life was recognized as legitimate: but even this concession to one of the constant factors of monastic experience now no longer sufficed. Already at the beginning of the eleventh century, Leo II, abbot of Nonantula and afterwards archbishop of Ravenna from 999 to 1004, had been obliged to write at length to some monks who had become hermits, to remind them of the sanctifying value of the cenobitic life[2]; and the whole spiritual movement of which St Romuald and St Peter Damian were the servants encouraged the life of solitude. Towards 1030 St John Gualbert founded the monastery of Vallombrosa, in Tuscany, which became the centre of a congregation. His biographer says of him that "all his fervour went towards the cenobitic life",[3] and yet in common with the reformers of his time he wished his monks to live away from the world, and his monasteries to be really poor. The same tendencies lay behind the foundations of Monte Vergine and Pulsano by St William of Vercelli and St John of Matera; these in their turn gave rise to two congregations whose characteristics were solicitude for poverty, solitude and austerity.[4]

In France John of Fécamp was the spokesman of the crisis. He wrote a *Complaint for the peace and rest which he has lost*, an admirable and moving piece of writing in which he sings a hymn to the desert and the spiritual joys he had known here.[5] Though in a letter to some monks who had become hermits without permission he reminds them that no one may go away to a life of solitude without the guarantees that obedience and a long probation give,[6] yet his *Complaint* reveals that he must have faced the same conflict as Leo of Ravenna between the duty of living in community

[2] Ed. F. Ughelli, *Italia sacra*, II, Venice, 1717, pp. 355–9.

[3] Andrea de Sturmi, *Vita S. Joannis Gualberti*, 12, *Acta SS Boll.*, Jul. III (1723), p. 345.

[4] Giovanni de Nusco, *Vita B. Guilielmi*, *Acta SS Boll.*, Jun. VII (1867), pp. 101–105 and *passim*; a better edition is that of Mercuro, Rome, 1907 (from *Rivista di storia benedettina I–II*, 1906–7). Anonymous *Life* of St John of Matera, *Acta SS Boll.*, Jun. V (1867), pp. 36–7, and *passim*; a better edition is that of a monk of Cava, Puteani, 1938.

[5] Ed. J. Leclercq and J. P. Bonnes, *Un maître de la vie spirituelle au XIe siècle, Jean de Fécamp*, Paris, 1942, pp. 184–97. See *supra*, p. 125.

[6] Ed. *ibid.*, pp. 218–20.

and the longing for the eremitical life. He himself overcame it with a serenity which did not, however, prevent him from denouncing a state of affairs which he considered inconsistent with the monastic ideal: in a letter to a friend he regrets that abbots and some of their monks are so often travelling about or engaged in lawsuits, and busy protecting their financial interests. "They are wealthier than bishops . . . there is no longer a great enough difference between the great ones of this world and the abbots who cultivate their friendship." Moreover, there is no difference between the monks and the secular clergy: too often their occupations and behaviour are identical[7]; John wishes to see a distinction made between their respective functions, so that the monks, freed from tasks which do not belong to their order, may give themselves more to prayer and penance.

In the last years of the eleventh century a great and profound "eremitical movement" suddenly made its appearance in several places, particularly in those regions in the west of France where there were still great tracts of uncultivated forest, favourable to the solitary life. It was a movement of some complexity in which women played a great part; it has even been spoken of as a "feminist movement". That there was at this time an individual religious vitality among women is shown by the considerable place they took in these eremitical groups, sometimes even in their government; as well as by the increase of vocations in monasteries of nuns.

This is not the place for a discussion of the social, economic, and institutional causes which lay behind the movement[8]; the facts connected with it are important because for two generations they left their mark on the asceticism of many Christians, and were, moreover, not without influence on the direction taken by certain foundations which were soon to blossom into "schools" of spirituality. These new kinds of "hermits" were often laymen, living first alone, and then in little groups; sometimes there was a community of women living separated from them as in the double monasteries. The hermits' desire was for true monastic poverty, and they worked to keep themselves and to have enough for alms. Their form of prayer seems to have been simple, borrowed either from the liturgies of the canons or monks, or from the vocal prayer of some group of lay ascetics and penitents. They never ate meat, their fasts were frequent and severe, and bodily mortification was much in

[7] Ed. *ibid.*, pp. 201–3.

[8] Cf. E. Delaruelle, R. Morghen, H. Grundmann, "Movimenti popolari ed eresie nel medioevo", in *Comitato internazionale delle scienze storiche X Congresso Internazionale, Relazioni*, III, Florence, 1955, pp. 307–402; *Atti del X Congresso Internazionale*, Rome, 1957, pp. 345–71; E. Werner, *Pauperes Christi, Studien zu social-religiösen Bewegungen im Zeitalter des Reform papsttums*, Leipzig, 1956.

favour. Very early in the movement, whether in order to beg, or impelled by genuine apostolic fervour, many of these solitaries left their hermitages and travelled about the countryside and then into the cities. As itinerant preachers they were exposed to various temptations and provoked opposition by denouncing abuses among the clergy; but they were listened to by multitudes among the people, and even found hearers among the great; their prestige was strengthened by their austerity and their ragged clothes. They based their preaching on the Bible and especially on the Gospel, and sometimes paid little attention to the traditions of the Church, yet their teaching, which was vague and at times even incorrect, often showed a real spirituality. This was the case with certain popular movements (sometimes called *pataria*) in various parts of Italy in the eleventh century, and of the wandering preachers in the west of France from the end of the eleventh century onwards. Monks and clergy often justly accused these "travelling hermits" of being vagabonds,[9] but they at least bore witness to the fervour of the generation they benefited. This "lay movement" had its dangers and was to meet with failures, but to the clergy and religious too it brought a sense of the responsibilities inherent in each state of life,[10] and so was one of the results of the crisis in monasticism which bore fruit.

2. *The Crusades and the Pilgrim Spirit*

In 1095 Urban II proclaimed the first Crusade at Clermont, and in 1145 St Bernard in the name of Eugenius III proclaimed the second at Vézelay. The same spirit lay behind this new kind of *peregrinatio* during that half century as that which had brought about the monastic crisis and the advent of the wandering hermits, though it was of course only one of the factors which led to the first Crusade. Since the ninth century the Church had tried to keep warlike activities within bounds, and to sanctify those she could not suppress, or that she herself was forced to encourage. The Crusades were a continuation of the religious policy of the popes—to reconquer Christendom by reforming national institutions and by a war against Islam in the Iberian peninsula; they were also seen as a means of re-establishing unity between Rome and Constantinople,[11] and as a chance of ending "fratricidal wars" between Chris-

[9] Cf. J. Leclercq, "Le poème de Payen Bolotin contre les faux ermites", in *Rev. bénéd.*, LXVIII (1958), pp. 52–86; L. Raison and R. Niderst, "Le mouvement érémitique dans l'ouest de la France à la fin de XI siècle et au début du XII", in *Annales de Bretagne*, LV (1948), pp. 1–46.

[10] Cf. H. Wolter, "Aufbruch und Tragik der apostolischen Laienbewegung im Mittelalter", in *Geist und Leben*, XXX (1957), pp. 357–62.

[11] Cf. C. Erdmann, *Die Entstehung des Kreuzzugsgedankens*, Stuttgart, 1955;

tian princes by turning their warlike ardour towards distant and more valuable ends, especially the freeing of the Holy Sepulchre. It is nevertheless true that the religious spirit which broke forth at Clermont gave these "holy expeditions" a fresh impulse, and the Church did her best to canalize this fervour.

The Crusades, for the Pope, for their moving spirits, and for the majority of those who took part in them, remained essentially a pilgrimage, a form of that *peregrinatio* which is found in all the stages of Western asceticism[12]; but this time it took on two new characteristics. Firstly it was a pilgrimage in arms, though its object was to bring peace, tranquillity and security for the Christians in the Holy Land, reconciliation between the Eastern Church and the Church of Rome, peace between God and all those who took up arms in the Holy War. It has been said that the Crusade is more than the result of an aggression complex, being in its way a war for peace, and as such the last of the wars, a war to end war; and it has been noted that the Council of Clermont which proclaimed the Crusade also organized the truce of God.[13]

It was a collective pilgrimage, not only because it was undertaken by great numbers of Christians at the same time, but because it united all classes of society, from nobles to churls, in one and the same effort, and since they became brothers in common poverty, the symbol of humility and charity, it made for a certain equality.

The religious value of this pilgrimage lay in its aim and in the demands it made. Its aim was the Holy City, the earthly Jerusalem which is the image of the heavenly one, the scene of the mystery of our redemption, the centre of the world and "the middle of the earth" (Ps. 73.12), the place around which the Churches are to be united, the promised land where the Lord will appear to judge the living and the dead. St Gregory, and after him St Odo, and those who were alive in the year 1000 believed, as have others at various time,[14] that the return of the Lord was imminent: many at the time of the Crusades shared their view and were seized with a longing to live and die in the land where God awaited them: they wished to be "faithful to the rendezvous with God".[15] This eschatological

---

L. Boehm, "'Gesta Dei per Francos' oder 'Gesta Francorum'. Die Kreuzzüge als historisches Problem", in *Saeculum*, VIII (1957), pp. 43–55.

[12] See *supra*, pp. 42, 58, 117. E. Delaruelle, "La Croisade comme pélérinage", in *Mélanges Saint Bernard*, Dijon, 1954, pp. 60–4.

[13] A. Dupront in *Atti dell X Congresso*, Rome, 1957, pp. 372–5.

[14] See *supra*, pp. 22, 107.

[15] A. Dupront in *Atti del X Congresso*, p. 373. Cf. P. Alphandéry and A. Dupront, *La Chrétienté et l'idée de Croisade*, I. *Les premières Croisades*, Paris, 1954, pp. 18–31. A thought-provoking work, in spite of the well-founded reservations made about it by G. Miccoli in *Bolletino della scuola normale superiore di Pisa*, XXVI (1957), pp. 294–303, where he very justly underlines the part played by the

idea appears in all the writings occasioned by the Crusade: letters, sermons, *chansons de geste*, marching songs and battle hymns. This pilgrimage in arms, this war of salvation, was a new and final Exodus. It was likened to those wars of liberation which had led the people of God to that very land where the Crusaders were going. The biblical happenings of the Old Testament played a large part in the spirituality of the Crusade, though its aim came from the Gospel itself. To go on the Crusade was a way of answering the call of Christ, of taking up one's cross and following him; it was an opportunity to imitate Jesus in his sufferings and death. For this reason the relics of the Passion assumed a great importance, especially the Holy Spear and the Cross itself, the emblem of the crusaders, the symbol of their renunciation, the ground of their confidence.[16]

Since the Crusade was a pilgrimage, asceticism and prayer were part of it. The separations required by a voluntary exile, the battles, the sufferings inherent in so long a journey, and caused by the heat and lack of water, were already a severe mortification, offering the opportunity of great destitution and a sort of martyrdom; indeed the crusaders were often known simply as *pauperes*. But in addition there were, before a battle, fasts, watchings and giving of alms, and afterwards processions in thanksgiving, and new acts of penance to obtain perseverance. Long ceremonies took place at the halting-places and at the end of the journey, and there were devotional practices like being baptized in the Jordan. It was true that booty and the wealth to be gained by pillaging was a continual temptation to the powerful, yet among the people there was often a murmur of protest against the greed of the leaders who quarrelled among each other for the principalities; though indeed the first of their sovereigns, Godfrey of Bouillon, refused to wear a royal crown because he wished to imitate our Lord Jesus Christ in his poverty. There was constant need of a reminder of the duty of conversion; preachers, often hermits, as was the greatest of them, Peter the Hermit, were ever insisting on an inward reformation,[17] for the crusader is by definition a man of abnegation. There were sometimes fanatics or visionaries who encouraged an unhealthy fervour

---

hierarchy of the Church in fostering and conducting the Crusades, seeing in them a means of reform, by enabling the laity themselves to co-operate actively in the life and works of the Church.

[16] Cf. P. Rousset, "L'idée de Croisade chez les chroniqueurs d'Occident", in *Relazioni*, III, 547–63; H. Wolter, "Elemente der Kreuzzugsfrömmichkeit in der Spiritualität des Hl. Ignatius", in *Ignatius von Loyola*, 1956, pp. 117–35; B. Bligny, *op. cit.*, pp. 182–9.

[17] A. Waas, in *Geschichte der Kreuzzüge*, Freiburg, 1956, I, pp. 76–85, points out in connection with Peter the Hermit the link between the Crusades and the movement towards poverty.

in a people already obsessed by the eschatological idea of a meeting-place; and the clergy, both those who went with the expedition and those who watched over it from a distance, strove to purify it, reminding the crusaders that above all they must serve the Church by fighting for Christ the King. The increasing number of defeats after the first victories made for weariness and discouragement, and this and greed led many, especially among the leaders, to lose the spiritual fervour which had marked their beginnings. Though during the twelfth century it gradually became degraded, the spirit of the Crusade never completely disappeared, and what was essential in it was re-echoed by St Bernard when he called for volunteers for the Second Crusade. In his encyclical letter to the princes he showed them the Holy War as a means of expiation, perhaps of martyrdom; the way to win heaven, to possess surely the Jerusalem which is above, an opportunity to show their faith, hope and love.[18] When the expedition was a failure he saw in this defeat a new motive for purity of intention.[19]

3. *The Military Orders*

St Bernard's task was not only to keep souls in order; he had to occupy himself with an institution sprung from the Crusade, one of the first "specialized" religious orders, the Knights Templar. About 1118 a community of laymen had been founded in the court of the Temple at Jerusalem; they were a kind of third order attached to the Canons Regular of the Holy Sepulchre, and their members undertook the defence (by arms if needs be) of the Christians in the Holy City and in the Frankish states in Syria and Palestine. What is definitely known about them, especially of their spiritual programme, comes from three sources. The first is a long letter written to them, probably by their Master Hugo de Payns, when he was in Europe.[20] In it he justifies their vocation in their own eyes: in peace they are to conquer themselves by asceticism, and in war to fight against "the enemies of peace": he exhorts them to remain humble laymen, and emphasizes that they must sanctify themselves by the works proper to their state, one in which prayer takes a lesser place than in the life of monks or canons regular. The second is a treatise written by St Bernard for Hugo and his Knights. A military order was something new, and the saint makes it his business to justify

[18] *Epist.*, 363. P.L., 182, 564–8.
[19] *De consideratione*, II, 1–4, P.L., 182, 741–5.
[20] J. Leclercq, "Un document sur les débuts des Templiers", in *Rev. d'hist. ecclés.*, LII (1957), pp. 81–90. The same text, but attributed to Hugh of St Victor, has been published since by Cl. Sclafert in *Rev. d'ascet. et de myst.*, XXXIV (1958), pp. 275–99.

its existence. The book was called *In praise of the new militia,*[21] and began with the words *Novum militia genus.* Bernard points out that the warlike activities of these monk-soldiers are lawful, because they are fighting for Christ's cause and to protect his servants and members; he reminds them that the very places where their lives are passed, since they have been made holy by the acts of our Lord, will provide them with ample matter for contemplation. The largest part of the treatise is taken up with elevations on the mysteries, and is an admirable guide for the pilgrim to Jerusalem. In the course of it, he shows that the Templars practised obedience, absolute chastity, and poverty—"nothing of evangelical perfection is lacking to them"; they are truly religious, and each one must unite the gentleness of the cloister with the courage of the battlefield: *monachi mansuetudo . . . militis fortitudo.* The third source is their Rule, drawn up after the Council of Troyes in 1128: it shows that their observances were taken in part from those of the Canons Regular, and in part from the Rule of St Benedict and Cistercian uses. They were to assist at the whole of the Divine Office, and if they were prevented from doing so they made it up by reciting Paternosters; they were bound to fasting and abstinence, and to avoid any superfluity in their clothing.[22] In short they were to keep the spirit of regulars in the midst of what were to a great extent secular occupations.

At about the same time the community of Hospitallers or Johannites, later known as the Knights of Malta, were founded in Jerusalem to look after the hospital of St John the Baptist. Less is known of their foundation, but it is clear that they were attached to the Canons Regular: the letter of Lucius II approving their Rule, "which it appears was confirmed by Eugenius III", makes express mention of the Rule of St Augustine and the Canons Regular.[23] In their Rule, which cannot be dated exactly, there is an actual quotation from the Rule of St Augustine,[24] in it can be seen that the Hospitallers were divided into two groups, clerics and laymen. They undertook to observe perfect chastity, obedience and poverty, and as a general rule lived in community, though on occasion they went on journeys to beg, or on other obediences. Their rule insists

[21] Ed. J. Leclercq, C. H. Talbot, H. Rochais, *S. Bernardi opera*, III, Rome, 1959, pp. 213–39. Recent translation by E. de Solms, collection, "Les écrits des saints", *Saint Bernard*, Namur, 1958, pp. 149–92.

[22] Ed. H. de Curzon, *La règle du Temple*, Paris, 1888; G. Schnürer, *Die ursprüngliche Tempelregel*, Freiburg im Breisgau, 1903, pp. 130–53. Cf. *Un document*, *loc. cit.*, note 20, *supra*.

[23] P.L., 201, 1364 (Jaffé L., 15455).

[24] Ch. IV, ed. J. Delaville Le Roulx, *Cartulaire général des hospitaliers*, vol. 1, Paris, 1894, pp. 62–8. It quotes the *Regula Tertia* (see *infra*, p. 137), P.L., 32, 1380–1.

on moderation and obedience in all things, on the avoidance of luxurious clothing or acquisition of any kind of personal wealth. Many of its prescriptions appear to aim at avoiding certain of the objections levelled at the "hermit preachers" at the beginning of the twelfth century. Both in Europe and in the East, other institutes of Hospitallers, some military in character, some not, depended on abbeys of monks or Canons Regular.[25] In a short time both the Templars and the Knights Hospitallers spread throughout Europe, particularly in the Iberian peninsula where they were useful in the reconquest from the Moors. There also came into being during the twelfth century in Spain and Portugal institutes which in some ways resembled them, but differed in that their members were not, strictly speaking, religious; they might marry and, if already married, were not obliged to continence, except on certain feasts and times of fasting. The rule of the Knights of St James gives some information about "*conversi*" of this kind[26]: men who had hitherto lived evil lives submitted to an authority and accepted Christian morality, deciding to use their swords for the protection of Christians and all ecclesiastical persons—including the Templars and the Hospitallers—and in the war against the Saracens "henceforward for Christ's sake exposing their bodies to a continual martyrdom". They lived either in community or at home: they were obliged to go to church at the sound of the bell for divine service, though not to assist at the whole Office. They also said a certain number of Paternosters. One of the last points of their rule is the following: "Let their whole mind be set on defending the Church of God and attacking the Saracens."

Other orders of chivalry, like those of Calatrava,[27] Alcantara and Avis, were in the ambit of Cistercian monasteries,[28] adopting to some degree the obligations of the religious life. Some allowed their members to marry; others, and among them some that were simply confraternities of knights, did not.

In the case of all of them, however, the historian of spirituality

[25] Cf. C. Dereine, art. "Chanoines", in *Dict. d'hist et de géog. ecclés.*, XII (1963), col. 385–6. A particular mention must be made of the Order of Saint Antoine in Viennois, founded about 1100 at the time of the translation of the relics of St Anthony the Great, about 1095, to a dependent priory of the Benedictine Abbey of Montmajour. Cf. Maillet-Guy, "Les commanderies de l'ordre de S. Antoine en Dauphiné", in *Rev. Mabillon*, XVI (1926), p. 1; J. Rauch, "Der Antoniter Orden", in *Archiv. für mittelrheinische Kirchengeschichte*, IX (1957), pp. 33–50.

[26] J. Leclercq, "La vie et la prière des Chevaliers de Santiago d'après leur Règle primitive", in *Liturgia*, II, Monserrat (*Scripta et Documenta*, 10), 1958, pp. 347–57.

[27] Cf. F. Gutton, *L'Ordre de Calatrava*, Paris, 1955.

[28] Cf. M. Cocheril, "Essai sur l'origine des ordres militaires dans le péninsule ibérique", in *Collectanea Ord. Cist. Ref.*, XXI (1959), pp. 239–50.

is faced with the same problem: given the cruelty of warfare in the Middle Ages, the pitiless retaliation upon prisoners, the occasional appalling fate of even the innocent "useless mouths", how could the disciples of Christ, the upholders of the Rules of St Benedict and St Augustine, reconcile the mildness of the Gospel with the laws of war? One thing must be noted: the military orders were conceived and founded solely for the purposes of religious war, and a defensive one against the Moslems of the East or of Spain; even the Teutonic Knights had been instituted in the Holy Land before being ordered to drive back the pagan Slavs. Since armed warfare appeared to the Church the only way to protect the Christian nations against a new and vigorous thrust by Islam, the religious knights, like the crusaders, were to some extent placed above the normal laws.[29] St Bernard, who forbade killing, even in lawful defence,[30] taught that the Templars "when they are fighting for the Lord are to fear neither the danger of being killed nor the sin of killing an enemy".[31] On the other hand, the death which they risked was not generally considered to be a martyrdom, in spite of the impression given by some literary phrases: when they were about to go into battle they sought absolution in order not to die in their sins. War itself remained an evil, a bitter necessity, and their state of life as Christian knights did not sanctify it, though they themselves were sanctified by asceticism and a life of prayer. In this way the monastic rules made the warriors themselves, and therefore the wars which they fought, milder.

"You are", said Peter the Venerable, "monks in virtue and soldiers in deed: *monachi virtutibus, milites actibus*". Therein, he added, was "a double combat",[32] since victory over the enemies of the faith depended on their arms and leaders, but victory over themselves on their own observance. The Knights Hospitallers were founded for humanitarian reasons before becoming soldiers, as were the Templars in their beginnings; and these very soldiers had as their object the protection of the weak and the enforcement of a respect for the rights of charity. No doubt they often fell below their ideal, but it remained, as an ideal, an exclusively religious one.[33]

[29] That the right to kill Saracens could give rise to a case of conscience is shown by the fact that the patriarch of Jerusalem wrote to Peter of Troyes to ask for an opinion, and received an answer from him. Ed. J. Leclercq, "Gratien, Pierre de Troyes, et la seconde Croisade", in *Studia Gratiana*, II, Bologna, 1954, pp. 584–593.

[30] *S. Bernardi opera, ed. cit., de laude novae militiae*, note 2, p. 215; *ibid., De praecepto et dispensatione*, note 13, *ibid.*, p. 262.

[31] *De laude . . .*, note 4, p. 217. [32] *Epist.*, VI, 26, P.L., 189, 434.

[33] Cf. M. Cocheril, "Essai sur l'Origine . . .", in *Collectanea Ord. Cist. Ref.*, XX (1958), pp. 346–61.

4. The Rise of the Canons Regular

The institute of Regular Canons took shape throughout the whole of the second half of the eleventh century, and from the beginning of the twelfth developed very considerably, being one of the results of the Gregorian reform of the clergy. It was also connected with the intense religious growth of the period, and gave stability to what was best in the "eremitical movement". The communities of canons founded or organized at this time came from various sources and therefore differed considerably from each other in their personnel and recruitment.[34] Cathedral chapters and colleges of clerics adopted the regular life, and when opposition prevented this reform a group would retire into solitude; in some places the canons had started as a hospital founded by penitents, often laymen, for the poor or the sick or travellers; on occasions hermit clerics came together to form a community, and were joined by laymen, sometimes by children and women too; gradually these latter—*conversae, sorores*—became nuns, either as an autonomous group or forming a double monastery of canons and nuns. There was no juridical connection between these various foundations, whose observances differed and whose work varied from place to place. Yet all the houses had this in common, that they referred themselves to some extent, or more often wholly, to the Rule of St Augustine. This could mean one or other of the following documents: the letter to nuns, number 211 of the epistles of the saint[35]; the *ordo monasterii*, a brief monastic rule which goes back to St Augustine or at least to his times[36]; or the *Regula Tertia*, that is the letter 211 transposed into the masculine and followed by a commentary.[37] This last was the most widespread at the time of the rise of the Canons Regular. Many documents bear witness to it,[38] and a commentary on it is attributed to Hugh of St Victor.[39] There also appeared gradually, as in the Benedictine tradition, *ordines* and *consuetudines* defining and completing the three documents[40];

[34] Cf. C. Dereine, *art. cit.*, col. 379–86; B. Bligny, *op. cit.*, pp. 163–228.

[35] P.L., 33, 958–65. On these texts see *Augustinus Magister*, III (1955), pp. 65–69; A. Manrique, "La vida monastica en S. Augustin", in *Escurial*, 1959, pp. 415–476.

[36] P.L., 32, 1449–52.

[37] P.L., 32, 1377–1434. Cf. C. Dereine, "Enquête sur la Règle de Saint Augustin", in *Scriptorium*, II (1948), pp. 28–36.

[38] J. Leclercq, "Documents pour l'histoire des chanoines réguliers", in *Rev. d'hist. ecclés.*, XLIV (1949), pp. 556–9.

[39] P.L., 176, 881–924. On its authenticity see R. Baron in *Recherches de science religieuse*, XLIII (1955), p. 360.

[40] C. Dereine, "Coutumiers et Ordinaires de chanoines réguliers", in *Scriptorium*, V (1951), pp. 107–113.

many of these collections owed much to the Rule of St Benedict and to monastic observances.[41]

The common features of the whole canonical movement were borrowed in great part from the monastic tradition, in its ideals as well as in its occupations. The canons wished to live, as monks had always done, the "apostolic life" in the sense of living in community and renouncing all private property: a life modelled on that of the Apostles round our Lord and the early Christian community in Jerusalem[42]: their ideal was "the primitive Church". These two essential demands of the life were formulated at the beginning of what may be called "the commandments of the regular Canon" and they recur in many manuscripts: *"Primum ut concorditer vivat—non dicat nec habeat proprium"*[43]; they are reminded of it again in the fragment of a widespread though anonymous document,[44] in a letter of Lietbert of Saint-Ruf,[45] in the Rule of Peter of Honestis,[46] in the commentary on the Rule of St Augustine,[47] and in the *De claustro animae* of Hugh of Fouilloy.[48] Taken as a whole, the documents written by or for the Canons Regular emphasize simplicity of life and humility, the renunciation of all personal property, and of one's own will: submission to a superior and sharing in the common life are often shown to be a consequence of poverty. Thus there came about the paradox that in these foundations, of which many were eremitical in origin, there is a ceaseless insistence on "concord", "unity" and "unanimity". The "cloister" is the symbol and guarantee both of the common life and of separation from the world.

The occupations of this "life of the cloister" are much the same as those of the monastic life. First comes conventual prayer, which is arranged in every detail by the *ordines* and customaries. To this is added prayer in private, made on traditional lines by meditating on the Scriptures: let the canon "be given to prayer: when he prays let him have in his heart what he says with his lips"[49]; his "exer-

[41] This is specifically the case in the *Regula Clericorum* of Peter de Honestis (†1119). P.L., 163, 703–48—an example of a foundation which later became wholly Benedictine, but which in its earliest tendencies is connected with the movement outlined here, has been studied by C. Dereine, "La spiritualité 'apostolique' des premiers fondateurs d'Afflighem (1083–1100)", in *Rev. d'hist. ecclés.*, LIV (1959), pp. 41–65.

[42] Text in J. Leclercq, *La vie parfaite*, Turnhout–Paris, 1948, pp. 82–105.

[43] Ed. in *Documents . . ., loc. cit.*, p. 567.

[44] Ed. *ibid.*, p. 566.

[45] P.L., 157, 718.

[46] Book I, ch. 1, P.L., 163, 703–5.

[47] Ch. 1, P.L., 176, 881. Cf. also Robert of Bridlington, *The Bridlington Dialogue; An exposition of the Rule of St Augustine for the life of the clergy*, London, 1960.

[48] P.L., 176, 1034, 1053 and *passim*. Cf. R. Grégoire in *Studia monastica*, 1962.

[49] Text in *Documents . . ., loc. cit.*, p. 567.

cises" are to be "reading, psalms, hymns, canticles and the other good works".[50] The Rule of St Augustine and the commentary on it ordains that at the end of the Offices the brethren "may pray privately and silently, *secrete et quiete*".[51] It is the same principle as that of St Benedict and Hildemar[52]: "the heart must meditate on what the lips are saying". In order to preserve this fervour and liberty it is essential that recollection, so favourable to "purity in prayer", should be a habit of the mind.[53] Prayer, however, is the Church's prayer, and in the chant and the ritual nothing may prevail over the laws of the Church. "In all things we must follow the authority of the Church rather than reason: for the former gives us an opportunity of humility and submission, whereas the latter may be an occasion of presumption."[54] Austerity must characterize the canon's life, but it must be kept within bounds; there is an insistence on *discretio* and *temperantia*.[55] As the communities of Canons became more and more communities of clerics, the dignity of the priesthood is brought into prominence: in the canon who is a priest is at last fully realized the priesthood of the Old Testament; Christ himself is their founder and remains their Rule.[56] By adding to the celibacy common to all priests the further obligations of poverty and obedience, the Canons Regular bring the institution of the priesthood to its perfection.

Not that they all, or indeed as a whole, undertook the duties of the *cura animarum*. In their earliest days this task was neither universal among them, nor considered essential to an individual vocation: in fact on occasion communities of canons actually refused parishes and other means of apostolic works,[57] showing once again that the "apostolic life" did not necessarily and primarily include apostolic activity. However, the rival interests of the communities of canons and abbeys led to each asserting their rights to pastoral duties and the revenues attached to them. There resulted a controversy which, doctrinally speaking, was not without result. The monks justified their claims on the grounds of tradition, and because by now the majority of them were priests.[58] Certain canons

[50] Pierre de Honestis, *Reg.*, Bk I, ch. II. P.L., 163, 708.
[51] *Exposit. in Reg. S. Aug.*, ch. 2, P.L., 176, 891.
[52] See *supra*, p. 80.
[53] *Exposit. in Reg. S. Aug.*, ch. 2, P.L., 176, 892.
[54] *Ibid.*
[55] Documents . . ., *loc. cit.*, p. 567; Ponce of Saint-Ruf, *Epist.*, ed. P.L., 163, 1477–80, and C. Dereine in *Rev. bénéd.*, LIX (1949), pp. 167–70; Hugh of Fouilloy, *De claustro animae*, Book II, 3, P.L., 176, 1052.
[56] Lietbert of Saint-Ruf, *Epist.*, I, P.L., 157, 717; Peter de Honestis, *Reg.*, I, 1. P.L., 163, 703.
[57] This has been emphasized, following many texts, by C. Dereine, *art. cit.*, col. 391 *et seq.*
[58] R. Foreville–J. Leclercq, "Un débat sur le sacerdoce des moines au XII

worked out a theory of the connection between the active and contemplative life. Anselm of Havelberg (†1158) in particular, in his *Apologetic epistle*, showed that the two lives can be harmonized in the same person by an alternation of the occupations they involve.[59] Thus lived the saints of the Old Testament and the Lord, "the head of contemplatives, the leader of those whose life is active", and many others like St Jerome, who as a monk belongs to the monastic order, and as a priest to the canons. In the same way St Paul was the apostle who preached and the monk who worked with his hands, did penance and gave the example of the eremetic life—indeed the monastery is a desert, *eremus*. In their own way monks imitate Mary and Martha if, while "writing, reading, chanting, making melody", they care for the poor and do all the good works their observance allows of. The Canons, in their way of life in which the *cura animarum* takes a greater place, also harmonize the two lives. Both, therefore, have their place in the Church: the ways in which they differ should only encourage humility and charity in mutual esteem for one another.

Finally, the place taken by the solitary life among some of the canons is an indication of their faithfulness to their eremitical origins. In this point, too, they followed the Benedictine tradition. Peter de Honestis, for example, showed very distinctly that a vocation to the desert, if rare, is perfectly normal, though certain conditions are necessary if it is to remain under the yoke of obedience.

> If there be brethren who wish, while wearing the canon's habit, to lead a more austere, a solitary life, let them lay the matter before their respective prelates. It will be for these to see whether they are fit for it, for this kind of life must not be undertaken by men who by weakness, temperament, age, or lack of practice would not be able to bear the weight of the unaccustomed fasts and vigils. This being understod, we do not oppose permission being granted to those who are strong enough for it. However, if the Church would suffer injury by it, or if it would be to the spiritual or material prejudice of the other brethren, we consider that such a request must be met with an absolute refusal. But for those to whom it is to be allowed, whether temporarily or permanently, there must be in a secluded place a church surrounded by a wall, with cells built round it; and there those of whom we have been speaking shall dwell. They must live under

---

siècle", in *Analecta monastica*, IV, Rome (*Studia Anselmiana*, 41), 1957, pp. 8–118.

[59] P.L., 188, 1132–8. In Anselm is seen the beginning of the theoretical basis of what was later to be called "the mixed life". Cf. M. Vetri, "L'idéale di vita sacerdotale presso Filippo di Harveng", in *Analecta Praemonstratensia*, XXXVII (1961), pp. 5–30.

the authority of the prior, and conform themselves to his decisions in all things.[60]

The various monasteries of the Canons Regular were organized into congregations, either by affiliation to some already existing house, or by new foundations. Thus came into being the congregations of Arrouaise, Saint-Quentin, Beauvais, Rottenbuch, Springiersbach, Saint-Ruf and others. The best known were those of St Victor and especially that of Prémontré which will be spoken of further on, but they all played a part in raising the spiritual level of the clergy in the twelfth century. The Church never made the common life obligatory for the clergy, yet that she considered it both useful and beneficial is shown by the encouragement she gave it.

All the spiritual literature of the canonical movement is admirable in tendency, its writers expressing with skill and sincerity their fervent seeking of the "inward man". One of the most widely read authors was Hugh of Fouilloy, whose treatise *De claustro animae*, though rather long-winded, is full of the thought of St Gregory and monastic tradition, and was copied on all sides. Its three first books set forth a very exalted programme of the spiritual life; the fourth consists of a discourse on the heavenly Jerusalem, the perfect monastery, the image of the paradise of the cloister. God, the supreme abbot, sent his Son to us: Christ, the prior, is the canons' superior, going before them in the path of labour and voluntary suffering, and leading them on to the eternal rest which is their goal.[61]

Thoughts and aims such as these were common to all who lived the monastic life, to all *claustrales*. There might be different observances, but the ideal was the same, in spite of the difference in the institutes and the oppositions which may have marked their beginnings. It remained essentially that of a life consecrated to prayer and penance, lived in common and conditioned by separation from the world. This is the sense in which the collection of sermons *Ad fratres in eremo*, which was so often copied among the regular canons and read everywhere in the twelfth century,[62] shows clearly the two elements inherent in every search for perfection: solitude and the love of the brethren.

5. *Some New Foundations*

At the time when the congregations of Canons Regular were developing most rapidly, various monasteries were coming into

[60] *Reg.*, I, 30. P.L., 163, 719–20.

[61] Book IV, ch. 42–3; P.L., 176, 1180–2. Cf. J. Leclercq, "Spiritualité des chanoines réguliers", in *La vita commune del clero nei secoli XI e XII*, Milan, 1962.

existence whose observances differed from that of Benedictine tradition. The most famous, and the one which had the greatest influence, was Cîteaux, which will be described at length in a later chapter. But there were others who also had an influence and a spiritual programme of their own. Vallombrosa, Pulsano and Monte Vergine, which developed into congregations,[63] have already been mentioned; some like Savigny and her daughters ultimately joined Cîteaux; others disappeared or joined the canons of Prémontré, or the monks of Cluny or some other older monastery. Of the foundations of the period, two of them, Fontévrault and Grandmont, were original in that they gave to two sections of the monastic order a preponderant place that they had never before enjoyed: in ever-increasing numbers women were developing a spiritual life of great intensity. This was true of every class: even public sinners, whether noble ladies or harlots, were touched by a longing for God if a favourable opportunity offered itself. As a reaction against a certain pessimistic attitude towards women—or rather towards woman—Blessed Robert of Arbrissel (†1116–17) founded, first at Fontévrault, and then in other places, communities of nuns devoted to the contemplative life under the Rule of St Benedict. So that they might live untroubled by material anxieties he added to each monastery of women a community of men living under the Rule of St Augustine. In the latter the brothers or *conversi* worked to support the nuns, while the clerics undertook the celebration of the liturgy and the administration of the sacraments. All were subject to the authority of the prioress of Fontévrault and her representatives, the superiors of the other houses. It was an arrangement which involved certain risks, and was strongly criticized in some quarters, but the popes, realizing the usefulness of such an institute, took it under their protection and direct jurisdiction; indeed the extraordinary spread of the order, which soon had several thousand nuns, showed that it answered a real need.[65] In England St Gilbert of Sempringham founded a similar order, whose only rule, however, was that of St Benedict, and whose constitutions were influenced by those of the Cistercians.[66]

The order of Grandmont was founded in the Limousin by St

[62] P.L., 40, 1235–1358; cf. *Documents . . ., loc. cit.*, p. 558, note 4.

[63] See *supra*, pp. 127, 128.

[64] The link between the "eremitical movement" and the "Frauenfrage" has been brought out by E. Werner, *op. cit.*, pp. 53–77.

[65] R. Niderst, *Robert d'Arbrissel et les origines de l'ordre de Fontévrault*, Rodez, 1952.

[66] Jean de la Croix Bouton, "Bernard et les Gilbertins", in *Bernard de Clairvaux*, Paris, 1953, pp. 327–38. On the double monasteries in general, and on recluses, cf. P. Schmitz, *Hist. de l'ordre de Saint Benoît*, VII, Maredsous, 1956, pp. 45–58.

Stephen of Muret (†1124). Our knowledge of its early days comes from the *Considerations* (*Liber sententiarum seu rationum*) of its founder, which were drawn up by his favourite disciple Hugh of Lacerta (†1157)[67] from the *Rules* drawn up by Stephen of Liciac, the fourth prior (1139–63)[68]; and by the *Lives* of Stephen of Muret which are later than these documents.[69] What chiefly differentiated Grandmont from other orders was the exclusive authority given to the lay brothers in administration, work, and even in relations with the outside world, with the object of guaranteeing absolute reclusion to the clerics. St Stephen compares the two categories of religious to Martha and Mary. The ideal set before all, which the lay brothers were to make possible for the clerics to realize to the fullest extent, was that of a solitary life lived in common: the Grandimontains were "hermits", lived in "deserts", and took St John the Baptist as their model. In order to unite themselves with God they renounced all things, even begging, or hearing or preaching sermons. Their essential work was prayer in its two traditional forms, liturgical and "secret"[70]: their aim was the *oratio continua*.[71] Great stress was laid on material poverty, and it was probably to safeguard this aspect of it that St Stephen excluded women from his Order. In the event the pre-eminence of the lay brothers over the clerics, though they were all under the authority of the prior of Grandmont, led to a series of crises in the relationships of the two categories of religious, each side in turn carrying off the victory. During the second half of the twelfth century the Grandimontains adopted a monastic observance similar to that of the Canons Regular or the monks of reformed monasteries, though their lay brothers still had more authority than they had elsewhere. By this time the Order had spread widely and many had sanctified themselves in it.

One of its characteristics was to recognize no rule except that of the Gospel, which was called "the Common Rule", and of which all others, St Augustine's or St Benedict's, were held only to be applications.[72] St Stephen personally used the discipline and wore iron chains and a breastplate, but his Order had not a very markedly penitential character. His *Considerations* show that he was chiefly

[67] P.L., 204, 1086–1136. [68] P.L., 204, 1135–62.

[69] Cf. J. Becquet, "Les institutions de l'ordre de Grandmont", in *Rev. Mabillon* XLII (1952), pp. 31–42; "Les premiers écrivains de l'ordre de Grandmont" *ibid.*, XLIII (1953), pp. 121–37; "La règle de Grandmont", in *Bull. de la soc. hist. et archéol. du Limousin*, LXXXVII (1958), pp. 9–36; art. "Étienne de Muret", in *Dict. de spirit.*, IV (1961), pp. 1504–14.

[70] *Sententiae*, ch. v, 2, P.L., 204, 1128.

[71] *Regula*, 46; P.L., 204, 1154.

[72] *Ibid.*, prol. P.L., 1135–8; partly translated by J. Leclercq in *La vie parfaite* pp. 113–14.

concerned with humility, purity of intention and the prayer which is directed to that intimate and "secret" converse with God, in which man may partake of his sweetness. For this reason each must be free to choose the position in which he will converse with God, and how he will speak or listen to him: the only thing which matters is the love which brings about an interior attitude of self-abandonment and simplicity,[73] and a prayer of acquiescence and praise.[74] In the same way, when he receives the Body of Christ in Holy Communion, if he offers himself entirely to God he receives him fully. God gives to each one this invitation. "Give thyself wholly to me and I will give myself wholly to thee."[75]

In every sphere the devotion of the period is marked by this need for "interiority", for complete generosity. The forms of life may vary, but prayer was still made on traditional lines, though psychologically it had a more personal *nuance*, a reflection of the increasing sensitivity which was beginning to appear in every domain, whether of spirituality, sacred art, or courtly literature. Yet prayer is still linked everywhere with the celebration of the liturgy and the reading of the Bible. The customaries of Vallombrosa, written in the eleventh century and amplified later, lay down that after Matins of the dead, all shall give themselves together in the dark to "private" prayer; "its length shall depend on the will of the abbot or the prior."[76] During the day there are more times for "reading or prayer",[77] and again before Compline and the confession that precedes it, "a brief and private prayer is to be made kneeling".[78] Here, then, as at Grandmont and elsewhere, there is besides public prayer, a "secret" or "private" prayer which is short when made in common, but to which a monk can give himself for longer when alone: such prayer is part of the ordinary occupations of every religious of every observance whether monk or canon.[79] William Firmat, who was, in the contemporary sense of the word, a "hermit", but who wrote for monks, composed a long *Exhortation* which reveals the spiritual tendencies common to the period. In it he speaks of solitude, of the common life in the paradise of the cloister,

[73] *Ibid.*, 102–4; P.L., 204, 1127–8.

[74] *Ibid.*, 106, P.L., 204, 1129.

[75] *Ibid.*, 94, P.L., 204, 1123.

[76] Ed. B. Albers, *Consuetudines monasticae*, IV, Monte Cassino, 1911, p. 226.

[77] *Ibid.*

[78] *Ibid.*, p. 229.

[79] There are similar prescriptions in the *De ordine canonicorum* of Anselm of Havelberg, ch. 21, P.L., 188, 1107, and in the customs of Marbach, ch. 4, 19, 46—ed. by Martène *De ant. eccl. rit.*, III, Antwerp, 1764, pp. 306, 311, 318. C. Dereine in *Rev. bénéd.*, LIX (1949), p. 177, has pointed out the resemblances between these and the customs of Saint-Ruf. In the customaries of the canons, as in those of the monks, recurs that *trina oratio*—a formula of prayer addressed in succession to each of the three persons of the Blessed Trinity—whose frequent repetition must have given the devotion of all *claustrales* a markedly trinitarian character; e.g. see Martène, *loc. cit.*, pp. 306–7.

and above all of the love of that "holy reading" which is the food of prayer: the chest in which are the volumes of the Bible and the commentaries on it, is the source of the doctrine of our salvation. If a man desires to taste of the sweetness of God, he must despise all things for the sake of contemplation, which is contained in and upheld by holy reading: *contemplatio lectionis divinae*.[80]

6. *St Norbert and Prémontré*

The most successful example of the rise of the canonical movement was Prémontré, whose foundation and development is an illustration of all that was best in it. The life and mission of St Norbert and the history and teaching of his early disciples are rich in content. Here they must be seen and their importance noted for the development of the spirituality of the period.

Norbert Gennep, a secular canon of Xanten, in the diocese of Cologne, was "converted" in 1115.[81] He retired into solitude and gave himself up to contemplation and austerities, and then began to preach barefoot. Like so many others, the priest hermit became a wandering preacher, denouncing the abuses of which clergy and laity were guilty. After the death of Pope Gelasius II who had encouraged him, he went in 1119 to the Council of Rheims to obtain the approval of the new pope, Callixtus II. The bishop of Laon, Bartholomew, wished to use Norbert for the benefit of his own diocese, and persuaded him to found a monastery at Prémontré, a short distance from his episcopal city, and to form a group of disciples there. They consisted of clerics and laymen, and their life of contemplation was marked by rigorous poverty, manual labour, and austerity in food and clothing. Preaching and the care of souls were not excluded, especially in Norbert's own case, but they were not then a predominant part of the life. In 1126 Norbert was made archbishop of Magdeburg, and proceeded to use his religious to reform his diocese and for missionary expansion in the North of Germany. From this time onwards and especially in those parts, the apostolate took a greater place. He died in 1134.

His first successor, Hugh of Fosses (who had already been elected in 1128), maintained the contemplative bent of the order in the French and English foundations; but from now on in varying degrees (which depended on places and circumstances) there was a

80 Ed. J. Leclercq, "L'exhortation de Guillaume Firmat", in *Analecta monastica*, II, Rome (*Studia Anselmiana*, 31), 1953, pp. 28–44.

81 On the life of St Norbert in its connection with the beginnings of Prémontré see C. Dereine, "Les origines de Prémontré", in *Rev. d'hist. ecclés.*, XLII (1947), pp. 352–78, and H. M. Colvin, *The White Canons in England*, Oxford, 1951, pp. 1–25.

harmonization of the two essential components of Norbert's own ideal: the life of the cloister with its separation from the world, and the exercise of the functions of the clergy; that is "the eremitical life according to the canonical profession".[82]

The Order developed. The *Statutes* codified between 1131–34, which owed much to those of Cîteaux, specified the lines on which the *Ordo monasterii*[83] was to be applied. In these statutes no place is given to the apostolate; the aim is to "attain to priestly perfection by the monastic ascesis".[84] However, they do not contain everything. The saints and writers of Prémontré give a complete picture of its ideal both by their example and by their spiritual writings.[85] Luke, abbot of Mont Cornillon, a disciple of Norbert, composed *Moralities on the Canticle of Canticles*, and Anselm, bishop of Havelberg, wrote at great length. In his *Apologetical Letter* he defends Canons Regular against the objections raised by certain monks, and in the first of the three books of his *Dialogues*, dedicated to the Cistercian Pope Eugenius III, he shows himself equally favourable to the Cistercians.[86] The programme he set forth was spread abroad and illustrated by the "heroes of the apostolic movement".[87] Garenbert, a hermit and a layman, became the father of a community of canons and founded a monastery of nuns; whole families, like those of the deacon Nicholas of Soissons, gave themselves to the canonical life; a girl of noble birth, the generous Oda of Bonne Espérance, whose story reminds one of a beautiful legend, became a prioress, and so austere was her life that she died of exhausion in 1158. In the next generation Blessed Frederick Feikone (†1175) founded two monasteries in Germany and took particular care of that of the nuns: like Norbert and all his disciples, he had a particular love of the poor. The *Lives* of several of these saints were written, and the canons also wrote theological works; Vivien wrote a treatise on *The Harmony between grace and free will*, which drew its inspiration from St Bernard[88] Zacharias of Besançon composed a *Commentary on the concordance of the Gospels*[89]; Blessed Hermann Joseph, who lived from 1150 to 1241,

[82] This expression is used in connection with St Norbert in a charter of 1124 ed. C. L. Hugo, *Annales Ord. Premonstr.*, Nancy, 1734, I, prol. ch. XLII.

[83] Ed. P. Lefèvre, *Les statuts de Prémontré*, Louvain, 1946. Cf. also C. Dereine, "Coutumiers et ordinaires . . .", *loc. cit.*, p. 111, and "Le premier ordo de Prémontré", in *Rev. bénéd.*, LVIII (1948), pp. 84–92.

[84] The expression is that of F. Petit, *La spiritualité de Prémontré au XII et XIII siècles*, Paris, 1947, p. 46. The pages which follow owe much to this well-documented piece of work; on it see C. Dereine in *Rev. belge de philol. et d'hist.*, XXVI (1948), pp. 667–70.

[85] P.L., 203, 480–584 (among the works of Philip of Harvengt).

[86] His writings are in P.L., 188, 1091–248.

[87] The expression is that of F. Petit, *op. cit.*, p. 65.

[88] P.L., 176, 1319–36.

[89] P.L., 186, 11–621.

wrote poems in honour of our Lady[90]; Philip de Harvengt, the abbot of Bonne Espérance, wrote still more. His great book is *A treatise on the formation of the clergy*,[91] in which he works out for their benefit a huge *exposé* of spirituality. He reminds them how great is their dignity and what duties it brings with it—detachment, absence of all kinds of avarice, the duty of studying the Holy Scriptures, the practice of poverty, continuence and obedience, as well as silence and recollection and the community spirit. These are the virtues of regular clerics, and Philip shows how in addition their vocation is to the service of souls, in which they differ from monks. He agrees with Rupert of Deutz that the latter may legitimately exercise clerical functions, but this is not the object of their institution; their proper functions are penance, compunction, work and prayer. On the other hand, a cleric, even one separated from the world, must to some extent be in contact with the world so that he may serve it. Philip also wrote some theological treatises, letters full of teaching and moral exhortation, and a *Commentary on the Canticle of Canticles* which he interprets in a Marian sense.[92]

Finally in 1150 there was born in England the most important of the Premonstratensian writers, Adam Scot.[93] He received his training in the schools and then entered the abbey of Dryburgh of which he was abbot in 1184 and which he ruled till he became a Carthusian at Witham shortly after 1189. He wrote much: an alphabetical anthology of *Allegories of Holy Scripture*; a small work which has been lost, *On the sweetness of God*; a series of sermons *On the order, the habit, and the religion of Prémontré*; a treatise in three volumes *On the Tabernacle*, in which he speaks in turn of the tabernacle of Moses, of the Church, and of the soul; a book on *The three kinds of contemplation* which begins with a *Confessio* inspired by the *Confessions of St Augustine*, as had been that of John of Fécamp, and goes on to speak of hell, and then at much greater length of heaven; *A soliloquy on the instruction of the Soul*, in which he points out the means of overcoming the temptations of the life of the cloister. He has particularly in mind (it was before he became a Carthusian) the case of conscience which the vow of stability gives rise to, and he resolves it in the sense dictated by his "soul", in spite of the objections urged by his "reason". "By desir-

[90] Cf. F. Petit, *op. cit.*, pp. 102–15. K. Koch–E. Hegel, *Die Vita des Praemonstratensers Hermann Joseph von Steilfeld—Ein Beitrag zur Hagiographie und zur Frömmichkeits geschichte des Hochmittelalters*, Cologne, 1958.

[91] P.L., 203, 665–1206.

[92] P.L., 203, 182–490. The *Moralities on the Canticle of Canticles*, published under his name in P.L., 203, 489–584, are by another Premonstratensian, Luke of Mont Cornillon; on whom cf. F. Petit, *op. cit.*, pp. 53–6.

[93] The greater part of his work is in P.L., 198, 20–872. For his life and work cf. J. Bulloch, *Adam of Dryburgh*, London, 1958.

ing a higher perfection and a more austere order, a man will amend his life and confirm his conversion."[94] His last work as a Premonstratensian was a long collection of *Sermons*, some on the feasts of the liturgy and others on the religious life. All his work is not on the same level; in some places he is tedious or makes an excessive use of allegory, but on the whole his style is sound. His writing is steeped in the Bible and much influenced by the Fathers, especially St Augustine and Origen; his thought on the subjects of the canonical life and contemplation is firm and precise, yet he unites with this an exquisite sensibility and a strong poetic feeling.[95] His teaching and deepest trends of thought, which are reflected in his style, have more in common with monastic tradition, whether Cistercian or Benedictine, than with scholasticism, and he bears witness to what the Premonstratensians and the regular Canons as a whole had in common with all the *claustrales*.

The characteristics of Norbertine spirituality can best be seen in relation to the whole movement from which it sprang. It arose as the result of the monastic crisis. It was eremitical in the sense that the word often had at the time, that is, a life lived in common but in solitude and far from the towns. On this point there were exceptions, but everywhere there was the same insistence on recollection, solitude of heart, and interior silence: the statutes speak of *multa quies*, and Adam Scot wrote, *vigor claustralium quies eorum*.[96] Another mark of the Premonstratensian spirit was an insistence on poverty. Not only were the poor cared for and given hospitality, but in the Order's beginnings the communities themselves, like the individual religious, enjoyed a certain degree of poverty, symbolized by the habit of coarse stuff. Its whiteness, due in the first place to its being made of undyed wool, became for Adam Scot a symbol of resurrection. Such a conception of poverty carried with it the need for intellectual or manual work: bringing waste land into cultivation was at first the usual form such labour took. One of St Norbert's titles to fame had been the huge number of women of every class that he converted.[97] He had formed them into religious communities joined to the houses of Canons; usually the clerics and the lay brothers occupied one side of the church, and the nuns the other. Many saints, like Oda of Bonne Espérance, blossomed in these double monasteries, but they gradually moved further away from the communities of men, though they remained connected with them.

94 II, 1, P.L., 198, 861.

95 Ed. F. Petit, *Ad viros religiosos, quatorze sermons d'Adam Scot*, Tongerloo, 1934.

96 Text in F. Petit, *La spiritualité . . .*, p. 217.

97 *Miracula Sanctae Mariae Laudunensis*, P.L., 156, 996.

One of the marks of Prémontré's reaction against monasticism is shown in the care taken to preserve its independence of the monastic traditions which had grown up. The Rule of St Augustine, that is the *ordo Monasterii* or *Regula secunda*, was to be applied literally. Though in fact the order's essential trends did come from this rule, the *statutes* which amplified it owed much to those of Cîteaux, which in their turn depended on Cluny.

Prémontré was contemporary with the Crusades and the military orders and shared their spirit.[98] In 1141 Hugh of Fosses, at the suggestion of St Bernard, agreed to found a house in Palestine, where in 1136 a swarm from the monastery of Floreffe had already settled. In Palestine the canons preached to all alike, Muslims and schismatics, as well as to crusaders. Several of these preachers became bishops, and some of the crusaders they had helped entered the Order; Henry Sdyck, bishop of Olmütz, wished to introduce the Premonstratensians into Bohemia, having had occasion to admire them on his visit to Jerusalem in 1136. The Order adopted the office of the Blessed Virgin[99] (which Urban II had prescribed to the clergy to be recited as a prayer for the success of the Christian arms), and their liturgy was also influenced by that of the Holy Sepulchre. Devotion to the Holy Places, especially to the Holy Sepulchre and to Bethlehem and the mysteries fulfilled there, found its expression in the writings of Philip of Harvengt and Adam Scot: it also took a considerable place in St Bernard's treatise *In praise of the new militia.*

As there is a connection between the rise of the canonical movement and the monastic renewal, so there are other points of contact between St Bernard and St Norbert, between Cîteaux and Prémontré. The aim of the largest of the new orders was to harmonize openly and fully, in the form of an institute, two elements which actually existed together in the monastic tradition, not necessarily but as the result of circumstances: the life of the cloister and the exercise of clerical functions. With regard to the first, there was no great difference between the life of the Premonstratensians and that of monks: there was the same emphasis on charity in the common life, the same austerities, the same love of that heavenly life of which the life of the cloister is an anticipation, the same conception of prayer in which the celebration of the liturgy alternated with the *lectio divina*, meditation, and pure prayer; the same guarded attitude towards too intellectual a knowledge, to which is to be preferred an understanding brought about by love, a "tast-

[98] Cf. F. Petit, *op. cit.*, pp. 79–90.
[99] Cf. P. Lefèvre, *La liturgie de Prémontré*, Louvain, 1957.

ing", an "experience"[100]; and finally the same devotion to the Mother of God,[101] and the same bringing of the new sensibility to bear on the contemplation of the mysteries of our salvation. The originality of the order lies therefore more in the balance between the spirituality of the cloister and the *cura animarum*; in its early days the latter was not as prominent everywhere, but it was always an essential part of the ideal of Prémontré, and gradually became more explicit. In their pastoral trend, as in giving the first place to poverty, the Premonstratensians were a foreshadowing of the mendicant orders of the thirteenth century. They showed that the crisis in monasticism had borne fruit in that it encouraged the appearance in the Church of more and differing states of life; it was not only that there were various ways of fulfilling the ideal of the Gospel: now the differences were recognized and justified on doctrinal grounds, a two-fold progress. Controversies had of course arisen, but in spite of them, and indeed because of them, many writers like Arnold of Reichersberg urged monks and canons to show mutual reverence and respect for each other's different ways.[102] It was generally agreed, as Hugh of Rouen says, that monastic life tends more towards contemplation, and that of the canons towards action,[103] but by now the varying nuances which still existed within the two institutions had taken shape and been approved. In his *De diversis ordinibus ecclesiae* Raimbaud of Liège distinguished two classes among those who had renounced the world; those who dwell "near to men"—monks like the Cluniacs, and canons like the Victorines—and those who go far from men: and among them are the Cistercians and the Premonstratensians; and differing from all these religious who lead the common life are the hermits few in number but lawful too, and admirable.[104]

7. *St Bruno, Guigo and the Chartreuse*

Of all the orders which came into being at this time, the newest and most original was an order of hermits in which solitude was to be tempered with a certain amount of common life. The Carthusians were founded by St Bruno, and their lawgiver was Guigo I or Guigo the Ancient. There is a good deal of explicit evidence about them and their work,[105] yet there are points in St Bruno's own life which

100 Texts in F. Petit, pp. 169, 173, note 3, and *passim*.

101 Cf. N. L. Reuviaux in *Maria, études sur la Sainte Vierge*, II, Paris, 1952, pp. 713–20.

102 *Scutum canonicorum*, P.L., 194, 1493–528.

103 *Dialogi*, VI, P.L., 192, 1218.

104 P.L., 213, 814–50.

105 They have been studied by A. Wilmart, "La chronique des premiers Chartreux", in *Rev. Mab.*, XVI (1926), pp. 77–112; C. A. de Meyer–J.-M. de Smet,

have been until recent times fairly obscure.[106] What is certain is that he was wholly engaged in choosing God alone in every circumstance and absolutely. He was chancellor of Rheims Cathedral, having first been master of its school; he remained uncorrupted in surroundings undermined by simony, and was considered a man of peace and of a "rare equanimity" of character. One day, on fire with love of God, he and two companions decided to leave the world and put on the monastic habit, and from then onwards nothing was to prevent his answering that inward call which his integrity had fed, and which had ripened, in long years of disinterested work. When they wished to make him bishop of Rheims he refused, and between 1080 and 1083 with two friends, Peter and Lambert, went away to live as a hermit in the forest of Sèche-Fontaine. It was near Molesmes and belonged to it, and St Robert allowed them to settle there. Soon other companions joined them, and a cenobium was built. But already by 1084 Bruno had chosen the wilderness and solitude: he went to Hugh, bishop of Grenoble since 1080, a man who was always to be the counsellor and protector both of himself and his successors. The bishop had spent two years in trying to reform his diocese in the face of the opposition of the clergy: he had then fled to the abbey of Chaise-Dieu to become a monk, but was obliged to come back a year later by the command of Gregory VII, and until his death in 1132 he was an unfailing help to all who were aiming at the life of contemplation which had been denied to him.

His first service to Bruno was to take him to a remote place, austere and sunless, where in a harsh climate and with few means of support he would find nothing but God. There, over 1,000 feet up in the Alps of the Dauphiné, Bruno and a few companions lived in separate cells: they agreed on certain observances similar to those followed in monasteries of monks and canons, but from the beginning they decided that a part of the Divine Office should be said privately, an innovation indicating their intention that solitude should have a large place, indeed the greatest place, in their life.

At the beginning of 1090, Urban II, who before his election to the papacy had been a pupil of Bruno's at Rheims, called his old master to Rome, to be his adviser and the servant of the Apostolic See. Bruno and his companions left the Chartreuse and went to Rome. After a few months all except the founder himself were

"Notes sur quelques sources littéraires relative à Guiges I[ier]", in *Rev. d'hist. ecclés.*, XLVIII (1953), pp. 168–95; B. Bligny, *Recueil des plus anciens actes de la Grande Chartreuse*, Grenoble, 1958, and *L'Eglise et les Ordres religieux dans le royaume de Bourgogne au XI*[e] *et XII*[e] *siècles*, Paris–Grenoble, 1960, pp. 245–318.

[106] The most recent and clearest account is in the *Vies des Saints et Bienheureux publiées par les Bénédictins de Paris*, X (1952), pp. 164–75. The following pages owe much to the help given me by the Carthusians, for which I am most grateful.

allowed to go back, with one of them, Landwin, as their prior; the pope wished to make Bruno bishop of Reggio in Calabria: he refused the bishopric, but it seems that in the autumn of the same year he went to Calabria. There, in the wilderness of La Torre, he took up his solitary life again with at least one companion, probably called Lanwin. He was, however, still in touch with the pope, and some of the Norman princes. The Church at La Torre was dedicated, like that of the Grande Chartreuse, to our Lady and St John the Baptist, and was solemnly consecrated on 15 August 1094, and Bruno and his companions, who had increased in number, led a purely contemplative life there. It was from there that he sent to Raoul le Verd, a friend of his youth, a pressing call to the life of solitude,[107] and through Landwin, who had come to visit him, he exhorted his brethren of the Grande Chartreuse to cherish their way of life.[108] He died on the 6th of October 1101, and nearly a hundred and eighty communities in Europe bore witness to their admiration for him, praising his kindness and equanimity, in the circular letter by which his monks announced his death.[109]

His work survived him, but developed on different lines in France and in Calabria. There Lanwin, who succeeded him as *Magister eremi*, founded a monastery of the Benedictine observance twenty-seven miles from La Torre. Some time after 1120 his successor drew up the Constitutions "for anchorites" and "for cenobites": on some points he was faithful to the practices of St Bruno, but in others followed his own ideas or took his inspiration from the customs of Camaldoli. Little by little, however, solitude gave way to the cenobitic life: by the end of the twelfth century the hermitage which Bruno had founded no longer existed.

At the Chartreuse on the other hand, his example and teaching during the few years he had spent there were wholly followed; they were the same as those which he had given them towards the end of his life. Only two letters, among all the writings attributed to him, are certainly authentic, but they suffice for his fame. In them he praises joy, obedience and poverty, and the "chaste love of God". He is full of a sense of the goodness of God, he shows himself very gentle, measured in his asceticism, careful of the health of Landwin the prior, sensible of the beauty of a quiet place. These qualities are of course found in others as well, though Bruno unites them to an exceptionally well-balanced mind; but what is particular to him is his sense of solitude, his attachment to a life in which God is sought alone, and shared with nothing else, from which every occupation not centred directly and immediately on

[107] Ed. P.L., 153, 420–3.
[108] P.L., 153, 418–19.
[109] P.L., 152, 553–606.

him is excluded. Unlike the majority of the hermits of the period, Bruno gave no place in his life and teaching to preaching or the active service of the Church. He was a man of silence, of that dwelling in the presence of God that is learnt in the wilderness "and of which only those who have experienced it can speak.... There is acquired that untroubled gaze whose love wounds the divine Spouse, and that pure love which contemplates God".[110]

This was the ideal which was cherished by the little group of hermits that he had trained at the Chartreuse. Owing to the harsh climate they had joined the cells to the chapel by a covered way. In 1132 an avalanche which killed seven of them obliged them to move a little lower down the valley, where the monastery of the Grande Chartreuse stands to this day. But the observances adopted in the beginning have not changed. St Bruno's fifth successor, Guigo, who was prior from 1109, wrote them down in the form of *Consuetudines* between 1121 and 1128. He also wrote some *Letters*, a life of *St Hugh of Grenoble*, and some *Reflections*.[111] He is one of the most remarkable spiritual writers of his century, the conciseness of his style making him unique of his kind; and he too is a man of silence. He became the lawgiver only at the instance of St Hugh and the priors of the hermitages which had adopted the Carthusian way of life. Portes was founded in 1115, Les Écouges in 1116, and by 1128 there were six houses each with no more than thirteen monks and sixteen lay brothers, a number which was not doubled either at the Grande Chartreuse or elsewhere till the end of the thirteenth century. In 1135 Mont-Dieu was founded, in the diocese of Rheims. All the hermitages were independent of each other and under the authority of the bishops, until in 1141 St Anthelm, prior of the Grande Chartreuse, summoned the general chapter which marks the beginning of the Carthusians as an order. Guigo's *Customs* were never imposed; they were so wise that the priors at whose instance they had been drawn up adopted them.

They are written soberly, in a style that appears severe, even authoritative; but in fact, because it is characterized by such balance and even sweetness, this short code of laws is one of the finest pieces of spiritual writing of the Middle Ages. Guigo says himself that he wished "to lay down wise laws, full of mercy".[112] The ideal and example was Bruno's, but he was not an organizer or admini-

110 Letter to Raoul le Verd, P.L., 152, 421 B.

111 His works are in P.L., 153, 593–784; and one of his letters was published by A. Wilmart, "L'appel à la vie cartusienne selon Guiges l'Ancien", in *Rev. d'ascet. et de myst.*, XIV (1933), pp. 337–48.

112 He applies this expression to himself in *Medit.*, 309; see *infra*, note 119. On the *Coutumes de Guiges* cf. C. A. de Meyer–J.-M. de Smet, *Guigo's "Consuetudines" van der erste Kartuizers*, Brussels, 1951.

strator: that part was to fall to Guigo, who shared the founder's love of solitude, about which he expresses himself enthusiastically.[113] He makes use of the legislative writings of the Benedictine and Camaldolese traditions, and in the Prologue refers explicitly "to St Jerome, to the Rule of St Benedict, and other authentic writings". We know him to have been learned, a lover of books,[114] and a great reader[115]: but the freedom with which he handles his sources makes his work unique. It is clear why the *Customs*, slightly added to by the prior Basil in the twelfth century, became the "Institutions" of the Carthusians—that is, their Rule.

In common with all customaries, it begins with prescriptions relating to the Divine Office; but even in the first paragraphs the emphasis is on simplicity in ceremonial, on poverty, silence and the keeping of the cell. There are to be two kinds of religious—monks and lay brothers—but they are all "hermits". He speaks of their house as the "hermitage" or "house", never the "monastery". Words like *quies*, *stabilitas* and *pax*, and phrases like *sine strepitu, sine sollicitudine et perturbatione*, recur occasionally. Guigo never uses the term *discretio*, dear to monastic legislators from St Benedict and St Columbanus to St Peter Damian, and yet one is conscious that he is always concerned not to overburden the brethren: *ne fratres graventur*.[116] He admits of the discipline and other practices of penance, but wishes them all to be submitted to the prior for his approval.[117] Like St Bruno, he leans to moderation; he knows that essential asceticism for a Christian lies in the very thing that is his joy, an active and laborious solitude; and his aim is to safeguard it. His achievement was to give a definitive form to a state of life which implied no *cura animarum*, and not even the education of children or future monks. "Our chief anxiety and the object of our life is to care for silence, and the solitude of the cell".[118]

In the *Customs* Guigo lays down the direction Carthusian life was to take, and its occupations, the "exercises" of the cell. In the *Reflections* or *Meditations* he insists on the necessity of interiority in the soul of a solitary, starting with his own. He is almost too concise: his writings are so finely chiselled that they are a crux for translators.[119] Sometimes he produces partly developed "maxims"

[113] This in *Consuet.*, LXXX, and in the letter published by A. Wilmart, "L'appel à la vie . . .", which has been translated with a commentary by G. Hocquard, "La vie cartusienne d'après le prieur Guiges I[ier]", in *Rev. des sciences rel.*, XXXI (1957), pp. 364–82.

[114] As is shown by letter I, 24, of Peter the Venerable, P.L., 189, 106.

[115] As his letter to the brethren at Durbon shows, P.L., 153, 593.

[116] *Consuet.*, XI, 4. [117] *Ibid.*, LXV, XXXV. [118] *Ibid.*, XIV, 5.

[119] The text is edited and translated by A. Wilmart in *Le recueil des pensées du B. Guiges*, Paris, 1936. A new edition and translation by G. Hocquard is promised in the collection entitled "Sources chrétiennes".

or "sentences" on God and his mysteries, sometimes paradoxical epigrams powerfully directed against himself. Then his aim is straight and true; he knows and accuses himself with inexorable clearness. The word "truth" is often on his pen: he looks at his spontaneous self in all its wretchedeness:—"Look at thyself—*vide —attende*"—and blushes for it, yet he establishes the facts and draws conclusions, or rather puts forward suggestions; for the lessons he scarcely adumbrates are borne in upon the reader. The first is humility. How can a man be proud of that love he has for himself, that care for his reputation, that longing for fame, that natural tendency towards his grosser instincts? This wretchedness is common to all men, and therefore piety, indulgence, kindness to others, all these forms of charity are linked with humility. But more than that, the sight of our own limitations brings to birth in us a desire for God; for detachment, obedience and patience, the putting aside of all vainglory, the acceptance of all the demands that asceticism makes on us; finally for that purity which makes us love "God alone" and see all things in him as the angels do, though we, unlike the angels, go to him by the Cross, by imitating Christ in his sufferings and cleaving to the mysteries in faith. The brethren must never put aside the will to save their brothers by loving them: "Christ is called Jesus, and therefore if for any reason you lose the will to save any one soever you cut yourself off from the members of Christ".[120]

Solitude is not isolation; the solitary plays his part in the Church by cleaving to God alone, by keeping his heart pure from all that is not God; his duty is to adore. Guigo teaches him this in a thousand ways in these *Reflections*, which defy analysis because each one is loaded with experience. In them the highest degree of interiority is condensed in the fewest words. Even his *Life of St Hugh* is shorter than the general run of similar *Lives*. Guigo's writings in their brevity and profundity symbolize the silence of the Carthusian, and in them was handed down the essential part of St Bruno's teaching. Later on in the twelfth century other Carthusians left behind them various works.[121] One of the best of these authors, and yet one of the least known, was Bernard of Portes whose letters,[122] particulary one written to the recluse Rainaud, breathe a spirit of moderation and fervour and reveal a keen sense of the trials which can torment a solitary.[123]

Guigo the Second († *c.* 1193) wrote a short treatise on the *Scale*

[120] *Médit.*, 236, translated by G. Hocquard, "La vie cartusienne", p. 380.
[121] A list of them is given by Y. Gourdel in the article "Chartreux" in the *Dict. de spiritual.*, II, 1 (1953), col. 760.
[122] P.L., 153, 885–910.
[123] See especially *ibid.*, 897–8.

of Paradise,[124] and *Meditations* which are of an affective rather than profound character.[125] Adam Scot, after he had entered the Charterhouse at the end of the thirteenth century, wrote his last book, the *Quadripartite exercises of the cell*.[126] In it he shows the qualities which made his Premonstratensian writings so valuable, but one misses the note of simplicity found in those who have always dwelt in solitude. The finest piece of writing on the Carthusian life, after those of St Bruno and Guigo, is that of a Cistercian, William, once the Benedictine abbot of St Thierry, who had gone to live at Signy. It is the *Letter to the brethren at Mont-Dieu*, known as the Golden Letter,[127] which he finished in 1145. In fact the Carthusians remained a centre of interest for the greatest spiritual men of the age. St Bernard, Peter the Venerable, Peter of Celle, Geoffrey of Auxerre and others visited them and wrote for them. The number of Carthusians was never to be very high compared with the monks of Fontévrault, the Cistercians or the Premonstratensians, but the light of their ideal shone on all the other observances and gained them the friendship of the most notable among the cenobites. They in fact fulfilled perfectly, and to the highest possible degree, the aspiration which is the essence of monasticism: to live for God, and God alone. By asserting the primacy of the relation of the soul with God they became the term of the eremitical movement of the time; they were the answer to the monastic crisis; a life from which all could draw inspiration without necessarily going so far as to adopt it. For it is an exceptional life, and for that very reason is able to bring together all who share the same interior vocation, however different may be the response they legitimately make to it. The smallest of the orders was the most adequate synthesis of the contemplative ideal, an absolute love of God.

8. Solitude recovered

In the Prologue to his *Customs* Guigo mentions St Jerome and St Benedict, and their names sum up what was new in the Carthusians' way of life. Its solitude did not altogether exclude the cenobitic life, and while it was a return to the aims of the Fathers of the desert it was not merely an imitation of their life; it took into account tradition and the accumulated experience of the Benedictine centuries. Yet to Peter the Venerable and William of St Thierry

[124] P.L., 184, 475–84. A French translation called *L'échelle du Paradis* was published in Paris (Éditions du Cerf) in 1935.

[125] Ed. by M. M. Davy in *La Vie spirituelle*, Suppl., 1932–4.

[126] P.L., 153, 787–884; see *infra*, p. 160.

[127] P.L., 184, 307–54.

it appeared something new, a renewal of "the ancient fervour of Egypt".[128] Carthusian life is distinguished from other forms of monastic life by the keeping of the cell; in its vocation to solitude and contemplation it takes as its models the ancient fathers of monasticism. What it has of the common life is in order to a solitude whose end is prayer.

St Bruno wrote: "The children of contemplation are fewer than the children of action",[129] and Guy justifies the fact that there are only thirteen monks in each house—*numeri paucitas*—on the grounds of avoiding the necessity, of which he has a horror, of their going abroad or begging: "*Quaerere et vagari . . . quod horremus.*"[130] In the life of this little group everything was organized in order to favour solitude in the cell: government, forms of work—copying being one of the principal—the ways of giving alms and receiving guests, for these great Christian duties are not disclaimed, only they are adapted to the Carthusians' essential aim.[131] Each monk "has to hand in his dwelling everything needful for his use, so as to avoid his having to go out of it".[132] In the beginning the Carthusian looked after his own needs completely—cleaning his cell, cooking for himself, doing his own washing (for which he was given a large tub).[133] His life is not as completely solitary as that of a recluse; the share given to the common life avoids the dangers inherent in reclusion, but in the economy of the Carthusian observance solitude takes the largest place. The *Customs* pile up precautions against the monk having to go abroad, not only outside the hermitage, but within it, and Guy repeats *vagandi omnino horremus.*[134] It is in this that consists the greatest hardship of the life; it is not difficult to understand the rather reserved attitude adopted towards additional penances.[135] It is in solitude and by solitude that the Carthusian sanctifies himself—Guy goes so far as to say saves himself. "We have fled into the secret places of this desert for the eternal salvation of our own souls, not to come to the aid of others in their bodily needs."[136] "Let him who dwells in it look upon his cell as necessary for his salvation and his life . . . the more he dwells in it, the more he will love it."[137] William of St Thierry and Adam Scot

[128] Peter the Venerable, *de Miraculis*, II, 28, P.L., 189, 945; William of St Thiery, *Ad fratres de Monte Dei*, I, P.L., 184, 945.

[129] Letter to Raoul le Verd. P.L., 152, 421.

[130] *Consuet.*, 79. P.L., 153, 753.

[131] Carthusian poverty and its relation with the Order's spirituality has been described by B. Bligny, *Recueil*, p. xx; see also, by the same author, "Les premiers Chartreux et la pauvreté", in *Le moyen âge*, LVII (1951), pp. 27–60.

[132] G. Hocquard, "La solitude cartusienne d'après ses plus anciens témoins" in *Bull. des Facultés Catholiques de Lyon*, V (1948), p. 11.

[133] *Ibid.*, cf. *Consuet.*, XXVIII, 5.

[134] *Consuet.*, XIX, 2.

[135] *Ibid.*, XXXV.

[136] *Ibid.*, XX.

[137] *Ibid.*, XXXI, 1.

also sang the praises of that *cella* which at once hides (*celare*) the monk from the world, and opens heaven (*coelum*) to him.[138] Separation and detachment from the world, however, do not mean contempt for it: the solitary has a love for the whole world,[139] and his apostolate is in the books he writes[140]; but nothing must turn him away from his own vocation. Adam Scot makes the "seductive voice"—the one which was the cause of Dina's shame—formulate an objection which is as old as monasticism itself: "Show thyself in the world wherein thou mayest live, if thou hast a mind to, as not belonging to it. Shut thyself up no longer in thy house. . . . Thou knowest it is more fruitful and of greater worth to save many souls than to save thyself alone".[141] But to some God has given another vocation. He wishes them to forget all things, in order to think on him alone, and to find in this rest, this "true sabbath",[142] the most fruitful of labours. "This is what we think, that among all the exercises of regular discipline, nothing is harder than the silence and repose of solitude."[143]

But this solitude is not an end in itself, as William of St Thierry explains: the aim of the solitary is not to be alone, but to be with God.[144] Guy ends his *Customs* by recalling all those who before the coming of Christ, and since, have chosen solitude in order to pray more freely—"*liberius orare*". Jesus himself several times retired "to pray alone", "thus making it very clear by his example how favourable to prayer is solitude".[145] From the beginning the only Office which the Carthusians sang in common was the long night Office, with a small part of the day Office, and both their rite and their calendar are extremely simple. Since about the middle of the twelfth century they have all been priests though in the early days each monk rarely said Mass.[146] Guigo himself wrote: "We rarely sing Mass", and had justified this custom by the preference given to solitude.[147] The priesthood of the Carthusian then was not "ministerial", nor was it "liturgical" to the same extent as with other

138 William of St Thierry, *Ad fratres de Monte Dei*, I, 10, P.L., 184, 314; Adam Scot, *De quadripart. exerc. cellae*, 5, P.L., 153, 810; other similar testimonies are quoted by G. Hocquard, "Solitudo cellae", in *Mélanges Louis Halphen*, Paris, 1951, p. 329.

139 See *supra*, note 120.

140 *Consuet.*, XXVIII, 4.

141 *De quadripart. exerc. cellae*, 10, P.L., 153, 818, translated by G. Hocquard, "La solitude cartusienne . . .", p. 10.

142 *Meditat.*, note 292, of A. Wilmart's edition, p. 118.

143 *Consuet.*, XIV, 5.

144 *Ad fratres de Monte Dei*, II, 23, P.L., 184, 352.

145 *Consuet.*, LXXX.

146 On the Carthusian liturgy see Y. Gourdel, *art. cit.*, col. 716–17. A long description of the Carthusian Mass is given by Peter of Celle, ed. J. Leclercq, "Nouvelles lettres de Pierre de Celle", in *Analecta monastica*, V, Rome (*Studia Anselmiana*, 43), 1958, pp. 160–79.

147 *Consuet.*, XIV, 5.

monks. They went to confession each week.[148] Contrary to what was laid down in many other monastic customaries, no time was given to mental prayer after Compline, which was recited privately: the Carthusian went to rest at once, and to sleep "so as to have more energy during his waking hours".[149] It was in solitude that the monk gave himself up as often and as long as he could to the activities of prayer. Guy advises "the economus" of the lower house "to return to his cell whenever his work allows of it", there to restore his mind to quiet by "reading, praying and meditating".[150] Nowhere does he elaborate a theory of prayer, but that he neglects none of its elements is clear from the allusions to it in his writings. Thus he proposes Mary as an example, who had the better part: "she kisses the feet of Christ, considering his Godhead, she empties her mind of other thoughts, she chastises her spirit, she recollects herself in prayer, she listens to what the Lord says within her; thus within the limits of her power, in figures and as in a mirror, she tastes and sees that the Lord is good, Her prayer is both for herself and for others in like condition."[151] The lay brothers in their spare time "give themselves to prayer as much as they can—*quantum possunt*"[152] on feast days they "keep their cell" and give to prayer the time between Terce and Sext.[153] The monks interrupt their manual labour to "utter short prayers—*quasi iaculatas*".[154] All forms of monastic life tend towards the *oratio continua*: in the Charterhouse solitude gave it a particular nuance, as well as being an additional guarantee of it.

The Carthusian writers at the end of the twelfth century slightly elaborated the principles laid down by their fathers, without losing the early simplicity of their teaching. Guigo II in his *Scale of Paradise* distinguishes "four degrees of exercises of the spirit", reading, meditation, prayer and contemplation[155]; then he defines each of them, showing that they are necessary to one another, and in the distinction which he draws between the last two he gives the traditional teaching on the subject greater precision. "Prayer is the lifting up of the heart to God to drive away what is evil and obtain what is good: contemplation is the raising up into God of the soul enraptured by the taste of eternal joys."[156] This rapture and the pain which is caused by the subsequent departure of the Bridegroom are

148 *Ibid.*, VII, 2. 149 *Ibid.*, XXIX, 4–5. 150 *Ibid.*, XVI, 2.

151 *Ibid.*, XX, 2. On the character of the *Devotio* in Guigo cf. J. Châtillon in *Dict. de spirit.*, III (1957), col. 711.

152 *Consuet.*, XLIII, 4. 153 *Ibid.*, LXX. 154 *Ibid.*, XXIX, 3.

155 P.L., 184, 475; extracts and a commentary in *L'oraison* (*Cahiers de la Vie spirituelle*), Paris, 1947, pp. 23–5. Cf. also J.-M. Déchanet, art. "Contemplation", in *Dict. de spirit.*, II (1953), col. 1959–61.

156 P.L., 184, 476; p.8 of French translation. See note 124, *supra*.

described in terms which come near to those of St Gregory and St Bernard: the alternation of immense spiritual joy with profound sorrow purifies the soul and increases her desire for God. St John of the Cross describes it in the same terms and borrows one of Guigo's happiest formulas: "Seek in reading and you will find in meditation; knock by prayer and it will be opened to you in contemplation."[157] Guigo's book had the advantage of distinguishing the four phases common to every life of prayer, and yet, like all authentic spirituality, respecting the mystery surrounding the last. In Adam Scot there are further distinctions over meditation: he describes eight different kinds, which gives a slightly artificial effect, but refrains from analysing contemplation with equal precision. He makes it particularly clear that contemplation is the goal of all the other exercises. In him may be found the elements of a doctrine of a "method of prayer", but fortunately he realized that contemplation is beyond all method.

William of St Thierry had also emphasized the exclusively contemplative turn of Carthusian life: "It behoves others to serve God, you to unite yourselves with him. The work of others is to believe, to know, to love, to revere: yours is to taste, to understand, to recognize and to enjoy."[158] In the actual body of the Golden Letter, he puts forward his own mystical theology, which is not that of the Carthusians: but everything he says in the first few pages, of life at Mont-Dieu, sums up perfectly what was new in the Charterhouse. "Few in number", "simple", "poor", lovers of "the secret places", the Carthusians carry out the ideal of every age, and like the Lord himself will always have detractors and admirers. They must be as indifferent to the one as to the other: they must tend toward a purity like that of angels, and remain as profoundly humble as their vocation is exalted. To the "rigour" of their observances let them unite "fervour of spirit, overflowing peace and the grace of simplicity". William ends by showing them that their path leads them from solitude to unity; they are one with God; let this assurance suffice them. Each monk can engrave on his soul, and at the entrance to his cell, the words of Isaias with which the *Letter to the brethren of Mont-Dieu ends*: "My secret to myself, my secret to myself."[159]

It is a very fine thing that a cenobite should have paid such a tribute to the eremitical life, and that this work of his should have found so many readers among all the observances, a fact which is

[157] *Ibid.*, St John of the Cross, *Avis et Maximes*, translation by Fr Gregory of St Joseph, Paris, 1947, p. 1217, note 256.
[158] *Ad fratres de Monte Dei*, I, 5, P.L., 184, 311.
[159] *Is.*, XXIV, 16.

attested by the number of manuscripts of varying provenance.[160] His spiritual teaching is valid for all religious, but nowhere was it put into practice as completely as among the Carthusians; their programme of a rigidly contemplative life was held in general esteem, even by those unable to carry it out. The life of the Carthusians was the occasion of the *Golden Letter*'s being written, and was its perfect illustration. There were none but saw the Charterhouse as a height at which it was good to aim, even if its exceptional nature made it inaccessible to the majority. If every form of the monastic life is in a sense a mystery,[161] yet it is true that the life of the Carthusian is the most hidden of mysteries, a secret known to God and to a very few.

160 Cf. J.-M. Déchanet, "Les manuscrits de la lettre aux Frères du Mont Dieu", in *Scriptorium*, VIII (1954), pp. 236–58.

161 See *supra*, p. 101.

VII

THE BENEDICTINE TRADITION

THOUGH, as the result of a monastic crisis, new Orders had come into being, traditional monasticism continued to bear fruit in the spiritual life. The new Orders did not change the forms of monastic life—observance was not modified to any considerable extent—but rather renewed its fervour. The twelfth century was that of the greatest and most numerous Benedictine and Cistercian spiritual writers. Several of them were thinkers of some originality, whose teaching had a markedly personal character; and in nearly all of them their teaching on the spiritual life was one with their theology. It is not easy to fit them into a few pages, which therefore will be limited to a description of their teaching on asceticism and prayer, though at the same time an endeavour will be made to show the link between this teaching and the general outlook of which it forms part.

1. A Monk and a Genius: St Anselm

St Anselm is the bridge between an earlier period and the great rise of monasticism in the twelfth century. He was born in 1033 near Aosta and trained by the Benedictines of that city. When he was twenty-seven he went to be a pupil of Lanfranc at the abbey of Bec in Normandy, and in 1060 became a monk there. As master of the school and later prior of the monastery he wrote several important doctrinal works. He became abbot of Bec in 1078, and archbishop of Canterbury in 1093. He was persecuted and exiled, but returned to England in 1106 and died in 1109, having written various other books. In his works, as in his life, there are so to speak two men: the father of souls and the teacher of minds. As monk, abbot and bishop he is a devoted friend, a shepherd of souls solicitous for the progress of those under his charge, particularly of the monks to whom most of his letters were written. At the same time he is a powerful thinker; men came from a great distance to learn from him. Later on, in the midst of the cares of the episcopate, he was to continue "to try and understand" the mysteries of God and to explain them. This is not the place for a study of his particular theology, though it is because he has one that it is necessary to see to what degree his spiritual doctrine is linked with it, first by describing his spirituality and then by attempting to answer the questions to which it gives rise.

His line of action and several of his letters show him as the father of souls. His whole life is characterized by what Eadmer, his biographer, calls "benevolence, kindness, love, gentleness, meekness, pardon, smiling exhortation",[1] and the same characteristics are found in his letters, his prayers, his conversations, his *dicta*. These, drawn up by the monk Alexander, are the sources for Eadmer's *Similitudes*[2] in which he mingled his own ideas with those of his master: St Anselm takes it for granted that observances are of themselves sanctifying, while Eadmer places more emphasis on the value of intention. The treatise is, however, faithful to Anselm's thought: its asceticism is all directed towards contemplation, which he speaks of several times. Cheerfully, not without humour, and with much good sense, he puts forward a doctrine which makes great demands. A man must above all give up his own will; by this his heart will be opened to an ardent longing for the heaven whose joys Anselm contemplates with delight. His prayer and his teaching on prayer is found in the *Prayers and Meditations* which he wrote at the request of some of his friends.[3] In his choice of words he shows his debt to St Augustine and St Gregory; the literary tricks which make each of his writings "a masterpiece of rhetoric"[4] do not conceal the intense fervour with which they were written. Anselm is seeking a certain experience of God; he uses the words *experiri, experientia* and *experimentum*.[5] His themes and his ideas are traditional ones, but what is personal in his emphasis is the new sensibility of the age.

Monastic asceticism, in St Anselm's eyes, is austere: he speaks of "the rigour of discipline" and the "rigour of the monastic

[1] *Vita*, I, 30, 31, P.L., 158, 68.

[2] Ed. F. S. Schmitt–R. N. Southern, in preparation; the question of authorship has been touched on, and extracts from the text are given by F. S. Schmitt in *Studi Gregoriani*, V, Rome, 1956, pp. 1–18.

[3] Ed. F. S. Schmitt, *S. Anselmi opera*, III, Edinburgh, 1946, pp. 1–91. On its authenticity see A. Wilmart, introduction to French translation by A. Castel, coll. "Pax", 1923; and *Auteurs spirituels*, Paris, 1932, pp. 147–216.

[4] F. S. Schmitt in "Des Hl. Anselm von Canterbury, Gebet zum Hl. Benedikt", in *Studia Benedictina*, Rome (*Studia Anselmiana*, 18–19), 1947, p. 307.

[5] Texts in A. Stolz, "Das Proslogion des Hl. Anselm", in *Rev bénéd.*, XLVII (1935), pp. 336–46.

order".[6] He did not lay great stress on exercises of corporal penance: the asceticism of a monk lies in the faithful, exact and unfailing practice of claustral observance. The *peregrinatio* which had been a means of sanctification for so many monks in earlier times was so no longer: St Anselm, as later on St Bernard, laid great emphasis on stability in the monastery, and discouraged all toying with the idea of going to the Holy Land, even to help on the Crusade which was being undertaken with such enthusiasm. The *peregrinatio* is a salutary mortification, but only for the clergy and for laymen.[7]

For Anselm it is the fear of God that the monk must cultivate, the religious spirit, that attitude of loving reverence towards the Lord which is one of the aspects of compunction. He exacts a high standard of obedience: it must be thorough, true and really interior. He speaks of fidelity to the Rule, to the monk's profession and the vows which he made then; they imply a total renunciation, humility, purity of intention, the offering of oneself. The reward of such austerity will be a feeling of inward peace and security, of confidence and love. Anselm, in a period which was one of preparation for the Cistercians and the other new Orders and which saw their beginnings, made clear how great an esteem he had for the traditional form of monasticism, and his writings give an idea of the high level of spiritual life which it fostered.

His views on prayer are altogether in the old tradition. In the Prologue to his *Prayers* he makes clear the relations which in earlier centuries existed between the *lectio*, the *meditatio* and the *oratio*: "I have set forth these meditations and prayers in order to arouse the reader to a love and fear of God, and to a scrutiny of himself. He should not read them in a hubbub, but in peace; not hurriedly but slowly, and a little at a time, reflecting attentively on what he reads; he need not read each one all through, but let him continue as long as they please him and he feels that with the help of God they excite him to fervent prayer."[8]

These prayers are the food of a solid piety in which a sense of sin is compatible with a contemplation of God's mysteries: they propose to the readers loving meditation on Christ and our redemption: the Mass and holy Communion; the Virgin Mother; the witnesses to our Lord—St John the Baptist, the *"monstrator Dei"*, the Apostles, particularly St John, the loving and beloved disciple,

[6] Texts in H. de Sainte-Marie, "Les lettres de S. Anselme de Cantorbéry et la règle bénédictine", in *Mélanges bénédictins*, St Wandrille, 1947, p. 300, and in the *Vita, loc. cit.*, 76.

[7] Cf. J. Leclercq, "Monachisme et pérégrination du IXe au XIIe siècles", in *Studia monastica*, III, 1961, pp. 32–52.

[8] Ed. Schmitt, p. 3.

dilector et dilectus; St Benedict and other saints. They also suggest prayers for those friends who played so large a part in St Anselm's life and in his letters.

Anselm has an important place in the realm of Mariology. In him doctrine and devotion are in harmony, and through his prayers and doctrinal writings and his influence on his disciples he may be said to be at the beginning of a development whose results were seen in St Bernard. The intuitions of the time were to prove fruitful, and it was Anselm's part to give them shape and balance. He uses the words *cor* and *affectus* in his writings, but though he gives a place to "the heart's affection", he is careful to keep rigidly to doctrine. For this spiritual father is a powerful thinker, and the historian's greatest difficulty in his regard is "to determine the proper function of speculation in the spiritual life".[9] Extreme answers have been proposed: some have considered certain of his writings purely philosophical; others have seen them as entirely mystical. It seems more than ever certain that the answer lies in a mean between these two views.[10] In the *Proslogion*, the *Monologion*, and other treatises on doctrine, there are various elements, some in the tradition of patristic "knowledge", others already in line with the method of the schools. Anselm brought these elements together, even tried to make them one, particularly in the *Proslogion*: the framework made by the prayers at the beginning and end, and throughout the treatise, is still that of "knowledge", and it might well be thought that the *intellectus fidei* to which Anselm tries to attain is a "wisdom", flowering into an "experience" of a mystical order. Yet into this Augustinian framework which resembles John of Fécamp's *Confessio*, the master of the school of Bec introduces a completely new and original element; the "ontological" argument which in itself is purely philosophical. The end is of course an experience, a gladness of the spirit, an enjoyment, but the means is of a conceptual order, the work of the intellect. St Anselm takes this work of the intellect (which was to be the essence of scholasticism) further than did St Augustine. He did not know the great works of Aristotle, and uses the dialectic inherited from Boethius, but there is already a definitely metaphysical tendency. In the *Pros-*

9 A. Forest in Fliche-Martin's *Histoire de l'Église*, XIII, Paris, 1951, p. 52.

10 Various answers have been put forward by several authors from differing points of view; in particular see E. Gilson, "Sens et nature de l'argument de Saint Anselme", in *Archives d'hist. doct. et littér. du moyen âge*, IX (1934), pp. 49–51; M. Cappuyns, "L'argument de Saint Anselme", in *Rech. de théol. anc. et médiév.*, VI (1934), p. 323; J. Bayart, "St Anselm's concept of mystery", *ibid.*, IX (1937), pp. 144–66; L. Baudry, "La présence divine chez St Anselme", in *Arch. d'hist. doct. . . .*, XIII (1942), p. 236; J. Leclercq–J. P. Bonnes, *Un maître de la vie spirituelle au XIe siècle, Jean de Fécamp*, Paris, 1946, pp. 78–9; J. P. Bonnes in *Rev. bénéd.*, LVI (1945–6), pp. 186–8; A Forest, *loc. cit.*, pp. 49–66.

logion and the *Monologion* especially, St Anselm transposes St Augustine's argument on the Trinity from the psychological to the philosophical plane: what for Augustine were "images" become for Anselm "analogies". One is sometimes conscious of his slightly ingenuous, possibly exaggerated, confidence in reason. It disappoints him finally in his longing to love God, yet it is a help to the spiritual man in him, turning him to fervent prayer. In his various writings the thinker and the mystic both show themselves at different times, one sometimes to the exclusion of the other. This alternation shows the intensity, the anguish of the conflict in so great a genius: Anselm is not like John of Fécamp, torn between action and contemplation, but rather between love and the intellect's search; a new form of Christian warfare, the austere asceticism of the thinker always hungry for knowledge and ever unsatisfied.[11]

Anselm is unique in his period: he declares that every problem he raises had been put to him by his disciples, friends or monks, yet what he had learnt in the school of Lanfranc was in no way a preparation for the solutions he proposed; and no one was to inherit his vigorous dialectic, nor did his teaching quickly find a place in the schools. His was not an attempt to make a synthetic whole of the mysteries of Christianity; he had turned his attention to particular, albeit fundamental, questions. As a thinker his influence lay less in his ideas than his ideal, and that confidence in reason which earned him the title of "the father of scholasticism". He believed in the compelling force of what he called "necessary reasons", and occasionally his arguments do not take account of the *auctoritas*. In the world in which the new forms of monastic life were developing he was on good terms with Ivo of Chartres and the Canons Regular, and in the same way he was sensitive to the ideas that were making their way in the world of doctrinal research; he may indeed be said to have adumbrated them. Though he combated the excesses of certain "dialecticians", yet dialectic plays a considerable part in his own thought. It was his monastic spirit that enabled him to keep an equilibrium which was far from simple. As a spiritual father he was profoundly traditional in outlook; he was the typical Benedictine, devoted to the Rule and ever giving the first place to contemplation, harmonizing all the values inherited from the past. At the same time the gifts of God had made of him a thinker of great power, an exception, a Benedictine of genius.

[11] This has been underlined by R. Perino, *La dottrina trinitaria di Sant'Anselmo*, Rome (*Studia Anselmiana*, 29), 1952, pp. 31–5.

2. Peter the Venerable and Cluny

Cluny in an earlier period had been a centre in which asceticism and prayer were in high esteem, and during the long abbacy of Peter the Venerable (from 1122 to 1156) the abbey and the Order were still important in this realm. Peter's delicate humanism and peaceful character were formed by the Cluniac life, and his life and actions bore witness to the vitality of its tradition. His ideal was one of great purity: he saw the life of the monk as one "hidden with Christ in God", and had a great admiration for all who lived thus, and particularly for the Carthusians. Though new orders were coming into being he did not consider the observance of Cluny to be less valuable,[12] though he increased the demands of "mortification" and reduced what he called "the great and continuous labour of the convent of Cluny". In short, he upheld what his biographer calls "the severity of the Order".[13] Among certain of his religious he encouraged various forms of the solitary life in the monastery itself or in hermitages in its neighbourhood: he even wrote, for one of them who had become a hermit with his permission and under his rule, a treatise which became a classic of the eremitical life.[14] His was that sense of the Church which had made Cluny fruitful during a period of reform, and it led him to devote himself to the papal service, to play a part in efforts at re-uniting the churches; he also exhorted the Jews to a conversion and set on foot a kind of intellectual crusade whose aim was to further a *rapprochement* between Christians and Mahometans. Yet his conception of monasticism was purely contemplative: its means of sanctification are penance, a life of prayer which consists in the exact and assiduous carrying out of the "psalmody", that is the Divine Office and its traditional additions, and in reading and mental prayer. The proof of the high level at which the life of prayer stood at Cluny was that all read or listened "daily and almost uninterruptedly" to the writings of St Gregory the Great.[15] Communion and confession were frequent, and "devotion" thus nourished flowered in the liturgy itself. The devotions themselves were both traditional and those of

[12] J. Leclercq, "Pierre le Vénérable et les limites du programme clunisien", in *Collectanea Ord. Cist. Ref.*, XVIII (1956), pp. 84–7: D. Knowles, "Peter the Venerable", in *Bulletin of the John Rylands Library*, XXXIX (1956), pp. 132–45. Until the end of this chapter references not preceded by an author's name are to works by the author in which questions which are only referred to in passing have been dealt with at greater length.

[13] *Pierre le Vénérable*, St Wandrille, 1946, pp. 92–149, and *passim*; art. "Contemplation", in *Dict. de spiritualité*, II (1953), col. 1944–5.

[14] "Pierre le Vénérable et l'érémitisme clunisien", in *Petrus Venerabilis*, Rome, 1956, pp. 108–20.

[15] Cf. *Pierre le Vénérable*, p. 261.

the period: to Christ, to our Lady, to the angels and saints.[16] Peter the Venerable wrote a long and beautiful treatise on the Resurrection, about the Holy Sepulchre for which the Crusaders were fighting; he also drew up the office of the Transfiguration, a feast which had long since been celebrated in the East, and which he now introduced into Cluny.

There is not a great deal of writing from Cluny, where the monks listened more than they wrote. The monk Ralph in his poems sings the praises of Cluny[17]; Bernard of Morlaix in his *De contemptu mundi* sets forth the traditional ideas on renouncing the world and longing for God[18]; Peter of Poitiers praises Peter the Venerable.[19] In Normandy, at Saint-Evroult, Ordericus Vitalis wrote his *Ecclesiastical History*, a work which has been called "the Cluniac way of writing history"[20]—the way being that of interpreting historical events from the point of view of religion. At Cluny, as no one can deny without flying in the face of the evidence, there was a harmonious union between the life of culture and the life of worship.[21] It was, however, true that on more than one point the institutions were beginning to show signs of age; there were those who wished to free themselves from some of the customs accumulated throughout the centuries, and they therefore shortened the psalmody and increased the austerity. Peter the Venerable's statutes were themselves in this sense.[22] His former prior, Matthew of Albano, showed that the solemn celebration of the long Offices harmonizes in itself asceticism and prayer and gives occasion for much self-abnegation.[23]

16 There is a translation of a beautiful prayer to Mary by Peter the Venerable in *La spiritualité médiévale*, by L. Genicot, Paris, 1958, p. 64.

17 Ed. M. B. Ogle–D. M. Schullian, *Rodulphi Tortarii Carmina*, Rome, 1933, pp. 447–53.

18 Ed. T. Wright, *Anglo-Latin Satirical Poets of the Twelfth Century*, London, 1872. Bernard of Morlaix is also the author of a treatise on the Redemption, the Blessed Eucharist and the desire for heaven (*Instructio sacerdotum*, P.L., 184, 771–792) and other writings (cf. *Dict. d'hist. et de géog. ecclés.*, VIII (1935), col. 699–700); possibly also of the *Mariale* published under the name of St Anselm by P. Ragey, Tournai, 1885; cf. A. Wilmart in *Rev. bénéd.*, XLV (1933), p. 250.

19 P.L., 189, 47–62.

20 H. Wolter, *Ordericus Vitalis. ein Beitrag zur kluniazensischen Geschichtschreibung*, Wiesbaden, 1955.

21 The latest contribution to the subject is that of H. Rupp, *Deutsche Religiöse Dichtungen des 11 und 12 Jahrhunderts*, Freiburg im Breisgau, 1958, pp. 284–94; cf. J. Leclercq, "Cluny fut-il ennemi de la culture?", in. *Rev. Mabillon*, XLVII (1957), pp. 172–82.

22 D. Knowles, "The reforming decrees of Peter the Venerable", in *Petrus Venerabilis*, Rome, 1956, pp. 1–20.

23 Text in U. Berlière, *Doc. inéd. pour serv. à l'hist. ecclés. de la Belgique*, Maredsous, 1894, pp. 93–110.

3. "*Turba Magna*"

St Anselm and Peter the Venerable were each in his own way exceptional, but the Benedictine milieu of the twelfth century was made up of ordinary men. Our knowledge of its spirituality comes from many writers, some of whom were not on the same level as Anselm and Peter, but who should be noted in any general sketch of the period. They existed in many different places.

Anglo-Norman monasticism was developing rapidly on a large scale.[24] Eadmer, the biographer and secretary of St Anselm, carried on his master's mariological work[25]; Gilbert Crispin explained the great value of the monastic life[26]; an obscure monk, possibly called Ralph, justified the custom of giving the monastic habit to the dying, whether clergy or laymen, who desired to receive the grace it symbolizes.[27] Odo of Canterbury showed that monastic profession is a "baptism of penance",[28] and from the writings of a monk of Bec can be learnt the devotions of the period.[29] The *Life* of Christina of Markyate by an anonymous author bears witness both to the fervour of the recluse and to that of the Abbey of St Albans. Thirteen miles away from the abbey there lived a religious called Roger, in whose praise it was said, "he was monk of our community, but lived in a hermitage, in obedience to his abbot".[30] A monk, almost certainly from Canterbury where he must have known Anselm, went to live near Ratisbon under the name of Honorius of Arles: he has left various catechetical, moral, and even spiritual writings.[31] It was in England, too, that Ralph d'Escures composed his homilies[32] and Osbert de Clare his prayers[33] and letters,[34] and Bishop Herbert de Losinga wrote letters[35] and

[24] Cf. D. Knowles, *The Monastic Order in England*, Cambridge, 1950, pp. 83–190 and 267–330.

[25] *De conceptione S. Mariae*, ed. Rome (*Classici Mariani*) 1959; cf. G. Geenen, O.P., "Eadmer, le premier théologien de l'Immaculée Conception", in *Virgo Immaculata Actus congressus Mariologici*, vol. V, Rome, 1955, pp. 90–136.

[26] *Analecta monastica*, II, p. 117–23.

[27] *Ibid.*, pp. 158–68. [28] *Ibid.*, pp. 124–39.

[29] *Ibid.*, pp. 150–73, cf. p. 144.

[30] Ed. C. H. Talbot, *The Life of Christina of Markyate*, Oxford, 1959, p. 80; on the eremitical life at St Albans and in English monasticism in the twelfth century, cf. *ibid.*, introduction pp. 16–18. Cf. J. Leclercq, "Sur le statut des ermites monastiques: les leçons du passé", in *La Vie spirituelle*, Suppl. 58, (1961), pp. 384–94.

[31] His works are in P.L., 172, 40–1270. On his life see R. Bauerreiss in *Studien und Mitteilungen zur Gesch. der Ben. Ordens*, LXVII (1956), pp. 306–13.

[32] One of them is in P.L., 158, 1505–8; cf. A. Wilmart, "Les homélies attribuées à Saint Anselme", in *Archives d'hist. doct. et litt. du moyen âge*, II (1927), pp. 16–22.

[33] Cf. A. Wilmart, *Auteurs spirituels*, pp. 261–86.

[34] Ed. R. Anstruther, *Epistolae Herberti de Losinga, Osberti de Clara, et Elmeri Prioris*, Brussels, 1846, pp. 109–200.

[35] *Ibid.*, pp. 1–102.

sermons.[36] Several of the meditations attributed to St Anselm are the work of anonymous monks of these milieux.[37] One of them is from the pen of Elmer of Canterbury who is also the author of the *Excitatio mentis in inquisitionem Dei*, a sermon, and sixteen letters on spiritual subjects.[38] In all these writings can be seen the great esteem in which traditional observance was held; in them the doctrines about profession and what it implies are stated with great precision.[39] Everything was seen from the point of view of "seeking for God", "pure love", "simplicity" in looking towards God. This is to be attained by "the exercise of devotion"—prayer in all its forms. These are called "spiritual exercises" to distinguish them from "corporal exercises", that is manual or exterior mortification. From these exercises comes an atmosphere of peace, gentleness, amiability, interior joy. This contemplative outlook, which owes much to St Gregory, is eminently favourable to certain kinds of development in the field of doctrine (for example on the Immaculate Conception), such as Eadmer brought about as a result of his reflection on the faith.[40]

At Monte Cassino Peter the Deacon developed at length Smaragdus' commentary on the Rule, taking his inspiration from the Fathers, St Gregory in particular. He also speaks much of simplicity,[41] compunction, and the longing for God; of the union of the soul with the Spouse, Christ, who hides himself that she may seek him more earnestly[42]; of the purity that the psalmody requires; of the necessity of the *lectio divina* and the prayer for which it is a preparation.[43] The *affectus** of which St Benedict speaks in connection with prayer he defines as "a love", "a desire".[44]

In the Empire it was a monk of St Laurent of Liège, later abbot of Deutz near Cologne, where he died in 1129, who was described by a good judge as "the great Rupert, the best representative of the ancient spirituality".[45] He wrote long commentaries on the

36 Ed. E. M. Goulburn–H. Symonds, *The Life, Letters and Sermons of Bishop Herbert de Losinga*, Oxford–London, 1878, vol. II, pp. 3–430.

37 They are the *Meditations* IV–VI and XIX. Cf. Wilmart, *Auteurs spirituels*, pp. 193–9.

38 Ed. *Analecta monastica*, II, pp. 45–117.

39 "Une doctrine de la vie monastique dans l'École de Bec", in *Spicilegium Beccense*, I (1959), pp. 477–88.

40 Cf. *L'amour des lettres et le désir de Dieu*, Paris, 1957, pp. 199–201, 209–10.

41 Ed. *Bibliotheca Casinensis*, V, Monte Cassino, 1894. *Florilegium*, p. 84 and *passim*.

42 *Ibid.*, p. 103.

43 *Ibid.*, p. 135.

* [*Rule of St Benedict*, ch. xx: "et ideo brevis debet esse et pura oratio; nisi forte ex affectu inspirationis divinae gratiae protendatur".—Trans.]

44 *Ibid.*, pp. 171, 172.

45 The expression is that of J. Huijben, "Les origines de l'École Flamande. L'École bénédictine", in *La Vie spirituelle*, Suppl., LIX (1939), p. [175]. The whole article, pp. [170]–[186], is excellent. The best study of Rubert of Deutz is by M.

Bible, some of which have significant titles: *On the Trinity and on its work, The victory of the Word of God, The glory and honour of the Son of Man, The glorifying of the Holy Trinity.*[46] He took occasion to express his great sense of the value of the traditional monastic ascesis,[47] but his scriptural writings are themselves a witness to the fruitfulness of the *lectio divina*. Rupert, reacting against the view of certain masters of the schools, held that the Scriptures suffice to nourish religious thought. His idea was to consider the mysteries of our salvation as they were developed in sacred history. His example, the quality of his works and the readers they found show that this conception corresponded to the needs of the monastic world. He was a contemplative, yet was among those who contributed most to what has been called "the patristic works of the twelfth century",[48] and to monastic theology.

His profound respect for the mysteries moved him to undertake a biblical synthesis of what he calls "the majesty of the Scriptures".[49] One feels that he is familiar with Origen and penetrated with the thought of St Gregory and St Augustine. The ardour of his writing is on a level with his enthusiasm. He seeks for and finds a "delectable" knowledge, he desires to "taste", to savour the realities of faith, and in order to express what he feels he frequently uses the language of conjugal love. He knows that it is a grace to be able to approach God thus; the Most High "touches" the soul in order to teach it,[50] "visits"[51] it, and at the same time gives it a certain "experience" of himself. All these terms, *tactus, contactus, visitat, officit, experimentum*,[52] will soon be found again in St Bernard. Rupert, however, is less concerned with the effects of grace in himself than with the divine work by which that grace was acquired for him. He considers with wonder the divine plan, the victory of the Word, the wonders of the Church. It is not so much the visible circumstances of Jesus' life that hold his attention as the mysteries of salvation that he accomplished. He suggests, and this for the first time in the history of exegesis or spirituality, a Marian interpretation of the Canticle of Canticles[53]: his commentary on it is a

---

Magrassi, *Teologia e storia nel pensiero di Ruperto di Deutz*, Rome, 1959. On Rupert's exegesis see H. de Lubac, *Exégèse médiévale*, II (1961), pp. 219–38.

[46] His works are in P.L., 167–70.

[47] *In Reg. S. Benedicti*, P.L., 170, 477–538.

[48] Cf. E. Gilson's preface to M. D. Chenu, *La théologie au XIIe siècle*, Paris, 1957, p. 9.

[49] *In Apoc.*, III, P.L., 169, 208 A.

[50] *Ibid.*, II, 2, P.L., 169, 881.

[51] *In Mt.*, XII, P.L., 168, 1604.

[52] They are brought together in a wonderful passage of the *De victoria Verbi Dei*, I, 3, P.L., 169, 1219 D–1220, which seems to derive from Origen, *Comment. in Cant.*, Bk I, ed. Baehrens, Berlin, 1925, pp. 105–6.

[53] P.L., 168, 839–962.

long colloquy with our Lady, in which he reflects that with Mary he is one with Christ, and through Mary with the Church. He also gives a considerable place to what he calls "the mystery of the psalms"[54] and holds that the assiduous reader, if he wishes to keep himself in the joy of the knowledge of God, that *dulce studium,*[55] that "Sabbath and leisure with the Word",[56] must learn the Scriptures by heart.[57] Without love, however, there can be no understanding: that is only given in the inner sanctuary, *in templo cordis.*[58] It can be seen how entirely traditional was this biblical spirituality.

At Liège, too, towards the middle of the twelfth century Wazelin of St Laurence wrote a *Concordia et expositio quattuor Evangeliorum* in which can be seen his own deep attachment to the Scriptures,[59] and a desire to encourage the same love in his readers. William of St James wrote a treatise in favour of the institution of a feast of the Holy Trinity[60]; Françon of Afflighem (†1135) sings of "the epic of grace"[61]; a century later the spiritual teaching of Rainier of Liège (†1230)—in a book *"On tears"*, in the lives of various holy persons and in other *opuscula*—is still traditional but more tender and expansive in style.[62] In the diocese of Trèves, Egbert, a monk (†1184), wrote *Letters, sermons, and meditations and prayers* on the childhood and Passion of our Lord and on our Lady[63]; and Abbot Emmecho († *c.* 1197) spread abroad the memory of St Elizabeth of Schönau.[64] In the Black Forest Werner of St Blaise (†1174) put together a long liturgical *florilegium*[65]: in Bavaria Idungue of Prüfening maintained the right of monks to exercise the priestly ministry, provided their life remained a monastic one[66]; in Carinthia Geoffrey of Admont (†1165) wrote some *opuscula* on biblical subjects and a long series of sermons which are too little known, as they contain treasures in the way of for-

54 *De Trin.*, IV, 5, P.L., 167, 1674.

55 *In Mt.*, X, P.L., 168, 1555 D.

56 *In Reg. S. Benedicti*, III, 8, P.L., 170, 515 D.

57 *In Apoc.*, IV, 5, P.L., 169, 925 C.

58 *In Johannem*, XI, P.L., 169, 709 A.

59 Cf. H. Silvestre in *Rev. bénéd.*, LXIII (1953), pp. 310–25.

60 "Le traité de Guillaume de St Jacques sur la Trinité", in *Arch. d'hist. doctr. et litt. du moyen âge*, XVIII (1950–51), pp. 89–102. On Guilbert of Gembloux see *infra*, p. 179.

61 J. Huijben, *art. cit.*, p. [174]. There are in P.L., 166, 717–814, in addition to the treatise *De gratia Dei*, two of Françon's letters.

62 His works are in P.L., 204, 15–212. J. Huijben, *art. cit.*, has described these writings which, like those of other noteworthy authors, can only be mentioned here.

63 Ed. F. W. E. Roth, *Die visionen der Hl. Elisabeth und die Schriften der Aebte Ekbert und Emecho von Schönau*, Brün, 1884, pp. 230–342.

64 *Ibid.*, pp. 343–59.

65 *Deflorationes*, P.L., 157, 725–1256; cf. P. Glorieux in *Mélanges J. de Ghellinck*, Gembloux, 1951, II, pp. 699–721.

66 Ed. Pez, *Thes. anecd. noviss.*, vol. II, part II, 505.

mulas on contemplation,[67] reading, meditation, and mental prayer,[68] and on the Sacred Heart of Jesus as the source of light whereby we may interpret the Scriptures.[69] Here, too, St Gregory's influence can be seen on every page.

There was no lack of spiritual writers in the part of France influenced by Cluny. Some of them, like Martinian,[70] Hervé du Bourg-Dieu,[71] and Drogo,[72] left little behind them, though the writings of the two last were to be well known as suppositious works of St Bernard. Others, like Arnold of Bonneval,[73] Geoffrey of Vendôme,[74] Julian of Vézelay[75] and Peter of Celle[76] wrote longer works. Abelard's Rule, addressed to Héloise and the nuns of the Paraclete, is an admirable example of monastic doctrine: its principles, securely based on tradition, are expressed in the language of humanism.[77] There were others, anonymous or little known—writers of letters,[78] sermons,[79] poems,[80] and treatises on the formation of novices,[81] all of whom show a true fervour. One of the most fruitful, and perhaps also one of the most disconcerting to the modern mind, was Peter of Celle (†1183), who wrote treatises, biblical commentaries and letters.[82] His is a very pure idea of the monastic life, and he illustrates it by biblical images of an astonishing exuberance. The monastery, since it is altogether ordered to contemplation, is a "foretaste" of heaven, and in it men anticipate the occupations of

67 P.L., 174, 91 D, 218, 422–3, etc.

68 *Ibid.*, 388–9.

69 *Ibid.*, 339.

70 H. Roux, "L'écrit spirituel du moine Martinien", in *Mélanges bénédictins*, St Wandrille, 1947, pp. 321–47.

71 His Homilies are in P.L., 158, 585–673; cf. Wilmart in *Arch. d'hist. doctr. et litt. du moyen âge*, II (1927), pp. 7–8.

72 *Meditatio in passionem et resurrectionem*, etc., P.L., 189, 1733–60. Cf. "Drogon et St Bernard", in *Rev. bénéd.*, LXIII (1953), pp. 117–28.

73 *De VII verbis Domini in Cruce, de laudibus beatae Mariae*, etc., P.L., 189, 1513–734; cf. *Rev. bénéd.*, *loc. cit.*, pp. 116–17, and "Les méditations eucharistiques d'Arnaud de Bonneval", in *Rech. de théol. anc. et médiév.*, XIII (1946), pp. 40–56.

74 P.L., 157, 33–289.

75 M. M. Lebreton, "Les sermons de Julien, moine de Vézelay", in *Analecta monastica*, III, pp. 118–37.

76 P.L., 202, 405, 1146.

77 Ed. T. P. McLaughlin, "Abelard's Rule for Religious Women", in *Mediaeval Studies*, XVIII (1956), pp. 241–92. The best account of Abelard's humanism is still E. Gilson's charming and penetrating book *Abélard et Héloïse*, 2nd ed., Paris, 1948, tr. L. K. Snook, *Heloïse and Abelard*, London, 1953.

78 *Analecta monastica*, I, pp. 91–123.

79 *Ibid.*, II, 18–27; *Rev. Mabillon*, XXXIII (1943), pp. 48–73; XXXVI (1946), pp. 1–12; *Mediaeval Studies*, XV (1953), pp. 95–106.

80 For example, Ralph Tortaire, a monk of Fleury, puts the *Life of St Maurus* and the *Miracles of St Benedict* into verse, ed. Ogle–Schullian, *op. cit.* pp. 349–442.

81 *Rev. d'asc. et de myst.* XXXIII (1957) pp. 387–99.

82 *La spiritualité de Pierre de Celle* Paris, 1946. "Nouvelles lettres de Pierre de Celle", in *Analecta monastica*, V, pp. 160–79.

that blessed life, which even now the saints and angels are performing: praising, adoring and thanking God and praying to him. It takes for granted a life of peace—within, the *quies mentis*; without, the *quies claustri*—and of leisure, that *otium* which is the difficult mean between idleness and *negotium*, a restlessness which is the negation of leisure. The aim of monastic study is to form the monk rather than to give him information, to give him a clearer knowledge rather than to add to his learning. This study is the foundation of the "sacred reading" which leads him by way of meditation and prayer to that height where he rests in God once more—*quies contemplationis*. God had once "formed" man in his own likeness, and it is the part of asceticism to "reform" that image which sin has "deformed". Then the soul joins itself to Christ as to its Bridegroom, the King of Love, and may undergo an unutterable experience only to be expressed in the poetry of the Bible, whose study was the soul's point of departure towards that mystical union.

Peter of Celle wrote for Benedictines, Canons Regular, Cistercians and Carthusians: every monastic milieu could understand his simple though difficult teaching, because they were united by ideals which were essentially the same.

4. *The Nuns*

The same monastic ideal held sway among religious women. Their numbers were increasing and they had become a spiritual world about which as yet little is known. They wrote less than the monks, but what the latter wrote for them or about them gives some idea of their interior life. This is especially true of a *Speculum virginum* written in the twelfth century by an anonymous writer, probably from the Middle Rhineland: it was widely read and recently its study has been made the occasion of a preliminary synthesis of feminine piety at the height of the Middle Ages.[83] The *Speculum* itself is a monastic writing, but its themes are elaborated in other writers of the time,[84] particularly in the *Hortus deliciarum* of the abbess of the Canonesses of Mont Saint-Odile in Alsace, Herrade of Landsberg.[85] Without precisely despising woman, it was taken for granted that her physical and moral weakness rendered her efforts at perfection more meritorious. From the Old and New Testaments were taken examples of holy women who had made illustrious the three states of life—that of wife, widow and virgin, whose spiritual fruits were compared with the yield of thirty, sixty

[83] M. Bernards, *Speculum virginum*, Cologne, 1955. In it are references to themes and passages that can only be mentioned here in passing.

[84] For a list of these, *ibid.*, p. 35.

[85] The latest edition is that of J. Walther, Strasbourg, 1952.

and a hundredfold of the parable. In itself virginity is the highest state, though a personal perfection greater than that of a nun can be attained in the other two. With regard to monastic vocation, it was loudly declared that freedom of choice was the condition of a true vocation, though in practice things were sometimes rather different. The Blessed Virgin, St John the Baptist, the virgin disciple St John the Evangelist, St Agnes, St Thecla and the other virgins and martyrs of antiquity were proposed to the nuns as models. Like the wise virgins in the Gospel, they are to await the return of Christ; they are privileged in that their existence points towards the last things. The writers of the time, when speaking of their virtues, freely make use of biblical allegories borrowed from descriptions of flowers, and the anonymous *Mirror*, like Abbess Herrade's *Garden*, is copiously illuminated. One nun is reminded that her humility should be as profound as her state of life is exalted, and that greatness lies in virginity of soul rather than of body. She will have to fight, to go to God as by the steps of a ladder, helped by that doctor of souls, her confessor, and frequently strengthened by the Blessed Eucharist—let her take care never, like Judas, to make an unworthy communion.

In some countries it was necessary to point out that all are equal in Christ, and to emphasize the consequences of this fact where charity is concerned. There were monasteries where only women of noble birth could enter, others being received merely as servants with very limited opportunities for the contemplative life; and even in communities where noble birth was not absolutely necessary, the others were made to feel the lack of it. These differences of degree, particularly in the countries with Germanic institutions, lay not so much in the wealth as in the feudal position of the family. St Hildegarde was in favour of maintaining what was in fact the position,[86] but more and more there grew up a wish for freedom. The author of the *Speculum* insists on equality. "As far as ancestry is concerned, we have but one father on earth. Adam, and one in heaven, Christ."[87] St Odo had said, "Go to ancient history and you will find that the most powerful are always the most wicked."[88] In any case the situation gave scope for humility to some and charity to all. Obedience was sometimes practised in the form of submission to our Lady as abbess, and her statue presided over the Office and the life of the community.[89] It was laid down that all should be poor and none should enjoy a *peculium*. The pretended *sanctimonialis*,

[86] *Epist.*, CXVI, P.L., 197, 336–7.
[87] Text in Bernards, *op. cit.*, p. 147, note 109.
[88] *Collat.*, III, 30, P.L., 133, 613.
[89] "Notre Dame Abbesse", in *Priez sans cesse, Trois cents ans de prière*, Paris, 1953, pp. 175–7.

who lived near the monastery but outside it, was reminded of the necessity of enclosure, separation from her family and stability[90]: the nuns themselves indeed were taught to make their own the spiritual advantages of the *peregrinatio*[91] without leaving their cloister.

A great measure of reserve was required in the relations between them and the *praepositus* who had charge of their souls: examples and warnings reminded him of the dangers and responsibility of his position.[92] The end of all this asceticism was union with the heavenly Bridegroom, the birth of Christ in the soul. The Word is to be conceived, and Mary is the perfect model of that spiritual motherhood.[93] All this teaching was calculated to encourage a purely contemplative life, which was held to have reached its fullness in that of the recluse.[94] The *Lives* of some of these, and devotions written for others, were generally read, and kept up an esteem for their vocation. Paul Bernried in the first half of the twelfth century tells with satisfaction how the Blessed Hercula left her native land to come and settle at Epfach, where she lived for thirty-six years, some of them with a companion. She was in touch with other hermits, and used to exhort her visitors to conversion. She died in 1127.[95] Joscelin of St Bertin († *c.* 1118) wrote a *Liber confortationis* full of advice and encouragement for one of his friends, Eva, a nun who had fled from the monastery of Wilton to come and live by a chapel on the land of the Benedictine priory of l'Évière in Anjou. Like Abraham and so many others, down to St Martin and St Augustine of Canterbury, hers was the grace of exile, of the *peregrinatio*.[96] Joscelin sends her the praises of the solitary life,[97] where she may feed from "the table of the Holy Scriptures".[98] She should especially nourish her prayer with the Psalter, because "in the mystery of the Psalms the Saviour himself, in virtue of his human nature, intercedes for us". She must meditate on them, attune her soul to them, and in them and by them speak heart to heart with God: when she finds a word which touches her, *affectuosius verbum*, let her pause and repeat it lovingly.[99] Every day she is to go to Holy Communion,[100] and she

[90] Bernards, *op. cit.*, p. 161. [91] *Ibid.*, p. 166.

[92] *Ibid.*, p. 168 and see the same author's "Zur Seelcsorge in den Frauenklöstern des Hochmittelalters", *Rev. bénéd.*, LXVI (1956), pp. 256–68.

[93] Bernards, *op. cit.*, pp. 185–92.

[94] P. Schmitz, *Hist. de l'Ordre de S. Benoît*, VII, Maredsous, 1956, pp. 53–8. Recluses, like other *sanctimoniales*, adopted either the Benedictine tradition or some other, according to the observance of the monastery in whose neighbourhood they dwelt; but the ideals of reclusion and the institution itself did not vary.

[95] *Acta. SS Boll.*, Aprilis II, 549–54.

[96] Ed. C. H. Talbot in *Analecta monastica*, III, pp. 37–8.

[97] *Ibid.*, p. 72. [98] *Ibid.*, pp. 79–80.

[99] *Ibid.*, pp. 82–3. [100] *Ibid.*, p. 90.

must grow in humility and longing for God. Joscelin ends his exhortation with a long discourse on heaven.

5. St Hildegarde and St Elizabeth of Schönau

These two nuns were not only contemporaries and friends, but both were visionaries. Their writings tell us much about themselves, but also about the circles in which they lived. Hildegarde was born at Bingen in Hesse in 1098.[101] She was brought up from the time she was eight years old among the nuns, by a recluse; she became abbess in 1136 and died in 1179. She was always ill. She declared that from the age of three she had been favoured with visions which continued all her life, and when she was forty an interior voice bade her write them down. From then onwards her reputation grew and spread. She travelled all over Germany, giving counsel and settling conflicts; prelates and princes, priests and religious, communities of nuns, all begged her prayers and asked her advice. She became a guide of souls as well as a prophetess: she consoles and cheers the sorrowful, calms the fears of the anxious, preaches perseverance to all, exhorting each to the virtue his letter shows him to require most. She is not afraid to speak plainly and to reprove iniquity, thus actively contributing to the reform of the Church. The huge collection of three hundred letters, each with Hildegarde's answer to it, is a sort of ascetical formulary unique of its kind. In it, as in all her works—of which the principal one is the *Scivias*—she set down in the form of "visions" what others said in a different way.[102] Her writings are sometimes obscure because of their literary *genre*, and her artistic use of words—the vocabulary of the "celestial harmony" or the allegories of flowers—and it is not clear what part her secretaries played in writing them down. But her profound humility of soul is always apparent, and though the Church has never taken up a definite position about her message, there is no reason to suppose that her gifts were not extraordinary and supernatural.

Her teaching embraced various domains, and belongs to a history of physics,[103] metaphysics[104] and apocalyptic,[105] which cannot be

[101] The best biographical account and bibliography is in the *Vies des saints et bienheureux* by the Benedictines of Paris, IX, Paris, 1950, pp. 336–71. There is also a good article by F. Vernet in *Dict. de théol. cathol.*, VI (1920), col. 2468–80.

[102] St Hildegarde's works are in P.L., 197, and J. B. Pitra, *Analecta sacra*, VIII, Monte Cassino, 1882. The authenticity of her works as a whole has been established by M. Schräder–A. Fürkötter, *Die Echtheit des Schriftums der Heiligen Hildegard von Bingen*, Cologne–Graz, 1956; see their conclusions, p. 184.

[103] Bibliography in H. Schipperge's, *Hildegard von Bingen, Heilkunde*, Salzburg, 1957.

[104] Cf. M. Ungrend, *Die metaphysische Antropologie der Hl. Hildegard*, Münster, 1938, and M. Böckler, *Hildegard von Bingen wisse die Wege* (a German

entered into here. On several points her intuitions were in advance of later scientific progress. Her theology was that of the mysteries, particularly the Trinity, the Incarnation, the Redemption, the Blessed Eucharist, the Church, the maternity of Mary and the last things. She would not admit that men should seek to know, even through her, the secrets of God, and more than once moderated the excessive curiosity of those who came to consult her. Her interpretation of the history of salvation by all that has come down to the faithful by tradition, was on a vast scale, and she attributed all her lights to the grace she had received of interpreting the Scriptures. The influence of other sources, sometimes distant ones, is, however, apparent. She may have read authors who handed down Greek or Neo-Platonic ideas, or have been able to profit by the symbolism which abounded in medieval work, particularly in the monasteries.[106] The liturgy left a profound impression on her, and this explains some of her modes of expression. Hildegarde wrote commentaries on the story of the creation, the prologue to St John's Gospel which frequently inspired her, and on certain passages in the psalms. She quotes much of other books of the Bible, especially the Canticle of Canticles, the Apocalypse and St Paul's epistles, but her favourite book seems to have been the Psalter, with which she was familiar from the Divine Office. All the resources of tradition were thus used in the service of God and the Church, *ad gloriam Dei et profectum ecclesiae*,[107] by this "contemplative soul", this *speculativa anima*, as Guibert of Gembloux called her.

Her teaching on asceticism is marked with that commonsense which enabled her own monastery to prosper under her rule. She calls all to penance. She conjures up a picture of the conflict of virtue and vice in the form of a cosmic drama in which demons and angels take part, and Christ is the final victor. This war between good and evil is described in terms of the elements which take part in it, and yet the lesson that emerges is always one of peace, of self-mastery gained with the help of grace, through efforts which weaknesses and even sins must not check. Hildegarde was opposed to that *vagatio* which prevents tranquility, the *quieta stabilitas*,[108] but on the other hand she does not object to all forms of *pere-*

---

translation of the *Scivias* with illustrations, an introduction, and a bibliography), Salzburg, 1954.

[105] Cf. Ray C. Petrie, *Christian Eschatology and Social Thought*, New York, 1956, pp. 133–6.

[106] Cf. B. Widmer, *Heilsordnung und Zeitgeschehen in der Mystik Hildegards von Bingen*, Basle, 1955; M. M. Davy, *Essai sur la symbolique romane*, Paris, 1955, pp. 104–13.

[107] *Epist.*, XX, Pitra, *op. cit.*, p. 394.

[108] *Liber vitae meritorum*, V, 4–5, 30, 45. Pitra, *op. cit.*, pp. 185–6, 196, 206.

grinatio, especially if they end in the monastic life. She pointed out that with the two saints whose lives she wrote, St Rupert and St Disibod, the exile they had chosen was, as it were, a retreat which prepared them for the choice of a state of life. The first felt a call to renounce all his possessions, which were great, and to go away and imitate the Lord of whom it was said "art thou only a stranger in Jerusalem".[109] The second left Ireland and journeyed about Germany for ten years doing penance and preaching, then with his disciples settled on a mountain where they lived the life of solitaries in cells which afterwards became a *coenobium*.[110] Hildegarde recommends to the bishop of Bamberg a girl who, like Abraham, had left her country to become a *peregrina*.[111] One of her correspondents, Guibert of Gembloux, takes a similar line, praising the quiet, the security and the watchful rest of St Benedict at Subiaco: in imitation of Abraham and the patriarchs of whom the Epistle to the Hebrews speaks, saying "they wandered in deserts"; for separation from the world is a necessary condition of contemplation.[112]

Hildegarde described very exactly the psychic state in which her visions took place: they were neither ecstasies nor hallucinations; she was neither asleep nor rapt out of herself; they took place in her soul without the normal use of her senses being suspended.[113] She declared that contemplation was possible for "whoever shall triumph over his vices, and on fire with the Holy Spirit shall fix the eye of his heart on God". This contemplation, however, "the fruit of the heart's devotion",[114] does not bring an immediate perception of God,[115] he is only seen "through the windows of faith".[116] As a preparation it is as well to fix in one's mind by reading and rumination passages which one will then meditate on spontaneously without any book, and even in the dark.[117] But the conventual Office comes before all: "Before the Hours greet God briefly, lest being tired by long prayer you pay less attention to the psalmody."[118] Despite a certain obscurity in her visions, St Hildegarde's counsels are in the sane monastic tradition.

Elizabeth, a nun of Schönau in the diocese of Trèves, played a similar part, though her visions were of a different nature, being ecstasies. They were accompanied by extraordinary manifestations

109 P.L., 197, 1087–8.
110 *Ibid.*, 1100–4.
111 *Epist.*, CLVIII, Pitra, p. 573.
112 *Sermo de laudibus S. Benedicti*, Pitra, pp. 593–7.
113 *Epist.*, II, Pitra, p. 332.
114 *Liber div. operum*, p. 1, visio I, c. 6, P.L., 197, 745.
115 *Scivias*, p. III, visio XI, P.L., 197, 718.
116 *Liber vitae meritorum*, Bk II, ch. 35, Pitra, p. 78.
117 *Explanatio Reg. S. Benedicti*, P.L., 197, 1057.
118 *Ibid.*, 1058.

and great sufferings of body and soul. The whole community was associated with them, together with the abbot and monks of the neighbouring Abbey of Saint-Florin. She received these mystical graces during the liturgical offices, and their object was the solemnities celebrated and the saints venerated in the office. To receive the Blessed Eucharist daily was beginning to be thought of more as a means of uniting the soul with the Bread of Life than as a participation in the sacrifice of Redemption, though faith in its supernatural efficacy still played a larger part than considerations of a psychological order. Elizabeth wrote down her visions by her confessor's order; she also wrote a book on *The ways of God*, and epistles and prayers.[119] The friends of God of whom she speaks most are St John the Baptist, "whose faith was made glorious by his solitary life", St John the Evangelist, *heremita praecipuus*, the Apostles, St Mary Magdalene, and the Magi whose relics are held to be in Cologne. The Blessed Virgin comes into her writings frequently: many of Elizabeth's "salutations" are addressed to her and commemorate her joys. One of the votive offices which Elizabeth wrote was that of the Blessed Trinity. She counsels the abbots of the Rhineland to walk "in the way of contemplation",[120] as she holds that the life of monks is contemplative as is that of nuns. She does not speak of the pastoral duties of the clergy, but to all who have renounced the world, and to the laity—"those who are surrounded by its cares"—she recommends the faithful keeping of the commandments of the Lord. She has a message for each state of life—for the married, for the continent, widowers, prelates, hermits, young men and children. Thus, on the morrow of the feast of St John the Baptist an angel instructs her on "the life of hermits and solitaries", and she addresses herself to them as to an important category of Christians. She counsels discretion in all things, and particularly in practices of mortification and obedience. Let them love solitude not because of the liberty it gives, but because of the works of religion it enables them to do.[121] Elizabeth's writings spread far and wide[122]; she was more like St Gertrude than St Hildegarde and indeed in some ways was akin to certain mystics of modern

[119] Ed. F. W. Roth, *op. cit.*, and *Das gebetbuch der Hl. Elisabeth von Schönau*, Augsburg, 1886. On Elizabeth see D. Besse, *Les mystiques bénédictins*, Paris, 1922, pp. 202–15.

[120] Ed. Roth, *Die visionen . . .*, pp. 141, 143, etc.

[121] *Ibid.*, pp. 118–19.

[122] K. Köster in *Archiv. für Mittelrhein Kirchengesch.*, III (1951), pp. 243–315, enumerates 130 mss. *Ibid.*, IV (1952), pp. 79–119 shows that there is evidence all over Europe for this *corpus* of writings which was brought together between 1159 and 1184. R. J. Dean, in *Modern Philology*, XLI (1943–4), pp. 209–20, has shown that the edition of Elizabeth's writings known in England at the end of the twelfth century included variants and interpolations.

times. Yet she was traditional because of the link between the graces she received personally and the Church's worship. Her mystical life was sustained by the liturgy, and used in the work of reformation.

6. *Attachment to the Monastic Ideal*

There are certain characteristics which are common to all the authors sketched above, and to their circles, but a distinction must be made between what is peculiar to them as monks and what they contributed to the general spirituality of the Church. There is firstly in all of them a love of their state and of traditional observance that no criticism can shake. They defend it against the objections formulated by the "Innovators", the men of the new Orders which came into being as a result of the crisis in monasticism. Towards 1135 Ordericus Vitalis, a monk of Saint-Evroult in Normandy, described this new growth which he had before his eyes: he recognizes what is authentic—*vera religio*—in the new movements, though they have other less noble aspirations too, but his conclusion is in favour of the Benedictine way of life as it has come down through history.[123] The anonymous author of a reply to Theobald of Étampes[124] and Rupert of Deutz[125] gives a similar answer to the criticisms made by the secular clergy and the Canons Regular; but the attacks made by St Bernard and the Cistercians were those which gave the black monks occasion to take a stand. With serene moderation and uprightness Peter the Venerable asserts the sanctifying value of the Benedictine life inherited from previous centuries;[126] Hugh of Reading does so with aptness and verve,[127] as does the anonymous writer —probably English—of a true and penetrating retort,[128] and the poet whose verse has come down in a manuscript from Anchin.[129] Payen Bolotin[130] and Peter of Sens, who were not themselves monks, also claim that the life of Cluny and of many other abbeys is a sure path to salvation: *sufficere potest Cluniacus ad salutem omni homini quaerenti Deum.*[131] In all this can be found, if not a theory, at least a firm and precise conception of the religious life as a state

[123] *Historia ecclesiastica*, VIII, 25–6, P.L., 188, 636–45.
[124] Ed. R. Foreville–J. Leclercq in *Analecta monastica*, IV, pp. 8–118.
[125] *In Reg. S. Benedicti*, IV, P.L., 170, 525–44; *De vita vere apostolica, ibid.*, 611–64; *Epist. ad Liezelinum, ibid.*, 663–8.
[126] *Epist.*, I, 28, P.L., 189; cf. *Pierre le Vénérable*, St Wandrille, 1946, pp. 169–178.
[127] Ed. Wilmart in *Rev. bénéd.*, XLVI (1934), pp. 296–344.
[128] "Nouvelle réponse de l'ancien monachisme aux critiques des Cisterciens", in *Rev. bénéd.*, LXVII (1957), pp. 77–94.
[129] Ed. E. de Méril, *Poésies inédites du moyen âge*, Paris, 1854, pp. 319–25; cf. *Rev. bénéd.*, LXVIII (1958), p. 74, note 2.
[130] *Rev. bénéd.*, LXVIII (1958), pp. 76, 84.
[131] Peter of Sens, ed. G. Constable in *Petrus Venerabilis*, Rome, 1956, p. 50.

of perfection. In the next century the discussions brought about by the mendicant Orders were responsible for an advance in theology on that point; in the same way controversy between the black monks and their various opponents was fruitful in statements of doctrine. Light was thrown on the distinction between "precepts" and "counsels", and the essential importance of obedience in all seeking after perfection is emphasized very clearly. Some of the arguments put forward may have been unsound, and some of the interpretations of the Rule not very valuable, but behind them lay the evolution of a definite body of ideas.[132] Round St Anselm,[133] at Vézelay[134] and at Admont,[135] at Vendôme[136] and elsewhere, a theory of monastic profession was being worked out: it was shown to be an irrevocable engagement, making the *conversio* a second baptism, a baptism of repentance, which, differing from the first, remits sin in virtue of the labour of mortification of which it is the beginning.[137] Inevitably there were failures, but in a general way there was no lack of regularity and even fervour,[138] and the ideal itself remained a very high one. In its formulation recourse was had to themes which can only be touched on here: they were nearly all taken from the Bible. The monastic life is an imitation of Christ, a bearing of the Cross, an undertaking "naked to follow the naked Christ".[139] By it the monk is able to carry out to some extent the examples of sanctity proposed in the Scriptures. It is a paradise where the fruits of the Redemption restore to man even more than he had in the first paradise and are a beginning of the paradise to come;[140] it is an exile wherein is accomplished in spirit that flight from the world that was required of Abraham, and that conquest of the promised land which cost so many battles[141]; it is the "royal way" which leads straight to the city of the King of Glory[142]; in it a man may imitate the

132 See particularly *la Nouvelle réponse . . ., loc. cit.*

133 *Analecta monastica*, III, pp. 166–7.

134 *Ibid.*, pp. 132–6.

135 Geoffrey of Admont, *Serm.*, XI, P.L., 157, 276.

136 Geoffrey of Vendôme, *Epist.*, II, P.L., 157, 147.

137 *La vie parfaite*, Paris–Turnhout, 1948, pp. 133–41.

138 Cf. P. Schmitz, "Le monachisme bénédictin au XIIe siècle", in *Saint Bernard*, Milan, 1954, pp. 1–13.

139 M. Bernards, *Speculum virginum*, pp. 153–6, 178–82. J. Leclercq, "La séparation du monde dans le monachisme au moyen âge", in *Problèmes de la religieuse d'aujourd'hui: La séparation du monde*, Paris (ed. du Cerf), 1961, pp. 75–94. These ideas are not peculiar to the Benedictine tradition, but are common to all *claustrales*; they are mentioned here because the new Orders took them from the traditional monasticism in which they had been preserved.

140 "Le cloître est-il un paradis?" in *Le message des moines à nos temps* (*Mélanges A. Presse*), Paris, 1958, pp. 141–60; *La vie parfaite*, pp. 161–9.

141 M. M. Lebreton in *Analecta monastica*, III, pp. 129–30.

142 "La voie royale" in *La Vie spirituelle* (Suppl.), November, 1948, pp. 339–352; *L'amour des lettres . . .*, pp. 102–5.

"monks of the Old Testament" and those of the New.[143] "A prophetic life", it consists in waiting for the coming of the Lord like Elias, Eliseus, and St John the Baptist,[144] in prayer and penitence: "an apostolic life", having nothing of one's own, renouncing all selfishness, living the common life in charity as did the disciples round the Lord and in the Cenacle, and in the first community in Jerusalem.[145] "A life of martyrdom", for monks are an army always engaged in battle with the obstacles to love[146]: "the life of the angels", for by it man takes a part in the prayer of the angels, and the desire of complete detachment is kept up in asceticism and purity of life.[147] Finally it is an evangelical life, in which every rule has for its sole object to enable a man to walk, as St Benedict says, "in the way of the Gospel".[148] These themes are elaborated according to the tradition of ancient monasticism and those who were its exemplars, particularly St Anthony.[149] All bear witness to a conception of the Benedictine life as one of contemplation.[150] Monks, of course, had their share in certain pastoral works,[151] even at this period when the task of preaching the Gospel fell more and more on the Premonstratensians and the religious whose profession included the *cura animarum*; but nowhere is it stated that this was essentially part of their calling: their life was shaped by its vocation to prayer and penance.[152] Its tendency was eschatological; it was looked on as the "noviceship of eternity": and a devotion to heaven, a longing for God, and a great love for that state where the soul is united with him for ever was one of its dominant traits.[153] The perfect *coenobium* will be that Jerusalem, where under the rule of Christ the supreme Shepherd and Abbot of abbots, the monks will be reunited with the angels and the apostles and all who have renounced this world.[154]

[143] *Analecta monastca*, II, pp. 18–27; cf. Geoffrey of Admont, *Sermo*, XI, P.L., 157, 279.

[144] *La vie parfaite*, pp. 59–81.

[145] *Ibid.*, pp. 82–105.

[146] *Ibid.*, pp. 125–60.

[147] *Ibid.*, pp. 19–56.

[148] *Ibid.*, pp. 109–21; cf. *The Rule of St Benedict*, prologue.

[149] "St Antoine dans la tradition monastique médiévale", in *Antonius Magnus eremita*, Rome, 1956, pp. 229–47; *L'amour des lettres . . .*, pp. 87–107.

[150] "On monastic priesthood according to the ancient mediaeval tradition", in *Studia Monastica*, III, 1961, pp. 137–55. *L'amour des lettres . . .*, pp. 87–107.

[151] P. Hofmeister, "Mönchtum und Seelesorge bis zum 13 Jahrhunderts", in *Studien und Mitt. z. Gesch. des Benediktiner-Ordens*, LXV (1953–4), pp. 209–73.

[152] Art. "Contemplation", Conclusion, in *Dict. de spirit.*, II, 2, col. 1946–8. See the definition of monasticism given by the author of the reply to Thibault of Étampes (who is nevertheless in favour of monks being also priests). *Analecta monastica*, IV, p. 90, note 45.

[153] *L'amour des lettres . . .*, pp. 55–69.

[154] *Analecta monastica*, IV, pp. 100–1.

7. Devotion

The traditional method of prayer went on in the Benedictine world, and, enriched by the contributions of the new writers, it satisfied the needs of the new generations. There had always been formulas of private prayer, and now they become more numerous and longer. "Their authors expressed the sentiments of a repentant soul, or simply of one busy about the work of her Creator and Saviour, and in doing so gave free rein to the outpourings springing up from the depths of their being... without *arrière pensée* or restraint they poured out their feelings to God, sometimes slowly and sometimes fast, telling him the movements of that intimate love through which they lose themselves in him."[155] These "free prayers",[156] as Dom Wilmart calls them,[157] were expressions of compunction, and as such were not susceptible of a "method" strictly speaking, yet because of the sequence of the mysteries contemplated and the texts meditated on, it is possible to see in some of the formulas, if not the theory, at least an outline of the practice of what later became "methodical prayer". There is as yet no ordered scheme of prayer itself, or of its degrees, but the elements of such a systematization can be found: compunction, reading, meditation, prayer and contemplation; appeals to reflection, sentiment and the imagination. All this activity is nourished by Holy Scripture with its commentaries and the devotional formulas which explain it. "The monk in his cloister is like the Samaritan cared for in the stable: he ruminates constantly on Jesus Christ as the other on the hay brought to his manger."[158] Prayer has no other end than to express and nourish and increase the love we owe to our Lord; it is an indispensable means of stimulating mortification, but it must be for ever turned towards contemplating God in his mysteries.

There was also a balance kept between doctrine and piety: thanks to "monastic theology",[159] to the constant reading of the Fathers—particularly Origen, of whom it was said that "the monks were less afraid of him than were the accredited theologians"[160]—thanks too to the atmosphere of the liturgy, there was no difficulty in uniting the thoughts of antiquity with the new sensibility. This is seen particularly in the forms taken by devotion to Christ. The mystery of Christmas was honoured with special tenderness at Cluny, for the

155 A. Wilmart, *Introduction aux Méditations et prières de Saint Anselme*, translated by A. Castel, Paris, 1923, p. XII.
156 Cf. "Culte liturgique et prière intime dans le monachisme au moyen âge" in *La Maison Dieu*, LXIX (1962), pp. 39–55.
157 A. Wilmart, *loc. cit.*
158 An anonymous *Mariale*, ms. Paris, B.N. lat. 594 (XII century), f. 58v.
159 *L'amour des lettres* . . ., pp. 179–218.
160 O. Lottin in *Bull. de théol. anc. et médiév.*, VII (1955), p. 435, note 1715.

immense love of God for man is seen in the Incarnation. At Saint Wandrille, Tournus, Saint-Vaast Mass was celebrated "in memory of the humanity of the Son of God", though the monks did not stop to consider the interior dispositions of Jesus, but passed on to consider the mysteries accomplished by them.[161] Towards the end of the century, however, there is a foreshadowing of an evolution in which little by little psychology won the victory over doctrine, although still, as in the earlier part of the century, the aim of devotion was above all to sustain a solid and explicit faith. When Drogo and Arnold of Bonneval wrote *Méditations* on the Passion (which were attributed to St Bernard and much enhanced his reputation); when Joscelin of St Bertin counselled men to "consecrate the hours of the day to the Passion", and to sing psalms in honour of the Five Wounds[162]; when Anselm, Rupert, Honorius of Arles, Geoffrey of Admont, Elizabeth of Schönau and others showed in the pierced side of Jesus the fountain whence flow the treasures of his Sacred Heart,[163] it was a union of the theology inherited from the Fathers with a fervent interior piety.[164] In Benedictine monasteries as elsewhere there was the same definite advance: traditional "devotion" was enriched with a new note of intimacy.[165] There was the same broadening out and increasing "interiority" in the attitude to the Blessed Virgin. The old homilies, the verse which found a place in the liturgy, and the various prayers added to the Office still spoke of Mary in the language of the East, and these symbols and metaphors developed in a similar way.[166] Practices of devotion to Mary became more numerous and took a larger place.[167] Anselm and other monastic theologians, Eadmer in particular, reached a further stage of precision on the subject of her conception and privileges, and all this doctrine was accompanied by a tenderness unknown in past centuries. In the same way the rational basis of frequent confession and daily communion was made clear, and they were not only recommended as salutary practices. Confession was shown to be a means of anticipating the great public avowal at the Last

161 "Sur la devotion à l'humanité du Christ", in *Rev. bénéd.*, LXIII (1953), pp. 128–30.

162 Ed. C. H. Talbot in *Analecta monastica*, III, pp. 83–4.

163 "Le Sacré Cœur dans la tradition bénédictine au moyen âge", in *Cor Jesu*, Rome, 1959, II, pp. 1–28.

164 H. Rahner, "Grundzüge einer Geschichte der Herz-Jesu-Verehrung", in *Zeitschrift für Aszese und Mystik*, XVIII (1943), pp. 69–73.

165 This evolution of the meaning of *devotio* has been described by J. Châtillon in *Dict. de spirit.*, III (1957), col. 710–11, and is exemplified among the Benedictine writers; cf., e.g., *Pierre le Vénérable*, pp. 317, 331, 332.

166 G. G. Meersseman, *Der hymnos Akathistos im Abendland*, Fribourg, 1958, pp. VI–VII.

167 "Dévotion et théologie mariales dans le monachisme au moyen âge", in *Maria*, II, pp. 557–63.

Judgment; as that will bring the elect to the joy of heaven, so here below a spontaneous confession and the grace of the sacrament purifies our sight and prepares us for contemplation.[168]. The Blessed Eucharist unites the Church and each individual soul with the Bridegroom,[169] with the King who for our sakes willed to be "humble, mild, tender and accessible. By his death the Lord redeemed the slave; by making his Body our daily bread he feeds his Church, by the Holy Communion he makes his Church one body with himself and he is one with her."[170] Tears must spring from the eyes of those who approach the chalice of his Blood; the sacrifice they lay on the altar must be that of a contrite heart, of feelings of love which well up from the depths of the soul.[171]

[168] Cf. *La spiritualité de Pierre de Celle*, Paris, 1946, pp. 120–4.
[169] *Ibid.*, pp. 124–38.
[170] Julian of Vézelay. See *Analecta monastica*, III, p. 130.
[171] *Ibid.*, pp. 125–8.

VIII

THE SCHOOL OF CÎTEAUX

THE spirituality of Cîteaux is treated last of all because in it medieval monasticism reached its fullest development. To realize its significance as a term one must look both at what went before it and at the religious movement contemporary with it. Thanks to Cîteaux the old monastic tradition provided, until the beginning of the thirteenth century, works which were comparable to those of the great epoch of the past; and it was one of the most fruitful solutions of the crisis through which the cenobitic ideal was passing and one of the most successful examples of the common life. The Cistercians harmonized the real values of the old monasticism and the new Orders. From its earliest beginnings, then, perhaps most of all, it made a living synthesis of the two. For the first time in history there is seen a "school" (the term was dear to the Cistercians themselves) of spirituality, because at its beginning or near it a master appeared who was both a genius and a saint. The whole achievement of Cîteaux is bound up with St Bernard, and his teaching was to direct the minds of all who formed part of this highly organized institution. There can, of course, be no question of a full history[1] of the Order in its early days or analysis of St Bernard's doctrine.[2] The two preceding chapters have sketched the surroundings in which it came into being, yet it may be useful to describe the tendencies common to the whole Order, to show what was peculiar to its chief representatives, and to make clear in what lay its originality.

1. The New Monastery

The three original founders of the Cistercian order were St Robert who, having founded Cîteaux in 1098, went back to the Benedictine

[1] The latest and most accurate general study is that of L. J. Lekai, *Les Moines blancs*, Paris, 1957. B. Bligny, *L'Église et les ordres religieux dans le Royaume de Bourgogne aux XIe et XIIe siècles*, Grenoble, 1960, pp. 326–94.

[2] The latest and most thought-provoking general study is that of L. Bouyer, *La spiritualité de Cîteaux*, Paris, 1955.

Abbey of Molesmes of which he was abbot; St Alberic, his prior who succeeded him as abbot of Cîteaux until 1109; and St Stephen Harding, his successor, who died in 1134. The story of their beginnings is today still the subject of research, but it is held that the abbots of the first four daughters of Cîteaux drew up in 1114 the first code, the *Carta caritatis*,[3] and before 1119 the first body of laws, called from its opening words the *Exordium parvum*.[4] These two documents were added to by successive General Chapters.

The idea which gave birth to the foundation was a conviction that it was possible to lead a monastic life without any compromise with the world. Cîteaux was at first called the "New Monastery", a name which symbolized its distinction from monasteries that by now were old: the very fervour of their abbots and religious, and the prestige they enjoyed, had brought them a material prosperity which to a greater or less extent involved them in temporal affairs; and from these the fathers of Cîteaux were determined to disengage themselves. At this period, when Cluny under St Hugh was at the height of its regular observance and influence, they reacted against a development which they had witnessed at Molesmes and which led from prosperity to relaxation, though not necessarily to decadence; simply that the fundamental obligations of monastic observance had, in traditional monasticism, gradually slackened and broadened. In order to restore them to their original vigour, a return was to be made to solitude and poverty. Cîteaux was connected with the whole "eremitical movement", not in the sense that it sought personal solitude as in the Charterhouse, but because its aim was separation from the world and society.[5] Cases of Cistercian hermits were not quite unknown,[6] but the aim was a common life, a *unanimitas*[7] of which the Order's writers were soon to sing the praises, and about which they theorized; moreover, the wish for a poverty that should be real[8] brought in its train a renewed esteem for manual labour,[9] and a return to simplicity in clothing, food, buildings and forms of worship. Many of the liturgical uses were

[3] The text is translated by J. Lefèvre in Lekai, *op. cit.*, p. 311, note 1.

[4] Cf. *ibid.*, pp. 37–50.

[5] See *supra*, p. 129. Gerhoh de Reichersberg in *De simoniacis*, in *M.G.H.*, *Lib. de lite*, II, 242–3, in the same way describes the life of the Cistercians as "prophetic" because it is eremitical.

[6] The case of "B. Conrad, disciple of St Bernard and hermit" as he is called in the *Menologium Cisterciense*, Westmalle, 1952, p. 37, is a sufficient proof. Cistercian reclusion will be studied elsewhere.

[7] Cf. J. Morson, "The 'De cohabitatione fratrum' of Hugh of Barzelle", in *Analecta monastica*, IV, pp. 127–40; J. Leclercq, *Sermon sur l'unité dans un manuscrit des Dunes*, in *Cîteaux*, XI (1960), pp. 212–13.

[8] Cf. R. Folz, "Le problème des origines de Cîteaux", in *Mélanges St Bernard*, Dijon, 1954, pp. 284–6.

[9] This is positively stated in *La constitution primitive de Cîteaux*, ch. xv, text in Lekai, p. 318.

taken from Cluniac tradition[10]: the daily Office of the Dead was one either taken over or adopted early on[11]: but many of Cluny's additional prayers were dropped, as were many ceremonies on solemn days. This desire for detachment and an interior spirit was seen in the architecture, and in the statutes of the General Chapters; and St Bernard in his *Apologia* gave complete expression to it.[12] The motive put forward was a wish to live in accordance with the authentic sources of monasticism, the first of which was the Rule of St Benedict. This attachment to the Rule was common to all forms of monasticism; Peter the Venerable used to say that it was kept with "rectitude at Cluny.[13] At Cîteaux as elsewhere it was acknowledged that the observance was not literal. The Office of the Dead was added to the prescribed offices; children were not accepted in the monastery in spite of the fact that the Rule makes provision for them; there were lay brothers, a class never mentioned by St Benedict; and other examples could be brought forward. Moreover, the limitations of the power of the abbots of Cistercian monasteries imposed by the powers of the abbot of Cîteaux and the General Chapters were, to say the least of it, quite foreign to the Rule.

No commentary on the Rule was written by any of the foremost Cistercian authors,[14] nor did the writers of the order mention it more frequently than others did: and yet in their own eyes and in those of their contemporaries they seemed specially faithful to St Benedict.[15] They did not pretend that theirs was not a particular interpretation of the Rule—that was done in every monastery—but the interpretation given by the first fathers of Cîteaux[16] was to be adopted by the whole Order.[17] Their aim had been to adopt a particular form of fervour and regularity whose characteristic was to be a return to the fundamental requirements of monasticism: a solitude and an austerity guaranteed by the Rule alone, rather than by the additional observances which had become part of monastic

[10] This has been shown by Bruno Schneider in "Cîteaux und die benediktinisch Tradition", in *Anal. Sac. Ord. Cist.*, XVI (1960), pp. 169–254; cf. *Collect. O. C. R.*, XXIV, 1962.

[11] Cf. J. Leclercq "Une ancienne rédaction des coutumes cisterciennes" in *Rev. d'hist. ecclés.*, XCVII (1932), p. 175. Until the end of this chapter references not preceded by an author's name are to works by the author, etc.

[12] On this point the reader is referred to the interesting suggestions of P. Deseille, "La liturgie monastique selon les premiers Cisterciens", in *La Maison-Dieu*", 51, 1957, pp. 82–6.

[13] *Epist.*, I, 28, P.L., 189, 149 C.

[14] C. H. Talbot in "A Cistercian Commentary on the Benedictine Rule", in *Analecta monastica*, V, pp. 101–58, has published extracts from a commentary preserved in a manuscript by an unidentified author at Pontigny.

[15] Texts in *Bernard of Clairvaux* (a collective work), Paris, 1963, pp. 61–2.

[16] *Charte de charité*, Lekai, p. 311, note 1.

[17] *Petit exorde*, IX, *ibid.*, p. 317.

tradition, especially since the Carolingian period.[18] They wanted to keep the Rule better and more thoroughly than it was kept at Molesmes, not "literally"—but "purely", "simply", "strictly" and "perfectly". They wanted to restore the monastic ideal in all its purity, and to this end to use no other means than the Rule itself, whose aim is a *monastica puritas*.

It was once more St Bernard who worked out the theory of the aims of all who before him had contributed to bring about "a renewal in the observance of the Rule", as Geoffrey of Auxerre described it.[19] The Cistercians held that the perfection of charity might be reached by putting into practice its chief prescriptions. They went beyond the letter, sometimes indeed deviated from it, but they rediscovered the spirit of the Rule.

St Stephen Harding went to great pains to obtain a revised and amended text of Holy Scripture, but this Bible had no particular influence on the Order,[20] whose love for the Scriptures was no different from that of other *claustrales*. There is no evidence that the Fathers of the Church or the ancient monastic writings were more read at Cîteaux than elsewhere, though it may well be that the austerity and simplicity of the ideals of Cassian and the desert Fathers were held in greater esteem among the Cistercians than among other monks. All the characteristics of Cîteaux might have been found elsewhere, either in the traditional monasticism or among the new orders: its originality lay in the happy conjunction of these different elements, though no one of them was peculiar to Cîteaux.[21]

Two factors made for the Order's success and encouraged its growth: its sound organisation and the coming of St Bernard in 1112. Later Cistercian hagiographers put him forward as the second founder without whom the first beginnings would not have lasted,[22] and it is true that this youth, athirst for the absolute, found at Cîteaux the surrounding he needed,[23] and which he was to cover with a quite unforeseen glory. Success brought with it a risk of

[18] This has been emphasized by D. P. Salmon, "L'ascèse monastique et les origines de Cîteaux", in *Mélanges St Bernard*, pp. 268–82; M.-A. Dimier in *Studia monastica*, I (1959), pp. 399–418.

[19] "Le témoignage de Geoffroi d'Auxerre sur la vie cistercienne", in *Analecta monastica*, II, p. 193, 3–4.

[20] Cf. *Études sur St Bernard et le texte de ses écrits*, Rome (*Analecta S. Ord. Cist.*, IX, I–II), 1953, pp. 194–7.

[21] On "the direction taken by various forms of spirituality . . . whose convergence may be said to characterize Cîteaux", see the balanced conclusions of P. Deseille in "Cîteaux et la tradition monastique", in *Christus*, VII (1960), pp. 128–129.

[22] On the value of these allegations cf. J. Winandy in *Rev. bénéd.*, LXVII (1957), pp. 54–5; A. H. Bredero, *Études sur la "vita prima" de St Bernard*; *Anal. Sac. Ord. Cist.*, XVII (1961), pp. 3–72, and XVIII (1962).

[23] Cf. A. H. Bredero in *Petrus Venerabilis*, Rome, 1956, pp. 53–71.

deviation, if not from the ideals and the institution itself, at least in practice. As time went on the huge number of monks, and the inevitable wealth, endangered the purity and generosity which had been the greatness of its heroic age. In the generations which followed the founders, the upholders of traditional monasticism could point to a certain self-satisfaction, a touch of pharisaism, among some of the Cistercians; it was necessary to remind them of the primacy of the spirit, and the respect they owed to Orders less austere than their own.[24] As Nicholas of Clairvaux[25] was to point out, the "gentler way" and the "more courageous way" are both legitimate, and there are difficulties to be met with in either of them. At Cîteaux itself, as elsewhere, prosperity threatened to make the initial success a short-lived one. Soon even he who had been its chief maker, and then the abbots to whom it fell to safeguard its constitution, would have to fight to keep the Order up to the level of its ideals.[26] Their efforts were not fruitless, since in spite of weaknesses and violations of the rules fervour showed itself in an abundant output of literature of a high level. The Cistercian writers of the first hundred years of the Order's existence (known since the thirteenth century as the "Cistercian Fathers") are, in common with the other monastic writers of the period, the last representatives of the age of the Fathers.

2. *St Bernard, the last of the Fathers*

The greatest of these, he without whom none of the others would have been what they were, has been called "the last of the Fathers, and not inferior to the earliest".[27] So significant were St Bernard's acts and works that it is not easy to touch on him briefly. He has, moreover, recently been the object of very able studies, sometimes so detailed that no more can be done in these few pages than to give their titles and sub-titles.[28] Many of these are concerned as much with his theology as with his spirituality, though he himself never separates one from the other. He wrote the theology of the spiritual life, and consequently of the mysteries to which it unites man's soul.[29] His contemporaries considered him a saint. His *Life* was

24 Cf. H. Farmer in *Analecta monastica*, V, pp. 187–207.

25 *Epist.*, XL, P.L., 196, 1639 B.

26 "Épîtres d'Alexandre III sur les cisterciens", in *Rev. bénéd.*, LXIV (1954), pp. 70–82.

27 On the origin and meaning of the phrase, cf. O. Rousseau in *St Bernard théologien*, Rome (*Analecta S. Ord. Cist.*, IX, III–IV), 1953, pp. 300–8.

28 On all these points see *Bernard of Clairvaux*. On the mass of literature about St Bernard in the last few decades see John of the Cross Bouton, *Bibliographie bernardine, 1891–1957*, Paris, 1958. [See also A. J. Luddy, *The Life and Teaching of St Bernard*, Dublin, 1927.—Trans.]

29 *Epist.*, II, P.L., 151, 284–5.

begun during his lifetime; in fact the authors of the *Vita Prima*, William of St Thierry and Arnold of Bonneval, were to die before him.[30] Those who knew him loved him; his friends praised the delights of his company, his "joyous devotion", of which we have an idea in some unaffected passages of his writings.[31] Looking back across the centuries and across the rhetoric of a period very different from our own, he may seem headstrong, immoderate and at times violent; yet Gerhoh of Reichersberg found him moderate, too much so for his liking, in his attitude towards Abelard,[32] and could say to him, "You habitually take the middle way between the various parties opposed to one another".[33] The truth lies in Bernard's inner conflict: he had to be the master of an exceptionally many-sided nature, to reconcile different talents, and with many gifts to remain single-minded. This resulted in his being able to take up various attitudes and different activities. His was the nervousness of a sick man, the ardour of the man of action, and an exaggerated sensibility coupled with the acuteness of a brilliant intelligence. Above all, in the midst of these contrasts, and thanks to the conflict they imposed, he lived intensely the mystery of Jesus Christ. His health caused him acute physical suffering and daily humiliations; to these were added exterior and interior conflicts, and the great anguish of not possessing God in the full measure of his desire. The power of Christ shone forth in Bernard, giving him a supernatural prestige and an influence which can only be explained in terms of a testimony to the resurrection of him in whose Passion he shared profoundly.[34]

One of the marks of his genius is his talent as a writer. Though he elaborated his works, and even rewrote[35] some of them to improve them, they were masterpieces when they came from his pen. In his first years as abbot he wrote letters and sermons, and the collection of both these increased as time went on. Bernard wrote more letters than anyone else of his century.[36] The first of his works that is dated

[30] The *Vita Prima* is in P.L., 185, 225–368. The later books are by Geoffrey of Auxerre who will be spoken of later on.

[31] "St Bernard et la dévotion joyeuse", in *St Bernard, homme d'Église* (collective work), La Pierre-qui-Vire, 1953, pp. 237–47. Cf. *Lettres de St Bernard* (Coll. écrits des Saints), Namur, 1962.

[32] *Études sur St Bernard et le texte de ses écrits*, Rome (*Analecta S. Ord. Cist.*, IX, I–II), 1953, p. 105.

[33] *De simoniacis*, in *M.G.H. Lib. de lite*, II, p. 243.

[34] *St Bernard mystique*, Paris–Bruges, 1948.

[35] "Aspects littéraires de l'œuvre de St Bernard", in the *Cahiers de civilization médiévale*, I (1958), pp. 425–50; *Recherches sur les sermons sur les cantiques*, VII; "St Bernard écrivain", in *Rev. bénéd.*, LXX (1960).

[36] *Études sur St Bernard*, pp. 83–103. St Bernard's works are in P.L., 182–3. Vols. I and II, *Sermones super cantica*, Rome, 1957–8, of a critical edition of St Bernard's works by J. Leclercq, C. H. Talbot and H. Rochais have already appeared. A list of translations and "How to read St Bernard" is given in *La Vie*

is a treatise on *The degrees of humility and pride*, written about 1124. This was followed by the *Apologia to William of St Thierry* (before 1125), the treatises on *The love of God* (1126–1141), *On grace and free will* (before 1128), *To the Knights Templar in praise of the new militia* (1128–1136). *On the commandment and the dispensation* (before 1144). From 1135 onwards, at the suggestion of Bernard, a monk of the charterhouse of Portes, he undertook the great work which became the series of 86 *Sermons on the Canticle*, and in spite of the interruptions caused by his other activities he worked at it till the end of his life. His latter years were also employed in writing a huge treatise in five volumes *On consideration*, dedicated to Pope Eugenius III, and a *Life of St Malachy*, an Irish bishop who had died suddenly while staying at Clairvaux. In spite of the variety of the subjects he treats of and the different literary forms he adopts, there is an underlying unity in all St Bernard wrote, which derives from his attachment to certain fundamental themes and his faithful adherence to the chief sources of his inspiration.

His conceptions are those of tradition and the Fathers. He thinks like the Scriptures and speaks like them,[37] and he puts forward no other teaching. He wrote no sustained commentary, but drew from everywhere in the Bible light on the one mystery—the divine life communicated to us in Jesus Christ. He is convinced of what he calls "the unity of the Scriptures"; that everything in them is meaningful and can be discovered by an ingenuous love. The Bible is for him who is willing to read it assiduously and meditate lovingly on it. Bernard reaches a sort of Biblical "experience", a "lived" comprehension of the truths it teaches[38]: the experience of sin, our grafting into Christ, the spirit which leads us back to the Father and bids us taste of love and sing its praises.[39]

It is in these themes of shining spirituality that Bernard excels. He is "mellifluous"[40] in the sense that he makes a hidden sense "flow" from the text itself. His is the method of Origen and St Augustine, of the age of the Fathers to which he is so much akin

---

spirituelle, April, 1960, pp. 440–7. [See also the following English translations of St Bernard's works: *On the Love of God*, tr. T. L. Connolly, London, 1937; *Of Conversion*, tr. W. Williams, London, 1938; *The Twelve Degrees*, tr. B. R. V. Mills, London, 1929; *Concerning Grace and Freewill*, tr. W. Williams, London, 1920; *The Letters of Bernard of Clairvaux*, tr. B. James, London–Chicago, 1953; and *The Life and Works of St Bernard*, S. J. Eales, London, 1896.—Trans.]

37 M. Dumontier, *St Bernard et la Bible*, Bruges–Paris, 1953; "St Bernard et la tradition biblique", in *Sacris erudiri*, XI (1960), pp. 225–48.

38 "St Bernard et le XIIe siècle monastique", in *Dict. de spirit.*, art. "Écriture sainte", fasc. XXV, Paris, 1958, col. 187–94.

39 C. Bodard, "La Bible, expression d'une expérience religieuse", in *St Bernard théologien*, pp. 24–45.

40 "Mellifluus", in *Études sur St Bernard*, pp. 184–91; H. de Lubac, *Exégèse médiévale*, pp. 586–620.

that he seems to be a continuation of it.[41] Yet he writes as a man of his period with all the resources of an intense and refined sensibility, and in the light of those mystic graces whose sublime nature he sometimes admits. The seductive originality of his work comes from his own gifts—a mixture of enthusiasm and clear seeing, vigorous speculation and simplicity of outlook, emotion and self-mastery; it is literary art of a high order, and yet spontaneous. He did not experience visions; he knew ecstasy, the *excessus*, but he describes it with great reserve, and there is no evidence that it involved parapsychological phenomena. He was simply an exceptional man who lived with a deep and complete generosity the mystery of Christ. As one reads his writings, the judgment of his contemporaries is confirmed; Bernard was a man of God: with all his gifts he had renounced all things, and though he had certain weaknesses, he was a man moved by the power of the Lord.[42]

3. St Bernard and the Journey from Humility to Ecstasy

The place for an account of the dogmatic and moral teaching in St Bernard's writings, that which gives them their unity and strength, is in a history of theology.[43] His doctrine of asceticism and prayer, which will be given here, cannot of course be entirely separated from his theology because it follows from it, it is its practical application and its full flowering. As no synthesis has yet been made which takes account of recent work or that in progress, and is as impartial, precise and full as the subject demands, an endeavour will be made to set forth here the place of spirituality in St Bernard's teaching. The programme he puts forward can be considered as a "return to God", a journey which leads from sin to glory, from the knowledge of self to the possession of God. The same weight of love moves the soul at every stage in its unceasing and interior pilgrimage. St Bernard is always a *doctor monasticus*; even when he is not writing for monks he looks at everything from the point of view of a monk, of a Cistercian who sees in his own Order complete success; he therefore does not look with favour on some of the traditional forms of asceticism, such as the solitary life or the *peregrinatio*. For him everything is moved on to the plane of the life of the soul, and he gives it a purely spiritual interpretation. He loves to quote the words of St Paul: *spiritualibus spiritualia comparantes*.[44]

[41] J. Daniélou, "St Bernard et les pères grecs", in *St Bernard théologien*, pp. 46–55 and *passim*. J. Leclercq, "Aux sources des sermons sur les cantiques", in *Rev. bénéd.*, LIX (1959), pp. 237–57.

[42] *St Bernard mystique, passim.*

[43] E. Gilson, *The Mystical Theology of St Bernard*, London, 1940; *St Bernard théologien, passim*: P. Delahaye, *Le problème de la conscience morale chez St Bernard*, Namur, 1957.

[44] I Cor. 2. 13, quoted at the beginning of the *Serm. super cant.*, I, i, etc.

The first of St Bernard's treatises is the one in which he lays down his fundamental attitude, the preliminary to all the others: humility. It is "a most true knowledge of self by which man becomes lowly in his own sight". It makes him realize how much there still is in man of the flesh, of "wretchedness", of a tendency to sin. But since humility is a gift of God, gained for us by Christ and shed abroad in our hearts by the Holy Spirit, it becomes a fruitful knowledge, a compunction made up of fear, desire and love. It is the source of charity, for man understands that his wretchedness is shared by his fellow men and so he needs must have pity and charity towards his neighbour. This wretchedness calls forth the mercy of God; the Son of God came to save us; it is for us to love him in return, and to prove our love by imitating that humility which in him was voluntary humiliation. Man's whole greatness consists in his being able thus to restore within himself that image of God which sin has deformed and darkened, though not done away with.

Starting from this twofold realization of his poverty, and his dignity as a Christian, he will go on from one experience to another[45] until in heaven he comes to partake in soul and body of the glory of God. To do this he must once more (as a result of efforts made possible by grace) be quite free to love God; this freedom has three degrees[46]; firstly free will, the absence of compulsion—*libertas a necessitate*, the possibility of choosing, even of choosing to sin; then freedom from sin, *libertas a peccato*: the possibility of not sinning was given to man in paradise, and love of God can win it back again so that in fact we do avoid sin, that we are able not to sin, *posse non peccare*. Love can even confer on us such a union of our spirit with God that we desire nothing but him, and therefore actually cannot sin: *non posse peccare*. Only in heaven will man reach the third degree of this progressive freedom. It will consist in complete and final liberation from all wretchedness, all possibility of sinning: *libertas a miseria*. Bernard conceives the mystic life as an anticipation of heaven—his thought, like that of the Fathers, is eschatological—and holds that in it man has some taste of that *turbari non posse*, that absence of even the disorder left by original sin. But what is the motive power common to each stage of the return to God, making them as it were necessarily follow one another? It lies in the only unchanging and unchangeable reality: love. Charity is at the heart of St Bernard's teaching: it explains all he says about God and man.[47] For God is love, the source of all love; his very

[45] J. Mouroux, "Sur les critères de l'expérience spirituelle d'après les sermons sur le Cantique des cantiques", in *St Bernard théologien*, pp. 253–67.

[46] *De gratia et libero arbitrio*.

[47] P. Delfgaauw, "La nature et les degrés de l'amour selon St Bernard", in *St Bernard théologien*, pp. 234–52.

life is love. He is the cause of our love for him, and love and the reasons for loving are his gift. On man's side the whole work of salvation consists in nothing else but the restoring of this order of charity, *ordinatio caritatis,* by which he proceeds from "the region of unlikeness" to the likeness of God, whom he has found once more; which substitutes for selfishness—the *proprium*—union with God, a will in common with his, a *voluntas communis.* He will pass from natural affection, "fleshly love", that he has for himself and which bends him back on himself, although it turns him towards God in the sense that it makes him realize his need of God, to a love which is both fleshly and "social", being only a widening out of natural affection which opens his heart to his neighbour; indeed, he even reaches a certain "fleshly" love for Christ, whose flesh reveals the Godhead to the creatures of flesh that we are. As man journeys further in his return to God he reaches the love of God for himself alone, then the love of self for God's sake. The degrees of love, humility and liberty are parallel, for with Bernard it is always a continuous movement, ever the same, towards deification, a life which is one with the life of God. It is when he speaks of love that his fervour, his gifts as a writer and his acuteness as a theologian are seen to the full. For him love is all: "the law", "righteousness",[48] desire and possession, a going out from self and an ecstasy. It explains God, who is goodness gratuitous and creative; and man, made in the image of that love which is God. It is the highest mode of knowledge, the only one which allows of the kiss, the *osculum,* of contemplation, and of fruitful service to the Church.

4. *St Bernard and the Concrete Approach to the Christian Mystery*

All this teaching has a general bearing and is valid for every Christian. St Bernard always takes it for granted, and in fact sometimes says, that it can best be put into practice in the monastery, the school of charity. He does not merely state this in his treatise *On the commandment and the dispensation,* which is too little known; he works out a whole doctrine of monastic charity for Benedictines.[49] He shows that the obligations of the Rule are ordered and subordinated to the primacy of charity; that obedience leads the monk into the infinite spaces of charity, *in latitudinem caritatis.* Bernard held that there was no observance of the life of perfection

[48] P. Delfgaauw, "La lumière de la charité chez St Bernard de Clairvaux", in *Coll. Ord. Cist. Ref.,* XVIII (1956), pp. 42–69, 306–20; J. M. Déchanet, art. "Contemplation", in *Dict. de spirit.,* II (1953), col. 1948–59.

[49] B. Calati, "Alcuni aspetti della dottrina monastica di San Bernardo", in *Camaldoli,* VII (1953), pp. 101–18. P. De Seille, "Théologie de la vie monastique selon St Bernard", in *Théologie de la vie monastique,* Paris, 1961, pp. 503–25.

which was not capable of attaining these blessings, and in the *Apologia* he declares that he esteems every order, and belongs to it by charity, *unum opere teneo, ceteros caritate.*[50] It is still true that, having said this, he shows in the *Apologia* itself and in various other places so absolute a preference for his own observance that it has been said "for him the Cistercian life is the only sure road of salvation",[51] and "No salvation outside Cîteaux".[52] It is in fact true that though the monastic ideal was essentially the same in every Order, Bernard was convinced that the institute of Cîteaux, and the whole movement of return to poverty and solitude from which it sprang, offered a better guarantee of its fulfilment.

Without completely excluding the possibility of the solitary life for the individual—as is seen in the favour he showed to Blessed Conrad[53]—he dissuaded those who wished to become hermits "from abandoning a certain good for a doubtful solution".[54]

He tended to be friendly towards the Carthusians and the Premonstratensians, in spite of the choice of personal solitude in the former, and the fact that the *cura animarum* had a place among the latter which it had not at Cîteaux. For Bernard monastic life, and that of Cîteaux in particular, was purely contemplative, ordered to prayer and penance. He speaks frequently of manual labour, but action and the fruitful service of our neighbour are for exceptional cases—as was his own—or refer to the mutual services the brethren, and especially the abbot, can render in the monastery. Bernard struggled throughout his life to safeguard the purity of the Cistercian programme, to ensure that the observances of the Order should be kept; and in spite of the growing wealth of the monasteries and the ever-increasing number of monks, he succeeded at least at Clairvaux.[55] He laid down once and for all, and in admirable and lasting form, the theory of what Cistercian monasticism should be. He was for the monks of Cîteaux what St Peter Damian had been for those of St Romuald.

In practice, what was to be the approach, monastic or otherwise, to the mystery of God who is love? There is but one way—Christ—and Bernard sums up in two words what man's attitude to him is

[50] *Apologia*, 8.
[51] A. Fliche in *Bernard de Clairvaux*, p. 359.
[52] A. Dimier, "St Bernard et le droit en matière de transitus", in *Rev. Mabillon*, XLIII (1953), p. 80.
[53] See *supra*, note 6.
[54] Texte in *Études sur St Bernard*, pp. 138–9.
[55] From the very year of his death the cartulary of Clairvaux reveals breaches in the observances, as has been noted by R. Fossier in *Bernard of Clairvaux*, p. 113.

to be: remembrance and imitation[56]—*Memor ero . . . Recordabor*. The whole point of meditation is there. On this subject Bernard's is the traditional teaching; he suggests the method he followed himself—to read the Bible with care, accompanying this reading by reflection and prayer in the atmosphere of the liturgy.[57] He is of his time in recognizing the lawfulness of the part played by the affections in any consideration of the life of Jesus; he enumerates for our loving compassion the sufferings of our Lord, adding that the safeguard of this love is the imitation of Christ, that is the practice of mortification in our daily duties, and the renouncing of every form of self-seeking. Then the cross itself becomes a joyful mystery: "the grace of devotion softens the crosses of penance".[58] *Devotio* comes to the help of generosity; it is an inner fervour which inflames the soul, enlightens the mind, and brings with it peace, gentleness and recollection.[59] Bernard holds that during the Divine Office the monk should think of nothing but the mystery which he is celebrating, and the words he is pronouncing. He defines pure prayer in this connection as "purely, that is, thinking of the psalmody and of nothing else".[60] Apart from the liturgy, in private prayer, and even while working, the soul should keep itself in loving and peaceful contemplation; and then the Word, when it pleases him, will grant to the spirit one of those ineffable visits which are the summit of Christian experience, the highest act of contemplation, the most sublime food of love.[61]

There is no space here to elaborate or fully to analyse this contemplative activity, nor to describe its object in all its requisite shades of meaning. This object is the person and work of Jesus Christ, by whom the Blessed Trinity is revealed to us, and we receive the divine life; the other mysteries, those of the Church, the Blessed Virgin, the sacraments, the angels, and eternal life, are all related to it.[62] Bernard's devotion to Jesus must, however, be seen in its true light: it rests neither in a sensible love for his humanity, nor in mystic contemplation of the Word.[63]

[56] *Sermo in Fer. IV hebd., sanctae*, n. 9–14, P.L., 183, 267–70.

[57] H. Wolter, "Meditation bei Bernard von Clairvaux", in *Geist und Leben*, XXVIII (1956), pp. 206–18.

[58] *Sermo in Dedic. eccles.*, I, 5; P.L., 183, 520.

[59] Texts in J. Chatillon, art. "Devotio", in *Dict. de spirit.*, fasc. XX–XXI, Paris, 1955, col. 711.

[60] *Serm. sup. Cant.*, 47, 8.

[61] Texts in *St Bernard mystique*, pp. 181–9, 224–32.

[62] St Bernard's teaching on these and other points is the object of various studies in *St Bernard théologien*.

[63] This problem has been studied by A. van den Bosch in a thesis, *La personne du Christ dans l'œuvre de St Bernard*, Rome (St Anselmo), 1957. The passage which follows is quoted from the summary of the thesis given in *Coll. Ord. Cist. Ref.*, XIX (1957), p. 393.

It would be truer to say that St Bernard points out above all the divine condescension by which the Word, who since the fall of Adam was beyond our reach, is offered us in the flesh, thus once more becoming accessible to us. By Christ in the flesh the treasures of lovingkindness hidden in the bosom of the Father are made manifest, to excite us to confidence, to give us a greater knowledge of the goodness and mercy of God and to draw us to imitate him and love him. All this is connected with Christ "according to the flesh" in his first coming. The Ascension leads us to a more spiritual love, since Christ is no longer there in the flesh to converse with us, except as the liturgical feasts bring him before us, or we meditate on him in his passion. More than this, it leads us higher still, to the contemplation of Christ in glory, and, reminding us of his second coming, to a conformity and union with his spirit.

That is why Christ is said to have become one flesh with us, that we might be one spirit with him. In this dynamic exchange "Christ in the flesh" and "the spirit of Christ" are to be taken in different senses, as also is the passage from one to the other. On the one hand faith was needed even by the centurion on Mount Calvary, if he was to see beyond the "flesh" and to reach the spirit, God. On the other the *excessus*, the highest degree of union possible within the bounds of faith in this world, never reaches the spiritual perfection of a soul after its resurrection. It is worthy of note that St Bernard in another connection praises an affective union, not only when, as in the beginning of the life of faith, we compassionate Christ in his sufferings, but also at the heights of spiritual union when the Spirit of the Son cries within us *Abba, Father*, and the glorified Christ leads us into the inmost dwelling of the Father.

St Bernard's devotion to the Blessed Virgin must not be exaggerated. He did not refer to her more often or at greater length than his contemporaries, nor was his teaching more precise nor his doctrine more exact than theirs. Yet in this sphere he had an originality and was not without influence. His personal genius found expression in traditional ideas and well-known symbols. It has been said

> there is a true unity between the Marian themes he makes use of because they are all in agreement with his predominant line of spirituality. He chose them instinctively because they are in accordance with the ways of his soul: virginity of heart and Mary's humility; the joys of the Virgin Mother and the pain of the Mother of Sorrows; the wound of love and the meeting with the Beloved in glory; the part of a mediator and the tenderness of the Mother of Mercy; devotion to her service and care to

imitate her virtues. Thus he loves to find in her his whole monastic ideal, and also the incomparable succour that his human frailty stands constantly in need of. Along these lines in particular his Mariology is in harmony with all his doctrine and mysticism.[64]

Bernard, because of the strength of his personality and the remarkable graces he received, is the perfect reflection of his period. In him can be found in their greatest intensity all the ideas of his time as well as those that were current before him. He made no new discoveries, but he threw a fresh light on the experience and teaching of his predecessors. With Cîteaux and the Knights Templar and with many other institutions he elaborated the theory of what in practice had come into existence before his own time; but his energy is such and his literary gifts so great that he seems to have been its instigator. Bernard in fact is tradition come to life in one who is a genius, a saint, and a mystic, whose incomparable style lends a brillance, hitherto unknown, to all he says. Everything he wrote was a masterpiece, and his example spread widely. All through his life and after his death he had an immense influence in the Church, and especially in his Order and on all who knew him or read his works. All his friends, disciples and admirers were to pass on, each in his own way, an echo of his teaching.

5. *William of St Thierry and Trinitarian Mysticism*

It is not clear whether William of St Thierry should be considered a representative of the order of Cîteaux or not, but he shows more clearly than anyone else that the Cistercians shared the ideals common to all the monasticism of the day. In his own way he belonged to every Order, and like them all he profited by St Bernard's influence. His first master was Anselm of Laon, and he made use of his teaching, though he carried it further.[65] Easily moved to enthusiasm and sometimes to passion, his care was always for the faith: to safeguard it if it seemed to be endangered, and analyse its action and progress in the soul. His teaching is one of the most difficult to summarize because of its closeness and its subtle overtones. In

[64] H. Barré in "St Bernard docteur marial", in *St Bernard théologien*, p. 112. The article, pp. 92–113, contains, besides an objective summing up of the mariology of St Bernard, a critical estimate of the bibliography on the subject. See also "St Bernard et la dévotion médiévale envers Marie", in *Rev. d'ascét. et de myst.*, XXX (1954), pp. 361–75. In a fine passage of *De laudibus Virginis Matris* (Hom. 2, 16; P.L., 183, 69) St Bernard exalts the virtues and merits of St Joseph. P. Pourrat, in *La spiritualité chrétienne*, II, Paris, 1921, pp. 92–4, sees in this the forerunner of what was later to be devotion to St Joseph.

[65] The pioneer of research in this field was J. M. Déchanet whose work is fundamental; especially his *Guillaume de St Thierry: l'homme et son œuvre*, Bruges–Paris, 1942.

pointing out the themes which are the essence of his doctrine there is a danger of overlooking the fact that their richness is due to his elaboration of them. William possibly had a more constructive mind than St Bernard, but was less of a genius; he synthesizes less, is a greater believer in method. At times he is more acute than Bernard, but his outlook and heart are narrower; they take in less of reality at the same time.[66] He was born at Liège, and after studying at Laon entered the Benedictine abbey of St Nicaise at Rheims. There he was brought up on the *lectio divina* and nourished with the Scriptures and the Fathers. In 1119 when barely thirty-four he was elected abbot of St Thierry in the diocese of Rheims. During the next three years he wrote two treatises which were among the most widely read of his works: *On the nature and dignity of love*[67] and *On the contemplation of God*.[68] Their teaching was different from that of St Bernard, but they were to circulate under his name, which may account in part for their success. Shortly after 1128 William wrote a book *On the Sacrament of the altar*, and then started on three more: *On the Canticle of Canticles, On the nature of the body and the soul, On the epistle to the Romans*—and a collection of meditations.[69]

At the end of 1118 while he was still at St Nicaise, he met St Bernard. He visited Clairvaux and came back full of admiration for the abbey and its abbot. A few years later in 1124 he sought admission to the community, but St Bernard refused and would never change his mind. Eleven years later William gave up his abbacy and retired to the Cistercian monastery of Signy in the diocese of Rheims. But even there he did not escape the doubts and trials that he had known earlier: he was a sick man and seems to have been a prey to worry. More and more, however, he reflected on the mystery of love; it was his life, and its joys were the theme of his song. He asserted, against Abelard, the transcendence of the life of faith over all rational knowledge of the mysteries of God,

[66] A parallel between the two authors has been drawn by J. Hourlier, "St Bernard et Guillaume de St Thierry dans 'Liber de amore Dei'", in *St Bernard théologien*, pp. 223–33.

[67] P.L., 184, 379–408.

[68] P.L., 184, 365–80. The other works of William of St Thierry are in P.L., 180, 205–726. A translation of the *Méditations et prières*, Brussels, 1945, and the *Miroir de la foi* with a critical edition of the text, Bruges, 1946, have both been made by J. M. Déchanet. J. Hourlier has published a critical edition with an introduction and translation of *De Contemplando Deo*, Paris (coll. "Sources chrétiennes"), 1959. [*The Epistle to the Brethren of Mont Dieu*, ed. Justin McCann, O.S.B., London, 1930; *On contemplating God, On the nature and dignity of love, The mirror of faith*, tr. G. Webb and A. Walker, London, 1955, 1956, 1959.—Trans.]

[69] One of these, hitherto unpublished, has been brought out by J. M. Déchanet, *Méditations . . .*, pp. 192–9. Another has been published by J. Hourlier, *op. cit.*, pp. 122–9.

and all undue reliance on dialectic. He wrote two works between 1139 and 1144—*The mirror of Faith* and *The enigma of Faith*—which were never widely known, though probably the latter represents his teaching at its highest. In 1144 he went to the charterhouse of Mont-Dieu, and there again was full of admiration. At the request of the Carthusians, on his return he wrote for them the *Golden Letter* which was to be so widely read in monastic circles.[70]

This Benedictine, who later became a Cistercian, who was a friend of the Canons Regular and wrote for the Carthusians, symbolizes what was common to all *claustrales*: their manner of life might differ, but they had the same way of loving and serving God. William died in 1148, before St Bernard, whose *Life* he had begun to write.[71] His own was written soon afterwards and is a document which throws light on some aspects of his teaching.[72] This contemplative, this weighty thinker, was a theologian, above all a theologian of the mystical life; his preoccupation was with the problems raised in the mind of Christians by pure love and the life of faith. It may be asked what effect his theology had on spirituality. He seems to have been as strongly influenced by Origen, St Gregory of Nyssa and Erigena[73] as by St Augustine.[74] The main outlines of his teaching are already to be seen in his earliest book, *On the nature and dignity of love*. In it he studies the three periods of the love by which the image of God is restored in man. It is the love which is realized in monastic charity in the school of St Benedict, in poverty, obedience and silence; a love whose end is in itself since it is a participation in the divinity; it is at one and the same time possession and desire, a tendency and a gift of God, the spirit of the Father given to us by Jesus Christ. This love is the end of man's creation, and he tends towards it by his very "nature" as it was created by God and adorned with grace. The aim of all asceticism is to carry into effect this tendency by which man turns towards God. To achieve this, "memory", "reason", and "love" must be sanctified, and man must pass from the "animal" to the "rational" life, and finally to the "spiritual life", which is union with God. This last will reach its perfection in eternal life, but man has a foretaste of it in contemplation through a progressive enlightening of his faith, or rather of his whole self acted on by faith.[75] The senses and the understanding are freed from all that is of the

[70] See *supra*, pp. 160–1. [71] See *supra*, p. 192.

[72] Edited by A. Poncelet in *Mélanges Godefroid Kurth*, Liège, 1908, I, pp. 85–96.

[73] See *supra*, pp. 93–4.

[74] Cf. J. M. Déchanet, *Aux sources de la spiritualité de Guillaume de St Thierry*, Bruges, 1940. In some unpublished notes which he kindly communicated to me Dom Déchanet points out the influence of Erigena.

[75] On "the scrutinizing of faith" according to William cf. H. Jaeger, art. "Examinatio", in *Dict. de spirit.*, IV, II, col. 1863–5.

flesh as soon as the soul shares in the mystery of the cross of Christ. This programme, which from the way in which William explains it appears at times to be very speculative in character, is conditioned and safeguarded by daily obedience to the word of God, to the truths it teaches and the moral laws it imposes. Obedience, which is to begin with "necessary", becomes an expression of love and finally a means of union. Both in the realm of faith and of love the most perfect expression of this obedience is participation in the mystery of the holy Eucharist. There, in complete certitude, man has a part in the Redemption, and theology itself becomes an act of adoration. William's means of preparation are found in the *meditativae orationes* in whose very title are united the two activities which since the days of St Gregory the Great have been the traditional components of contemplation. The reading of the Scriptures is taken for granted, and the mode of knowledge is that formulated by St Gregory: *Amor ipse notitia.* William, of course, explains more fully why love is identified with knowledge: this love within us is none other than the Spirit of God: our spirit adheres to him by faith and by that cleaving of the whole being which is the *affectus*, and the Spirit introduces it into the life of the blessed Trinity itself.

At the summit of all William of St Thierry's teaching is a mysticism of the Trinity.[76] The goal of the journey from the "region of unlikeness" to the restoration of the image of God in man is a certain experimental apprehension of the Holy Trinity: the Holy Spirit grants this knowledge in love in proportion to the degree of likeness to the Trinity which the soul has reached. The "image" of God in man—his natural tendency towards God, his capacity for God—becomes a "likeness". By it he possesses God and is made like to him. William's is not so much an analysis of the presence and action of the Holy Trinity in the soul as of the latter's movement towards the Trinity. He connects memory with the Father, reason with the Son, and the love which comes from both with the Spirit who proceeds from the Father and the Son.[77] Man, since his creation, tends towards his archetype, God, and this movement is supernaturalized by the Three Persons, who thus raise him above what he is by his own nature.

At her highest, the soul is not only "with God", it is "like unto

[76] This has been studied by O. Brooke, "The Trinitarian Aspect of the Ascent of the Soul to God in the theology of William of St Thierry", in *Rech. de théol. anc. et médiév.*, XXVI (1959), pp. 85–127, and "The Speculative Development of the Trinitarian theology of William of St Thierry in the 'Aenigma Fidei'", *ibid.*, XXVII (1960), pp. 193–211, XXVIII (1961), pp. 26–58.

[77] *De nat. et dig. am.*, II, 3, P.L., 184, 382 D.

God."[78] William's whole teaching is the history of the soul's ascent from sin to union and oneness with God, until it is moved by the influence of the Spirit alone. Then in faith it has a foretaste of the beatific vision. The Incarnation and the whole economy of salvation were necessary to bring it to this point. Christ came to reveal the mystery of the Trinity to man who was still under the sway of things of sense.[79] The divine activity at work in the bosom of the Trinity, then *ad extra* in the economy of redemption, and in the Spirit sent by the Son, is one and the same. Man is united to God first *per Filium*, then *in Spiritu*, but the sequence is a logical one, for since the Son is one with the Spirit, the soul is united at the same time to both. These distinctions, however, help the soul to realize what is happening within it. William constantly appeals to spiritual experience, like all theologians. It is by a rational process that he analyses the content of revelation, but his continual recourse to experience turns his theology into a spiritual doctrine and his method into a kind of mystical dialectic.

In his teaching, which is not merely theoretical, an important place is taken by the Scriptures and the sacraments, chiefly the Holy Eucharist, through which we come to Christ. In his writings can be recognized themes from the Greek and Latin Fathers, particularly from St Augustine, and others that were dear to "the last of the Fathers", but his way of putting them together was quite his own. For centuries men had had an experience of God, but William contributed more than any other writer to the theology of that experience, and was more explicit on the subject, if not more profound, than Bernard himself. His terminology is more precise, less variable, and he goes so far as to elaborate a *ratio fidei* which differs both from that sought by St Anselm or the one desiderated by Abelard.[80] For him faith is a creative power which transforms the inmost nature of the soul, adapting it to its end, the possession of God. Only vision can take the place of faith; and until that happens, faith itself progresses, develops, becomes a superior form of knowledge, a sort of "reason", whose method of knowledge is love. The Trinity is not "explained" by faith; in fact by faith it is seen to be a mystery. William does not try to explain it: in that field his work is less fruitful than that of the scholastics such as Abelard and Gilbert de la Porrée. The title of the work in which he expresses his thought most completely, *Aenigma fidei*, is an illustration of every stage of his teaching. He always clings to "the simplicity of Scripture". He brings the soul back to the point from which it

[78] *In Cant.*, P.L., 180, 503–4.
[79] *Aenigma fidei*, P.L., 180, 426 C.
[80] *Ibid.*, P.L., 180, 417.

started, after having proved to it—not by demonstration but by experience—that its goal transcends all natural knowledge and is attainable by love alone. The Holy Spirit is the union of the Father and the Son, and therefore, as they are, both knowledge and love: he communicates to the soul that mutual love of the Father and the Son which renders it like to the three divine Persons.[81] When the soul has been brought by the life of faith and by asceticism to the *unitas spiritus*, in one sense "it is itself the Holy Spirit".[82] It is no longer a question of a reality in the psychological order but of an ontological fact.

The mystery lies in the harmony in God of unity in Trinity: the soul which shares in this mystery is no longer troubled by it. It simply passes from one to the other of these two aspects, harmonizing them in itself under the action of the Holy Spirit who moves it to consent, to love, and to long to see. This mysticism of the Trinity was William of St Thierry's most original contribution and one which enriched both theology and traditional spirituality.

6. *Aelred of Rievaulx, Father and Abbot*

In one of Cîteaux's daughter abbeys Bernard's disciples were training the man who was to be most like him, though he always kept his own personality. Learned and used to the life of a court, Aelred entered Rievaulx at the age of twenty-four. Walter Daniel, his disciple, has described his life, which was a simple one[83]: he became, as others did, successively novice, monk, master of novices and then abbot of two monasteries, Revesby and Rievaulx, where he died in 1167 after being its superior for twenty years. The interest of the biography lies in its confirmation af what Aelred's own writings reveal of his moral aspect.

He was delicate, and ill over a long period of time, yet was ever amiable. From the infirmary where his monks crowded round the door, he administered a great property, ruled a community which at one time consisted of six hundred religious, and above all was a director of souls. More than anything else Aelred was a spiritual father and guide; his writings map out the monastic way. He is one of those who succeeded in giving to the traditional theme of the *peregrinatio* a purely spiritual meaning, that of the inner journey by which the monk follows in the steps of all who have known an exodus. It is a question of a going out from self and sin, to find God once more in the community of the brethren, under an abbot.

[81] *Speculum fidei*, P.L., 180, 391–3.
[82] *Epist. ad frat. de Monte Dei*, II, 16, P.L., 184, 349.
[83] Edited by F. M. Powicke, *The Life of Aelred of Rievaulx by Walter Daniel*, London, 1950.

Aelred wrote some short historical works in which legend and fact are equally mixed,[84] but he does not reach his highest level in these. Of his other writings, the longest and most beautiful, the majority and the fullest are monastic. They are mostly sermons[85] and treatises. The most notable and one of the earliest (the only earlier one is a short *Disceptatio* on the end of monastic life)[86] is the *Mirror of charity* (1142 or 1143); ten years later he wrote an explanation of the Gospel, *When Jesus was twelve years old*;[87] then a work *On spiritual friendship*,[88] a *Pastoral prayer*[89] and a dialogue *On the soul*.[90] About 1160 he dictated a book *On the formation of recluses* for his sister, showing his interest, in common with other Cistercians, in the solitary life. The second half of the book consists in a series of meditations on the mysteries.[91] Aelred understood reclusion, the extreme form of the eremitical life, and yet all his teaching is bound up with the cenobitic life, and his expression of its theology, which will not be summed up here,[92] cannot be separated from his spirituality. The whole of asceticism, for him as for St Bernard, for Peter of Celle, and for so many others, consists in restoring in man that image of God which sin has darkened. Man is a wanderer in the country of his own "wretchedness", in the "land of unlikeness"[93]; in Christ he may and must be "made like to God". His whole nature longs for this union because God left in him the gift of desiring and tending towards him. Man was made to enjoy God in eternal happiness, but "God is friendship" and "who dwells in friendship dwells in God, and he in him".[94] Jesus must be loved as the dearest of friends, *familiarissimum amicum*.[95] Every friendship among men, as long as it is a spiritual one and according

[St Aeldred's *Letter to his Sister* and the meditations *On Jesus at Twelve Years Old* are translated into English by G. Webb and A. Walker, London, 1957, 1956. —Trans.]

84 Except where otherwise noted, Aeldred's works are in P.L., 195, 210–796.

85 In addition to the sermons in P.L., 195 there are the *Sermones inediti* published by C. H. Talbot, Rome, 1952.

86 Edited by A. Wilmart in *Rev. d'ascét. et de myst.*, XXIII (1947), pp. 265–73.

87 P.L., 184, 849–70; edited by A. Hoste, Paris (Coll. "Sources chrétiennes"), 1958.

88 Translated into French by J. Dubois, Bruges, 1948.

89 Edited by A. Wilmart, *Auteurs spirituels*, Paris, 1932, pp. 287–98.

90 Edited by C. H. Talbot, London, 1952.

91 P.L., 32, 1465–71; edited by C. H. Talbot in *Analecta S. Ord. Cist.*, VII (1951), pp. 167–217. The fairly considerable number of manuscripts which contain works of his are evidence of the influence of Aelred's writings. Cf. A. Hoste, *Bibliotheca Aelrediana*, Steenbrugge–The Hague, 1962.

92 This has been the object of a study, *Un éducateur monastique, Aelred de Rievaulx*, by A. Hallier, Paris, 1959.

93 On the theme of the *Regio dissimilitudinis*, its sources and its spread, cf. G. Dumeige, art. "Dissemblance", in *Diction. de spiritualité*, XXII–XXIII (1956), col. 1330–46.

94 *De spirituali amicitia*, I, P.L., 195, 670 A.

95 *Serm. de temp.*, I, P.L., 195, 212 B.

to Christ, is a means to God; it is in itself "the most excellent degree leading towards perfection".[96] "As soon as a man is the friend of another, he is the friend of God".[97]

Aelred was influenced by the common ascetic teaching of his time as well as by St Bernard and William of St Thierry. His own contribution was a certain new emphasis and different shade of meaning. In his eyes the interior life is a social one, a communion. The monastery is "the school of love" where under the abbot, who holds the place of Christ, the brethren are initiated together into that great friendship with God which they have found again. It is for the abbot to adapt himself, to stimulate, to forgive, to uphold and encourage; for monks will never lack suffering. That Aelred knew from his own experience, since his frail body was very often worn out by the patience he needed with so many monks. He occasionally speaks of the austerity of the life, of the weariness which comes from labour and the observances; but more than this, he surely shows us, in the form of answers to questions put by novices, the temptations which had been confided to him.[98] In these Cistercian houses, as at all times and in all monasteries, men asked themselves whether their daily suffering had any value: not all the monks by any means lived in a continual state of sensible joy and enthusiasm. A life which seemed to be a failure had to be lived each day, unseen by anyone, in the darkness of faith and in frequent dryness. Yet Aelred believed in the fruitfulness of a life spent imitating Christ and the apostles who suffered persecution for him. There cannot be a monastic life without pain, but it is a sure and straight way to the happiness of heaven, and even here below obtains for the monk an interior and truly spiritual joy which is not incompatible with both physical and psychological trials.[99]

This union of the spirit with God is kept up by contact with the Holy Scriptures, by the celebration of the mysteries of the liturgy, as well as by writings on the monastic tradition. Aelred owed much to the *Confessions* of St Augustine,[100] and also made considerable use of Cicero[101]; this he had in common with all the monastic authors of his time, Cistercian or not. He was less affective than Benedictines such as Anselm, Drogo and Arnold of Bonneval, and more imaginative. Like Peter the Venerable he had a feeling for the concrete, he liked "things seen"—psychological observations, ex-

[96] *De spirit. am.*, II, P.L., 195, 672 A.
[97] *Ibid.*, 671 D.
[98] *Speculum caritatis*, II, 17–20, P.L., 195, 562–70.
[99] *Ibid.*, 22, 570–1; II, I, P.L., 195, 547, *passim.*
[100] Cf. P. Courcelle, "Aelred de Rievaulx à l'école des 'Confessions'", in *Rev. des études augustiniennes*, III (1952), pp. 163–74.
[101] Cf. P. Delahaye, "Deux adaptations du 'De amicitia' de Cicéron au XIIe siècle", in *Rech. théol. anc. et médiév.*, XV (1948), pp. 304–31.

amples and tales, even those full of wonders. Like all *claustrales* he took the realities of community life for granted, loving and praising them, but he theorized about them more than anyone else, even St Bernard. He sees the *congregatio monastica* as having its place in the body of the Church, in the history of the salvation of mankind, in the great collective pilgrimage towards heaven on which the redeemed communicate to each other the gifts which God has given to each one for the benefit of all, and together are united in Christ to this one God. At the end of the journey they will again be united to each other: now suspicions, envy, detraction and the other vices which spring from the fund of covetousness and self-will that the Lord has left alive in them threaten to slow down their march. It is everyone's affair by charity, and the abbot's by his counsels, to prevent anyone straying from the path, or any delay on the journey. This peaceful confidence in the monastic life is not peculiar to St Aelred, but he sets it forth with a charm, a good humour, and at times a humorousness, that are entirely his own. St Bernard, his master, is a doctor of the Church, whereas St Aelred is only a doctor of the monastic life; and yet his teaching has a universal value, because monasticism is part of the Church, and he himself lays stress on unity of spirit. Still, he is thinking first of all of monks. The theologian is always the pleasant Father Abbot.

7. *In the Wake of St Bernard*

There were other Cistercian abbots who were theologians and masters of the spiritual life. Some simply handed on the common teaching, the monastic and Cistercian tradition; others left their own mark on it, sometimes one of great originality. Like the representatives of Benedictine spirituality, the Cistercians were in the twelfth century a *turba magna* in which all were not equally great. It is not possible here, any more than in the preceding chapter, to give a detailed account of these masters of holiness. The most that can be done is briefly to describe the two most significant, and to sketch the others in an effort to see whether their teaching develops as the generations succeed each other.

The nearest to St Bernard, whom he calls "his master",[102] is Guerric of Igny. He did in fact spend fifteen years at Clairvaux after his conversion in 1125. Like the greatest of the other Cistercian abbots, he was trained in the schools and had indeed been master of the cathedral school at Tournai. But he chose the monastic life, first with St Bernard and then at Igny in the diocese of Rheims, where he was abbot until his death in 1157. He had become abbot

[102] *Serm. in nat. SS Petri et Pauli*, III, 1, P.L., 185, 183.

in 1138 when he was already sixty and in bad health—in this latter he is like St Bernard, Aelred and William of St Thierry. He left fifty-four sermons for the liturgical year, [103] and a short treatise *On the languors of the loving soul.*[104] In it he tells of the mysteries of God and the joys of the monastic life where a wholly spiritual philosophy is taught, a wisdom which is already that of heaven.[105] Guerric was amiable and indulgent, not given to reproof,[106] and he wrote with grace and elegance; his delicacy of touch is more evident than his brillance, yet he saw in manual work one of the paths on which we meet Jesus,[107] and regretted that he could not give himself to it as his monks did.[108] In common with the preachers of his day he spoke of our blessed Lady, and loved to contemplate the childhood of Jesus. The great difference, however, between him and minds more given to speculation is that he emphasizes the mysteries celebrated by the liturgy, and the forming of Christ in the souls of those who take part in them; for by receiving the sacraments and imitating our Lord they bring Christ to birth in themselves.[109] Their soul becomes the "mother of Christ" and receives true life from him, by the gift of the Holy Ghost who proceeds from the Father and himself. Guerric loves to reflect on the interior states of Christ, on the heart and body in which he underwent them, on the actions he performed for us. The Blessed Virgin, the perfect model of spiritual motherhood, is associated with him in all this; following her example the soul grows in the light of Christ, in faith and wisdom, in a contemplation which is both a cleaving in love to God, and a desire to experience him as intensely as it is possible before the glory of heaven.

Isaac de Stella, like Guerric, had received his training in the schools before his conversion. He gave them up, not without difficulty, but never lost a certain taste for speculation, which gave a depth, vigour and originality to his work as a theologian.[110] Yet this

[103] P.L., 185, 11–214. Cf. "La collection des sermons de Guerric d'Igny", in *Rech. théol. anc. et médiév.*, XXIV (1957), pp. 15–26.

[104] Edited by D. de Wilde, *De Beato Guerrico*, Westmalle, 1935, pp. 189–96; the text had already been published by J. Beller, *Le bienheureux Guerric, disciple de St Bernard, et second Abbé de Notre Dame d'Igny*, Rheims, 1890, pp. 337–47.

[105] "Guerric et l'école monastique", in *Collectanea Ord. Cist. Ref.*, XIX (1957), pp. 238–47.

[106] On his personality see A. Frachebout, "Le charme personnel du B. Guerric d'Igny", *ibid.*, pp. 222–37. Other studies, *ibid.*, pp. 249–99, are devoted to his teaching.

[107] *Serm. in Resurrec.*, III, 4, P.L., 185, 150; other writings on manual labour will be found in the sermons *In Pentecost*, II, 4; *In Assumpt.*, III, I; IV, 3, 4.

[108] According to the *Exordium Magnum*, III, 7, P.L., 185, 1058.

[109] On this aspect of Guerric's teaching cf. de Wilde, *op. cit.*

[110] Isaac, as A. Frachebout has shown, draws his inspiration from the Pseudo-Dionysius—a thing rare in the monastic tradition. See articles which appeared in *Coll. Ord. Cist. Ref.* in 1947, 1949, 1950. Isaac's own writings—sermons, *De*

strong and hearty Englishman worked assiduously and energetically in the fields. He theorized, almost theologized, over this work, giving it a place in his conception of the spiritual life.

For Isaac it was a means of obeying the law of God, of expiating sin, of making possible a charity which took the form of almsgiving and hospitality. He liked to remark in his sermons that he was speaking during a pause in his labour. He was aware that this work was hard and even wearying: yet it must not be allowed to become exhausting; if the soul is to be upheld by attending to God, the work of the spirit must alternate with that of the body, for thus labour can be the means of "meeting Jesus".[111] Isaac lived in various monasteries before he became in 1147 abbot of L'Étoile in the diocese of Poitiers, and died there about 1169. He recalled having met St Bernard and having been enchanted by the man himself and his writings.[112] He has his own way, however, of reflecting on the Christian mystery and describing it.[113] An account of his thought belongs to a history of theology: here it is enough to say that his emphasis is particularly on the social aspect of dogma. He does not, like Rupert of Deutz, trace it in the history of the development of our salvation, but works out in a speculative way biblical themes such as the marriage of God with mankind in the Incarnation and in the Church, of which the Blessed Virgin is the type and perfect fulfilment, in the sacrament of the Eucharist, and in mystical union. But he is too well balanced and moderate to consider these mysteries on a purely intellectual level: with his customary cheerfulness and common sense he joins his forceful ideas to a fervent love; his theology is the handmaid of spirituality.

Among those who approached St Bernard, Guerric and Isaac are, with Aelred and William of St Thierry, the most prominent Cistercian writers; but there are others who, without having produced work of the same originality, witness to a milieu marked by the teaching and example of the last of the Fathers. First of all are

---

missa, *De officio missae*—are in P.L., 194, 1689–1896. See also M. R. Milcamps, "Bibliographie d'Isaac de l'Étoile", in *Coll. Ord. Cist. Ref.*, XX (1958), pp. 175–186.

111 *Serm. 10*, P.L., 194, 1716; other writings on manual labour in *Serm.*, I, 3, 7, 14, 15, 20, 24, 34, 37.

112 *Serm. 52*, P.L., 194, 1869. Cf. J. Debray-Mulatier, "Biographie d'Isaac de Stella", in *Cîteaux*, X (1959), pp. 178–98.

113 An analysis will be found in *La spiritualité de Cîteaux* by Louis Bouyer, Paris, 1954, pp. 205–32. A. Piolanti, "La nostra solidarità sopranaturale nel pensiero di Isacco della Stella", in *Palestra del clero*, 1956, n. 7, pp. 1–18, notes the writings on the theology and philosophy of Isaac de Stella that have been published. On his mariology see H. Barré in *Études mariales*, IX (1951), pp. 61, 75, 86–7, 118–23. C. Balič, *Testimonia de Assumptione B.M.V.*, Rome, 1948, I, pp. 191–2, points out the reticent position taken up by Isaac on the doctrine of the Assumption.

Bernard's own converts. In the first flight is Geoffrey of Auxerre who was his secretary, confidant and biographer and became successively abbot of Clairvaux and several other monasteries.[114] He had been a disciple of Abelard, but gave him up for Bernard in 1140. After the latter's death he devoted all he had learnt in the schools and in the cloister to his service: he continued the series of sermons on the Canticle of Canticles[115]; his own sermons were studded with anecdotes he had heard from St Bernard; he finished the *Vita Prima* and the *Corpus* of writings which enshrines the ideal picture of the saint which it was desired to perpetuate. These documents, which are hagiographical rather than historical, had a lasting influence in the Order. Geoffrey was also a friend of the Carthusians and wrote and preached for their benefit.[116] He was deeply attached to the common life, but did not underestimate a vocation to the solitary life, and admires in the Carthusians the happy combination of the hermit and the cenobite.[117] He advised the abbots of his Order to show patience and discretion in the exercise of their authority. More than once he shows a certain anxiety at the prosperity of the Order and the resulting dangers to its original spirit.[118] There is no doubt that he did more than anyone else to consolidate St Bernard's position as father of the Order. Nicholas of Clairvaux, a Benedictine of Montieramey, for some years Bernard's notary, was also greatly attached to his memory. He may have been a discreditable secretary, but as a faithful admirer he handed on in his sermons and letters St Bernard's ideas in his own style. Not that he lacks certain happy touches of his own, especially on the subject of the Blessed Virgin.[119] One of Bernard's converts, Hugh of Pontigny, wrote sermons on the liturgy.[120]

Blessed David Himmerod, a Florentine who came to Clairvaux in 1131, was typical of the first generation of monks.[121] ... Gervase of Louth Park, who says he met St Bernard, was one of those who resigned or wished to resign his office; a common attitude in the

[114] The latest biographical notice is that of A. Dimier in *Catholicisme hier et aujourd'hui*, IV (1956), col. 1849.

[115] "Les écrits de Geoffroy d'Auxerre", in *Rev. bénéd.*, LXII (1952), pp. 274–291.

[116] "Les souvenirs inédits de Geoffroy d'Auxerre sur St Bernard", in *Études sur St Bernard*, pp. 151–70.

[117] "Le témoignage de Geoffroy d'Auxerre sur la vie cistercienne", in *Analecta monastica*, II, pp. 174–201, esp. p. 179.

[118] *Ibid.*, p. 196; cf. *Sermo in anniv. obitus S. Bernardi*, n. 2, 17, P.L., 185, 574–584.

[119] "Les collections de sermons de Nicholas de Clairvaux", in *Rev. bénéd.*, LXVI (1956), pp. 269–302.

[120] C. H. Talbot, "The Sermons of Hugh of Pontigny", in *Cîteaux in de Nederlanden*, VII (1956), pp. 5–33.

[121] A. Schneider, "Vita B. Davidis monachi Hemmerrodensis", in *Analecta S. Ord. Cist.*, XI (1955), pp. 27–44.

Order, and one of the forms of spirituality peculiar to its abbots.[122] Roger of Byland, the friend of St Bernard, was before all things a master of novices: sensible and with a great heart.[123] Galland of Rigny was a monk with a sense of humour: in order to cure the boredom which threatened some of his brethren he composed *Proverbs*[124] and *Parables*,[125] dedicated to St Bernard, which inculcate in a pleasing way lessons of generosity in the Lord's service. As for Peter of Roye, he was formerly a canon of Noyon and tells in rhetorical style of his earlier excesses, his conversion, and his years at Clairvaux when Bernard was his abbot. He draws an idealistic picture of the sons of the great abbot, describing them in all their occupations: prayer and work, in the oratory and hoeing in the fields, in the meadows and forests. What he writes bears witness to the influence of Bernard and his community.[126] Serlo induced St Bernard to join the Order of Savigny to that of Cîteaux, and wrote sermons, mostly for liturgical feasts.[127] Amédée of Lausanne, who was one of Bernard's admirers at Clairvaux, wrote sermons on Mary[128]; and an anonymous monk also has left some sermons which owe their inspiration to Bernard.[129]

Gilbert of Hoyland, abbot of Swineshead in Lincolnshire, possibly came to Clairvaux. He knew Aelred and undertook to continue St Bernard's series of sermons on the Canticle of Canticles, using some of the exhortations he had already written for nuns.[130] He laid particular stress on virginity.[131] According to him, in the body of Christ contemplatives are the heart.[132] Like Bernard and the other Cistercian writers, and unlike Rupert of Deutz or Honorius of Arles, his commentary on the Canticle is not a Marian one. In the spirit of St Bernard's teaching he emphasizes the part played by love. He works out a complete spirituality of the reciprocal duties of an abbot and his monks. He reminds the brethren of the obligation of manual labour, and of private prayer which must always be contemplative: *privatim . . . sed privata non petunt.*[133] He reacts in

122 C. H. Talbot, "The Testament of Gervase of Louth Park", *ibid.*, VII (1951), pp. 32–45.

123 C. H. Talbot, "A letter of Roger, Abbot of Byland", *ibid.*, pp. 218–31.

124 Edited by J. Châtillon in *Rev. du moyen âge latin*, IX (1953), pp. 5–152. With a translation by M. Dumontier and an excellent introduction.

125 "Les paraboles de Galland de Rigny", in *Analecta monastica*, I, pp. 166–80.

126 Letter to the provost of Noyon, P.L., 182, 706–13.

127 A. Wilmart, "Le recueil des discours de Serlon Abbé de Savigni", in *Rev. Mabillon*, XII (1922), pp. 26–38.

128 P.L., 188, 1304–46. Cf. A. Dimier, *Amédée de Lausanne*, St Wandrille, 1949.

129 "Sermons de l'école de St Bernard dans un manuscrit d'Hauterive", in *Analecta S. Ord. Cist.*, XI (1955) pp. 3–26.

130 P.L. 185, 11–298; cf. *Rev. bénéd.*, LXII (1952), pp. 289–90.

131 E.g. *In Cant*,, 17, 5–6, P.L., 185, 90, 18, 2, 5, 93, 95 and *passim.*

132 *Ibid.*, 21, 6, 113.

133 *Ibid.*, 23, 3, 120.

every possible way against the danger of lukewarmness. He is of course not to be compared with St Bernard—*quis sustinebit*? The Chronicle of Clairvaux says "he wrote in the style of St Bernard",[134] yet he was not merely a skilful imitator who carried on Bernard's work honestly: he was also his fervent disciple. Another English abbot, John of Ford, also took up the completion of the sermons on the Canticle of Canticles.[135] Alcher of Clairvaux, who probably also had known Bernard, was a compiler.[136] The Blessed Fastrede, abbot first of Clairvaux and then of Cîteaux (†1163), quotes two sentences which he had heard from the lips of Bernard himself; there is a letter from him to another abbot in which he defends austerity with an insistence which gives the impression that it was tending to lessen. He appeals not only to Bernard's words on the subject, but to the example he gave; he fears lest the wealth of the Order should lead the abbots into a life of pomp and greed, and notes that one among them has already given way to the danger. The whole letter—it is not known to whom it was written—has the appearance of being an open letter, a public not a private one, and it was kept and published as though it were to the address of all.[137] From this time onwards recollections of the times of St Bernard and the first generation of Cistercians became a means of reawakening fervour: Herbert of Mores (†1180) wrote three books of *Miracles*[138] for that purpose, and Conrad of Eberbach (†1221) in his *Magnum Exordium* stored up stories of the heroic age, idealized pictures of the austerity, poverty and simplicity in the time of St Bernard.[139] Henry of Marcy, abbot of Hautecombe in 1160, of Clairvaux in 1176, and then cardinal bishop of Albani (†1189), carried on Bernard's work by preaching as he had done against the heretics of the south of France. His letters reveal the depths of his attachment to Bernard,[140] and his zeal for the interests of his Order, temporal as well as spiritual. He dedicated to the monks of Clairvaux his great work *De peregrinante civitate Dei*[141] in which he works out an ecclesiology in a vast scale.[142] Later on two English Cistercians, Matthew of Rievaulx[143] († *c.* 1215) and a monk of

[134] P.L., 185, 1247, ad ann. 1172.

[135] The Prologue has been published in *Coll. Ord. Cist. Ref.*, V (1939), pp. 252–261.

[136] They have been studied by C. J. Holdsworth, "John of Ford and English Cistercian Writings 1167–1214", in *Trans. R. Hist. Soc.*, Series 5, vol. X, 1960, pp. 117–36.

[137] P.L., 182, 704–6.

[138] P.L., 185, 1273–1384.

[139] P.L., 185, 995–1198.

[140] *Epist.*, VI, P.L., 204, 220.

[141] P.L., 204, 251–402.

[142] Cf. Y. Congar, "Henri de Marcy", in *Analecta monastica*, V, pp. 1–90, and "Église et cité de Dieu", in *Mélanges E. Gilson*, Toronto–Paris, 1959, pp. 173–202.

[143] A. Wilmart, "Les Mélanges de Mathieu préchantre de Rievaulx", in *Rev. bénéd.*, LII (1940), p. 54.

Rufford,[144] writing of the glories of their Order, give Bernard a special place in it.

The two last representatives of Clairvaux are not the least engaging. Blessed Helinand was a Flemish *trouvère* who after a rackety and wandering youth entered the monastery of Froidmont in the diocese of Beauvais. He became its prior and died about 1235. He wrote *Sermons*, two short treatises on *Self-knowledge* and *The good government of the prince*, an *Epistle to Gauthier*, a *Chronicle* and some poems of which the only ones to come down to us are those concerned with death.[145] He threw himself into his new life with unparalleled zest in spite of the burden of experience which he frankly admits that he had acquired in too gay a past. With admiration he discovers in his writings him whom he calls "our Bernard": he carries on his teachings, adapting them to his own milieux and times. He is not a thinker but a poet; he does not create so much as adorn everything he touches. He is contemporary with St Francis and sings in his way, a biblical one, of the sun and the flowers. He likes the Cistercian life, penance, prayer and work. He takes up and works out more completely the idea of feudal homage to our Lady[146] which had been suggested nearly two centuries before by St Odilo of Cluny.[147] Yet like many other Cistercians who followed St Bernard he avoids pronouncing himself in favour of the Immaculate Conception. In his writings are some of Guerric's ideas —such as that of the spiritual motherhood of the soul—and Bernard's—that of the "region of unlikeness". Helinand puts his mountebank's liveliness and his taste for proverbs and stories to the service of his tender love for him whom he calls, in an enchanting phrase, *Dominus humanissimus*, "our most human master, the most sweet Lord Jesus Christ".[148] Both the man and the style are delightful.

Adam of Perseigne, who had been formerly a Canon Regular and then a Benedictine abbot, is of a more serious bent. Though he had never been a Cistercian novice himself, he became master of novices at Pontigny and then abbot of Perseigne for thirty-three years, till his death in 1221. He wrote letters, some friendly and some of direction, to Carthusians, to monks and nuns, and to abbots and the great ones of this world—several are positive treatises—and he also composed sermons.[149] All his work is coloured by the writings

144 "Documents sur le mort des moines", in *Rev. Mabillon*, XLVI (1956), p. 77.

145 P.L., 212, 481–1081. Cf. M. J. du Halgouët in *Coll. Ord. Cist. Ref.*, XX (1958), pp. 131–5. *Les vers de la mort* have been translated into modern French with a commentary by J. Coppin, Paris, 1930.

146 *Serm. in Nativ.*, I, 495.

147 See *supra*, p. 109.

148 *Epist. ad Galterum*, P.L., 212, 757.

149 His writings are in P.L., 211, 583–754. A critical edition of his letters has

of St Bernard whose ideas on the image of God, the degrees of humility, and the harmonizing of humility and virginity in the Mother of God he reproduces; but specifically monastic or Cistercian allusions are rare. He delights to speak of the gifts of thc Holy Spirit, drawing a comparison between them and the seven days of the week, the last being that of contemplation, the *sapientiae sabbatum.*[150] He passes on St Bernard's teaching through a psychology of nearly a hundred years later, in no very original way, but with unction and affection, in a style more fervent than profound. His writings reflect, too, the progress which devotion to the Blessed Virgin had made everywhere.

8. *Cistercians not of Clairvaux*

There were, among the Cistercian writers, particularly towards the end of the twelfth century, some who had not known St Bernard and did not profess any connection between their writings and his. One of the earliest is Burchard of Balerne, abbot of Bellevaux (†1163). The humour of his *Apologia for beards* is not to everyone's taste,[151] but it is one of the rare spiritual writings which speaks at length of lay brothers, though fortunately many of these *conversi* are known to us from hagiography. It seems that in spite of deviations against which the General Chapters were continually legislating,[152] there was among the brothers a real spirit of prayer and penance.

Odo of Ourscamp, who became a cardinal in 1170, speaks of Cistercian nuns and appeals to the abbots of the Order in favour of "the original vigour of the observance".[153]

Thomas of Froidmont († *c.* 1170) wrote for his sister, who seems to have been a Cistercian nun, a treatise *On leading a good life* which had a wide circulation.[154] Garnier of Rocheford, abbot of Clairvaux till 1192, then bishop of Langres, wrote sermons both for feasts of the Church and for the General Chapter,[155] and was possibly the author of *Distinctiones, sive liber qui dicitur Angelus.*[156]

Arnold of Bohéries wrote, about 1200, a short directory in which

---

been published by J. Bouvet in *Archives historiques du Maine*, 1952–8; cf. J Bouvet, "Biographie d'Adam de Perseigne", in *Coll. Ord. Cist. Ref.*, XX (1958), pp. 16–26, 145–52.

150 *Epist.*, VII, P.L., 211, 803.

151 Edited P. Goldschmidt, Cambridge, 1955.

152 Cf. A. Dimier, *St Bernard "pêcheur de Dieu"*, Paris, 1953, pp. 128–38.

153 "Lettres d'Odon d'Ourscamp, Cardinal cistercien", in *Analecta monastica*, III, pp. 149 and 157.

154 P.L., 184, 1199–1300.

155 P.L., 205, 559–828.

156 Cf. J. C. Didier, "Garnier de Rochefort, sa vie et son œuvre", in *Coll. Ord. Cist. Ref.*, XVII (1955), pp. 145–58.

he sums up the whole of ascetic practice,[157] following the monk through his day. He speaks of manual labour, and the teaching of his few pages is entirely practical. It is a short, stimulating work, simple, clear, and without flights of fancy, and was one of those most often copied. The same is true of the treatise *On the interior dwelling-place* which was probably also written by a Cistercian.[158] One fact which reveals the climate of the times is that mystical writings were not the most widely read, though there was no lack of them. An Englishman, Gilbert of Stanford, in his *Commentary on the Canticle of Canticles*, wrote much on the soul and on love; he asserts his belief in the absolute value of contemplation and the contemplative life. These are self-sufficient and do not require to be completed by action, although the contemplative must, if necessary, be prepared to renounce contemplation for action.[159]

Thomas of Perseigne († *c.* 1190) compiled two works *On the soul's preparation* and *On the Canticle of Canticles*[160] in which he elaborates in distinctions, divisions and sub-divisions the themes of a thoroughly traditional spirituality. Baldwin of Ford (†1190) is far more original: his short works had spiritual vigour,[161] and his long treatise *On the sacrament of the altar* earned him an honourable place in theological history[162]: his theological method, however, is ordered entirely to contemplation. Ogier of Locedio (†1214) left a fine commentary *On the Supper of the Lord*,[163] some sermons *On the praises of the Mother of God*,[164] and a *Complaint of Mary* inspired by the writings of Godfrey of St Victor.[165] He puts the Cistercians on their guard against various abuses, especially the attraction of the parlour. He shows an exquisite sensibility in his tender outpourings of friendship for Jesus. The influence of scholasticism is already discernible in the work of Gunther of Pairis († about 1220). His slightly systematic (he had indeed been a teacher) exposition *On prayer, fasting and almsgiving*[166] reveals a true piety, and his pages on God and the love of God, if they are not particularly original, are full of fervour; he makes no allusion to

157 *Speculum monachorum*, P.L., 184, 1175–8.

158 P.L., 184, 507–52; 177, 145–70; cf. P. Delhaye, *Le problème de la conscience morale chez St Bernard*, Namur, 1952, pp. 91–110.

159 "Le commentaire de Gilbert de Stanford sur le Cantique des cantiques", in *Analecta monastica*, I, pp. 205–30.

160 P.L., 206, 17–862. "Les deux compilations de Thomas de Perseigne", in *Mediaeval Studies*, X (1948), pp. 204–9.

161 P.L., 204, 403–640.

162 P.L., 205, 641–774. There is a critical edition with a translation and introduction published in the collection "Sources chrétiennes".

163 P.L., 184, 879–950.

164 Edited by Adriani, Turin, 1873.

165 H. Barré, "Le 'planctus Mariae' attribué à S. Bernard", in *Rev. d'ascét. et de myst.*, XXVIII (1952), pp. 245–66.

166 P.L., 212, 99–222.

monasticism in it. Odo of Morimond wrote sermons[167]; the most noteworthy is a sort of treatise on the *Stabat iuxta crucem*, in which he adopts a position against the Immaculate Conception[168]; but in other points his thought, expressed in sonorous prose, is as true as it is beautiful.

Folcuin of Sittichenbach exhorts monks to be true to the chief meaning of the word *claustrum*, which comes from *claudere* not *claudicare*: let them not limp, divided between the preoccupations of the cloister and the world.[169] A last representative of the end of the first century of Cîteaux was Alan of Lille: he spent nearly the whole of his life in the schools and probably wrote nothing in the monastery which he entered in old age; but what he wrote before his conversion has the flavour of his generation and reveals its devotional outlook, which was already in line with that of his Order.

Finally, among the evidence of the spiritual outlook and practices of the Cistercians a place must be given to works of hagiography. They are not particularly useful as factual history, but are extremely valuable as giving a picture of ideas and ideals. Lives like those of Amadeus the Old[171] or Christian of l'Aumône,[172] or a late compilation like *The Book of Miracles* of Caesar of Heisterbach (†1245)[173] reflect the pictures and the recollections which abbots, monks and brothers left in the collective memory of their Order. Many of the abbots became great prelates, cardinals, papal legates; one even became pope, Eugenius III; others travelled about in the Church's service preaching against heresy, or undertaking missionary labours. None of this had been foreseen in the primitive institute. Caesar does not hide weaknesses or even scandals, but on the other hand he lingers over examples of extreme austerity such as could only have been accomplished, if indeed they ever were, by that "singularity" which had been reprobated by St Bernard.[174] Moderation and the community sense seem to have been sacrificed to a wish to rival

[167] M. Bernards, "Zu den Predigten Odos von Morimond", in *Cîteaux in de Niederlanden*, IV (1953), pp. 101–23.

[168] Cf. *Analecta S. Ord. Cist.*, VII (1951), pp. 61–2. The homily referred to *ibid.*, p. 61, note 6, has been attributed to Albert the Great and edited by M. von Loë, Bonn, 1916. Number IV of the *Coll. Ord. Cist. Ref.*, XXIII (1961), is devoted to Odo of Morimond.

[169] Cf. *Analecta S. Ord. Cist.*, VII (1951), p. 57, and "Une homélie de Volcuin de Sittichenbach", in *Studi medioevali*, II (1962).

[170] On his life and writings see A. le Bail, art. "Alain de Lille", in *Diction. de spiritualité*, I (1937), col. 270–2. His works are in P.L., 210. Cf. also G. Raynaud de Lage, *Alain de Lille*, Paris, 1951.

[171] Edited L. P. d'Hozier, *Armorial général de la France*, Registre V, 1st part (1764). Cf. A. Dimier in *Petrus Venerabilis*, Rome, 1956, pp. 88–94.

[172] "Le texte complet de la vie de Christian de l'Aumône", in *Analecta Bollandiana*, LXXI (1953), pp. 21–52.

[173] Edited Strange, Cologne, 1851.

[174] Cf. *Études sur Saint Bernard*, pp. 199–201.

the eccentricities of some of the Fathers of the Desert. Yet through all these wonders and marvels can be seen the confidence of each and all in the Cistercian way of life; which was also among the ways of being faithful to St Bernard.

9. Cistercian Spirituality

With the Cistercian school as with monasticism of the traditional kind, it would have been agreeable to linger over authors who have barely been mentioned, each of whom in his own way expresses the spiritual tendencies of the period. In looking at the spirituality of the twelfth century as a whole, the question arises whether there is to be found in the Cistercian institutions, and the writers who lived according to them, anything which is not found among all representatives of the monastic tradition. No simple answer can be given. It is clear that devotion to Christ and his Mother is the same at Cîteaux as elsewhere: that is equally true of the psychology of devotion, in which a similar note of tenderness is found everywhere, but possibly earlier outside Cistercian circles. The fundamental notions of the life of prayer and of asceticism and the subjects which relate to the monastic life are identical in every place.[175] Any differences there may be are in observance. As has been seen by the fact that supererogatory prayers had been reduced at Cîteaux,[176] actual practices of devotion to the Blessed Virgin had a smaller place. Again, there is a great stress laid on poverty and simplicity, but the fact that its importance had so often to be insisted upon proves that the temptation to stray from it was as strong at Cîteaux as everywhere else. The monastic ideal was the same there, and had to contend with the same human frailties. There is, however, one point to which Cistercian writers recur with a vigour and constancy peculiar to themselves, and that is manual labour. This was not a practice in any way foreign to the monasteries of the old tradition, though in them it usually took the form of "fraternal services" inside the enclosure of the monastery rather than field work outside it, but at Cîteaux it was a fundamental of asceticism; and in this point Cistercian spiritual writing constantly reflected the outlook of the primitive institution, whose aim had been a return to poverty.[177]

Prayer was not conceived differently at Cîteaux than it had ever been elsewhere. In a commentary on the Rule from Pontigny the passages referring to prayer are explained along the lines of Hilde-

175 See *supra*, pp. 182–3.

176 This fact was pointed out by A. M. Dal Pino in *Studi Storici dell'Ordine dei Servi di Maria*, V (1953), p. 235.

177 Ed. C. H. Talbot, "The Commentary on the Rule from Pontigny", in *Studia monastica*, III (1961), p. 100.

mar's commentary. Aelred in his *Rule for recluses* also emphasizes the need for alternating occupations, and variety in prayer. He adds: "After Matins is the time for prayer, which should be prolonged or shortened according to the help which the Holy Spirit gives, taking care, however, that lengthy prayer does not engender boredom. It is better to give oneself to prayer for a short while and often than for a long time on end, unless, in a fervour inspired by God's grace, your prayer is prolonged in spite of yourself."[178] Further on he says: "Take good care not to make a rule that you will say a certain number of psalms. Use the psalms as long as they suit you; if they begin to weigh on you, turn to reading; when that begins to pall, rise and pray. When wearied of these various exercises, work with your hands. Thus by a healthy alternation you will recreate your spirit and drive away accidie." And on the subject of commemorations: "Never bind yourself by vow or oblige yourself to say a fixed number: but follow your own devotion in the matter."[179] It is true of course that this work is thought to have been written for a recluse; but Aelred knew that it would become public, and its title shows it to have been written for recluses in general, and we know that Stephen of Jalley[180] advised that it should be read by the Cistercian novices.

Cistercian spirituality was therefore in the line of the whole monastic tradition with the shades of difference proper to the twelfth century. On the other hand, if there is no properly Cistercian spirituality, that is, one clearly distinct from all monastic tradition, from Cîteaux came a theology of spirituality. One theological legacy of Benedictine monasticism has been that of the mysteries: the Cistercians cultivated a theology of the mystical life, under the influence of two great spirits, St Bernard and William of St Thierry, especially the former. The great problem that these two doctors and their most eminent disciples concentrated on was that of man and his relations with the Blessed Trinity. A definite step forward is taken in writings on the mystical states. Without St Bernard monastic doctrine would have developed—as it did outside Cîteaux with Rupert, Eadmer and Geoffrey of Admont, to name but a few—in the direction of a harmony between the new, more affective devotion and dogmatic progress. St Bernard's achievement was to enrich this homogeneous progression with certain profoundly traditional ideas—those of the image of God, of the region of unlikeness, of the degrees of love—to which his genius gave a freshness; and because of him they took a larger place in the writings of his Order

178 Ed. C. Dumont, *Aelred de Rievaulx, La vie récluse*, Paris, 1961, p. 65, note 9.
179 *Ibid.*, p. 67.
180 Cf. E. Mikkers, "Un 'speculum novitii' inédit d'Étienne de Salley", in *Coll. Ord. Cist. Ref.*, VIII, 1946, p. 52.

than elsewhere. It is in this sense that one speaks not of a spirituality but of a Cistercian theology which could more properly be called that of Clairvaux. To stress such differences, however, is to run the risk of forgetting the profound unity of all *claustrales.* Like the Cistercians, the Benedictines, the Carthusians, the Canons Regular, all read St Bernard and those writings of William of St Thierry which were soon to be attributed to him, together with the meditations of Drogo and Arnold of Bonneval which underwent a similar attribution. The *claustrales* had in common a conception of asceticism wholly ordered to contemplation, and a contemplation nourished on the mysteries of faith.

From St Gregory to St Bernard the objective content of revelation was unchanged, as were the practical demands which union with God makes on the soul; only men themselves had changed to a certain extent. A new sensibility, a more affective outlook, had gradually appeared; men had turned their minds to aspects of the work of our salvation which had been less the object of their thought at the beginning of the Middle Ages. St Gregory showed men the way to Christ, but he spoke of a reuniting of man with God by the way of knowledge, though by one which was truly a knowledge of love. St Bernard was to speak more of Christ himself, of the soul which is his bride, and of love which is a love by knowledge. From either point of view the Christian lives in faith, in the longing for God, but every increase in the acuteness and fullness of his psychological perceptions enlarges the human resources with which he loves.

PART TWO

New Milieux, New Problems

FROM THE TWELFTH TO THE SIXTEENTH CENTURY

by

DOM FRANÇOIS VANDENBROUCKE

Benedictine of Mont-César

I

THE SCHOOLMEN OF THE TWELFTH CENTURY

1. Medieval Monasticism and Scholasticism

THE twelfth century was one of intellectual renaissance and humanism,[1] in contrast with its predecessors: not that it was in any absolute sense a starting-point for something fresh, for what was new in it had been in preparation, and there was no break with the past. The Renaissance of three centuries later was to break with the genius of the Middle Ages in almost every sphere, going back to antiquity for its conception of man: in the twelfth century, on the other hand, men of learning felt themselves to be carrying on the monastic and patristic culture of the generations before them; it was a reawakening[2] rather than a renaissance.

Some, indeed, were full of enthusiasm for the ancient culture (among them Hildebert of Lavardin [1056–1133], bishop of Mans in 1096 and of Tours in 1125): not that they themselves enjoyed its charms so much as that they saw in its thought a useful instrument for Christianity. In any case, the mentality of the century was too Christian for a culture pagan in inspiration, like that of the Italian renaissance,[3] to take root in it.

What was new was not so much the flowering of literature, art and thought, but rather the fact that new milieux, new social strata, shared in it. This was also true of the spiritual life; even in its highest forms it was no longer almost exclusively the portion of monks and of the clergy, but was open to an ever-widening circle of the laity. The spiritual awakening of the period is seen to be an

[1] See C. H. Haskins, *The Renaissance of the Twelfth Century*, Cambridge, 1928; H. Pirenne, G. Cohen, H. Focillon, *La civilisation occidentale au moyen âge du XIe au milieu de XVe siècle* (*Histoire générale, Histoire du moyen âge*, VIII, Paris, 1933), p. 220.

[2] Cf. M. W. A. Nitze in "The so-called Twelfth-Century Renaissance", in *Speculum*, XXIII (1948), 464–71.

[3] Cf. M. N. Scivoletto, *Spiritualità medioevale e tradizione scolastica nel secolo XII in Francia*, Naples, 1954. This work summarizes the literary production of the twelfth century in France.

opening out of the ways leading to holiness, before becoming a discovery of forgotten truths or of those that were really new.

Among these new social groups in which the ferment of an intense spirituality was beginning to work, were first the schools, the universities which were coming into being, and the countless laymen, individually or in groups, who longed to lead a completely evangelical life.

There are various aspects of this emergence of the laity, some of which will be touched on in a later chapter. To turn for the moment to the schools: in the eleventh century the monasteries were the only centres of Christian thought. "The abbeys remained the repositories of the great Christian ideas."[4] Thinkers still drew their inspiration from the liturgy and from the traditional *lectio divina* of monasticism, that is, from Scripture and the Fathers.

But in the twelfth century, although intellectual life in the monasteries was still very strong, theologians and thinkers appear outside it, criticizing the monks as mere classifiers and copyists who spent their time drawing up lists and rehearsing old opinions. It was a method of work the new men considered limited to "reading the Bible and the Fathers, in the liturgical setting of monastic life".[5] Side by side with medieval monasticism the age of the Schoolmen was coming into being.

The new movement aimed first and foremost at a more systematic method of research and greater precision, and it was stimulated by the new sources at hand: the philosophical works of antiquity were being read afresh. The Greeks, the Arabs and the Jews were beginning to be translated into Latin, opening unknown horizons. There was need of a new synthesis which should integrate all this, and the twelfth century saw the birth of a scientific theology which was to reach its highest point in the thirteenth. *De facto*, if not *de jure*, the new science leaned more to reason and dialectic than to faith, the word of God, truth received without discussion as coming from the Truth. Scholasticism has been variously defined: some have seen it as a new method, taken from Aristotle's logic[6]; for others, its specific note lies in its content, its systematization of the Church's doctrine.[7] Again, in the view of some recent writers, it

[4] J. Leclercq, O.S.B., "Mediévisme et unionisme", in *Irenikon*, XIX (1946), p. 20; cf. his "Pour une histoire humaine du monachisme", in *Studia Anselmiana*, XLI (1957), pp. 1–7; and "Y a-t-il une culture monastique", in *Settimane di studio del Centro italiano di studi sull' alto medioevo*, IV, Spoleto, 1957, pp. 339–56.

[5] Cf. J. Leclercq, *L'amour des lettres et le désir de Dieu*, Paris, 1957, p. 10 and *passim*.

[6] Cf. M. Grabmann, *Geschichte der scholastischen Methode*, 2nd ed., Graz, 1956, 2 vols.

[7] Cf. M. de Wulf, *Histoire de la philosophie médiévale* (up to the 5th ed.).

consists in the use of methods of exposition called "scholastic", chiefly that of the *quaestio* applied to Scripture, to the *sacra pagina*.[8]

Theology henceforward claimed to be a science, and according to the Aristotelian ideal took on a speculative and even deductive character. Like all sciences, it was disinterested; it was no longer concerned with nourishing the spiritual life, as the monastic theologians would have it do. The Scriptures were read, studied and taught with the view of the mind rather than the heart acquiring knowledge, and theological activity assumed a more purely intellectual character, less contemplative, less dependent on the atmosphere created by the liturgy.[9] The study of the Bible had markedly a twofold aim: theological interpretation, and literal exegesis; the thirteenth century was to reap the fruit of these efforts.

The twelfth century, then, theologically speaking, without going into the other aspects of spiritual life, appears somewhat complex. It was indeed still a monastic age, but at the same time it was already a scholastic one. It will be seen later what theology owed, besides, to the various evangelical movements that were springing up everywhere at the time, and in a more general way, to the whole enrichment of culture and of human activity that took place during the century.[10]

The reawakening of studies in the twelfth century was not confined to the domain of the *sacra pagina* but went far beyond it. The newly discovered sources revealed the possibility of a broader field of human knowledge than had ever been suspected. As men came in contact with these sources they broke through the traditional framework of thought. It foreshadowed the movement that was to end, three or four centuries later, in a much more radical renaissance; one which would destroy the Church's monopoly of intellectual life.[11] This is not the place to describe the tremendous surge forward in philosophy, history, theology and canon law, though it is worth emphasizing its significance. The new develop-

[8] Cf. J. Leclercq, *op. cit.*, p. 10.

[9] Cf. M.-D. Chenu, O.P., *La théologie au XIIe siècle*, Paris, 1957, ch. IX (*L'Ancien Testament dans la théologie médiévale*).

[10] On this last point the following general works should be mentioned: H. Pirenne, *Histoire économique de l'Occident médiéval*, Paris, 1951, especially the second part, "Le mouvement économique et social au moyen âge du XIe au milieu du XVe siècle"; G. de Lagarde, *La naissance de l'esprit laïque au declin du moyen âge*, 3rd ed., vol. I, Louvain, 1956.

[11] In this connection, see the works mentioned in note 1; also M.-D. Chenu, *op. cit.*, ch. 1 ("La nature et l'homme: La renaissance du XIIe siècle"); P. Delhaye, "L'organisation scolaire au XIIe siècle", in *Traditio*, V (1947), pp. 211–68; A. Fliche, *La chrétienté médiévale* (*Histoire du monde*, VII), pp. 473–83. In addition, the following may be consulted: P. Vignaux, *La philosophie au moyen âge*, Paris, 1958; G. Cohen, *Le mouvement intellectuel, moral et littéraire* [of the Middle Ages], in the *Histoire générale* (Glotz), vol. VIII.

ments came into being in a world in which the Church alone, and even for a very long time the monasteries alone, were the guide of intellectual life; she made humanism her own (before that word had been invented) and at the same time continued to lead souls towards God and perfection. She was able to assimilate the new aspirations and to welcome, in the words of St Paul: "Whatsoever things are true, whatsoever holy, whatsoever just, whatsoever lovely, whatsoever of good fame" (Phil. 4. 8). She did this boldly while keeping to her traditions and her proper mission, and as a result four centuries more were to be able to strike a balance between strictly supernatural values and human ones.

The men of that age loved the authors of antiquity; they wrote more and more, in Latin and even occasionally in the vernacular; they translated Greek,[12] Arabic and Hebrew texts; the writings of the Schoolmen on grammar,[13] rhetoric, metaphysics,[14] law, poetry and history[15] spread one after the other, and this in its turn brought about a great output of new literature. Events as diverse as the Crusades and the creation of new intellectual centres such as the universities complete the picture of a century that admired the masterpieces of the past and of nature and, reflecting upon them, could read in them the handwriting of God.[16]

2. *The Schools and the Universities*

In this flowering the schools in the cities[17] played a leading part. Several of them shone with a brilliance previously unknown: Laon with Anselm,[18] Chartres, Rheims, Bourges, Canterbury, Toledo. France had no monopoly of intellectual life, but the extent of her influence was unequalled; the schools of Paris, especially, stood

[12] Cf. M.-D. Chenu, *op. cit.*, ch. 5 ("Les platonismes au XIIe siècle"), ch. 6 ("Aetas Boetiana"), chs 12 and 13 ("L'entré de la théologie grecque" and "Orientale lumen").

[13] *Ibid.*, chs 4 and 17; P. Delhaye, "Grammatica et Ethica au XIIe siècle", in *Rech. théol. anc. méd.*, XXV (1958), pp. 59–110.

[14] Chenu, *op. cit.*, ch. 14 ("L'éveil métaphysique").

[15] *Ibid.*, ch. 3 ("Connaissance de l'histoire et théologie"). On the whole body of non-theological and non-spiritual literature of the twelfth century, see J. de Ghellinck, S.J., *L'essor de la littérature latine au XIIe siècle*, 2nd ed., Brussels, 1955.

[16] Chenu, *op. cit.*, ch. 1, "La nature de l'homme", gives the principal texts on "the discovery of nature" and that of man as "microcosm" and "master of nature". One may note especially here the names of Godfrey of St Victor, Honorius Augustodunensis, Alan of Lille, William of Conches, etc. For Honorius, see above, Part I, ch. 7, p. 169.

[17] On the organization of these schools, see P. Delhaye, *Organisation Scolaire au XIIe siècle*, pp. 238–68; M.-D. Chenu, *op. cit.*, chs 15 and 16.

[18] Works in P.L., 162. His *Sentences* and his *Commentaires bibliques* have been edited by O. Lottin, O.S.B., *Psychologie et morale au XIIe et au XIIIe siècle*, vol. V, Gembloux, 1959.

out because of a series of illustrious masters: among them Peter Abelard,[19] whose correspondence with Héloise has earned him a rather second-rate fame, but whose theological works, daring as they may have been for their day, had a considerable influence[20]; William of Conches,[21] Gilbert de la Porrée,[22] William of Champeaux, Peter Lombard (who will be discussed further on), Alan of Lille,[23] Peter the Cantor[24] and several others.

Their intellectual standing and the quality of their teaching attracted students to Paris from every corner of Europe.[25] At first the school of Notre Dame was simply one school among others: its principal competitor was St Geneviève, where Abelard shone. The chancellor of Notre Dame was unable to assert his authority over the rival school, and the masters who chose to move to Mount St Geneviève did so without his "licence", *licentia docendi.* The tension went on till the beginning of the thirteenth century when, thanks to the support of Pope Innocent III, a statute was enacted that decisively removed both masters and students from the authority both of the chancellor of Notre Dame and of the abbot of St Geneviève. This statute made of the *universitas magistrorum* (as it would later be called) an association dependent on Rome alone.[26] A little later, before 1221, the students grouped themselves, with their masters, into the *universitas magistrorum et scholarum Parisiensium.* They were divided into four "nations": French,

[19] Works in P.L., 178; ed. V. Cousin, 3 vols, Paris, 1836–59; B. Geyer, 4 vols, Münster, 1919–33; *Oeuvres choisies*, translated into French and arranged by M. de Gandillac, Paris, 1945.

[20] E. Gilson, in *Héloïse et Abélard*, new ed., Paris, 1948, believes this correspondence to be authentic, as against B. Schmeidler, "Der Briefwechsel zwischen Abälard und Heloise als eine literarische Fiction Abälards", in *Zeitschr. Kirchengesch.*, LIV (1935), pp. 323–38; and against C. Charrier, *Héloïse dans l'histoire et la légende*, Paris, 1933, See also G. Truc, *Abélard avec et sans Héloïse*, Paris, 1956 (a popularization). For Abelard's controversies with St Bernard, see A. Borst, "Abälard und Bernhard", in *Histor. Zeitschr.*, CLXXXVI (1958), pp. 497–526.

[21] Editions by C. Jourdain and J. Holmberg.

[22] Works in P.L., 64 and 188. Several editions or revised editions by A. Landgraf and A. Heysse.

[23] Works in P.L., 210; ed. by R. Bossuat and A. J. Creighton.

[24] Works in P.L., 205; ed. by Pitra.

[25] A summary of the teaching of the principal masters is given by A. Forest in "Les doctrines dans les écoles urbaines du XIIe siècle", in *Histoire de l'Église* (Fliche–Martin), XIII, pp. 69–110; "La théologie des Sommes et des Sentences", *ibid.*, pp. 147–78; A.-M. Landgraf, *Dogmengeschichte der Frühscholastik*, 5 vols, Ratisbon, 1952 and following years. R. W. Southern, in *The Making of the Middle Ages* (London, 1953), puts forward the hypothesis that Paris attracted students especially by its teaching of logic (ch. 4, "The Tradition of Thought", p. 221).

[26] See H. Rashdall and F. M. Powicke, *The Universities of Europe in the Middle Ages.*, 3 vols, Oxford, 1942; L. Halphen, *A travers l'histoire du moyen âge*, Paris, 1950, Part VI, ch. 2: "Les origines de l'Université de Paris"; cf. L. Halphen, G. Le Bras, G. Dupont-Ferrier, C. Samaran, *Aspects de l'Université de Paris*, Paris, 1949.

Picard, Norman and English. From 1200, we find at Paris the four "faculties": theology, arts, canon law and medicine.

Similar intellectual centres grew up in Italy: Milan, Pavia, Padua, Naples and Palermo. Salerno, like Montpellier, specialized in medicine. At Bologna there was a renaissance of the study of law; by the side of the school of civil law shone one of canon law. It was there that Gratian, by his *Decretals*, made his name in the middle of the twelfth century; his work is a source for almost any point of doctrine, ecclesiastical law, or even of religious practice,[27] in the Middle Ages. Later, the schools of France and Italy were to be rivalled in England by Oxford and Cambridge, in Bohemia by Prague, in Spain by Salamanca, in Portugal by Coimbra; and by the thirteenth century the change is completed; the universities take their place in the foreground of the intellectual life of Europe.[28]

The new methods of scholarship—the use of Aristotle, the arrangement of the "sentences" of the Fathers and theologians around each "question" put by the "master"—were thus the means of a remarkable intellectual flowering. But it is not clear that the result was always happy from the point of view of the spiritual life. Men's minds were working on new methods of theological investigation, inspired by pagan philosophy: might not their activity lose sight of the Gospel? Did it occur to the men of the time that the new methods might wither men's hearts?

This method was popularized by "the Master of the Sentences"—Peter the Lombard († *c.* 1160). His most famous work, entitled *The Four Books of the Sentences*, did in fact take the place which had formerly been given in the city schools and universities, and was still being given in monastic schools, to the Bible and the Fathers. The Lombard enjoyed unlimited authority in theology. He stood in the front rank, with Gratian and Peter Comestor. In these three masters, twelfth-century theology, canon law and exegesis reached their highest point—so much so that for a time there was a legend that they were not only brothers but triplets. Reservations can be made about the doctrine of the *Sentences* on the Trinity, their "christological nihilism", and even about their identification of the theological virtue of charity with the Holy Spirit,[29] but for

[27] There are countless editions, of which we may mention P.L., 187; and a critical edition by E. Friedberg, 2 vols, Leipzig, 1879. A number of excellent studies have been published in *Studia Gratiana* (Bologna, 1953 and following years), of which seven volumes have appeared up to date.

[28] On teaching and the universities, especially in the thirteenth century, see the synthesis by C. Touzellier in *Histoire de l'Église* (Fliche-Martin), X, pp. 341–86. Cf. also L. Halphen, *A travers l'histoire du moyen âge*, Paris, 1950, Part VI, ch. 3: "Les Universités au XIIIe siècle".

[29] On his teaching on charity (cf. *I Sent.*, dist. 17), see G. C. Meersseman, O.P., "Pourquoi le Lombard n'a-t-il pas conçu la charité comme amitié?" in *Miscell.*

several centuries they were the basic text of all theological teaching,[30] universally adopted and commented upon.

The danger of this rigidly technical work was that henceforth it would come between the churchman and the Gospel. The theologian would forget the word of God and rely for his whole spirituality on the *Sentences*. Clearly there had to be some sort of systematization in the twelfth century: the new sources and the new methods of research were bound to end in a new synthesis. But there was a real danger that the word of God would no longer be given to souls who longed to hear and live by it.

3. *Hugh of St Victor*

There was, however, in the schools of the twelfth century a very happy attempt at spiritual synthesis, the work of the Chapter of St Victor, at the gates of Paris. The school owed its origin to William of Champeaux. After years of teaching at Notre Dame, where he had a famous controversy with his pupil Abelard, he retired in 1108 with several disciples to the hermitage of St Victor. There in 1113 he adopted the rule of St Augustine and resumed his teaching. St Victor soon became one of the best-known theological and spiritual centres and at the same time the birthplace of a congregation of canons regular which spread rapidly; it absorbed even the renowned collegiate church of St Geneviève. William was made bishop of Châlons-sur-Marne, and died in 1122,[31] but the school, known as that of St Victor, owed its glory not to its founder but to some of his disciples.

Among these the most prominent was Hugh. He entered St Victor about 1115 or 1118, taught there from 1125, and about 1133 succeeded William of Champeaux as Master of the school. He re-

---

Lombardiana, pp. 165–74; A.-M. Landgraf, *Dogmengeschichte der Frühscholastik*, Part I, vol. I, 1 (Ratisbon, 1952), ch. 7, pp. 220–37. This doctrine was derived from St Augustine and was to be found in Paschasius Radbertus and even in William of St Thierry; cf. A. Landgraf in *Dict. de spirit.*, III, col. 573–4; also, by the same, "Anfänge einer Lehre von Concursus simultaneus in XIII. Jahrh.", in *Rech. théol. anc. méd.*, I (1929), pp. 202–28, 338–55.

30 P.L., 191 and 192; also ed. Quaracchi, 2 vols, 1916. A number of studies on this edition have been published. On his commentators (more than 500 of them, of whom half were Dominicans and a third were in England), see F. Stegmüller, *Repertorium commentariorum in Sententias Petri Lombardi*, 2 vols, Würzburg, 1947; V. Doucet, O.F.M., *Commentaires sur les Sentences. Supplément au repertoire de M. F. Stegmüller*, Quaracchi, 1954; and J. de Ghellinck, S.J., art. "Pierre Lombard", in *Dict. théol. cath.*, XII, col. 1941–2019. A considerable number of valuable studies were published in the collection *Miscellanea Lombardiana*, Novara, 1957.

31 Works in P.L., 163. The *Sententiae vel quaestiones* have been edited by G. Lefevre, in *Travaux et mémoires de l'Univ. de Lille*, VI, Lille, 1898. On the school of St Victor at its origin, see P. Delhaye, "L'organisation scolaire au XIIe siècle", *art. cit.*, pp. 241–6.

mained in that office until his death in 1140 or 1141.[32] Theologian, philosopher and teacher, he was also a contemplative: for him there were no divisions between learning, study and contemplation; both in his life and his writings they met together.

Hugh carried on—as did, after him, the whole school of St Victor—the monastic way of reading and studying the Bible and the Fathers.[33] Unlike his contemporary Abelard, and unlike Peter the Lombard later on, his idea was to treat theology as the Fathers had done, *more Patrum*, making it the art of reforming the soul and leading her to salvation. He owed to the atmosphere of the Paris in which he lived an astonishing breadth of view, which led him to touch on a great variety of subjects.[34] "Learn everything: you will see afterwards that nothing is superfluous and that there is no joy in a knowledge that is cramped and narrow."[35] His delight was to study and comment upon the Scriptures,[36] whose object is precisely the one he took as the centre of his own theological and spiritual ideas—the restoration of fallen man. He explored several branches of dogmatic and moral theology[37]; he even sketched the

[32] He was a native of Saxony, according to J. Taylor, *The Origin and Early Life of Hugh of St Victor, An Evaluation of the Tradition*, Notre Dame, Ind., 1957. According to R. Baron in *Rev. d'hist. eccl.*, LI (1956), pp. 920–34, he came from Ypres. On the literary, historical, and doctrinal questions raised by Hugh of St Victor, see R. Baron, *Science et sagesse chez Hugues de St Victor*, Paris, 1957.

[33] Works in P.L., 175–7. There were many other editions and translations; cf. R. Baron, *Science et sagesse . . .*, pp. 231–42. For a bibliography of studies devoted to Hugh of St Victor, see *ibid.*, pp. 243–63. There is an anthology of mystical writings of Hugh, Richard and Adam of St Victor translated into German by P. Wolff, *Die Viktoriner Mystische Schriften*, Vienna, 1936. Cf. R. Baron, "Hugues de St Victor: contribution à un nouvel examen de son œuvre", in *Traditio*, XV (1959), pp. 223–98; D. van den Eynde, O.F.M., *Essai sur la succession et la date des écrits de Hugues de St Victor*, Rome, 1960.

[34] Among many other works may be mentioned an introduction to the study of the liberal arts and of Holy Scripture, the *Eruditio didascalia* or *Didascalion*, P.L., 176, c. 739–812; critical edition by C. H. Buttimer, Washington, 1939.

[35] *Eruditio didascalia*, P.L., 176, c. 800–1.

[36] *De scripturis et scriptoribus sacris praenotatiunculae* (P.L., 175, 9–28); *Adnotationes elucidatoriae in libris Regum* (*ibid.*, 95–114); *In Salomonis Ecclesiasten homeliae 19* (*ibid.*, 113–256); *Adnotationes elucidatoriae in Threnos Jeremiae* (*ibid.*, 255–322); *Explanatio in Canticum B. Mariae V.* (*ibid.*, 413–32); *Orationis dominicae expositio* (*ibid.*, 774–89); a commentary on the Epistle to the Hebrews, 4. 12–15, 2 (P.L., 177, 289–94). There are many exegetical portions in the seven books of the *Miscellanea* (P.L., 177, 469–900; Books I and II alone are authentic).

[37] See especially his *Institutiones in decalogum legis dominicae* (P.L., 176, 9–18); the *De B. M. Virginitate* (*ibid.*, 875–6); the *De annunciatione* and the *De assumptione B. M.* (P.L., 177, 656–7 and 1209–22); the *Egredietur* (ed. R. Baron, *Rev. d'ascét. et myst.*, 1955, pp. 269–71); and the *De quinque septenis seu septenariis* (P.L., 175, 405–14), in which he connects the seven deadly sins, the seven requests of the *Pater*, the seven gifts of the Holy Spirit, the seven principal virtues, and the seven beatitudes. In this connection it is to be noted that Hugh, following the tendency that was general until about 1235, makes no distinction between gifts and virtues (see O. Lottin, *Psychologie et morale aux XIIe et XIIIe siècles*, III, Louvain, 1949, pp. 330–59 and 455). The *Summa Sententiarum* (P.L., 176, 41–174) certainly does not appear authentic; see R. Baron, "Note sur l'énigmatique

outline of a *summa* of the whole Christian faith, in the dialogue *On the Sacraments of the Natural Law and the Written Law*[38] and above all in his major work, *On the Sacraments of the Christian Faith*,[39] a sort of introduction to the understanding of Scripture. These "sacraments" are all the holy things spoken of in the Bible and revelation, the economy of salvation, including what we mean today by "sacraments". In the latter work, Hugh sets forth first the *opus conditionis*, that is, all that preceded the Incarnation—God, creation, original sin, the Law; then, the *opus reparationis*, that is, Christ, the Church,[40] the sacraments, eschatology. Hugh's theological thought was strongly christocentric, ecclesial, and sacramental; in this it ran counter to that of the schools and universities, which were preoccupied with problems of metaphysics, anthropology, psychology and morals. Hugh viewed the Christian economy in its historic dimension—and in this he was followed by the Victorines as a group—rather than under these intemporal aspects.[41]

But his theological teaching was not an end in itself; with this theology, deeply rooted in Scripture, was integrated a wealth of spiritual experience. To describe this experience, Hugh had turned to the Pseudo-Dionysius and wrote a commentary on the *Celestial Hierarchy*.[42] His writings also reflect, sometimes with marked emphasis, his preoccupation with the monastic ideal and monastic life. He wrote for the novices a sort of guide book, the *De institutione novitiorum*,[43] explaining that they ought to acquire and possess the "science of true discretion" and to apply it in their use of speech, at table, at study and in obedience. Hugh's chief concern is with prayer[44] and the interior life.[45]

Summa Sententiarum", in *Rech. théol. anc. méd.*, XXV (1958), pp. 6–41; O. Lottin, O.S.B., "A propos des sources de la Summa Sententiarum", *ibid.*, pp. 42–58.

[38] *De sacramentis legis naturalis et scriptae*, P.L., 176, 17–42.

[39] *De sacramentis christianae fidei*, P.L., 176, 173–618. Various aspects of Hugh's theology have been studied especially by H. Weisweiler, S.J.

[40] Cf. J. Châtillon, "Une ecclésiologie médiévale: l'idée de l'Eglise dans la théologie de l'école de St Victor au XII° siècle", in *Irénikon*, XXII (1949), pp. 124–131. The author mentions the relatively inconspicuous place given to the Holy Spirit and to the Blessed Virgin in this ecclesiology.

[41] Cf. M.-D. Chenu, O.P., *La théologie au XIIe siècle*, ch. 3: "Conscience de l'histoire et théologie". Cf. W. A. Schneider, *Geschichte und Geschichtsphilosophie bei Hugo von Sankt Viktor*, Münster, 1933.

[42] *Commentarium in Hierarchiam coelestem s. Dyonisii Areopagitae*, P.L., 175, 923–1154. Cf. R. Roques, "Connaissance de Dieu et théologie symbolique d'après l'In Hierarchiam coelestem de Hugues de St-Victor", in *De la connaissance de Dieu* (*Recherches de Philosophie*, III–IV, Paris, 1958), pp. 187–266.

[43] P.L., 176, 925–75. There is also an *Expositio in Reg. S. Augustini* (c. 881–924) which, like the *De institutione novitiorum*, is probably authentic.

[44] *De meditando* (P.L., 176, 993–8), on the objects of meditation—creatures, Scripture, virtues and vices; *De modo orandi* (*ibid.*, 977–88); on conditions and degrees of prayer; *Soliloquium de arrha animae* (*ibid.*, 951–70; ed. K. Müller in

His doctrine of contemplation is derived from St Augustine[46] and from the Pseudo-Dionysius. The primacy of love, which he lays down as a principle, is thoroughly Augustinian: "One loves better than one understands, and love comes close to the goal while knowledge remains on the threshold."[47] But this love—*o bona caritas! o cara caritas!*[48]—in a way which recalls the Dionysian mysticism, carries us above anything that can be given us by *cogitatio, meditatio, oratio* or *operatio*. Love makes us enter into *contemplatio*, and "Contemplation is a penetration of the intellect which embraces everything in a clear vision", *cuncta in palam habens manifesta visione comprehendit.*[49]

Contemplation must rest on foundations which today we should call "natural", and Hugh, as he considered it, was led to work out a psychology—one that was far richer than that of William of Champeaux or Anselm of Laon, or even that of Peter Abelard.[50] He also linked up contemplation with philosophy, as well as with theology. For him the latter were not purely speculative sciences; they were stages through which a man would pass, leading to an even more faithful reproduction in himself of the divine perfection. Thus Hugh conceived of philosophy as a "wisdom" which participates in God's wisdom, and not as mere knowledge: a wisdom which includes love. Hugh comes to look on philosophy as a meditation on life and death; and if it is that, it is the road that leads to our last end. Philosophy is concerned with the world, which is a mirror

---

the collection *Kleine Texte*, Bonn, 1913), a discourse on the spiritual favours that the soul may experience while awaiting eternity (French translation by M. Ledrus, *Le gage des divines fiançailles*, Bruges, 1923); *De contemplatione et eius speciebus*, of which Hugh may have been the principal author (critical edition by R. Baron, Tournai–Paris, 1958).

45 *De vanitate mundi et rerum transeuntium usu* (P.L., 176, 703–40) treats of the love of God as a remedy for the evils caused by this "vanity" and this "use". In *De arca Noe morali* (P.L., 176, 617–80) the ark is the soul, the Church, and especially wisdom. In the *De arca Noe mystica* (P.L., 176, 681–704) Hugh explains the same doctrine by a symbolism which never varies; the word mystical is often equivalent to "symbolic" or "allegorical". *De operibus trium dierum* (P.L., 176, 811–38) also uses the symbolism of the mystical ark. *De amore sponsi ad sponsam* (*ibid.*, 987–94) describes the mystical union, as does *De laude caritatis* (*ibid.*, 969–76). On Hugh's allegorical expression of certain of his characteristic moral and mystical doctrines, see F. L. Battles, "Hugh of St Victor as a Moral Allegorist", in *Church History*, XVIII (1949), pp. 220–40.

46 In a more general way, his doctrine of salvation, and the fact that he recognizes no theoretical distinction between the natural and the supernatural, are Augustinian in character, according to H. Köster, *Die Heilslehre des Hugos von Sankt Viktor*, Emsdetten, 1940.

47 *In Hierarchiam caelestem*, 6; P.L., 175, 1038.

48 *De laude caritatis*, P.L., 176, 976.

49 *Homilia*, I, 10, 2; P.L., 175, 117.

50 Cf. J. P. Kleinz, *The Theory of Knowledge of Hugh of St Victor*, Washington, 1944. See also R. Javelet, "Psychologie des auteurs spirituels du XIIe siècle", in *Rev. sciences relig.*, XXXIII (1959). Also published Epinal, 1959.

reflecting the perfections of God; and with man, body and soul, in whom all is a harmony (*musica*), reflecting creative wisdom. For that reason philosophy embraces the arts, logic, moral philosophy, and the purely theoretical sciences like mathematics, physics and natural theology. It is a *sapientia inferior*, and as such it is subordinate to the *sapientia superior*, theology proper.

At the centre of the latter is Christ as redeemer, come to heal in us the wounded image of the divine wisdom, and to lead us straight to our goal. Theology is therefore a school of perfection, and so neglects neither reason nor faith. As one reads Hugh, one feels that while his is still a thoroughly monastic theology, yet it also heralds the systematic theology of the thirteenth century.[51]

His philosophy and theology lead spontaneously to mysticism; so much so that at times the two vocabularies seem to be one. The terms—*contemplatio, sapientia,* even *sacramentum*[52]—ascend like Moses climbing Sinai, until they come to signify contact with God.[53] Strictly speaking, contemplation, towards which man tends "on the level of thought as much as on that of life", is of the order of "the experience of divine Reality".[54] The steps in this transition from "knowledge" to "wisdom" are classified and designated differently in Hugh's writings, sometimes even in the same work.

Thus the *De contemplatione et eius speciebus*, a "sort of synthesis of Hugh's thought"[55] (it is not certain that it is his), speaks successively of "seven sendings", "three paradises", "six bonds", "four inspirations", "four winds" and so forth. The reader is tempted to say that Hugh is overdoing symbolic arithmetic. In the last chapter Hugh speaks of the fifth mode of knowing God. Without defining it, he describes the mystical life, chiefly in its effects:

> In that blessed sight, the few who have the happiness of enjoying it in this present life are ravished by the extreme sweetness of tasting God, and no longer look at anything but God. . . . The whole soul is lit up with the splendour of eternal light; it hates sin with a constant and absolute hatred, puts the world into the background, renounces itself, and tends wholly towards God, . . . freed from matter, stripped of all form, freed from every limitation.[56]

[51] Cf. D. Lasič, O.F.M., *Hugonis a Sancto Victore theologia perfectiva. Eius fundamentum philosophicum ac theologicum*, Rome, 1956.

[52] Cf. R. Baron, *Science et sagesse . . .*, pp. 222–3; and, on the various senses of *contemplatio*, p. 192.

[53] Cf. J. Châtillon, "Moïse figure du Christ et modèle de la vie parfaite. Brèves remarques sur quelques thèmes médiévaux", in *Moïse, l'homme de l'alliance*, Tournai, 1955, pp. 305–14.

[54] R. Baron, *Science et sagesse . . .*, pp. 199–200.

[55] *Ed. cit.*, p. 33.

[56] Translated by R. Baron, *De contemplatione . . ., ed. cit.*, appendix, p. 42; Latin text, p. 87.

Three types of contemplation, in which the soul experiences at once both the delights of the spirit and its nakedness, are represented by Job, John and Solomon: suspension, silence, sleep. In each of these stages the *De contemplatione* sees various degrees: suspension (or recollection) of the soul in itself, then in the consideration of what it is, then above itself; next, silence of the mouth, silence of the spirit, and silence of the reason; finally, sleep of the powers, the soul, the memory and the will. The summit to which this ascension leads reminds one of what was later to be called the spiritual marriage; the vocabulary in which it is described is that of the *Canticle of Canticles*, that of the "mystical nuptials" or *Brautmystik*. This contemplation leads to the threshold of the vision of God face to face, *facie ad faciem*.[57]

According to Hugh, the soul mounts in contemplation by illumination and by love, but he lays greater stress on the Augustinian theme of love:

> Faith consists in two things: knowledge and *affectus*. In the latter is found the *substantia* of faith, and in knowledge its *materia*. Faith, by which one believes, is one thing; and the object of faith is another. Faith is found in love, and what it believes in knowledge. That is why the *substantia* of faith is in the *affectus*, for this *affectus* is faith.[58]

This text, which is difficult to translate, says in short that the end of all Christian life is union with God by "affective" faith, in an experience which ultimately is one with love. It would be possible, however, to quote a great many other texts from Hugh's works according to which the soul's intimate contact with God is not a solitary one. The soul, in achieving union, does not lose its essential quality of being a member of Christ and of the Church. It still nourishes its faith, *fides*, on Scripture and the "sacraments" which are given it by Christ and incorporate it in the Church, and this *fides* is, at the same time, *affectus*. There were very few in his time whose genius for synthesis equalled that of Hugh.

4. Richard of St Victor

Richard of St Victor perhaps comes more readily to mind than Hugh when speaking of the school of St Victor, because in fact this

57 There is an analysis of the *De contemplatione* in R. Baron, *Science et sagesse* . . ., pp. 205–8.

58 *De sacramentis*, I, x, 3; P.L., 176, 332. "Duo sunt in quibus fides constat: cognitio et affectus. In affectu enim substantia fidei invenitur; in cognitione materia. Aliud enim est fides qua creditur, et aliud quod creditur. In affectu invenitur fides, in cognitione id quod fide creditur. Propterea fides in affectu habet substantiam, quia affectus ipse fides est."

newcomer made mystical theology his speciality. Although in several aspects of his teaching he did not follow his master he was still, on the whole, a faithful disciple of him whom he called "the chief theologian of our time".

According to some sources Richard seems to have been born in Scotland, and it is not known when he entered St Victor. He became prior in 1162 and died in 1173.[59] His learning and knowledge of antiquity were as encyclopaedic as those of Hugh. But Richard strikes us as being a much more original mind, in the sense that he quotes his predecessors much less, though as a matter of fact he is indebted to them for a great deal—to Hugh above all, but also to Hugh of Fleury, Rhabanus Maurus, the Venerable Bede, Isidore of Seville, Gregory the Great and Augustine.[60]

As a theologian, Richard wrote various *opuscula*,[61] among which the treatise *On the Trinity* is particularly noteworthy.[62] The Trinity is the supreme object of contemplation (he says this also in the two works in which he condensed his spiritual doctrine, the *Benjamin minor* and the *Benjamin major*[63]); but before contemplation must come speculation. Even though the mystery is beyond our power

[59] There is a discussion of the biographical sources and of the known facts by G. Dumeige in his *Richard de St Victor et l'idée chrétienne de l'amour*, Paris, 1952, pp. 165–7.

[60] P.L., 196. To this must be added the *Liber exceptionum*, fragments of which are to be found elsewhere in P.L. (177, 191–284; 175, 633–774 and 789–828; 177, 901–60); critical edition by J. Châtillon, Paris, 1958. It is a sort of treatise which touches upon the liberal arts, geography, history, and exegesis. Richard also left the *Sermones centum* (P.L., 177, 899–1210; cf. J. Châtillon, in *Rev. moyen âge lat.*, IV, 1948, 23–52, 343–66); and the *Tractatus super: Misit Herodes rex manus* (P.L., 141, 277–306). The *De IV gradibus violentae caritatis* (P.L., 196, 1207–24) and the unauthentic *Epistola ad Severinum de caritate* or *De gradibus caritatis* (P.L., 196, 1195–1208), which seems to be by a "Brother Ivo" who was perhaps a Cistercian, have been edited by G. Dumeige, Paris, 1955. A sermon, "Super exiit edictum", often entitled "De tribus processionibus", has been edited, with a French translation, by J. Châtillon, W. J. Tulloch, and J. Barthélemy in *Richard de St Victor, Sermons et opuscules spirituels inédits*, vol. 1, Paris, 1951.

Among the translations that are available are also *Les quatre degrés de l'amour ardent* (French translation by E. Leclef, Paris, 1926) and *Selected Writings on Contemplation* (partial English translation of the two *Benjamin* treatises and other extracts, by C. Kirchberger, London, 1957).

For bibliographies on Richard, see G. Dumeige, *Richard de St Victor . . .*, pp. 171–85; and Châtillon–Tulloch–Barthélemy, *op. cit.*, pp. xv–xviii.

[61] P.L., 196, 991–1074.

[62] P.L., 196, 887–992. Critical edition by J. Ribaillier, Paris, 1958. The treatise has been studied by A.-M. Ethier, O.P., *Le "De Trinitate" de Richard de St Victor*, Paris–Ottawa, 1939; by F. Guimet, "Notes en marge d'un texte de Richard de St Victor" ("*De Trinitate*", Book III, ch. 2; P.L., 196, 916 C–917 B), in *Arch. hist. doctr. litt. moyen âge*, XIV (1943–5), 371–94; by the same, "'Caritas ordinata' et 'amor discretus' dans la théologie trinitaire de Richard de St Victor", in *Rev. moyen âge lat.*, IV (1948), 225–36 (on the *De Trinitate*, Book III, ch. 7); and by T. de Régnon, *Etudes de théologie positive sur la Sainte Trinité*, IV, Paris, 1892, pp. 235–335. French translation by G. Salet, S.J., in the collection "Sources chrétiennes", Paris, 1959.

[63] P.L., 196, 1–202.

of comprehension, *supra et praeter rationem*, nevertheless Richard in the *De trinitate* undertakes to investigate it by the light of reason. In 1153, following Anselm of Canterbury, he began to construct a theology in which he lays down the "necessary reasons" which reveal to the intellect the mysteries of the life of the Trinity. These "reasons" are, actually, arguments from congruity, developments of certain principles: the existence of God, uncaused, *a semetipso*; his supreme perfection, including the existence in himself of every perfection in the highest degree; and finally the fact that God is love. Now, love presupposes plurality. The procession of the Second Person thus becomes a procession of love. That of the Third Person results from the common desire of Father and Son to communicate the delights of their mutual love. This kind of theology is clearly very far from that of Augustine for whom the mode of procession of the Word is intellectual. Richard is thought by some to have been influenced by St Gregory,[64] but even more by Achard, another Victorine whose works as yet are almost all unpublished.[65]

Richard—thorough mystic though he was, and inclined to carry his contemplation to the highest degree—based his description of contemplation on a very shrewd analysis of the faculties of the soul. He studied their mutual relationships and their respective roles in both the mystical life and the moral.[66] His two best-known treatises, the *Benjamin minor* and the *Benjamin major*, describe the journey of the soul towards contemplation.

Love is the starting-point: love rooted in a will wounded by original sin but able with the help of grace to regain its first purity and reach God. This love is none other than the reflection of the supreme love which is the life of the Trinity. This is the connection between the *De trinitate*, the two *Benjamin* treatises, and the treatise (probably authentic) *De quatuor gradibus violentae caritatis*. Love can better be described than defined. "Being the all and the truth of God, it must also be the all and the truth of man."[67] And just as God, supreme love, gives himself to himself and to his creation, so charity, which is a reflection of divine love, gives itself to God and to the creatures to whom God has given himself. The love of God wounds the soul, binds it, makes it languish, and finally causes it to

[64] F. Guimet, *Notes . . ., art. cit.*

[65] Cf. M.-T. d'Alverny, "Achard de Saint-Victor. De Trinitate—De unitate et pluralitate creaturarum", in *Rech. théol. anc. méd.*, XXI (1954), pp. 299–306.

[66] Cf. C. Ottaviano, *Riccardo di Santo Victore. La vita, le opere, il pensiero* (Rome, *Reale Acad. Naz. dei Lincei*, Ser. VI, 4, 1933), pp. 447–501. See also E. Kulesza, *La doctrine mystique de Richard de St-Victor*, Saint-Maximin, 1924 (and in *La Vie spirit.*, Suppl., vol. X, 1924); J. M. Déchanet, art. "Contemplation au XIIe siècle", *Dict. de spirit.*, II, col. 1961–6; J. Beumer, "Richard von Sankt Viktor, Theologe und Mystiker", in *Scholastik*, XXXI (1956), pp. 213–38.

[67] G. Dumeige, *Richard de St-Victor . . .*, p. 157.

swoon. These are the four degrees of a life that transforms the wretched condition of man, appeases the wrath of God, creates an intense spiritual tension and a thirst for God, unites the powers of the soul, kindles the affective powers, binds the memory to the point of paralysing thought, attracts the soul towards recollection and solitude, begets in it a wonder which goes so far as to make it swoon away, so insatiable is its desire, and finally absorbs it in God, transforming it into him by a union of wills[68]:

> All this is wonderful and astonishing. The more a soul dares to hope for from the Lord, the more it humbles itself for the Lord. The higher its boldness takes it, the lower is it brought by humiliation. As the height to which it has dared to rise is far above man, so the depth to which its patience brings it is far below him. As I have said, in the first degree the soul enters within itself. In the second it rises to God. In the third it enters into God. In the fourth it sinks down beneath itself. In the first and second case, it rises up. In the third and fourth it is transformed. In the first it ascends to what it is; in the second it goes beyond this; in the third it is re-formed [*elle se modèle*] according to the splendour of the Divinity; in the fourth it is conformed to the humility of Christ. Or again: in the first is return; in the second, transport; in the third, transformation; in the fourth, resurrection.[69]

Richard's thought was fed by the Bible; even the title of the two *Benjamin* treatises was taken from Psalm 67. 28, "Benjamin in ecstasy of mind", *Benjamin in mentis excessu*. It owed little to philosophy.[70] Even Platonism does not seem to have had much influence on it, unless through Boethius' first commentary on the *Isagoge* of Porphyrus, and perhaps through Proclus.[71] In Richard, nevertheless, love is not a sort of blind affectivity: there must be a thorough preparation for contemplation, and in this a very large place is given to a deep and progressive understanding of the world, the soul, and God. Such a preparation is a "free and wondering

[68] Cf. J. Châtillon, "Les quatre degrés de la charité d'après Richard de St-Victor", in *Rev. d'ascét. et myst.*, XXI (1939), pp. 237–64.

[69] *De quatuor gradibus violentae caritatis*, 47; ed. G. Dumeige, pp. 176–7.

[70] On Richard as an exegete, see B. Smalley, *The Study of the Bible in the Middle Ages*, 2nd ed., Oxford, 1952, pp. 106–11; C. Spicq, O.P., *Esquisse d'une histoire de l'exégèse latine au moyen âge*, Paris, 1944, pp. 128–31.

[71] This was noticed in connection with the *Benjamin major* by J.-A. Robilliard, O.P., "Les six genres de contemplation chez Richard de St-Victor et leur origine platonicienne", in *Rech. Sc. Phil. théol.*, XXVIII (1939), pp. 229–33. Cf. E. von Ivanka, "Zur Ueberwindung des neuplatonischen Intellektualismus in der Deutung der Mystik: intelligentia oder principalis affectio", in *Scholastik*, XXX (1955), pp. 185–94.

penetration of the mind into the realm of wisdom", as *Benjamin major* defines it.[72]

Before becoming "penetration", *perspicacia*, contemplation demands a sustained effort of purification and of training in the virtues. This ascesis is described in the *Benjamin minor* or *De preparatione anima ad contemplationem*. It requires especially self-knowledge, *discretio*, which is the art of guiding oneself; and this art is acquired either by experience in virtue or by the grace of revelation.[73] Discretion takes its origin in reason, as Joseph was born of Rachel: *Joseph de Rachel, discretio de ratione*. Its utility, its properties, its tasks, and even its difficulties show why it is the way of access to contemplation. *Consilium*, which allows one to distinguish what is fitting from what is not, is also important.[74] Contemplation itself consists first in *cogitatio*, then in *meditatio*, and finally in the *contemplatio* of the lower creatures and of the soul itself. Then and only then can the soul lift itself up to God.[75] Richard enumerates in this way six kinds of contemplation, according to the increasing degree of dignity of their object and the mode of knowledge by which they operate.[76] The contemplation of God, before becoming *alienatio* or *excessus mentis*, which is the fruit of grace alone, is *dilatatio mentis*, the fruit of human industry; then *sublevatio mentis*, requiring at once both divine grace and personal effort.[77]

Thus love and knowledge go hand in hand in the *Benjamin* treatises and in the *De quatuor gradibus caritatis*. Because of this Richard's mysticism is "speculative"; a foreshadowing of that of the Rhineland mystical writers almost two centuries later. His spiritual influence was immense; all the later authors who wrote on the "degrees" of the love of God had read him.

But there were deeper resemblances between Richard and Hugh. Neither of them distinguished, as we should do, between the natural order and the supernatural. They take for granted a fundamental continuity between the degrees of the interior life, from its ascetic or strictly intellectual basis to mystical knowledge and love, and to the vision of God. Contemplation, in Hugh's view as in Richard's,

[72] Book I, ch. 4; P.L., 176, 67: an approximate translation of "*libera mentis perspicacia in sapientiae spectacula cum admiratione suspensa*". In almost the same place there is a definition that is a little more intellectualist: "*perspicax et liber animi contuitus in res perspiciendas*". This is the one quoted by St Thomas (*S. Theol.*, II^{a}–II^{ae}, q. 180, a. 3, ad 1).

[73] *Beniamin minor*, ch. 67–71; P.L., 176, 48–51.

[74] *Ibid.*, ch. 48. Cf. *De statu interioris hominis*, I, 24–9; c. 1133–8.

[75] *Benjamin major* or *De gratia contemplationis*, Books 1–4.

[76] Cf. J. Maréchal, S.J., *Essai sur la psychologie des mystiques*, II, Brussels, 1937, pp. 257–61; M. Lenglart, *La théorie de la contemplation mystique dans l'œuvre de Richard de St-Victor*, Paris, 1935.

[77] *Benjamin major*, Book 5. Cf. J. Châtillon, "Les trois modes de la contemplation selon Richard de St-Victor", in *Bull. litt. eccl.*, XLI (1940), pp. 3–26.

has as its object the truth: any truth, not supernatural truth alone. Yet in opposition to scholastic methods that were beginning to appear in their time, truth was not to be reached by induction, still less by deduction, but by meditation and contemplation.

5. *The other Victorines*

After Hugh and Richard, the abbey of St Victor had no more masters of their stature; far from it. Most of the later Victorines turned to fields of learning lower than mystical knowledge: theology and philosophy, the latter including, of course, the whole area of secular knowledge.

Achard (†1171), who became the second abbot of the famous monastery and then bishop of Avranches, was a contemporary of the two great Victorines. As a theologian he wrote chiefly on the dogmas of the Trinity and of christology, and he tended to defend the union of the two natures in Christ against opponents of various schools of thought, chiefly the nominalists, whose teaching had caught men's attention at that time.[78] Until all his works are published it is not possible to estimate his place in the mystical tradition of St Victor. At present the only writings easily available are the *De discretione animae, spiritus et mentis*[79] and two *Epistolae*.[80]

Godfrey of St Victor († after 1194) left a philosophical work in an original form, the *Fons philosophiae*. It is a poem of 836 verses,[81] composed after 1176, in which he goes back over the stages of his education at the University of Paris and gives a picture of his studies in the seven liberal arts and in theology. To this he adds the story of his entrance to St Victor and a description of the stages of his religious life. When speaking of the liberal arts, he is particularly interested in the *trivium*, and above all in dialectic; at the same time, he records that the students preferred the *quadrivium*, which led to more remunerative careers. He reduces the study of theology to the exegesis of the Bible, according to the four classical meanings, and to the study of the Fathers. The *sententiae* and the *quaestiones* do not as yet appear in the curriculum. His allegorical

[78] Cf. J. Châtillon, "Achard de Saint-Victor et les controverses christologiques du XII° siècle", in *Mélanges Cavallera*, Toulouse, 1948, pp. 317–38. There is a note on Achard in P.L.; 196, 1371–4. In connection with these controversies, attention should be called to Gauthier de St-Victor (cf. J. Châtillon, *op. cit.*, p. 321, note 14).

[79] G. Morin, O.S.B., in *Aus der Geisteswelt des Mittelalters, Stud. u. Texte M. Grabmann gewidmet*, Münster, 1935, vol. I, pp. 251–62. Dom Morin had prepared the material for a complete edition and it is to be hoped that those who are carrying on his work (M.-T. d'Alverny for the *De trinitate* or J. Châtillon and Dom Bauer for the *Sermones*) will soon make Achard better known.

[80] P.L., 196, 1381–2.

[81] Edited by P. Michaud-Quantin, Namur, 1956. Some very short fragments are to be found in P.L., 196, 1417–22.

style is not always easy to understand, but the work is worth reading as it gives an idea of the intellectual and spiritual environment of the abbey. It shows, once again, that the school of St Victor was humanistic in its outlook; in this respect, the *Fons philosophiae* is very like Hugh's *Didascalion* and Richard's *Liber exceptionum*.[82] Godfrey wrote also, towards 1185, a *Microcosmus*.[83] In it he reacted against a certain Christian pessimism fairly widespread in his time, which tended to stress the vanity of earthly things and the perversity of fallen man. He holds that the works of the Creator, the dignity of man and his potentialities, do not deserve this contempt, since grace brings man the gifts of faith, interior purification and charity. Though the *Microcosmus* has the outlook of Christian humanism, it is based on the Bible and not on philosophy: it is simply an allegorical exegesis of the first chapters of Genesis. Though it resembles a number of other works of the period it differs from them by its optimism and by its tendency to reconcile Christian humanism with the demands of the mystical life.

The school of St Victor produced no more noteworthy works in the twelfth century, unless we include the *Sequences* of Adam of St Victor (†1192).[84] It was not until the thirteenth century that a spiritual work of some importance appeared there, that of Thomas of St Victor, or Thomas Gallus. He was one of the community of the abbey before 1218, but by 1219, at the request of Cardinal Guala Bicchieri, he, with three other religious, had founded the monastery of St Andrew at Vercelli, and he became its abbot in 1225. In the quarrel between the Guelphs and the Ghibellines, he succeeded in remaining neutral until 1243, but then he was obliged to take refuge in the neighbouring village of Ivrea. He probably died there in 1246.[85]

Almost all his writings are on mystical theology, including his scriptural commentaries, notably the one on the *Canticle*[86]; but his

[82] Cf. P. Delhaye, "L'organisation scolaire au XIIe siècle", *art. cit.*, pp. 242–3.

[83] Edited by P. Delhaye with a theological study, 2 vols, Lille, 1951; this is the best study on the life and work of Godfrey. In addition, the latter left some sermons; in that connection, see P. Delhaye, "Les sermons de Godefroi de Saint-Victor", in *Rech. théol. anc. méd.*, XXI (1954), pp. 194–210.

[84] P.L., 196, 1421–1534. Edited, with a German translation, by F. Wellner, *Adam von S.-V. Sämtliche Sequenzen*, Münich, 1955. There are other editions by C. Blume and H. Bannister, *Anal. Hymnica*, vols LIV–LV, Leipzig, 1914–22; by L. Gautier, Paris, 1894; etc. On the date and on Adam's works, see J. Châtillon, "De Guillaume de Champeaux à Thomas Gallus", in *Rev. moyen âge latin*, VIII (1952), pp. 247–72.

[85] Cf. G. Théry, O.P., "Thomas Gallus. Aperçu biographique", in *Arch. hist. doctr. litt. moyen âge*, XIV (1939), pp. 141–208.

[86] Edited by Pez, *Thesaurus anecdot. noviss.*, II, Augsburg, 1721, col. 501–690. The date of this commentary seems to be about 1223. It was followed by two others. The one in P.L., 206, 18–286 is by another Thomas, the Cistercian Thomas de Vaucelles (1173–89).

chief interest was in commenting upon, and summing-up, the work of the Pseudo-Dionysius. As yet, none of his commentaries are published. The work that has been undertaken to bring them to light is still at the preliminary stage. An inventory of manuscript sources is being drawn up, their authenticity is being studied, and their dates are being established.[87] It is to be hoped that good editions and translations will be published soon.

The importance of the work in progess lies in the fact that it is making clear the place occupied at the time, both in spirituality and in theological research (there are indications of this in the work of the first great Victorines), by a *"Dionysian corpus"*, which was added to from the twelfth to the fourteenth centuries.[88] The *corpus* in question includes a *vetus translatio* of Dionysius by Erigena; the glosses of Anastasius the Librarian; the commentaries of Hugh of St Victor and John Sarrazin; the *Extractio* of Thomas of Vercelli; a commentary and extracts of the *De divisione naturae* of Duns Scotus. In this development Thomas Gallus holds no negligible place. Up to his time the Dionysian mysticism is unadulterated, whereas later the commentators were inevitably influenced by having read Aristotle. In his commentaries, Thomas, following Dionysius, emphasized (as Hugh of St Victor had already done) total darkness, the renouncing of every image in the mind, the "emptiness of the understanding as a condition of union with God".[89]

[87] These studies are those of G. Théry, O.P.: "Les œuvres dionysiennes de Thomas Gallus", in *La Vie spirit.*, Suppl., XXXI (1932), pp. 147–67; XXXII (1932), pp. 22–43; XXXIII (1932), pp. 129–54; "Chronologie des œuvres de Thomas Gallus, abbé de Verceil", in *Div. Thom.* (*Piac.*), XXXVII (1934), pp. 265–277, 365–85, 469–96; "Thomas le cistercien, Le commentaire du Cantique des cantiques", in *New Scholasticism*, XI (1937), pp. 101–27; "Commentaire sur Isaïe de Thomas de St-Victor", in *La Vie spirit.*, Suppl., XLVII (1936), pp. 146–62 (ed. of an extract). There are also, by P. Théry, "Saint Antoine de Padoue et Thomas Gallus", in *La Vie spirit.*, Suppl., XXXVII (1933), pp. 94–115, 163–78; XXXVIII (1934), pp. 22–51; "Thomas Gallus et Egide d'Assise. Le traité De septem gradibus contemplationis", in *Rev. néoscol.*, 1934, pp. 180–90. More recent studies have been by D. A. Callus, O.P., "An Unknown Commentary of Thomas Gallus on the Pseudo-Dionysian Letters, in *Dominican Stud.*, I (1948), pp. 58–73; and by A. Dondaine, O.P., "Un manuscrit de l''Expositio' de Thomas Gallus sur les cinq premières lettres du Pseudo-Denys", in *Rech. théol. anc. méd.*, XVII (1950), pp. 311–15. An edition of this *Expositio* by M.-T. d'Alverny is in preparation. See also her study on "Le second commentaire de Thomas Gallus, abbé de Verceil, sur le Cantique des cantiques", in *Arch. hist. doctr. litt. moyen âge*, XIII (1940–2), pp. 391–402. A good summary of what was known about Thomas Gallus was published in 1946 by P. Glorieux, O.P., in *Dict. théol. cathol.*, XV, 773–7.

[88] In this connection, see H. F. Dondaine, O.P., *Le corpus dionysien de l'Université de Paris au XIIIe siècle*, Rome, 1953. Cf. G. Théry, O.P., "Denys au Moyen Âge. L'aube de la 'nuit obscure'", in *Etudes carmélitaines*, XXIII, II (1938), pp. 68–71; U. Gamba, "Commenti latini al 'De mystica theologia' del Pseudo-Dionigi Areopagita fino al Grossatesta", in *Aevum*, XVI (1942), pp. 251–71.

[89] G. Théry, O.P., "Denys au Moyen Âge . . .", p. 71.

This way of looking at mystical theology presages the anti-intellectual tendency which is found in the *Cloud of Unknowing* in the fourteenth century. At the same time, paradoxically, it is the herald of that negative theology—sprung from Aristotle, his Arabian and Jewish commentators, and the Neo-Platonists—which characterized the speculative mysticism of the Rhineland at the same period; Nicholas of Cusa owned the commentaries of Thomas Gallus. At the beginning of the thirteenth century these new trends, which had a common origin, were closely linked together; the fourteenth century saw here, as in many other fields, a cleavage and a clearly defined opposition between them.

A question which was to become acute a hundred years later can already be asked at the beginning of the twelfth century: to what extent is the tendency towards "rationalism" and a taste for dialectic reconcilable with the spirit of the Gospel?

The scholastic method of theological research which was born in this century was, in fact, a new one. The Master of the Sentences became the chief authority, or at least the necessary starting-point. Hence came the formidable threat, a danger only too real, that the actual reading of the Bible and the Fathers would be forgotten or relegated to a lower level; a foreshadowing of the divorce between theology (now definitely a science) and mysticism, or at least the spiritual life. The province of the latter would then be purely religious sentiment which, at this time, had still a penetrating insight and "taste" of the object of faith; but it was to become a value in itself even to the point of rejecting the intellectual foundations on which it had formerly rested. Soon it would consist in an "unknowing" with a Dionysian flavour, and this would be laid down in principle as a necessary condition for the spiritual ascent.

The case of the Victorines raises, in this respect, a genuine problem, both historical and spiritual. Despite their sincere attachment to the Scriptures, despite a fruitful attempt at an encyclopedic synthesis at every level, they opened the way—no doubt without suspecting it—to a very debatable tendency when they gave so large a place to the teaching of the Pseudo-Dionysius. That they took this position is explained by the extraordinary authority then enjoyed by the Areopagite, that supposed disciple of St Paul. But we today, better informed and with a better knowledge of the Dionysian *corpus* and its origins, may wonder whether they were not unconsciously engaging spiritual tradition on a most perilous course.

II

LAY SPIRITUALITY IN THE TWELFTH CENTURY

1. Devotion to Christ

ONE of the chief characteristics of medieval piety was that it was deeply biblical. In the twelfth century especially, there was a passion for reading the Scriptures, but men were a little on their guard against the spiritual exegesis once so highly esteemed; they took a greater interest in its literal meaning and the historical aspect of salvation. It was therefore natural that devotion to Christ should take a new direction. Historians of spirituality have often held that sensible devotion to the humanity of Christ, and especially to the mysteries of his earthly life that most appeal to the human heart—his birth, his passion, his death on the cross—was in a sense a discovery of the twelfth and thirteenth centuries, above all by St Bernard of Clairvaux, and especially St Francis of Assisi.[1] This view overlooks the fact that there was as ardent a devotion to the Humanity in the early ages of Christianity; it existed also in the East[2] and is particularly notable in Origen.[3]

As has been already noted, the first documentary evidence of a tender devotion to Christ's humanity is found in monastic circles. It even took, at times, forms that seem to us exaggerated, such as

[1] See, for example, P. Pourrat, *La spiritualité chrétienne*, II, pp. 76 and 256. Attention should be called in general to the collection of medieval texts in C. G. Coulton, *Life in the Middle Ages*, 4 vols, Cambridge, 1928–30 (religion, folklore and superstition; chronicles, science and art; men and customs; monks, friars and nuns). There is much useful information in C.-V. Langlois, *La vie en France au moyen âge, de la fin du XIIe au milieu du XIVe siècle*, 4 vols, Paris, 1926–8; and in M. Bloch, *La société féodale*, 2 vols, Paris, 1939–40. In addition there may be mentioned, once and for all, G. Le Bras, "Institutions ecclésiastiques de la chrétienté médiévale", in *Histoire de l'Église* (Fliche–Martin), XII, Paris, 1959.

[2] Cf. A. Dumon, O.S.B., "Grondleggers der middeleeuwse vroomheid", in *Sacris erudiri*, I (1948), pp. 206–24.

[3] Cf. F. Bertrand, *Mystique de Jésus chez Origène*, Paris, 1951. For the history of the devotion to Christ's humanity, see C. Richstätter, S.J., *Christusfrömmigkeit in ihrer historischen Entfaltung. Ein quellenmässiger Beitrag zur Geschichte des Gebetes und des mystischen Innenleben der Kirche*, Cologne, 1949. For the twelfth century, he studies especially St Bernard and the Victorines.

the devotion to the "maternity" of Jesus.[4] It would have been surprising if the faithful had remained untouched by this new trend. Among other convincing indications that they did not, the *Treatise on Sacramental Confession* may be cited. This book was the work of a secular controversialist of the late twelfth century, Peter of Blois (†1200). A passage from it shows how deeply some kinds of sermons on Christ touched their hearers, but the author is a shrewd psychologist. He distrusts the kind of emotion that can be aroused equally well by profane writings: it is not necessarily a proof that the soul is living in the love of God! In this, Peter of Blois is still faithful to the spirit of the Fathers.

> There is no merit in any feeling of devotion [he says] unless it proceeds from the love of Christ. Many of the characters in tragedies and other poems and songs are wise and illustrious and powerful, and excite our love: they have every gift. The actors put before us the trials they endured, the injustices they suffered—as for example those of Artus, Gangan and Tristan—and the audience is moved to tears. Thou art touched by these fables. When thou dost hear our Lord spoken of devoutly and art so moved, hast thou truly the love of God? Thou hast compassion for God: and also for Artus! And in either case thy tears are in vain if thou dost not love God, and thy tears of devotion and penitence flow not from the sources of our Saviour, that is from hope, faith and love.[5]

Devotion to the name of Jesus developed in the Middle Ages: it had not been unknown to antiquity, though in a less explicit way. Up to the time of Francis of Assisi, it was the spoken name of Jesus, to which St Bernard was much devoted. Later it was to be the written name whose liturgical cult in the thirteenth century was propagated by England and most of all in the fifteenth by St Bernardino of Siena (†1444).[6] It may well be that this devotion came into the liturgy because it was more and more widespread among the masses. The celebrated hymn *Iesu dulcis memoria* did much to popularize the love of Christ and the veneration of his holy Name.

[4] This devotion, of which there are hints in ancient times, was made popular by St Augustine's *Oratio* 65. It is found in St Mechtilde of Hackeborn (†1298), Marguerite d'Oyngt (†1310), Juliana of Norwich (†1373), and the Carthusian Helio in the fifteenth century. See A. Cabassut, O.S.B., "Une dévotion médiévale peu connue: la dévotion à 'Jésus notre mère'", in *Rev. d'ascét. et de myst.*, XXV (1949), pp. 234–45.

[5] *Liber de confessione sacramentali*, P.L., 207, 1088–9. Cf. A. Landgraf, "Zeitgenössische Dichtung und Kunst in den theologischen Werken der Frühscholastik", in *Theologica catholica slovaca*, I (1941), pp. 7–15.

[6] Cf. R. Biasiotto, O.F.M., *History of the development of devotion to the Holy Name* (St Bonaventure, N.Y., 1943), especially pp. 27–30 and 35–40.

It is not by St Bernard as was once thought, but by an English Cistercian of the twelfth century.[7]

Dulcis Iesu memoria
Dans vera cordi gaudia
Sed super mel et omnia
Eius dulcis praesentia.

Nec lingua potest dicere
Nec littera exprimere
Expertus novit tenere
Quid sit Iesum diligere.

Then again, the devotion of the laity towards Christ may be deduced from the increasing veneration with which the Blessed Sacrament was surrounded. The custom of the elevation was introduced in the twelfth century. The first juridical mention of it is probably a canon of a synod held at Paris under Bishop Odo (1196–1208),[8] but it seems to be established that this practice was already in existence by then; the *Life* of Elizabeth of Schönau († 1155), in connection with a vision of Christ on the cross, speaks of the elevation of the chalice, doubtless after the consecration[9]; Guibert of Nogent (†1124) seems to allude to an elevation of the Host, in an account which tells of a child who saw the Child Jesus in it.[10] The introduction of this new rite has been interpreted as a reaction against the views of Berengarius or Peter the Cantor, or as a consequence of controversies on the sacraments,[11] though the general public of the twelfth century hardly took a passionate interest in theological discussions. It may well be, however, that a deeper impression was made by the attacks of the Albigensians and by their practices, and that this was one of the factors which made for an increase in devotion to the sacred species.[12] The rite, however, was not adopted at Rome until distinctly later.[13]

There were other signs of devotion to the Eucharist among the

[7] Cf. A. Wilmart, O.S.B., "Le 'jubilus' sur le nom de Jésus, dit de saint Bernard", in *Ephem. Liturg.*, LVII (1943), pp. 3–285. The original poem had only forty-two stanzas; later eighteen others were added. Translations soon became general. According to the manuscripts, the first line is *Dulčis Jesu memoria.*

[8] Cf. Mansi, *Ampl. coll. conc.*, XXII, col. 682, can. 28.

[9] Ch. 4; P.L., 195, 147.

[10] *De pignoribus sanctorum*, I, 2; P.L., 156, 616.

[11] Cf. E. Dumoutet, *Le désir de voir l'hostie*, Paris, 1926. His opinion is followed by P. Browe, S.J., "Die Elevation in der Messe", in *Jahrb. f. Liturgiewiss.*, IX (1929), pp. 20–66; by the same author *Die Verehrung der Eucharistie im Mittelalter*, Munich, 1933; A. Wilmart, O.S.B., *Auteurs spirituels et textes dévots du moyen âge latin*, Paris, 1932, pp. 370–8.

[12] Cf. G. G. Grant, S.J., "The Elevation of the Host: A Reaction to Twelfth Century Heresy", in *Theolog. Studies*, I (1940), pp. 228–50; and G. Barbiero, *Le confraternite del SSmo Sacramento prima del 1539*, Vedelago, 1944.

[13] As is seen in the *Ordo Romanus XIV* (of 1311), ch. 61; P.L., 78, col. 1176.

laity: there were the confraternities of the Blessed Sacrament, the first of which date from the twelfth century; a *Company of Grey Penitents* existed at Avignon in 1226, with the intention of making reparation for the outrages committed against the Blessed Sacrament by the Albigensians; then again, some historians consider that the famous story of the Quest of the Holy Grail, dating from the beginning of the thirteenth century, is to be understood in a eucharistic sense, the Grail being the Eucharist and the quest being the avid seeking after it.[14] It is not at all necessary, however, to explain it in this sense: it is possible to see in it a picture of Cistercian life,[15] or to give it a Marian interpretation.[16]

In spite of their devotion, the people as a whole rarely went to Holy Communion. Their sense of respect for the Eucharist, their fear of sacrilege, and their consciousness of sin kept them away from the altar. This was so marked that the Fourth Lateran Council had to make communion at Easter strictly obligatory.[17] Even on Good Friday the faithful no longer communicated, which was contrary to the prescriptions of the old liturgical books, though at the beginning of the thirteenth century it became the custom by the rubric *"communicat autem solus pontifex* [*et*] *sine ministris."*[18]

Communion seemed so great an act that a long preparation was needed. To prepare himself well, a Christian went to confession, even if the state of his soul did not make this indispensable. Confessions of devotion became more and more general.[19] At the same

[14] Cf. W. Hamilton, "L'interprétation mystique de 'La Queste del saint Graal'", in *Neophilologus*, XXVII (1942), pp. 94–110.

[15] A. Pauphilet, *Études sur la Queste del saint Graal attribuée à Gautier Map*, Paris, 1921. There can be detected in it at least the influence of St Bernard's ideas, according to E. Gilson, *Les idées et les lettres*, Paris, 1932, pp. 55–91.

[16] M.-M. Davy, *Essai sur la symbolique romane* (*XII*e *siècle*), Paris, 1955, pp. 195–201. On *Les Romans du Graal aux XII*e *et XIII*e *siècles*, see the volume of the *Colloques internationaux du Centre national de la Recherche Scientifique*, No. 3, Strasbourg, March 29 to April 3, 1954 (Paris, 1956). See also H.-J. Koppitz, *Wolframs Religiosität*, Bonn, 1959, on Wolfram von Eschenbach († *c.* 1220), the author of the German *Parzival*.

[17] Denz, 437. Local councils had already prescribed communion three or four times a year; e.g. the synod of Gran (Strigonia, Hungary) in 1114 (cf. Mansi, XXI, 100).

[18] Thirteenth-century pontifical, a revision of previous usages made by Innocent III (1198–1216). Cf. M. Andrieu, *Le pontifical romain au moyen âge*, II, Vatican City, 1940, pp. 467–9; B. Capelle, O.S.B., "Le vendredi saint et la communion des fidèles", in *Nouv. Rev. Théol.*, LXXVI (1954), pp. 142–54; P. Browe, S.J., *Die häufiger Kommunion im Mittelalter*, Münster, 1938.

[19] Cf. P. Browe, S.J., "Die Kommunionvorbereitung im Mittelalter", in *Zeitsch. f. Kathol. Theol.*, LVI (1932), pp. 375–415. On the *Adoro te*, A. Wilmart, *Auteurs spirituels . . .*, pp. 361–414. V. Miano, "La confessione di devozione nella scolastica pretridentina", in *Salesianum*, VIII (1946), pp. 177–255. B. Bott–C. Mohrmann, *L'ordinaire de la messe*, Paris–Louvain, 1953, p. 26. G. Le Bras, *Introduction à l'histoire de la pratique religieuse en France*, 2 vols, Paris, 1942–5, gives information on the Middle Ages, especially vol. 1, pp. 36–40, 58–63 and 84–93.

time, there was a great increase in the number of prayers (the *Adoro te* is one of them) bringing out the meaning of every gesture of the Mass; several of them have survived in the present Roman missal, notably at the Offertory.

Faith in the Blessed Sacrament was very strong, and is witnessed to by the increase in the number of "eucharistic miracles", although there had been some previously. According to the accounts of eye-witnesses, they were answers to extraordinary petitions; they confounded priests who were lukewarm, unbelieving, sacrilegious, or blasphemers; they revealed the sacrilegious intentions of Jews bent on profanation; or, again, they protected the Sacred Host in the midst of tempest, fire or flood. One of the most celebrated of these miracles took place at Bolsena in 1263 and was immortalized by Raphael in a fresco in the Chamber of Heliodorus in the Vatican.[20]

As for devotion to the Sacred Heart, in the twelfth century it seems still to have been confined to the monasteries. In one sense, the devotion is as old as Christianity. Since all grace comes from Christ and flows from his love, some of the Fathers had applied the much-debated text of St John: "Out of his belly shall flow rivers of living water" to this mystery, It must be admitted, however, that this text, as far as regards the heart of Christ, is not very pertinent.[21] Not until the twelfth century, with St Bernard, William of St Thierry, and above all Richard of St Victor, was it more explicit.[22] In their way of speaking of it, these writers did not disassociate Christ and his Heart. They knew nothing of that sentimentalism which was to characterize the devotion after the thirteenth and fourteenth centuries. The impetus was then to come from the Cistercian nun Luitgard of Aywières (†1246) and from the nuns of Helfta; Mechtilde of Magdeburg, Gertrude and Mechtilde of Hackeborn, and St Gertrude the Great.[23] It is not at all clear to what extent the

[20] Critical catalogue of these facts by L. Birot, "Apologétique de l'eucharistie", in *Eucharistia*, Paris, 1934, pp. 709–17. Cf. P. Browe, S.J., "Die eucharistische Verwandlungswunder des Mittelalters", in *Römische Quartalschr.*, XXXVII (1929), pp. 137–69; B. Pesci, O.F.M., "Il miraculo di Bolsena", in *Eucaristia*, Rome, 1957, pp. 1025–33.

[21] John 7. 38. In favour of this interpretation, see H. Rahner, S.J., "Grundzüge einer Geschichte der Herz-Jesu-Verehung", in *Zeitschr. Asz. Myst.*, XVIII (1943), pp. 61–83; by the same, "Flumina de ventre Christi. Die patristische Auslegung von Joh. 7. 37–38", in *Biblica*, XXII (1941), pp. 269–302, 367–403.

[22] William of St Thierry, *Meditativae orationes*, 6; P.L., 180, 225–6; Richard of St Victor, *De Emmanuele*, I, 21; P.L., 196, 655. On the history of the devotion to the Sacred Heart, the best recent study is that of Fr P. Debongnie, C.SS.R., "Commencement et recommencement de la dévotion au Cœur de Jésus", in *Le Cœur*, Paris (*Etudes carmélitaines*, 29), 1950, pp. 147–92. On the Sacred Heart in Benedictine tradition, see J. Leclercq O.S.B., "Le Sacré-Cœur dans la tradition bénédictine au moyen âge", in *Cor Jesu*, II, Rome, 1959, pp. 3–28.

[23] See *infra*, ch. VI, §1 (Mechtilde of Magdeburg); ch. VIII, §1 (Gertrude and Mechtilde of Hackeborn, Gertrude the Great).

great mass of the laity was affected by these trends; they are not necessarily evidence of the religious outlook of the ordinary Christian.

The literature of the period, with its mystery plays, miracles and liturgical dramas, tells us more: it shows the underlying tastes of a world which did not have, as ours does, other forms of entertainment. The mysteries, the plays, and the miracles developed particularly during the course of the fourteenth and fifteenth centuries. Their themes were the birth and passion of our Lord Jesus Christ, the miracles of our Lady, or events in the lives of the saints. In these the people, who provided both audience and authors, recognized their own devotion. Before the thirteenth century, religious plays were chiefly liturgical or semi-liturgical, their principal themes being furnished by the mysteries of Easter and Christmas. For liturgists their interest lies not so much in the appearance of the vernacular as in the fact that they were performed in the nave of the church—indeed, even in the sanctuary—by clerics in liturgical dress. They were short, and were made up almost exclusively of fragments borrowed from the liturgy, into which they gradually made their way, skilfully reinforcing its teaching.[24] The events of our redemption, the temporal cycle of the liturgy, were still in the foreground, with no serious competition from the cycle of our Lady's feasts, or devotion to the saints.

The best sculpture and architecture of the period also reflected devotion to the person of Christ. The artists of the time were mostly monks and clerics, and one of them, Suger (†1151), the illustrious abbot of St Denis, described the construction of his abbey church and the means employed, and explained his ideas.[25]

The monks drew their inspiration above all from the Bible, but they did not hesitate to express in their art all that they knew of the world and of nature.[26] The Black Monks were principally respon-

[24] Cf. G. Cohen, *Le théâtre en France au moyen âge*, Paris, 1948; by the same, *Anthologie du drame liturgique en France au moyen âge*, Paris, 1955 (an edition, with commentary, of six plays for the Easter cycle, ten for Christmas, two on lives of the saints, the play of the wise and foolish virgins, and an Easter play); J. Leclercq, O.S.B., "Dévotion privée, piété populaire et liturgie au moyen âge", in *Études de pastorale liturgique*, Paris, 1944, pp. 149–83. In English, see K. Young, *The Drama of the Medieval Church*, 2 vols, Oxford, 1933; for Spain, see R. B. Donovan, *The Liturgical Drama in Mediéval Spain*, Toronto, 1958.

[25] *De consecratione Ecclesiae a se aedificatae*, P.L., 186, 1239–54. This treatise dates from 1143. It has been translated into French by J. Leclercq, O.S.B., *Comment fut construit Saint-Denis*, Paris, 1945.

[26] Cf. E. Mâle, *L'art religieux du XIIe siècle en France*, Paris, 1922. This work is still the source of most of the recent studies in this field. The literature on the subject is very extensive. For bibliographies, see Vol. II of the report of Congrès archéologique of France in 1935, and D. Duret, *Architecture religieuse*, Paris, 1950. See particularly E. de Bruyne, *L'esthétique au moyen âge*, Louvain, 1947; by the same, *Études d'esthétique mediévale*, II, Bruges, 1946; and M.-M. Davy, *op. cit.*

sible for this encyclopaedic trend, and they came into conflict with Cistercian aesthetic ideals, which were dictated primarily by austerity and poverty. The Victorines, following in the footsteps of the Pseudo-Dionysius and of Scotus Erigena, came to have an aesthetic theory of a mystical character, in which the invisible is perceived through what is sensible. The art of the twelfth century reflected the teaching of Scripture and the Fathers.

France was far from being the only country where this development can be seen. In Germany, from the twelfth century to the end of the Middle Ages, writers and artists expressed themselves in a similar way. They respected the human body and the symbolism of nature, and they regarded the Redemption with confidence.[27] Several German poems, some of them very long, were really a synthesis of the history of salvation. They are put forward as illustrations of the *Credo*, or as a kind of *Summa Theologica* in verse.[28] One well-known example of this way of looking at human life and the scriptural account of salvation was the famed *Hortus deliciarum* of Herrade of Landsberg, the Alsatian abbess of Mt St Odile (1167–1195). Its 336 miniatures were unfortunately destroyed in 1870, by the great fire in Strasbourg, and are now known only by descriptions and reproductions. A few modern enlargements can be seen on the walls of the abbey. This particular work does not, of course, reflect a lay mentality, but it shows the general direction that Christian piety was taking. Like the Bible, Herrade's work begins with the Creation, moves to the events of the Old Testament, then treats of Christ and the life of the Church, and closes with the end of the world and the last judgment.[29]

There were many similar works of art and they did not come only from monasteries. Furthermore, the monks, nuns and clerics who produced sculptures, buildings, paintings and verses did not work only for their brethren. The greater part of the time, they were ornamenting the churches frequented by the crowds of the faithful. Their literary works, too, were read in other milieux than their own. All this reveals that devotion to Christ in the monasteries was at

[27] Cf. W. Stammler, "Allegorische Studien", in *Deutsche Vierteljahrsschr. Lituraturwissensch. Geistesgesch.*, XVII (1939), pp. 1–25; A. Landgraf, "Zeitgenössische Dichtung und Kunst in den theologischen Verken der Frühscholastik", in *Theologica catholica slovaca*, I (1941), pp. 7–15.

[28] Cf. H. Rupp, *Deutsche religiöse Dichtunger des 11, und 12. Jahrhunderts*, Freiburg-im-Breisgau, 1958.

[29] Reproductions were published in 1879–99 by A. Straub and G. Keller. A selection of them appears in *Hortus deliciarum. Le "Jardin des délices" de Herrade de Landsberg. Un manuscrit alsacien à miniatures du XIIe siècle*, Strasbourg, 1945; cf. R. Will, "Le climat religieux de l'"Hortus deliciarum' d'Herrade de Landsberg", in *Rev. hist. Philos. relig.*, XVII (1937), pp. 522–66. See *supra*, p. 240, note 84.

bottom very much like that in the world outside. The romanesque painting of the twelfth century has been called "popular liturgical art", in which the dominant note is "the contemplation of the King of Glory, the risen Christ, surrounded by the homage rendered to him by the city of God"[30]; and this is true of other arts besides painting.

2. *Devotion to Mary*

Devotion to Christ brought with it as a matter of course a fresh increase of devotion to Mary. Although this was more popular in character, it nonetheless exercised a real influence on the conceptions of the theologians and great spiritual writers. Mary's pre-eminent place in the Redemption seemed to them to give her a unique title to a special[31] veneration. This was not a case of being carried away by unreflecting piety: that of course was avoided by the more wary spiritual writers and theologians. St Bernard and St Thomas Aquinas even rejected Mary's privilege of the Immaculate Conception. Yet the liturgical cultus of this mystery spread among the people,[32] in spite of the controversies that divided the ranks of the monks.[33] The twelfth-century writers who admitted the privilege differed among themselves in their way of presenting the doctrine, especially in regard to the moment when Mary was sanctified, but all of them conceded to her the state of innocence that existed before the sin of Adam.[34] The doctrine and cultus of the Assumption, for

[30] J. Leclercq, O.S.B., "Un art liturgique populaire", in *Cahiers de l'Art sacré*, II: *Peintures romanes françaises*, Paris, 1945, pp. 17–23.

[31] The veneration called "hyperdulia". Cf. St Thomas, *Summa Theologica*, IIª IIªᵉ, q. 103, a. 4; St Bonaventure, *In III Sent.*, d. 9, a. 1, q. 3.

[32] For all that concerns the history of the cultus of Mary, see *Maria. Études sur la sainte Vierge*, under the direction of H. du Manoir, S.J., Paris, 1949–58 (5 vols have already appeared); the synthesis by J. Leclercq, O.S.B., "Grandeur et misère de la dévotion mariale au moyen âge", in *La Maison Dieu*, XXXVIII (1954), pp. 122–35; and T. Meier, *Die Gestalt Marias im geistlichen Schauspiel des deutschen Mittelalters*, Berlin, 1959. For the Immaculate Conception, see *Maria*, I, pp. 853–4; G. Geenen, O.P., "De voorgeschiedenis van de toewijding der wereld aan het Onbevlekt Hart van Maria", in *De toewijding aan O. L. Vrouw*, Tongerloo, 1944; X. Le Bachelet, art. "Immaculée Conception", in *Dict. théol. cathol.*, VII, col. 995–1042; L. Frias, "La antiguedad de la fiesta de la I.C. en las Iglesias de España", in *Miscell. Commilas*, XXII (1954), pp. 27–88; XXIII (1955), pp. 81–156; R. Laurentin, "L'action du Saint-Siège par rapport au problème de l'Immaculée Conception", in *Virgo Immaculata. Acta congressus mariologici-mariani Romae anno 1954 celebrati*, II, *Acta magisterii ecclesiastici de Imm. B.M.V. Conceptione*, Rome, 1956, pp. 14–18.

[33] A treatise by the monk Eadmer (†1124), the *De Conceptione B.M. Virginis*, had considerable repercussions; P.L., 159, 301–18. It has been translated into French by B. del Marmol, Maredsous, 1923. See H. Barré, "Deux sermons du XIIᵉ siècle pour la fête de la Conception", in *Sciences ecclés.*, X (1958), pp. 341–359 (Rhineland monasteries).

[34] Cf. L. Modrič, O.F.M., "Illustratio privilegii Immaculatae Conceptionis per eiusdem consectaria iuxta doctrinam theologorum saeculi XII", in *Antonianum*, XXXI (1956), pp. 3–24.

which there was the support of authorities that were already time-honoured, was also developing. The manuscripts, a good many unpublished, contain a number of sermons on this subject.[35]

The growing devotion to Mary was reflectetd in the art of the period. A real flowering of such art had taken place as early as the second half of the eleventh century, at the period of Cluny's triumph. Soon, bishops were to build, with the help of whole cities, great cathedrals dedicated to Mary—Romanesque first, then Gothic.[36] Countless churches on a more modest scale, humble chapels in the fields, or at the street-corners, reminded everyone of her watchful presence. The basilicas and places of pilgrimage of Notre-Dame du Puy and Notre-Dame du Port at Clermont[37] are only a few examples among the most famous.[38] The sculpture and painting of this century, too, drew a notable part of their inspiration from Mary.[39]

There, too, Mary was acclaimed "with the same magnificent language as that of the Liturgy",[40] and her divine motherhood[41] was always its centre. Mary and her Son were never separated. Sometimes she is seated in majesty at the side of Christ, as in the mosaic in the apse of S. Maria in Trastevere, set up by Pope Innocent II about 1140; sometimes the Mother is offering the Child to the faithful to be worshipped. The Epiphany, in which she appears as the *Sedes Sapientiae*, became a favourite scene. Stained glass, bas reliefs, tympanums, and statues showed her as the Mediatrix, as the Mother of mercy, dispensing "miracles" like that of the renegade Theophilus. The Assumption and the Coronation began to appear in Western art during the twelfth century, but even in these Mary remains still gentle and accessible to all.

In literature, the same flowering took place.[42] The legends of Mary, the "miracles", had their golden age from the twelfth to the

[35] See *Maria*, I, pp. 645–6. C. Balič, O.F.M., "Codices manuscritos de las bibliotecas españolas en torno a la muerte y asunción de la Virgen", in *Actas del Congresso mariano*, Madrid, 1948, pp. 245–61 (more than 170 Spanish sermons of the thirteenth to fifteenth centuries); by the same, *Testimonia de assumptione B. Virginis Mariae ex omnibus saeculis*, 2 vols, Rome, 1948–50.

[36] Cf. *Maria*, V, pp. 781–90 (Y. Delaporte).

[37] Cf. *Maria*, IV, pp. 113–36 (A. Mabille de Poncheville) and pp. 271–380; M. Vloberg, *Bibliographie des pèlerinages marials de France*.

[38] Cf. *Maria*, IV; E. Baumann, *Histoire des Pèlerinages de la Ste Vierge*, Paris, 1941.

[39] Cf. M. Vloberg, *La Vierge et l'enfant dans l'art français*, Paris, 1954; by the same, "Les types iconographiques de la Vierge dans l'art occidental", in *Maria* I, pp. 483–540, especially pp. 499–502 (an excellent summary); E. Sabbe, "Le culte marial et la genèse de la sculpture médiévale", in *Rev. belge archéol. et hist. de l'art*, XX (1951), pp. 101–25.

[40] Cf. M. Vloberg, "Les types iconographiques . . .", p. 501.

[41] Cf. M. Vloberg, *Les Noëls de France*, Paris, 1953.

[42] Cf. *Maria*, II: various notes on the most important Western literature.

fourteenth centuries: the most famous collection was that of Gautier de Coincy.[43] Mary is of course still a creature, and it would be an exaggeration to see in these sometimes rather naïve tales a sort of deification. Powerful as her mediation and intercession are, it is God who works the miracles.[44] She is the *Sponsa Christi*,[45] the matchless Lady. She is queen, and reigns with Christ:

> The flower is she, she is the rose;
> Of archangels is Queen.
> Mistress is she of heaven and earth,
> Of the air and of the sea.
> Loved will she be of all the world.[46]

There is no doubt of the profound faith of the Christendom of those days in Mary our Mother, ever protecting us. It may well be that devotion to the heart of Mary grew up along these lines.[47]

To this evidence we may add that of the popular prayers to Mary which were ever more widespread about the twelfth century. The *Ave Maria* was possibly derived both from the account of the Annunciation and Visitation according to St Luke and the Offertory for the fourth Sunday of Advent, which was already in the antiphonaries of the eighth and ninth centuries.[48] It then became the type of popular prayer in exaltation of Mary and her motherhood —so much so that the Council of Paris, held at the end of the twelfth century under Bishop Odo, directed the clergy to teach it

[43] Cf. A.-P. Ducrot-Granderye, *Etudes sur les Miracles Nostre-Dame, de Gautier de Coincy*, Helsinki, 1932 (with a good bibliography). There is a rather mediocre translation by A. Poquet, *Les miracles de la Sainte Vierge . . . par Gautier de Coincy*, Paris, 1857. Another collection of similar miracles, of the twelfth and thirteenth centuries, from the manuscript Barcelona Arch. Couronne d'Aragon, Ripoll 193, has been published by C. Baraut, O.S.B., "Un recueil de miracles de Santa Maria", in *Maria-Ecclesia, Regina et mirabilis* (Scripta et Documenta, 6, Montserrat, 1956), pp. 127–60. See also R. W. Southern, "The English Origins of the 'Miracles of the Virgin'", in *Mediaeval and Renaissance Studies*, 4 (1958), pp. 176–216.

[44] Cf. M. V. Gripkey, *The Blessed Virgin Mary as Mediatrix in the Latin and Old French Legend prior to the Fourteenth Century*, Washington, 1938.

[45] Cf. A. Pidanti, "'Sicut sponsa ornata monilibus suis . . .' Maria come 'Sponsa Christi' nella teologia fino all'inizio del sec. XIII", in *Euntes docete*, VII (1954), pp. 299–311.

[46] Gautier de Coincy.

[47] Cf. A. Piolanti, "Mater unitatis. De spirituali Virginis maternitate secundum nonnullos saec. XII scriptores", in *Marianum*, XI (1949), pp. 423–39; H. Barré, "Une prière d'Ekbert de Schönau au saint Coeur de Marie", in *Ephem. mariologicae*, II (1952), pp. 409–23 (twelfth century); *Maria*, I, pp. 825–73 (G. Geenen, O.P.), 573–618 (T. Koelher, G.-M. Roschini).

[48] Cf. R.-J. Hesbert, *Antiphonale missarum sextuplex*, Brussels, 1935, p. 11; see also pp. 8–9 and 44–5. This offertory may have been composed in the seventh century for a new feast of the Annunciation (pp. xxxviii–xxxix). On the history of the *Ave Maria*, see H. Thurston, S.J., *Familiar prayers. Their Origin and History*, London, 1953, ch. VI.

to the people, with the *Pater* and the *Credo*.[49] The "Psalter of Mary", the origin of our rosary, began to spread at this time.[50] The themes of the *Ave Maria* were expressed in a series of hymns. Other compositions—sequences, antiphons, "salutations" to Mary—were influenced by the celebrated Byzantine Akathistos, which had been translated at the end of the eighth century: its themes of *Ave, Gaude, Salve* appear again in these hymns. This was especially the case from the eleventh century onwards, when the antiphons of our Lady that we still read in the breviary were composed: the *Alma redemptoris Mater* by Hermanus Contractus, a monk of Reichenau (†1054); the *Ave regina caelorum*; and especially the *Salve Regina*, long attributed to the Bishop of Puy, Adhémar de Monteil (†1094). The *Regina caeli* is of later date.[51]

Among medieval French poems, one of singular delicacy is the trope *Quant li solleiz*, which sings of the meeting of Mary and Christ at the time of the Assumption. Its setting and its inspiration were taken from some of the themes of the Canticle of Canticles and the liturgy. It extols the beauty of Christ and of Mary. For the latter, it draws the old parallel between her and Eve, and sees her prefigured in the Old Testament.

Li miens amis, il est de tel parage
que neuls om n'en seit conter linnage
de l'une part.
Il est plus genz que solleiz en ested,
vers lui ne pued tenir nulle clartez,
tant par est bels.[52]

[49] Mansi, *Ampl. coll. conc.*, XXII, col. 681, can. 10. The second part of the *Ave Maria* would seem to have originated in Italy in the fourteenth century; cf. Thurston, *loc. cit.*, and C. Cecchelli, *Mater Christi*, IV, Rome, 1954, pp. 374–6.

[50] C. Cecchelli, *loc. cit.*, pp. 391–5. The little office of our Lady and the consecration of Saturday to her veneration seem to date from the ninth to the eleventh century. In the twelfth, her litanies appear; cf. L. Gougaud, O.S.B., *Dévotions et pratiques ascétiques du moyen âge*, Maredsous, 1925, ch. IV.

[51] See Thurston, *op. cit.*, ch. VII–VIII. On the whole medieval literature derived from the *Akathistos*, see G. Meersseman, O.P., *Der Hymnos Akathistos im Abendland*, I, Akathistos-Akoluthie und Crusshymnen, Fribourg, 1958; by the same *L'hymne acathiste en l'honneur de la Mère de Dieu* (Greek text, translation, and introduction), Fribourg, 1958. On the Byzantine *Akathistos*, cf. *Maria*, I, pp. 259–65. Texts of medieval hymns to our Lady are to be found in F. J. Mone, *Lateinische Hymnen des Mittelalters*, II, Freiburg-im-Breisgau, 1854; and in G. M. Dreves, *Analecta hymnica medii aevi*, vols 30 and 31.

[52] Ed. H. Lausberg, "Zum altfranzösischen Assumptionstropus 'Quant li solleiz'", in *Festschrift J. Trier*, Meisenheim, 1954, pp. 88–147. Attention should be called to the texts and poems collected and translated into modern French by R. J. Hesbert, O.S.B., and E. Bertaud, O.S.B., *L'Assomption de Notre-Dame*, I, *Des origines au XVIe siècle*, Paris, 1952; for the twelfth century and the end of the Middle Ages, pp. 109–425. On the interpretation of the Canticle in the twelfth century, see the excellent work by F. Ohly, *Hohelied-Studien. Grundzüge einer Geschichte der Hoheliedauslegung des Abendlandes bis um 1200*, Wiesbaden, 1958.

Twelfth-century devotion never separated Mary from Christ, but it became a little more tender and full of wondering awe when there is a question of her who is all-beautiful, who was greeted by the angel as full of grace, and whom Elizabeth called blessed among women. As yet, this admiration was wholly governed by its object. The psychological echoes it could awaken were not yet as important as they were soon to become.

3. Saints, Angels and Demons

Popular medieval piety was very superstitious in what concerned saints, angels and demons, and in this respect the twelfth century was no different from any other. The saints still "took possession of places as they were converted, and became their patrons. Sometimes the place already had a native name which disappeared; elsewhere, the name of the saint is the first known one; in other places, one saint succeeded another in the same spot."[53] Countless localities thus received names that testify to the devotion of their inhabitants to particular saints. The popularity of certain patrons, like St Martin, St John the Baptist, and St Michael, was tremendous; that of others was local. The pilgrimages to St James of Compostela, to Vézelay, and to the Saintes-Maries were inspired by ardent devotion. Too often, however, more or less sordid interests were mingled with it—the avarice of the clergy and the monasteries, and the legitimate claims of the laity; for in the trade that grew up around these centres of pilgrimages laymen found some compensation for the services rendered to the clergy. Crowds were drawn to tombs like that of St Thomas Becket at Canterbury. Devotion to the angels, to St Michael in particular, make up part of the same picture. As with Mary, there was an abundance of sculptures, paintings, bas-reliefs and stained-glass windows exalting the saints and angels, depicting their striking acts and their miracles.

In the twelfth century, the golden age of the *Vitae* had passed. Although they were still being written, and often with greater artistry than in the past, yet they are stereotyped and of no great historical value.[54] They are, however, evidence of great faith in the intercession of the saints, as well as enthusiastic admiration for them, but also, unfortunately, of a mentality that degraded legitimate venera-

---

It is noteworthy that the principal commentators at that time were to be found in France and in England.

[53] P. Séjourne, art. "Saints (culte des)", in *Dict. théol. cath.*, XIV, c. 939. Cf. R. Foreville, *Du premier concile du Latran à l'avènement d'Innocent III* (*Histoire de l'Église*, Fliche–Martin, vol. IX, 2, Paris, 1944), pp. 355–6.

[54] On the hagiographical literature of the twelfth century, cf. J. de Ghellinck, S.J., *L'essor de la littérature latine au XII*[e] *siècle*, 2nd ed., Brussels, 1954, pp. 388–394 and 403–11.

tion to the level of a superstition, where the only motive was strictly utilitarian. Relics were looked on as a concrete form of supernatural aid, and became mascots to be carried on one's person, or touched. Hence the traffic carried on in them. Owing to the Crusades, Constantinople became the great centre of this lucrative business, and the Holy Land an inexhaustible mine of relics. The Holy Blood of Bruges, for example, was brought back from there in 1149 by the Count of Flanders, Thierry of Alsace. It was only a step from this to the theft of relics and then to the production of bogus ones.[55] Their veneration sometimes gave rise to festivities disapproved of by ecclesiastical authority: a council at Avignon in 1209 had to forbid dances, races and games unsuitable to churches.[56]

The *Vitae* of contemporary saints, on the other hand, have the advantage of being more reliable. There were people alive who had known St Bernard and St Norbert, and their accounts restrained biographical fantasies. This was also true of Thomas Becket who was murdered on 29 December 1170 for having opposed Henry II and for having faithfully done his duty as archbishop. Before long many miracles took place at his tomb, the most spectacular of which was the public repentance of Henry II himself. The day after this memorable scene took place, 13 July 1174, his armies won a brilliant victory over the Scots, which was taken as a sign of heaven's forgiveness. Very soon Thomas's secretary, John of Salisbury (†1180), and many others, recorded the tragedy in writing.[57] There were other biographies produced by dependable witnesses, such as the *Vita Caroli comitis* written by Gautier of Thérouane the year after the murder of Charles the Good, Count of Flanders (†1127), and the *Passio Caroli* by Gualbert of Bruges.[58]

Sermons to the praise of the saints naturally were not as much concerned with historical accuracy: they simply adapted a scriptural or liturgical text to some aspect of the saint's personality or to some episode of his life.[59]

[55] Cf. H. Silvestre, "Commerce et vol de reliques au moyen âge", in *Rev. belge philolog. hist.*, XXX (1952), pp. 721–39.

[56] Mansi, XXII, col. 791, can. 17.

[57] Cf. R. Foreville, *L'Eglise et la royauté en Angleterre sous Henri II Plantagenet (1154–1189)*, Paris, 1943, pp. 163–368; by the same, in *Histoire de l'Église* (Fliche–Martin), IX, 2, pp. 83–126. There is a literary treatment of the theme by R. Speaight. The *Vitae* are to be found in *Rolls Series*, 67, vols I–IV, London, 1875–9 (J. C. Robertson); and in P.L., 190. Cf. J. de Ghellinck, *op. cit.*, pp. 172–7; M. Walberg, *La tradition hagiographique de saint Thomas Becket avant la fin du XIIe siècle*, Paris, 1929. On the veneration of this saint in the Middle Ages, see R. Foreville, *Le Jubilé de saint Thomas Becket, du XIIIe au XVe siècle (1220–1470). Étude et documents*, Paris, 1958.

[58] P.L., 166, 901–1046; or *Acta Sanctorum*, March, I, pp. 163–219; cf. J. de Ghellinck, *op. cit.*, pp. 187–95; J.-M. de Smet, art. "Charles le Bon", in *Dict. hist. géogr. eccl.*, XII, pp. 483–6.

[59] On preaching in the twelfth century, see J. de Ghellinck, *op. cit.*, pp. 173–230.

There were more holidays of obligation. Sundays, feasts of our Lord and our Lady, the apostles, John the Baptist, Stephen, the Holy Innocents, Sylvester, Laurence, Michael, Martin, All Saints, the Dedication, and the Rogation Days became part of people's devotional life by the mere fact that there was no work done on these days; yet at this stage the feasts of the saints had not begun to compete with the feasts of the seasons in the Church's year: it was only later that there was the abnormal growth in the number of feasts of saints, against which the reforms of Pius V, Pius X and Pius XII reacted so energetically. Processes of law were coming into force with regard to the culture of the saints; in the twelfth century the norms for canonization were being laid down. The *vox populi* no longer sufficed, as it had done in ancient times and during the early Middle Ages; nor did episcopal approval suffice, as in the tenth and eleventh centuries. The popes were beginning to reserve the matter to themselves.[60] Alexander III, in 1170, declared that the privilege of decreeing public veneration of a saint belonged to Rome alone. He did not intend, however, to give dogmatic force to such decrees, as though they constituted a positive declaration that the person concerned was in heaven. His aim was only to check abuses such as the canonization of a "martyr" who had been killed or executed when he was drunk, *in potatione et ebrietate occisus*. The measure was simply a disciplinary one. It is clear also that the theologians avoided the tone of the *Vitae* and the popular preachers. All that they actually say is that the saints have merited for us and that they intercede for us.[61]

If the veneration of saints can easily degenerate, the fear of the devil lends itself even more readily to superstition. As Marcel Bloch has pointed out:

> How could it be supposed that the explanation of a nature so decried could be inherent in itself? Its appearance down to the last detail was held to be illusory, and its phenomena the work of hidden wills. "Wills," not a will, if one was to believe the simple-minded, and even many of the learned. For below the one God, and subject to his almighty power—though usually it was not altogether clear how far that subjection went—the ordinary run of men saw a crowd of saints, angels, and devils especially in a perpetual warfare of opposing wills. "Who is there who does not know", wrote the priest Helmold (*Chronica Slavorum* I,55),

[60] Decretal *Audivimus* (ed. Friedberg, II, col. 650). On the history of canonizations, see E. W. Kemp, *Canonization and Authority in the Western Church*, Oxford, 1948; S. Kuttner, "La réserve papale du droit de canonisation", in *Rev. histor. droit français et étranger*, XVII (1938), pp. 172–228.

[61] So Hugh of St Victor, *De Sacramentis*, II, pp. 16, 7–11 (P.L., 176, 594–6); Peter Lombard, *IV Sent.*, dist. 45.

"that wars, whirlwinds, pestilences, and indeed all the evils which fall upon mankind happen by the ministry of demons?" Wars, be it noted, are put side by side with storms: social misfortunes and what we should call natural accidents are on the same level. Whence an attitude of mind which has already been revealed by the history of invasions: not precisely a renunciation, but a turning towards what are thought to be more effective means of action.[62]

Thus a legitimate veneration of the saints and a well-justified fear of Satan were mingled in the Middle Ages with popular superstition; the fact is not surprising, considering that superstition has not disappeared today. The theologians of the time, and their predecessors, spoke of the devil in very sober terms. Peter Lombard confined his teaching on the subject to a few points: the incorporeity of the angels, whether fallen or not; the original goodness of the demons; their trial; their fall through pride, and their action upon men, permitted by God.[63] Clear-headed writers, without actually attacking the more degraded forms of religion, deliberately ignored them; they did not forget the real meaning of dogma, or lose plain common sense.

4. *Towards the Poverty of the Gospel*

Ardent reading of the gospels and fervent meditation upon them went side by side with a tender devotion to the sacred Humanity. Reflection on the mysteries of Christ's nativity and passion led a good many of the faithful to examine their own personal response to his teaching. Parallel with this movement of the laity, and affecting it, were the Gregorian reforms and the new religious foundations. All tended towards a purer Christianity and a more naked spirituality, less involved in institutions and a traditional framework that had become conventional and factitious.

Here and there the idea sprang up that, after all, the Gospel is the only norm, the only *regula*, for a Christian. The moralist Gerhoh of Reichersberg (†1169), while fighting for an obligatory, common life for the clergy, laid this down in his first work, *De aedificio Dei*:

> Every man who at his baptism has renounced the devil with his pomps and his suggestions, even if he never becomes a clerk or a monk, has nevertheless renounced the world which is alto-

[62] M. Bloch, *La société féodale. La formation des liens de dépendance*, Paris, 1939, pp. 134–5.

[63] See the article "Démon" in *Dict. de spirit.*, III, col. 212–31. For Peter Lombard, see *II Sent.*, dist. 3–8.

gether of the Evil one, his very "pomp" itself. Yet every Christian has renounced his pomps. Thenceforward let those who use this world be as though they used it not. Thus rich and poor, noble and serf, merchant and peasant, all and every one who professes himself a Christian, must cast away everything inimical to that name, and follow what is conformable to it. Every class, every profession without exception, possesses in the Catholic faith and the teaching of the apostles a rule suited to his own circumstances, and, by fighting as it behoves it under this rule, will obtain the crown.[64]

Stephen of Muret, who founded the "Poor men of Christ"—the group that was later to become the Order of Grandmont—for his part taught, "If anyone asks what is your religious profession, your rule, your order, answer that it is the first and principal rule of the whole Christian religion: the Gospel, the source and principle of all the others."[65] This was echoed a few decades later by Jacques de Vitry (†1240): "We consider as Regulars not only those who renounce the world and enter religion, but all the faithful of Christ who serve the Lord under the rule of the Gospel and under the one supreme Abbot."[66]

This new consciousness had tremendous consequences in every field. From that time on, moral and pastoral theology was to distinguish the duties pertaining to the different states of life,[67] and Christian perfection would no longer be exclusively for spiritually privileged castes.[68]

The spiritual was, however, only one aspect of a wider movement. In the feudal society of the twelfth century, the municipalities were beginning to be conscious of their power, and both individuals and corporations were determined to assert their rights.[69] The

[64] Ch. 43; P.L., 194, 1302. This version of the treatise seems to date from 1138–1139; cf. D. van den Eynde, O.F.M., *L'œuvre littéraire de Gerhoh de Reichersberg*, Rome, 1957, pp. 13–19.

[65] "Sermo de unitate diversarum regularum", in Martène, *De antiquis Ecclesiae ritibus*, IV, Venice, 1783, p. 308. There is an analysis by J. Becquet, "La règle de Grandmont", in *Bull. Soc. archéol. et histor. du Limousin*, LXXXVII (1958), pp. 9–36. Extracts have been translated into French by L. Génicot, "Présentation de saint Etienne de Muret et de la pauvreté", in *La Revue Nouvelle*, XIX (1954), pp. 578–89.

[66] *Libri duo, quorum prior Orientalis ... alter Occidentalis Historiae nomine inscribitur*, Douai, 1597, p. 357.

[67] On the precise meaning of *ordo* and *status*, see M.-D. Chenu, O.P., *La théologie au XIIe siècle*, Paris, 1957, pp. 241–3.

[68] Cf. P. Delhaye, "La place de l'éthique parmi les disciplines scientifiques du XIIe siècle", in *Miscellanea moralia ... A. Janssen*, I, Louvain, 1948, pp. 29–44; by the same, "L'enseignement de la philosophie morale au XIIe siècle", in *Med. Studies*, XI (1945), pp. 77–99.

[69] Cf. E. Werner, *Pauperes Christi: Studien zur sozial-religiösen Bewegungen im Zeitalter des Reformpapsttums*, Leipzig, 1956; the author writes as a "historical materialist" (see esp. p. 10); his point of view therefore is one which does not

organization of the land and serfdom were not simply feudal questions. The lands owned by the Church, and particularly those of the Cistercians, played an important role in the transformation of agriculture. Often this was beneficent: the white monks carried on work of clearing the land that had been begun by their Benedictine forebears.[70] But, like the black monks, their property became too great.

There are innumerable writers of the period who denounce the most obvious and most detestable vices of the clergy, both secular and regular. Greed comes first,[71] and only too often it is accompanied by incontinence.[72] This is not to say that the mass of the faithful were any better. In his youth the future Pope Innocent III (†1216) viewed his contemporaries with a very pessimistic eye. His treatise *On the misery of man's condition* (before 1195) describes, from birth to death, the moral wretchedness of man—his vices, his pride, and the punishment that awaits him in the next world. All this did not prevent Innocent from working courageously to reform the Church, organizing the Fourth Crusade, calling the Lateran Council of 1215, and approving the mendicant orders.[73]

Thus the popular reactions of the twelfth century, which were sometimes violent, had not only a political bearing: the Church was too much bound up with the ruling and money-making classes. The ground-swell that was rocking them was bound to affect her too; the same mobs who crowded round the walls of the castles also surrounded the cathedrals, the bishops' palaces, and the abbeys.

---

command universal agreement. See also A. Mens, O.F.M. Cap., "Innerlijke drijfveeren en herkomst der kettersche bewegingen in de Middeleeuwen. Religieus ofwel sociaal oogmerk?" in *Miscellanea historica . . . L. van der Essen*, I, Brussels, 1947, pp. 299–313; and vol. III of the *Relazioni . . . del X Congresso Intern. Scienze storiche*, Florence, 1955, section on *Movimenti religiosi popolari ed eresie nel medioevo*.

[70] Cf. H. Pirenne, *Histoire économique de l'Occident médiéval*, Paris, 1950, pp. 219 *et seq.*: A. Mens, *art. cit.*

[71] Cf. *Histoire de l'Église* (Fliche–Martin), X, pp. 388–9.

[72] Cf. can. 21 of the First Lateran Council (1123), declaring null the marriages of clerics (subdeacons and higher orders) and monks, and forbidding their concubinage (Mansi, XXI, 286; cf. Friedberg, I, col. 100); can. 7–8 of the Second Lateran Council (1139) (Mansi, XXI, 527–8; Friedberg, I, col. 1059). Gratian collected all the testimony on the subject from the Fathers and councils, sometimes exaggerating their real bearing. The obligation of celibacy for clerics *in majoribus* began to be established in his time. This was to be repeated by Alexander III (†1181; Friedberg, II, 684–5) and Celestine III (†1198; P.L., 206, 1254). On the situation in England, see C. N. L. Brooke, "Gregorian Reform in Action: Clerical Marriage in England, 1050–1200", in *Cambridge Histor. Journal*, XII (1956), pp. 1–21; cf. *ibid.*, pp. 178–88.

[73] *De miseria humane conditionis*, ed. M. Maccarone, Lugano, 1955. Cf. W. Will, "Innocent III und sein Werk 'Uber das Elend des menschlichen Daseins'", in *Humanismus*, Leyden, 1953, pp. 125–36; E. Binns, London, 1931; A. Fliche, *Histoire de l'Église*, X, pp. 11–215. Innocent's works are in P.L., 214–17; A. Luchain, 6 vols, Paris, 1904–8.

Their various reactions were not always bad for the Church; a great many of the faithful were seeking to practise the Gospel better while remaining within the limits of orthodoxy, of the social structure, and of that minimum of conformity that is presupposed by tradition, sacramental life and hierarchy. The leaders of the Church were themselves stimulated to a more evangelical life. On the whole, the Christians of the twelfth century were tending towards a "new balance between nature and grace".[74] What were the influences that led them in that direction? It has been suggested that they were haunted by the ideal of evangelical poverty, of the "apostolic life" of the early Christians, and certain historians have claimed that this return to poverty was the common denominator of all the new movements, from Robert of Arbrissel and Norbert of Xanten to Francis of Assisi, including Stephen of Muret and the various confraternities (to be discussed later) and other more suspect groups.[75] There is certainly a great deal of truth in this interpretation of the facts, and it may be accepted provided we admit that there were other influences of a secular nature—economic and social contingencies.

Wherever the normal pattern of communities in the Church persisted—dioceses, parishes,[76] monasteries, chapters, confraternities—it seems undeniable that orthodoxy was not seriously threatened. On the other hand, wherever the faithful were seeking to escape from it, they were in danger of losing their spiritual balance and ultimately their orthodoxy. People often tended towards a "private interpretation" of the Gospel. This explains why Western Christianity, when confronted by poverty or, possibly, by the Gospel and its ideal of absolute nakedness, presents a complex picture. On the one hand there were the solid religious organizations; they remained perfectly orthodox, and those of the faithful who did not belong to them were very ready to accuse them of betraying the Gospel. On the other hand, there was a swarm of small groups who wished, for various reasons, to practise the Gospel in all its purity but who easily foundered in heresy. Their

[74] Cf. M. D. Chenu, O.P., *op. cit.*, pp. 244 *et seq.*

[75] Notably H. Grundmann, *Religiöse Bewegungen in Mittelalter. Untersuchungen über die geschichtlichen Zusammenhänge zwischen der Ketzerei, den Bettelorden und der religiösen Frauenbewegung im 12. und 13. Jahrhundert und über die geschichtlichen Grundlagen der deutschen Mystik*, Berlin, 1935. See also E. W. McDonnell, "The 'Vita Apostolica': Diversity or Dissent", in *Church History*, XXIV (1955), pp. 15–31.

[76] Among many studies on medieval parishes—often of a local nature—may be mentioned R. A. R. Hartridge, *A History of Vicarages in the Middle Ages*, Cambridge, 1930; much information in E. Lesne, *Histoire de la propriété ecclésiastique en France*, 8 vols, Lille, 1910–43; G. le Bras, *op. cit.* (see *supra*, note 19); and the works mentioned in note 1.

spirit was not altogether sound, and they were much in the limelight, as can be seen from references to them in contemporary documents.

The tendency to break away from social patterns infected everyone to a greater or lesser degree. Some of the foremost writers of the period declared that charity at a certain level in the soul, by the mere fact that it is present by grace, has nothing to fear from temptation. This comes close to the "illuminism" which eliminates all effort on the part of the soul and rejects the sacraments and the society of brethren as its support in spiritual warfare. A man like Stephen Langton, seeing the danger, while he reaffirmed the part played by divine grace and charity,[77] demanded of the Christian an unceasing vigilance and a constant effort. It is easy to see where such optimism could lead. To many, the Holy Spirit, one of whose gifts is the fear of the Lord,[78] set men free from all fear, all servitude, and all conflict.

5. *Unrest and Heresy*

A detailed study of the various heretical movements of the twelfth century does not properly belong to a history of spirituality, but rather to the general history of the Church[79]; if they are mentioned here, it is because they reveal a certain spiritual trend. There was a sense that something was lacking: men were seeking for the life of the Gospel in the Church, the "apostolic" life of primitive Christianity, and were not finding it. Parallel with the pursuit of this ideal ran other motives: an antagonism to the clergy, and demands for reforms in the social sphere: the movements were not therefore solely spiritual. Moreover, though the agitators were not wholly in the wrong, their persistence unfortunately degenerated into pride. By accusing others of betraying the Gospel one ends in betraying it

[77] Cf. A. Landgraf, "Caritas und Widerstand gegen die Versuchungen nach der Lehre des ausgehenden 12. und beginnenden 13. Jahrhunderts", in *Gregorianum*, XXIV (1943), pp. 48–61, 327–46.

[78] Cf. A. Landgraf, "Die Lehre der Frühscholastik von der knechtischen Furcht", in *Div. Thomas (Fr.)*, XV (1937), and XVI (1938).

[79] There is a collection of documents on these heresies, especially those of the Waldensians and Cathari, in I. von Döllinger, *Beiträge z. Sektengeschichte des Mittelalters*, 2 vols, Munich, 1890. Survey by H. Grundmann, *Religiöse Bewegungen ...*; E. Aegerter, *Les hérésies du moyen âge*, Paris, 1939; E. Dupré-Theseider, *Introduzione alle eresie medioevali*, Bologna, 1953; R. Manselli, *Studi sulle eresie del secolo XII*, Rome, 1953; R. Morghen, *Medioevo christiano*, Bari, 1951, pp. 212–86; by the same, "Movimenti religiosi popolari nel periodo della riforma della Chiesa" [especially the eleventh century], in *Relazione del ... X Congresso Intern. Sc. storiche*, III, Florence, 1955, pp. 333–56; H. Grundmann, "Eresie e nuovi ordine religiosi nel secolo XII" [in German], *ibid.*, pp. 357–402; *Histoire de l'Église* (Fliche–Martin), IX, 1, pp. 91–102; 2, pp. 330–51; X, pp. 112–138 and 291–340.

oneself. One forgets that it teaches humility and love, and the human means it employs are often unexpected ones. If, then, those accused of betrayal retaliated and with a good conscience set in motion the machinery of human justice, the result was bound to be fratricidal conflicts and wars of religion or the Inquisition.

Those who were discontented did not immediately question any dogmatic truths, as had been done in the past, or more recently by Berengarius of Tours, who attacked the dogma of the Eucharist. At first they were not interested in abstract discussions; that came later. Their only desire was to go back to primitive Christianity. Gregory VII, Bernard of Clairvaux, and later Francis of Assisi and Dominic, believed it was possible to bring this about inside the Church, and this saved them from error and illuminism. Others were less wise. The heretics were not exclusively laymen; more than one of their leaders was a cleric or a monk.

In the north of Italy, as early as the eleventh century, religious movements called *Pataria* had come into being. They wanted to reform the Church, but they spoilt their case by taking a decidedly independent line towards the hierarchy.[80] Here it was, at Brescia, that one Arnold[81] was born at the end of the eleventh century. A pupil of Abelard at Paris between 1115 and 1119, he returned to Italy to be ordained priest. Very austere towards himself, he became superior of a community of canons regular. He took the side of the municipality of Brescia against his bishop, even though the latter, like himself, was striving to reform his clergy. Arnold demanded that the bishop strip himself of all his possessions in favour of laymen and transfer all civil authority into their hands. "He declared that salvation was impossible for clerics who possessed property, for bishops, lords, and monks who held lands. All their goods should revert to the prince and must, with his approval, pass into the use of laymen alone."[82] The end of all this was a revolt on the part of the city and the condemnation of Arnold at the Second Lateran Council in 1138.

Sent into exile, the reformer rejoined Abelard in France; but he did not follow the example of his master, who withdrew into a monastery after the Council of Sens in 1140. Instead he began to teach at Mont St Geneviève, setting himself up as a prophet,

[80] Cf. C. Violante, *La Pataria milanese e la riforma ecclestiastica*, I, Le premesse (1045–57), Rome, 1955; R. Morghen, in *Relazione del . . . X Congresso*, *op. cit.*

[81] The sources on Arnold of Brescia are in the *Historia Pontificalis*, a work of John of Salisbury, ed. Pertz, *Monum. Germ. Histor.*, *Script.*, XX, pp. 517–45; ed. M. Chibnall, in Nelson's Medieval Texts (in preparation); *Gesta Frederici I Imperatoris* by Otto of Freising, ed. G. Watz, in *Monum. Germ. Hist.*, *Script. rerum german. in usum scholarum*, Hanover, 1912, pp. 1–161; several letters of St Bernard. For a bibliography, see A. Suraci, *Arnolpho da Brescia*, Asti, 1952.

[82] Otto of Freising, *loc. cit.*, p. 133.

reproving bishops for their cupidity, their shameful money-making, and their disgraceful lives. He even accused St Bernard of vain-glory. On the advice of the latter, Louis VII in his turn exiled Arnold, who proceeded to wander about first in Switzerland and then in Bohemia. In 1146, overcome perhaps by some grace of humility, he cast himself at the feet of Pope Eugenius III at Viterbo. Arnold's repentance did not last long; in 1147 he resumed his preaching in Rome, and his listeners soon formed an organized group, a real sect, called the "Lombards". They combined the greatest austerity and chastity of life with the most resolute opposition to the pope and the clergy. They rejected a corrupt priesthood, holding it to be useless, together with the sacraments it administered. Placed by the Romans at the head of their republic, Arnold tried to set Frederick Barbarossa against Adrian IV, but the peace concluded by the two sovereigns in 1155 was fatal for him. He was denounced as a "heretic" by the pope, imprisoned by order of the emperor, and finally burned alive. There were still redoubtable "Arnoldists" to be found at the end of the century.[83] Some historians have seen in them the origin of certain groups of "Humiliati" which appeared in Italy in the twelfth century and were recognized as a religious order in the thirteenth.[84] This is probably an error. The "Arnoldists" were tending in much the same direction as the Cathari, and moreover St Bernard and Otto of Freising had definitely considered Arnold a heretic. The Italian revolutionaries of the nineteenth century made him into a martyr for liberty and a hero of freedom of thought against the papacy.

Hugo Speroni, who inherited Arnold's point of view, taught in 1175–85. His themes were those of his master: the rites of the Church are inventions of the priests and idolatrous materializations of the true religion, which should be spiritual; the disciple of Christ is justified by the mere desire to be such, even though he sin; exterior works such as fasting, liturgical worship or communion are useless; what counts is the interior baptism, spiritual communion with the Word, and inner compunction.[85] But the underlying motive of their doctrines was the rejection of the established order. Their dogmatic errors were common to many heretics of the times: Arnold of Brescia and Hugo Speroni have been held re-

[83] Cf. the decretal *Ad abolendum* of Lucius III, at the Council of Verona in 1184 (ed. Friedberg, II, 780).

[84] Cf. P. Guerrini, *Gli Umiliati a Brescia*, Miscellanea Pio Paschini, I, Rome, 1948, pp. 187–214.

[85] Cf. Ilarino da Milano, O.F.M., *L'eresia di Ugo Speroni nella confutazione del Maestro Vacario. Testo inedito del secolo XII con studio storico e dottrinale*, Vatican City, 1945. The only original source for the account of Speroni is this "confutazione" entitled *Liber contra multiplices et varios errores*, manuscript Vatican Chig. A.V. 156.

sponsible for heretics prosecuted at Arras, at Cologne and elsewhere, or for the Petrobrusians whom Peter the Venerable refuted.[86]

The Arnoldi and Speronii were not the only sects to attract attention. Pope Lucius III mentions the "Humiliati" or "Poor Men of Lyons".[87] It is still uncertain how they started; our knowledge of them really begins with Peter Waldes or Waldo, a merchant of Lyons (†1218). He embarked on a life of penance and poverty about 1170[88]: with a few companions, he preached to his humble neighbours the love of poverty and the example of Christ. The authorities did not intervene at once; it was only in 1184 that Lucius III forbade the Poor Men to preach.[89] Like the Lombards, with whom they were in touch, they denied the value of the hierarchy and the sacramental economy. The validity of the sacraments, according to them, depended on the sanctity of the minister. Waldo, although not a priest, assumed the right to confer not only baptism but confirmation, penance (at that period it was still considered that confession could be made to any layman), and the Eucharist. The condemnation of their views weakened the force of their teaching, and they even became infected with some of the errors of the Cathari, but they organized themselves into a sect.

Waldo's authoritarian attitude soon led to a break with the Lombards, about 1210, and the return of some of his disciples to the Church. After his death, the sect survived in the Vaudois, in the region of Pignerol and Torre Pellice, and there was to come a time when the reformers of the sixteenth century would see in the Waldenses their forerunners. It is important to notice that this movement was of lay origin,[90] as was another heresy of that century, Catharism.

86 Cf. D. Cantamori, "L'eresia di Ugo Speroni", in *Riv. storia della Chiesa*, I (1947), pp. 95–9. See *supra*, pp. 167–8.

87 See note 83, *supra*.

88 On the *Humiliati*, see the art. "Humiliés" by F. Vernet in *Dict. théol. cath.*, VII, 311–21. For the Waldensian movement the principal sources are: Walter Map, *De nugis curialium distinctiones quinque*, ed. T. Wright, London, 1850; *Chronicon Univ. anonymi Laudunensis*, ed. O. Holder-Egger, in *Monum. Germ. Histor., Script.*, XXVI, pp. 447–9; Etienne de Bourbon, *Tract. de septem donis S. Spiritus*, ed. Lecoy de la Marche, Paris, 1877; Innocent III, *Epistulae*, P.L., 215–216; Raynier Sacconi, *Summa de Catharis et Leonistis seu pauperibus de Lugduno*, ed. Martène–Durand, *Thes. nov. anecd.*, V, col. 1759–75; and *Liber adversus Waldenses*, ed. J. Gretser, *Bibliotheca Patrum*, XXV, Lyons, 1613; Bernard Gui, *Practica inquisitionis*, ed. C. Douais, Paris, 1886; trad. and ed. G. Mollat, 2 vols, Paris, 1926–7. For a bibliography, see A. A. Hugon–G. Gounet, *Bibliografia Valdese*, Torre Pellice, 1953.

For the history of the Waldensians, see J. Marx, *L'inquisition en Dauphiné*, Paris, 1914; art. "Vaudois" by L. Cristiani in *Dict. théol. cath.*, XV, col. 2586–2600; E. Comba, *Storia dei Valdesi*, 4th ed., Torre Pellice, 1950.

89 See note 83.

90 Cf. H. Wolter, S.J., "Aufbruch und Tragik der apostolischen Laienbewegung

Another leader, Amalric of Bène, also wanted to escape from the hierarchical and sacramental pattern. Born in the neighbourhood of Chartres, he studied and taught in Paris but quickly became suspect there. He made a journey to Rome in an effort to obtain the protection of Innocent III but did not succeed. He was obliged to return to Paris and died there about 1205 or 1207, leaving a group of sympathizers, the "Amalricians", who were often taken to task in the theological writings of the thirteenth century.[91] It seems that Amalric added a kind of pantheism to the usual stock of the heresiarchs of the period. In the Middle Ages this was sometimes confused with that attributed to Scotus Erigena, which affirmed that the formal principle of all beings was identical with God. "What absurdity is there in saying that God is stone in a stone, or Godin in Godin? Let men worship Godin, then! . . . let them worship a mole or a bat, too, for God is there?"[92]

Amalric was above all a reformer, but he was also a prophet. His disciples added to his pantheism the theory of the three ages of the world associated with Joachim of Flora. A good example of how they distorted the message of the Gospel is to be seen in their translation of the Paternoster. It was found in the record of an interrogation of four Amalricians. It puts the emphasis on the presence of God on earth as much as in heaven. Temptation seems to be, in their eyes, an exterior snare rather than an interior struggle, and for Evil they substitute accidental evils. Instead of the prayer of the Gospel that God may be glorified, they ask only for the strengthening of something which already exists—the divinization of the human heart. They slip almost imperceptibly from *thy kingdom come* to *give us thy kingdom*. which has a quietist flavour."[93]

> Great Father who art in heaven and on earth,
> strengthen thy name in our hearts; give us

---

im Mittelalter. Die Anfänge der Waldenserbewegung im Urteil der Quellen", in *Geist u. Leben*, XXX (1957), pp. 357–69.

[91] For lack of other sources, one must have recourse to an anonymous "Contra Amaurianos (*c.* 1207–1210)", ed. C. Baeumker, in *Beitr. z. Gesch. Philos. d. Mittelalters*, XXIV, pp. 5–6, Münster, 1926. The propositions condemned in 1210 will be found in Martène–Durant, *Thes. Nov. Anecd.* IV, pp. 163–4, reproduced by Denifle-Châtelain in *Chart. Univ. Paris*, I, 71; a few documents have been published by M.-T. d'Alverny, in *Arch. hist. doctr. litt. moyen âge*, XVIII (1950–1951), pp. 325–36. Cf. G. C. Capelle, *Autour du décret de 1210. III. Amaury de Bène. Études sur son panthéisme formel*, Paris, 1932; M. del Pra, *Amaury de Bène*, Milan, 1951.

[92] *Contra Amaurianos*, IX; *ed. cit.*, p. 24. Saint Thomas mentions this pantheism in the *Summa Theologica*, I[a], q. 3, a. 8.

[93] M.-T. d'Alverny, *art. cit.*, p. 335. The text quoted is in *ibid.*, p. 330; from the manuscript *Paris nat. lat.* 2702, f. 129–30.

thy kingdom, may thy will be done on earth
as it is in heaven; give to every soul each
day what it needs, forgive us our faults as we
forgive others, keep us from the wiles of the
[*devil*? word illegible owing to erasures] deliver
us from every evil.

The Joachimites took a different direction. The movement, in its beginnings, could not be called a heresy. Faced with the unhappy spectacle of the present world, instead of turning towards the past, like the others, it looked to the future. Perfection is not of this world, and never will be! It will become a reality in an age to come, that of the Spirit and of liberty, after the age of the Father (the Old Testament, a time of servitude and fear) and following that of the Son (our own time). This "trinitarian" conception of history was the work of a Cistercian. Joachim (*c.* 1130–1202), formerly abbot of Corazzo in Calabria, founded in 1192 the monastery of San Giovanni in Fiore, near Cosenza, in the same part of Italy, which soon had numerous daughter houses. Joachim was attached to monastic life, as is shown by his treatise recently published on St Benedict and the divine office.[94] But he was also a seer. He envisaged in the near future a Church, pure at last, under the leadership of spiritual men, *viri spirituales*. "In the third age of the world, the Scriptures are to be renewed spiritually as though in those days Christ were being born, as though he were raising the dead to life and breathing into his disciples the gift of the Holy Spirit, as though he were sending his apostles to preach to the nations, as though the apostles were establishing and building up new churches. All this, as I have said, is to be consummated at the beginning of the third age, in the Spirit." Thus his *Expositio* on the Apocalypse.[95]

[94] Ed. C. Baraut, O.S.B., "Un tratado inedito de Joaquin de Fiore: De vita S. Benedicti et de officio divino secundum eius doctrinam", in *Anal. sacra Tarrac.*, XXIV (1951), pp. 33–122. On Joachim's foundations, see F. Russo, *Gioacchino da Fiore e le fondazione florensi in Calabria*, Naples, 1959.

[95] The authentic works which specially reveal his thought are the *Concordia Veteris et Novi Testamenti*, Venice, 1519 (extracts translated into French in E. Aegerter, *L'Evangile éternel*, II, Paris, 1928, pp. 25–86); the *Expositio in Apocalypsim*, Venice, 1527 (extracts trans. in Aegerter, II, pp. 89–145); and the *Psalterium decem chordarum*, Venice, 1527 (extracts trans. in Aegerter, II, pp. 149–67). The *Tractatus super quatuor Evangelia* have been edited by E. Buonaiuti, Rome, 1930; as has a *Liber figurarum* which Mgr L. Tondelli (*Il libro delle figure*, Turin, 1940; 2nd ed., 1953) considers authentic, as against F. Foberti and F. Russo. For a bibliography, see F. Russo, *Bibliografia gioachimita*, Florence, 1954; cf. H. Grundmann, *Neue Forschungen über J. von. F.*, Marburg, 1950; B. Hirsch-Reich, "Eine Bibliographie über J. von F. und dessen Nachwirkung", in *Rech. théol. anc. méd.*, XXIV (1957), 27–44.

The best recent study on the life, work, sources and influence of Joachim is that of M. W. Bloomfield, "Joachim of Flora. A Critical Review of his Canon, Teachings, Sources, Biography and Influence", in *Traditio*, XIII (1957), pp. 249–311. On his doctrine of the Spirit, E. Benz, "Creator Spiritus, Die Geistlehre des

The present era, forty-two generations of thirty years each, was to come to an end soon afterwards, in 1260.[96] Some of his disciples interpreted this date as that on which the "Franciscan era" was to open. But St Francis died in 1226. Others thought that the time had been fulfilled on the appearance of Gerard Segarelli, an obscure preacher who stirred up the mob at Parma in 1260, and organized a sect which survived him; he himself was burnt at the stake by the Inquisition in 1300. Another name mentioned was that of a certain Guillelmina, a woman of Milan who gathered a group of followers around her about 1260; these "Guillelmites" were convinced that she was the incarnation of the Holy Spirit.[97]

Although this way of looking at the present life and the course of history originated in a monastic milieu, it spread rapidly among the masses through preachers and *illuminati* who announced the imminent coming of the kingdom of God. It is important to note that Joachim never wished to separate himself from the Church: he died recommending to his monks submission to the Pope.[98] It seems, too, that in his lifetime his conception of history was not held to be dangerous. It kept alive in men's souls a genuine fervour and a longing for the world to come. It was only his doctrine of the Trinity that was condemned by the Fourth Lateran Council in 1215.[99]

Joachim's cause was injured by his own admirers—not, of course, by the best of them such as St Bonaventure and Dante and others, whose views were not disturbed,[100] but by more sinister characters, some of whom have already been noticed, who were ill content with the established order.

"Joachimism" combined, in fact, several quite different currents, which had nothing in common except a trinitarian conception of history. Among the best known of its supporters we find certain "Spiritual" Franciscans of the thirteenth and fourteenth centuries.

Joachim von Fiore", in *Eranos-Jahrbuch*, XXV (1956), pp. 285–355, should be read with caution.

96 *Concordia, lib.* II, tract. I, cap. 16.

97 Cf. E. Jordan, art. "Joachim de Flore", in *Dict. théol. cath.*, VIII, 1446–7.

98 At least, he did so according to the *Chronologia Joachimi Abbatis et ordinis Florensis*, published at Cosenza in 1612 by Giacomo Greco, a monk of San Giovanni. Part of this appears in the *Acta Sanctorum*, May, vol. VII, col. 92–109; esp. col. 102.

99 Cf. Mansi, XXII, 982 *et seq.*; Denz., 431–3. The Council condemned his *Libellus de essentia Trinitatis contra Lombardum* (lost). The *Liber contra Lombardum* (Peter Lombard), published by C. Ottaviano after the manuscript *Oxford Balliol 296*, Rome, 1934, seems to be a recapitulation of the authentic treatise.

100 Cf. M. E. Reeves, "Studies in the Reputation and Influence of the Abbot Joachim of Flora, Chiefly in the XVth and XVIth Centuries", in *Bull. Inst. Histor. Research*, X (1932–3), pp. 190–2.

Nevertheless, it would be a mistake to see primitive Franciscans in a Joachimite light.[101]

A curious treatise known as *The Eternal Gospel*, by an intransigent Franciscan, Gerard of Borgo San-Donnino, was connected with the spread of these ideas, which it distorted.[102] A syllabus of thirty-one propositions was extracted from the work by the theologians of Paris in 1254. St Thomas was wiser; he confined himself to pointing out, in a passage of the *Summa Theologica*, the "vanity of certain persons", *quorumcumque vanitas*, who look for a new age. As Scripture implies (Hebrews 10.19), he says, no age better than the present one is to be hoped for in this world.[103] The whole movement reached a climax in the condemnation of Pierre Jean Olivi at the Council of Vienne in 1311–12[104] and the censure of the errors of the "Spirituals" by John XXII in 1318[105]; and thus those who still held more or less to Joachim's theories were reduced to a sect.

The extraordinary success of this apocalyptic and spiritual vision of history was a symptom of the prevailing mentality of large sections of the faithful. The Church's doctrines seemed too favourable to the existing state of things, which was a lamentable one, in spite of the efforts of Gregory VII and several religious founders to reform it. No doubt there was a good side to this spiritual movement; it paved the way for the providential success of Francis of Assisi and Dominic Guzman. But neither of these saints saw salvation in terms either of future hopes or of a return to past forms. It is true that all things pass, preparing the way for a better era—there Joachim was right. It is also true that the Church of the apostles and martyrs is the model to which we must ever turn; the other "heretics" of the period—Arnoldists, Speronists, Amalricians—had clearly seen this, and there they too were right. These divergent, and indeed opposed, ideals were to be reconciled by the mendicant orders of the thirteenth century, who provided a solution that satisfied them both—poverty. A poverty which is truly that preached by Christ detaches men from passing things and directs their gaze beyond this world, and at the same time it is a return to the way of life of the first Christian community.

101 As was done by E. Benz in *Ecclesia Spiritualis. Kirchenidee und Geschichtstheologie der franziskanischen Reformation*, Stuttgart, 1934; cf. L. Salvatorelli, "Movimento francescano e Gioachimismo", in *Relazione . . . del Congresso Intern. Sc. stor.*, III, pp. 415–16. See *infra*, ch. III, pp. 295 *et seq*.

102 French translation by E. Aegerter, *L'Evangile éternel*, *op. cit.* Cf. H. S. Denifle, "Das Evangelium aeternum und die Commission zu Anagni", in *Archiv. f. liter. u. Kirchengesch. des Mittelalters*, I (1885), pp. 49–164.

103 Iª IIªᵉ, q. 106, a. 4, c. et ad 2ᵘᵐ.

104 Denz., 480–3.

105 Denz., 484–90. Cf. *infra*, ch. III, pp. 299–300.

6. The Catharist Menace

This was a much more formidable heresy, perhaps even a new religion. The Cathari, too, wanted to go back to the purity of primitive Christianity, but their religious conceptions were dominated by doctrines unacceptable to the Church. The basis for their teaching was an over-simplified metaphysic which tried to explain the problem of evil by the old Asiatic dualism of Manes (†276). Even St Augustine had been seduced by this system before his conversion, so attractive was it. The Cathari of the south of France had predecessors—the Bogomils, concentrated in the Balkan peninsula from the tenth century.[106] The eleventh-century Patarines in the north of Italy doubtless also had an influence on them.[107]

The success of Catharism, especially in the twelfth century, is sometimes thought to have been due to its easy-going morality, which tempted those who were dismayed at the austerity of the Gregorian reform. Such an explanation is obviously inadequate. We must look to the causes that were operative in the cases of similar movements of the time: abuses and dissolute lives of the hierarchy, the scandal of the wealthy, the gross superstitions of the people. One should beware of facile generalizations; real Catharist sources are very rare both because they were systematically destroyed and because of the violence with which the sect was repressed, and Christian sources are not wholly impartial and must be read in a critical spirit.[108]

The dialectic of the Cathari was logically bound to lead them to belief in two Gods: a principle of good and a principle of evil. As we read in an anonymous Catharist treatise, *De duobus principiis*:

[106] Cf. D. Obolensky, *The Bogomils. A Study in Balkan Neo-manicheism*, Cambridge, 1948; H.-C. Puech, "Catharisme médiéval et bogomilisme", in *Convegno di scienze morali, storiche e filologische 1956*, Rome, 1957, pp. 56–83.

[107] See *supra*, p. 262.

[108] The sources have been collected by J. Guiraud, *Histoire de l'Inquisition au moyen âge*, 2 vols, Paris, 1935–8; cf. vol. I, pp. xi–xliii. They are too extensive to be cited here in their entirety. A bibliography (to the year 1935) will be found in *ibid.*, I, pp. xliii–xlviii; cf. A. Borst, *Die Katharen*, Stuttgart, 1953, pp. 1–58 and 319–40; S. Runciman, *Le manichéisme médiéval. L'hérésie dualiste dans le christianisme*, French translation, Paris, 1949, pp. 197–206; H. Söderberg, *La religion des cathares*, Uppsala, 1949, pp. 273–88. The treatise *De duobus principiis* has been edited by A. Dondaine, O.P., *Un traité neo-manichéen du XIIIe siècle*, Rome, 1939, and has been translated into French, together with other texts, by R. Nelli, *Ecritures cathares*, Paris, 1959. See also D. Roché's apologetic works: *Etudes manichéennes et cathares*, Arques, 1952, and *Le catharisme*, Toulouse, 1947; the *Cahiers d'Etudes cathares*, 1949 and following years, is of the same nature. The *Revue de synthèse*, XXIII (1948), devoted one number to Catharism and its influence. On the Albigensian crusade, cf. P. Belperron, *La croisade contre les Albigeois et l'union du Languedoc à la France, 1209–1249*, Paris, 1942. There is a popular pamphlet by F. Hayward, *Que faut-il penser de l'Inquisition?*, Paris, 1957.

There is no need to learn that good and evil oppose one another: it is a fact that we have experienced in our inmost self. What is the cause of evil? If there were but one God, and he good, nothing that exists would be evil; yet evil is everywhere in the world!

It is not enough to attribute to the creature the power of failing, for in the last resort he would have this unhappy power from the Creator. God would again therefore be responsible for evil. Thus there is another principle, the cause of the creature's imperfection and of evil.

The activity of this evil principle does not merely affect the working of created beings, but also that of the good God, since it is opposed to the perfection of his works; the good God is not *all-powerful*. The evil principle is eternal. . . .[109]

The consequence of this doctrine in the ascetical order is the renunciation of evil and escape from the sphere of the earthly, the carnal, the impure. This escape is more the work of man himself than of grace gradually penetrating him by means of the sacramental economy, according to Christian teaching. Ultimately there was even the negation of whatever is good in man—sacred suicide, the *endura*.

As for points of contact with Christian ritual, only the *consolamentum* really resembled a sacrament. It was a kind of liturgical committal to the sect, with a laying on of hands and of the gospels.[110] Those who were liberated from earthly things were the "perfect"; they were *veri* and *boni Christiani.*[111] An absolute indifference enabled them to endure, "through the justice of Christ", hunger, thirst, scandal, persecution, even death[112]; but according to the unanimous testimony of their contemporaries, it also freed them from the most elementary rules of sexual morality, despite the exhortation to live in purity—*toto tempore vite vestre cum puritate cordis et mentis*[113]—which formed part of the Catharist ritual. For them, worship was reduced to the *Pater* and to the reading in common of the New Testament; there was at times an *agape* or a confession, in imitation of the sacraments of the Eucharist and penance.

The Cathari were not confined to the south of France, or indeed to the diocese of Albi (whence their name of "Albigensians"). They were to be found also in the rest of Languedoc, in Provence, and in

109 A. Dondaine, *op. cit.*, pp. 21–2. The texts of the *De duobus principiis* corresponding to this summary are too long to be given here but will be found chiefly *ibid.*, pp. 118–31.

110 On the *consolamentum*, cf. *ibid.*, pp. 45–57; and the ritual as edited by Dondaine, *ibid.*, pp. 149–65.

111 "Rituel cathare du consolamentum", Dondaine, *ibid.*, pp. 159, 162.

112 *Ibid.*, p. 163.

113 *Ibid.*

the north of Italy.[114] Outside these areas, their doctrine had no very considerable influence except in what concerned their moral teaching and their criticism of the hierarchy. In this diluted form, Catharism was merged in practice with the movements already discussed. People readily held it responsible for the impiety and deplorable morals of men like the preacher Tanchelin, or Tanshelm, who was making a stir among the masses in the Netherlands about 1100[115] or the Breton layman Eudes de l'Étoile († after 1148), who recognized himself in a passage of the ritual of exorcism, "*per eum qui venturus est judicare vivos et mortuos*". He was so sure that *eum* referred to him that he changed his name to Eon. It is unlikely, however, that he was in touch with Catharism except indirectly.[116] The same may be said of Peter de Bruys (†1140) and Henry of Lausanne († after 1145), who were attacked by Peter the Venerable, St Bernard, and a monk named William who may have been William of St Thierry.[117]

Languedoc and northern Italy were the area most favourable to Catharist doctrine. Repression was not long in coming, first by the pen[118] but very soon by judicial intervention as well. In the twelfth century it did not yet, as a rule, take an extreme form; the canonist Gratian was in favour of imposing exile or a fine rather than prison or capital punishment.[119] The Third Lateran Council in 1179 allowed the ecclesiastical authorities to remit the punishment, the *salutare remedium*, to the judgment of princes, in order to avoid itself inflicting corporal punishment or the death penalty.[120]

Seeing that Languedoc was lost to the true faith, Alexander III organized the repression there. This was the origin of the Inquisition,[121] which at first was dependent on the authority of the bishops.

[114] Cf. S. Savini, *Il catarismo italiano ed i suoi vescovi nei secoli XIII e XIV. Ipotesi sulla cronologia del catarismo in Italia*, Florence, 1958. The name "Cathari" may come from the Greek, or it may be derived from the *Pataria* and the patarines mentioned above.

[115] Cf. E. de Moreau, S.J., *Histoire de L'Église en Belgique*, II, 2nd ed., pp. 410–425.

[116] Cf. E. Jarry, art. "Eon de l'Étoile", in the encyclopedia *Catholicisme*, IV, pp. 278–9.

[117] Peter the Venerable, *Ep. adv. Petrobrusianos*, P.L., 189, 719–850. For St Bernard, cf. Vacandard, *Vie de saint Bernard*, 4th ed., II, pp. 226–44. On Henry, see R. Manselli, *Il monaco Enrico e la sua eresia*, in *Bull. Istit. Storico Italiano per il medioevo*, LXV, Rome, 1953 (with a critical edition of "William's" refutation).

[118] We have the sermons *Contra Catharos* of Ekbert, abbot of Schönau in the diocese of Trèves (1166–84), P.L., 195, 11–98. There is also a *Contra hereticos* by Ermangaud, abbot of St-Gilles (1179–95), P.L., 204, 1235–72; a *De fide catholica contra haereticos sui temporis*, by Alan of Lille, P.L., 210, 306–430.

[119] *Decretum*, sec. pars, c. XXIII, especially qq. 4–6; ed. Friedberg, I, col. 899–950.

[120] Can. 27; Mansi, XXII, col. 231–2; Friedberg, II, 779–80.

[121] Cf. J. Guiraud, *op. cit.*; H. Maisonneuve, *Études sur les origines de l'In-*

It turned over to the "secular arm", *saeculari judicio,* cases of clerics and monks convicted of heresy.[122] Later, under Innocent III, the Inquisition became "legatine", that is, exercised by papal legates. When guilt had been proved, it was they who pronounced the sentence of banishment and the confiscation of goods. They went no further, except when it was necessary to punish obstinacy in the case of relapsed heretics, or infractions against previous sentences. At this time (the beginning of the thirteenth century) there arose in Livonia, Prussia, and Languedoc "militia of Jesus Christ", derived from the tradition of the military orders and from the Cistercian spirit; only one such body, an Italian one, was organized on the initiative of a Dominican. The one in Languedoc took up the "crusade" against the Albigenses and was prepared to support the Inquisition by effective military action.[123]

The legates were Peter of Castelnau and Raoul of Fontfroide, both Cistercians: their sermons and discussions had been unsuccessful when there came on the scene Diego d'Azevedo and Dominic Guzman.[124] After a decisive interview at Montpellier in 1206, they persuaded the two legates to renounce the pomp with which they surrounded themselves[125] and to set an example of evangelical poverty. The success of this move was extraordinary. The persistent opposition, however, of Count Raymond VI of Toulouse, and especially the murder of Peter of Castelnau at St Gilles, on the Rhone, on 15 January 1208, aroused the indignation of Christendom. The result was the terrible and bloody "Albigensian crusade", described by Peter Vaux-de-Cernay.[126]

It degenerated into an interminable war, which dragged on through the whole of the thirteenth century and was often poisoned by political dissensions. Little by little, peace returned, in spite of dramatic episodes like the famous siege of Montségur in 1243–1244.[127] Boniface VIII celebrated the victory of the Church by

---

quisition, Paris, 1942; A. Dondaine, O.P., "Le manuel de l'inquisiteur 1230–1330", in *Arch. Fratr. Praedic.*, XVII (1947), pp. 85–194.

[122] According to the decretal *Ad abolendum* of Lucius III, in 1184. Cf. Friedberg, II, 781.

[123] On this history of these militia, see G. G. Meersseman, O.P., "Les milices de Jésus-Christ", in *Arch. Fratrum Praedic.*, XXIII (1953), pp. 275–308.

[124] Cf. ch. IV, p. 315.

[125] Cf. C. Touzellier, "La pauvreté, arme contre l'albigéisme", in *Rev. Hist. Religions* (1957), pp. 79–92.

[126] Ed. P. Guébin–E. Lyon, *Hystoria Albigensis*, 2 vols, Paris, 1926–30; translated into French by P. Guébin–H. Maisonneuve, *Histoire albigeoise*, Paris, 1951. Cf. P. Belperron, *op. cit.* Among the sources translated into French, see the *Chanson de la croisade albigeoise*, written in Provençal verse, by E. Martin-Chabot, 2 vols to date, Paris, 1931–57.

[127] Cf. Z. Oldenbourg, *Le bûcher de Montségur*, Paris, 1959. On this period, see Y. Dossat, *Les crises de l'Inquisition toulousaine au XIIIe siècle (1233–1273)*, Bordeaux, 1959.

proclaiming the great jubilee of 1300. The work of the Inquisition, however, was not finished, as is shown by the *Manual of the Inquisitor* by the Dominican Bernard Gui, published at the beginning of the fourteenth century.[128]

Between 1231 and 1234, the Inquisition passed into the hands of the mendicant Orders and became "monachal". It is astonishing to find such work undertaken by those who preached the Gospel in all its purity; and indeed the price paid for the repression was enormous. The misdeeds of the Inquisition must not, however, be exaggerated; only four or five per cent of those against whom charges were prepared were handed over to the secular arm by the inquisitor Bernard Gui. One must also take into account the mentality of the times: to the Church's noblest sons, it seemed to be the one and only means of defeating the threat to Christian unity. When one realizes that the Gospel requires gentleness and charity toward those who have gone astray, and that even after the peace of Constantine coercion by the civil power was fairly rare, one can only believe that the danger must have seemed fearful indeed. The toleration on principle of earlier ages was temporarily forgotten in the thirteenth century, and it would not be remembered until the fifteenth, when we find a certain return to it with Nicholas of Cusa, and in the sixteenth, with Thomas More and Erasmus.[129] But by that time the use of force had become customary, and Christendom was threatened by a crisis of a very different order of gravity—that of the Reformation—and the voices of More and Erasmus found no answering echo.

Men's aspirations to live according to the Gospel in its purity had one consequence that was far from being in the spirit of Christ. They tended to create among those who pursued them a real sense of caste. The "pure", the "holy", the "true Christians", the "true poor men", the "*humiliati*" too often set themselves above the rest of mankind. The Gospel, after all, is not addressed to the "elect", especially not to those who are conscious of being so; it is offered to all, including those least favoured by nature or by grace. Then too, quite apart from any questions of dogma, the secret pride of the heretics constituted a danger. It was a danger of which they were probably unconscious, but it was comparable to that of the

[128] Ed. C. Douais, Paris, 1886. Part of it has been edited by G. Mollat, 2 vols, Paris, 1926–7. Cf. A. Thomas, "Bernard Gui, frère prêcheur", in *Hist. litt. France*, XXXV (1921), pp. 139–232; A. Dondaine, O.P., *Le manuel de l'Inquisiteur* (*1230–1330*), pp. 85–199.

[129] Cf. A. Cherel, "Histoire de l'idée de tolérance", in *Rev. hist. Église de France*, XXVII (1941), pp. 129–64; XXVIII (1942), pp. 9–50; J. Lecler, *Histoire de la tolérance au siècle de la Réforme*, 2 vols, Paris, 1955 (Books I and II give some information on ancient and medieval times; there is an excellent bibliography).

scandal given by the abuses and vices in Church and society. The true reformers, on the other hand, were saints, humble and obedient in charity.

7. *Hermits and Recluses*

There is a spontaneous desire in men to escape from a world whose vileness they see and feel that they are powerless to remedy. Thus the same cause, and sometimes the same disappointments, that provoked the movements just discussed drove certain laymen to make the experiment of seeking holiness alone, outside the ordinary conventual setting, or at the most within the sphere of influence of a monastery or a church. There was, of course, nothing new in the eremitical life; it had been known in ancient times, even before cenobitical communities had been formed. St Benedict permits a monk who has been purified by the common life to withdraw into solitude. The characteristic thing about this life at the period with which we are concerned was that it was often embraced by laymen who desired the contemplative life but did not believe that they could find it in a monastery.

Some hermits had begun by leading the monastic life in a cenobitical setting; several monasteries and certain foundations of the eleventh and twelfth centuries were thus surrounded by hermitages.[130] Others had sought an independent solitude, and it was for these that the councils, the bishops, and the abbots were anxious to give Rules: certain guarantees were needed, for "the habit maketh not the hermit",[131] as the saying went, and solitude can become for some a danger to humility, charity, and purity—just as, of course, the common life can for others. It would be a mistake, however, to conclude from this that all the hermits were vicious, misanthropic or eccentric; that they were semi-savages, prudish and at the same time weak in the face of temptation. More than once they were represented as being good-natured and affable, and as wise men offering sound advice. We have only to remember Tristan and Isolde, who were kindly received by the old hermit Ogrin, despite the fact that they were living in sin. He exhorted them to repentance and finally to separation.

L'ermite Ogrins mot les sarmone,
du repentir consel lor donne.
Li hermites sovent lor dit
Les profecies de l'escrit

[130] See *supra*, Part I, ch. VI, p. 127.

[131] Rutebeuf († *c.* 1285), *Le dit de Frère Denise* (*Oeuvres complètes*), ed. E. Faral and J. Bastin, vol. II, Paris, 1960, p. 283.

et mot lor amentoit sovent
l'ermite le Dé jugement[132]

(Ogrin the hermit admonished them, advising them to repent: often would he tell them of the prophecies of Scripture and many a time bring to their minds the judgment of God.)

There is a contrast between the twelfth-century hermits and what had been seen previously. Formerly they deliberately kept away from inhabited places and were often reduced to a primitive and almost savage level of existence. Now they were again becoming more sociable—and, it must be conceded, more Christian. When they lived in the vicinity of a monastery, as they often did, they were really cenobites who returned periodically to the desert. The disadvantage, however, of this life of solitude, even when tempered by the neighbourhood of a monastery, was that the hermit, unless he possessed a solid spiritual foundation, tended towards exercises of devotion which could easily take the place given in monasteries of the traditional type to the *opus Dei* and the *lectio divina.*

Women, for whom the eremitical life presents particular dangers, practised it by preference under the form of reclusion[133]; there were also some men who undertook this manner of life. It was not in itself new, but what was new was the anxiety to give the recluses a stable constitution. Among others, there were the rules drawn up for the recluse Rainaud,[134] by Bernard, prior of the Charterhouse of Portes in Burgundy (†1153), and the twelfth-century *Ordo inclusorum* for the lay recluses of the monastery of Baumburg in Bavaria.[135]

The best-known of these rules is an English one, the *Ancrene Riwle.*[136] There has been much discussion over its authorship, its

[132] Béroul fragment, ed. Muret (4th ed., Paris, 1947), lines 1393–8. Cf. L. Gougaud, O.S.B., *Ermites et reclus. Etudes sur d'anciennes formes de vie religieuse,* Ligugé, 1928, pp. 36–40; P. Doyère, O.S.B., art. "Ermites", in *Dict. Droit Canon.,* V, pp. 412–29. An investigation of medieval eremitism in France has been made by J. Sainsaulieu. For England, see R. M. Clay, *The Hermits and Anchorites of England,* London, 1914. There is a bibliography in Doyère, *loc. cit.,* col. 429.

[133] J.-K. Huysmans, in *L'Oblat,* Paris, 1903, pp. 123–35, is better informed than Victor Hugo in *Notre-Dame de Paris* (the chapter on the Trou-aux-Rats).

[134] P.L., 153, 892–900.

[135] Cf. Benoît Haeften, *Disquisitiones,* I, 8, p. 83; or ed. Matteus Raderus, *Bavaria Sancta,* III, Munich, 1704, pp. 117 *et seq.* For a list of rules for recluses, see Gougaud, *op. cit.,* pp. 62–5; L. Oliger, O.F.M., *Speculum inclusorum,* Rome, 1938, pp. 9–12.

[136] There are editions of the English text, from various manuscripts, by M. Day, London, 1952 (2 vols), and A. C. Baugh, London, 1956; of the Latin text, by C. d'Evelyn, London, 1944, and R. M. Wilson, London, 1954. The medieval French text has been edited by J. A. Herbert, London, 1944, and W. H. Trethewey, Oxford, 1958. There is a translation into modern English by M. B. Salu, London, 1955, and Notre Dame, Ind., 1956. On the problems of criticism, see

place of origin, and its date. It has been held that it was written about 1235 by the Dominican Robert Bacon (1180–1240)[137]; or again, by Godwin of Kilburn (near London) in the first half of the twelfth century.[138] The thirteenth century seems more probable, because of the points of resemblance between the rules for confession and temptation and those in the manuals for confessors that were then being widely circulated. Also in one passage there is a reference to the figure on a crucifix having one foot over the other; a style which does not appear before the thirteenth century. The *Ancrene Riwle*, therefore, seems to be of later date than the English rule for recluses written in Latin by Aelred of Rievaulx; though it may depend on it here and there.[139]

The *Ancrene Riwle* was written as a kind of handbook of the spiritual life—lively, wise and discreet. The gospels must take first place, says the introduction, and the eight books that follow review the devotional practices which the recluses are to observe: the Mass, the Divine Office, other vocal prayers, litanies and various exercises, the custody of the exterior and interior senses, the advantages afforded for this purpose by the solitary life, confession, penance, the love of God, and external rules. On the whole little importance is attached to the liturgy; the spiritual life is directed towards those practices and prayers that today would be called private; for example repetitions of the *Pater* in honour of the Holy Trinity, the five Wounds, the seven Gifts of the Holy Spirit, or to preserve oneself from the seven deadly sins, etc.[140] It emphasizes the ascetic character of the recluse's life and does not lay stress on contemplation as a higher state and the goal of spiritual effort.[141] The love of God is conceived chiefly as the response of the recluse, in her life of penance, to the suffering of Christ.

It is as though the idea of progressing towards contemplation, which was a favourite subject and an innovation of the Victorines, had not yet touched the piety of these milieux. Then again, if they were not near a monastery, the recluses' spirituality was not formed

---

H. Käsmann, *Zur Frage der ursprünglichen Fassung der A.R.*, in *Anglia*, LXXV (1957), pp. 134–56.

[137] P. McNable, O.P., "The Authorship of the A.R.", in *Arch. Fratr. Praed.*, IV (1934), pp. 49–74.

[138] H. E. Allen, "On the Author of the A.R.", in *Public. Modern Lang. Assoc. of America*, XLIV (1929), pp. 635–80. See C. H. Talbot, "Some Notes on the Dating of the A.R.", in *Neophilologus*, XL (1956), pp. 38–50.

[139] Cf. C. H. Talbot, "The 'De institutis inclusarum' of Ailred of Rievaulx", in *Analecta Sacri Ord. Cisterc.*, VII (1951), pp. 167–217.

[140] Cf. the English translation by M. B. Salu, *op. cit.*, pp. 193–6 (appendix by G. Sitwell, O.S.B.).

[141] Cf. G. Sitwell, O.S.B., "The Mysticism of the A.R.", in *Ampleforth Journal*, XXXVII (1932), pp. 194–202.

by the liturgy and the *lectio divina*, except more or less in the same way as the *conversi*, who recited *Paters* in place of the Office. Of the current of piety towards Christ, his Mother and the saints, which was fairly general from the twelfth century onwards, the hermits really only adopted practices of private devotion. On the other hand, when monks became hermits or recluses their spirituality was more ecclesial, liturgical, and eschatological. Their life, said Peter the Venerable, anticipates the state of resurrection which will be that of every Christian at the end of time. "Pouring forth ardent prayers, they serve the Church of God."[142]

Little by little the life of the recluses, because of its great dignity and because of its dangers, like that of the hermits, was surrounded with safeguards. There was a ceremonial for the entrance into reclusion, regulation of contacts with the outer world, spiritual direction, and the obligation of living in the vicinity of a monastery or a church.[143]

The number of recluses must have been considerable at times; 260 of them were known in Rome in 1320! At the end of the Middle Ages, however, their numbers declined, and in any case, the influence they exerted on their contemporaries must always have been somewhat limited. In the twelfth century hermits and recluses caused much less talk than did heretical agitators: the fact that they chose to live completely separated from the world preserved them from the temptations of success and influence. They believed that their life of penance and their prayer were serving the Church, as well as giving them entrance, even in this life, to the kingdom of God.

8. *Chivalry and Courtly Love*

As the result of a clearer sense of spiritual vocation, among the laity chivalry came to be looked upon as something truly sacred. In some ways this followed naturally from the Crusades, whose primary aim was undeniably religious. This hallowing of the profession of arms bears no uncertain witness to the extent to which the Christian ideal had penetrated the ruling classes of feudal lords and princes. Thus chivalry, one of the pivots of medieval social structure, came to have its religious character sanctioned by a rite of blessing approved by the Church.[144]

[142] Letter to Gilbert, a recluse of Cluny; P.L., 189, 100.

[143] Cf. L. Gougaud, *op. cit.*, pp. 66–114; P. Schmitz, *Histoire de l'Ordre de Saint-Benoît*, VII, Maredsous, 1956, pp. 53–8.

[144] Cf. G. Cohen, *Histoire de la chevalerie en France au moyen âge*, Paris, 1949; U. T. Holmes, *Daily Living in the Twelfth Century. Based on the Observations of Alexander Neckam in London and Paris*, Madison, Wis., 1952, especially chs VII

The ideal of the Christian prince was sketched out in a series of writings on political ethics. The first in order of date is from the eleventh century: the *Policratus* of John of Salisbury (1059).[145] The most representative among them, apart from the *Policratus*, were the *Liber de principis instructione* of Giraldus Cambrensis,[146] an important *Speculum regale* of Norwegian origin which appeared about 1260, the *Summa collationum* of John of Wales[147] (second half of the thirteenth century), the *De regimine principum* of St Thomas Aquinas, and that of Giles of Rome, coming down to the *De officio regis* of John Wyclif (1379) and the *Basilikon Doron* of King James I of England.[148] These "mirrors of princes" formed a literary *genre* distinct from that of the political treatise, the pamphlet, and the utopia. They sought to give advice on the upbringing of the prince, on whom the happiness of the State depends. Their whole teaching is dominated by the ideal of the Christian knight, the man of honour. But their authors also dealt with problems of State, the limits of power, and relations between states. The treatises of the end of the Middle Ages and during the Renaissance are written from a more humanistic point of view. Several of them derived from a mysterious *Secretum secretorum* of oriental origin known from the twelfth century in various translations,[149] which purported to be a letter from Aristotle to his disciple Alexander the Great. Nor were these ideals purely theoretical: one has only to remember the examples of sanctity given by King Louis IX of France (†1270), Elizabeth of Hungary (†1231) and Alfonso of Castile (†1284).[150]

The knight was blessed during a religious ceremony which had some points in common with the consecration of virgins and the coronation of kings. The "dubbing" (the blessing of the knight's arms and his investiture) was preceded by a bath of purification, by confession and communion, and sometimes by a vigil of prayer.

---

and VIII. On the crusades, see P. Alphandéry–A. Dupront, *La chrétienté et l'idée de croisade*, II, *Recommencements nécessaires* (*XIIe–XIIIe siècles*), Paris, 1959.

145 Ed. C. J. Webb, 2 vols, Oxford, 1909; P.L. 199, 379–823.

146 *Opera*, VIII, *Rerum Britan. Script.*, 21, London, 1891.

147 This work exists only in a very rare edition of 1493 with no indication of the place of publication.

148 Cf. W. Berges, *Die Fürstenspiegel des hohen und späten Mittelalters*, Leipzig, 1938 (pp. 291–356 are an analysis of forty-six writings, from John of Salisbury to Petracrch); W. Kleinke, *Englische Fürstenspiegel von Policraticus Johanns von Salisbury bis zum Basilikon Doron Jakobs I*, Halle, 1937.

149 Three versions were edited by R. Steele, London, 1898.

150 Cf. C.-V. Langlois, *Saint Louis, Philippe le Bel, les derniers Capétiens directs* (*1226–1328*) (*Coll. Histoire de France* [E. Lavisse], III, 2), Paris, 1901. There is a biography of St Elizabeth of Hungary by J. Ancelet-Hustache, Paris, 1947. For Alfonso, see J. A. Sánchez Pérez, *Alonso X el Sabio*, Madrid, 1935.

According to an *ordo* of the tenth century,[151] the bishop first blessed the standard, the lance, and the sword; he then went to the new knight and girded him with the sword; last of all came the shield; the whole ceremony was accompanied by prayers and by the chanting of various antiphons. This ceremony, very simple as can be seen, approves the *defensor's* using his arms against his own enemies and those of the Church. It gives him as models Gedeon and David, St Martin, St Sebastian, and St George, who were soldiers. It may well be imagined, however, that in that rough and uncultivated society the purpose of the profession of arms was not always limited to combating the "adversaries of the holy Church of God"—far from it.

At the end of the thirteenth century in the *Pontificale* of William Durand, bishop of Mende, the dubbing was given a more or less definite ritual.[152] The bishop blessed the sword, then the other arms, and presented the bare sword to the knight, who brandished it three times. After this, the bishop received him to the kiss of peace, saying, "Be thou a peaceable soldier, diligent, faithful and devout." He then gave him a light buffet and put the standard into his hand. The other knights present put on his spurs, where that was the custom. There were prayers that he might use these arms to defend himself and to protect the Church against the enemies of the cross of Christ and of the Christian virtues. The bishop admonished him to do this without committing injustice, and in the spirit of those same virtues, for in the exercise of the profession of arms the knight was not to forget that he was a Christian, and the Church forbade him to give way to the savagery of barbarism. It did not lay upon him the duty of killing, but only to defend himself and the weak. The Church, rather than be indifferent to the profession of arms, wanted the knight to see his duty as one of religion in such a way that he would act as a Christian in exercising his right of legitimate defence, especially if the cause of the faith or the Church was at stake.

The dubbing of knights had, however, one regrettable consequence. It gave rise to a caste mentality, exactly as in the case of the "pure" of all sorts that appear in the various heretical movements. The universal character of the Gospel message, offered to

[151] In the *Ordo Romanus Antiquus*, ed. M. Hittorp, *De catholicae ecclesiae divinis officiis ad ministeriis*, ed. Rome, 1591, pp. 115–16. The formulas of blessing were in fairly general use; cf. M. Andrieu, *Les Ordines Romani du haut moyen âge*, I, Louvain, 1931 (tables).

[152] Ed. M. Andrieu, *Le Pontifical romain au moyen âge*, III, Vatican City, 1940, pp. 447–50 and 549–50. It is to be found, with little modification, in the present Pontifical, Part I, *De benedictione novi militis*, and Part II, *De benedictione armorum, De benedictione ensis, De benedictione et traditione vexilli bellici*. There is a historical commentary on the *benedictio novi militis* by J. Catalano in his edition of the *Pontificale romanum*, Part I, tit. XXIII; Paris, 1850, vol. I, pp. 642–56.

everyone without distinction, became obscured in this case too. In principle, knighthood was accessible to anyone, but in fact from the end of the twelfth century it became a privilege reserved to the sons of knights. "The highest order that God has made is the order of Chivalry, which must be without baseness."[153]

The same time that the Church was trying to christianize the profession of arms saw also the rise of "courtly love". It was the result of the improvement that had taken place in the position of women. It has been said in this connection that love as we know it in modern literature and art—if not in the current conception of it—may be called "a French invention of the twelfth century" (C. Seignobos, G. Cohen). In that century society, aided by the Church, had become accustomed to see woman as the *dame* instead of a plaything of the passions and the slave of the home, and to respect in her a reflection of the purity and maternity of the Blessed Virgin. Human love took over the language of divine love and borrowed, for example, from the *Canticle of Canticles*. Some have seen in this a consequence of the piety towards our Lady to which a saint like Bernard is so fervent a witness.[154]

This new attitude towards women took the form of a code of politeness, of fidelity, of "courtesy" which was to have considerable influence in the West.[155] It originated in the south of France, where "courts of love" were held. At the same time a literature of courtly love was gradually coming to the fore.[156] On their side, certain romances of chivalry rose to a high contemplation of the Christian mysteries[157] as well as to a new understanding of the deep reality of love. Of these, the *Quest of the Grail* was the most mystical. Under-

[153] Chrétien de Troyes, *Perceval le Gallois*, line 2831 (ed. C. Potvin, vol. I).

[154] Cf. M. de Montoliu, "San Bernardo, la poesia de los Trobadores y la 'Divina Comedia'", in *Spanische Forschungen*, I, 12, Münster, 1956, pp. 192–9.

[155] For the history of courtly love, see M. R. Bezzola, *Les origines et la formation de la littérature courtoise en Occident (500–1200)*, I, Paris, 1944; P. Belperron, *La joie d'amour. Contribution à l'étude des troubadours et de l'amour courtois*, Paris, 1948. There is a sketch by A. Jeanroy in *Anthologie des Troubadours*, Paris, 1930.

[156] The bibliography of these works and of the studies that have been devoted to them is very extensive; R. Boussuat's *Manuel bibliographique de la littérature française du moyen âge*, Paris, 1951, gives more than 1300 titles. Among the texts may be mentioned the treatise of André le Chapelain (chaplain of Marie de Champagne), lines 1182–6; Latin text, with two Italian translations, by S. Battaglia, *Andrea Capellano. Trattato d'amore*, Rome, 1947; English translation by M. J. J. Parry, New York, 1941; there is also a study by F. Schlösser, *A. C., Seine Minnelehre und das christliche Weltbild um 1200*, Bonn, 1960. Selected texts will be found in A. Jeanroy, *op. cit.*; A. Barry, *Florilège des Troubadours*, Paris, 1930; R. Gout, *Le miroir des dames chrétiennes*, Paris, 1935. Studies by P. Remy, *La littérature provençale du moyen âge*, Brussels, 1944; J. Huizinga, *Le déclin du moyen âge*, Paris, 1948.

[157] Cf. E.-R. Labande, *Le "Credo" épique. A propos des prières dans les chansons de geste*, collection presented to M. C. Brunel, Paris, 1955, pp. 62–80.

lying the narrative is found the aspiration to purify the love of woman, to elevate and sublimate it. Perceval learns that he must keep himself pure if he wishes to become the guardian of the Grail and so attain to divine love. His son Galahad is the example and model of perfect holiness, and he it is who guards the Grail.[158]

Tristan and Iseult gives a more realistic picture of human love with its weakness, its faults, and its remorse, though one must not forget the words of mercy addressed to the lovers in the name of Christ by the hermit who reproved them.[159] The *Romaunt of the Rose*, a later work, also exalts (at least in the first part, by Guillaume de Lorris) the quest for the "rose", that is, for love, for woman. She becomes the object of a real worship and of pure desire which ennobles the virtuous man; a foreshadowing of Dante's Beatrice, who reveals to him something of the beauty of God himself. But the author of the second part, Jean de Meung, repudiated this exalted love.[160] For him the teaching on love, which is the essence of the *Romaunt*, includes a whole philosophy and theology, a view of the world and of human nature, whose law is fecundity. This alone is enough to justify fleshly love, and continence and virginity are just as much to be blamed as free love.[161]

This exaltation of woman was very far from being merely platonic. The end of the twelfth century was not notable for its morality, as we see in the works originating from other milieux, like the *Fabliaux* and the *Roman de Renart*.[162] "Love in the sense of passion", says Denis de Rougemont, "appeared in the West as one of the repercussions of Christianity (and especially of its doctrine on marriage) in souls in whom paganism, natural or inherited, was still alive."[163] There were obviously more general causes for this rather low morality, such as "the emergence of the lay spirit" or, more simply still, the fact that the level of civilization in many countries of Europe was not very high. The infection of Catharism, which developed in precisely those regions in which the literature of courtly love originated, is also a possible cause, and even more the possibility of Arabic influence.

It has been said that "love in the sense of passion, glorified by

158 For other interpretations, see *supra*, p. 246.

159 See *supra*, p. 274.

160 The first part was circulated in the second half of the thirteenth century; the rest seems to date from about 1280. Ed. E. Langlois, 5 vols, Paris, 1914–24.

161 Cf. G. Paré, *Le Roman de la Rose et la scolastique courtoise*, Paris, 1942; by the same, *Les idées et les lettres au XIII*e *siècle. Le Roman de la Rose*, Montreal, 1947.

162 The latter is thought to derive from the *Ysengrinus* of the Fleming Nivard (ed. F. J. Mone, 1832; E. Voigt, Halle, 1884), which seems to date from 1152 (L. Willems, *Etudes sur l'Ysengrinus*, Ghent, 1895).

163 *L'amour et l'Occident*, Paris, 1939, p. 68.

myth, was in the twelfth century (the date when it appeared) really a *religion* in the full sense of the term; specifically, it was a Christian heresy, historically determined",[164] but this seems unlikely, if the word "heresy" is to keep its meaning. The troubadours were not harassed; there is nothing to prove that they suffered from the Albigensian Crusade or from the Inquisition. The decline in the poetry of courtly love that took place in the thirteenth century was not caused by suppression; it was the result of a social evolution and of new literary tastes.[165] When we compare the traditional conception of human love with that of Catharism, dehumanized to the point of paradox in its requirement of purity and in its indulgence toward the flesh, and then with that of courtly love, it seems clear that the latter is Christian in origin.[166]

A new proof of this has recently been brought forward by showing how Provençal literature, from the twelfth to the fourteenth century, expresses in lyrical terms the fundamental Christian dogma of the Holy Trinity. The troubadours, of course, were always quite outside the debates of the schools, and their language is not very precise. For example they sometimes applied the term Trinity to Christ! They had a certain preference for devotion to the Holy Spirit, the *dulcis hospes animae* of the liturgy, and this devotion persisted even in the period of decline—the *Leys d'amor* and the *Breviari d'amor*. With this they combined a vivid sense of God who creates out of his sheer goodness, and whose fatherly "sweetness" is experienced by the believing soul.[167] The process by which Christian piety was refined is shown here with rare delicacy. The assiduous reading of Scripture as a source, together with the progress of civilization, was slowly creating a new equilibrium of the human and the supernatural. It was a prelude to the one that was soon to be worked out by the great Christian thinkers.

164 *Ibid.*, p. 119.

165 Cf. M. R. H. Gere, "The Troubadours' Heresy and the Albigensian Crusade", in *Abstracts of Dissertations*, XVI (1956), p. 738 (résumé of a thesis); A. J. Denomy, *The Heresy of Courtly Love*, New York, 1947; by the same, "An Inquiry into the Origins of Courtly Love", in *Mediaeval Studies*, VI (1944), pp. 175–260.

166 Cf. P. Belperron, *op. cit.*, pp. 220–35; E. Gilson, *The Mystical Theology of St Bernard*, Paris, 1947, p. 214. The *Revue de synthèse*, XXIII (1948), includes several studies on the relationship between Catharism and the troubadours, but they should be read with caution.

167 Cf. D. Zorgi, *Valori religiosi nella letteratura provenzale. La spiritualità trinitaria*, Milan, 1954. Devotion to the Trinity, however, was already long established. The feast and the office were observed at Liège in the tenth century, at the time of Bishop Stephen (903–20), in a form almost identical with that of the present Roman breviary (cf. A. Auda, *Etienne de Liège*, Brussels, 1923, pp. 67–84). Liturgical prayers and Masses in honour of the Trinity were in use from the eighth century (cf. A. P. Frutaz, art. "Trinità", in *Encicl. cattol.*, XII (1954), col. 541–4.

III

THE FRANCISCAN SPRING

1. The State of Religion at the Beginning of the Thirteenth Century

The twelfth century as a whole gives the impression of being a return to the sources. These were, first of all, the monastic sources, as seen in Cîteaux and the Chartreuse. But the sources of Christianity itself, the Bible and the Fathers, were being read anew; the teaching of tradition could now be more exactly determined, thanks to the system and technique, the categories and frames of thought, derived from the Greeks. Finally there was appearing, almost everywhere, a kind of passionate straining towards the pure ideal of the Gospel. Writers, artists and theologians were stressing the unrivalled place held in it by Christ and his Mother. Revolutionaries, social, political and religious, on their side, were pushing to extremes its requirement of absolute poverty and its opposition to all formalism or legalism. This attitude implied a sharp criticism of the monastic Rules. Were they necessary? Was not the Gospel put into practice enough? Could not others besides monks reach a high level of spiritual life?

Thus some men were no longer satisfied with the old monastic life—those that sought spiritual support adapted to their condition and to their conception of the perfect life, and those who demanded a purer preaching of the Gospel and a more vigorous reaction against abuses, especially against the wealth of the monasteries and the higher clergy. There were also those who wanted to make contact with the new scientific learning.

It was in this context that the Franciscan Spring arose, like a heavenly answer to the longings in the depths of the Christian soul. Poverty seemed to be a remedy, if not, indeed, *the* remedy. For all—rich and poor, clergy and laity—it was the living reminder of what Christ expected of them. At about this same time, the "Dominican crusade" took as its object, from 1206 on, a more direct fight against heresy. This has already been discussed in connection with the Albigensian crisis. The surprising thing, even on the doctrinal level, is that the remedy which Diego d'Azevedo and Dominic Guzman at length applied was not controversy, which had proved so ineffective; it was the life of poverty. Dominic and Francis were united not only in the end at which they aimed, the well-being of the Church, but also in their means: poverty and the active life.

The Orders which they founded provided a solution to the monastic and canonical aspirations of the period, but only by creating a new form of religious life, the Mendicants. At the same time they corresponded to the new intellectual tendencies, though indirectly, sometimes even unintentionally. Some of their members were soon to be found among the most shining lights of the universities, and would take their place among the doctors of the Church.

Francis and Dominic, then, gave to the spiritual problems of their time two not dissimilar answers. But although to begin with the two Orders shared the same ideal of service to the Church and practised the same poverty, although their theologians soon became masters of the first rank and the leaders of the schools, there was nevertheless a clear distinction between their ways of life. The spirituality of each, the theological teaching of their disciples and even the atmosphere they created (their form of religious life, in the conventional sense of the word) were sufficiently different to justify a separate study of each.

2. *Francis of Assisi*

The story of St Francis is one of the best known among Christians. To Catholic and non Catholic, believer or agnostic, his life and the Umbrian setting of the beginnings of the Order have a poetic quality which has always touched the imagination. They have all felt that in it they were rediscovering the Gospel in all its purity: it has even been said that no other saint has come as close to Christ as Francis. What makes him so attractive, today especially, is that he led, uncompromisingly, the life of the Gospel, even in a world where the Church had grown old and entangled in inextricable partisan conflicts and scandalous abuses.

No life of St Francis could be written which does not include a sketch of his own spirituality. He left little in writing—two Rules, a Testament, a few letters, a few exhortations and prayers,[1] but

[1] Ed. *Opuscula S. P. Francisci Assisiensis*, 3rd ed., Quaracchi, 1949; French translation, D. Forreux and P. Bayart, Paris, 1956; Willibrord, O.M.Cap., *Le message spirituel de Saint François d'Assise dans ses écrits*, Blois, 1960. Among the sources should also be mentioned the *Expositio quatuor Magistrorum super Regulam Fratrum Minorum (1241–1242). Accedit eiusdem Regulae textus cum fontibus et locis parallelis*, ed. L. Oliger, O.F.M., Rome, 1950. The *Opuscula* have been translated into most languages. For an Italian translation of the second rule and the *Testament*, see A. Levasti, *Mistici del Duocento e del Trecento*, Milan, 1935,

these themselves are only lit up by their author's life. It is the principal source, the one to which one must always go back, and it is therefore worth stopping a little while to reflect on it.

It is a difficult life to write. It is not enough to reproduce, just as they stand, the assertions of his too numerous biographers. Often they simply copy from one another. With no critical sense whatever, they draw upon the *Fioretti* (very debatable from a historical point of view) and then proceed to embroider. Fortunately, some recent historians have felt the need of exact and reliable documents and have devoted themselves to a real criticism of sources.[2] The first of them was the Protestant, Paul Sabatier, at the end of the last century[3]; since then the critics have scrupulously examined the ancient biographies and the works of St Francis and have tried to reconstruct the early days of the Order and to draw the authentic spiritual portrait of the *Poverello*.[4]

The difficulty arises chiefly from the first biographers of St Francis. Despite their authority, which is sometimes that of direct witnesses, they are consistently tendentious. The first of them was Thomas of Celano, an immediate disciple of Francis, received into the Order in 1214. He composed a *Vita* of which two versions are extant. That of 1229 was begun the day after the canonization of Francis (16 July 1228) and constitutes a source of the greatest value for the historian, as does that of 1247. But Thomas of Celano is suspected of having sought to reconcile the primitive Franciscan ideal with what it had later become in the Order, and so of having given an inaccurate picture of Francis. He also wrote a *Legenda chori* (1230) and a *Tractatus de Miraculis* (1250–3).[5]

---

pp. 107–20. We refer the reader, once and for all, to this excellent anthology of Italian spiritual writers of the thirteenth and fourteenth centuries; also to the anthology *Mystiques Franciscains* by I. Gobry, Paris, 1959.

[2] The principal biographies are those of J. Joergensen (translated into all languages), Fr Cuthbert, O.S.F.C. (London, 1912), O. Englebert (Paris, 1947), and I. Gobry's *Saint François d'Assise et l'esprit franciscain*, Paris, 1957. The most valuable popular publication—which is also the most dependable, letting the old texts speak for themselves—is A. Masseron's *La légende franciscaine. Textes choisis, traduits et annotés*, Paris, 1954. See also A. G. Little, *Guide to Franciscan Studies*, London, 1920; J. R. H. Moorman, *Sources for the Life of St Francis*, Manchester, 1940; D. Knowles, *The Religious Orders in England*, vol. I, Part II (esp. chs XI, XII and XV), Cambridge, 1956. For bibliographies, see Englebert, pp. 396–426; Masseron, pp. 49–54; Gobry, pp. 186–91. Also see *infra*, note 15.

[3] *Vie de saint François d'Assise*, 1st ed., Paris, 1894.

[4] There is a summary of recent studies by L. Salvatorelli, "Movimento francescano e gioachimismo", in *Relazione . . . del X Congresso Intern. Sc. stor.*, III, Florence, 1955, pp. 403–18.

[5] These works by Thomas of Celano are to be found in *S. Fr. A. Vita et miracula*, ed. Ubald d'Alençon, Rome, 1906. There are French translations of the *Vitae* by M. J. Fagot, Paris, 1922 and D. Vorreux, Paris, 1952. See also note 6. The *Vita* by Julian of Speyer, written between 1232 and 1239 (ed. *Analecta franciscana*, vol X), is an abridgment of Thomas's first biography.

The second important biographer, though he was later by a generation, was St Bonaventure. He also left two versions. The second, the *Legenda maior* (1263), became the official biography, and by this very fact is suspect to many historians. It was approved in 1266 by the chapter of Paris, which ordered at the same time that all other "legends" should be suppressed; among these was Bonaventure's first version, the *Legenda minor* (1261).[6]

There are, however, other sources of information: the writings set down or inspired by the fervent disciples of the early days, especially Brother Leo. To help Thomas of Celano in composing his second *Vita*, the minister general Crescentius had a memoir drawn up, the *Legenda trium sociorum*, the "legend of the three companions"—Leo, Angelus and Rufinus. It had scarcely any circulation on account of the ban of 1266, and what can be reconstructed of it today is of debatable value; some consider that in its present form it dates from the end of the thirteenth century.[7] A *Legenda antiqua* is more dependable and can be considered to be really the work of Brother Leo.[8] A *Speculum perfectionis*, "mirror of perfection", has been the object of lively controversies. Sabatier held it to be a testimony of capital importance, which must date from 1227 and must be attributed, like the *Legenda antiqua*, to Brother Leo. The date may be contested, but some good historians admit that this document, together with the "legend of the three companions", represents the "Leonine" tradition, or that which stemmed from Brother Leo.[9] The poem known under the title of *Sacrum commercium sancti Francisci cum domina Paupertate* would seem to date from 1227 and so belongs to the same period.[10]

These are the three groups of sources to which cautious and discerning reference must be made. Bonaventure, the latest in time, was concerned with appeasing the rivalries that were dividing St Francis' disciples, and with minimizing their deviations from the primitive ideal. As for Thomas of Celano and Brother Leo, each

[6] A learned edition of Bonaventure's two *Legendae* and those of Thomas has been published in *Analecta franciscana*, vol. X, Part I, Quaracchi, 1926–41 (*Legendae S. F. Ass. saeculis XIII et XIV conscriptae*). There are French translations of Bonaventure by M. J. Fagot, Paris, 1926 and D. Vorreux, Paris, 1952.

[7] Ed. *Acta Sanctorum*, October, II, pp. 723–42; Mgr M. Faloci-Pulignani, Foligno, 1898. There is a French translation by L. Pichard, Paris, 1926.

[8] Ed. F. M. Delorme, Paris, 1926 French translation by M. J. Fagot, Paris, 1927.

[9] Cf. L. Salvatorelli, *loc. cit.*, p. 409. The *Speculum* was published by P. Sabatier, with the *Acta B. Fr. et sociorum eius*, the *Chronicle* of Jordanus of Giano, and various other texts, in the "Collection de documents pour l'histoire religieuse et littéraire du moyen âge", Paris, 1898 and following years. Others have been published in *Analecta franciscana*, vols. I to V. There is a French translation of the *Speculum* by P. Budry, Paris, 1911.

[10] Ed. Édouard d'Alençon, Rome, 1900; ed. Quaracchi, 1919. French translation, Paris, 1913.

must be corrected and completed by the other. Thomas neglects those aspects of Francis' personality that would offend the mentality of his present disciples, such as the practice of manual labour and the refusal to accept favours or ecclesiastical charges. Leo, on the other hand, is rigid in his fidelity to the primitive traditions. The least that can be said is that the assertions of all these sources must be compared with one another and with the writings of Francis himself.

Before long there were other attempts at biography. The *Vita* of Jacopo de Voragine (1265–80) depends on Thomas of Celano and St Bonaventure.[11] The *Legenda sanctae Clarae virginis* was written in 1256 at the order of Alexander IV and seems also to be by Thomas of Celano.[12] The best known of these late writings, and the one from which a number of modern writers have drawn their inspiration, is known under the title of *Fioretti*, "little flowers". Its fifty-three chapters were set down later than 1322, a century after the death of Francis. They appear to be the work of "Spiritual" Franciscans of the Marches of Ancona. Here, as has been said, "we are at the somewhat vague borderline between history and legend, taking the latter word in its present-day and not its medieval sense".[13] In short, the *Fioretti* throw more light on the history of the Order after a century of existence than they do upon its origins.[14]

These preliminaries are not superfluous; they make it easier to understand what caution is needed in accepting even the data that comes from the sources nearest to Francis himself. The principal stages of his extraordinary life are known, but the accounts that are given of them must be carefully checked.[15]

Francis was born in 1181 or 1182, the son of a rich cloth merchant of Assisi, Pietro Bernadone, and his wife Pica who, according to a trustworthy tradition, came from Provence. Assisi was an imperial town and at that time was very prosperous, which accounts for the fact that Pietro Bernadone was travelling in France on business at the time when his son was born. Pica had named him Giovanni; Pietro, on his return, nicknamed him Francesco. If we

[11] Ed. *Analecta franciscana*, X. [12] Ed. F. Ponnacchi, Assisi, 1910.

[13] A. Masseron, *op. cit.*, p. 46. The *Fioretti* have been edited, with other texts, by P. Bughetti, O.F.M., Florence, 1926. On the sources from which they were derived, see G. Petrocchi, *Ascesi e mistica trecentesca*, Florence, 1957, ch. IV, pp. 85–146. There have been many translations of the *Fioretti* into all languages.

[14] On the history of the Order at its origin, the principal work is that of Gratien, O.S.F.C., *Histoire de la fondation et de l'évolution de l'Ordre des Frères Mineurs au XIIIe siècle*, Paris, 1928; cf. R. M. Huber, *A Documented History of the Franciscan Order, 1182–1517*, Washington, 1944.

[15] On modern biographies, see the summary by F. van den Borne, O.F.M., "Het probleem van de Franciscus-biografie in het licht van de moderne historische Kritiek", in *Sint Franciscus*, LVII (1955), pp. 241–320; also *ibid.*, LVIII (1956), pp. 31–80.

are to believe the *Legenda prima* of Thomas of Celano, Francis' youth was worldly and given up to sin.[16] This was not denied till Bonaventure's *Legenda* and the chapter of 1260, which had two lines of the Matins hymn revised: *plus suis nutritoribus/se gessit insolenter* became *divinis charismatibus/preventus est clementer.*[17] Francis took part in his father's business. He was prodigal of the money he handled, and not all of it went in alms. All the accounts, even when stripped of their rhetoric, confirm his own avowal in the Testament: *cum essem in peccatis*, "when I was still in sin".[18] Nevertheless, Francis always kept a fundamental decency, the honourable behaviour of a well-bred man; he even showed considerable sympathy for the sufferings of others.

He was a youth when Assisi dreamed of throwing off the imperial yoke. The *Rocca*, a fortress which overlooked the town, was defended by an imperial garrison. At the end of 1199 or the beginning of 1200, the burghers and townspeople took it by storm and destroyed it. They then built massive walls, parts of which still exist. The nobles of Assisi, who had fled to Perugia, succeeded in unleashing a war in which, for ten years, the two towns wore themselves out. In the course of this struggle there took place, on 12 September 1202, the battle of the Ponte San' Giovanni on the Tiber, in which Francis was taken prisoner and carried off to Perugia. He remained there until November 1203 and then, thanks to a provisional peace, returned to Assisi. He was ill, he had possibly already contracted the tuberculosis which, according to some, carried him off prematurely. In any case, he recovered only slowly from the effects of his captivity. The ordeal did not cause him to abandon his dreams of pleasure and chivalry.

Yet it was now that his conversion began. A prophetic dream at Spoleto made him give up the plan of rejoining the papal forces, and one day he began to muse aloud, before his companions, of "plighting his troth to a Lady so noble, so rich, so fair and so wise, that none of you ever saw anyone like her".[19] This "Lady" to whom he wanted to give himself was the Poverty of him who demands that a man leave all things to follow him. On a pilgrimage to Rome he put on the livery of that Lady, and on his return "I was impelled by the Lord", he says, "to go to the lepers, and mercifully did I care for them. When I left them, what had seemed to me bitter was changed for me into sweetness both of spirit and body. A short

[16] I, I, 1–2 (French translation by A. Masseron, *op. cit.*, pp. 56–9). The *Legenda secunda* gives a slightly different picture (*ibid.*, pp. 59–61).

[17] "He behaved insolently toward those who brought him up" was changed to "He was mercifully favoured with divine charismata".

[18] *Testament*, 1; D. Vorreux and P. Bayart, *Opuscules* . . ., p. 147.

[19] *Vita prima*, 7; *Tres Socii*, 7.

time afterwards, I left the world."[20] These words from the *Testament* throw light on the story of the kiss given to the leper, in a lazar-house to which Francis had taken a poor wretch whom he met along the road.

He then took up the rebuilding of churches, among which was the dilapidated chapel of San Damiano. Had not the Byzantine crucifix there said to him, "Francis, see to the repair of my house, which is falling to ruin"? But he made the mistake of using his father's money for the purpose. Everyone knows the scene in which, called before the bishop of Assisi, he gave back to his father not only his money but all his clothes, renouncing even his sonship, "having no longer any father but him who is in heaven". After a sojourn at Gubbio, and another with the lepers, he came back to San Damiano and began again to rebuild churches; this time he begged the money needed for the work. He probably continued this way of life for two or three years. One day he attended Mass in the restored chapel of St Mary of the Angels, which was later to be called the Portiuncula,[21] some little distance from Assisi, on the Umbrian plain. There, at the reading of the Gospel, he heard this order from Christ: "Do not possess gold, nor silver, nor money in your purses: nor scrip for your journey, nor two coats, nor shoes, nor a staff; for the workman is worthy of his meat. And into whatsoever city or town you shall enter, inquire who in it is worthy, and there abide till you go thence."[22] This episode must have taken place in 1208 or 1209. Francis now understood that his vocation was not to rebuild churches but to rebuild the Church, and that the means was to be none other than the Gospel itself and its charter of poverty. In the preceding century too there had been men who wanted to return to radical poverty; Stephen of Muret, for example, wished to do so, but he conceived this poverty as being for monks, apart from the world. Francis made it the instrument of his work for the Church. He then began to preach, and disciples began to gather about him. Among these companions of the early days, Bernard of Quintavalle, Peter of Cattaneo, and Giles are the best known. Later came Leo, Elias, Juniper and many others. Unfortunately there were also Judases among them. This band of "brothers" in no sense adumbrated a new Order. Possibly, at least at the be-

[20] *Testament*, 2–3.

[21] It is said to have been so called by St Benedict, who was supposed to have acquired an adjoining property (*portiuncula terreni*). The chapel was served by the Benedictines of Monte Subasio.

[22] Matt. 10. 9–11. It is difficult to fix the exact date on which the Gospel was read. There are evangeliaria which show that, before the thirteenth century, these verses came on the feasts of St Luke and St Mark (according to Luke, ch. 10, as today) and in Masses of martyrs (according to Matthew and Mark).

ginning, they were hardly distinguishable from certain bands of penitents, and adopted their usages.

When the disciples numbered eleven, Francis gave them (in 1209 or 1210) a first Rule, very short, which is unfortunately lost today. It was approved orally by Innocent III, after the well-known dream in which he saw the Lateran basilica, on the point of collapsing, upheld on the shoulders of the frail beggar.[23] Francis then made a promise of obedience to the pope, which was followed by the tonsure of the first brethren and possibly by the ordination of Francis to the diaconate.

Despite papal approval, Francis encountered difficulties, as may well be imagined. After all, he and his disciples were given to extreme ascetic and apostolic practices which would appear to identify them clearly with the heretics who were pullulating all over Italy.[24] Their Rule so emphasized humility, poverty and even mendicancy that such a suspicion could not fail to arise in men's minds. But its emphasis was no less on charity and on the strictest obedience to the authority of the Church. "Let the brethren, under pain of being expelled from the brotherhood, always behave as good Catholics. They are to follow the customs and teaching of the Roman Church, and to rely on the teaching of the clergy, secular and regular, in all that is not contrary to their rule. Let them go to confession to any priest approved by the Church."

This zeal and this love of the Church did not exclude any of Christ's representatives, not even the most unworthy. The *Testament* expresses, in moving language, what Francis thought of priests, "even if they were to persecute me".[25] This attitude is characteristic of the true reformer. Francis had what enables a man to do a lasting work in the Church: love, humility and obedience. He was to go so far as to let another man be put at the head of his Order and to submit himself to him.

Now came the enchanted years of the life of the first brethren. They came from all parts and bound themselves by a vow of obedience to the Poverello. Sometimes they were sent out to preach, to work on the farms, to beg, or to tend the lepers. Sometimes they lived a life of prayer and penance in the wood that then surrounded the Portiuncula (the Benedictines of Monte Subasio had ceded it to Francis in perpetuity, at a low rental) or, later, at the Carceri, at Rivo Torto, Monte Alverna, Fonte Colombo and elsewhere.

The recruits included women as well as men. Of those who came

[23] It has been possible to reconstruct the Rule of 1209 in accordance with the *Testament*, 15; see O. Englebert, *op. cit.*, pp. 117–18.

[24] See the table of these in L. Salvatorelli, *loc. cit.*, pp. 418–24. For an account of the heretics, see previous chapter.

[25] *Testament*, 6–13.

in contact with the life and preaching of Francis, the best known is Clare, who belonged to the patrician family of the Offreducci of Cocorano.[26] Francis gave her the religious habit at the Portiuncula in March 1212, and so began the Order of the "Poor Ladies". Francis drew up a rule for them, a fragment of which was incorporated in the "Rule of the sisters of St Clare". In his "last counsels to St Clare",[27] it is not surprising to find him insisting on the poverty that his spiritual daughters had undertaken to practise at San Damiano.

Francis' preaching, according to unanimous testimony, touched the most hardened hearts. The wonderful fascination that emanated from his whole person acted even on irrational creatures. The conversion of the wolf of Gubbio and the sermon to the birds (mentioned as early as the first *Legenda* of Thomas of Celano, though in very brief form) are the best known of many episodes in which all creation was subject to his mysterious charm. His holiness seems to have somehow restored the atmosphere of the earthly paradise, in which man lived in friendship with nature.

As a consequence of his passionate love of Christ and the Gospel, Francis was also a passionate apostle of the Church, like Dominic Guzman. To the latter he left, perhaps deliberately, the urgent task of preaching in the areas tainted with the Albigensian heresy.[28] He himself dreamt always of devoting himself to the conversion of Islam. In 1212 he started for the East for the first time, with this end in view. His ship was driven by the wind on to the Dalmatian coast, and he went back to Italy by land. The plan took shape again, however, and two years later Francis tried to reach Morocco. Again his way was barred, this time in Spain by illness, and again he returned to Italy. Possibly he saw, in this double failure, a sign from Providence. In the meantime, in May 1213, a hermitage on Monte Alverno had been given him by Count Orlando of Chiusi; perhaps this too seemed to him a sign that his vocation did not lie in far-off lands. As it was, he decided, at least provisionally, that he was still called to devote himself to the salvation of his neighbours,[29] yet without altogether giving up the plan of converting the Moslems. In 1219 he again took the road for the East. But the unworthy conduct of the crusaders at Damietta, after they took

[26] See the biographical sketch by E. Longpré, O.F.M., "Sainte Claire d'Assise", in *Études franciscaines*, 4 (1953), 5–21 (bibliography); ed. Schneider, *Sainte Claire d'Assise*, Paris, 1959; A. M. Berel, Paris, 1960.

[27] See D. Vorreux and P. Bayart, *Opuscules* . . ., pp. 142–3; A. Masseron, *op. cit.*, pp. 168–9.

[28] Cf. K. Esser, O.F.M., "Fr von A. und die Katharer seiner Zeit", in *Arch. francisc. histor.*, LI (1958), 225–64.

[29] In the *Fioretti*, 16, we find a slight reflection of this hesitation on Francis' part.

that city on 5 November 1219, the failure of his efforts to convert the Sultan, and the difficulties that were beginning within his Order in Italy made him decide to retrace his steps, after having made a detour through the Holy Places.[30]

Little is known as to Francis' presence (which is, in any case, doubtful) at the Fourth Ecumenical Council of the Lateran in 1215; *a fortiori*, still less of any activity of his there. The question of the new religious orders was examined at the Council. The thirteenth canon forbade the creation of any more of them, and declared that henceforth anyone wishing to enter religion or to found a religious house must choose an institute and rule that had already been approved. Innocent III made it known that the Friars Minor had received his verbal approval.[31] As for Dominic, he chose the rule of St Augustine. It was probably in this year that Francis and Dominic, the two chief founders of Orders in the thirteenth century, met one another. A little later—in 1216, it would appear, under Honorius III—Francis obtained the celebrated indulgence known as that of the Portiuncula, for all those who should visit the chapel of that name on 2 August of that year, the day of the solemn dedication of St Mary of the Angels. Only later was this indulgence extended to each anniversary of the event.

As the Order continued to spread, it became necessary to have rules, a controlling organization, and a more precise juridical constitution. The Franciscan movement owed its birth to a great spiritual fervour, and at the beginning its character was distinctly charismatic. But human beings remain weak, though they may be capable of sanctity when they are following in the footsteps of a real saint who leads them on beyond their ordinary potentialities. Francis, therefore, in order to ensure the cohesion of the Order and to maintain its fervour, organized the chapters—a sort of periodic camp to which all the brethren came. There were first the chapters of Pentecost, then those of St Michael.[32] The chapter of Pentecost in 1217 established the provinces and the provincial ministers. That of 1219, called "the chapter of the mats", created missions in all countries except England, where there was no mission until 1224.[33] A few years later, in 1223, the chapter approved the Rule and

[30] On the hardening of Francis' attitude after Damietta, see L. Massignon, "Mystique musulmane et mystique chrétienne au moyen âge", in *Convegno di scienze morali, storiche e filologiche*, Rome, 1957, pp. 32–4.

[31] See *Legenda antiqua*, ed. M. Delorme, *Arch. francisc. histor.*, XV (1922), p. 311; cf. Mansi, *Ampl. collect. concil.*, XXII, pp. 1002–3.

[32] The only general chapters of which we have certain knowledge are those of 1217, 1219, 1221 and 1224. After 1221, they were called only every three years, and a limited number of friars took part.

[33] In this connection, see the *Tractatus de Adventu Fratrum minorum in Angliam* of Thomas of Eccleston (ed. A. G. Little, Manchester, 1951).

solemnly confirmed it. This was the "second" of the rules contained in the "opuscula of St Francis"; it is still in force today. The "first", that of 1221, had been the rough draft of it, and was itself preceded by the lost rule of 1209 or 1210. The text of 1221 was a patchwork of various provisions, chiefly juridical, and of scriptural quotations collected by Caesarius of Spires at Francis' request. The Rule of 1223 bears in addition the mark of "the modifications which the papal chancellery quietly imposed on the text before its final approval by Honorius III on November 29".[34] Divided into twelve chapters, it is considerably more condensed than the preceding version, which had twenty-three. We find in it the themes that had always been dear to Francis: poverty, manual labour, preaching, missions to the heathen, and the balance between action and contemplation.

During Francis' journey to the East, the Order was shaken by its first serious disturbance. The vicars-general whom he had left in Italy, Matthew of Narni and Gregory of Naples, introduced innovations that were foreign to Francis' idea: study, more frequent fasting and abstinence, strict discipline, and the building of churches and convents. These were not altogether bad things and they tended, moreover, to bring about a greater cohesion among the friars, who were now several thousand in number, often wandering about with fantastic notions. Besides, the vicars had the excuse that there had been a rumour of Francis' death in the East. But directly Francis returned, he went to the pope and asked him for an assistant to govern the Order; Honorius III designated Cardinal Ugolino. At the chapter of St Michael (probably that of 1220) the saint resigned and appointed Peter of Cattaneo as minister general. But Peter died on 10 March of the following year. He was then succeeded by the notorious Brother Elias.

Francis, whose health was becoming more and more precarious, devoted himself henceforth to preaching, penance and prayer. On 17 September 1224, in the hermitage of Monte Alverno, he received the grace of the stigmata. This miracle, which was without precedent in the Church, was a sign that Francis, by his humility and his suffering, had united himself to the Redeemer who looks to men to collaborate in his work of redemption by penance, by prayers, by holiness and by love.

At the same time, his weakness and his blindness were increasing. More and more frequently he vomited blood. Neither the sisters at San Damiano nor physicians of great repute were able to relieve him. At this painful time, when his physical strength and his sight

[34] D. Vorreux and P. Bayart, *Opuscules . . .*, p. 119.

were deserting him and when his Order was passing into other hands—hands that were sometimes so strangely harsh and uncomprehending towards the Poverello and Lady Poverty—he composed at San Damiano the unforgettable Canticle of the Sun. In an hour of cruel suffering, before the *Testament* of April, 1226, and that of his very last days,[35] he drew up this other spiritual testament, this joyful masterpiece of religious poetry:

Most high, most powerful and good Lord,
To thee be praise and glory,
Honour and all blessing.

They become thee alone,
O thou most high.
No man is worthy to pronounce thy name.

Blessed be thou, my Lord, with all that thou hast made,
Especially my Mother Sun
By whom thou givest us light, and the
day which thou hast made.

One of the stanzas dates from July, 1226, and sings the praises of pardon and peace, for Francis wished to put an end to the strife between the bishop of Assisi and its mayor.

Blessed be thou, my Lord, for those who forgive,
for love of thee bearing injustice and
tribulation.

Blessed are they when they persevere
in peace, for it is thou, Most High,
who shall crown them with glory.

Meanwhile his strength continued to decline. He gathered the brethren together and spoke to them once more of Lady Poverty. He encouraged Clare and her sisters, Jacoba of Settesoli, and his first disciple, Bernard of Quintavalle. He made them lay him naked on the earth, to await death. He accepted a garment made of woollen stuff brought him by "Brother Jacoba". He added a new stanza to the Canticle of the Sun:

Blessed be thou, my Lord, for our sister
the death of the body,
from whom no man alive escapes.

Wretched alone are they who die in mortal sin.

[35] D. Vorreux and P. Bayart, *Opuscules . . .*, pp. 145–55 and 328–9. On the *Testament*, see K. Esser, O.F.M., *Das Testament des hl. Fr. von Ass. Eine Untersuchung über seine Echtheit und seine Bedeutung*, Münster, 1949. Akin to the *Testament* is the letter *ad omnes clericos de reverentia Corporis Domini*, Vorreux and Bayart, *Opuscules . . .*, pp. 183–7. There is a study on it by B. Cornet, O.F.M., in *Études franciscaines*, VI (1955), pp. 65–91, 167–80; VII (1956), pp. 20–35, 155–171; VIII (1957), pp. 33–58.

Blessed are they who have fulfilled
thy most holy will, for the second death
can no longer harm them.

Praise and bless my Lord; give thanks to him,
and serve him with great humility.[36]

On the evening of 3 October 1226 he intoned Psalm 141, *Voce mea ad Dominum clamavi*, and his brethren chanted with him those haunting words which sum up all Francis' longings for contemplation, and all his joy; *Educ de custodia animam meam ad confitendum nomini tuo!*—"Bring my soul out of prison, that I may praise thy name!" One of them read, at his request, Chapter 13 of St John, *Ante diem festum Paschae*. As he listened to it the saint breathed his last. The *vox populi* had already canonized him in his lifetime; Gregory IX was only confirming its verdict when, on 16 July 1228—less than two years after his death—he enrolled him in the calendar of saints.

3. *The Critical Episode of the Spirituals*

Men have often wondered what it was that St Francis intended. In the beginning he was simply a fervent Christian, full of love for Christ and intransigent in his fidelity to the gospel of poverty and to humble manual labour: "everything was to recall pilgrimage and exile."[37] His desire to imitate Christ made him embrace the cross with passion. Periodically he was seized with a yearning for the eremitical life. At the same time, he looked at nature with the eyes of a child and a poet. He wanted to put himself at the service of the Church, to devote himself to preaching the kingdom of God, to vow every tenderness to the poor, the wretched and the lepers. The number of disciples who flocked to him soon made necessary at least a minimum of organization, and here Cardinal Ugolino gave a new aspect to Francis' work: chapters, provinces, a Rule, the appointment of a Superior.

From this time also dates the first known rule for associations of layfolk, *fratres et sorores*, "living in their own houses", "continents", "penitents".[38] But the existence of such associations goes

[36] Cf. G. Sabatelli, O.F.M., "Studi recenti sul Cantico di frate Sole", in *Arch. francis. histor.*, LI (1958), pp. 3–24; E. W. Platzeck, *Das Sonnenlied des hl. Fr. von Assisi*, Munich, 1957.

[37] Second *Vita* by Thomas of Celano, ch. xxx. On Franciscan poverty, see F. Leclercq, O.F.M., "La pauvreté de saint François", in *La pauvreté*, Paris, 1952, pp. 71–84; and K. Esser, O.F.M., "Die Lehre des hl. Fr. von der Selbstverleugnung", in *Wiss. u. Weisheit*, XVIII (1955), pp. 161–74.

[38] Text of the *Manuale propositi Fratrum et Sororum de Penitentia in domibus propriis existentium*, of 1221, ed. B. Bughetti, O.F.M., in *Arch. franc. hist.*, XIV (1921), pp. 109–21.

back much further than Francis' time,[39] and he certainly never dreamed of creating a "third order" in the shadow of the first two, his own and Clare's. His own Brotherhood in the beginning must have been of this kind. In any case, the *Manuale* of 1221, composed for such confraternities, does not imply affiliation with the Franciscans, unless it be in the repeated mention of the "minister" who supervises them. There are papal bulls officially recognizing them from this date, but they do not speak of an Order in this connection until after 1249. In the thirteenth century the sovereign pontiffs tended to put these associations, which were sometimes unruly, under the direction of important Orders. The example of the Franciscans was very soon to be followed by the Dominicans. It was about fifteen years, then, before a clear distinction began to be made between religious and seculars living by the same Franciscan ideal.

There had been an evolution in the Order properly so called, even in Francis' lifetime. That was why he preferred to leave to others the government of his thousands of disciples, while he himself chose to bear witness with obstinate fidelity, by his preaching and example, to Lady Poverty; he went on doing so before seculars as well as before the Friars Minor, up to his last moments when he lay on the bare earth. That there was an evolution is quite clear. To give only one indication of it, it may be recalled that the immediate disciples of Francis built, in a few years, the two magnificent basilicas, one upon the other, of the *Sacro Convento* at Assisi. To glorify Lady Poverty and her troubadour, they called upon the most celebrated artists and architects. Francis himself had disapproved of a building that was too sumptuous for his liking, built near St Mary of the Angels, and had had it demolished.[40] What would he have said of the basilica which now shelters the Portiuncula and which reminds one slightly of St Peter's in Rome? In spite of this lack of understanding among his most immediate disciples, the authentic Christian message was saved at the time by a few saints, chief among them Francis himself. And this despite the fact that he belonged to thirteenth-century Italy, with all that was peculiar to it, and also despite his undeniable kinship of spirit with the suspect sects of his day. Francis succeeded in extracting from

[39] Cf. G. Meersseman, O.P., and E. Adda, "Pénitents ruraux communautaires en Italie au XIIe siècle", in *Rev. d'hist. eccl.*, XLIX (1954), pp. 343–90. A true religious order "of penance", derived from the Franciscan Order, had a somewhat ephemeral existence between 1248 and 1274; see G. M. Giacomozzi, O.S.M., "L'Ordine della penitenza di Gesù Cristo. Contributo alla storia della spiritualità del secolo XIII", in *Studi storici dell'Ordine dei Servi di Maria*, VIII (1957–8), pp. 3–60.

[40] Celano, *II Legenda*, II, 27, 57; French translation in A. Masseron, *op. cit.*, pp. 144–5.

all these longings what was timeless and supra-national in them, and in giving them a positive content by remaining "a good Catholic" (to use his own expression) in the love of Christ and the Gospel, of the Church and her hierarchy. He saw that this was the sure way to renew the Church "from within". His was, therefore, a much bigger work than the mere foundation of a new Order. His own laying down of all authority and the treacheries of his disciples have never been able to suffocate the message.[41]

Of course one must not underestimate the tremendous difficulties involved in the practice of this ideal in a very large Order, devoted to extensive apostolic labours, and soon to undertake the intellectual work inevitably demanded by the training of young recruits, and by the priesthood.[42] The brethren were not to possess anything; they were not to receive coin or money "either directly or through an intermediary", according to the express terms of the second Rule; according to the *Testament*, "neither churches nor humble dwellings, nor anything built for them, if it is not in conformity with the holy Poverty which we have promised in the Rule". It would be difficult to realize this ideal in the concrete! This explains both the mitigations which were soon made in the Poverello's sacred precepts and also the reactions in the direction of strict fidelity to them. These reactions were embodied in Brother Leo, and they passed into the writings, which are attributed to him or use his name, where the reader sometimes senses the passion with which they were charged. It is well known that the reform known as the "Observants" brought together all the brethren who felt as Brother Leo did; but their connection with the Spirituals (who will be discussed presently) rendered them suspect for a long time. It was not until the end of the fourteenth century that they received authorization to leave the convents in the towns and to live in hermitages. Thus they were distinguished from the "Conventuals" who lived in the "convents" and who, not accepting the reform, permitted the holding of collective property including revenues and lands. The Council of Constance, in 1415, gave the Observants an independent hierarchy.[43]

41 In this connection, see L. Salvatorelli, *loc. cit.*, pp. 424–37. For St Francis' influence on popular piety, see the study by R. Delaruelle, "L'influence de saint François d'Assise sur la piété populaire", in *ibid.*, pp. 449–66. See also Fr. Cuthbert, O.S.F.C., *The Romanticism of St Francis*, 2nd ed., London, 1924; Knowles, *op. cit.*, ch. xv, "The Evolution of the Franciscan Ideal".

42 See S. Clasen, O.F.M., "Priesterliche Würde und Würdigkeit. Das Verhältnis des hl. Fr. zum Priestertum der Kirche", in *Wiss. u. Weisheit*, XX (1957), pp. 45–58.

43 Other reforms appeared in the fifteenth and sixteenth centuries. The only one that survives today is that of the Capuchins. All the others (Recollects, Alcantarins, etc.) were attached to the Observants by Leo XIII in 1897 (the "Leonine Union").

The trouble with the Spirituals had begun very early. From the first days of the Order, and even more after the founder's death, it had seemed necessary to modify the primitive ideal. Inevitably, difficulties arose: a violent reaction broke out at the end of the thirteenth century and the beginning of the fourteenth, on the part of one section of the Friars Minor, later called the "Spirituals". In their intransigent fidelity to the Poverello, they ended up by setting poverty above obedience—including obedience to the pope —and even above charity. In one sense they were right to defend the radical poverty which had been Francis' ideal. But a certain tone betrays them. For example, one of the most famous of them, Angelo da Clareno, in his *Chronicle of the Troubles of the Order of Minors*, did not hesitate to accuse Brother Elias in these terms:

> He caused to fall into disuse a great many of the prescriptions which he had received by the words and the example of Francis the man of God, judging them to be without value and contemptible. Carried away by the false words of his flatterers and partisans, raised to honour by the renown and favour that he enjoyed with the emperor, the pope, and the other masters, who considered him far superior to all the rest on account of his knowledge, his natural prudence, and the apparent integrity of his life, he began to impose his views on all the brethren as being sound, salutary, easy of execution, and full of discretion.[44]

Elsewhere the situation was complicated by quarrels with the secular clergy and with the University of Paris.[45] The Spirituals accepted certain theses of Joachimism and believed that the era of the Holy Spirit had begun with Francis, or at least that it would begin soon. After Francis' death, as has been seen, the attitude of the minister general Brother Elias was not such as to calm the anxieties of Brother Leo's disciples. Nor could the bull *Quo elongati* of Gregory IX (28 September 1230) satisfy them, since it recognized as legitimate the use of money, at least through an intermediary. And mitigations continued to increase. In the eyes of the Spirituals, the *Testament* of the Poverello took on the aspect of a pathetic appeal, authorizing insubordination towards superiors in the Order and even towards the authority of Rome, and condemning in advance, as bastard works, those of Thomas of Celano and St Bona-

[44] *Second Tribulation.* The first two of these *Tribulations* were published by F. Tocco in *Rendiconti della R. Accademia dei Lincei*, XVII (1908); the last five, by Fr Ehrle in *Archiv. f. Literatur u. Kirchengesch.*, II (1886). Another document that is interesting in connection with the episode of the Spirituals, the *Expositio regulae fratrum minorum* of Angelo of Clareno, has been published by Fr L. Oliger, O.F.M., Quaracchi, 1912.

[45] On St Bonaventure and the disputes with the seculars, see S. Clasen, O.F.M., *Bonaventura und das Mendikantentum*, Werl in Westphalia, 1940.

venture, who sought to reconcile what was essential in the Franciscan ideal with the powers of the average human being.

Such, then, were the dramatic events of the time: if poverty was losing ground in the Community, obedience and charity were in danger among the Spirituals. In 1294 Celestine I officially sanctioned the division of the two branches and recognized the existence of the Spirituals, who then formed three quite distinct groups (the Marches of Ancona, Provence and Tuscany). Boniface VIII, however, re-established unity, to the obvious advantage of the Community,[46] and the Spirituals took up a defensive attitude. The names associated with this phase of their history are those of Pierre Jean Olivi (†1298), Ubertino of Casale († after 1329), Angelo de Clarena (†1337), and even the holy Brother Conrad of Offida, *alter Franciscus* (†1306). Clement V granted the Spirituals their own convents, despite their juridical union with the Community. John XXII, however, wanted to lessen the tension that persisted between the two groups; the decretal *Quorumdam* of 7 October 1317 sharply reminded the Spirituals of the duty of obedience, and of the right possessed by superiors of defining the manner in which poverty was to be observed in the Community of Friars.[47] It was not, as yet, a condemnation, but that was to follow in the bulls *Sancta Romana* (30 December 1317) and *Gloriosam Ecclesiam* (23 January 1318). The first of these was aimed at all the Spirituals, Fraticelli, Brothers of the Poor Life, Beghards, etc., whatever their names might be[48]; the second was aimed specifically at certain Tuscan Spirituals who had taken refuge in Sicily.[49] Angelo da Clareno nevertheless continued to regard himself as general of the "Fraticelli," as they were henceforth to be called, and to act accordingly. In 1334, John XXII issued a warrant for his arrest, which was never executed. Angelo does not seem to have had any successor, but there were still Fraticelli in the fifteenth century.[50] Moreover, the Order as a whole always retained a yearning for more radical poverty, often tinged with an eremitical tendency. It has already been mentioned that this

[46] The Community's point of view is expressed in a little treatise *De usu paupere*, which has been edited, with other useful texts from *Rome, Arch. of Coll. of S. Isidore 1/146*, by F. M. Delorme, in *Collect. francisc.*, XV (1945), pp. 5–91.

[47] *Bullarium franc.*, vol. V, No. 289.

[48] *Ibid.*, No. 297.

[49] *Ibid.*, No. 302.

[50] See Gratien, O.S.F.C., *Histoire de la fondation et de l'évolution de l'Ordre des Frères Mineurs au XIIIe siècle*. Among recent studies, the following may be consulted: L. Oliger, O.F.M., art. "Spirituels", in *Dict. théol. cath.*, XIV, col. 2522–2549; M. D. Chenu, O.P., "L'expérience des Spirituels au XIIIe siècle", in *Lumière et vie*, No. 10 (1953), pp. 75–94 (in which the "episode of the Spirituals" is taken, not unreasonably, as beginning with the Third Lateran Council, 1179); E. Benz, *Ecclesia spiritualis*, Stuttgart, 1934 (to be read with caution). There are French translations of the texts in A. Masseron, *op. cit.*, ch. XVI. On Angelo of Clareno, see L. von Auw, *Angelo Clareno et les Spirituels franciscains*, Lagny, 1952.

ideal resulted, at the beginning of the fifteenth century, in a separation to some extent of the Conventuals from the Observants.

What lay behind this critical episode? Was it intransigence—poverty at any price—even, if necessary, at the expense of charity and obedience? The question is an agonizing one. In the light of the Gospel, absolute poverty is certainly the ideal proposed by Christ to the rich young man, and of course to anyone who asks himself that question. Also, renunciation of all earthly possessions is the necessary interior disposition of anyone who wishes to be Christ's disciple. Obedience too seems to be a precept of general application; it is binding upon every Christian, committed as he is to a Church whose life presupposes an authority derived from Christ himself. It is no more a matter of choice than is renunciation. The conflict between the ideal of poverty, and obedience, among the disciples of the Poverello, lay in the fact that some were led, by their adhesion to poverty, to minimize obedience; the others, for the sake of obedience, to sacrifice something of Francis' precepts.

This serious crisis made it clear that absolute poverty—difficult enough to practise even for the hermit, who must possess at least the indispensable clothing and food—is not meant for community life. Still less is it possible in an Order with thousands of members, whose corporate organization necessarily entails possessions of every kind. The question is reduced then to one of interior detachment, even with regard to these indispensable possessions. Here the message of the Gospel is intransigent. Francis realized it by contenting himself personally with what was strictly necessary, and by inducing his disciples so far as possible to do the same, renouncing all, even collective, possessions—being without any lands, estates, or property whatsoever. But the measure of what is strictly necessary is itself a relative matter. This crisis therefore led thinking men to discover the decisive norm in obedience, the only way to give certainty to a subordinate. Already in the Acts of the Apostles, Ananias and Sapphira's fraud shows up in a society set up by the Apostles among the Christians of Jerusalem, in which all goods were in common: that is to say, the Church has always considered that she has a certain jurisdiction over the use of material goods.[51] And Christ himself had given his disciples sweeping authority: "He that heareth you, heareth me". This latitude was taken by the popes and by the superiors of the Franciscan Order to authorize a modification of the Poverello's ideal, so as to make it capable of survival,

[51] The Jerusalem experiment had, practically speaking, no "tomorrow". The discipline of the Church has always recognized the difficulties involved in ecclesiastical interference in this province. Only in the religious life has the model of Jerusalem been revived; the Rule of St Benedict refers to it explicitly (chs 33, 34 and 56).

while at the same time respecting those evangelical requirements which were an essential part of it.

Immediately the perennial question arises: is it then impossible to practise the *letter* of the Gospel? And if the spirit dispenses with the letter, is it not in danger of becoming a shadow without substance?

4. *The Franciscan Theologians*

This was a problem which occupied the minds of the Franciscan "doctors" of the thirteenth and fourteenth centuries, notably St Anthony of Padua, St Bonaventure and John Duns Scotus. These three names are merely the chief ones in an impressive line of theologians, many of whom left a considerable body of work. Among these were Alexander of Hales (†1245); later, John Pecham (†1292); Roger Bacon († *c.* 1292), still celebrated as the originator of the scientific method[52]; Petrus Aureolus (†1332); Francis Mayron († after 1328); Nicholas of Lyra (†1349); and William of Ockham († *c.* 1348), the *venerabilis inceptor* who was criticized for his deliberately voluntarist philosophy and his revolutionary logic, called "nominalist"; with them was John de Ripa, who taught at Paris between 1350 and 1370 and who was blamed by Gerson for his intemperate dialectic.[53]

The Franciscans, because of the needs created by the constant growth of their Order, had soon launched into study and even occupied chairs at the universities. The spirit of Brother Elias was dominant among them. Like their Dominican rivals, they adopted the method of the schools and took their place among the scholastics. This was especially the case with Alexander of Hales, who left

[52] Roger Bacon, *Opera inedita*, ed. J. S. Brewer, London, 1859 (including the *Opus tertium* and *Opus minus*); *Opus maius*, ed. J. H. Bridges, 3 vols, Oxford, 1897–1900; *Opera hactenus inedita*, ed. R. Steele *et al.*, Oxford, 1909—in progress. Biographies by E. Heck, Bonn, 1957; T. Crowley, O.F.M., *Roger Bacon*, Louvain and Dublin, 1930. See also *Roger Bacon: Commemoration Essays*, ed. A. G. Little, Oxford, 1914; D. E. Sharp, *Franciscan Philosophy at Oxford in the Thirteenth Century*, Oxford, 1930, pp. 115–71. On his scientific conceptions, see P. Duhen, *Le système du monde*, III, Paris, 1915, pp. 260–76, 411–41; V, Paris, 1917, pp. 375–411.

For the Franciscan theologians, the reader is referred to the bibliographies published regularly by *Collectanea franciscana*; also to P. Glorieux, *Répertoire des maîtres en théologie de Paris au XIIIe siècle*, II, Paris, 1933, pp. 1–248.

[53] On his works, see A. Combes, *Présentation de Jean de Ripa*, in *Arch. hist. litt. doctr. moyen âge*, XXIII (1957), pp. 145–242; *Determinationes* and *Conclusiones*, 2 vols, Paris, 1957. For Ockham, see D. Knowles, *op. cit.*, I, Part II, ch. xx, "The Friars from the Council of Lyons to William of Ockham"; also P. Boehner, "A Recent Presentation of Ockham's Philosophy", in *Franciscan Studies*, IX (1949), pp. 443–56. Ockham's *Opera Politica* have been edited by J. G. Sikes, Manchester, 1940.

an impressive commentary on the Sentences.[54] On the whole they did not forget the spiritual life. When they speak of it, they do indeed keep to the message of their founder, St Francis, but the question of evangelical poverty was not the only problem to which they addressed themselves, and they accepted the way of thinking and working characteristic of the schools.

Like all the other theologians, the Franciscan masters grounded their work upon Scripture. It took pride of place among the sources, studied and commented upon before other works, such as the Sentences. Like many others, the Franciscans emphasized the spiritual dispositions necessary for the study of the Scriptures. A biblical course drawn up by John of Rupella opens with this text (Apoc. 10. 10–11): "I took the book from the hand of the angel and ate it up . . . and he said to me: Thou must prophesy again." The author gives this interpretation of the text: "By this, the Evangelist teaches his duty to whoever teaches Holy Scripture. Three things are required: knowledge, life and doctrine. The first is shown by the words "I took", the second by "I ate", and the third by "thou must prophesy".[55]

St Bonaventure, in the prologue of his *Breviloquium*, emphasizes the necessity of faith in Christ for those undertaking the study of Scripture. This faith, more than any other knowledge, is a true illumination. It is a gift from God; knowledge of Scripture, then, is not acquired in the same way as other learning. By a "supernatural light", *lumen supernaturale*, it encompasses the totality of all that exists: *describit totum universum*. And the fruits of this knowledge is life and eternal happiness. Scripture, therefore, can only be approached in an attitude of prayer, "bending the knees of our heart", *flectendo genua cordis nostri*—an admirable phrase. We need humility, purity and assiduity.[56]

The theme of the "two tables", the Bible and the Eucharist, seems to have originated with the Franciscans. The germ of it is found as early as David of Augsburg (†1272) in his treatise on "the pattern of the exterior and interior man", *De exterioris et interioris hominis compositione*.[57] It appears again, further developed, in the treatise of Rudolph of Biberach († *c.* 1360), "On the seven gifts of the

[54] *Glossa in Quatuor Libros Sententiarum*, 4 vols, ed. Quaracchi, 1951–7. The *Summa Theologica* (5 vols, ed. Quaracchi, 1924 and the following years) is the work of Alexander and his disciples, though Book IV is certainly not authentic.

[55] Ed. F. M. Delorme, in *France Francisc.*, XVI (1933), pp. 345–60.

[56] *Breviloquium*, prol.; *Opera*, vol. V; ed. Quaracchi, 1891, pp. 201 *et seq*. Cf. A. Kleinhans, "De Studio S. Scripturae in ordine Fratrum Minorum saec. XIII", in *Antonianum*, VII (1932), pp. 413–40; and *Dict. de spirit.*, I, col. 1819–1820. The Dominican masters put more emphasis on intellectual qualities.

[57] Part III. *De processibus*, ch. LIII, ed. Quaracchi, 1899, pp. 296–300. See also *infra*, p. 312.

Holy Spirit".[58] In this treatise we read, in connection with the gift of knowledge (not that of wisdom, as it has been generally understood in the West), a chapter on "the table of the Scriptures, or knowledge, and the food that is found there", "*De mensa divinae Scripturae, sive scientiae, et de ferculis quae in ea apponuntur*".[59] The inner man, he says (drawing upon Hugh of St Victor), must be nourished just as the outer man is fed in the refectory. This takes place at a threefold table, the "three understandings", *tres intellectus*, of Holy Scripture: the table of history, that of mystery, and that of morals (*mensa historialis, mysterialis, et moralis*). At the first of these, the faith of the simplest men is nourished with "examples" and with the miracles of Christ. At the second our hope is fed, and this one is more for the learned, *doctoribus*; it includes "the love of mysteries" and teaches us their figurative meaning. The third offers "gentleness of life" and nourishes our love with the words of Christ; this one is for all. Rudolph declares (drawing upon Thomas Gallus) that the Eucharist is to be referred to the third of these tables. The gift of knowledge "enlightens us to know the truths of Holy Scripture and to love them". It opens to the understanding what we now call the typology of Scripture (with Rudolph, it often borders on verbal coincidence). He gives a more penetrating explanation of the gift of understanding "which brings us to the clear contemplation of truth." "It leads", he says, "to the lights and contemplation of pure truth that are concealed in the Scriptures, even to the discovery of the naked truth."[60] In short Rudolph teaches, without actually saying so, that we are nourished at two "tables", Scripture and the Eucharist—a truth which was to be clearly formulated in the *Imitation*.[61]

In the early days of the Order other Franciscan masters also held to the method of biblical interpretation and application. Among those whose sermons have come down to us were John Pecham[62] (†1292), David of Augsburg[63] (†1272), Berthold of

[58] Formerly published among the works of St Bonaventure; cf. the edition of Vivès, vol. VII, Paris, 1866, pp. 583–652; see also *Dict. de spirit.*, I, col. 1846.

[59] Part II, Sec. 3, ch. 4, pp. 611–13.

[60] *Ibid.*, Sec. 6, ch. 4, pp. 629–31. Somewhat analogous ideas are found in the *De septem itineribus aeternitatis*, 6, especially dist. 7 (among the works of St Bonaventure, ed. Vivès, vol. VIII, pp. 472–3).

[61] Book I, chs v and xx. See *infra*.

[62] See L. Douie, "Archbishop Pecham's Sermons and Collations", in *Studies in Mediaeval History*, Oxford, 1948, pp. 269–82; M. D. Knowles, "Some Aspects of the Career of Archbishop Pecham", in *English Historical Review*, LVII (1942), pp. 1–18, 178–201; and the article by C. L. Kingsford in *Dictionary of National Biography*. For a bibliography, see C. L. Kingsford, A. G. Little, and F. Tocco, *Fratris Johannis Pecham Tractatus Tres de Paupertate*, British Society of Franciscan Studies, II.

[63] He also wrote ascetical and mystical treatises; among others, *De triplici statu religiosorum* or *De interioris et exterioris hominis reformatione*, *De septem*

Ratisbon[64] (†1272), and the most famous of them all, St Anthony of Padua (†1231).[65] He was born at Lisbon in 1195, became a canon in 1210 and a Friar Minor in 1220. He preached in various towns in France and Italy, and finally (after 1229) at Padua, after having been the first lector of the Order at the *Studium* of Bologna.[66]

St Anthony's spiritual teaching is known only from his sermons,[67] the collection of which forms a sort of manual of preaching. In them is found, as would be expected, a review of the Christian virtues, whose end is to restore the life of God in the soul. Three enemies, pride, concupiscence, and avarice, are to be combated by contrition of heart, purification of the soul, and the practice of humility, obedience, purity and poverty. All this should be placed under the dominion of love, which assures the spiritual progress of the soul. This fundamentally Augustianian spirituality is shot through with the spirituality of the early Franciscans. Popular and

---

processibus religiosi status, and *De septem gradibus orationis*; ed. Quaracchi, 1899. Cf. J. Heerinckx, "Theologia mystica in scriptis fratris David ab Augusta, in *Antonianum*, VIII (1933), pp. 49–83, 161–92; J. Clark, *Great German Mystics*, Oxford, 1949, pp. 98–109; D. Stöckerl, O.F.M., *Bruder D. von A. Ein deutscher Mystik aus den Franziskaner Orden*, Munich, 1914; and *supra*, p. 302. There is an edition of the *Canticum pauperis*, Quaracchi, 1949.

64 His Latin sermons have been edited by G. Jakob, Ratisbon, 1880; his sermons *ad religiosos*, by F. Hoetzl, Munich, 1882; his German sermons by F. Pfeiffer and J. Strohl, 2 vols, Vienna, 1862–80. There is an anthology by O. H. Brandt, Leipzig, 1924; see also F. Göbel, *Die Missionspredigten des Franziskaners B. v. R. in jetziger Schriftsprache*, 5th ed., Ratisbon, 1929.

On Berthold of Ratisbon and the role of the Bible in medieval preaching, see R. Leuensberger, *Die Bibel in der deutschen Predigt des Mittelalters von den Anfängen der Mystik*, Münsingen (Switzerland), 1955. Aspects of his preaching are mentioned in E. W. Keil, *Deutsche Sitte und Sittlichkeit im 13. Jahrh. nach den damaligen deutschen Predigten*, Dresden, 1931; and R. J. Ianucci, *The Treatment of the Capital Sins and the Decalogue in the German Sermons of B. von R.*, Washington, 1942.

65 When St Anthony was proclaimed a doctor of the Church (1946), a number of works were published which called attention to his life, work, and teaching. Among these were *S. Antonio dottore della Chiesa. Atti delle Settimane antoniane tenute a Roma e a Padova nel 1946*, Vatican City, 1947; *S. Antonio di P., Dottore Evangelico. Volume commemorativo . . . dei FF. Min. Conventuali* (Padua, 1946); *Doctor evangelicus* (Bois-le-Duc, 1949). Among the many biographies may be mentioned those by Willibrord de Paris, O.M.Cap., Paris, 1947; G. Herzog-Hauser, Lucerne, 1947; M. A. Habig, Paterson, N.J., 1954; F. F. Lopes, Braga, 1954; L. Arnaldich, O.F.M., Barcelona, 1958.

66 The first life of St Anthony of Padua, the *Legenda prima* or *Legenda assidua*, was composed by an unknown Friar Minor shortly after the canonization (1232); it deals chiefly with the saint's apostolate at Padua. This valuable source has been translated into Italian and compared with other documents by A. F. Pavanello Padua, 1946. There is a Latin edition by L. de Kervan, Paris, 1904.

67 *Sermones dominicales et in solemnitatibus*, edited by Locatelli and others, Padua, 1895–1913. There is a French translation by P. Bayart, Paris, 1944. Other sermons exist which are doubtfully attributed to St Anthony. Fr S. Doimi has made a study of his teaching in *La dottrina della predicazione in S. A. di P.*, Padua, 1952. His *Sermones in psalmos* are probably not authentic; cf. A. Callebaut, in *Arch. franc. hist.*, XXV (1932), pp. 161–74; G. Piccoli, in *Miscell. francesc.*, LII (1952), pp. 461–513.

simple though this preaching is, it does not ignore the fact that contemplation is the full flowering of the spiritual life, and many pages of the sermons are devoted to setting forth its nature, its degrees, and the conditions for its attainment. It is noteworthy that the principal object[68] of the sermons is God and Christ, and that the Bible and its various meanings are frequently referred to.[69]

The great Franciscan doctor of the spiritual life was St Bonaventure. Born in 1221 at Bagnorea, near Viterbo, he became a master of arts at Paris, and probably entered the Franciscan Order in 1243 in that city. He studied under Alexander of Hales, and after proceeding bachelor of theology in 1248, he began his teaching by commenting on St Luke. Beginning in 1250, he expounded the Sentences. His *Quaestiones disputatae* and a preliminary sketch of a *summa theologica* known as the *Breviloquium* are both later than 1253. In that year he was made a doctor, at the same time as Thomas Aquinas but, unlike the latter, he was not admitted as a fellow of the University of Paris until 1257, and then only by order of Alexander IV. This delay was caused by the rivalry between the Mendicants and some of the secular masters, William of St Amour in particular. Meanwhile, Bonaventure had been elected Minister General of the Order on 2 February 1257.

His generalship, which was a very active one, was monopolized from the start by the business of the Order. His predecessor, John of Parma, was suspected of Joachimism; Bonaventure probably presided at the trial that acquitted him. He also had to deal with the problem of poverty, and succeeded better than Brother Elias, whose outlook had not been spiritual enough, in giving the Order a viable adaptation of the primitive ideal. As has been shown, he did not put an end to the resistance of the intransigents, but he succeeded in providing a sound doctrinal base for discussion. At the same time he had to fight for the recognition of the new Order's rights. His influence was such that Clement IV wanted to make him archbishop of York in 1265. Bonaventure declined the honour, only to receive the cardinalate in 1273, with the bishopric of Albano. He accompanied the pope to the Council of Lyons, and there, on

[68] In this connection, see A. Blasucci, O.M.Conv., "La spiritualità di S. A. di P.", in *S. Antonio dottore evangelico*, pp. 121–32; and, by the same author, "La teologica mistica di S. A.", in *S. Antonio dottore della Chiesa*, pp. 195–222; J. Heerinckx, "S. A. P. auctor misticus", in *Antonianum*, VII (1932), pp. 39–76, 167–200; L. Meier, "De contemplationis notione in sermonibus S.A.P.", in *Antonianum*, VI (1931), pp. 361–80. G. Théry, O.P., in *La Vie spirit., Suppl.*, XXXVII (1933), pp. 94–115, 163–78; XXXVIII (1934), pp. 22–51, shows what St Anthony's mystical teaching owes to Thomas Gallus.

[69] See L. F. Rohr, O.F.M., *The Use of Sacred Scripture in the Sermons of St Anthony of Padua*, Washington, 1949. See also J. M. Cummings, *The Christological Content of the "Sermones" of St A.*, Padua, 1953.

20 May 1274 he resigned as general of the Order. On 6 July his skilful diplomacy obtained the recognition of the Roman pontiff by the Greeks. The next day he fell ill, and he died in the night of the 13th to 14th.[70]

In spite of his activity at the head of the order and the short time he taught at Paris, St Bonaventure left a considerable body of work.[71] His theological and exegetical writings, most of them earlier than 1257, have given him a place among the best theologians. Though their technique is less elaborate than that of Thomas Aquinas, they have earned their author the right to stand beside him, not only as his contemporary, his fellow student, his rival, and his colleague in teaching at Paris, but also—and especially—as a doctor of the Church.[72]

Bonaventure also left, as one would expect, a considerable number of oratorical works, *collationes* and *sermons*.[73] Among his spiritual writings, one of the most important is the *Itinerarium mentis ad Deum*, "The Mind's Road to God", in which the reader's thought is raised up, step by step, as resting successively on the three orders— sensible, psychological and metaphysical.[74] Also of

[70] There are biographies by E. Bettoni, Brescia, 1945; S. Clasen, Werl in Westphalia, 1940. See also the articles in *Dict. de spirit.*, *Dict. hist. géogr. eccl.*, and *Encyclopedia cattolica.*

[71] The *Opera omnia* have appeared in several editions, often including writings of doubtful authenticity or by other authors. The best edition is that of Quaracchi (10 vols, 1882–92); it replaces all the others, including that of Vivès (15 vols, Paris, 1864–71). The *Opera theologica selecta* have been edited in 4 vols, Quaracchi, 1934–49. There are many editions of single treatises, chiefly of the *De triplici via*, of the *Itinerarium mentis in Deum*, and of the *Breviloquium.* A collection of *Decem opuscula ad theologiam mysticam spectantia* was edited at Quaracchi in 1900. Among the translations must be mentioned the *Obras de San Buenaventura* (text in Latin and Spanish), 6 vols, Madrid, 1945–8. Among the collections of texts translated into French are those of V. M. Breton in *Maîtres de la spiritualité chrétienne*, Paris, 1943; and of Jean de Dieu de Champsecret, 3 vols, Paris, 1930–1932. The *Breviloquium* has been translated into English by E. E. Nemmers, St. Louis and London, 1946.

[72] These works are a commentary on the Sentences (ed. Quaracchi, *Omnia opera*, vols. I–IV); the *Breviloquium*, a fairly short *Summa Theologica* (vol. V, pp. 199–291; and in a small edition by P. Barbaliscia, Pompei, 1934); the *Quaestiones disputatae* (V, pp. 1–198), of which the four *De perfectione evangelica* (pp. 117–98) must be specially mentioned here; the *De reductione artium ad theologiam* (V, pp. 317–25); the *Collationes in Hexaëmeron* (V, pp. 327–454; small edition, Quaracchi, 1934); and commentaries on Ecclesiastes, Wisdom, St Luke and St John (vols VI and VIII). *Prolegomena ad sacram theologiam ex operibus eius collecta* has been published by T. Soiron (Flor. Patrist., Bonn, 1932).

[73] *Collationes* on St John (VI, pp. 532–634) and the *Hexaëmeron* (see note 72). Seven others on *De septem donis Spiritus Sancti* and seven on *De decem praeceptis* (V, pp. 455–532). *Sermones*, to the number of 475, *de tempore*, *de Sanctis*, *de B. Maria V.*, *de diversis* (vol. IX); an *Ars concionandi* (IX, pp. 8–21); and five theological sermons (V, pp. 532–79). Cf. E. Eilers, *Gottes Wort. Eine theologie der Predigt nach B.*, Freiburg-im-Breisgau, 1941; P. Glorieux, "La collection authentique des sermons de saint Bonaventure", in *Rech. théol. anc. méd.*, XXII (1955), pp. 119–25.

[74] Vol. V, pp. 293–316. There are many other editions and translations, including

importance is the treatise "On the threefold way", *De triplici via*,[75] and there are nine other spiritual *opuscula* that are considered authentic.[76]

Bonaventure's aim is to help souls in their progress towards contemplation by the way of love. The Franciscan spirit gave this approach an affective tone, one that may be called "subjective", even "devotional", directed towards Christ and the appealing mysteries of his birth and passion. Even more distinctly Franciscan were the great doctor's *Life* of St Francis, the official nature of which has been mentioned,[77] and his two defences of the Mendicants, *De paupertate Christi* and *Apologia pauperum*.[78]

Bonaventure's[79] doctrine is of interest to us chiefly for its spiritual value.[80] All his works are directed to the union of the soul with God; they form one great directory leading to that end. Among the practices calculated to ensure the soul's progress, Bonaventure emphasizes humility, examination of conscience, and frequent confession. He does not consider frequent spiritual direction indispensable, except at the beginning, because the gift of "discretion" should take its place.[81]

The way to religious understanding and to contemplation is

---

a French translation by E. Clop, Paris, 1924 and an English one by P. Boehner, St Bonaventure, N.Y., 1956. Another English translation is that of G. Boas, *The Mind's Road to God*, New York, 1953.

[75] Vol. VIII, pp. 3–27; sometimes called *Incendium amoris* or *Itinerarium mentis in seipsum*. French translations by V. M, Breton, Paris, 1942, F. Bonnefoy, Paris, 1945 and Jean de Dieu de Champsecret and L. de Mercin, Paris, 1956. There is a commentary by J. Bonnefoy, Paris, 1934.

[76] *Sollloquium de quatuor mentalibus exercitiis*, *Lignum vitae*, *De V festivitatibus Pueri Jesu*, *Tractatus de praeparatione ad missam*, *De perfectione vitae ad sorores*, *De regimine animae*, *De sex alis seraphim*, *Officium de passione Domini*, and *Vitis mystica* (vol. VIII; this volume also contains some writings of doubtful authenticity).

[77] *Legenda maior*, VIII, pp. 504–64; *Legenda minor*, pp. 565–76. See *supra*, p. 286.

[78] The *De paupertate Christi* appears in the *Quaestiones disputatae*, vol. V; the *Apologia pauperum* in vol. VIII, pp. 230–330. In this connection, see *infra*, ch. IV, §5, pp. 337 *et seq.*

[79] There seems to be no final survey of his doctrine, unless perhaps it be the essays of E. Gilson, *La philosophie de S. B.*, Paris, 1924, and of F. Imle and J. Kaup, *Die Theologie des hl. B.*, Werl in Westphalia, 1931. There are many separate studies of his philosophy and theology.

[80] His spiritual doctrine is studied in Jean de Dieu de Champsecret, "L'intuition sans concept et la théorie bonaventurienne de la contemplation", in *Études francisc.*, VII (1956), pp. 63–74, 133–54; E. Longpré, "La théologie mystique de S. B.", in *Arch. francisc. histor.*, XIV (1921), pp. 36–108; J. F. Bonnefoy, *Le Saint-Esprit et ses dons, selon S.B.*, Paris, 1929; D. Phillips, "The Way of Religious Perfection according to S.B.'s De triplici via", in *Essays in Medieval Life and Thought*, New York, 1955, pp. 31–56; G. Grünewald, *Franziskanische Mystik . . . des hl. Bonaventura*, Munich, 1932; F. Imle, *Das geistliche Leben nach der Lehre des hl. B.*, Werl in Westphalia, 1939. See also the introduction to the collection by V. M. Breton, *op. cit.*

[81] *De sex alis Seraphim*, chs 1–2.

necessarily that of *ascesis*.[82] In this connection, the problem of poverty was bound to arise. We have seen the efforts that he made to get all the brethren to accept a form of religious life in which the renunciation of all goods, the refusal of money, and living on alms would be combined with a certain abandonment of manual labour, with study and apostolic work. In this connection Bonaventure cites the example of Christ and gives an exegesis of the Gospel texts concerned with poverty.[83] These efforts have earned him the right to be called the second founder of the Franciscan order. "How many painful and regrettable breaches would have been avoided if only this spirit of tolerance had been maintained, if the hermitage and the convent had been able to live in harmony, as St Bonaventure wished.... When anyone wishes to adapt the Rule of St Francis to various times and circumstances, he must steep himself as Bonaventure did in the holy founder's thought, rather than in his personal practices."[84]

Spiritual progress, as conceived by Bonaventure, is an integral part of a whole theology, which starts from the original condition of man and his fall, and culminates in the new creation in Jesus Christ. This "re-creation" of the soul, as it has been called on the strength of a number of passages, is the work of grace. The theological virtues work together to "rectify" the soul, the use of the sacraments heals and nourishes it, and it develops to its full extent by the gifts of the Holy Spirit and the "beatitudes".[85]

The ascent of the soul towards contemplation, viewed as the normal prolongation of the life of grace, is described in the *De triplici via*, "Bonaventure's *summa* of mystical theology".[86] This threefold way —purgative, illuminative and unitive—was to become the classical formula of spiritual literature. It is not a question of successive stages: the activity proper to each "way" always remains concomitant with that of the others, although the proportions vary. "Purification" disciplines the outer man, the "old man"; it regulates the life of the senses and passions and leads him to interior peace by means of examination of conscience, meditation on his last end, remembrance of Christ's passion, *ascesis*, humility, and mortification. "Illumination" disciplines the activity of reason, enlightens the soul, and teaches her to know Christ and follow him even to

82 See T. Soiron, "Die Aszese der Erkennens nach S. B.", in *Wiss. u. Weisheit*, I (1934), pp. 310–16.

83 See Gratien, *op. cit.*, pp. 247–320; S. Clasen, *Bonaventura und das Mendikantentum*, Werl in Westphalia, 1940.

84 Gratien, *op. cit.*, pp. 319–20.

85 Cf. E. Longpré, art. "Bonaventure", in *Dict. de spirit.*, I, col. 1777–91.

86 "*Somme bonaventurienne de théologie mystique*" is the title of a commentary on this *opusculum* by J. F. Bonnefoy, Paris, 1934.

the cross and, through him, to know the Father and herself. The "consummation" finally brings man to an experimental knowledge, an awareness of God, which is at once both wisdom and love; it is not an immediate knowledge, but the contemplation that wisdom gives (*contemplation sapientielle*), before being beatitude in the other world.

This outline of spiritual progress, or rather of its aspects, is really the object of the first part of the *De triplici via* only. The second part deals with prayer and briefly describes three acts, of a distinctly affective character, proper to it: avowal of one's own wretchedness, imploring of God's benevolence, and homage of adoration, all of which more or less correspond with the stages outlined in the first part. The third and last part treats of contemplation alone and of its degrees—there are seven—which lead to peace, truth and love.

St Bonaventure never fully defines contemplation, and this explains the lack of agreement among his commentators. He certainly depends on Hugh of St Victor, whose description he accepts: "a free, penetrating, and fixed gaze", *liber ac perspicax ac defixus intuitus*. Contemplation, which is an act of the will, unitive love, is at the same time an act of the intellect. It is an affective gaze directed to God.[87] But it is not to be confused with the ecstasy of the immediate experience of God, which is comparable to that of taste and especially of touch.[88] It is not the same thing as *raptus*, which implies the light of glory, nor the same as "the knowledge of God in the inner effect of grace". Again, it is not the same as the beatific vision, because in contemplation the *affectus* is first and the intellectual act is second.[89] Moreover, the "gaze" of contemplation is not turned away from creatures; God is present in them, and the religious significance of creation is disclosed to the contemplative, assisting his flight towards God.[90]

At the end of the *De triplici via*, St Bonaventure summarizes the

[87] Cf. J. Bissen, O.F.M., "La contemplation selon S.B.", in *France francisc.*, XIV (1931), pp. 175–88; Jean de Dieu de Champsecret, O.M.Cap., "Contemplation et contemplation acquise d'après S.B.", in *Études francisc.*, XLIII (1931), pp. 401–9. Bissen published a series of articles on the degrees, effects and conditions of contemplation according to St Bonaventure, in *France franciscaine*, 1931–6.

[88] Cf. K. Rahner, S.J., "La doctrine des sens sprituels au moyen âge, surtout chez S.B.", in *Rev. d'ascét. et de myst.*, XIV (1933), pp. 263–99.

[89] See K. Rahner, S.J., "Der Begrift der Ecstasis bei B.", in *Zeitschr. Asz. Myst.*, IX (1934), pp. 1–19.

[90] This is especially the teaching of the treatise *Itinerarium mentis in Deum*. See E. Sauer, *Die religiöse Wertung der Welt in Bonaventuras Itinerarium mentis in Deum*, Werl in Westphalia, 1937; F. Imle, *Gott und Geist. Das Zuzammenwirken des geschaffenen und des ungeschaffenen Geistes . . . nach B.*, Werl in Westphalia, 1934).

steps that lead from purification to illumination, and thence to union:

"Thus do thou distinguish the steps that lead to the way of union:
let vigilance make thee attentive, for the Bridegroom passeth swiftly;
let confidence make thee strong, for he cometh without fail;
let desire enkindle thee, for he is sweet;
let fervour raise thee up, for he is sublime;
let delight in him give thee repose, for he is beautiful;
let joy inebriate thee, for he is the fullness of love;
let attachment unite thee to him, for his love is full of power.
And mayest thou ever, O devout soul, say to the Lord with all thy heart:
I seek thee, I hope for thee, I desire thee, I raise myself up toward thee,
I lay hold on thee, I exult in thee, at last I cleave to thee."[91]

St Bonaventure succeeded in disengaging himself from the narrow limits of the controversies of his time: those about poverty within the Franciscan Order, those between the mendicants and the seculars, and finally those which sprang up in the schools and universities on the introduction of Aristotle's philosophy. He was extraordinarily open-minded, thanks to his very active life, devoted to study and teaching for fifteen years and during the last twenty directed to spiritual and pastoral problems. His work left an enduring mark on the Christian spirituality of the centuries to come. It is one of the links that connects the monastic spirituality of St Bernard with that of the *Imitation.*

His own Order, particularly, preserved some characteristic traits of his spirituality. The Franciscans liked to draw upon the *Itinerarium mentis in Deum* and the *De triplici via* to describe the progressive ascent of the soul through the stages of prayer. In the first stages, a prominent place was given to meditation. Devotion to Christ took on, in their Order—as already often outside it—an affective, "subjective" colouring, which simply accentuated a tendency that can already be seen in St Bernard and St Francis.[92] Finally, the Order remained—and in this it was being faithful to its Augustinian tradition—the defender of love and of its primacy in Christian

[91] *De triplici via*, Part II, ch. III, §5.

[92] On "devotion" in the spirituality of St Bonaventure, see J. Châtillon, art. "Dévotion", in *Dict. de spirit.*, III, col. 713. On the place of Christ in it, see N. Simovelli, O.F.M., *Doctrina christocentrica Seraphici Doctoris S. Bonaventurae*, Aesii, 1958; and on devotion to the Sacred Heart, see L. Di Fonzo, O.M.Conv., and G. Colasanti, O.M.Conv., "Il culto del Sacro Cuore di Gesù negli Ordini francescani", in *Cor Jesu. Commentationes in Letteras Encyclicas "Haurietis aquas"*, II, Rome, 1959, pp. 97–137.

life. On this point, the standpoint of the Franciscans and those of the best Dominican theologians were often to diverge.

Among the Franciscan theologians of the late thirteenth and early fourteenth centuries, John Duns Scotus († 1308) had a considerable influence, at least within his own Order. His teaching on contemplation derived from his idea of the beatitude of the blessed: although both the intellect and the will play an active part in it, beatitude consists of a single act, the final act of the will, *fruitio* or joy in the possession of the good.[93] The happiness of man during his earthly life, of *homo viator*, also consists in the enjoyment of God. Scotus describes the object of contemplation, which is for him all that concerns salvation; and he makes its intrinsic nature consist in a complete and perfect cleaving of the soul to God, in and by charity.[94] The Scotist notion of contemplation must be understood from this point of view of charity.[95] In accordance with the Franciscan tradition, for Scotus meditation on Christ and his example is always of the first importance in the development of contemplative love.[96]

5. *Franciscan Mystics*

The distinction between Franciscan theologians and Franciscan mystics, in the thirteenth century and the beginning of the fourteenth, is in reality a somewhat artificial one. Even for those doctors who left a considerable body of theological work, like Alexander of Hales and Duns Scotus, the essential thing was not to know but to live and to love. This was even more true of Bonaventure. Nevertheless, the distinction can be made, because the men discussed in the preceding section, while they were spiritual writers, also commented on the *pagina sacra*, taught theology as *scolares*, and adopted the methods of the schools of their time. Those to be

[93] *In IV Sent.*, dist. 49, q. 5, No. 1; ed. Vivès, vol. XXI, Paris, 1894, pp. 171–7.
[94] *Ibid.*, No. 2, pp. 177–80.
[95] Cf. J. Klein, *Die Caritaslehre des Joh. D. Sc.*, Münster, 1926; J. Heerinckx, "De momento caritatis in spiritualitate franciscana", in *Antonianum*, XIII (1938), pp. 19–32, 135–70, 475–88.
[96] Cf. Déodat de Basly, *Scotus docens*, Paris, 1934, pp. 293–312. The primacy of love, and for that matter of all the theological virtues, is so clear to Scotus that he firmly denies the distinction between the virtues and the gifts, the latter being no longer necessary to one perfectly exercising the theological and cardinal virtues. Cf. O. Lottin, *Psychologie et morale aux XIIe et XIIIe siècles*, IV, Louvain, 1954, p. 705; cf. pp. 693–704: the original texts according to the *reportata* of his *Commentary on the Sentences* written at Oxford, Book III, dist. 34, q. unica, according to the text of the manuscript *Assisi 137*; in the Vivès edition, vol. XV, Paris, 1894, pp. 464–587. Cf. J. Reuss, "Die theologische Tugend der Liebe nach der Lehre des J.D.S.", in *Zeitschr. Kathol. Theol.*, LVIII (1934), pp. 1–39, 208–42; E. Bettoni, *L'ascesa a Dio in D.S.*, Milan, 1943. See also C. R. S. Harris, *Duns Scotus*, 2 vols, Oxford, 1927; A. G. Little, "Chronological Notes on the Life of Duns Scotus", in *English Historical Review*, XLVII (1932), pp. 568–82.

discussed here are remarkable more for their life than for their learning.

A few of them may simply be mentioned in passing. Of these, David of Augsburg (†1272), has already been noted.[97] Adam Marsh (†1258), a friend of Robert Grosseteste, left a body of work of which is unpublished; his vast correspondence is accessible, however, and this reflects his spirituality.[98] Conrad of Saxony (†1279) was the author of a *Speculum B. Mariae Virginis*, a commentary on the Hail Mary.[99] The mystical poet Jacopone da Todi (†1306) is known for his *Laude*,[100] the most famous of which is the *Stabat Mater*, still found in the present Roman missal. Bertram of Ahlen, who was a professor at Münster from 1308 to 1315, wrote a mystical work on the knowledge of God, *De Laude Domini novi saeculi* (*c.* 1304–9), which shows a marked dependence on the Pseudo-Dionysius.[101]

Blessed Angela of Foligno (*c.* 1249–1309) deserves more attention. At the age of about forty, after a thoroughly worldly life, she was converted and became a Franciscan tertiary, living thenceforward as a recluse. Her life of prayer was accompanied by extraordinary mystical phenomena.[102] Her writings have been published in their original purity.[103] One of her "teachings" distinguishes three ascending stages in prayer: bodily prayer, "which is made with the sound of words and with bodily exercises, such as genuflections"; mental prayer, in which the soul "thinks of nothing other than God"; and supernatural prayer, "in which the soul is carried away by God's mercy, and by meditation on him, as it were beyond the bounds of nature".[104] These three stages lead to the knowledge of God and of oneself,[105] a knowledge which begets love and is at the

[97] See pp. 302 and 303, and note 63, *supra*.

[98] There are 247 letters; ed. J. S. Brewer, London, 1858. Cf. G. Cantini, "A. de Marisco, O.F.M., auctor spiritualis", in *Antonianum*, XXIII (1948), pp. 441–74.

[99] Ed. Quaracchi, 1904.

[100] Ed. F. Ageno, Florence, 1953. There is a French translation by P. Barbet, Paris, 1935. A critical note by L. Russo appeared in *Rittrati e disegni storici*, Bari, 1951, pp. 36–68. For a biography, see A. Barolo, *Jacopone da Todi*, Turin, 1929.

[101] Long extracts have been edited by M. Bihl, with an analysis and an examination of sources, in *Arch. francisc. histor.*, XL (1947), pp. 3–48. Many other Franciscan spiritual writings might be mentioned here. Among these is the *Stimulus amoris* of James of Milan (French translation by Ubald d'Alençon, Paris, 1921); cf. R. Loenertz, "Frère J. de M., missionaire en Orient au XIIIe siècle", in *Arch. Fratr. Praedic.*, VIII (1938), pp. 274–84. Another is the anonymous *Meditatio pauperis in solitudine*, ed. F. M. Delorme, Quaracchi, 1929.

[102] For a biography and a sketch of her doctrine, see T. Biondi, *Angela da Foligno*, Foligno, 1950; cf. J. Ferré, *La spiritualité de S.A. de F.*, Paris, 1928.

[103] *Le livre de la Bienheureuse A. de F.*, ed. P. Doncoeur, S.J.; Latin text, Paris, 1922; French translation, Paris, 1926. There is a literary analysis by G. Petrocchi, *Ascesi e mistica trecentesca*, Florence, 1957, ch. 1, pp. 3–19.

[104] Ed. P. Doncoeur, 1922, pp. 123–4.

[105] *Ibid.*, pp. 124 and 136.

same time its fruit.[106] Thus is produced the transformation into Christ[107]—the true "book of life"[108]—in love, the embrace.[109] This spirituality is distinctly christocentric in character.[110] It has been stressed that, in connection with contemplation, "a streak of Dionysius appears belatedly in her thought (divine darkness, ineffability, the "all-ness" of God).[111] It is not surprising that she had, as her letters show, a great many disciples.

Raymond Lull (1235–1316), who was also a Franciscan tertiary, at first led a very reckless life. His conversion was such a decisive turning-point that it filled him with a rare missionary zeal, which led him to martyrdom.[112] When speaking of spiritual things, he too adopts St Bonaventure's schema of the ascending progress of the soul. Meditation is directed to man and the world, and then goes on to God and his attributes, redemption, the commandments, the sacraments, vices and virtues. This "contemplation" is described in the *Art de contemplacio*[113]; it is "carried on by the orderly and methodical application of the soul's powers, especially the memory, the understanding, and the will",[114] and, as Lull says elsewhere, of the interior senses.[115] All this must have had its influence on St Ignatius of Loyola, two centuries later.[116] Lull, like Angela of Foligno, distinguishes three stages in the ascent. The first two, the sensible and the intellectual, correspond as regards their object to Angela's first two; the third "multiplies good works".[117] This practical aspect is new. Nevertheless, union is achieved in the

[106] *Ibid.*, p. 165 and *passim*.
[107] *Ibid.*, p. 142. [108] *Ibid.*, p. 152. [109] *Ibid.*, p. 151.
[110] See A. Blasucci, *Il cristocentrismo nella vita spirituale secundo la B. Angela da Foligno*, Rome, 1940; and, by the same author, *Il cammino della perfezione negli scritti della B. A. da F.*, Padua, 1950.
[111] P. Doncoeur, S.J., art. "Angèle de F.", in *Dict. de spirit.*, I, col. 571. See, for example, the Latin text, *op. cit.*, pp. 193–5.
[112] There is an edition of his works, *Obras de R.L.*, 6 vols, Palma de Mallorca, 1932–50; *Obras literarias*, ed. M. Batllori, S.J., and M. Caldentey, Madrid, 1948; *Obres essencials*, vol. I, published Barcelona, 1957; *Opera latina*, ed. F. Stegmüller, vol. I published Palma de Mallorca, 1959. Cf. J. Avinyo, *Les obres autentiques del beat. R. L.*, Barcelona, 1935. Biographies by E. A. Peers, *R.L., a Biography*, London, 1929; by the same author, *Fool of Love. The Life of R.L.*, London, 1946; F. Sureda Blanes, Madrid, 1934; L. Riber, Barcelona, 1935; J. Soulairol, Paris, 1951 (in a popular style). Since 1957, the review *Estudios Lulianos*, Palma de Mallorca, has published a great many interesting studies. See also *R.L., docteur des missions*, with texts translated and annotated by R. Sugranyes de Franch, Schöneck-Beckenried, 1954.
[113] There is an edition of the Catalan text by J. H. Probst in *Beiträge z. Gesch. der Philos. des Mittelalters*, XIII, fasc. 2–3, Münster, 1914, pp. 1–126. For a study of his mysticism (in French) see *ibid.*, pp. 1–30.
[114] E. Longpré, art. "Lulle", in *Dict. théol. cath.*, col. 1130.
[115] *Cogitatio, perceptio, conscientia, subtilitas, animositas*. See the *Liber contemplationum*, Book 2, ch. 43, Nos. 1–3.
[116] Cf. J. de Guibert, S.J., "La 'méthode des trois puissances' et l'Art de Contemplation de Raymond Lull", in *Rev. d'ascét. et myst.*, VI (1925), pp. 367–78.
[117] Book 5, ch. 315, No. 4.

ecstatic meeting of "the Friend and the Beloved".[118] It has been said of this meeting, which is both affective and intellectual, that the psychology it depends on is "neither pantheistic, nor Freudian, nor abnormal".[119]

The "Meditations on the Life of Christ", *Meditationes vitae Christi*, was long attributed to St Bonaventure and published among his works.[120] They reflect all that was most characteristic of Franciscan piety; tender and affective meditation on Christ and especially on those mysteries of his life that are most apt to touch the heart—his birth, childhood, passion and death. This "mystical biography"[121] of Christ may perhaps be the work of a certain John de Caulibus at the end of the thirteenth century; or, according to others, of an unknown Tuscan Franciscan of the first third of the fourteenth.[122] Its aim is to lead the reader to Christ and to help him to know, love and follow him. "Take delight and rejoice. Compassionate with his sufferings. By familiar friendship, confidence, and love, imitate Jesus with all thy heart and with all thy strength." This way of seeking to move the soul foreshadows the "Lives of Christ," like that of Ludolph the Carthusian (†1370), that were to circulate widely later; and even the method of contemplation recommended by the *Exercises* of St Ignatius of Loyola. These *Meditations* direct the soul not only to Christ but also at the same time to Mary and Joseph.

This work brings out once again how much the spirituality that we call Franciscan, at the end of the thirteenth century and the beginning of the fourteenth, was a bridge between the spirituality of the twelfth century which was still almost exclusively the monopoly of the cloister, and the one that began to flourish at the end of the fourteenth, the *Devotio moderna*, which was for long to set its mark on the spiritual life of the Church. "Bernardine" and "Franciscan" devotion were still anchored, so to speak, to the "objective" contemplation of Christ's mysteries. The drift in the direction of "subjective" devotion was to take place during the fourteenth century. The twelfth had opened the spiritual life to new milieux; the fourteenth was to give it a new character, interior and "devotional", which would make its way into almost every circle of fervent Christians.

118 *Llibre d'Amic et d'Amat*, ed. E. M. Olivar, Barcelona, 1927. French translation by G. Etchegoyen, in *Études francisc.*, XLV (1933) and XLVI (1934); also by G. Lévis Mano and J. Palau, Paris, 1953.

119 J. H. Probst, "Ramon Lulls Mystik, ihre Grundlage, ihre Forme", in *Wiss. u. Weisheit*, II (1935), pp. 252–65; by the same author, "La mystique de R.L. et l'Art de contemplacio", in *Beiträge . . .*, XIII, 2–3, pp. 1–30 (cf. Note 113).

120 For example, in the Vivès edition, vol. XII, Paris, 1868, 509–628. There are many translations.

121 P. Pourrat, *La spiritualité chrétienne*, vol. II, edition of 1946, p. 278.

122 See C. Fischer, art. "Bonaventure (apocryphes)", in *Dict. de spirit.*, I, col. 1848–53; G. Petrocchi, *op. cit.*, ch. III, pp. 41–83.

IV

THE DOMINICAN CRUSADE

1. Dominic Guzman

St Dominic has already come into this history of spirituality. In their attack on the Catharist heresy, the Inquisition had reached a deadlock, and the discussions initiated by the Cistercian legates Peter of Castelnau and Raoul of Fontfroide were proving fruitless.[1] Neither force nor dialectic is of much use when it is a matter of convincing men, still less when it is a question of bringing them to the faith. At this point, in 1206, Diego d'Azevedo, the former prior of the canons regular of Osma, passed through Montpellier whilst on a journey, accompanied by Dominic Guzman. They approached the Cistercian legates with the proposal that the heresy should be combated by giving an example of poverty. The immediate results surpassed all hope, although they were not decisive, and the history of the suppression of the Albigenian heresy during the course of the thirteenth century was marked by sorrow and bloodshed.

Dominic was born about 1173 in the Castilian village of Caleruega, in the diocese of Osma.[2] From his childhood—which,

[1] See Part II, ch. II, §6, pp. 269 *et seq.*

[2] The sources relating to St Dominic are almost all collected in the *Monumenta ordinis Fratrum praedicatorum historica*, Rome, 1896 and following years, especially in vols XV and XVI, *Monumenta historica S.P.N. Dominici* (1933–5). These documents include, first, the *Libellus de principiis Ordinis praedicatorum*, by Blessed Jordan of Saxony, the first master general of the Order after Dominic. Then come the *Acta canonizationis* and the *Legendae* of Peter Ferrand, Constantine of Orvieto, and Humbert of the Romans. The Life by Thierry of Apolda has not yet been published in these *Monumenta*, but will be found in the *Acta Sanctorum* of the Bollandists, vol. XXXV, 4 August, pp. 558–628. For a bibliography and a French translation of all the important sources, including the process of canonization and Jordan's *Libellus*, see H. M. Vicaire, O.P., *Saint Dominique de Caleruega, d'après les documents du XIII*[e] *siècle*, Paris, 1955. There are French translations of the Lives of Peter Ferrand (*Frère Dominique, Père des prêcheurs*, Paris, 1934), by Gerard of Frachet (*Vies des frères*, Paris, 1912), and by Thierry of Apolda, Paris, 1887. The one by Gerard of Frachet has been translated into English by P. Conway, O.P., *Lives of the Brethren of the Order of Preachers, 1206–1259*, ed. with notes and introduction by B. Jarrett, O.P., London, 1924. Other useful documents are the *Bonum universale de apibus*, by Thomas of Cantimpré (Douai, 1627; translated into French as *Les abeilles mystiques* by M. de Waresquier,

unlike that of Francis of Assisi, was exemplary—he showed such evident signs of a vocation that he was entrusted to the care of an uncle who was an archpriest, and then sent to Palencia to be educated in the liberal arts; after which he took up the study of Holy Scripture. His charity towards the poor was already evident at this time: when a famine occurred in the neighbourhood, he sold his books and other belongings and gave the money to the poor. Soon after this, he became a canon of the cathedral of Osma. The milieu was a fervent one, in which the canons lived in common and devoted themselves assiduously to prayer under the leadership of the prior Diego d'Azevedo, who became bishop of Osma in 1201. Dominic soon became sub-prior, and it was in this capacity that between 1201 and 1206 he twice accompanied Diego on missions to Denmark which Alfonso VIII of Castile had entrusted to the prior. It was on their way back from the second of these, in 1206, that there occurred the meeting in Languedoc with the Cistercian legates.

For Dominic, the contact with the heretics was decisive. He understood the tragic situation in which the Church was involved, and, like Francis, he saw at once that the only efficacious remedy would be poverty in practice. For all that he did not neglect preaching; until 1215 he devoted himself to it almost unaided, Diego returning to his diocese to seek further aid, only to die there soon afterwards. About 1207, Dominic founded at Prouille, near Fanjeaux, not far from Carcassonne, a monastery intended to receive and assist noble women converted from heresy. This was his home port, one might say, until 1214, when he became parish priest of Fanjeaux. His companions during these years in Languedoc remained free and were not in any way linked with him.[3]

Dominic preached a course of sermons at Toulouse in 1215 with some of these companions, and they then received the official approbation of Bishop Fulk of Toulouse[4] and the Order properly so called began.[5] It was to obtain confirmation for "the title and

---

Paris, 1902); the *De quatuor in quibus Deus praedicatorum ordinem insignivit*, by Stephen of Salanhac and Bernard Gui (ed. T. Kaeppeli, *Monumenta O.P. historica*, XXII (1949); and the *Abbreviatio in gestis et miraculis sanctorum*, by Jean de Mailly (French translation by A. Dondaine, O.P., Paris, 1947). Extracts from the principal texts covering the whole thirteenth century have been translated into French and arranged by M. T. Laureilhe in *Saint Dominique et ses fils*, Paris, 1956.

[3] Among modern biographies of St Dominic, first place must be given to H. M. Vicaire, O.P., *Histoire de saint Dominique*, 2 vols, Paris, 1957. See also G. K. Brady, *Saint Dominic, Pilgrim of Light*, London, 1957.

[4] There is a French translation of this document according to the original text of the Rodez manuscript, by Vicaire, in *Saint Dominique de Caleruega*, pp. 127–8, and in *Histoire de saint Dominique*, I, pp. 337–8.

[5] For the history of the Dominican Order, see *Monumenta O.P. historica*; also A. Walz, O.P., *Compendium historiae O.P.*, 2nd ed., Rome, 1948, and D. A.

function of Preacher",[6] and not for the statutes of this embryonic organization, that Dominic went with the bishop to see Innocent III, at the beginning of the Lateran Council of 1215. It was also at Rome, and at this time, that he seems to have met Francis of Assisi. But while Francis had seen the definitive approbation of his rule, Dominic was obliged to choose a rule already in existence. As he had lived by the rule of St Augustine for twenty years, he naturally looked no further. From that day, the Dominican community conformed to the 10th and 13th canons promulgated by the council with regard to new religious establishments and to clerks or regulars who preached.[7] The definitive confirmation, however, was given not by Innocent III but by Honorius III, on 22 December 1216.[8] Meanwhile the first *Consuetudines* had been drawn up. They were derived from the *Institutiones* of Prémontré[9] and included many prescriptions of a monastic character, adapting religious life to the canonical form and to the aims of the new order: preaching, study and the practice of evangelical poverty. Fulk's charter of approbation already declared that the Brethren were to preach and study "in order to uproot the perversion of heresy, to expel vices, to teach the rule of faith and to inculcate sound morals". As for poverty, it remained that adopted in 1206, but the house accepted an income from the bishop.

The bull of 1216 granted to the friars "preachers", in addition to the chapel of St Romain at Toulouse near which Dominic's companions lived, the church of Prouille, those of our Lady at Lescure, of the Holy Trinity at Loubens, the hospice at Toulouse known as Arnaud Bernard's and their dependencies, as well as some lands and tithes.[10] It can be seen that the new Order admitted, from the beginning, the principle of collective ownership. Although St Dominic's disciples remained "mendicants", they were less intransigent than the Franciscans on this point, and by this fact they

---

Mortier, *Histoire des Maîtres généraux de l'Ordre des Frères Prêcheurs*, 8 vols, Paris, 1903–14. A number of documents relating to the history of the Order have been published in *Archivum Fratrum Praedicatorum*, Rome, 1931 and following years, *Archives d'histoire dominicaine*, Le Saulchoir-Etiolles, 1946, and *Année dominicaine*, 1860 and following years. See also G. R. Galbraith, *The Constitution of the Dominican Order, 1216–1360*, Manchester, 1925; and D. Knowles, *The Religious Orders in England*, I, Cambridge, 1956, Part II, esp. chs XIII and XIV.

[6] Vicaire, *Histoire de saint Dominique*, II, p. 17.

[7] Mansi, vol. XXII, c. 998–1003.

[8] There is a French translation by Vicaire in *Saint Dominique de Caleruega*, pp. 129–33.

[9] According to Vicaire, they form the prologue, §1, and the first "distinction" of the "primitive Constitutions" in the Rodez manuscript. See *Saint Dominique de Caleruega*, pp. 116–17; French translation, *ibid.*, pp. 140–61.

[10] For a French translation, see *Saint Dominique de Caleruega*, pp. 129–30.

avoided the prolonged crises and bitter controversies that divided the ranks of the Friars Minor.

In 1217, Dominic decided to send his friars on the mission although there were only about twenty of them. It is said that he was led to make this decision by a vision that he had of St Peter's basilica in Rome, in which he saw his sons going forth and preaching throughout the world.[11] A certain Brother Matthew was elected "abbot", that is, superior of St Romain. He was, however, the only one to receive this title, which was used among the canons in France.[12] Thenceforth the local superiors were to be called "priors", according to the southern usage, while the general was to be designated by the name "master of the Order". Immediately afterwards, in 1218, the two principal convents were founded, that of Paris and that of Bologna. These were destined to play a leading role in the doctrinal and apostolic mission of the Friars Preachers.

Dominic was only to live three years more. Those years were filled with journeys—to Italy, to Spain, to France. They were fruitful to a degree that is astounding when we consider the difficulties of communication of that period. They sufficed for the saint to give his Order, which was growing rapidly, a solid statutory basis. General chapters, similar to those of the Franciscans, but annual, became the masterpiece of the organization. The first, which was held at Bologna on 17 May 1220, was of great importance, for there it was decided that all property, even collective, should be renounced, and the communities committed to mendicancy. It is possible that this more decisive move in the direction of poverty was the fruit of the meeting between Dominic and Francis which probably took place either at the Lateran Council or elsewhere. In any case, from that time onwards, as Thierry of Apolda says, "the foundation stone was evangelical poverty. The friars did indeed reject all possessions and temporal revenues by a perpetual statute, renouncing even those which they held in the region of Toulouse, preferring the poverty of Christ to the riches of the Egyptians."[13] This general chapter also drew up a considerable portion of the second part (*secunda distinctio*) of the "primitive Constitutions"[14];

[11] Story told by Constantine of Orvieto, *Mon. O.P. hist.*, XVI, p. 304.

[12] According to Jordan of Saxony, *ibid.*, p. 48; cf. Vicaire, *Histoire de saint Dominique*, II, p. 90.

[13] Ch. XVI of his life of St Dominic, *Acta Sanctorum*, August, vol. I, p. 590.

[14] See Vicaire, *Saint Dominique de Caleruega*, p. 115. The passages concerned are chs XVII–XVIII; XIX, §2; XX–XXI; XXVI, §1; XXVIII, §1; XXIX; XXXI, §3; XXXII, §2; XXXIII, §1; XXXIV, §§ 1–4; XXXV, §1; XXXVII, §1 and 3. The refusal of property is explicitly mentioned in ch. XXVI, §1. Ch. XXXV, §1, demands "simple houses". Ch. XXXVII lays down a special statute for the lay brothers. For a French translation, see *ibid.*, pp. 171–83.

it can be presumed that many of the passages in it are the work of Dominic himself.

In spite of a request made by Dominic to this chapter, it did not proceed to name a new master general. The saint was worn out by a life of intense activity and deep-seated inner tension. The last year of his life was devoted to organizing the two convents in Rome—St Sixtus for the nuns, and St Sabina on the Aventine, which was to become the residence of the master general of the Order. When the general chapter of 1221 met on 30 May, Dominic once more sought to be relieved of his charge, and once more he failed. From that time on, his chief work was to divide the Order into "provinces", from England to Poland, and from Scandinavia to the furthest limits of Spain and Italy.

In the course of this chapter of 1221, Jordan of Saxony had been made prior of the Province of Lombardy. A few months later he succeeded to the office of Dominic himself. But it was too late: the saint died on 6 August of that year.

2. *Dominican Spirituality*

Dominic left very little in writing. His correspondence must have been extensive, but only three letters have survived, and those are brief and administrative in tone. He certainly had a part in drawing up the primitive Constitutions—those which date from 1216 and 1220—but it is impossible to determine just how great it was. We can at least be sure that the Constitutions as a whole were not written without his approval, and that they reflect the spirit which he wanted to inculcate in the Friars Preachers.[15] His personal spirituality, however, and that of the Order in its beginnings are not easily defined.[16]

In any case, when one speaks of the "spirituality" of St Dominic, or of his Order, or of any school in the Church, it does not mean that it is distinguished from others by a particular combination of elements. Neither does it mean that it is cut off from the dogmatic and moral whole which is the common property of all Christians. It is simply that the ideals of the Gospel set before all men are

[15] In order to reconstruct the spiritual aspect of Dominic, this lack of personal writings must be made up by reference to the records and biographies relating to the beginnings of the order which have been published in *Monumenta O.P. historica.* A French translation of the principal documents will be found in Vicaire, *Saint Dominique de Caleruega.*

[16] In this connection, see H. Clérissac, O.P., *L'esprit de saint Dominique*, Saint-Maximin, 1924; A. Lemonnyer, "Les prières secrètes dans la vie dominicaine", in *Année dominicaine*, LXIII (1927); M. V. Bernadot, *La spiritualité dominicaine*, Paris, 1938; P. Philippe, "L'oraison dominicaine au XIIIe siècle", in *La Vie spir., Suppl.*, February 15, 1948, pp. 425–54.

embodied in a way which may take on a particular colouring and form according to the men, the civilization, the period or the place —characteristics that belong specifically to these and not to Christianity itself. Dominic did not escape, any more than did Francis of Assisi, from the law by which the evangelical ideal, in itself timeless, takes on quite distinct forms according to concrete circumstances.

In determining how Dominic and his disciples of the first generations reacted to the ideal of the Gospel, we find first of all a fixed determination to be poor. This was expressed more distinctly in 1220, of course, than in 1216. But it would be a mistake to see the practice of poverty as the very purpose of the Order. It was rather a method of apologetics, as can be seen in Dominic's attitude at the time of the repression of the Albigenses, as early as 1206. It was also—and here the father of the Preachers is at one with St Francis—a protest against, a refusal to countenance, the abuses that were then rampant in the Church: against the traffic in benefices and tithes and other such practices.[17] It would seem obvious to any unprejudiced mind that Dominican poverty took a less absolute form than Franciscan; yet it is hardly surprising to learn that each of the two Orders, at a period when theological quarrels were vehement and impassioned, claimed for itself the merit of a more perfect poverty. They went so far as to compare their respective customs, not only over property in general but even with regard to such petty details as the use of meat and of shoes![18]

The Order's real object was to preach. There are few texts as revealing as Chapter 31 of the *secunda distinctio* in the primitive Constitutions. The principal passage is as follows[19]:

> Those who are able to go out preaching, when they are about to leave the convent for that purpose, shall receive from the prior the *socius* that he shall deem suitable to their habits and their position. Having received the blessing, they shall set forth and shall everywhere comport themselves as men who seek to obtain their own salvation and that of their neighbour, in all perfection and the spirit of religion; like evangelical men following in the

[17] In this connection, see M. D. Chenu, O.P., "La pauvreté mendiante: saint Dominique", in the miscellany *La pauvreté*, Paris, 1952, pp. 61–70. See also B. Altaner, "Der Armutsgedanke beim hl. D.", in *Theologie u. Glaube*, XI (1919), pp. 404–17; H. C. Lambermond, *Der Armutsgedanke des hl. D. und seines Ordens*, Zwolle, 1926.

[18] In this connection, see the interesting article by F. Pelster, S.J., "Eine Kontroverse zwischen englischen Dominikanen und Minoriten über einige Punkte der Ordensregel", in *Arch. Fratrum Praedic.*, III (1933), pp. 57–80. See also Knowles, *op. cit.*, pp. 221–4.

[19] Ch. 31, §3. This section dates from 1220. The translation given here is from the French in Vicaire, *Saint Dominique de Caleruega*, pp. 179–80.

> footsteps of their Saviour, speaking with God or of God, either within themselves or with their neighbour; they shall avoid familiarity with any questionable groups. When they thus set forth to exercise the ministry of preaching, or to travel for any other reason, they are not to receive or to carry any gold, silver, or coin or any other gift except food, clothing, and other necessary equipment, and books. None of those who are appointed to the ministry of preaching and to study shall receive any office or temporal administration, so that in greater liberty they may become capable better to fulfil the spiritual ministry entrusted to them; unless by chance no other person be found who can take charge of the necessary business, for it is not a bad thing to be detained occasionally by daily necessities. They shall not take part in litigation or lawsuits unless it be for the cause of the faith.

What stands out most of all in this text is zeal for souls. This end may be attained by actual preaching, or by study: both of these ways of instructing one's neighbour are equally the vocation of a Dominican. The Preacher "speaks with God or of God"; he gives to others, but after having heaped up treasure in contemplation. That is the fundamental difference between this new religious institute and the old monastic Orders. The monks "spoke to God", and frequently even "of God", but the aim of their life was not directly apostolic in the modern sense of the word; the contemplative life was an end in itself. In the Dominican order, on the other hand—and to some extent, in the Franciscan—the apostolate and contemplative go hand in hand, though to a certain extent the latter is subordinate. It is the Church that matters, although the Order of course looks to the end of each of its members in person, their own sanctification.

Among the Dominican apostles of the thirteenth century, there are a number of attractive figures, such as Jordan of Saxony (†1237), Hugh of St Cher (†1263) and Humbert of the Romans (†1277).[20] The one who best represents the apostolic bent of the Order was St Raymond of Pennafort, who was born about 1180 or 1185. His *Summa iuris* dates from the time when he taught at Bologna. Recalled to Barcelona by his bishop and promoted to provost of the chapter, he entered the Friars Preachers in 1222. There he continued his legal career: his *Summa casuum* or *Summa de poenitentia* must be placed between 1232 and 1235, and in 1234, by order of Gregory IX, he published a collection of all past decretals. This Pope had brought Raymond to Rome in 1230 in the capacity of confessor and penitentiary, but, exhausted by his labours, he soon

[20] His *De oratione* has been edited by H. M. Hering, O.P., Rome, 1960.

returned to Spain. He did not, however, long remain free from the burden of office: the chapter of the Order chose him in 1238 as master general, to succeed Jordan of Saxony. In 1240, he resigned the charge and devoted himself thenceforth, until his death in 1275, to the apostolate among the Jews and Moors of Spain and Africa.[21]

At the end of the thirteenth century, the Dominican Order was to provide missionaries to the East. These were the "Friars Pilgrims", a sort of congregation in which several houses were united under a vicar of the master general. Their field of action extended to Armenia, Azerbaijan, Turkestan and to India and China.[22] The wide scope of this missionary effort is remarkable and indeed admirable.

In the European sphere, the activity of a great Dominican pope must be mentioned. Peter of Tarentaise (born before 1225) was a master at Paris from 1259 to 1265, then provincial, archbishop of Lyons (1272), cardinal bishop of Ostia, and finally pope (January-June 1276) under the name of Innocent V. Of his works there have been preserved some scriptural commentaries, some sermons (unpublished), and a commentary on the *Sentences*. His great concerns were the peace of the Church and the danger from the Moslems.[23]

In spite of their definitely apostolic bent, the Preachers kept many usages of canonical life; they were clerics, and they were regulars. As yet their conception of the apostolate had not called in question the recitation of the Divine Office in common, except for individuals or classes of friars sent on a mission of study or preaching; for them, the principle of dispensation is clearly laid down in the primitive Constitutions from the Prologue onwards.[24] Their Office, in comparison with that of the Benedictines, Cistercians or Carthusians, was an abridged one. Manual labour was only

[21] Sources in *S.R. de P. Diplomatorio*, ed. J. Rius Serra, Barcelona, 1954; and in *Raymundiana, Monumenta O.P. historica*, IV, 1–2, 2 vols, Rome, 1898–1901. *Summa juris*, ed. J. Rius Serra, Barcelona, 1945. Raymond drew up a version of the Constitutions of the Friars Preachers; see R. Creytens, O.P., in *Arch. Fratrum Praedic.*, XVIII (1948), pp. 5–68.

There are various biographies, including those by F. Valls-Taberner, Barcelona, 1936 (republished in his *Obras selectas*, I, Barcelona, 1952); and by M. Durán y Bas, in *Galeria de Catalanes illustres*, II, Barcelona, 1951, pp. 225–68 (a new edition of a biography written in 1888). On Raymond as well as the other masters general of the order, see A. Mortier, *Histoire des Maîtres généraux de l'Ordre des Frères Prêcheurs*, Paris, 1903 and following years.

[22] Cf. P. R. Loenertz, O.P., "Les missions dominicaines en Orient au XIVe siècle et la Société des Frères Pérégrinants pour le Christ", in *Arch. Fratrum Praedic.*, II (1932), pp. 1–83 (historical study and documents).

[23] Ed. Toulouse, 1640–52. On Peter of Tarentaise, see P. Glorieux, O.P., *Répertoire des maîtres en théologie de Paris au XIIIe siècle*, I, pp. 107–12; M. H. Laurent, O.P., *Le Bienheureux Innocent V*, Vatican City, 1947; and the collection *Beatus Innocentius PP. V, Studia et documenta*, Rome, 1943.

[24] Prologue, §2; this passage dates from 1220. There is a French translation in Vicaire, *Saint Dominique de Caleruega*, p. 139.

undertaken where it was actually necessary, and then only by those not bound to apostolic work. With these divergences from the old monastic usages, there were points of contact that must not be overlooked. Thus the training of novices in the early days of the Order (throughout the thirteenth century) was still in conformity with the tradition of Augustine, Gregory, Bernard and the Victorines; even at the end of the century, the writings of the great Dominican scholastics, including St Thomas, had no privileged place in their studies.[25] Dominic himself had shown a positive predilection for the *Conferences* of Cassian,[26] as had his disciples for a devotion to our Lady which was to have some influence in the devotional life of the period.[27] The Order played a definite part in the spread of the Rosary and its confraternities.

It is also characteristic of the Dominican spirit that the direction of souls should have taken on the importance of a direct aim in the Order. In the twelfth century, indeed, spiritual direction was usually conceived according to the old monastic pattern, in which the abbot, the superior of the community, was normally the director of his subjects' consciences; in any case, a fervent spiritual life outside the cloister was hardly to be thought of. In the thirteenth century, however, the interest of spiritual masters turned towards the laity. This was to be one of the glories of the Dominicans, although the Franciscans also did much in the same direction. The guidance given by the Preachers consisted in giving the lives of laymen as monastic an outlook as possible, taking into account their state of life; that was the whole point of the "third orders". Confraternities of St Dominic and of St Peter Martyr, parallel to those of St Francis, and congregations of the Blessed Virgin, were organized as early as the middle of the thirteenth century.[28] We even find simple laymen acting as spiritual directors, completely

[25] In this connection, see R. Creytens, O.P., "L'instruction des novices dominicains au XIIIe siècle d'après le ms. Toulouse 418", in *Arch. Fratrum Praedic.*, XX (1950), pp. 114–93. On life in Dominican houses in the thirteenth century, see the documents in M. T. Laureilhe, *op. cit.*, Part III, pp. 189–282.

[26] Jordan of Saxony, *Libellus*, n. 13. For a French translation, see Vicaire, *Saint Dominique de Caleruega*, pp. 32–3.

[27] In spite of the fact that St Thomas Aquinas, and the entire Order after him for two centuries, denied the privilege of the Immaculate Conception. See A. Duval, O.P., "La dévotion mariale dans l'Ordre des Frères Prêcheurs", in *Maria*, II, Paris, 1952, pp. 737–82. See also A. Walz, O.P., "De Corde Mariae testes dominicani", in *Angelicum*, XXXI (1954), pp. 307–51; the testimony from the fifteenth century is the most significant.

[28] See the studies by G. G. Meersseman, O.P., "Etudes sur les anciennes confréries dominicaines", in *Arch. Fratrum Praedic.*, XX (1950), pp. 5–113; XXI (1951), pp. 51–196; XXII (1952), pp. 5–176; XXIII (1953), pp. 275–308. Later, Thomas of Siena wrote a *Tractatus de ordine fratrum de paenitentia S. Dominici*, which has been edited by H. M. Laurent, O.P., and F. Valli (*Fontes vitae S. Cather. Sen. historici*, XXI), Siena, 1938.

outside the structure of the hierarchy and moved by an impulse that can only be called charismatic. This was true of Hadewijch and of Catherine of Siena, who will be discussed further on. In moving away from the "conventual" pattern of spiritual direction, these laymen were unconsciously going back to the primitive monastic pattern, in which an "abbot", without having received any commission from the hierarchy, gathered disciples about him.

The Dominican Order was prepared to undertake the spiritual direction of fervent laymen. The principle had been laid down as early as 1220 in the prologue of the primitive Constitutions, when dispensations were permitted not only for the sake of study and preaching, but also for the good of souls in general, because "our Order was specially instituted, from the beginning, for preaching and the *salvation of souls*, and because on principle our efforts must be directed with ardour and with all our energies, toward rendering ourselves capable of being *useful to the souls of our neighbours*".

Another sign of this special bent is to be found in the *Summa magistri Pauli*, the work of Paul of Hungary, a professor of canon law, which reveals "the preoccupations, intellectual and apostolic, of the Preachers of Bologna in 1220 and 1221. It reflects their state of mind and, we may confidently add, that of him who was their leader, St Dominic."[29] This *Summa* includes a *Summa de Confessione* and a *Tractatus de vitiis et virtutibus*.[30] It "has reference to, and is directly attached to, the great reform undertaken by the Fourth General Council of the Lateran of 1215 . . . , which made it obligatory for all the faithful to go to confession and communion at least once a year."[31] Consequently, the Council recognized the possibility of turning to confessors other than one's parish priest (though with the latter's authorization) and defines the role of such confessors.[32] This was clearly meant to designate the Friars Preachers. A few years later, on 4 February 1221, Honorius III addressed "all the prelates of Christendom, and after earnestly commending to them the ministry of the Preachers, whose whole object it is to preach the word of God, he exhorted them also to confide to them the ministry of confession."[33]

The Dominicans carried out these tasks faithfully. The ideal

[29] P. Mandonnet and H. M. Vicaire, O.P., *Saint Dominique. L'idée, l'homme et l'œuvre*, I, Paris, 1938, p. 268. On the *Summae confessorum*, see texts quoted by S. Kuttner, "Pierre de Roissy and Robert of Flamborough", in *Traditio*, II (1944), pp. 492–9.

[30] Ed. R. Duellius, *Miscellanea*, Book I, Augsburg and Gratz, 1723, pp. 29–83. There is a more recent edition in *Bibliotheca Casinensis*, series IV, Monte Cassino, 1880, pp. 191–215; cf. Mandonnet, *op. cit.*, I, pp. 249–69.

[31] Mandonnet, *op. cit.*, I, p. 253. Cf. Mansi, XXII, col. 1007–10.

[32] *Ibid.*, col. 998, 1010.

[33] Mandonnet, *op. cit.*, I, pp. 254–5.

portrait of the confessor and spiritual director was sketched by Paul of Hungary in the *Summa* just mentioned. The author states, of course, that he is drawing upon St Augustine:

> Let him be inclined to correct kindly, and to bear the weight himself. He must be gentle and affectionate, merciful to the faults of others. He shall act with discernment in different cases. Let him aid his penitent with prayer, alms, and other good works. He is to help him by calming his fears, consoling him, giving him back hope, and if need be, by reproving him. Let him show compassion in his words, and teach by his deeds. Let him take part in the sorrow, if he wishes to share in the joy. He must inculcate perseverance.[34]

The Friars Preachers were very soon to be faced with the question of the *cura animarum* of nuns. St Dominic had known and organized only three monasteries of women, those of Prouille, St Sixtus in Rome, and Madrid. Shortly after his death, these convents multiplied to such an extent that the general chapter of 1228 inserted into the primitive Constitutions a provision forbidding this ministry which had become burdensome to the point of interfering with the most urgent of apostolic duties.[35] In vain did Jordan of Saxony, then master general, protest against the measure, as well as the nuns of St Agnes in Bologna.[36] More than once, in the years that followed, the Preachers were explicitly excluded from all ministry to nuns, whether in directing their souls or in administering their houses. Little by little, however, the Holy See granted exemptions, notably in favour of Prouille and St Sixtus. The entreaties of the nuns finally led to a bull of Clement IV, issued on 6 February 1267, which put an end to the long discussion and regulated, once and for all, the juridical status of the Dominican Sisters.[37] Very soon after this date, we find many examples of spiritual direction given by the Preachers to *mulieres religiosae*. Not only Dominican nuns but also

[34] Ed. *Bibliotheca Casinensis*, p. 196.

[35] Dist. II, ch. XXVII. For a French translation see Vicaire, *Saint Dominique de Caleruega*, pp. 176–7.

[36] Cf. Mandonnet, *op. cit.*, II, p. 290, n. 22. Nevertheless Jordan exercised a profound influence as a spiritual director; see his letters to the community of St Agnes and to the Dominican nun Diana d'Andalo. Cf. *Dict. de spirit.*, III, pp. 853–5; M. Aron, *Bienheureux Jourdain de Saxe: lettres à la Bienheureuse Diane d'Andalo*, Lille–Bruges, 1924. There is a critical edition of his letters by B Altaner, *Briefe J. v. S.*, Leipzig, 1925. Cf. A. Walz, O.P., "Intorno alle lettere del beato Giordano di Sassonia", in *Angelicum*, XXVI (1949), pp. 143–64, 218–32; H. C. Scheeben, "Der literarische Nachlass Jordans von Sachsen", in *Histor. Jahrb.*, LII (1932), pp. 56–71; by the same author, *J. der Sachse*, Vechta, 1937, and *Beiträge z. Gesch. J. v. S.*, Vechta, 1938.

[37] See O. Decker, O.P., *Die Stellung des Predigerordens zu den Dominikanerinnen (1207–1267)*, Leipzig, 1935; R. Creytens, "Les Constitutions primitives des Sœurs dominicaines de Montargis", in *Arch. Fratrum Praedic.*, XVII (1947), pp. 41–3.

Béguines and religious of other orders benefited from their aid, particularly in the Netherlands.[38]

The influence of the mendicant Orders in the Church was bound to encounter lively opposition here and there. Between 1252 and 1270, the mendicants and the seculars were engaged in a real conflict, of which more will be said further on. Even literature entered the fray: one of Rutebeuf's poems, the *Dit des Règles*, is thought to have been an attack on the place which the Preachers claimed for themselves in the Church and on the abuses for which they were held responsible.[39]

Such opposition shows that the new orders presented a problem. Some, taking their stand on the New Testament, held that their very existence was unlawful. Since the structure of the Church is that of a hierarchy, the degrees of which go from the baptized to the bishops, they asked what place there was for the friars in it.

This phenomenon is perfectly understandable if one takes into account the needs of the Church at the time. Francis and Dominic had come to her aid in the most providential manner. But it is to be noted that their vocations were different in character. All that Francis wanted, at the beginning, was to gather together a band of fervent Christians who would go forth to announce, or to recall, the message of the Gospel. He probably did not even foresee that his friars would normally be priests, for in many passages of his rule he says that they are to be subject to the priests who have jurisdiction in the places where they are visiting and preaching. Dominic's case was different; he was a priest and a canon of Osma, and he became parish priest of Fanjeaux. The community of preachers which he organized at Toulouse was a canonical and sacerdotal one, and the mission on which he sent it extended across the whole of Europe.

The real innovation, then, was made not at San Damiano but at Toulouse. But there too the problem began to arise. Though the debate was not carried on at the highest level (it was over new observances, superiority of one state of life over another) and although it does not seem to us to have got to the bottom of the

[38] See G. Meersseman, O.P., "Les Frères Prêcheurs et le mouvement dévot en Flandre au XIIIe siècle", in *Arch. Fratrum Praedic.*, XVIII (1948), pp. 69–130. There has been preserved a letter of spiritual direction from the Dominican Henri of Louvain († *c.* 1302) to a devout lady. A Latin translation of this letter, known as the *Epistola aurea*, was incorporated by St Peter Canisius in a collection of the sermons of John Tauler and thus was given a very wide distribution. See S. Axters, O.P., "De zalige Hendrik van Leuven O.P. als geestlijk auteur", in *Ons geestelijk Erf*, XXI (1947), pp. 225–56.

[39] See E. Faral, "Pour le commentaire de Rutebeuf, Le dit des 'Règles'", in *Studi medievali*, XVI (1943–50), pp. 176–211; *Œuvres complètes*, ed. by E. Faral and J. Bastin, Paris, 1959–60, vol. I, pp. 267–76.

question, still one cannot help thinking today that the mendicants' opponents were not entirely wrong. In the eyes of the secular clergy, the Franciscans and Dominicans had the same defect; to have created a regular clergy parallel to the only authentic one. The two orders joined in retaliating—which only shows once again that the disciples of St Francis had gravitated towards the clerical state.[40] Many of the Dominican doctors of the thirteenth century, however, were far from concerning themselves with this question. As will be seen, St Thomas succeeded, thanks to his theological and spiritual genius, in rising above these limited problems, just as St Bonaventure had risen above that of the evolution of the Franciscan Order.

The difficulty was more practical than theoretical. The monastic Orders had indeed kept a certain tradition of fervent spiritual life; the secular clergy, on the other hand, were not zealous in the performance of their duties. Now, Orders such as the Franciscans and Dominicans were not in competition with the monastic Orders, but the secular priests, who could have looked on them as a valuable aid, inevitably feared their competition in the ministry to the faithful, in obtaining university chairs, etc. Consequently, though they were welcomed, they sometimes met with contradiction and sarcasm from some of the intellectuals and opposition from certain bishops and parish priests.

3. St Albert the Great

The first great Dominican doctor[41] was St Albert the Great. He is renowned chiefly as the master of St Thomas, and that is indeed one of his many titles to glory. Born of a noble family about 1206 in the diocese of Augsburg, from his youth he showed great interest in the natural sciences. While studying at Padua, he was won to the life of perfection by Jordan of Saxony and entered the Dominican Order at the age of sixteen. Soon he was teaching in the German convents, chiefly at Cologne, and after about 1240 at Paris. He was superior of the new *Studium generale* at Cologne from 1248 to 1252, where he wrote commentaries, notably on Dionysius. Among his disciples between 1245 and 1252, first at Paris and then at Cologne, was St Thomas Aquinas. In 1254, he was elected provincial of Germany. He remained in office until 1257 and then returned to Cologne. In 1260 Albert's life took a

[40] For the details of this episode, see *infra*, §5, pp. 336 *et seq*.

[41] It would be impossible to give here a complete list of the great Dominican teachers of the thirteenth century. On the Dominican masters at Paris in the first century of the Order, see P. Glorieux, *Répertoire des maîtres en théologie de Paris au XIIIe siècle*, I, Paris, 1933, pp. 27–222.

very different turn. He had been above all a man of study, except during his term as provincial; now he was made bishop of Ratisbon. He soon resigned his see to return to his studies, but his intellectual activities did not prevent his undertaking countless missions, notably at Wurzburg and Strasbourg. In 1271 he was again at Cologne, having been sent to make peace between the city and the archbishop, Engelbert von Falkenberg. In 1274 he was present at the Council of Lyons. During a stay in Paris in 1276–77, he had an opportunity to defend his Aristotelian position and that of his disciple Thomas. This life of extraordinary labours came to an end on 15 November 1280 at Cologne.[42]

Albert's written work is immense.[43] It includes, first of all, what we should now call "philosophy", but a considerable part of it is devoted to the natural sciences. This portion of his work includes commentaries on Aristotle, Porphyry and Boethius. Albert also wrote commentaries on most of the books of the Bible, on the Pseudo-Dionysius, and on Peter Lombard. He wrote a *Summa Theologica*; various treatises on dogmatic and moral questions; sermons on the Eucharist and on the Sunday gospels; a *De laudibus Beatae Mariae Virginis*; commentaries on the *Pater* and the Creed; the *Paradisus animae*, a famous ascetic treatise; and finally the *De adhaerendo Deo*, a mystical treatise on union with Christ through the renouncing of all things.[44]

[42] There is a recent biography of Albert by H. C. Scheeben, Cologne, 1955. No contemporary biography exists; it has been necessary to reconstruct the stages of his life from his own writings and other documents. Many biographical writings have been based on Quétif-Echard, *Script. O.P.*, I, Paris, 1719, pp. 162–71. Cf. H. C. Scheeben, *A. der Gr. Zur Chronologie seines Lebens*, Leipzig, 1931; P. Mandonnet, art. "Albert le Grand", in *Dict. hist. géogr. eccl.*, I, pp. 1515–24. Bibliographies will be found in *Rev. thomiste*, XXXVI (1931), pp. 260–92, 422–68; and *Angelicum*, XXI (1944), pp. 13–40.

[43] P. Glorieux, *Répertoire . . .*, I, pp. 62–77. Albert's works were published in 21 folio volumes at Lyons in 1651 and in 38 quarto volumes at Paris in 1890–9. In spite of its defects, the latter edition is the one more often cited. The "Albertus-Magnus-Institut" of Cologne, under the direction of Professor B. Geyer, is republishing the *Opera Omnia*; vols XII, XIX, XXVI and XXVIII appeared between 1951 and 1958. The problems of authenticity, editions, etc., have been studied by G. Meersseman, O.P., *Introductio in Opera omnia B. Alb. Magni, O.P.*, Bruges, 1931; this work should be supplemented or corrected by the facts summarized by W. Kûbel in *Prolegomena* of vol. XXVI of the Cologne edition (1958). Several writings on the Blessed Virgin, such as the *Mariale super "Missus est"*, are not authentic; cf. A. Fries, C.SS.R., "Die unter dem Namen des A. Magnus überlieferten mariologischen Schriften", in *Beiträge z. Gesch. Philos. Theol. Mittelalters*, 37, 4, Münster, 1954.

[44] This treatise (vol. 37 in the Paris edition, pp. 523–43) was completed by some chapters (chs XVII–XXIII) which are not authentic. They are probably the work of John of Castel, a Bavarian Benedictine of the fifteenth century. The *Sermones de tempore et sanctis* and the *Commentarium super Ave Maria* are not authentic; cf. A. Fries, *op. cit.*

A good anthology of texts translated into French is A. Garreau's *Saint Albert le Grand*, Paris, 1957.

His spiritual writings give an impression of a piety whose object is to arouse fervour and devotion in the reader's soul rather than to provide him with doctrine. This is in contrast to his scientific and theological works. He was even one of the few authors of the twelfth century who was acquainted with the cultus of the Sacred Heart,[45] whether envisaged in its physical reality or in its spiritual significance, as the seat of the soul's faculties, of the virtues, and especially of love and intimate contemplation. Albert takes up themes that are to be found as far back as Origen: he sees the redeeming blood springing from that Heart, and with it the Church and the sacraments, especially Baptism and the Eucharist. This Heart gives life to the mystical Body of Christ. But the approach is not purely devotional; he is careful to connect this outlook with the redemption. On this point, Thomas Aquinas is more sober than his master. Albert was of German origin, and it was chiefly in the Empire that this devotion spread.

One has the impression that Albert did not keep himself apart from the devotional channels of his century, but his theology remains lucid. Though he chose to comment on the Pseudo-Dionysius and to admit with the mystic that "all that we know of God is the *quia est*" and that "we still do not know his *quid est*"; nevertheless, he also knew that "God is he who is proved to be, more than he is he who is experienced."[46] He therefore has reservations as to what mystical contemplation can do, though without falling into agnosticism on the point. In contemplation and by it, of course, the soul "sees" God, in the sense that it is raised above all created objects. But it does not "see" God in himself: it is not an immediate vision, like that of heavenly glory or of rapture. It takes place by means of an abstract *species*, the finite limitations of which are set aside by the intellect so that it may rise, by this *species*, towards the Infinite "by a certain supernatural knowledge, but with a certain confusion".[47] This mode of defining contemplation

[45] See R. Erni, *Die Herz-Jesu-Lehre Alberts des Grossen*, Lucerne, 1941; A. Walz, O.P., *De veneratione divini Cordis Iesu in Ordine Praedicatorum*, 2nd ed., Rome, 1937; by the same author, "Dominikanische Herz-Jesu-Auffassung", in *Cor Jesu. Commentationes in litteras encyclicas "Haurietis Aquas"*, II, Rome, 1959 pp. 49–95.

[46] M. M. Gorce, O.P., *L'essor de la pensée au moyen âge. Albert le Grand—Thomas d'Aquin*, Paris, 1933, p. 128. In this connection see *ibid.*, pp. 127–37.

[47] *Quadam supernaturali cognitione sub quadam confusione.* Cf. G. Meersseman, O.P., "La contemplation mystique d'après le bienheureux Albert est-elle immédiate?", in *Rev. thomiste*, XXXVI (1931), pp. 408–21. See particularly Albert's commentary on the *De mystica theologia* of Dionysius (vol. XIV in the Paris edition, pp. 834–5); J. Maréchal, S.J., *Etudes sur la psychologie des mystiques*, II, Brussels, 1937, pp. 265–8.

prepared the way for that of St Thomas, and of the German mysticism of the following century.[48]

4. *St Thomas Aquinas*

Thomas was born in 1225 at Rocca Secca, of the family of the counts of Aquino, and received his first education at the Benedictine abbey of Monte Cassino. His family wished him to have a brilliant career in the Benedictine Order, but he resisted their ambitions and entered the order of Preachers, probably in 1244, after studying philosophy at Naples. He was sent to the *Studium generale* at St Jacques in Paris, where he remained from 1245 to 1248; then to Cologne, where he studied until 1252. It has been seen how much he owed to Albert the Great during this formative period. He returned to Paris to take his master's degree in theology and received it on 15 August 1257 at the same time as Bonaventure. Thenceforth he devoted himself exclusively, until his death, to his task of teaching. During this period he spent little time in Paris; he was in Italy from 1259 to 1269, and again from 1272 to 1274 while he was organizing the *Studium generale* at Naples. He set out for the Council of Lyons, but fell ill on the way, at the castle of Maenza, the home of his niece. He was carried to the Cistercian monastery of Fossanova, between Naples and Rome, and there he died at the age of forty-nine, on 7 March 1274.[49]

His work is comparable in extent to that of his master, Albert the Great.[50] In a history of spirituality like this, it is impossible to give even a brief review of his teaching or of his positions in matters of

[48] On this influence, see M. Grabmann, "Der Einfluss Alberts des Grossen auf das mittelalterlichen Geistesleben", in *Zeitschr. f. Kathol. Theologie*, XXV (1928), pp. 153–82, 313–56; W. Stammler, "A. der Grosse und die deutsche Volksfrömmigkeit des Mittelalters", in *Freib. Zeitschr. Philos. u. Theol.*, III (1956), pp. 287–319.

[49] The principal biographies are: in English, by G. Vann, O.P., London, 1940, New York, 1947; in French, by E. Gilson, 2nd ed., Paris, 1925, E. de Bruyne, Paris, 1928, and L. H. Petitot, O.P., Paris, 1929; in German, by M. Grabmann, Munich, 1946 and A. Walz, O.P., Basle, 1953; in Italian, by I. Taurisano, Turin, 1941. There is a bibliography by P. Mandonnet and J. Destrez, Kain, 1921; and in the *Bulletin thomiste*. The sources have been edited by O. Prümmer, O.P., *Fontes vitae S. Th.A*, Toulouse (no date). A French translation of part of these Fontes, notably of the life by Guillaume de Tocco, has been made by T. Pègues and X. Maquart, Paris–Toulouse, 1925.

[50] See P. Glorieux, *Répertoire* . . ., I, pp. 85–104. The complete works [of St Thomas] have been published several times: the "Leonine" edition (*Jussu Leonis XIII P.M.*), which is well done, in general, but unwieldy (16 vols, Rome, 1882–1948); that of Paris (Vivès, 34 vols, 1871–80; 2nd ed., 1889–90); of Parma (1852–1872); and of Rome (1570–1). There have been countless partial editions, especially of the *Summa Theologica*. The *Summa Theologica* was translated into English by the Fathers of the English Dominican Province, and a small popular edition (Everyman's Library) gives English translations of extracts from the *Summa Theologica* and other works, edited by M. C. d'Arcy, S.J.

philosophy, of dogmatic or moral theology, or of exegesis. It has been said again and again how much he owed not only to Aristotelianism but also to Neo-Platonism and the Arabian philosophers. Nevertheless, even in philosophy, he thinks as a Christian and, as such, he accepts the message of the Bible, on which he commented at length, and that of the Fathers of the Church, among whom he puts St Augustine in the front rank. It is interesting from the point of view of this book to note that he read Cassian every day and that more than once he drew inspiration from his teaching. The great doctor's words in this connection are recorded by his biographer William of Tocco[51]: "From this reading I reap devotion, and that makes it easier for me to lift myself up into speculation. So, the *affectus*, attachment to God, widens into devotion, and thanks to it, the intellect ascends towards the highest summits."

Naturally, Thomas knew the teachings of the Church's *magisterium*, the councils and the popes. He also knew and discussed what had been taught by his immediate predecessors and his contemporaries: Albert, Bonaventure, Alexander of Hales, William of Auxerre and others. But where he differs from them is in the great vigour of his thought and his more exact method—that "scholastic" method which in the schools of the twelfth century had begun to take on precision, but which in his hands became a perfect instrument—and finally by his more rigorous systematization, which reached its height in the *Summa Theologica*. In all this, he reveals himself not merely as a compiler, however endowed with genius, but as a powerful and original thinker.

His doctrine is distinguished from that of the Franciscan masters by a definite "intellectualism". By this must be understood, not his use of an intellectual method, for that had become common to all the schools of the time, but rather his affirmation of the primacy of the intellect over the will. He had inherited from Aristotle an unlimited confidence in the possibilities of the human intellect, "capable of God", *capax Dei*. But it goes without saying that he far surpassed his master in rational speculation on God, as well as in psychology and in moral philosophy.[52]

[51] Cf. *Vita* by Guillaume de Tocco, in *Acta Sanctorum*, March, vol. I, p. 665; or *Fontes vitae S. Th. Aq.*, ed. cit., pp. 65–160. Cf. J. Leclercq, O.S.B., in *La Vie spirit.*, XCVIII (1958), 658–9.

[52] The best general studies of Thomism in French are those by A. D. Sertillanges, O.P., Paris, 1910; E. Gilson, 4th ed., Paris, 1942; and R. Garrigou-Lagrange, O.P., *La synthèse thomiste*, Paris, 1947. There may also be mentioned the little introduction by P. Grenet (series "Que sais-je?", 587, Paris, 1953), and the one by M. D. Chenu, O.P., entitled *Introduction à l'étude de saint Thomas d'Aquin*, Paris, 1950; as well as Chenu's *Saint Thomas d'Aquin et la théologie* (series "Maîtres spirituels", XVII, Paris, 1959) The last-mentioned cites a number of texts, but presents St Thomas in so "modern" a manner that it should be read critically.

This progress was made possible by his acceptance of the fact that God had spoken. Aristotle gave him the structure of a deductive science of God, to be deduced, like all rational sciences according to the ancients, from first principles. He gave him a "logic" and the principles of a metaphysical system. When it is a question of the sacred science of the word of God, the first principles are the "articles of faith", *articuli fidei*. These are known by faith, which is itself based on Scripture; but theology goes on from them by the work of deductive reason.[53] As for the authority of these articles of faith, it did not constitute any special problem for Thomas. The reasons for believing them and their intrinsic fittingness caused him no more difficulty than the postulates of geometry This is a point that distinguishes his attitude—and, indeed, that of the Middle Ages as a whole—from our modern theology, which begins by carefully establishing the foundations of revealed truth.[54]

When Thomas was obliged to establish those foundations, however, he proceeded carefully. Probity marks his exegesis of the word of God; moreover, he demands *longum studium et exercitium*,[55] "long study and practice" of one who would devote himself to that task—without overlooking, for all that, either grace or the "light of divine wisdom" or the preparation provided by the moral and intellectual virtues. He who listens to the exegete's teaching, on his side, must have an upright judgment and the "fertility which will enable him, in his turn, to set forth much after having heard but little", *ex paucis auditis multa*.[56]

Thomas uses the spiritual sense comparatively rarely, but occasionally his exegesis fails when he sets out to seek the literal sense. This is of course due rather to a lack of knowledge in the vast fields ancillary to exegesis (Hebrew, Greek, philology, history, archaeology, etc.), than to any lack of critical sense on his part or any free rein given to fantasy.

For our purpose it is not so much this summary view of his intellectual genius that is interesting, as the way in which he reacted in the face of spiritual problems themselves. In his religious psychology there are a few fundamental traits that are distinctively his, and they are bound up with deep personal experience. First is his love of wisdom, which finds its fullest expression in the science of theology;

[53] See M. D. Chenu, O.P., *La théologie comme science au XIIIe siècle*, 3rd ed., Paris, 1957.

[54] See R. Aubert, "Le caractère raisonnable de l'acte de foi d'après les théologiens de la fin du XIIIe siècle", in *Rev. d'hist. eccl.*, XXXIX (1943), pp. 22–99.

[55] *Summa Theologica*, II[a] II[ae], q. 1, a. 9, ad 1.

[56] In this connection, see his discourse on receiving the degree of master of theology at Paris, known under the title of *De commendatione Sacrae Scripturae* (*Opuscula*, ed. R. A. Verardo, vol. I, Turin, 1954, pp. 441–3).

next his love of charity, which is the soul of morality.[57] Faithful to the Gospel, Thomas teaches that the perfection of Christian life consists in charity.[58] Another distinctive trait is his love of peace, the fruit of charity, which can overcome every difference, every controversy. All this takes concrete form in the love of Christ, whom Thomas loved passionately.[59]

Thomas was not simply an intellectual genius, distinguished from Aristotle by his acceptance of God's word in lively and unconditional faith. He was also a mystic who experienced, in some way, what he taught. It was said of him that he wrote or dictated when in ecstasy. Whether this be true or not, it is worth remembering: Thomas wrote only what he knew from experience.

Much has been written on St Thomas's mystical teaching.[60] When he speaks of contemplation, he starts by defining it. It is a light, a superhuman mode of knowledge; it is intuitive, and it is experimental like sensible knowledge—although in his early writings Thomas is less positive on this point.[61] It is impregnated with love; it is a wisdom, a knowledge full of delight, by which we attain to God and taste him. It is distinct from the knowledge of faith: its formal principle is a "light" which the generality of Christians do not possess. It is, then, characteristic of what is called the mystical life. To attain to it, the theological virtues are not sufficient: there must be perfect docility to God's leading. This docility is bestowed by the "gifts of the Holy Ghost", which tend to be summed up in the gift of wisdom, a replica of the Wisdom of the Word and a light specifically distinct from the light of faith. It seems, according to certain passages, that Thomas admitted two modes of action according to which the gifts could operate: an ordinary one, which is that of every Christian living in a state of grace; and an exceptional one, in which "the life of grace, as a whole, is ruled by

[57] See L. B. Geiger, O.P., *Le problème de l'amour chez saint Thomas d'Aquin* Montreal, 1952.

[58] See, for example, *S.T.*, IIª–IIªᵉ, q. 184, a. 1.

[59] Cf. M. Grabmann, *Das Seelenleben des hl. Th. v. A. nach seinen Werken und den Heiligsprechungsakten dargestellt*, 3rd ed., Fribourg (Switzerland), 1949. In this connection it should be remembered that the hymn to the Blessed Sacrament, *Adoro te*, is probably not the work of St Thomas, but rather is to be regarded as an example of a style which had become traditional since the ninth century; see S. Axters, O.P., "De ontwikkeling van het Adoro te van de 9ᵈᵉ tot de 16ᵈᵉ eeuw", in *Studia eucharistica*, Antwerp, 1946, 269–303.

[60] See particularly L. Roy, S.J., *Lumière et sagesse. La grâce mystique dans la théologie de saint Thomas d'Aquin*, Montreal, 1948; G. Turbessi, O.S.B., *La vita contemplativa. Dottrina tomistica e sua relazione alle fonti*, Rome, 1944. St Thomas's mystical doctrine is set forth chiefly in *S.T.*, IIª–IIªᵉ, q. 179 to 182; and in *III Sent.*, d. 35.

[61] Cf. F. Vandenbroucke, O.S.B. "Notes sur la théologie mystique de saint Thomas d'Aquin", in *Ephem. Theol. Lovan.*, XXVII (1951), pp. 483–92.

passivity".[62] This second mode would then be characteristic of the mystical life. Not all historians accept this interpretation of St Thomas's doctrine. However that may be, the distinction between the two modes of action of the gifts simply clarifies his teaching on their superiority and their difference. It was current at Paris, at least after about 1235, in Franciscan circles as well as Dominican ones.[63]

When Thomas speaks of contemplation, he makes love its principle; he also makes it its term and its effect. He is committed, by his confidence in Aristotelianism and by the primacy that he attributes to the intellect in man, to seeing contemplation as being "formally" an intellectual act. This "intellectualist" point of view governs his replies to the questions that can be raised in connection with contemplation. Is the vision of God's essence possible for the human intellect, and, if so, under what conditions? What are the degrees of contemplation? And how is it related to love?[64] This intellectualism does not go so far as to admit the possibility of man's seeing the essence of God, at least not normally; Thomas makes an exception only for St Paul's rapture.[65]

In any case, he had found, in the writings of the masters of the mystical life, sufficient justification for his intellectualist point of view. St Augustine, the doctor of love, had left that famous aphorism, "greatly Love understanding", *Intellectum valde ama*; and St Anselm, "Faith seeking understanding", *Fides quaerens intellectum*. Thomas's thought was relatively independent of the negative theology so dear to the Pseudo-Dionysius,[66] so that he combined a deep faith in the activities of the human intellect with the pure tradition of the "monastic" Middle Ages. His harmonious synthesis only loses by being commented upon, systematized and scrutinized. It is sufficiently explained by being set forth in its simplicity.

The Aristotelian starting-point of Thomist teaching—that is, the primacy of the intellect over the will—is not admitted by the Franciscan school. The mystical doctrine which gravitated around the *Devotio moderna* during the last two or three centuries of the Middle Ages seems much more indebted to the Franciscan school than to the Thomist one. The Franciscans, faithful to St Augustine, laid down as a principle the primacy of love in contemplation. Man's beatitude consists of loving possession, enjoyment, rather

[62] L. Roy, S.J., *op. cit.*, p. 196.

[63] Cf. O. Lottin, *Psychologie et morale au XIIe et XIIIe siècles*, vols. III and IV, Louvain, 1949–54. See also *Dict. de spirit.*, III, col. 1587–1635.

[64] See G. Turbessi, *op. cit.*, pp. 34–75; cf. *S.T.*, II^a–II^ae, q. 180.

[65] Cf. *S.T.*, II^a–II^ae, q. 180, a. 5.

[66] Cf. M. Waldmann, "Th. von A. und die 'Mystische Theologie' des Pseudo-Dionysius", in *Geist u. Leben*, XXII (1949), pp. 121–45.

than in understanding; it is *frui* and not *intelligere*. This view indeed carries on, more faithfully than that of the Dominican school, the movement of christocentric and affective piety that touched the heart of Europe in the twelfth and thirteenth centuries, in the steps of Bernard of Clairvaux[67] and especially Francis of Assisi. Their conception of affective and pious "devotion" had become very general, but for the Thomist devotion is "the interior act of the virtue of religion, distinct from *oratio*, by which a being consecrates himself to the service of God".[68] This *devotio* gives rise to understanding of the divine realities.[69] The "objective" aspect of the contemplative life—and, more generally, of the Christian life—again prevails over the subjective and psychological aspects. Here again, it is clear what separates Dominic's disciples from the others.

Now, a century earlier, Richard of St Victor had defined contemplation in a formula that epitomized the knowledge acquired in preceding centuries. It is, he said, 'the clear gaze of a free spirit, suspended in wonder, on the marvels of wisdom," *libera mentis perspicacia in sapientiae spectacula cum admiratione suspensa*.[70] Thomas Aquinas never quoted that definition literally, but he must have known it, for he cites another that is to be found in almost the same place in the *Benjamin major*—the one that is more intellectualist: "The soul's clear and free dwelling upon the object of its gaze", *perspicax et liber animi contuitus in res perspiciendas*.[71]

When one weighs these words carefully and compares them with the definitions formulated by the two great schools of the thirteenth century, it seems as though Thomas's adoption of the dialectic and the philosophical principles of Aristotle—that adoption for which St Bernard so violently reproached Abelard in the century before—led him to lay the stress on the first words, *mentis perspicacia*, "the clear gaze of the spirit": while the Franciscan masters, more faithful to the Augustinian spirit, accentuated the last ones, *cum admiratione suspensa*, "suspended in wonder". These particular nuances certainly did not lead either school to forget the rest of the definition, but one can see the danger. There is always a risk that what is a mere preference may become exclusive. Each of the parties concerned is tempted to emphasize the "specific difference" that separates it from the other, until finally the difference in question takes on the aspect of an inalien-

[67] Cf. J. Châtillon, "L'influence de saint Bernard sur la pensée scholastique au XIIe et au XIIIe siècle", in *Saint Bernard* théologien, Rome, 1953, pp. 281 *et seq.*

[68] Cf. J. Châtillon, art. "Devotio", in *Dict. de spirit.*, III, col. 714.

[69] *Vita* by Guillaume de Tocco, *loc. cit.*, n. 22, p. 665.

[70] *Benjamin major*, I, 4; P.L., 196, col. 67.

[71] *S. T.*, IIa–IIae, q. 180, a. 3, ad 1.

able principle, to be maintained, demonstrated, and vindicated at all costs—or else the exact spirit of each tendency will be falsified. Theories of contemplation have been no exception to that law.

Thomas Aquinas seems to us a man with an extraordinarily balanced mind. While holding firmly to the rights of the intellect, he succeeded in avoiding the "cerebral" tone of the pure intellectual. To take only one instance among many, he sets forth with perfect exactitude all that concerns the devil and his fall, as well as the problem of temptation. As a man of his century, he is not concerned with the mode of action by which the devil's *impugnatio* reaches and upsets the psychological mechanism of a human being and, through it, the will itself.[72] But he avoids, better than his contemporaries—better, needless to say, than certain monastic circles and *a fortiori* better than the mass of Christians—any sort of anthropomorphism.[73]

With St Thomas, theology is not the work of the mind alone. The scholastic method, frankly accepted and worked out to its fullest extent, does not go so far as to cut it off from experimental knowledge of God, from contact with the word. Thomas lived in an age when the door between theology and the experimental knowledge of God was not yet closed. He succeeded in keeping himself free, in his interior life as well as in his teaching on contemplation, of the pietistic trends which had grown up in the last hundred years. In a word, his "religion" was something completely virile: he was not led into exaggeration either by his deep piety or by his keen intellect. This is as true in his austere and impersonal works such as the *Summa Theologica* as it is in his biblical commentaries and minor works of devotion like the commentaries on the *Pater* and the *Ave Maria*.

5. *The Conflict between the Mendicants and the Seculars*

The doctrinal controversies between the Dominicans and the Franciscans did not prevent their joining forces to defend their existence against the attacks of the secular masters. Between 1252 and 1270 there were lively polemics on the subject of religious observance and perfection. The first encounter took place from 1252 to 1256, the combatants being William of St Amour on one

[72] In connection with St Thomas's demonology, see A. Hayen, S.J., *Le péché de l'ange selon saint Thomas d'Aquin. Théologie de l'amour divin et métaphysique de l'acte d'être*, Teoresi, IX (1954), 83–176; Philippe de la Trinité, O.C.D., "Du péché de Satan et de la destinée de l'esprit d'après saint Thomas d'Aquin", in *Satan* (*Etudes carmélitaines*, XXVII, Bruges, 1948), pp. 44–85. (This article is not included in the English edition of *Satan* mentioned in ch. IX *infra*, note 35.)

[73] See particularly *II Sent.*, dist. 3–8; *S.T.*, I[a], q. 63, 64, 109 and 114; I[a]–II[ae], q. 80.

side and the Mendicants on the other.[74] William, echoing an opinion that must have been fairly general, attacked these new Orders and their unusual form of poverty. This was the chief object of his pamphlet, "On the perils of the latter times", *De novissimorum temporum periculis*. His statement of the case was injured by his immoderate language: he represented the Mendicants as the false prophets who herald the advent of Antichrist. St Bonaventure replied with the *De paupertate Christi*, which has already been mentioned.[75] Thomas Aquinas was assigned, by a general chapter of his order held at Agnani, the task of composing another reply. This was the *opusculum* written at the end of 1256 "against those who attack the worship of God and the religious life", *contra impugnantes Dei cultum et religionem*. In it, Thomas seeks to justify the developments by which the new Orders had modified monastic observance—the principle of dispensation, the abandonment of manual labour, collective poverty,[76] priestly ministry, study and teaching in the universities. The important thing, he says in effect, is not the worship of observance for its own sake, but the end for which it was instituted. Even before the *opusculum* was finished, however, 5 October 1256,[77] Alexander IV condemned William and ordered him to leave the University of Paris, in which Thomas and Bonaventure were soon to be masters in theology. To this censure of their adversaries the same pope added his praise of their own activity; in a bull of 23 March 1257:

> Their preaching goes forth to the uttermost ends of the earth. They are men of great renown and shining piety. As stars shining in the firmament of the Church, they point out to men by their enlightened doctrine the way of life. Vessels of gold, overflowing with perfume, they spread abroad the sweet odour of their holy lives; they exhort the faithful, leading them to shake off their torpor, to rise up and with all speed to betake themselves to good works.
>
> For this reason all the prelates of the Church and their faithful people should cherish them with particular affection. Fitting

[74] The chronology of the controversy is given in detail by P. Glorieux, "Le conflit de 1252–1257 à la lumière du Mémoire de Guillaume de Saint-Amour", in *Rech. théol. anc. méd.*, XXIV (1957), pp. 364–72. See also Knowles, *op. cit.*, pp. 188–9.

[75] See *supra*, p. 307. The *De periculis* will be found in William's *Opera Omnia*, Constance, 1632, f. 17–72; there are extracts in M. Bierbaum, *Bettelorden und Weltgeistlichkeit an der Universität Paris*, Münster, 1920, pp. 1–36.

[76] St Thomas's ideas on poverty and the "*régime de possession des religieux*" have been studied by R. Bellemare, "Pour une théologie thomiste de la pauvreté", in *Rev. Univ. Ottawa*, XXVI (1956), pp. 137*–64*.

[77] In the constitution *Romanus Pontifex*; the text is in Denziger, 458–9.

honour should be shown them, and favours should be showered upon them, as becomes such venerable servants of God.[78]

Between 1268 and 1270, there was a conflict in which something more serious than new observances was at stake—more even than the Dominicans' trend towards the *cura animarum*. St Thomas had said almost nothing on this last subject. He had mentioned it only incidentally, in connection with the preaching of the Apostles.[79] He did not need to defend this work of his Order. He had even declared that the contemplative life, considered in itself,[80] was superior to the active and that action must "proceed from the fullness of contemplation",[81] a formula that reflects the spirit of the Order's primitive constitutions. This time the battle was fought on different grounds: it was not a question (at least not directly) of the Mendicants' right to exist or their observances, but rather the "perfection" of their state of life. For Thomas, the religious as such is superior to the parish priest, not indeed by reason of his "office", or of the end common to all Christians, which is charity, or even of his personal holiness, but by reason of his vows and the complete consecration of his life to the pursuit of perfection.[82] For the secular masters, on the other hand—especially for Gerard of Abbeville,[83] then for his followers or *Geraldini*, Henry of Ghent, Godfrey of Fontaines, Nicholas of Lisieux—the office of the parish priest is a participation in that of the bishop, and this latter is of divine origin. By reason of this office, the priest too is established in a state of perfection, the *status rectorum*. At the same time, by accepting this office, the parish priest is obliged to fulfil the specific functions of his state; the obligation is not the result of a vow, but takes the place of one. Curiously enough, in this controversy neither the seculars nor St Thomas appealed to the consecration by which the bishop is established in the "state of perfection".

78 *Bullarium O.P.*, I, Rome, 1729–40, p. 338. For a French translation, see M. T. Laureilhe, *op. cit.*, pp. 284–5.

79 See, among others, *S.T.*, II^a–II^{ae}, q. 184, a. 2, ad 3, and a. 6; III^a, q. 64, a. 2, ad 3, and q. 72, a. 2, ad 1.

80 *S.T.*, II^a–II^{ae}, q. 182; cf. G. Turbessi, *op. cit.*, pp. 76–86.

81 *S.T.*, II^a–II^{ae}, q. 188, a. 6.

82 *S.T.*, II^a–II^{ae}, q. 184, a. 8.

83 See particularly his treatise *Contra adversarium perfectionis christianae*; it has been edited, with an analysis and an account of the circumstances in which it was written, by S. Clasen, O.F.M., in *Arch. Francisc. Histor.*, XXXI (1938), pp. 276–329; XXXII (1939), pp. 89–200. The documents and historical record of the controversy have been edited by P. Glorieux, "Les polémiques 'contra Geraldinos'. Les pièces du dossier", in *Rech. théol. anc. méd.*, VI (1934), pp. 5–41; by the same author, "'Contra Geraldinos'. L'enchaînement des polémiques", *ibid.*, VII (1935), pp. 129–55; and "Pour une édition de Gérard d'Abbeville", *ibid.*, IX (1937), pp. 56–84. A. Teetaert, O.M.Cap., has edited *Quatre questions inédites de Gérard d'Abbeville pour la défense de la supériorité du clergé séculier*, in *Archivio italiano per la storia della pietà*, Rome, 1951, pp. 83–178.

Thomas found it comparatively easy to answer the question at issue, formulated in terms of the notions of perfection and vow, of state, "order" and function.[84] First of all, perfection consists for him, according to the teaching of the Gospel, in the love of God and one's neighbour. As for the counsels of poverty and chastity, they are given clearly enough in the Gospel for anyone who is seeking, as was the rich young man or "he that can take it", how to be perfect and live only for the kingdom of God. With regard to obedience, the modern exegete is inclined to wonder whether the Scriptures do indeed make it optional; it appears in them as the portion of every Christian, an obligation rather than a counsel. Everyone who belongs to the people of God is subject to the authority exercised by men who have received their mandate from Christ. But Thomas did not go into this question; for him, the practice of the three counsels, to which the religious is bound by his "solemn" vow,[85] gives his individual effort a character of stability, of total self-abandonment, of irrevocability, and even of heroism,[86] which seems to Thomas to assure a higher perfection than that derived from any "office". This gift of himself causes the religious to enter a "state" that is admirably fitted to direct him towards perfection, whence the term "state of perfection" which became current after Thomas's time. In a sense, this state is comparable to that of the bishop, not to that of the priest, who has the cure of souls only in virtue of the bishop's commission. The bishop, however, is in a "state of perfection" as being a living source of perfection for his flock, *ut perfector*, says the *Summa*[87]; whereas the religious is in that state by the excellence of the means employed and by the true handing over of himself which constitutes his profession.[88]

In the *Summa Theologica*, Thomas adds another consideration to these. In religious profession, God effects a "spiritual consecra-

[84] In this connection, see *S.T.*, II^{a}–II^{ae}, q. 184; the *De perfectione vitae spiritualis* (1269); the *Contra pestiferam doctrinam retrahentium homines a religionis ingressu* (1270); and the *Quodlibet* 3. Cf. K. Scheyer, "Disputes scholastiques sur les états de perfection", in *Rech. théol. anc. méd.*, X (1938), pp. 279–93; F. Hirschenaueur, O.S.B., *Die Stellung des hl. Th. von A. im Mendikantenstreit an der Universität Paris*, St Ottilien, 1934. The *De perfectione vitae spiritualis* was attacked, together wih the *Quodlibet* 3, by Nicholas of Lisieux; cf. P. Glorieux, in *Bull. litt. ecclés.*, XXX (1938), pp. 121–9.

[85] By a "simple" vow St Thomas means only a *promise* of religious life; only a "solemn" vow causes a person to enter the religious *state*. Cf. *Contra pestiferam doctrinam retrahentium homines a religionis ingressu*, ch. 12.

[86] Cf., for example, *IV Sent.*, d. 38, q. 1, a. 2, qle 3, sol. 3.

[87] *S.T.*, II^{a}–II^{ae}, q. 184, a. 7.

[88] This explains why, for Thomas, the Church can dispense from a solemn vow but cannot annul it, as she can a simple vow (*IV Sent.*, d. 38, q. 4, qle 4, ad 3).

tion".[89] That is to say that the efficacy of profession derives from the spiritual power of the religious signs used by the Church to extend Christ's influence to us. Religious profession is not a legal formality, with merely human effects. Neither is it a mere symbol; it is not a sacrament either.[90] But by it the professed is marked out, designated, and permanently vowed to God's service; henceforth he is set apart from all secular employments. Religious profession is thus one of the most important sacramentals. As such, it confers holiness in proportion to the intensity of the recipient's faith and charity—dispositions which are required for any good work if it is to be truly supernatural. It is therefore meritorious, and its heroic value surpasses that of any other good work—any private vow, pilgrimage, or almsgiving[91]—giving it a value which, according to the great doctor, obtains the remission of all sins. "Hence we read in the *Lives of the Fathers* that by entering religion one receives the same grace as by being baptized."[92]

To us today, Thomas appears to have been right in reaffirming the place of the bishop in the structure of the Church. Any priest having the care of souls is only his representative, and this must be said just as emphatically today as in the past. Nevertheless, our modern mind has some difficulty in following Thomas when he ascribes a "state" to the bishop alone and does not admit that the priest, by his ordination, has entered such a "state". The priest appears to be irrevocably handed over and consecrated—so much so that, even if he apostatizes, is excommunicated, or reduced to the lay state, he remains a priest in virtue of his "character". Furthermore, this irrevocable nature of the priesthood seems to be much more real than that of the religious, even though the latter may have taken solemn vows. It may well be asked, in any case, whether the Church, as the scholastics thought, has not the power to annul those vows, but only dispense from them. All this comes

89 *S.T.*, IIª–IIªᵉ, q. 88, a. 7.

90 This consecration, without having the nature of a sacrament, "is simply the sign of a state of separation from the world and adhesion to God. But it is an efficacious sign, not only for the religious himself but also for those who witness his life, and as such it is endowed with a spiritual reality analogous to that of the characters" (I. Mennessier, O.P., "Le voeu solennel", in *La religion*, a French translation of the *Summa Theologica*, ed. *Rev. Jeunes*, Paris, 1934, vol. II, app. p. 434).

91 *Quodlibet* 3, q. 5, a. 13; and *passim*.

92 *S.T.*, IIª–IIªᵉ, q. 189, a. 3, ad 3. In writing these words, what St Thomas evidently had in mind was "satisfaction" for the punishment due to sin. After his time, others quite rightly excluded from profession any remission of sins *quoad culpam* (it is not the same thing as the sacrament of penance) and, of course, the remission of original sin (obtained once for all at baptism). Cajetan appears to have sought to avoid any ambiguity on this point (*In Sum. Theol.*, IIª–IIªᵉ, q. 189, a. 3, ad 3). Cf. F. Vandenbroucke, *Le moine dans l'Église du Christ*, Louvain, 1947, pp. 67–81.

down to the same question: even when one carefully distinguishes that which is proper to each, do the religious and the bishop have a monopoly of the "state", to the exclusion of the "simple" priest[93]?

To exalt solemn vows in this fashion, even to the point of denying that the Church can annul them, was the logical consequence of a doctrine of fixed and stable "states", according to the teaching of the canonists of the time. This logic led St Thomas to introduce into the theology of the vows the concept of "spiritual consecration", somewhat analogous to the sacramental characters. It is not clear to us today that this edifice is very solid, and that it is not simply a construction of the mind, raising more problems than it solves.

Yet another question arises. The religious who pronounces solemn vows thereby enters, according to St Thomas, into a "state of perfection", but of perfection to be acquired, *status perfectionis acquirendae*. This is precisely what distinguishes the state of the religious from that of the bishop, who possesses this perfection to the point of being able to communicate it to others, *status perfectionis acquisitae*.[94] Now, is not every Christian obliged to tend towards perfection—to seek to realize in the concrete circumstances of his life, and in the "state" in which Providence has placed him, that perfection of charity to which all men are called by Christ? Of course he is; St Thomas knows this, and he is therefore obliged to make the perfection proper to the religious consist in that of his state, by the vows which direct him towards charity.[95]

With all this in mind, one wonders whether Dominic Guzman had not taken his stand on firmer ground: that of the apostolic needs of the Church, which demanded specialized teams. The privilege of exemption, which removed these teams from the bishop's authority and made them dependent on the Holy See alone, created no problem, theoretically speaking. It matters little whether religious depend on the pope or on the bishops, provided they are serving the interests of the Church—although, according to the traditional way of envisaging the fundamental structure of the Church, the rights of the bishops in their respective dioceses must not be forgotten. This perfectly simple position is weakened as soon as one introduces the concept of state and of perfection. Not looking at it as Thomas did, one may wonder, especially today, whether the fact of entering one of those specialized teams that are

[93] Here it is a question of "states" in the ecclesiastical domain. St Thomas speaks elsewhere of the state of liberty, the state of servitude, etc.

[94] Cf., for example, *S.T.*, II^{a}–II^{ae}, q. 184, a. 7; q. 185, a. 8.

[95] Cf. *ibid.*, q. 184, a. 3.

called "Orders" or "religious congregations" is enough to place a man in a "state of perfection".

Faced with these difficulties, to which our contemporaries are particularly sensitive, it would seem that the grounds of the discussion should be altered. The religious life is specified by the vows—excellent means for attaining evangelical perfection: their character of complete self-abandonment, which makes them a heroic act on the part of the one who makes them, is a real test of his spiritual quality. To commit oneself, freely and irrevocably, to live the law of evangelical renunciation in order to follow Christ—and that by the practice of the counsels, freely accepted and promised by vow, *sub voto*—this is the religious life at its deepest level. In this sense, St Thomas is justified in speaking of a "state of perfection" and of a "spiritual consecration". To this basic attitude, which was that of traditional monasticism, the Mendicant Orders simply added a greater availability for the apostolic work of the Church. But what fundamentally consecrates religious profession (as St Thomas and many theologians after him emphasized) is unchanging: it is the absolute and exclusive nature of the gift of oneself.

In spite of this, the religious would be mistaken if he thought himself "more perfect" than others. The danger is obvious. The interior gift of self might not really be complete, and yet the religious might have passed the tests and trials that admit one to profession. If he then spoke of his own "perfection", it would be an abuse of words: true in themselves but misleading. He is not perfect simply by having entered this "state", but rather he finds the state an excellent help in his progress toward evangelical perfection. Unless the matter is viewed in this light, he will appear insufferably proud, intolerable to other Christians. And if ever he falls for a moment below the level of his vocation, and his practice of the vows becomes lukewarm even if not unworthy, at once they will make the inevitable comparison with themselves: many a Christian layman living in the world, without vows, is nearer to perfection than he.

It was precisely this state of things that became general in the religious Orders during the fifteenth and sixteenth centuries. Luther, who was a religious himself and saw these abuses, became the avowed enemy of vows to which life did not correspond. He ranked them with those "works" of the law by which, of themselves, no man is justified. He and his disciples attacked the monastic vows, and one cannot entirely blame them when one considers what their contemporaries had made of those vows: a mere label, covering a life empty of evangelical perfection. Too many monks and friars were blinded by a pharisaism which prevented their seeing that the religous state is in itself too noble to be measured by the scalc of men's weakness, or even by that of their attainment of holiness; the weak and the holy alike being still men, unworthy of the gifts of God.

V

LAITY AND CLERGY IN THE THIRTEENTH CENTURY

1. Popular Piety

IN the twelfth century, popular piety had been characterized by an effort to live the life of the Gospel more fully outside the traditional monastic setting. Christians for whom the old forms of religious life were impracticable, or who felt that they were called to another kind of work, had sought a new solution. It goes without saying that the same basic characteristics and the same tendencies are seen in the thirteenth century.

But the pastoral concerns of the clergy became more practical —those at least of those who were seeking, by the pen or the spoken word, to raise the moral and religious level of the people. This movement of reform was a fruit of the Fourth Lateran Council in 1215, and the foundation of the medicant Orders greatly contributed to it. A whole didactic literature appeared, both in Latin and in the vernacular, which sought to inculcate more deeply in the faithful and the clergy the dogmatic and moral teachings of Christianity. The truths necessary for salvation were abundantly popularized by sermons, "mirrors" and "dialogues". This was also the case with the *summas* and penitentials, such as the celebrated *Somme le roi* by a Friar Preacher, Lawrence of Orleans, who was confessor to the king. It treats successively of the ten commandments, the twelve articles of faith, the seven deadly sins, the virtues, the *Pater* and the seven gifts of the Holy Spirit. On a somewhat higher level, the circulation of the conciliar documents also tended to spread the truths of the faith and to aid moral reform.[1]

[1] On the *Somme le roi*, see C. V. Langlois, *La vie en France au moyen âges de la fin du XIIe au milieu du XIVe siècle*, IV, *La Vie spirituelle*, Paris, 1928, pp. 123–98. This whole volume should be consulted on the spiritual life in France from the twelfth to the fourteenth century. See also E. Faral, *La vie quotidienne au temps de saint Louis*, Paris, 1956. The conciliar texts have been assembled by H. J. Schmitz, *Die Bussbücher und die Bussdisciplin der Kirche. Die Bussbücher und das Kanonische Bussverfahren.* Nach handschriftlichen Quellen dargestellt, 2 vols, 1883–98; new edition, Graz, 1958.

One of the best-known works of the time is the *Manuel des péchés*, written in Anglo-Norman about 1260[2] and very soon translated into various languages.[3] In 1303 Robert Mannyng made an English adaptation under the title *Handlyng Synne*. A considerable portion of the manual consists of *exempla*, or edifying stories, often drawn from the *Lives of the Fathers*, the Dialogues of St Gregory, or other sources. The anonymous author, who was a churchman living in the world, also derived a good deal from the *Summa de vitiis et virtutibus* by William Peyraut.[4] Like other similar writings, the manual is interesting because of the picture it gives of the life of the times. It confirms and completes the information furnished by penitentials and conciliar and canonical documents. Its author had observed the world in which he lived and he points out to his readers (he seems to have been writing for the clergy) the vices, abuses, temptations and superstitions that afflict it—those that threaten society, the parish, the family, and the individual. Although this merciless picture of their moral life did not spare the laity, for whom the book was not originally intended, it nevertheless had a great success among them. The English adaptation, *Handlyng Synne*, is even explicitly dedicated to them.[5]

But the life of the people was not wholly lacking in Christian virtue: it had also its admirable side. Countless records have been preserved that testify to an ardent spirituality: one has only to think of St Louis, the king of France, who has always been the model of the fervent layman living in the world.[6] Christ was always the centre of popular devotion; many were the sermons preached on his kingship, as is seen in the Palm Sunday text *Ecce rex tuus venit tibi mansuetus*. The scriptural colouring of these documents is worthy of note.[7] The same is true of Latin poems like the *Philomena* of John Pecham (†1292), archbishop of Canterbury, which tells the whole life of Christ in 90 verses.[8]

Devotion to the Blessed Virgin was often lyrical in form, as for example in all the compositions inspired by the Byzantine

[2] Possibly the work of William of Waddington, or copied by him. Ed. E. J. Arnould, *Le manuel des péchés. Etude de littérature religieuse anglo-normande* (*XIIIe siècle*), Paris, 1940.

[3] For a study of the sources of this literature, its characteristics, and its influence, see E. J. Arnould, *op. cit.*

[4] Cf. A. Dondaine, O.P., "Guillaume Peyraut, Vie et œuvres", in *Arch. Fratrum Praedic.*, XVIII (1948), pp. 162–236.

[5] Cf. D. W. Robertson, "The Cultural Tradition of *Handlyng Synne*", in *Speculum*, XII (1957), pp. 162–85.

[6] See *supra*, ch. II, note 150.

[7] Cf. J. Leclercq, O.S.B., "L'idée de la Seigneurie du Christ au moyen âge", in *Rev. d'hist. eccl.*, LIII (1958), pp. 62–4.

[8] Cf. Maximilianus, O.M.Cap., "Philomena van John Peckham", in *Neophilologus*, XXXVIII (1954) pp. 206–17, 290–300.

Akathistos.[9] The poem *Rossignol* (1274), by Jean of Hoveden, extols the omnipotence of love as shown in the lives of Christ and his Mother, and ends with a long eulogy of our Lady.[10] Another "praise of Mary", from the Rhineland, the *Marienlob*, makes full use of the symbolism so dear to the Middle Ages, but soberly and with discretion. There is no allusion to the legends of our Lady that abounded at the time, and no recourse to apocrypha; poetry found sufficient nourishment in tradition. The poet contemplates the mystery in the affective spirit of a particular current of mysticism, rather than in the deliberately intellectual manner of the Victorines.[11] Jacob van Maerlant (†1299), who is sometimes considered a sort of Flemish Dante, also dedicated to Mary his composition of 34,000 verses, a sort of universal history, inspired by Scripture.[12]

There arose about this time a new devotion to the saints, with pilgrimages to their sanctuaries. Their lives and miracles were the stuff of religious drama. In the twelfth century this had been chiefly liturgical or semi-liturgical, the predominant theme being the mysteries that make up what today is called the temporal cycle. Now, however, the theatre turned to the *jeux* and to miracle plays drawn from hagiography. In France the principal productions were the *Jeu de saint Nicolas* by Jehan Bodel[13] and Rutebeuf's *Miracle de Théophile.*[14]

But the people were still responsive to the Bible. William Durandus, bishop of Mende, advised preachers to preach "the words of the Gospel and the creed, or else to expound the New

9 See *supra*, ch. II, p. 280; cf. G. Meersseman, O.P., *Der hymnos Akathistos im Abendland*, I, *Akathistos-Akoluthie und Crusshymnen*, Fribourg (Switzerland), 1958, pp. 86–98.

10 Cf. L. W. Stone, "Jean de Hoveden, poète anglo-normand du XIIIe siècle", in *Romania*, LXIX (1946–7), pp. 496–510.

11 *Das Rheinische Marienlob. Eine deutsche Dichtung des 13. Jahrh.*, ed. A. Bach, Lepzig, 1934. In addition there may be mentioned the *Mariale super "Missus est"*, or *De laudibus B.M. Virginis*, wrongly attributed to St Albert; see A. Fries, C.SS.R., *Die unter dem Namen des Albertus Magnus überlieferten mariologischen Schriften*, Münster i. W., 1954; and B. Korošak, O.F.M., *Mariologia S. Alberti Magni eiusque coaequalium*, Rome, 1954. Also the *Cantica canticorum Beate Marie*, in imitation of Pierre Riga's *Aurora*; cf. P. E. Beichner, in *Marianum*, XXI (1959), pp. 1–15.

12 Ed. J. David, Brussels, 1858–9. For extracts in French translation see R. J. Hesbert, O.S.B., and E. Bertaud, O.S.B., *L'Assomption de Notre-Dame*, I, Paris, 1952, pp. 243–5. Cf. J. van Mierlo, S.J., *Jacob van Maerlant. Zijn leven, zijn werken, zijn betekenis*, Turnhout, 1946. There is an edition of extracts (in Dutch) from the "strophic poems" by Fr Mierlo, Zwolle, 1954.

13 Ed. A. Jeanroy, Paris, 1925.

14 *Œuvres complètes*, ed. E. Faral and J. Bastin, vol. II, Paris, 1960, pp. 167–203. Adaptation by G. Cohen, Paris, 1948. Cf. G. Cohen, *Le théâtre en France au moyen âge* Paris, 1948, pp. 28–33.

Testament to them".[15] In his own explanations of the liturgy in all its aspects—the Mass, the sacraments, the liturgical year, even down to the setting and the furniture—he constantly has recourse to the Bible, though he uses it chiefly in an allegorical and symbolic sense. This attachment to the Bible is noticeable also in works of a more popular nature, such as the *Biblia pauperum*.[16] This book composed in the twelfth or thirteenth century, perhaps in Bavaria,[17] is a sort of summary of the Scriptures. Its author seems to have intended it as a weapon against the contagion of Catharism among the people.[18] Each of its woodcuts, which are rather crudely executed, shows a scene from the New Testament bordered by "prefigurations" taken from the Old.[19] The *Speculum humanae salvationis*, which is of a later date (it was probably composed by Ludolph the Saxon in 1324), also presents scenes from the Gospel paralleled by the Old Testament events which prefigured them. In the same vein are the "*Bibles moralisées*"—abridged editions of the Scriptures, often illuminated, whose aim was to give their readers moral teaching in an easily assimilated form.[20]

The visual arts also show the direction taken by popular piety. As in the twelfth century, they were much influenced by the Bible. Sculpture, painting and stained glass made the churches, especially the cathedrals, what the Dominican Vincent of Beauvais (†1264) called, in his *Speculum maius*, really "an historical mirror" of the Old and New Testaments from Genesis to the Apocalypse and the end of the world.[21] The churches became "pictorial Bibles" and, in their way, "the Bibles of the poor". Emile Mâle, in his *Art religieux du XIII*e *siècle en France*,[22] made a very happy use of

15 *Rationale divinorum officiorum*, IV, 26; ed. Venice, 1609, p. 90; French translation, vol. II, Paris, 1854, p. 168.

16 Reproduced in the works of St Bonaventure (ed. Peltier, vol. VIII, Paris, 1866, pp. 423–642).

17 Sometimes ascribed to Nicholas of Hanapis, O.P. (†1291); cf. *Dict. de spirit.*, I, 1847. But it appears to be of an earlier date.

18 This has been suggested by M. A. Weckwerth, "Die Zweckbestimmung der Armenbibel und die Bedeutung ihres Namens", in *Zeitschr. Kirchengeschichte*, LXVIII (1957), pp. 225–58.

19 Cf. H. Cornell, *Biblia pauperum*, Stockholm, 1925; H. Zimmermann, "Armenbibel", in *Reallexicon z. deutsch. Kunstgesch.*, Munich, 1937, col. 1072–1084; H. Rost, *Die Bibel im Mittelalter*, Augsburg, 1939, pp. 214–31; H. Engelhardt, *Der theologische Gehalt der B.P.*, Strasburg, 1927.

20 Cf. J. Lutz and P. Perdrizet, *Speculum humanae salvationis*, 2 vols, Paris, 1907–9; E. Breitenbach, *Spec. hum. salv.*, Strasburg, 1930; H. Rost, *op. cit.*, pp. 231–7. For the Dutch translation, see the edition of L. Daniels, O.P., *De Spieghel der menscheliker Behoudenese*, Tielt, 1949. From the artistic point of view, see E. Mâle, *L'art religieux de la fin du moyen âge en France*, Paris, 1908, pp. 229–46. On the *Bibles moralisées*, see *Hist. littéraire de la France*, XXXI, Paris, 1893, pp. 213–85 [L. Delisle].

21 Ed. Douai, 1624, 4 vols. The "moral mirror" was written at the beginning of the fourteenth century, but it formed part of Vincent's plan.

22 Paris, 1902; latest edition, 1948.

Vincent's treatise to reveal in the art of this century the fourfold mirror—natural, doctrinal, historical and moral—which made the places of worship a kind of pictorial encyclopedia of all the knowledge of the period. In this vast panorama, history takes the leading place, and the history of salvation before profane or legendary history.

In the centuries that followed, religious art became more realistic; a greater sensibility and even tenderness are characteristic in its development. Works inspired by the *Biblia pauperum* and the *Speculum humanae salvationis,* while they still made use of biblical typology, came to be more concerned with man and his destiny than with Christ and the mysteries of redemption. But although art became more anthropocentric—closer to the artist's emotions than to the object contemplated—until the end of the Middle Ages it remained the expression of a deep religious experience and at the same time eminently educational and "pastoral" (in the modern sense of the word) in its work. As early as about 1025,[23] a synod at Arras had already said that art "teaches the unlettered what they cannot learn from books". In the words of Daniel-Rops:

> The Cathedral, the people's house, made itself wonderfully comprehensible to them. There was of course the face it turned to scholars: that perceived only by the learned, those whose profound knowledge of the Holy Scriptures and theology enabled them to understand its symbolism; but there was also its simple, familiar, popular aspect which gave the poor and humble confidence. The forms which in their beauty could teach the learned at the highest spiritual level, could also touch the hearts of the simple minded, telling them of faith, hope and love; and they understood this language all the better because so much was taken from their own lives, and these symbols seemed close to their own experience.[24]

2. *Spiritual Groups*

The popular piety of the twelfth century, trying to find a new equilibrium, had its counterpart in anti-clerical movements, in

[23] Can. 14; Mansi, XIX, col. 454.

[24] Daniel-Rops, *L'Église de la cathédrale et de la croisade*, Paris, 1952, p. 480. The bibliography of recent works on the religious art of the thirteenth century is very extensive; many of them are based on E. Mâle, *L'art religieux du XIIIe siècle en France*. There are brief bibliographies in Daniel-Rops, *op. cit.*, pp. 791–2; and in vol. II of the report of the *Congrès archéologique de France* of 1935, by M. Aubert. Special mention should be made of C. Terrasse, *La cathédrale, miroir du monde*, Paris, 1954; J. Gimpel, *Les bâtisseurs de cathédrales*, Paris, 1958; and L. Réau, *Iconographie de l'art chrétien*, Paris, 1955 and following years (much of the information is inaccurate, and the bibliographies are not very up-to-date). On the Bible and its influence in all domains during the Middle Ages, an excellent survey is that of H. Rost, *op. cit.*

revolts against the hierarchy, and finally in heresies which directly attacked dogma. During the thirteenth century, these heretical movements continued to recruit followers and disquiet the Church. The history of the Cathari, the Waldenses, the Joachimites, not to mention others,[25] goes beyond the limits of the century in which they arose, and in some cases well into the next.

The thirteenth century witnessed no fresh eruptions of this kind; a real, if slight advantage over its predecessor. Only the agitation of the Fraticelli[26] must be set down as really new, and that was more a domestic quarrel than a controversy involving the Church or large sections of Christendom. One further sect, however, should be mentioned –or possibly several—known as the *Fideles Amoris*. Their existence and their true nature have been studied carefully during the last thirty years or so.[27] It has been held that they arose from the "courts of love" in Provence and France, but it certainly does not seem that these courts sheltered secret gatherings of heretics. Conventicles there were a purely literary fiction, whereas these sects had a real existence. The proof is to be found in the *Documenti d'Amore* of Francesco da Barberino (1264–1348). These *Documenti*, with the Latin commentary and illustrations that accompany them, were a real manual of initiation into the various degrees of the mystical ascent and of union with uncreated Wisdom. They are possibly significant as the remains of a certain Tuscan confraternity, of the time of Dante and Guido Cavalcanti, which had for its ensign the god of love. In France, indications of the same kind can be found in the *Fiefs d'amour* of Jacques de Baisieux, which dates from the second half of the thirteenth century. Although there was, as yet, nothing specifically heterodox in this, it shows the *Fideles Amoris* as knights in the tradition of the Holy Grail, united in a secret society as worshippers of the Lady (who was sometimes the Virgin, sometimes Wisdom). Documents, chiefly Italian, seem to show that there were degrees of initiation in the sect.

Still other groups, either at this time or later, were derived from those in the twelfth century that wished to return to the "apostolic" life. Gerard Segarelli of Parma, the Joachimite, has already been mentioned; his disciples' own name for themselves was "Brethren of the Apostles". The sect appeared in 1260, and when in 1300

[25] See *supra*, ch. II.
[26] See *supra*, ch. III, pp. 295 *et seq.*
[27] These studies were begun chiefly by L. Valli, *Il languaggio secreto di Dante e dei Fedeli d'Amore*, Rome, 1928; followed by A. Ricolfi, *Studi sui "Fedeli d'Amore" I. Le "Corti d'Amore" in Francia ed i loro reflessi in Italia*, Milan, 1933; and by a number of articles, chiefly in the *Nuova Rivista storica*, since 1932.

Gerard was condemned and burned at the stake,[28] it was taken over by a more violent agitator and one who was less naïve. This was Fra Dolcino of the diocese of Novara in Piedmont, whose history was written by an "Anonymus Synchronus".[29] He finally shared Segarelli's fate in 1307, but as usual the disciples and successors did not acknowledge defeat.[30] Their ideal was, in itself, worthy of nothing but respect; it was simply to go back to the way of life and outlook of the apostles. Segarelli suffered, however, from the measures of suppression which the Church was obliged to take against other similar movements which were quite rightly suspect. As for Fra Dolcino and his disciples they adopted the views of Joachim of Flora on the history of the Church, and their invective against the Church of Rome was unusually bitter. For them she is the whore of the Apocalypse, and a free and spiritual Church must now take her place; the consequences of such doctrines, particularly in the moral sphere, inevitably disquieted inquisitors like Bernard Gui.[31]

There were no new chapters in the history of heresy until Wyclif, John Hus, and later the Protestant "revolution"; which does not mean that the Church was not obliged to condemn various doctrines between the twelfth and fifteenth centuries. William of St Amour, whose exaggerated language was condemned by Rome,[32] has already been mentioned, and there was soon to be the condemnation of the Beghards and Beguines[33] and that of Eckhart.[34]

It seems as though the two new Orders that had arisen in the thirteenth century had given to Western Christendom a certain spiritual equilibrium. This lasted, despite the tremors that shook the Order founded by St Francis, for almost three centuries. In this way, they both rendered a great service to the Church. Moreover, the friars mixed more closely with the people than the monks had done and so exercised a marked influence on popular piety from the thirteenth century onwards. This was certainly one reason for the relative absence of important heretical movements before the

[28] See *supra*, ch. II, p. 267. A well-documented history has been written by L Spätling, O.F.M., *De Apostolicis, Pseudoapostolis, Apostolinis*, Munich, 1947, pp. 127–40.

[29] Ed. A. Segarizzi, in *Rerum Italic. Scriptores*, vol. IX, fasc. 51, Città di Castello, 1907. Cf. L. Spätling, *op. cit.*, pp. 141–55. On Fra Dolcino, see C. Vionini and M. I. Mazzone, *Fra' Dolcino e la setta degli Apostolici*, Turin, 1942; G. Miccoli, in *Annali di Scuola norm. sup. di Pisa*, XXV (1956), pp. 245–59.

[30] Cf. L. Spätling, *op. cit.*, pp. 156–64.

[31] *Ibid.*, pp. 165–79; for the text of Fra Dolcino's *De secta illorum qui se dicunt esse de ordine Apostolorum*, see Segarizzi, *op. cit.*, pp. 15–36.

[32] In connection with his controversy with the Mendicants, see *supra*, ch. IV, pp. 336 *et seq.*

[33] See *infra*, §4, pp. 353 *et seq.*

[34] See *infra*, ch. VI, §2, pp. 382 *et seq.*

fifteenth and sixteenth centuries. One of the principal means by which this influence was exercised was the Franciscan third order, which originated during the lifetime of St Francis.[35] By the end of the century, it was made up of a number of influential brotherhoods which had been given a new rule by Nicholas IV in 1289. There was a parallel development of Dominican confraternities, as has been said, and at the end of the Middle Ages, of those of other religious Orders.[36]

The "brothers" of the Franciscan third order sometimes called themselves *Apostoli* or *Fratres apostoli*. Their lives were marked by poverty and charity, but their affinity with movements, such as the Fraticelli, Béguines, and Beghards, sometimes got them into difficulties.[37]

A multitude of charitable institutions were also springing up. Some were distinctly religious, in the technical sense of the word, like the orders of the Hospitallers; the Antonines, in Dauphiné; the Order of the Holy Spirit in Montpellier; the Fratres Cruciferi, in Bologna; the Order of St Lazarus, for the care of lepers, in the East; the Croziers; the Trinitarians and Mercedarians, who devoted themselves to the ransom of captives. Other institutions, such as the Hôtels-Dieu, hospitals and lazar-houses, had only lay members. The "brothers" and "sisters" who served them had a rule, but were not religious: their rule simply gave them a form of life and a superior, who was usually a monk or cleric.[38]

Among the groups of devout laymen the old associations of the *Fratres* (and *Sorores*) *de paenitentia* may again be mentioned.[39] They soon constituted themselves into an *Ordo* officially recognized by the Church. Such brotherhoods existed almost everywhere in Italy,[40] in Germany,[41] and in France. Sometimes their object was to make reparation for the outrages committed against the Blessed Sacrament by the Albigensians; this was the case with the *Confraternity of Grey Penitents* at Avignon in 1226, of whom records

35 See *supra*, ch. III, pp. 295–6.

36 There are numerous "histories" of the third orders. A survey is given by S. da Romallo, art. "Terz'ordine", in *Encicl. Cattol.*, XI, 2044–8. See particularly P. Duparc, "Confréries du Saint-Esprit et communautés d'habitants au moyen âge", in *Rev. histor. Droit français et étranger*, XXXVI (1958), pp. 349–67, 555–85.

37 See L. Spätling, *op. cit.*, pp. 183–5.

38 Cf. J. Imbert, *Les hôpitaux en droit canonique*, Paris, 1947; L. le Grand, "Comment composer l'histoire d'un établissement hospitalier", in *Sources et Méthodes*, Paris (no date).

39 See *supra*, ch. III, pp. 295–6.

40 Cf. G. Meersseman, O.P. and E. Adda, "Pénitents ruraux communautaires en Italie au XIIe siècle", in *Rev. d'hist. eccl.*, XLIX (1954), pp. 343–90.

41 Cf. A. Simon, *L'Ordre des pénitentes de Sainte-Marie-Madeleine en Allemagne au XIIIe siècle* [thesis], Fribourg, 1918; K. Köster, "Mainz in der Geschichte des Renerinnen-Ordens", in *Jahrb. f. das Bistum Mainz*, IV (1948), pp. 243–72.

remain. A number of others were founded, up to the end of the Middle Ages, with the object of honouring the Blessed Sacrament.[42] Local confraternities of all kinds were founded not only for charity or penance but also for various pious purposes: venerating a patron saint, honouring some mystery of Christ or the Blessed Virgin, reciting the rosary, etc. Some were even organized to preserve the purity of the faith, like the famous *White Confraternity* organized at Toulouse by Bishop Foulques. Others aimed at nothing more than gathering together members of the same craft, so that it is sometimes difficult to determine the borderline between Confraternity and Guild.[43]

This tendency to form groups was, moreover, very general at that time. Among the secular clergy one of the fruits of the Gregorian reform had been to bring about the common life in many places, or at least spiritual association at the level of the deanery, region, or town; even laymen were sometimes affiliated to them.[44] On a larger scale in the whole of the thirteenth century society, feudalism was becoming less individual and new collective institutions were developing; the communes were becoming organized and conscious of their own power, and their organization was not unaffected by the example of the religious Orders[45]; the corporations were coming into being and they found support for their existence in the analyses of the canonists and jurists, while at the same time the great syntheses of the scholastics brought out the meaning of *multitudo* and *unitas* in human society.[46]

On the other hand, papal centralization was tending to absorb the civil power. The Church sensed that civil society was escaping from her, and there was an instinctive nervous reaction towards an exaggeration of authoritarianism, connected with the name of Boniface VIII, and the bull *Unam Sanctam* of 1302. Theocracy asserted itself more absolutely than ever before, just when history

[42] Cf. G. Barbiero, "Confraternite del S.mo Sacramento", in *Eucaristia*, Rome, 1957, pp. 935–42.

[43] Cf. G. Le Bras, "Les confréries chrétiennes. Problèmes et propositions", in *Rev. hist. Droit français et étranger*, XIX–XX (1940–1), pp. 310–63; J. Duhr, "La confrérie dans la vie de l'Eglise", in *Rev. d'hist. eccl.*, XXXV (1939), pp. 437–478; H. Durand, art. "Confrérie", in *Dict. Droit Canon*, IV, pp. 139–44.

[44] See *supra*, Part I, ch. VI; also G. Meersseman, O.P., "Die Klerikervereine von Karl dem Grossen bis Innocenz III", in *Zeitschr. f. Schweizerische Kirchengeschichte*, XLVI (1952), pp. 1–42, 81–112.

[45] Cf. L. Moulin, "La science politique et le gouvernement des communautés religieuses", in *Rev. intern. Sc. administratives* (1951), pp. 42–67; by the same, "Les origines religieuses des techniques électorales et délibératives modernes", in *Rev. internat. d'histoire politique et constitutionelle* (1953), pp. 106–48.

[46] In this connection, see G. de Lagarde, "Individualisme et corporatisme au moyen âge", in *L'organisation corporative du moyen âge à la fin de l'Ancien Régime*, Louvain, 1937, pp. 1–60. See also his *La naissance de l'esprit laïque au moyen âge*, 6 vols, Paris, 1934–46.

had come to the point of distinguishing the powers of the State from those of the Church in their origin, nature and end.[47]

The situation was paradoxical. On the one hand, Christian life appears as "communal" (and the pontifical theocracy unifying all Christendom, both spiritual and temporal, at the highest level cannot be excluded). On the other hand, facts belie the appearance. For one thing temporal rulers did not always recognize the pontifical claims—far from it. Then, the best among the laity, though they were indeed forming themselves into groups by means of the numerous associations or confraternities, by that very fact were beginning to lose something of the real communal life of the Church. Their spiritual life developed by the side of the authentic liturgical and parochial life. It seems as though the traditional communities of the Church, valid for all, were no longer sufficient to nourish their Christian life; as though they found, in the practices of their own associations, a better means of access to God's word and his grace.

As yet, this escape from the normal patterns only led to the setting up of new ones which gave fervent Christians a greater sense of support and comfort. In the course of the fourteenth century, however, the ordinary faithful slipped even further away and many of the laity developed a nostalgia for the solitary life, even if not the courage to practise it. That century saw the final divorce between theology and mysticism, but in addition the separation of mysticism from the life of the community, and private devotion from liturgical and sacramental life.

3. Béguines and Beghards

Among the spiritual associations of laymen that developed in the thirteenth century, those of the Béguines and Beghards have a special place. They too wanted something other than ordinary religious life; or else, being unable to enter it, they wanted to find an equivalent for it (this seems to have been the case with many of the Béguines in the Low Countries). Yet they did not feel called to the complete solitude of the hermits and recluses. Their mode of life was that of pious individuals living round a church or chapel, which was often served by a priest of a mendicant Order.[48]

[47] Cf. M. Pacaut, *La théocratie. L'Église et le pouvoir au moyen âge*, Paris, 1957.

[48] The sources have been collected by S. Axters, O.P., *Geschiedenis van de vroomheid in de Nederlanden*, I, Antwerp, 1950, pp. 306–7, 447–52; A. Mens, O.F.M.Cap., *Oorsprong en betekenis van de Nederlandse begijnen- en begardenbeweging. Vergelijkende studie: XII^de^–XIII^de^ eeuw*, Antwerp, 1947, pp. xii–xviii. Most of these sources have now been published; they consist chiefly in *Vitae* such as that of St Marie d'Oignies (†1213) by Jacques de Vitry, *Acta Sanctorum*, June, vol. V, pp. 547–72, and those of Ida of Louvain, Julienne of Mont Cornillon

Groups of Béguines and Beghards began to form towards the end of the twelfth century in the towns of the Low Countries and neighbouring regions—the Rhineland and the north of France. The Béguines, who were the more numerous, lived in little houses and met in the church at fixed hours for prayer. They took no vows but made a promise of chastity for as long as they stayed at the "béguinage". Their obligation of obedience was only that of submission to the statutes, to the ecclesiastical authorities, and to the "mistress general", "*grand'dame*" or "*demoiselle*". Poverty and the evangelical life were held in honour. They lived simply, each one supporting herself by her own work, unless the community had been endowed by pious foundations. The Beghards specialized in weaving; the Béguines, in the feminine arts of sewing, embroidery and the care of vestments; the care of the sick, also, and even the teaching of children, as well as serving the aged ladies who wished to end their days in peaceful surroundings. The novices were trained by an older Beghard or Béguine, but did not live in the béguinage until after a year and a half or two years of trial. They could not live alone until after six years, and then only on condition of having reached their thirtieth year. Their prayers and their ascetic practices, like those of the recluses, were coloured by the usages of their time, and by the tender devotion of the period to the persons of Jesus and Mary.

The life of the Beghards and Béguines showed an undeniable resemblance to that of the recluses, but unlike the latter they practised a measure of common life. The Béguines very soon gathered in an enclosed quarter of the town; béguinages of this kind are still to be seen in most of the towns of Flanders, and some of them still attract recruits.[49] These formed real parishes, and they were constituted as such by the approbation which Jacques de Vitry obtained from Honorius III in 1216.[50] The Beghards do not seem

(†1258), St Lutgarde of Aywières (†1246), St Christine the Admirable (†1235), Marguerite of Ypres (†1237), etc. There are also letters and episcopal, pontifical, and conciliar documents.

There is a considerable literature on the subject. For a bibliography, see A. Mens, *op. cit.*, pp. xvii–xxx. See also studies by S. Axters, *op. cit.*, I, pp. 306–35; A. Mens, *op. cit.*; J.B.P. [Porion], *Hadewijch d'Anvers*, *Poèmes des béguines*, Paris, 1954, introduction; H. Grundmann, *Religiöse Bewegungen im Mittelalter*, Berlin, 1935, pp. 319–54; and especially E. W. McDonnell, *The Béguines and Beghards in Medieval Culture*, New Brunswick, N.J., 1954. There is a short analysis of the last by A. Mens in *Le moyen âge*, LXIV (1958), pp. 305–15. For a more superficial treatment of the subject, see J. Huijben, O.S.B., "Le mouvement spirituel dans les Pays-Bas au XIIIe siècle", in *La Vie spirit.*, *Suppl.*, I (1947–8), pp. 39–45. There are articles in the *Dict. de spirit.* and *Dict. hist. géogr. eccl.*

[49] Cf. the history of them by L. J. M. Philippen, *De Begijnhoven*, Antwerp, 1918.

[50] Cf. "Briefe des Jacobus de Vitriaco", ed. R. Röhricht, in *Zeitschr. f. Kirchengeschichte*, XIV (1894), p. 103; S. Axters, *op. cit.*, I, pp. 315–18.

ever to have congregated in actual béguinages, but rather to have lived isolated in separate houses.

The spirituality of the Beghards and Béguines began fairly soon to appear suspect, despite the simplicity of their life and the absence of any pretensions to teach or to reform. It has been thought, but it would seem quite mistakenly, that an indication of this mistrust was to be found in their very name, *beguinus* and *beguina* being derived from *Albigensis*.[51] However that may be, the first evidence of the use of *beguina* seems to date from 1199: the *Dialogus miraculorum* of Caesar of Heisterbach (†1245) tells the story of a woman who cried out, *Quid vultis videre istas beguinas?* "Why do you want to see those béguines?"[52] referring to some Cistercian nuns. She may have used the word in a somewhat pejorative sense, as we might say "old bigots".

But it is a long way from that to a suspicion of Catharist heresy —a heresy which, moreover, was unknown in the Low Countries at the end of the twelfth century and even in the thirteenth. During the thirteenth century the pejorative sense of béguine began to disappear, and when, at the end of the thirteenth and during the fourteenth, the Beghards began to be harassed by the ecclesiastical authorities, the suspicions which bore upon them had only the most tenuous connection with the Albigensian heresy. It is more probable that their nickname came from the *beige* colour of their habits, which were made of raw undyed wool.[53]

There were more substantial reasons for the suspicions of the authorities. The first serious accusations appear in a little treatise *De scandalis ecclesiae*, by the Franciscan Gilbert of Tournai and intended for the members of the Council of Lyons in 1274. In a section entitled *De beghinis*, the author attacks their interpretation of Scripture and their use of the vernacular for Bible-readings at their meetings. As he finds nothing else to blame them for, the matter was evidently not very serious as yet.[54] Later, some of their errors were condemned by councils, like that of Cologne in 1306; the principal condemnation was by the ecumenical Council of Vienne in 1311, two decrees of which censured the institution of both Béguines and Beghards *in regno Alemaniae*.[55] The first decree

[51] In favour of this derivation, see J. van Mierlo, S.J., especially his article "Béguins", in *Dict. de spirit.*, I, col. 1341–3.

[52] Book VII, ch. 22; ed. J. Strange, Cologne, 1851, vol. II, p. 31.

[53] Lambert "li Beges" (†1177), who was among the advisers of these new groups, may have received his nickname from the colour of his habit and so contributed to spread the term.

[54] Ed. A. Stroick, O.F.M., in *Arch. francis. histor.*, XXIV (1931), pp. 61–2.

[55] Cf. E. Müller, O.F.M., *Das Konzil von Vienne, 1311–1312. Seine Quellen und seine Geschichte*, Münster, 1934, pp. 577–87.

attacked the Béguines[56]: in spite of their habit they are not religious, because they have neither obedience nor an approved rule; they lose themselves in foolish speculations on the Trinity and the divine essence, on other dogmas and points of doctrine, and on the sacraments. Their influence was denounced, and the Council considered it its duty to condemn them. Naturally this censure did not apply to all of them but only to those guilty of the errors stigmatized.[57] The second decree was aimed at both the Beghards and the Béguines, an "abominable sect" which was spreading in the German lands.[58] This document gives, in its eight propositions, the picture of a sort of quietism, only vaguely related to Catharism. The members of the sect, in their aberrations, profess that man can arrive at the perfection of Christ himself and so become incapable of sin, *impeccabilis*. He then has no further need of fasting and prayer; he has nothing more to fear from the weakness of his sensual nature. For one who has achieved this perfection, a sensual kiss loses all character of sin, as does the act of intercourse performed from concupiscence. No obedience is due either to human authority or to the Church: *ubi spiritus Domini, ibi libertas!* Moreover, final beatitude is accessible to our intellectual nature even here below. At this stage of perfection, there is no longer any question of striving to acquire virtue; and the Eucharist no longer requires such marks of reverence as might make a man descend from the level of contemplation at which he had arrived.

Certain of these theses, in a more acceptable form, are to be found in a treatise which was long considered as the anonymous work of a French or Flemish writer of the late thirteenth century, and is only known in its English version, *The Mirror of Simple Souls*.[59] The author says, for instance, "that the humble soul should cease to worry about the pursuit of virtue as it does not need to: virtue now works on the soul's behalf. Such a soul has no further need of the consolations of God or his gifts, should not be anxious about this and could not be anyway, for God is now its only object and such anxieties are obstacles." These are precisely the propositions that sent Marguerite Porete, a *dévote* from Valenciennes, to

[56] *Cum de quisbusdam mulieribus*, Clement, Book III, Title XI, ch. I (ed. Friedberg, II, col. 1169).

[57] As has been pointed out by J. van Mierlo, S.J., art. "Bégardisme", in *Dict. hist. géogr. eccl.*, VII, col. 433.

[58] *Ad nostrum*, Clement, Book V, Title III, ch. 3 (ed. Friedberg, II, col. 1183–4; Mansi, XXV, 358 and 410; Denz., 471–8).

[59] *The Mirror of Simple Souls*; ed. C. Kirchberger, Orchards Series, No. 15, London, 1927. The French original has recently come to light. As yet unpublished, it is contained in the manuscript *Chantilly, Musée Condé 986*.

the stake in Paris in 1310, which seems to justify considering her as the author of the *Mirror*.[60]

But the propositions condemned at the Council of Vienna are more or less the common basis of quietism in every period. They also show undeniable resemblances to the heresies of the twelfth and thirteenth centuries, except Catharism (at least as regards its dualistic metaphysics). Perhaps the Council, which had been put on the alert by the religious authorities of Germany, was too far away to form a balanced judgment. It may well be that it applied the common label of Beghards and Béguines to a considerable number of groups whose common denominator was made up of the following doctrines: a pantheism which went too far in identifying the mystic with God, refusal to accept the hierarchy, indifference towards the sacraments, and moral licence elevated into a virtue for the perfect. The "Brethren of the Free Spirit", the "Friends of God" and other similar groups to be discussed in connection with speculative mysticism in fourteenth-century Germany,[61] were there to keep up the confusion.

In spite of repression, the latent pantheism of the Beghards and Béguines seems to have become accentuated in the course of the fourteenth century, as also their moral aberrations. One should not forget, however, that in their beginnings both wanted to go back to a practice of the Gospel accessible to all, in poverty and chastity, but without the burden of a community life whose formalism they seem to have mistrusted. At the very threshold of the fourteenth century, there were several pontifical documents favourable to the Béguines, and the number of them who remained faithful was estimated at 200,000, if we are to believe a letter from John XXII to the bishop of Strasbourg (1321?).[62] It would therefore be a mistake to generalize from the condemnation of exceptional cases. Both Beghards and Béguines broke away from the traditional conventual pattern, probably often because of incompatibility of temperament, but their life in its simplicity could well lead them to the Gospel, to poverty and chastity, with a minimum of common life and common prayer. Unfortunately, that minimum does not seem to have been enough, in the long run, to preserve them from all the contagions that lay in wait for them at the end of the thirteenth century. What is astonishing is that they should have remained so long untouched. When they succumbed it was not due to the basic principles of their institute so much as to the ideas of the time.

[60] Cf. S. Axters, *op. cit.*, II, pp. 162–3; J.B.P. [Poriot], *Hadewijch d'Anvers*, pp. 12–13.
[61] See *infra*, ch. VI.
[62] Cf. *Documenta ecclesiastica ad perfectionis studium spectantia*, ed. J. de Guibert, S.J., Rome, 1931, No. 281.

4. *"Brautmystik" and "Wesenmystik"*

The spiritual life of the groups just mentioned is best seen in the concrete, in the lives of their finest representatives. Marie d'Oignies (†1213) was one of the originators of the movement, and she is still one of the best known. According to her *Vita*, written by Jacques de Vitry,[63] she undertook one day, out of fidelity to the Gospel, to become a beggar.

> The spirit of fear had given her so great a love of poverty that she deprived herself even of necessities. Once she wished to run away and beg from door to door, unknown and despised, *so as naked to follow the naked Christ*: putting aside the cloak of temporal riches like Joseph, leaving the water like the woman of Samaria, the shroud as John did. She often thought on the poverty of Christ, who was born without a shelter, who had no stone on which to lay his head, no money to pay tribute; who lived on alms and the hospitality of others. So great was her longing for poverty that she took nothing but a bag in which to put any alms or food that might be given her, a cup to drink from, and clothed herself in rags. Those around her could not forbear to weep. Torn between the desire to be free and live as a beggar for Christ's sake and to stay for the sake of her brothers and sisters, she chose to stay since she saw that they could not have borne her absence. But she did what she could, and remained so attached to poverty that she was wont to cut into pieces the cloth on which they had their meals and other linen too, so as to give at least part of them to the poor.[64]

The model of this absolute poverty was Christ. It was the better to follow and imitate him that she would have liked to beg and to live despised; *ut nudum Christum nuda sequeretur*, her biographer said of her, following St Jerome. One is inclined nowadays to condemn these beggars as parasites, but it is a fact, confirmed by the history of the Franciscan and Dominican Orders, that it was Christ the wandering beggar who was then taken as the model of poverty—not Christ the workman of Nazareth, nor yet the first Christians of Jerusalem, as the monks had done. In this connection Jacques de Vitry gives us a glimpse of his disillusionment in the face of the "poverty" of many a convent. "Woe to you, who accumulate goods, who take over a whole countryside! Did this poor one of Christ ever lack for anything?"[65]

The love of our Lord explains various other aspects of the spirituality of the Beghards and Béguines; for example, the great interest which they took in the Crusades and, in quite another domain, their

[63] *Acta Sanctorum*, June, vol. V, pp. 547–72.
[64] *Ibid.*, p. 557.
[65] *Ibid.*, pp. 557–8.

devotion to the mysteries of Christ's childhood.[66] There was also their devotion to the Eucharist. Juliana of Cornillon (†1258), with whom the institution of Corpus Christi is commonly connected, seems to have belonged to a community of Béguines,[67] and it seems clear that Marie d'Oignies[68] and Jacques de Vitry, and later the spiritual milieux of the principality of Liège, were already working in that direction. The feast was approved in 1246 for the diocese of Liège, and then by Urban IV in 1264 for the universal Church, but was not actually celebrated everywhere until after 1317.[69]

There are other names that can be connected more or less directly with the Béguines, among them Beatrice of Nazareth (†1268), who was taught first by the Béguines of Léau (between St Trond and Tirlemont, in Belgium) before becoming a Cistercian nun.[70] She died prioress of the monastery of our Lady of Nazareth at Lierre (between Malines and Antwerp). She was accustomed to put down in writing her reflections and the graces she received, and these notes enabled William of Afflighem (†1297?) to draw up her *Vita*.[71] One chapter of the life corresponds to a little mystical treatise which has come to light called "The Seven Degrees of Love", *Van seven manieren van minne*.[72] Love, according to Beatrice, comes from God and leads back to him. The seven degrees go from purification to the final attainment of eternal Love and the vision of God's essence. "It was granted her", says her biographer, "to see (*videre*) the divine essence in the fullness of its glory and very perfect majesty; that essence which contains every power, which governs the universe and disposes all things. She had a clear and penetrating contemplation (*clara contemplationis acie*) of it."[73] But

66 Cf. A. Mens, *op. cit.*, pp. 97–272; S. Axters, *op. cit.*, I, p. 319.

67 *Vita* in *Acta Sanctorum*, April, vol. I, pp. 435–76.

68 Oignies is the present Aiseau, in Belgian Hainault.

69 See F. Callaey, O.F.M.Cap., "Origine e sviluppo della festa del 'Corpus Domini'", in *Euntes docete*, X (1957), pp. 3–33; and in *Eucaristia*, Rome, 1957, pp. 907–33. On the history of the office, see C. Lambot, O.S.B., "L'Ufficio del S.mo Sacramento", in *Eucaristia*, pp. 827–35; by the same, *L'Office de la Fête-Dieu primitive*, Maredsous, 1945; by the same, "L'office de la Fête-Dieu. Aperçus nouveaux sur ses origines", in *Rev. bénéd.*, LIV (1942), pp. 61–123.

70 Cf. S. Roisin, "L'efflorescence cistercienne et le courant féminin de piété au XIIIe siècle", in *Rev. hist. eccl.*, XXXIX (1943), pp. 342–78. Mechtilde of Magdeburg also received her first training from Béguines; cf. ch. VI, §1, pp. 375 *et seq.*

71 Part of it was reproduced by C. Henriquez, in *Quinque prudentes virgines* Antwerp, 1630. The manuscript that contains the whole is *Bruxelles, Bibl. royale 4459–70*, f. 66–138. Extracts have been edited by L. Reypens, S.J., in *Ons geest. Erf.*, V (1931), pp. 430–3.

72 Ed. L. Reypens, S.J., and J. van Mierlo, S.J., Louvain, 1926. There are several versions in modern Dutch, and a French translation by J. Kerssemackers appeared in *La Vie spirit.*, *Suppl.*, 1939. Beatrice was also responsible for a version of the well-known legend of the sacristan; ed. R. Roemans, *Beatrijs* (Klassieke Gallerij, No. 21), Antwerp, 1945.

73 *Vita, ed. cit.*, p. 430 (MS. f. 111–13); cf. J. Maréchal, *Étude sur la psychologie des mystiques*, II, pp. 288–92.

to reach this it is necessary that the soul be free from all self-interest, having a desire for God which becomes at once torment, joy and inebriation before becoming stabilized in a security in which the soul is fully mistress of herself." The words describe an experience, that of Beatrice, one quite apart from all abstract theories. Yet she occasionally hints at a mystical life which is not exclusively "bridal", as is that said to be derived from St Bernard —that is, described in terms borrowed from the Canticle of Canticles, and expressing the ascent of the soul towards God in the vocabulary of human love and human marriage.[74]

This treatise, together with the writings of Hadewijch (to be discussed shortly), is one of the oldest known examples of Dutch prose. Can one deduce from it the existence at this time, though still in embryonic form, of a school of spirituality proper to the Low Countries? The documents of the thirteenth century certainly do not seem to justify recognizing one distinct from that of the neighbouring regions, France and the Rhineland. The language, to be sure, is already different from Middle German, but it is doubtful whether this is sufficient to establish the existence of a separate school of spirituality, especially when one considers the case of the *Book of Love* or *Discourse of the Fifteen Degrees*.[75] Written in Middle German in the Rhineland during the thirteenth century, it was very soon translated into Middle Dutch, probably by 1250.[76] It was distinctly in the tradition of St Augustine and the Victorines, but above all it was inspired by "bridal" mysticism. Now, in the circles of devout women, *mulieres religiosae*, of the thirteenth century, mysticism of that kind enjoyed considerable popularity, which shows that the spirituality of the Low Countries was not peculiar to itself; it was derived from a spiritual tradition which was developing in the Latin countries; going beyond that, it owed a great deal to St Bernard and the *Canticle of Canticles*. Yet it is true to say that, by its language and its allegorical style, it is more closely related to the spirituality of the Rhineland.[77]

[74] Another former Béguine who became a Cistercian nun, Mechtilde of Magdeburg (†1283), will be studied in the next chapter (pp. 375 *et seq.*). A token of the relationship between religious circles in the Low Countries and the Cistercian Order is to be found in the little treatise *Of the Daughters of Sion*, which derives from the *Filia Sion* of Guerric of Igny; cf. *Vander Dochtere van Syon*, ed. J. van Mierlo, S.J., Antwerp, 1941; and L. Reypens, S.J., "Het latijnsche origineel der allegorie 'Vander Dochtere van Syon'", in *Ons geest. Erf*, II, 1943, pp. 174–8.

[75] *Dat boec der Minnen* or *Die Rede von den 15 Graden.*

[76] There is an edition of this translation by J. M. Willeumier-Schalij, Leyden, 1946; see the introduction and chs I–III. There is a study by J. B. Schoemann, S.J., *Die Rede von den 15 Graden*, Berlin, 1930. The authorship seems to be the same as that of another mystical treatise, derived from the *Vitis mystica* often attributed to St Bonaventure, *Die Lilie* (ed. P. Wüst, Berlin, 1909).

[77] The existence of a Netherlands school of spirituality has been questioned by

The "bridal" tendency in the Béguine movement of the thirteenth century is apparent all through the work of Hadewijch.[78] Not much is known about her. Our information is limited to her name, the fact that she came from Antwerp, and the approximate period of her life (about the middle of the thirteenth century). That she was of noble birth and was superior of the Béguines at Nivelles (Brabant) is pure conjecture.

One thing is certain, that in her writings—*Visions, Letters* and *Poems*—the central theme is love. Hadewijch belonged to that stream of spirituality, at once affective and ecstatic, according to which the soul can only come into contact with God by a love which makes it go out of itself, which, indeed, drives it out of itself. This love is both its joy and its torment. In this, Hadewijch shows the same spiritual tendency as the author of the *Discourse of the Fifteen Degrees*. Once again, the influence of a particular current of spirituality can be detected. In it, the dogmatic content becomes more and more impoverished; affectivity and religious emotion come to be almost an end in themselves. But this love, which is expressed in language akin to that of the literature of courtly love, is directed to God or to Christ:

> Ah! dear Love, if any love I love,
> 'Tis Thee, my love.
> Who givest grace for grace
> The loved one to sustain.
>
> Ah! sweet Love, I would that I were love,
> And loved thee, Love, with love itself!
> Ah! sweet Love, for love's sake grant
> That love may wholly know her love.[79]

Dom J. Huijben, "Y a-t-il une spiritualité flamande?", in *La Vie spirit.*, L (1937) *Suppl.* [129–47]. It appears certain that such a school did not exist before Ruysbroeck. S. Axters, O.P., *op. cit.*, admits its existence but attributes its origin to Ruysbroeck; see also his *Spiritualité des Pays-Bas*, Louvain, 1948. The reasons for doubting this interpretation will be discussed in the next chapter (§6).

[78] J. van Mierlo, S.J., has edited the *Brieven* (letters), Antwerp, 1947; the *Visioenen*, Louvain, 1924; the *Strophische Gedichten* (strophic poems), 2 vols, Antwerp, 1942; and the *Mengeldichten* (poems of another type), Antwerp, 1952. See also *Hadewijch-Brieven*, original text and Dutch translation, by F. van Bladel, S.J., and B. Spaapen, S.J., Tielt–Hague, 1954.

The best study in French is that of J.B.P. [Porion], *Hadewijch d'Anvers*. It includes a translation of Hadewijch's *Spiritual Poems* written about 1250, and of the *New Poems* by another writer, as will be seen further on. For critical comments on this collection see C. Journet, "Note sur la spiritualité des béguines", in *Nova et vetera*, XXV, Fribourg, 1955, pp. 56–67. See also S. Axters, *Geschiedenis . . .*, I, pp. 335–82 and 452–6 (bibliography). Cf. J. van Mierlo, S.J., "Hadewijch, une mystique flamande", in *Rev. ascét. myst.*, V (1924), pp. 269–89, 380–404.

[79] *Mengeldichten XV*, trans. by J.B.P., *op. cit.*, p. 121. Cf. J. van Mierlo, S.J., *De "minne" in de strophische gedichten van Hadewijch*, Brussels, Acad. royale flamande de littérature, 1941, pp. 687–705.

Here and there, however, Hadewijch's spirituality takes a different form. From St Bernard—and, through him, from St Augustine—came the notion of exemplarism which "seems to be the very basis of her theology".[80] This it is that gives the return to God by way of love something other than a merely sentimental or moral flavour. It becomes above all a matter of restoring God's image in man—an image that has been defiled by sin. According to this speculative conception of the soul's ascent to God, which has been called "mysticism of the essence" (*Wesenmystik*), the whole of the spiritual life consists in this return. The doctrine rests on a very solid scriptural theology. The journey by which the soul returns to God, by which it will recover its lost likeness to him, is a dialectic. It is described in terms which are clearly intellectual and speculative, but side by side with them go a total stripping of self, a faith which becomes clear vision, a love which flowers into undivided possession, and a Unity into which disappear, as Ruysbroeck says, all "persons, modes and names" in the simplicity of God's essence. The Rhineland mystics and Ruysbroeck are foreshadowed in a sentence from Hadewijch's Letter XVIII: "For God, the soul is a free and open way, into which he can plunge from out of his furthest depths; and for the soul, in return, God is the way of freedom, towards the depths of the divine Being, which nothing can attain save the depths of the soul".[81]

This theme is found even more clearly in the writings which were put forth under the name of Hadewijch but which belong to a later period. These are poems XVII to XXIX in the collection known as *Mengeldichten*. They too, it would appear, were written by a Flemish Béguine. They may have been influenced by Meister Eckhart.[82] Their interest lies in the way they illustrate the doctrinal evolution which took place in the *milieux* of the Béguines within a few generations. Some of Eckhart's major themes—for example, that of spiritual nakedness, which is found in his famous sermon *Beati pauperes spiritu*—will be recognized in poem XXVI:

Naked love which spares nothing
In its wild death
When every accident is left aside
Finds itself again pure essence.

In love's pure abandon
No created good can subsist:

[80] S. Axters, *op. cit.*, I, p. 369.
[81] *Letter XVIII*, 1. 73–8; trans. in *Nova et Vetera*, 1952, No. 4, p. 295. A few other passages sound the same note; see J. Maréchal, S.J., *op. cit.*, II, pp. 285–8.
[82] Cf. J.B.P., *H. d'A.*, pp. 47–9. If these poems were not influenced by Eckhart, they are still good evidence of the evolution of spirituality.

For love strips of all form
Those whom it receives in its simplicity.

Freed from every modality,
Alien to every image
Is the life here below
Of the poor in spirit.

All is not found in poverty,
Exile, and all such ways:
The poor in spirit must dwell
Without notions in a vast simplicity,

A simplicity without end, and having no beginning
Neither form, modality, reason, nor object,
Without opinion, or thought, or intention, or learning:
One that is boundless and without any limit.

Here in this wild desert
Dwell in unity the poor in spirit.
Nothing is there for them save freedom in a silence
Ever answering to Eternity.[83]

It would be rash to assert that there had been a radical change in spiritual attitude between Hadewijch and the author of this poem. Many spiritual writers have echoed both tendencies, affective and speculative, and "the second Hadewijch" (as she is sometimes called) may have done so. It was true of St Bernard, and he seems to have been the master of the second Hadewijch as well as of the first, inasmuch as he speaks of the soul's journey as it strives to recover its lost likeness to God. But Bernard's description of this return was not that of the Rhineland mystics. It was here that his spiritual heirs revealed their weakness: affectivity so dominated their worship that, even when the necessary doctrinal support was there, they never dreamed of taking advantage of it. The theology underlying this spirituality had begun to be envisaged by the béguinages of the thirteenth century. The Rhineland mystics were their heirs; theologians and spiritual directors simply elucidated what they had learned from those they directed. Eckhart was not, strictly speaking, an initiator; he owed a great deal to the milieux of which the two Hadewijches are the best examples, together with the authors of the *Mirror of Simple Souls*, the *Discourse of the Fifteen Degrees*, and other similar writings.

One would have to go back further than the immediate sources of the two Hadewijches to determine the origin of the *Wesenmystik*. It is a difficult question, in which one must beware of fantastic simplifications and affiliations which prove very little. Here the

83 Trans. by J.B.P., *ibid.*, pp. 173–4.

causes that contribute to produce any given effect are difficult to distinguish precisely and equally difficult to isolate from one another. Among these causes, the Neo-Platonism of St Augustine can certainly be singled out, with that of the Pseudo-Dionysius; they left their mark on the whole thought of the Middle Ages. The *Wesenmystik*, however, perhaps shows more affinity with Plotinus' doctrine of the soul's ecstatic ascent towards the *nous* and her final return to the divine One. We know that William of St Thierry, who was much read by the spiritual-minded in the Low Countries, knew Plotinus through the Greek Fathers, and William is the only author from whom the first Hadewijch copied and adapted a passage,[84] though she developed it in a direction probably not envisaged by her sources[85]; we are to become, here below, what we are, by losing ourselves in the Abyss of the divine essence, and by keeping ourselves from all works save pure love alone. In this way Hadewijch, though clearly heir to the *Brautmystik*, had, better than Beatrice of Nazareth, opened a way for others.

5. *Dante: A Mystical Poet*

All that Christian life and thought had acquired and discovered during the last hundred years was brought together by a genius in an incomparable masterpiece. Dante Alighieri (1265–1321) was one of the six "Priors" of Florence. At the close of an era in which new milieux had become conscious of their spiritual vocation, on the threshold of a period in which the tension between religious knowledge and the spiritual life was to be stretched to breaking-point, Dante stands out as a poet in whom the harmony between theology and mysticism still reigned.

Yet unfortunately he is not usually given a great place in the history of spirituality. For one thing, he was neither a clerk nor a monk. Dante has suffered from that sort of exclusiveness which monopolizes all spiritual achievement for the clergy and religious, and which makes it difficult, even today, to describe the lay milieux of other times. Then he is reproached with having taken too definite a stand against Boniface VIII, that he thereby involved himself too completely in the affairs of this world, and that he was not afraid of saying what he thought of those in high places, of the hierarchy, of the monks and friars. To many, these facts were just so many in-

[84] Cf. *ibid.*, p. 24, note 1, and p. 40; J. van Mierlo, S.J., "H. en Willem van St Thierry", in *Ons geest. Erf*, III (1929), pp. 45–59; J. M. Déchanet, O.S.B., "Guillaume et Plotin", in *Rev. moyen âge latin*, II (1946), pp. 241–60; by the same, *G. de S. Th., l'homme et son œuvre*, Bruges, 1942, pp. 200–9 (on William's sources).

[85] Cf. J.B.P., *H. d'A.*, pp. 34–7.

dications that he lacked humility and that his interior life could not have reached the stage of being content with the "one thing necessary". He was also a poet; and that, it is felt, shows a too human concern for literary form. He sings the praises of Beatrice Portinari, with whom he had fallen in love at the age of nine, and whose death in 1290 left a void which does not seem to have been filled by his marriage a few years later. In 1300 he came to power in Florence, with the support of a party which was soon driven out by the opposition; at that point began his wandering life of an exile, and it was during this last period that he wrote the *Divine Comedy*; death cut him off in 1321 without his having seen his native Florence again.[86] A career so far removed from the accepted canons of the interior life was inevitably bound to compromise Dante in the eyes of many. It is only by putting certain prejudices on one side that one can see clearly the spiritual quality of what he wrote.

The important thing to note is the doctrine that emerges from this great work. It is impregnated with mysticism; it is impossible to understand the *Divine Comedy*, and especially the *Paradiso*, if that is not realized at once. Dante had been influenced by the Neo-Platonic ideas of the Pseudo-Dionysius; in fact he cites the *De caelesti hierarchia* as his source, with the *Liber de causis*, in the letter (of doubtful authenticity) to Can Grande della Scala.[87] He had also read the great doctors of his own time, Thomas Aquinas, Albert the Great, and Bonaventure—so much so, that both the Dominicans and the Franciscans have each claimed him as a disciple.

[86] The bibliography relating to Dante is very extensive; special volumes have been devoted to it. See M. Barbi, *Dante, vita, opere a fortuna*, Florence, 1933. U. Cosmo, *Guida a Dante*, Turin, 1947. A brief bibliography is given in *Encicl. Cattolica*, IV, 1209–12; and in the French translation of the *Divina Commedia* by A. Masseron, vol. IV, Paris, 1950, pp. 205–28.

Editions of the complete works include the Oxford edition, by E. Moore and P. Toynbee, 4th ed., 1924; and that of the Società dantesca italiana, Florence, 1921. There are a number of partial editions, chiefly of the *Divina Commedia*, the *Convivio*, and the *Monarchia*. There is a French translation of the *Vita Nuova* by H. Cochin, Paris, 1914; of the *Divina Commedia* by A. Masseron, 4 vols, Paris, 1947–50; and of the *Monarchia* by B. Landry, Paris, 1933. The reader of Masseron's translation will find his *Pour comprendre la Divine Comédie*, Paris, 1939 helpful; or G. Cohen, *Lettres chrétiennes du moyen âge*, Paris, 1957, pp. 64–119.

For a biographical sketch, see A. Valensin, S.J., *Regards sur Dante*, Paris, 1956. The principal recent works on Dante will be cited in the pages that follow. Some specialized reviews appear regularly, including *Studi danteschi* (Florence) and *Deutsches Dante-Jahrbuch* (Weimar).

[The passages from the *Divina Commedia* quoted in this section are taken from the translation by P. H. Wicksteed (for the *Paradiso*) and T. Okey (for the *Purgatorio*), edited by H. Oelsner, London, 1899–1901.—Trans.]

[87] *Epistolae*, ed. P. Toynbee (with English translation), Oxford, 1920, pp. 184–185.

According to a common interpretation of the *Divine Comedy*, the poet makes his way, by three stages, towards the vision of the Holy Trinity, which he chose to represent under the image of three interlaced circles; in this he was probably influenced by Joachim of Flora, but of course he goes far beyond him.[88] It has also been thought that the spiritual ascent of the *Divine Comedy* suggests, without describing them in detail, the three "ways" of the return to God: *purgatio*, *illuminatio* and *perfectio*. The poet passes throught these stages, led successively by Virgil, Beatrice and St Bernard. These guides were not chosen arbitrarily. Inevitably, the Virgil of the *Divine Comedy* is not the Virgil of history,[89] any more than Beatrice, the disciple of St Thomas, is the Florentine maiden with whom Dante had fallen in love as a child.[90] St Bernard, however, has a greater resemblance to the abbot of Clairvaux. In the poet's eyes the third guide symbolizes mystical theology. Speculative thought is no longer adequate to lead him to the goal of his journey; an experience of a new order is needed—contemplation—and of this St Bernard is the incarnation.[91]

When Dante speaks of contemplation in Canto XXXIII of the *Paradiso*, he may be drawing upon St Bonaventure's *Itinerarium*[92] and upon the *Benjamin major* of Richard of St Victor. Ultimately, however, beyond these one must go back to St Augustine. In the *Paradiso*, Dante adopts Augustine's division of knowledge into three species: *visio corporalis, visio spiritualis sive imaginaria*, and *visio intellectualis*,[93] and from him also he takes his conception of love.[94] Yet it is impossible to fit Dante into any category. He gave poetic expression both to mystical and to scholastic theology, and his work bears the mark of St Thomas as well as of St Francis,

[88] Cf. *Paradiso*, Canto XXXIII, lines 115–20. See G. Busnelli, S.J., "Interpretazione della visione dantesca della SS. Trinità", in *Civ. cattol.*, XCIV, III (1943), pp. 337–44; B. Hirsch-Reich, "Die Quelle der Trinitätskreise von Joachim von Fiore und Dante", in *Sophia*, XXII (1954), pp. 170–8. On the relationship between Joachim and Dante, see M. W. Bloomfield, "Joachim of Flora. A Critical Survey of his Canon, Teachings, Sources, Biography and Influence", in *Traditio*, XIII (1957), pp. 303–7 and 310–11; L. Tondelli, *Da Gioacchino a Dante*, Turin, 1944.

[89] Cf. J. H. Whitfield, *Dante and Virgil*, Oxford, 1949.

[90] E. Gilson (*Dante et la philosophie*, Paris, 1939, ch. I) and it is generally held today that the Beatrice of the *Divina Commedia* was the human Beatrice; whereas P. Mandonnet, O.P. (*Dante le théologien*, Paris, 1935) regards her as purely symbolic of the Christian supernatural order.

[91] Cf. A. Masseron, *Dante et saint Bernard*, Paris, 1953, especially ch. III.

[92] Cf. E. Jallonghi, *Il misticismo bonaventuriano nella Divina Commedia*, Città di Castello, 1935, pp. 117–36.

[93] Cf. C. Calcaterra, "S. Agostino nelle opere di Dante e del Petrarca", in *S. Agostino, Pubblicazione commemorativa del 15. Centenario della sua morte*, Milan, 1931, pp. 432–40.

[94] Cf. P. Chioccioni, *L'agostinismo nella Divina Commedia*, Florence, 1952, ch. IV. This is the best work on the subject.

though if he has a preference his "philosophy of love" would seem to be more Franciscan than Dominican, though it could be traced further back, in different respects, to the Gospel and even to Plato's *Symposium*.[95] These are the last lines of the *Paradiso*:

> Within its depths I saw ingathered, bound by love in one volume, the scattered leaves of all the universe. . . .
> The universal form of this complex I think that I beheld, because more largely, as I say this, I feel that I rejoice . . .
> Thus all suspended did my mind gaze fixed, immovable, intent, ever enkindled by its gazing.
> Such at that light doth man become that to turn thence to any other sight could not by possibility be ever yielded.
> For the good, which is the object of the will, is therein wholly gathered, and outside it that same thing is defective which therein is perfect. . . .
> To the high fantasy here power failed; but already my desire and will were rolled—even as a wheel that moveth equally—by the Love that moves the sun and the other stars.[96]

This context helps us to understand that for Dante the contemplative life is higher than the active. His thought on this point is best expressed in the *Convivio*. The contemplative life, "more divine and more beloved of God",[97] is the part of Mary, the better part.[98] It sets man on the road to the highest beatitude, "which cannot in any case be obtained here below", and goes far beyond the imperfect happiness to be gained by the active life and the exercise of the moral and intellectual virtues.[99] This doctrine comes entirely from Aristotle and St Thomas. For Dante—and here his thought recalls Aristotle more than St Thomas—"the only one of the three beatitudes [active, contemplative and supreme] that is strictly proper to man is also the lowest of them all; it is that of the active life of the human composite, of act according to virtue".[100] In the

[95] Cf. R. Resta, *Dante e la filosofia dell'amore*, Bologna, 1935; H. Ostlender, "Dantes Mystik", in *Deutsches Dante-Jahrbuch*, XXVIII (1949), pp. 65–98. The most important work on the parallels to the *Divina Commedia* in antiquity, paganism, the Bible, and Judaism is that of A. Rüegg, *Die Jenseitsvorstellungen von Dante und die übrigen literarischen Voraussetzungen der "Divina Commedia". Ein quellenkristicher Kommentar*, 2 vols, Einsiedeln, 1945. See also Y. Batard, *Dante, Minerve et Apollon. Les images de la Divine Comédie*, Paris, 1952; P. Renucci, *Dante, disciple et juge du monde gréco-latin*, Paris, 1954. On the Arabian sources, see E. Cerulli, *Il "Libro della scala" e la questione delle fonti arabo-spagnole della Divina Commedia*, Vatican City, 1949; M. Asin Palacios, *La escatologia musulmana en la Divina Comedia*, Madrid, 1943; L. Massignon, "Mystique musulmane et mystique chrétienne au moyen âge", in *Convegno di Scienze morali storiche, e filologiche 1956*, Rome, 1957, pp. 20–34.

[96] *Paradiso*, Canto XXXIII (Wicksteed translation).

[97] *Convivio*, Book II, 4. Critical edition by G. Busnelli and G. Vandelli, 2 vols, Florence, 1934–7.

[98] *Ibid.*, Book IV, 17.

[99] *Ibid.*, Book IV, 22.

[100] E. Gilson, *Dante et la philosophie*, p. 138. See the entire section entitled

Divine Comedy too, the contemplatives are accorded the better part.[101] St Bernard, as has been said, is chosen to be the poet's guide in the "unitive life", because he "by contemplation tasted of that peace" which he now enjoys.[102] And St Bonaventure is placed above St Thomas.[103]

Apart from these theories and their poetic expression, there is the question of Dante's own mystical experience, on which opinions remain divided. On the one hand, historians bring forward the authors from whom Dante said he had drawn his inspiration, but this argument does not prove that he had himself experienced that which the sources describe. In the letter to Can Grande, he cites various scriptural texts to explain the visions of the *Paradiso*[104]; those include the passage in which St Paul says that he was caught up to the third heaven, and the account of the Transfiguration. He then cites the *Benjamin major* of Richard of St Victor, St Bernard's *De consideratione*, and St Augustine's *De quantitate animae*.[105] All this gives him too the right to say:

> In that heaven which most receiveth of his light, have I been; and have seen things which whoso descendeth from up there hath nor knowledge nor power to re-tell;
> because, as it draweth nigh to its desire, our intellect sinketh so deep, that memory cannot go back upon the track.
> Nathless, whatever of the holy realm I had the power to treasure in my memory, shall now be matter of my song.[106]

If it be doubted, in spite of the support that might be given to such an interpretation by the letter to Can Grande, whether Dante was speaking of a personal experience in these lines, the fact remains that the great poet's life had been marked by at least two heavy trials; first the loss of Beatrice, and then exile. Dante had suffered intensely, with the sensibility of a man drawn both to ideal love and to action. Suffering is the school that God provides so that men may return to him, and Dante had passed through that school. It had taught him to understand the one thing necessary: Mary's part not Martha's; St Bernard's—the contemplative life.

But Dante had sinned. He had known the two most powerful seductions that a man can encounter, that of love and that of power,

"*Primat de la contemplation*" according to the *Convivio*, *ibid.*, pp. 130–43; also A. Valensin, S.J., *Le christianisme de Dante*, Paris, 1954, pp. 41–4.

101 *Paradiso*, Canto XXII.

102 *Ibid.*, Canto XXXI, 109–11 (Wicksteed translation).

103 *Ibid.*, Cantos X and XII.

104 On the scriptural language in the *Divina Commedia*, see G. Marzot, *Il linguaggio biblico nella Divina Commedia*, Pisa, 1956.

105 *Epistola* X. Ed. P. Toynbee, pp. 189–92.

106 *Paradiso*, Canto I, 4–12 (Wicksteed translation).

and he had not withstood them. When one reads, in Cantos XXX and XXXI of the *Purgatorio*, the stinging reproaches of Beatrice and the "confessions" by Dante which follow them, one begins to see that the whole poem is not simply a vision of the other world and a poetic figure of the last judgment. The *Divine Comedy* is the journey beyond the grave of a poet who had "fallen so low that all other means would have been powerless to set him again on the straight path which he had lost".[107] Dante had sinned, and it is easy to imagine what his disorders had been: he had yielded, apparently, to the temptations of the flesh, he had striven against the pope; but here his excuse is that he had risen up not so much against the vicar of Christ as against the political autocrat, and against those who were exploiting the bride of Christ, who "was not reared upon my blood, and that of Linus and of Cletus, that she might then be used for gain of gold".[108] There were also aberrations of the intellectual order. He had tasted pagan humanism under all the aspects of his time.[109] His religion, which was that of a faithful Catholic and a lucid theologian, did not prevent his putting forward opinions which must have seemed temerarious to the men of his day. He spoke at times, with no apparent concern for orthodoxy, of suicide, of the non-eternity of Limbo, of the salvation of infidels, and of the independence of Church and State.[110] In this last proposition, especially, he was in opposition to a large section of Christendom, and yet it seemed to him the only effective way of restoring to the Church her primarily spiritual mission. Was he wrong in preaching the separation of the two swords? We are much less inclined to think so today than were the prelates of the *trecento*.

These weaknesses do not seem to justify seriously questioning Dante's personal experience of the mystical life. Sin has never been an absolute obstacle to the merciful grace of God: so many saints—St Paul, St Augustine, and St Bernard, whom Dante himself often cites, among them—have proved this. Possibly Dante's own temperament may have been another obstacle, but here again this is not decisive. All one can say is that the poet was a man of action and at the same time highly emotional. Possibly he was not a mystic in the sense that is often given to the word—an exceptional being, who experiences God, so to speak, by virtue of a natural predisposition. Dante belongs to a different tradition, that of those great Christian spiritual writers who were at the same time men of action, of whom the leader was St Paul.

[107] A. Masseron, *La Divine Comédie*, II, *Purgatoire*, p. 268; *Purgatorio*, XXX, 136 (Okey translation).
[108] *Paradiso*, Canto XXVII, 40–2 (Wicksteed translation).
[109] See A. Renaudet, *Dante humaniste*, Paris, 1952.
[110] See A. Valensin, *Le christianisme de Dante*, Part II.

There is still the question whether the visions of Holy Week, 1300, those related in the *Divine Comedy*, are a pure literary fiction. The least one can say is that they are described in an extraordinary skilful and polished style (down to the placing of the key words and the number of lines). Beneath this slightly artificial form, however, lies a deep experience. Dante had become conscious of his own sin. He had understood the nature of the contemplative life and of Christian love. He had begun to see what that life is, to which our life on earth is leading us. He had grasped the place of Mary in Christian life.[111] His religion is pure and grave. It is joyful, even when he is speaking of purgatory or of the dying Christ.[112] All this reveals an unusual understanding of the Christian message. It is not that of the theologian who determines scientifically what a dogma is, and then examines its significance and its implications. Neither is it that of the devout man (or more frequently the devout woman) who records in verse his mystical experiences, or what he believes to be such. It is the intuition of a poet of genius, a master of his craft, a man who had experienced the agony of human life—its passions, its defects, its spiritual possibilities—and who was at the same time a contemplative, who could not stop at the appearance of things, but found their meaning in uncreated Love.

Perhaps he did not experience God in the sense in which we now speak of the mystical life, but he sang of the Truth and the Love that come from God.

This brings us to a final question, that of Dante's place in the spiritual history of the Middle Ages. It is not without interest, if one considers the various cross-currents that appeared in Europe at the end of the thirteenth century and the beginning of the fourteenth.

At the time Dante was writing the *Divine Comedy*, no suspicion as yet rested on the speculative mystics of the Rhineland; Eckhart was preaching north of the Alps in the valley of the Rhine, and the second Hadewijch was echoing his teachings. The spirituality of certain groups of Beghards and Béguines, however, was showing the tendencies which had been censured by the Council of Vienna. No reflection of all this seems to appear in Dante's work, nor yet of that bridal mysticism which characterized the first Hadewijch; such a form of spiritual life was quite foreign to him; yet he took as his guide to heaven St Bernard, the reputed originator of "bridal mysticism". But which St Bernard—the one who commented on the

[111] Cf. H. Schackenburg, *Maria in Dantes Göttlicher Komödie*, Freiburg in Breisgau, 1956; A. Valensin, *Le christianisme de Dante*, pp. 126–36; A. Masseron, *Dante et saint Bernard*, ch. II.

[112] A. Valensin, *Le christianisme de Dante*, pp. 117–26.

Canticle of Canticles and extolled the Spouse of the soul? Or the one who declared that the contemplative life of Mary is superior to the active life of Martha; who taught us to know ourselves in the *De consideratione* and to love ourselves for God alone in the *De diligendo Deo*; who described the twelve degrees of pride and humility, and who was the "faithful Bernard" of the Queen of Heaven?[113] There is no doubt about the answer. Though Dante spoke much about "the Love that moves the sun and the other stars", he does not belong to the *dévot* and affective stream of thirteenth-century feminine piety. His sources are quite different: the Franciscan and Dominican doctors, and antiquity—pagan, biblical and patristic.

It is in his power of synthesis that Dante's extraordinary genius appears. Through the medium of poetry, he described the same vision of Christianity as a whole that the theologians had expressed in their *summas*, the artists in the cathedrals, and the mendicant Orders in carrying out their apostolic and evangelical mission. If there was a "first renaissance" in the thirteenth century, then Dante was its poet, as Francis of Assisi and Dominic had been its missionaries, Bonaventure and Thomas its theologians, and, if you like, Joachim of Flora its prophet.[114]

In the history of spirituality possibly the last synthesis of genius was Dante's. One might almost say, with Daniel-Rops, that he was the last man to bear witness to Christendom,[115] in the sense that after his time Christendom no longer existed. That is, Christianity no longer impregnated the whole of civil society, and its various disciplines began to separate. After Dante, there were still eminent theologians; there were mystics and founders of Orders who left an enduring mark upon the Church. Certain great writers, like Denys the Carthusian and Nicholas of Cusa, still succeeded in uniting the science of theology with that of the soul making its way towards God. We even find, a few years after Dante, a Norman monk, William of Digulleville who, without knowing the *Divine Comedy*, wrote three poems on exactly the same theme (though far inferior in strength of inspiration): the *Pilgrimage of Human Life*, the *Pilgrimage of the Soul*, and the *Pilgrimage of Jesus Christ*.[116] Nevertheless, the fact is that at the beginning of the fourteenth century

113 *Paradiso*, Canto XXXI, 100–2.

114 That is the point made by E. Buonaiuti's book *La prima rinascità. Il profeta: Gioacchino da Fiore. Il missionario: Francesco di Assisi. Il cantore*; *Dante*, Milan, 1952. See also G. Toffanin, *Storia dell' Umanesimo*, Naples, 1933; by the same, *La religione degl' Umanisti*, Bologna, 1950.

115 *L'Eglise de la cathédrale et de la croisade*, pp. 750 *et seq.*

116 Ed. J. J. Stürzinger, 3 vols, London, 1893–7. There is a modern adaptation by J. Delacotte, Paris, 1932; for a biographical and literary note by E. Faral, see *Hist. litt. France*, XXXIX, I (1952), pp. 1–132.

a chasm opened irrevocably. The theologian became a specialist in an autonomous field of knowledge, which he could enter by the use of a technique independent of the witness of his own life, of its personal holiness or sinfulness. The spiritual man, on the other hand, became a *dévot* who cared nothing for theology, one for whom his own experience ultimately became an end in itself, without reference to the dogmatic content to be sought in it. There were still some who attempted a synthesis, but the reader is quick to dismiss them as mere compilers, whose work may be useful for anyone who wants to find out, quickly and accurately, what their predecessors thought about problems of theology, Scripture, morals or spirituality.

Dante was the poet who *saw* what he wrote of, saw it with the eyes of a believer as much as, and even more than, with the intuition of a poet. His intuition was that of "the Love that moves the sun and the other stars", and calls the sinner to the eternal light of the Trinity:

> O Light eternal who only in thyself abidest, only thyself dost understand, and to thyself, self-understood self-understanding, turnest love and smiling![117]

[117] *Paradiso*, Canto XXXIII, 124–6 (Wicksteed translation).

VI

GERMAN SPIRITUALITY IN THE FOURTEENTH CENTURY

1. *The Dawn of the Century*

TAKING a broad view, and subject to corrections of detail, one could say that the Latin countries, from the fourteenth century to the beginning of modern times, lost their spiritual hegemony. The two great movements of the thirteenth century, the Franciscan and the Dominican, originated in Italy and in the south of France. In the fourteenth, the spiritual centres of Christendom shifted towards the German countries and England, particularly towards Germany. (By "German" must be understood all the regions of Germanic language and culture, including Alsace, Austria, Switzerland, and the Low Countries.) Henceforth, it was there that new spiritual problems arose and that solutions to them were sought for. There were some notable exceptions to the general rule: it will be seen, for example, how much the spiritual history of this period owes to Catharine of Siena and to John Gerson.

In another respect the fourteenth century differed from the preceeding one: the thirteenth had been dominated by one critical issue, although its earliest signs had of course appeared before that—the question of Mendicant poverty. St Francis had succeeded in finding an answer that was new and at the same time orthodox, but it was not long before his own answer was itself in dispute. Hardly had the Poverello died than his sons were divided on the matter of a practical application, and this led to the intervention of John XXII at the beginning of the fourteenth century. The shift of the spiritual centre towards the Germanic regions was paralleled by a change in the problem under discussion; what was at issue was no longer poverty, but contemplation. The problem was to know what constituted its essential element, how to define it, and so to determine in practice how to attain to it. In one sense, poverty was involved in this debate. Eckhart and his disciples continued to preach the necessity of detachment as a basis for the return to the image of God;

they even did so with some intransigence.[1] But in fact this was something different from Franciscan poverty; what they had in mind was an interior condition rather than an exterior realization, though the latter was not excluded.

Apart from this question, one fact leaps to the eye: the Dominican Order, because of its intellectualist tendency—its theologians holding as a principle the primacy of the intellect over the will—plays the leading role in the questions at issue.

The problems raised by the *Wesenmystik*, or "mysticism of the essence", have already been discussed in connection with Hadewijch and writings akin to hers. This new movement appeared only unobtrusively in the thirteenth century, yet clearly enough for its traces to be clearly seen. From the amount and quality of the evidence available to the historian of spirituality, however, the year 1300 seems to mark the extraordinary preponderance of the *Brautmystik* in Germany.

This trend was influenced more and more by the Franciscans of those regions. David of Augsburg and Berthold of Ratisbon were certainly no strangers to it.[2] It was chiefly among women, however, that the *Brautmystik* was received with fervour.[3] Hildegarde of Bingen and Elizabeth of Schönau had cultivated it in St Bernard's

[1] Cf. H. Grundmann, "Die geschichtlichen Grundlagen der deutschen Mystik", in *Deutsches Vierteljahrsschrift Literaturwiss. Geistesgesch.*, XII (1934), pp. 400–29.

[2] See *supra*, ch. III, pp. 303–4.

[3] We may cite here, once for all, a few anthologies of German mystical texts: F. Pfeiffer, *Deutsche Mystiker des 14. Jahrh.*, 2 vols, Leipzig, 1845–57 (Hermann of Fritzlar, Nicholas of Strasburg, David of Augsburg, Eckhart); J. Quint, *Deutsche Mystikertexte des Mittelalters*, I, Bonn, 1929 (Mechtilde of Magdeburg, Hadewijch, Eckhart); J. Quint, *Textbuch zur Mystik des deutschen Mittelalters* (*M. Eckhart, J. Tauler, H. Seuse*), Halle, 1952; A. Spamer, *Texte aus der deutschen Mystik des 14. und 15. Jahrh.*, Jena, 1912 (Eckhart's circle); P. Strauch, *Paradisus animae intelligentis*, Berlin, 1919 (sermons by Eckhart and his disciples); W. Muschg, *Mystische Texte aus dem Mittelalter*, Basle, 1943 (a rather varied selection); W. Stammler, *Gottsuchende Seelen*, Munich, 1948; S. M. Gieraths, O.P., *Reichtum des Lebens. Die deutsche Dominikanermystik des 14. Jahrh.*, Dusseldorf, 1956; J. A. Bizet, *Mystiques allemands du XIVe siècle. Eckhart, Suso, Tauler*, Paris, 1957 (a selection of texts in *Mittelhochdeutsch*, with an excellent introduction in French, bibliography, grammatical notes and glossary).

The principal translations into modern German are: W. Oehl, *Deutsche Mystikerbriefe des Mittelalters 1100–1550*, Munich, 1931; A. Rozumek, *Vom inwendigen Reichtum*, Leipzig, 1937; L. Schreyer, *Deutsche Mystik*, Berlin, 1925; by the same, *Die Mystik der Deutschen*, Hamburg, 1933; O. Karrer, *Textgeschichte der Mystik*, 3 vols, Munich, 1926–7; *Deutsche Mystiker*, 5 vols, Kempten–München, 1910–19; H. Kunisch, *Ein Textbuch aus der altdeutschen Mystik*, Hamburg, 1958.

For translations into French, see the collections cited below in connection with Eckhart and his disciplies; also, H. S. Denifle, O.P., *La vie spirituelle d'après les mystiques allemands du XIVe siècle*, Paris, 1903.

An excellent recent bibliography of medieval German spirituality appears in F. W. Wentzlaff-Eggebert, *Deutsche Mystik zwischen Mittelalter und Neuzeit*, Tübingen, 1947, pp. 272–339. The thesis of this book will be discussed further on.

time. Later, Mechtilde of Magdeburg (1207–82 or 1298) carried on their tradition. She was first a Béguine at Magdeburg about 1230, where she came under the influence of the Dominicans. The last years of her life (probably from 1270) were spent at the monastery of Helfta, where she was a contemporary of Gertrude the Great (†1302) and of Mechtilde of Hackeborn (†1295).[4] The first six chapters of the treatise in which her spiritual experience is condensed, *The Flowing Light of the Godhead*, were written between 1250 and 1265, under the guidance of her spiritual director, the Dominican Henry of Halle.[5] The seventh chapter is later and dates from Helfta. The original was written in Low German, but all that we now possess of it is a revision in High German, for which we are indebted to Henry of Nördlingen and the circle of the "Friends of God" at Basle (1343–5).[6] There is also a Latin translation, which seems to have been made at the Dominican convent at Halle about 1280,[7] but it appears to be less faithful to the original than the High German revision.[8]

Taking her inspiration from the *Brautmystik* and even from the literature of courtly love,[9] Mechtilde describes her experience of ecstasy and seeks to express the nature of the mystical union in love.[10] *The Flowing Light of the Godhead* is a dialogue between the soul and her betrothed, Christ. Presumably this is merely a literary device and not the transcription of words really exchanged between two speakers. In the following passage, which dates from the period when Mechtilde was a Béguine, the soul describes the summit of her ascent in love:

> Then the beloved goes in to the Lover, into the secret hiding-place of the sinless Godhead. . . . And there, the soul being fash-

[4] Gertrude the Great and Mechtilde of Hackeborn will be discussed in ch. VIII, pp. 449 *et seq.*

[5] A biographical note by R. Hünicken, "Studien über Heinrich von Halle", appeared in *Thüringisch-sächsische Zeitschr. Gesch. u. Kunst*, XXIII (1934–5), pp. 102–17.

[6] *Das fliessende Licht der Gottheit*, ed. G. Morel, Ratisbon, 1869, after the MS *Einsiedeln 277*. Extracts were published by J. Quint in *Deutsche Mystikertexte des Mittelalters*, I, pp. 1–20. There is an English translation by L. Menzies, *The Revelations of Mechthild of Magdeburg (1210–1297), or the Flowing Light of the Godhead*, London, 1953. There are a number of translations in modern German; e.g., W. Schleussner, Mainz, 1929.

[7] Ed. by the monks of Solesmes, *Revelationes Gertrudianae et Mechtildianae*, II, Paris, 1877, pp. 435 *et seq.* The order of the chapters is not the same as in the German text.

[8] Cf. H. Neumann, "Problemata mechtildiana", in *Zeitschr. deutsch. Altert. deutsch. Literatur*, LXXXII (1948–50), pp. 153–72.

[9] Cf. R. Kayser, "Minne und Mystik im Werke Mechtilds von Magdeburg", in *Germanic Review*, XIX (1944), pp. 3–15.

[10] The best recent works on the subject are those of J. Ancelet-Hustache, *M. de M., Etude de psychologie religieuse*, Paris, 1926; and H. Tillmann, *Studien zum Dialog bei M. von M.*, Marburg, 1933.

ioned in the very nature of God, no hindrance can come between it and God.

Then our Lord said—Stand, O Soul!
SOUL: What wilt thou, Lord?
THE LORD: Thy SELF must go!
SOUL: But, Lord, what shall happen to me then?
THE LORD: Thou art by nature already mine!
    Nothing can come between me and thee!
    There is no angel so sublime
    As to be granted for one hour
    What is given thee for ever.
    Therefore must thou put from thee
    Fear and shame and all outward things.
    Only of that of which thou art sensible by nature
    Shalt thou wish to be sensible in eternity.
    That shall be thy noble longing,
    Thine endless desire,
    And that in my infinite mercy
    I will evermore fulfil.
SOUL: Lord! now am I a naked soul
    And thou a God most glorious!
    Our twofold intercourse is love eternal
    Which can never die.
    Now comes a blessed stillness
    Welcome to both. He gives himself to her
    And she to him.
    What shall now befall her, the soul knows:
    Therefore am I comforted.

    Where two lovers come secretly together
    They must often part, without parting.[11]

Here Mechtilde is using the language of love with a realism that does not hesitate to evoke the image of carnal union.[12] Two sentences in this passage, however, are expressed with less imagery. One is that in which the Lord says to the soul, "Thou art by nature already mine; nothing can come between me and thee"; the other, that in which he lays down the condition demanded for such a conformity, that is, total setting aside of all "fear and shame and all outward things". These two themes were soon to become, with Meister Eckhart, characteristic of the speculative mysticism of the Rhineland. Thus the *Wesenmystik*, of which there is already a

[11] *The Flowing Light of the Godhead*, L. Menzies, pp. 24–5.

[12] On Mechtilde's mystical vocabulary, see G. Lüers, *Die Sprache der deutschen Mystik des Mittelalters im Werke der M. von M.*, Munich, 1926. On the verbal influence of *The Flowing Light of the Godhead*, see H. Neumann, "'Der Minne Spiegel' und M. von M.", in *Zeitschr. deutsch. Philologie* LXXIII (1954), pp. 217–26; the article deals with a mystical poem of the first half of the fourteenth century.

glimpse in Hadewijch, is found again in Mechtilde. It may be asked whether the latter conceived the end of union as an assimilation of the soul to God, such that it could be called a true fusion of their natures. On this point the German text is almost untranslatable; it runs: *"Ir sint so sere genaturt in mich, das zwischent uch und mir nihtes nit mag sin."* To render this exactly, it would be necessary to say, "You are so en-natured in me that nothing may remain between you and me." This does not necessarily imply a fusion of the pantheistic type[13]; the idea is merely that every barrier between God and the soul disappears in mystical union. But Eckhart's imprudent use of such expressions was to lay him open to censure.

It was, then, among the Béguines of the thirteenth century, in the Low Countries with Hadewijch, and in Germany with Mechtilde, that the first evidence of the *Wesenmystik* is found; it was to develop in the next century. In the thirteenth century, however, the preponderance still lay with the "nuptial" vocabulary of mystical union. Many examples might be cited, but they would contribute little that is new. In this connection, an interesting test has been used by certain philologists. While studying the influence of this "nuptial" tendency on the Germanic vocabulary, they have succeeded in establishing a line of descent which goes from Mechtilde to a numerous progeny of illustrious disciples. Among these is Henry Suso, dependent upon Eckhart though he may be. The language they use for love, which is that of the *Brautmystik* itself, reveals a tongue that is still young, still taking shape, and trying (sometimes rather clumsily) to describe the inner world. The other tendency, that of speculative mysticism, was to have its first truly typical expression in Eckhart. Its vocabulary, too, would be gradually perfected in a similar way, and this process can again be traced by a succession of examples. There are, of course, points of contact between the two streams.[14]

There is a great variety of this mystical literature, regardless of which tendency it belonged to. Autobiographies,[15] biographies, letters, sermons, dialogues, meditations, prayers and mystical or speculative treatises were all apparently on the same themes. Well before Eckhart's time, there was already a considerable number of

[13] This was pointed out, and explained at length, by J. Ancelet-Hustache, *op. cit.*

[14] Cf. K. Berger, *Die Ausdrücke der Unio mystica im Mittelhochdeutschen*, Berlin, 1935. For an interpretation of the speculative vocabulary, see the posthumous work of H. S. Denifle, O.P., *Die deutschen Mystiker des 14. Jahrh. Beitrag zur Deutung ihrer Lehre*, Fribourg (Switzerland), 1951.

[15] For a selection of writings of this nature, from St Hildegarde to Nicholas of Cusa, see K. Bihlmeyer, "Die Selbstbiographie in der deutschen Mystik des Mittlelalters", in *Theol. Quartalschr.*, CXIV (1933), pp. 504–44.

them.[16] To these must be added another class of writings, little known and often unpublished even today: that of manuals for spiritual directors, and guidebooks for persons of different categories, laymen, priests, monks or nuns. These were to flourish especially at the end of the Middle Ages, but many examples are found as early as the thirteeth century.[17] This literature, taken as a whole, shows a preference for developing certain themes, such as the mirage of learning, the danger of ecclesiastical legalism, true knowledge and true wisdom, the various states of life, and the duties of pastors.[18]

The Dominican Order had received from its founder the mission of preaching and teaching. It was therefore able to undertake the spiritual direction of the fervent among the faithful.[19] In the Germanic countries, the Preachers were the directors of Béguines at least as much as of monastic communities and Dominican nuns. Mechtilde of Magdeburg was the spiritual daughter of the Dominican Henry of Halle, and hers was not an isolated case. But the Béguines and Beghards were sometimes suspect as to their orthodoxy and their moral life. In connection with them, much has been said of a sect that claimed to be that "of the Free Spirit", or *de novo spiritu*. According to a list of 97 heretical propositions, drawn up about 1270 and attributed to Albert the Great, the sect in question would appear to have recruited followers in Germany in the thirteenth and fourteenth centuries; its place of origin would seem to be Ries, in Swabia.[20] The documents that we possess do not justify calling it a separate group, and the origin of the movement, if one can use the word, remains obscure. It may have been subject to various influences: a kind of pantheistic monism, partly mystical in origin and partly philosophical; perhaps certain Catharist doctrines; the distress felt by the devout confronted by the unworthiness of many members of the clergy; and social emancipation.[21] The symptoms, however, are those of a state of mind which was not peculiar

[16] Cf. H. Wilms, O.P., "La mistica alemana", in *Ciencia tomista*, L (1934), pp. 166–95; K. Bihlmeyer, "Der Sog. St Georgener Prediger und anderes", in *Theol. Quartalschr.*, CXXIII (1942), pp. 79–97.

[17] Among the many examples that might be cited here, there may be selected for mention a short rule, rather moralistic in tone, for the Brigittines of Danzig in the thirteenth century, recently edited by T. Ahldén, *Nonnenspiegel und Mönchsvorschriften*, Göteborg, 1952.

[18] Cf. F. W. Oediger, *Über die Bildung der Geistlichen im späten Mittelalter*, Leyden, 1953; there is an excellent bibliography of printed works and unpublished manuscripts on pp. 138–48.

[19] See ch. IV, pp. 323–6.

[20] Proposition 88; cf. Preger, *Gesch. der deutschen Mystik im Mittelalter*, I, Leipzig, 1881, p. 469.

[21] Cf. W. Zippel, *Die Mystiker und die deutsche Gesellschaft des 13. und 14. Jahrhunderts*, Düren, 1935.

to the spiritual groups of the period, who were simply suffering from the general situation. So true was this that the Council of Vienne condemns under the name of Béguines and Beghards all the suspect groups of the time in Germany.[22] Moreover, they existed not only in those countries; documents show that they were also found in Umbria at the beginning of the fourteenth century[23]; and the condemnation, as so often happens, did not stop the excesses: there were Brethren and Sisters of the Free Spirit to be found in the middle of the fifteenth century.

2. *Meister Eckhart*

In this troubled atmosphere there arose the leader of "German speculative mysticism", the Dominican Meister Eckhart. Born about 1260 of a noble family at Hochheim near Gotha in Thuringia, he entered the Friars Preachers at Erfurt between 1275 and 1280. At the end of his noviciate and his studies, he was sent to Cologne, to the *studium generale* of the Teutonic province of the Order. Nothing precise is known of him until he was elected prior of Erfurt and at the same time named vicar of the province of Thuringia. This must have taken place before 1298, because a general chapter held in that year forbade the holding of the two offices together. Eckhart had, therefore, the confidence of his brethren and his superiors; he was always to remain a prominent member of the Order. From this period of his youth dates his commentary on the *Pater*, based on St Thomas,[24] as well as some "Spiritual Talks" (*Reden der Unterscheidung*) by which he sought to maintain the fervour of his community during meals.[25] Some rash expressions already appear in these, but no one seems to have taken alarm at them. His very brief *Collatio in libros Sententiarum* also dates from between 1297 and 1300.[26]

[22] For the history of the sects of the Free Spirit, see A. Mens, O.M.Cap., *Oorsprung en betekenis van de nederlandse Begijnen en Begardenbewegung*, Antwerp, 1947, pp. 198–206 and *passim*.

[23] Cf. L. Oliger, O.F.M., *De secta Spiritus Libertatis in Umbria saeculo XIV*, Rome, 1943.

[24] The publication of Eckhart's Latin works (*Opera latina*, cited henceforth as OL) has begun under the auspices of the Dominicans of Santa Sabina in Rome. They include the *Super oratione dominica*, OL, vol. I, ed. R. Klibansky, Leipzig, 1934. The monumental critical edition known as the "Stuttgart edition" (1936 and following years), which was still unfinished in 1960, includes *Deutsche Werke* (cited as DW) and *Lateinische Werke* (LW). The latter includes the *Super oratione Dominica*, vol. V.

[25] Ed. E. Diederichs, Bonn, 1913; to be published shortly in DW, vol. V. J. A. Bizet, in *Mystiques allemands*, also gives a critical edition of these discourses, as well as of the German sermons *Intravit Jesus in quoddam castellum* and *Quasi vas auri solidum*, pp. 123–86.

[26] LW, vol. V.

About 1300, Eckhart was sent to Paris to complete his studies, and in 1302 the title of *magister* was conferred on him directly by Pope Boniface VIII. At that time, Philip the Fair wished to appeal to the general council against the pope, and before the end of June 1303 all foreign religious who had not signed the appeal left or were expelled from France. Eckhart may have been among their number. At the period of this first sojourn in Paris, the primacy of the intellect or the will was the object of lively discussion in the schools. Eckhart upheld the primacy of the intellect, probably during the academic year 1302–3, against the Franciscan Gonzalvo of Balboa. Reflections of the controversy can be seen in the first three *Quaestiones parisienses.*[27] Eckhart's intellectualism is seen in them in all its intransigence. He lays it down as a principle not only that being and intellection are equivalent in God, but even that *intelligere* has the primacy over *esse*: "intellection is higher than being". This attitude inevitably influenced his purely spiritual teaching.

The chapter of the new province of Saxony, which had been separated from that of Teutonia, chose Eckhart for its provincial in 1304. He continued in this office until 1311, and in addition a chapter at Strasburg in 1307 named him vicar general of the province of Bohemia. Obviously his orthodoxy was not under suspicion. In 1311 the general chapter of Naples relieved him of the office of provincial and sent him to Paris, to the convent of St James, *ad legendum*, that is, to comment either on the *Sentences* of Peter Lombard or, more probably, on Scripture. He remained there until 1314 and perfected his Thomistic outlook; partly at the Order's wish, since the intellectual positions of the Dominicans were threatened by the disciples of Duns Scotus, and also at the wish of the master-general, Aymeric of Piacenza. The last two *Quaestiones parisienses* date from this period.[28] Eckhart's spiritual teaching, properly speaking, began with the *Liber benedictus,* which really includes two little treatises: the *Book of Divine Consolation* and *The Noble Man.*[29]

This second sojourn at Paris must have been fairly short, since Eckhart was at Strasburg again in 1314 as Master and professor of

[27] Those in the manuscript *Avignon Ville 1071.* Ed. A. Dondaine, OL, vol. XIII; and B. Geyer, LW, vol. V, and in a separate volume, Bonn, 1931. The *Sermo in die b. Augustini Parisius habitus* (ed. B. Geyer, *ibid.*) probably dates from this period.

[28] Those in the manuscript *Vatican lat. 1086.* Ed. A. Dondaine, *op. cit.*, and B. Geyer, *op. cit.*

[29] *Daz Buoch der goetlichen Troestunge* and *Von dem edeln Menschen*; ed. DW, vol. V, and J. Quint, Berlin, 1952. The *Liber benedictus* may be a little earlier, 1308–11; cf. G. Théry, O.P., in *Mélanges de Ghellinck*, II, pp. 905–35; and H. Roos, S.J., "Zur Abfassungheit von M. Es. Trostbuch", in *Orbis litterarum*, IX (1954), pp. 45–9.

theology, *Magister et professor sanctae theologiae.* Probably he directed the Dominican *studium* in that city. He devoted a considerable part of his time to the spiritual direction and supervision of a number of houses of Dominican nuns. He was still at Strasburg in 1322, when he was ordered to go to Cologne, it is thought to direct the *studium* there. He remained there until 1327. During this final period of his life, which was devoted to theological teaching and to spiritual direction, there appeared his scriptural commentaries,[30] probably most of his sermons (generally written down in summary form, or else taken down fragmentarily by his listeners),[31] and the minor spiritual works,[32] particularly the one treating of the soul's self-stripping, *Von Abegescheidenheit.*[33]

At the end of his life, Eckhart planned a synthesis of all his writings, the *Opus tripartitum.* According to his "general prologue",[34] this was to comprise three parts. The first a "book of propositions", the *Opus propositionum,* of which only the prologue is known. In it the author develops, perhaps by way of a model, the proposition *Esse deus est.* This was to be followed by more than a thousand others, divided into fourteen treatises. The second part was to be a "book of questions", the *Opus quaestionum,* which was to follow the plan of St Thomas's *Summa Theologica* and form a sequence of expositions on disputed questions. Finally the third part was to be called the "book of expositions", *Opus expositionum*; in this part, Eckhart's commentaries on Scripture and his sermons were to be brought together and completed.[35]

30 A faulty edition of the commentaries on Wisdom was published by G. Théry, O.P., in *Arch. hist. doctr. litt. moyen âge*, III (1928), pp. 321–443; IV (1929), pp. 233–394. For those on Genesis, Exodus, Ecclesiasticus (24. 23–31), Wisdom, and St John, see LW, vols I–III.

31 For the Latin sermons, see LW, vol. IV; for the German ones, DW, vols. I–IV. Of about 140 German sermons, only the first 24 have been published (vol. I). Until the complete edition appears, the old edition by F. Pfeiffer may be used: *Meister Eckhart*, 4th ed., Göttingen, 1924. Of the sermons in the latter edition, the following appear to be authentic: 6, 8, 10–14, 21, 25, 29, 31, 32, 40, 43, 45, 48, 55, 56, 65, 66, 82–4, 87, 90 and 96. A few others have been published in less accessible works.

32 Ed. of the *Traktate* in DW, vol. V.

33 Critical edition by E. Schäfer, Bonn, 1956.

34 LW, vol. I; and H. Bascour, O.S.B., O.L., vol. II.

35 There are many translations of Eckhart's works into modern German. Among the best may be mentioned those of the LW and DW; then that of J. Quint, *Meister Eckhart. Deutsche Predigten und Traktate*, Munich, 1955. There are numerous anthologies (see note 3); in addition, see E. K. Pohl, *M. E. Ausgewählte Predigten und Traktate. Von der Geburt der Seele*, Gütersloh, 1959.

In French, see the selection of texts translated by J. Molitor and F. Aubier, *Maître Eckhart. Traités et sermons* (introduction by M. de Gandillac), Paris, 1942; P. Petit, *Œuvres de Maître Eckhart*, Paris, 1942; A. Mayrisch Saint-Hubert, *Telle était Sœur Katrei . . .*, Paris, 1954; J. Ancelet-Hustache, *Maître Eckhart et la mystique rhénane*, Paris, 1956.

In English, R. B. Blackney, *M.E. A Modern Translation*, New York, 1957;

The German sermons were taken down, not very well, by the religious who listened to them: Dominican, Benedictine, and Cistercian nuns, Béguines, and others. Eckhart's style of oratory seems, in any case, to have been rather volcanic. And it must not be forgotten that he was one of the first to express the deepest truths of the spiritual life in the vernacular: hence certain imperfections in his language. It is not surprising, therefore, that some suspicion as to his orthodoxy arose during his time in Cologne. In addition, the sects of the Free Spirit and the heterodox Béguines and Beghards were creating an unfavourable atmosphere round him and contributing to increase the confusion. Finally, matters were envenomed by the rivalries between Friars Preachers and Friars Minor, between seculars and regulars, and between the partisans and enemies of the Avignon pope, John XXII.

The result was the notorious trial of Eckhart in 1326 at the instigation of the archbishop of Cologne, Henry of Virneburg. A syllabus of 49 articles was drawn up by two inquisitors named by him: Master Reynier, a canon of Cologne and doctor of theology, and Pierre de Estate, a Friar Minor and former prior of Cologne. Of these articles, fifteen came from Eckhart's *Liber benedictus*, six from an Apology now lost, sixteen from his sermons, and the others from his scriptural commentaries. On 26 September, Eckhart replied energetically to these accusations. He protested his fidelity to the Church, challenged the competence of his inquisitors—for he was himself exempt—and defended himself by explaining the true meaning of the impugned propositions. The minutes of this session, or *Rechtfertigungsschrift*, have been preserved,[36] and it is a document of the greatest importance. In it Eckhart's orthodox intention is manifest, and equally clear is the bad faith, the ill-will and deliberate misunderstanding of his adversaries. They then submitted to him 59 new propositions, taken from his sermons alone. Eckhart strove to demonstrate the correct sense which these bore in his thought. Some propositions from each of these groups later ap-

---

J. M. Clark and J. V. Skinner, *M.E. Selected Treatises and Sermons*, London, 1958.

Innumerable works on Eckhart have appeared in Germany in the last thirty years. For a bibliography, see F. W. Wentzlaff-Eggebert, *op. cit.*, pp. 301–9. There are surveys by K. Heussi, *Eckhart-Studien*, Berlin, 1953, pp. 5–28; G. Théry, O.P., in *La Vie spirit., Suppl.*, II (1948–9), pp. 304–37; J. Ancelet-Hustache, *M.E. et la mystique rhénane*, Paris, 1956; J. M. Clark, *M.E.*, London, 1957; and in several works of reference, notably the *Dict. de spirit.* (R. L. Oechslin) and the *Dict. d'hist. géogr. eccl.* (F. Vandenbroucke). The principal works will be cited in the following pages.

[36] In the manuscript *Soest Stadsbibl. 33 b*; ed. A. Daniels, in *Beitr. Gesch. Philos. Mittelalters*, XXIII, 5. Münster, 1923; and G. Théry, O.P., in *Arch. hist. doctr. litt. moyen âge*, I (1926–7), pp. 129–68. It is to be published in LW, vol. V, together with the other documents of the trial.

peared in the list condemned by John XXII. Subsequently the trial became more complicated.[37] Finally, in January 1327, Eckhart appealed to the Holy See, submitting in advance to its decision. John XXII took account of this humility in the bull of condemnation and the propositions were condemned only according to the plain sense of the words.[38] In the same year, 1327, in the course of a journey to Avignon which he undertook in his own defence, Eckhart died, probably in that city itself, without having seen the end of this wretched business. A memorandum was drawn up for the theologians at Avignon charged with the enquiry.[39] In it are to be found, practically word for word, the 28 propositions which were finally condemned on 27 March 1329.[40] But in this last list the terms of the memorandum are slightly softened. Credence is given to Eckhart's denial that he had taught the last two of the 28 offending articles. Only the first fifteen and the last two were censured as "containing errors or tainted with heresy". The others could "with considerable explanation, be understood in a Catholic sense".

What, then, was this dangerous teaching? In theology, Eckhart certainly owes much to St Thomas, but there were other influences at work. That of Maimonides, in his *Guide for the Perplexed*, with its central idea concerning the divine simplicity. It is more difficult to determine precisely how much Eckhart borrowed from Neo-Platonism, which he knew both through Albert the Great, founder of the *studium* of Cologne, and probably also the Pseudo-Dionysius.[41] *A fortiori* the influence of Oriental mysticism—of Shankara for example—can be confidently rejected. Such connections are too tenuous if one does not take dogmatic presuppositions into account.[42] In spiritual matters, Eckhart had read and reflected on Bernard of Clairvaux.[43] There are such points of resemblance between his works and many contemporary sermons, meditations, and spiritual

[37] The known documents have been edited by M. H. Laurent, O.P., "Autour du procès de Maître Eckhart. Les documents des Archives Vaticanes", in *Div. Thom.* (*Piac.*), XXXIX (1936), pp. 331–48, 430–47.

[38] *Ibid.*, p. 444.

[39] Contained in the manuscript *Vatic. lat. 3899*; ed. F. Pelster, S.J., "Ein Gutachten aus dem Eckhart-Prozess in Avignon", in *Aus der Geisteswelt des Mittelalters*, in *Beitr. Gesch. Philos. Theol. Mittelalters*, Suppl. III, 2, Münster, 1935, pp. 1099–124.

[40] Laurent, *op. cit.*, pp. 435–44; Denz., No. 501–29. The original is contained in the manuscript *Vatican. Arch. A.A. arm. I–XVIII, n. 3226.* For an account of the trial, see J. Koch, "Kritische Studien zum Leben M.E.", in *Arch. Fratrum Praedic.*, XXIX (1959), pp. 5–51; XXX (1960), pp. 5–52.

[41] See *supra*, ch. IV, pp. 329–30.

[42] Cf. R. Otto, *Mystique d'Orient et mystique d'Occident* (French translation), Paris, 1951.

[43] Cf. E. Wechssler, "M.E. und B. von Cl.", in *Euphorion*, XXX (1929), pp. 40–93.

opuscula originating in the same German milieu, that one begins to doubt his originality.

It was in the field of *Wesenmystik* that he showed the extent of his powers. *The Mirror of Simple Souls* by Marguerite Porete (†1310) had already taught that the soul must recover the image of the Trinity by a poverty, a detachment, and a nakedness that will make it conscious of its nothingness.[44] The first Hadewijch and Mechtilde of Magdeburg had caught sight of this idea, but had not developed it. Thus Eckhart, who was an eclectic, was able to develop ideas that were in the air and were already familiar to the spiritual circles of his time.[45] He allowed himself to be carried away, as he preached on nakedness and the birth of the Word in the soul, into extreme and paradoxical expressions, whose exact tenor, moreover, is not absolutely certain from the texts at our disposal. Because Eckhart was unable to complete the *Opus tripartitum*, he never gave final form to his teaching. It would be an exaggeration to see him simply as a spiritual writer and to reduce all his teaching, even the theological, to a speculative exposition of his own spiritual life and that of the persons he directed. His spirituality does indeed depend upon a theology, but the latter is not blindly at its service.

His theological teaching is definitely in conformity with the Thomist tradition in that it proceeds from a very marked intellectualism. The first of the *Quaestiones parisienses* asked whether, in God, being and intellection are the same thing, and the reply is in the affirmative.[46] From this is derived the intellectual perspective in which Eckhart saw creation and the return of creatures to God, they having been contained in the Word from all eternity. There is no other being except God: *esse est Deus*.[47] In relation to his being, the creature in itself is nothingness; *Preter esse et sine esse omnia sunt nichil, etiam facta*. But the being of the creature is not one with the being of God.[48] This is the basis of the fundamental attitude which the soul must take in its return to God. Its "self-stripping" takes on an aspect that goes further than psychological and ethical needs. It becomes an ontological necessity for a being, only nothingness in itself, which desires to participate in that being which alone is, and to let the Father "beget" the Word in it.

[44] See *supra*, ch. v, pp. 356–7.

[45] Cf. R. L. Oechslin, O.P., "Eckhart et la mystique trinitaire", in *Lumière et vie*, No. 30 (1956), pp. 99–120.

[46] Cf. P. Kelley, O.S.B., "M.E.'s Doctrine of the Divine Subjectivity", in *Downside Rev.*, LXXVI (1958), pp. 65–103.

[47] The only *propositio* in the *Opus propositionum*; LW, vol. I, pp. 41 *et seq.*

[48] Cf. *Prologus in Op. proposit.*, LW, vol. I, pp. 45–6; and *Expositio libri Genesis*, in cap. I, v. 6, LW, vol. I, p. 62.

Eckhart therefore preaches the radical necessity, in order to arrive at purely spiritual union and at contemplation, of leaving aside all created things (*Abegescheidenheit*).[49] He goes beyond the evangelical horizon of sin, redemption and grace, which was that of current theology, and puts himself on the plane of the essential unity of the Godhead and the soul.[50]

In his dialectical development of this theme lies the greatest difference between him and Bernard of Clairvaux, and the other representatives of the *Brautmystik*. His dialectic presupposes the primacy of the *intellectus*; from the time of his first teaching in Paris, Eckhart regarded this as a metaphysical axiom. From it he drew the conclusion that the highest part of the soul, that in which the contact with God takes place, is intellectual in its essence. This *Kraft*, this *virtus*, is a spark, *Seelenfünklein* or *vünkelin*,[51] *scintilla animae*, as earlier authors had said.[52] This "ground of the soul", *Grund der Seele*,[53] is "something", *etwaz*, both uncreated and uncreatable.[54] It is that which, in man, is equal to God. It is the seat of the divine life, and also of the contemplative life properly so called, to which the spirit or *vernünftichkeit* attains.[55] In this uncreated *etwaz* of the soul, the "birth" of the Word and the return to the likeness of God take place, in a Plotinian journey. This birth, which Eckhart describes chiefly in his commentary on St John, must be preceded by the liberation of the soul from sin. It transcends the moral, ascetic and sacramental life, and goes beyond the stage of active prayer.[56] It creates the "noble man",[57] and it is consummated in "identity". Henceforth, the soul is one with the Godhead, with that which is unknowable in God, that which con-

[49] See the treatise *Von Abegescheidenheit*, ed. E. Schäfer; or the German sermon *Beati pauperes spiritu*, ed. Pfeiffer, No. 87; French translation by P. Petit, *op. cit.*, pp. 134–9.

[50] R. Frick, "Meister Eckharts Predigt von der geistlichen Armut", in *Jahrb. theolog. Schule Bethel*, VIII (1937), pp. 195–210; P. Kelley, O.S.B., "Poverty and the Rhineland Mystics", in *Downside Rev.*, LXXIV (1956), pp. 88–96.

[51] Cf. H. Hof, *Scintilla animae . . . in M.E. Philosophie*, Lund, 1952; W. Frei, "Was ist das Seelenfünklein beim M.E.?" in *Theol. Zeitschr.*, XIV (1958), pp. 89–100; H. Wilms, O.P., "Das Seelenfünklein in der deutschen Mystik", in *Zeitschr. Asz. Myst.*, XII (1937), pp. 157–66.

[52] Cf. H. Wilms, O.P., "De scintilla animae", in *Angelicum*, XIV (1937), pp. 194–211.

[53] Cf. H. Kunisch, *Das Wort "Grund" in der Sprache der deutschen Mystik des 14. und 15. Jahrh.*, Osnabrück, 1929; B. Schmoldt, *Die deutsche Begriffssprache M. Eckharts*, Heidelberg, 1954; T. Schneider, *Der intellektuelle Wortschatz M. Eckharts*, Berlin, 1935.

[54] Cf. Sermon 12; DW, vol. I, pp. 197–8.

[55] Cf. Sermon 1; DW, vol. I, pp. 48–9.

[56] Cf. H. Piesch, *Eckharts Ethik*, Lucerne, 1935, ch. VI.

[57] Cf. E. Benz, "Über den Adel in der deutschen Mystik", in *Deutsch. Vierteljahrschr. Literatur Wiss. Geistesgesch.*, XIV (1936), pp. 505–35. On the birth of the Word in the soul, see K. G. Kertz, S.J., "Meister Eckhart's Teaching on the Birth of the Divine Word in the Soul", in *Traditio*, XV (1959), pp. 327–64.

stitutes his own being, above and beyond the God of whom we shape an image which we can comprehend, giving him ordinary and intelligible attributes.[58] That is true contemplation. Although it is intellectual in type, it unites vision and love in a single act, by which man finds "all beatitude, from God alone, by God alone, and in God alone".[59]

This teaching implies a doctrine, worked out by Eckhart, in which there can be found certain essential themes of Thomism, mingled with Neo-Platonic ideas. But his teaching cannot be reduced to a mere theological syncretism. It is also, and indeed far more, the reflection of his spiritual experience and that of his listeners. It is significant that his boldest themes—the transcendence of God, and total detachment in order to recover unity and the image of God—are to be found in his very earliest writings, for example, in the *Reden der Unterscheidung*. At that period, that is before 1300, no one saw anything in them to cause anxiety. Moreover, certain expressions used by Eckhart were fairly common among medieval mystics, although few authors before him had carried out to the full, as he did, the theme of the "essential" way. The *Rechtfertigungsschrift* of 1326 upholds his presentation of Catholic dogma, and his appeal to the Apostolic See ran foul, in the last resort, not of John XXII but of various political influences. Among these can be discerned, with the Franciscans, the partisans of Ludwig of Bavaria, who were hostile to the Avignon pope (whereas the Dominicans as a whole were faithful to him). Perhaps, too, his condemnation was the revenge of certain Franciscans who could not endure the canonization of the Dominican St Thomas.

The propositions noted by the preparatory commission concerned the eternity of the world (propositions 1–3), the distinction between the divine Persons (23–4), the transformation of the just man into the divine essence as the bread is transformed into the body of Christ (10, 13), the nothingness of creatures (26), the glory or praise of God shown forth even in sin (4–6), the uselessness of exterior acts (16–19) (in which the Protestants have seen an anticipation of Luther's doctrine), sin which does not impede the will of God (14–15), the importance of fraternal charity (25), and the necessity of absolute detachment (8–9). It can be seen that these theses could be interpreted in an orthodox sense, as John XXII himself declared.

As for the transformation of man into God (10–13 and 20–22)—

[58] Cf. G. Stephenson, *Gottheit und Gott in der spekulativen Mystik M. Eckharts*, Bonn, 1954.

[59] *Von dem edeln Menschen*; D W, vol. V, p. 117.

an essential point in Eckhart's mysticism—he himself explained his position on this point before his judges at Cologne:

> It is false to say that we are transformed and changed into God. Indeed, a holy and virtuous man does not become Christ himself nor the only Son, and other men are not saved by him; he is not the likeness of God, the only begotten Son of God, but he is in the likeness of God, a member and heir of the true and perfect only Son. We are his co-heirs, as it is written, and that is what the comparison (I have) used means. In the same way, indeed, as many hosts on different altars are changed into the same true and only Body of Christ, conceived and born of the Virgin, which suffered under Pontius Pilate, though the species of the bread remains; so is it with our soul by the grace of adoption: and we are united to the true son of God, we are made members of the one head of the Church, Christ. . . . To the extent that a man possesses grace and is a son of God, he has power over God, and over his works, because he wills nothing but what God wills and does.[60]

It may be asked whether Meister Eckhart was really a forerunner of the Reformation. Certain of the propositions condemned by John XXII (16–19) are akin to theses cherished by the Reformers of the sixteenth century, on the uselessness of exterior works: "God loves souls, not exterior works." It seems difficult, however, to show a direct influence. The Reformers do not appear to have read Eckhart or to have taken their inspiration from him. A recent historian of the sixteenth century has explicitly recognized this in one particular case.[61] Points of contact can doubtless be found between Eckhart's teaching and that of Luther,[62] but even supposing these points of contact to be really characteristic of the men in question, they would not for all that prove a direct line of descent. The coincidence is rather to be attributed to the fact that these ideas were commonly accepted in the Germanic world at the end of the Middle Ages.

There have been efforts to show Eckhart's influence on German thought under a different aspect. A contemporary historian[63] has found, in German mysticism from the Middle Ages up to our own time, a basic continuity of two themes which are opposed but complementary: speculation and union. The theme of "union" was pre-

[60] Ed. Daniels, *op. cit.*, p. 15; Théry, *op. cit.*, p. 199; French translation by J. Ancelet-Hustache, *op. cit.*, p. 136.

[61] W. Zeller, "M. Eckhart bei Valentin Weigel (†1588). Eine Untersuchung zur Frage der Bedeutung Meister Eckharts für die mystische Renaissance des 16. Jahrh.", in *Zeitschr. Kirchengesch.*, LVII (1938), pp. 309–55.

[62] For a comparison of their notions of God, see H. Bornkamm, *Eckhart und Luther*, Stuttgart, 1936.

[63] F. W. Wentzlaff-Eggebert, *op. cit.*

ponderant in the *Brautmystik* of Hildegarde of Bingen, Mechtilde of Magdeburg, and the various conventual milieux of the fourteenth and fifteenth centuries. That of "speculation" on the other hand, which seems to be that of the *Wesenmystik*, characterized the milieux of the Rhineland Dominicans of the fourteenth century, the Friends of God, and Ruysbroeck. At the end of the century, pure speculation was, according to this view, distorted by the *Devotio moderna.*

This last point is certainly true; in fact, that particular spiritual movement appears, as will be seen, in the light of a distinctly antispeculative reaction. But according to the thesis under examination, "speculation" persisted in German spirituality in spite of the Reformation, down to Fichte and Novalis, while the pietism-by-anticipation of the *Devotio moderna* developed into the Protestant pietism of modern times. This conception of spiritual history is true for the Middle Ages, but beyond that period it requires some qualification. It attaches too little importance to the dogmatic positions of the Reformers, who ended by breaking with Catholic tradition on many points. If one overlooks that break, it is possible to trace, if one likes, two streams in German spirituality, one speculative and the other pietistic. Again on the same presupposition, it is legitimate to consider Eckhart as the "father of German speculation", as was done in the last century by a work[64] whose thesis was again taken up by several historians at the time of National Socialism. Such theories should, though, be viewed with caution, because they fail to take account of the breach created by the Reformation.[65] This is the basic objection to them, but there are others, several of which have already been expressed here. They may be summed up briefly: Eckhart's lack of originality and his eclecticism; the ecclesiastical world in which he lived, which was far from being a purely German one; and finally his indisputable fidelity to the Church and to the Christian faith.

3. *John Tauler*

Little is known about the life of this Dominican from Strasburg. Born about 1300 of a well-to-do family, he entered the Friars Preachers in his native city at the age of about eighteen. There he knew Eckhart for a few years, and he may still have been his disciple at the time of the master's last sojourn at Cologne. Like Eckhart, Tauler was a renowned preacher and spiritual director, especially in the convents of Dominican nuns in the region of the

[64] J. Bach, *Der Vater der deutschen Spekulation*, Vienna, 1864.
[65] Cf. K. Heussi, *op. cit.*

Rhineland. Unlike his master, however, he was not *ex professo* a theologian, although his doctrine was solid. He died at Strasburg in 1361, without having published anything. His sermons, like those of Eckhart, were taken down by his listeners, with greater or lesser fidelity.[66] His letters of direction have not been preserved.

Tauler's doctrine is akin to that of his master. The *Vernunft* becomes the *Gemüt*, but this word is often untranslatable; "basic will" has been suggested.[67] The *Grund* of the soul has almost as important a role in his religious psychology as in Eckhart's, but he gives it a more local sense, so to speak; it is the place where the meeting takes place between the naked soul and God. There is the same doctrine of the Father's begetting of the Word in the *Gemüt* of the soul; of the soul's divinization by "the Gemüt which knows itself to be God in God, while being nevertheless created"[68]; the same doctrine of the necessity of self-stripping in order to attain to this divinization and finally to contemplation. But Tauler is more prudent than Eckhart in his assertions. He very rarely cites his master, probably because of the latter's condemnation.[69] In any case, he is more of a poet; he likes familiar images, drawn from daily life, and theological subtleties arouse his distrust. He speaks severely of those who merely study Scripture without living by it.[70] While he is reserved as to the possibility of complete abandonment, which "never succeeds, here below, except for a very brief time", he nevertheless emphasizes what has been called the "technique of detachment".[71] Man, as St Paul says, is flesh, soul and spirit—a tripartite division which explains the threefold self-stripping of the spiritual ascent. The "exterior man" must be purified by a life of virtue; the "rational man", by the training of his intelligence, his intentions, and his works. After these trials, the "interior man" too will be

[66] Critical edition by F. Vetter, *Die Predigten Taulers*, Berlin, 1910. Translation by Surius, ed. Cologne, 1548, etc. French translation by E. Hugueney, G. Théry and A. L. Corin, 3 vols, Paris, 1927–31. Translations into modern German by W. Lehmann, W. Oehl and others. In English, see S. Winkworth, *The History and Life of the Revd Dr John Tauler of Strasbourg*, London, 1857; *Signposts to Perfection, a Selection of the Sermons of John Tauler*, trans. by E. Strakosch, London, 1958.

[67] Hugueny, Théry and Corin, *op. cit.* See P. Wyser, O.P. "Der Seelengrund in Taulers Predigten", in *Lebendiges Mittelalter*, Festgabe W. Stammler, Fribourg (Switzerland), 1958, pp. 204–311.

[68] Sermon 64, ed. Vetter, *op. cit.*

[69] Cf. K. Müller, "Ein Zitat aus M. Eckhart bei T.", in *Zeitschr. deutsch. Altertum deutsch. Liter.*, LXXII (1935), pp. 94–6.

[70] Second Sermon for the Ascension, 19, 3; trans. by Hugueny, Théry and Corin, *op. cit.*, I, pp. 339–40.

[71] M. de Gandillac, "Tradition et développement de la mystique rhénane. Eckhart, Tauler, Suse", in *Mél. Sc. Relig.*, III (1946), pp. 69–72; cf. B. Lavaud, "Les épreuves mystiques selon J.T.", in *Rev. Thom.*, LXV (1939), pp. 309–29; by the same, "L'angoisse spirituelle selon J. T.", in *Études carmélitaines*, XXIII, 2 (1938), pp. 82–91.

purified, because God will dwell in him, and he will be instantly enlightened in contemplation and set afire with love.[72] Indeed, at this summit where man is deified, love is superior to knowledge.[73]

Unlike Eckhart and Suso, Tauler connects the ascent of the soul with the gifts of the Holy Spirit.[74] The highest of these, those of understanding and wisdom, lead men to contemplation:

> These two gifts truly lead man straight to the Ground (*Grund*) above all human mode of life, to the divine abyss where God knows himself, comprehends himself, and tastes of his own wisdom and the goodness of his essence. In this abyss the soul loses itself to such an extent and in so fathomless a manner that it knows itself no more. There it knows neither words, nor definite modes of thought, nor taste, nor feeling, nor reasoned knowledge, nor love: for naught but God is there in the absolute purity of his simplicity, an ineffable abyss, a (simple) Being, the one (only) Spirit. God gives to the soul by grace that which he is himself by nature, and then the soul is united to the nameless Spirit, who is formless and undetermined. There God will perform in this spirit (spiritual) works: knowledge, love, praise, enjoyment; in this (work) the soul is passive, it is in the divine *laissez-faire*. All this, and that which takes place in this state, is as impossible to speak of as to speak of the divine Being, and it is the more incomprehensible in that it is beyond the capacity (either by nature or by grace) of all created intelligences, whether of men or of angels.[75]

There was, as can be seen, a continuity between Eckhart's *Wesenmystik* and Tauler's teaching, and this fact is the more striking in that the latter was teaching after the condemnation of 1329. A few doctrinal themes are the common property of the two celebrated Dominicans, and these reappear in Suso and the other German spiritual writers of the fourteenth century: "The necessity of going beyond images and concepts; the definition of the *Grund* as pure simplicity and as an interior fortress; the 'hyperformation' of man in the Godhead; the emptiness of scholastic distinctions between grace and nature; the nothingness both of the creature and of the divine Abyss; the positive value of temptation, and even of sin; and finally that liberty which lies beyond the will."[76]

[72] Sermon 68, ed. Vetter, *op. cit.*

[73] Sermon 64, *ibid.*

[74] Sermon 26, *ibid.*

[75] *Ibid.*

[76] M. de Gandillac, *art. cit.*, p. 76. Tauler has been studied in a number of works, usually with Eckhart and Suso. The following may be mentioned here for both Tauler and Suso; M. de Gandillac, in *Histoire de l'Église* (Fliche et Martin), XIII, pp. 377–98; this text appears in more fully developed form in *Études germaniques*, V (1950), pp. 241–56; also J. M. Clark, *The Great German Mystics*, Oxford, 1949. There is a study of Tauler's spiritual teaching by M. de Gandillac, *Valeur du temps dans la pédagogie spirituelle de Jean Tauler*, Montreal, 1956. For a bibliography, see F. W. Wentzlaff-Eggebert, *op. cit.*, pp. 273–339. There is an anthology of texts in the critical edition by J. A. Bizet, *Mystiques allemands*,

4. *Henry Suso*

Henry Suso differs considerably from both Eckhart and Tauler, in that he really seems to have himself known by experience the stages of the mystical life of which he speaks, whereas the others were speaking chiefly of what they were told by those whom they directed. Suso was born at Constance about 1300 (perhaps a little earlier) and entered the Dominican Order while very young. He probably knew Eckhart at Strasburg and at Cologne. His life was devoted to preaching and to directing nuns, in the countries between the Danube and the Rhine. He lived mostly at Ulm from 1348 until his death in 1366.[77] One of his spiritual daughters, Elizabeth Stagel, wrote his *Vita* and incorporated into it fragments of his works. This is the source to which reference must continually be made in order to discover the spirituality of the man himself. It is not, properly speaking, a biography, but rather a treatise based on personal experiences.[78]

Suso was extremely austere, very sensitive by temperament, almost too intense. His *ascesis* is rather a sorrowful one, and his works reflect a personal evolution in which his inner life became more and more closely united with the cross of Christ. At the same time he was somewhat naïve, even credulous, as is particularly noticeable in his descriptions of hell and of the demons.[79] He was much more a poet and "knight of wisdom" than a theologian and thinker. Nevertheless he was prudent and tried to draw a clear distinction between the spiritual liberty of the false mystics and true detachment of soul. Thus in the *Little Book of Truth*, which was probably written after the condemnation of 1329, he tries to give solid teaching which will not be open to the suspicion that had fallen on Eckhart.[80] Beneath contemplation properly so called,

---

Paris, 1957, pp. 241–89. There are also several collections in German; see *supra*, note 3. A thesis on Tauler by C. Champollion is to be published.

[77] There is a biography by Mgr C. Gröber, *Der Mystiker H.S.*, Freiburg in Breisgau, 1941. See also the work by J. A. Bizet, *Le mystique allemand H.S. et le déclin de la scolastique*, Paris, 1946; and S.M.C., *H.S., Saint and Poet*, Oxford, 1947.

[78] Cf. B. de Gaiffier, S.J., in *Anal. Bolland.*, LXI (1943), p. 316. For the *Vita*, see note 80.

[79] For example, *Horologium Sapientiae*, I, 10; Sermon 1 (*Lectulus noster floridus*). Translated by B. Lavaud, Paris, 1946, vol. V, pp. 167–9, and vol. IV, pp. 154–5.

[80] Edition of the works and the *Vita* by K. Bihlmeyer, *H.S. deutsche Schriften*, Stuttgart, 1907. There is a version in modern German by E. Diederichs, Jena, 1911. French translation with introduction, by B. Lavaud, 5 vols, Paris, 1946; anthology with a valuable introduction by J. Ancelet-Hustache, Paris, 1943; a selection of texts, in a critical edition, is included in J. A. Bizet, *Mystiques allemands* . . ., pp. 187–240. Suso's works include *The Little Book of Eternal Wisdom* and *the Little Book of Truth* (trans. J. M. Clark, London, 1953), and the *Briefbuchlein* (11 letters). These writings, together with the *Vita*, which is partly by

with which this *Little Book* is concerned, Suso was acquainted with various "states of prayer" corresponding to the "recollection" and "ecstasy" of later authors.[81] Above ecstasy he puts "transport" (*Übervart*) and the "rapture" (*Abzug*), which St Paul experienced. Transport, he says, "is distinguished from rapture in that it leaves the spirit in its own form instead of ravishing it wholly into God".

At the point where the soul "loses the sense of being distinct from God" (admirably prudent words!), it arrives, according to Suso, at "union without distinction". The *Little Book of Truth* attempts to clarify Eckhart's thought on this point and render it more exact, especially in Chapter 5, but other valuable information is to be gleaned elsewhere in his works, particularly in the two collections of letters. Suso emphasizes the transformation of man into Christ,[82] and describes this transformation, as Eckhart had already done, as "generative", that is, as a birth. But Suso comes closer to Scripture[83]; his language is, more or less, that of the fourth Gospel. The new birth is that of man, not that of the Word in the *Grund der Seele*.

Like Eckhart and Tauler, Suso reminds his readers that self-stripping is indispensable for anyone who is aiming at the union of the soul with the "One", the "Eternal Nothingness". This paradoxical expression—and there are others to be found in his writings—betrays the influence of Dionysius, or at the very least of the Neo-Platonism that permeates the writings of Eckhart. The supreme union is above all comprehension: the powers of the soul attain God without the intermediary of "created species": it is a kind of intuition. "By unknowing, the Truth becomes known." By this "annihilating absorption into Nothingness", the soul and its faculties "are lost" in God, without losing, for all that, the distinction between the Creator and the creature. It is like the eye, which "becomes one with its object, and yet each of the two remains what it is". There is bliss, the soul contemplating "God the One" and loving him, without knowing that it knows and loves him; that very consciousness would be a screen. There it "rests" wholly and only in Nothingness, and knows nothing of the "being that God or Nothingness is." This knowledge "without any image or likeness"

Suso's spiritual daughter Elizabeth Stagel, make up the *Exemplar*. There are also the *Horologium Sapientiae* (a Latin version of the *Little Book of Eternal Wisdom*, perhaps of an earlier date) and the *Grosses Briefbuch* (28 letters).

[81] Cf. J. A. Bizet, *Le mystique allemand H.S. . . .*, pp. 263–6.

[82] Suso's Christology, however, does not appear to be very original. Cf. J. Bühlmann, *Christuslehre und Christusmystik des H.S.*, Lucerne, 1942; R. Schwarz, *Das Christusbild des deutschen Mystikers H.S.*, Greifswald, 1934.

[83] Cf. M. A. Fischer, *Die hl. Schrift in den Werken des deutschen Mystikers H.S.*, Spires, 1936.

of God, or of creatures in God, is the "morning knowledge", as opposed to the "evening knowledge" in which images and distinctions remain.

Suso goes on to emphasize, as against the heterodox mystics, that the possibility of sin remains in a man thus raised up, and that humility is necessary for all men, especially for those who have not yet attained to the understanding of "what the aforesaid Nothingness is". He wishes, in fact, to "hold fast to the common teaching of holy Church". "One sees many good and simple men who attain to a holiness worthy of praise without having been given a vocation to this."

The *Little Book of Truth* is certainly one of the most beautiful writings on contemplation that the fourteenth century produced. When one reflects upon it, one is amazed at the author's intellectual vigour and dialectic, and the singular art with which he has treated one of the most difficult of subjects—perhaps the most difficult of all. He was indeed, as P. Strauch has said, "the minstrel of German mysticism, a spiritual troubadour, the last poet of *Mittelhochdeutsch*".[84] As Francis of Assisi was the knight and troubadour of Lady Poverty, so Henry Suso was the liegeman of divine Wisdom, and his language takes more than a formal dress from that of courtly love. If, as Bergson observed, passionate love had first plagiarized mysticism—its fervour, its transports, and its ecstasies—then Suso was simply "recovering what belonged to the spiritual life when he used the language of the poets to sing the praises of the hypostatic Wisdom".[85] Suso rehabilitated the language of courtly love, which in his time was beginning to be thought archaic and decadent, if not suspect. He hymned the basic oneness of love, the nature of which remains essentially the same whether the object be man or God.

5. *The Rhineland School*

The great Rhineland mystics gave rise to a school. A certain number of the spiritual writers of the end of the Middle Ages in Germany can be regarded as their disciples. But with the exception of John Ruysbroeck (who will be discussed in the next section) they were not of the stature of their predecessors. A considerable number of them are very little known and their writings still unpublished. The gaps can be partially filled in by the anthologies

[84] *Allg. deutsche Biographie*, XXXVII, pp. 171 *et seq.* Cf. L. Heieck, *Das Verhältnis des Aesthetischen zum Mystischen dargestellt an H.S.*, Erlangen, 1936.

[85] J. A. Bizet, *Suso et le Minnesang, ou la morale de l'amour courtois*, Paris, 1947, p. 169.

of German texts of the fourteenth and fifteenth centuries which have been published in the last hundred years.[86]

The *Brautmystik* still had its fervent adherents. Among many examples, a characteristic one is that of the "Limburg Sermons" (*Limburgsche Sermoenen*). This collection dates from the end of the thirteenth century or the beginning of the fourteenth.[87] Originating partly in Germany and partly in Brabant, it depends to some extent on the commentary of Richard of St Victor on the Canticle of Canticles, perhaps through Hadewijch's Letter X.[88] Certain passages, however, recall the *Wesenmystik*.[89]

The theme of the *hortus conclusus*, again derived from the Canticle of Canticles, is found now and again, not only extolling the Church or the Blessed Virgin, but also describing the spiritual life of the Christian soul. Thus a little treatise on mystical symbolism, the *Lüstliche Würtzgarte*, gives the meaning of this garden and of the castle it encloses: the soul must enter it to consummate its union with God.[90]

In the notion of contemplation, love often holds the preponderant place, exactly as in St Bernard's mysticism or the *Brautmystik*. An example is the *Septililium* of Blessed Dorothea of Montau (†1394).[91] A number of mystical poems, chiefly emanating from feminine circles, took as their theme Christ the spouse of the soul, as frequently as they did that of the infant Christ or the Crucified.[92] In the same line of thought, there were a number of *opuscula* consisting of meditations on the passion of Christ, like the one entitled *Extendit manum*, which had a fairly wide circulation under the name of a certain Henry of St Gall (end of the fourteenth century). It was clearly derived from St Bernard, St Bonaventure, and

86 Besides the anthologies already cited, there may be mentioned A. Dempf, *Vom inwendigen Reichtum. Texte unbekannter Mystiker aus dem Kreise Meister Eckharts*, Leipzig, 1937.

87 Ed. J. H. Kern, Leyden, 1895; cf. J. van Mierlo, S.J., "Over den ouderdom van de Limburgsche Sermoenen", in *Kon. Vlaamsche Acad. Taal-en Letterkunde*, 1935, pp. 1081–93.

88 Cf. J. M. Schallij, "Richard van S. Victor en Hadewijchs 10de brief", in *Tijdschr. nederl. Taal-en Letterkunde*, LXII (1942–3), pp. 219–28; S. Axters, O.P., *Geschiedenis van de vroomheid in de Nederlanden*, II, Antwerp, 1950, pp. 138–49.

89 Cf. Sermons 15 and 42. Attention may be called here to the commentary on the beginning of the Canticle which has been studied by F. Landmann, "Johannes Kreutzer aus Gebweiler (†1468) als Mystiker und Dichter geistlicher Lieder", in *Archives de l'Église d'Alsace*, V (1953–4), pp. 21–67 (of the works, description of the commentary and edition of extracts).

90 Cf. K. Schmidt, *Der Lüstliche Würtgarte*, Wildenfels, 1932.

91 Ed. F. Hipler, *Anal. Bolland.*, II–IV, 1883–5; cf. H. Westphal, art. "D. de M.", in *Dict. de spirit.*, III, 1664–8.

92 Cf. E. Benary, *Liedformen der deutschen Mystik im 14. und 15. Jahrh.*, Greiswald, 1936.

the *Meditationes vitae Christi.*[93] There was another also that recounted a vision of the entire passion of Christ.[94]

These treatises take the form of historical narratives. To accentuate their realism, their authors frequently draw upon apocryphal writings: the Gospel of Nicodemus, the Life of Mary, etc. They also interpret the Old Testament allegorically, but they do this to support many concrete details of the passion. The end they have in view is the imitation of Christ, and only up to a certain point can one speak of "mysticism" in connection with their attitude of conformity to the suffering Christ. They were also concerned, in general, with giving a rational justification to the sufferings of the redemption. They ordinarily do this on the model of the *Meditationes vitae Christi,* imagining a farewell meeting between Jesus and his mother at Bethany, in the course of which the necessity of the passion is discussed. Their works thus become real treatises on the subject of satisfaction, based on the teaching of the great scholastics.[95]

The mystics of this period are also characterized by the increasing frequency of ecstasies, visions, and private revelations. Up to the time of Eckhart and Tauler, the men among them had remained spiritual directors—observers who guided the souls entrusted to them, and they do not seem to have shared their inward experiences. Suso, on the other hand, had himself experienced what was described to him by those he directed. Among the women, the picture takes on a distinctly unusual character. St Bridget of Sweden (†1373) is still celebrated for her "Revelations".[96] Among the nuns of Eckhart's group, the extraordinary had become the rule. This is found even among the Dominican nuns, although they were guided by the intellectual influence of the great spiritual men of their order. It was the case at the convent of Colmar,[97] and also at Töss, where the nun Elizabeth Stagel lived. She wrote the life of her spiritual father, Suso, and those of her sisters in religion,[98]

[93] K. Ruh, "Studien über H. von S. G. und den 'Extendit manum' Passionstraktat", in *Zeitschr. schweizer. Kirchengesch.*, XLVII (1953), pp. 210–30, 241–278.

[94] *Christi Leiden in einer Vision geschaut* (*A German Mystic Text of the Fourteenth Century*). Ed. F. P. Pickering, Manchester, 1952. An account of the Passion in Middle Dutch was published by A. Holder, *Dat lijden ende die Passie ons Heren Jhesu Christi*, Leyden, 1877.

[95] Cf. K. Ruh, "Zur Theologie des mittelalterlichen Passionstraktats", in *Theol. Zeitschr.*, VI (1950), pp. 17–39.

[96] Cf. F. Vernet, art. "Brigitte de Suède", in *Dict. de spirit*, I (1943–58); *Revelationes*, ed. E. and M. Wessen, Copenhagen, 1949–52; *Revelationes extravagantes*, ed. L. Hollmann, Uppsala, 1956. Cf. K. Adalsten, *Die hl. B.*, Freiburg, 1951; E. Peacey, *S.B. of S.*, London, 1934; de Flavigny, *Ste. B. de S.*, Paris, 1910.

[97] See "Les *Vitae Sororum* d'Unterlinden", critical edition by J. Ancelet-Hustache, in *Arch. hist. doctr. litt. moyen âge*, V (1930), pp. 317–509.

[98] Ed. Vetter, in *Deutsche Texte des Mittelalters*, VI (1906); cf. J. Ancelet-

many of whom led a life that was truly astonishing. The *Revelations* of Adelaide Langmann (†1375)[99] and those of Christina Ebner (†1356) are typical.[100] Christina's cousin, Margaret Ebner (†1351), also left an account of revelations,[101] the orthodoxy of which has recently been recognized.[102] The letters of her spiritual director, Henry of Nördlingen, are a valuable source for anyone who wishes to write her life and reconstruct the milieu in which she lived.

These nuns seem to have been influenced by the *Wesenmystik*, a view which is supported by the fact that certain of them were in touch with the groups of "Friends of God" which were formed in the course of the fourteenth century.[103] This was especially the case with Margaret and Christina Ebner, whose spiritual director, the secular priest Henry of Nördlingen, was a member of one of these associations. It is true that the name "Friends of God" was currently used to designate Christians who were leading a life of intense union with God, whether they were religious or layfolk. The writings of the great Rhineland mystics, especially those of Tauler, use the name, and there is no reason to suppose that they are referring to organized brotherhoods, even secret ones, still less to sects, though certain writings, such as the *Theologia deutsch*, distinguish between true and false Friends of God. There were some suspect groups which, about 1400, liked to use this title in the way they used the names "apostolic", "evangelical", etc. There is no doubt that such spiritual circles were to be found in certain parts of the Rhineland, particularly Strasbourg and Basle. They were more or less organized, and were much influenced by Tauler. Thus Margaret and Christina Ebner were Tauler's disciples, though indirectly, through the intermediary of Henry of Nördlingen and the group at Basle.[104]

These "Friends of God" still present an enigma to the historian. In particular, who was that "Friend of God of the Oberland" who

---

Hustache, *La vie mystique d'un monastère de dominicaines au moyen âge*, Paris, 1928.

[99] Ed. P. Strauch, Strasburg, 1878.

[100] Partially edited by G. Lochner, Nuremberg, 1872. She may have been the author of the *Büchlein von der Gnade*, a biography of the nuns of Engelthal, ed. J. von Schlumberger, Guebwiller, 1898.

[101] Ed. P. Strauch, Freiburg in Breisgau, 1882. Translated into modern German, together with the revelations of Adelaide Langmann, by J. Prestel, Weimar, 1939.

[102] In 1937. Cf. H. Bleienstein, "M.E. (1291–1351). Ein Hinweis", in *Zeitschr. Asz. Myst.*, XII (1937), p. 232.

[103] Cf. R. M. Jones, *The Flowering of Mysticism. The Friends of God in the XIVth Century*, New York, 1939.

[104] Cf. A. Walz, O.P., "Gottesfreunde um Margarete Ebner", in *Histor. Jahrb.*, LXXII (1953), pp. 253–65. For biographical data on Henry of Nördlingen, see H. Gürsching, "Neue urkundliche Nachrichten über den Mystiker H. von N.", in *Festgabe . . . K. Schornbaum*, Neustadt, 1950, pp. 42–57.

is mentioned in certain documents and who would appear to be the author of various *opuscula*? He has often been considered a fictitious character, but according to others he really existed.[105] Perhaps he is to be identified with a certain Rulman Merswin,[106] or possibly he is sometimes a fiction employed by Merswin to represent the voice of God.[107] This Rulman Merswin was a rich banker of Strasbourg who decided, with his wife, to renounce the world. About 1347 he placed himself under the direction of Tauler. He was in touch with Henry of Nördlingen and Margaret Ebner, and before long he was directing the community of Johannites of Isle-Verte, near Strasbourg, where he remained until his death in 1381. Of all the works attributed to him,[108] the only one that appears to be original is *Von den vier Jahren seines Anfangs*.[109] This is a fragmentary autobiography, covering about four years, the years that followed his conversion. All the others are merely compilations. When Merswin writes of his own experiences, he is somewhat commonplace, although he likes to use apocalyptic language. His vocabulary and his images are largely derived from Eckhart and Tauler. When he borrows from the writings of his predecessors, however, he does so in such a way as to impoverish their mystical content. It has been said that "in this class of 'literature for lay brothers, the spirit of mysticism is generally lacking."[110]

There are a few treatises that are exceptions. First, there is the "Book of Spiritual Poverty", *Buch von geistlicher Armut*.[111] Long attributed to Tauler himself, it seems to be the work of one of his disciples or friends. It was often called the "Imitation of Christ's Life of Poverty". It develops the Rhineland theme of spiritual poverty as a source of detachment, of liberty, of purity of action, which makes the soul a "friend of God". This is the way by which one attains to the imitation of Christ, to the perfection of the

[105] The arguments in favour of this view have been assembled by W. Rath, *Der Gottesfreund von Oberland*, 2nd ed., Stuttgart, 1955.

[106] A. Chiquot, art. "Ami de Dieu de l'Oberland", in *Dict. de spirit.*, I, 489–92.

[107] Cf. A. Jundt, *Rulman Merswin et l'ami de Dieu de l'Oberland*, Paris, 1890, pp. 94–5.

[108] Ed. P. Strauch, *Schriften aus der Gottesfreundliteratur*, Halle, 1927.

[109] Ed. A. Jundt, *Beiträge zu den theol. Wissenschaften*, V, Jena, 1854, pp. 54–76.

[110] E. Dehnhart, *Die Metaphorik der Mystiker Meister Eckhart und Tauler in den Schriften des R. M.*, Burg b. M., 1940, p. 118. On Rulman Merswin, the best study is that of J. M. Clark, *The Great German Mystics*, Oxford, 1949, ch. v.

[111] Ed. H. Denifle, Munich, 1877. There is an English translation, in archaic language, by J. R. Morell, *Following of Christ*, London, 1886; and a new translation by C. F. Kelley, *The Book of the Poor in Spirit by a Friend of God*, London, 1955. Similarly, some *Institutions* were published by St Peter Canisius in 1543 among the works of Tauler, which were really only a compilation of writings by Tauler and other writers of the Rhineland and Flanders. This work had some influence on the reading of the speculative mystics in modern times.

virtues, to peace of heart, to spiritual death, and finally to contemplation and union with God. The emphasis is constantly on "poverty of spirit"—that of the Gospel beatitude, with its promise of the kingdom of heaven. It is understandable that his *opuscula* should have been attributed to Tauler, who had such a predilection for describing "techniques of detachment" in his works.

Another treatise by an "*Anonymus Francofurtanus*" entitled "Germanic Theology" or *Theologia deutsch* (end of the fourteenth century) has been the subject of somewhat heated discussions among historians. There have been two questions at issue. The first is whether the text published by Luther in 1516 and 1518, or the one of 1497 (discovered in the last century and edited by F. Pfeiffer) is the original. At the present time, the discussion is still open, but it seems likely that the text of 1497 is the earlier of the two. In that case Luther used a truncated text, which he may have further modified in accordance with his reforming ideas.[112] This raises the question of the orthodoxy of the work, which is precisely the object of the second question. On this point, too, no agreement has been reached. Some find in the treatise a very definite leaning towards quietism and pantheism, while others see no difference, except one of tendency and spirit, between it and the accepted doctrine of scholasticism.[113] An unprejudiced reading would probably find it to contain nothing that had not already been said by other spiritual writers of the period and milieu; what is striking is its exceptional vigour of language. What Luther did was to transpose to the dogmatic level (for example, in his doctrine of the uselessness of works) expressions which embodied in a few words an interior experience of a very high order.

The author, who was custodian of the house of the Knights of the Teutonic Order at Sachsenhausen, near Frankfurt, appears to have belonged to the Rhineland school of mysticism. But if his writings are compared with those of the great Dominican spiritual writers of the fourteenth century, they have a more traditional and more classical aspect. The theme of the *Theologia deutsch* is the interior life. The end of man is union with God, and the way that leads to it consists first in detachment which purifies the soul,

[112] Luther's text, ed. Wittemberg, 1516 and 1518; French translation, Amsterdam, 1676. Text of 1497, ed. Pfeiffer, 1871; W. Ull, *Der Frankforter*, Bonn, 1912; French translation, J. Paquier, *Le livre de la vie parfaite* (*La théologie germanique*), Paris, 1928; German translation, G. Siedel, Gotha, 1929; J. Bernhart, Munich (no date). On the question of which is the original text, see G. Baring, "Neues von der 'Theologia Deutsch' und ihrer Weltweider Bedeutung", in *Archiv f. Reformationsgeschichte*, XLVIII (1957), pp. 1–11.

[113] This is the view of J. A. Bizet, "La querelle de l'Anonyme de Francfort", in *Études germaniques*, III (1948), pp. 201–7; J. Paquier, *L'orthodoxie de la Th. g.* Paris, 1922.

divests it of self-love, and sets it free. Next comes illumination "by the true light that is sown by God and produces the fruits of God",[114] but which cannot be attained without the complete abandonment of one's own will, joined to humility and spiritual poverty.[115] Finally, the man, enlightened by this divine light and afire with genuine love, is united to God; such a man is "deified, or divine".[116] In short the treatise keeps to the classic division of the three ways: purgative, illuminative, and unitive. It ends by emphasizing the aid that Christ gives us on our road towards the life of perfection. The last lines sum up the dominating thought in extremely strong terms:

> All that has been said up to now concerns the outward life; it is only a way, an introduction to the real life, the inward life. Now the inward life itself begins. When we begin, as far as we are able, to taste the Perfect, all created things and man himself seem nothingness: we realise that truly the Perfect alone is all things and above all things, so that all good must necessarily be attributed to the Perfect alone, and not to the creature: being, life, intelligence, knowledge, power etc. It follows that we attribute nothing to ourselves.... So that we feel ourselves to be very poor; everything becomes nothingness to us; ourselves and all that like us is partial and created. Then it is that the inward life really begins; God takes the place of ourselves.
>
> What this life is, what one learns and experiences in it, no words or song have ever expressed. The tongue has not found words for it, the heart itself has not really known or understood it.
>
> ...One must know which to choose: no man can serve two contrary masters. If the Creator is to enter, the creature must go forth. Let this be quite clear.
>
> Oh that we would then renounce ourselves: abandon all things for God, neglect our own will and die to it so as to live only for God and for the accomplishment of his will.[117]

6. *Groenendael and John Ruysbroeck*

The works of Eckhart and his disciples circulated beyond the present frontiers of Germany. Flanders, which was akin to Germany in language and in sensibility, was the first country to become acquainted with them and to translate them. We still possess a great many of these translations in Middle Dutch,[118] and it is in Flanders that we find, in the thirteenth century, the first traces of

[114] Ch. XL.
[115] Chs XXXIV–XXXV.
[116] Ch. XLI.
[117] Ch. LIV; J. Paquier's translation.
[118] For a bibliography, see M. A. Lücker, *Meister Eckhart und die Devotio moderna*, Leyden, 1950, pp. 156–65. See also G. I. Lieftinck, *De middelnederlansche Taulerhandschriften*, Groningen, 1936.

that *Wesenmystik* which was the major theme of the Rhineland spiritual writers. That country was, therefore, prepared to read their teachings and to propagate it.

The greatest mystic of the fourteenth century in the Low Countries was undeniably John Ruysbroeck, so called from the name of his native village, situated about ten kilometres south of Brussels. After his ordination in 1317—he was then twenty-four years old—he became one of the clergy of St Gudule's, the collegiate church of Brussels.[119] From that time he seems to have been concerned with the Béguines, their doctrines, and their sometimes curious behaviour; there was a certain Bloemardine who was attracting attention about that time. In 1343, he retired with a few friends into the forest of Soignes, at the gates of Brussels, to lead a solitary life in the hermitage of Groenendael (Green Valley, Vauvert). There he soon took the Augustinian habit. He became prior of the community and remained in that office until his death in 1381.[120]

On a number of points, the great mystic of Groenendael was influenced by Meister Eckhart, either directly or possibly through the second Hadewijch, who was herself a disciple of Eckhart.[121] However that may be, Ruysbroeck can be considered as belonging to the spiritual movement of the Rhineland, though he neither lived there nor belonged to the Dominican Order. It is an open question whether he should be regarded as the founder of a new school of spirituality in the Low Countries. The arguments in favour are solid ones, and they may be summarized as follows. Before Ruysbroeck there were few authors who, like Hadewijch, wrote in Dutch, which was then in the process of separating from Middle German. After him, on the other hand, there was a considerable flowering of mystics and spiritual writers in the Low Countries who left a permanent mark in the spirituality of the whole Church. Indeed, it will soon be seen how much we owe today, in our practice of the Christian life, to the movement in the Low Countries known as the *Devotio moderna*. But although a new line of spiritual writers may be said to have begun with Ruysbroeck, in the sense that he was the first to express the highest experience of the interior life in a language that was still in process of formation, so opening

119 On this period, see P. Lefèvre, O. Praem., "Le séjour du mystique brabançon J. de R. à Bruxelles", in *Rev. d'hist. eccl.*, XXIX (1933), pp. 387–98. An excellent synthesis of Ruysbroeck's doctrine will be found in S. Axters, O.P., *Geschiedenis . . .*, II, *De eeuw van Ruusbroec*, Antwerp, 1953, pp. 213–91; bibliography, pp. 517–26.

120 A valuable source for the history of Groenendael is *L'obituaire du monastère de Groenendael*, ed. M. Dijkmans, S.J., Brussels, 1940.

121 Cf. J. B. P. [Porion], *Hadewijch d'Anvers, Poèmes des béguines*, Paris, 1954, pp. 47–9 and 53–4.

the way to other writers, it must be said that these others did not follow him in what was most characteristic. They represent, in fact, a stream of affective spirituality—ascetic, moralizing, deliberately simple, and even anti-speculative. In all this, they were the reverse of Ruysbroeck; he has little in common with them except the language. He appears, therefore, much less a founder of a school than a disciple of the Rhineland mystics.[122]

Though Ruysbroeck was influenced by Eckhart, he nevertheless drew upon other sources: St Augustine, the Pseudo-Dionysius, the Venerable Bede,[123] Peter Comestor, St Bernard,[124] Beatrice of Nazareth, Hadewijch. His relative independence of the great Dominican should in itself make possible an unprejudiced interpretation of the passages in which he seems to share Eckhart's supposed pantheism. In addition, he himself deliberately left no doubt about his "dualism", that is, his doctrine of the distinction between God and the creature. There can be no question, with him, of pantheism in any form whatever.[125] He says this expressly in the "Book of Supreme Truth", *Dat boec der hoechster waerheit*: "No creature can be or become so holy as to lose its created nature and become God".[126] Nevertheless, certain expressions in Book III of "The Splendour of the Spiritual Espousals", *De gheestelijke brulocht*, provoked the criticisms of Gerson,[127] and there have been

[122] The arguments in favour of the thesis that Ruysbroeck was the founder of the Netherlands school have been put together by S. Axters, O.P., *La spiritualité des Pays-Bas*, Louvain–Paris, 1948, especially ch. v; and in his *Geschiedenis . . .*, II. For the opposite view see the work of Dom J. Huijben, especially the article "Y a-t-il une spiritualité flamande?", in *La Vie spirit., Suppl.*, L (1937), [pp. 129–147].

[123] His treatise *The Spiritual Tabernacle* was based on Bede's *De tabernaculo*, P.L., 91, 393–498; cf. P. van den Krabben, "Beda als bron van 'Van den gheesteliken tabernakel'", in *Ons. geest. Erf*, IX (1935), pp. 382–7.

[124] Cf. A. Ampe, S.J., "Bernardus en Ruusbroec", in *Ons geest. Erf*, XXVII (1953), pp. 143–79.

[125] Cf. A. van de Walle, "Is Ruusbroec pantheïst?" in *Ons geest. Erf*, XII (1938), pp. 359–91; XIII (1939), pp. 66–195. For the question of Gerson's criticisms of Ruysbroeck, see *infra*, ch. vii, §5, p. 441.

[126] The best recent edition of Ruysbroeck is the one known as the edition of the Ruusbroec-Genootschap, Malines, 1932; 2nd ed., Tiett, 1944–8. It will be cited here according to the 1st ed. The text quoted above will be found in vol. III, pp. 276–7. There is a French translation by the Benedictines of Wisque, 6 vols, Brussels, 1912–38.

There are anthologies by J. A. Bizet, Paris, 1947; and J. Alzin, Namur, 1958; see also F. Hermans, *R. l'admirable et son école*, Paris, 1958. All the works have been translated into modern Dutch by H. Moller, Bussum, 1914. The Latin translation by the Carthusian Surius of Cologne (Cologne, 1552, 1609, 1692) is valuable for the study of how Ruysbroeck's work was disseminated and interpreted. In English, see *Jan van Ruysbroek, the Spiritual Espousals*, trans. by E. Colledge, London, 1952: *The Seven Steps of the Ladder of Spiritual Love*, trans. by F. S. Taylor, London, 1952.

[127] Cf. A. van de Walle, *art. cit.*; A. Combes, *Essai sur la critique de Ruysbroeck par Gerson*, vols I–III published, Paris, 1945–59.

historians who exaggerated the opposition between Ruysbroeck's spiritual experience and the dogmas of the Catholic church.[128] It is true that the treatise "Of the Twelve Virtues", *Van den XII dogheden*, seems to have been influenced by Eckhart's *Reden der Unterscheidung*, but the work was in reality that of a disciple of Ruysbroeck, Godfrey of Wevel.[129]

Like the Rhineland mystics, Ruysbroeck tried to explain how, and in what measure, man can arrive at union with God. At the beginning of his career as a writer—in the *Spiritual Espousals*, for example—he admitted the possibility of an intuitive vision of the divine essence.[130] Later he showed greater reserve on this point, as in the *opusculum* entitled *The Ring or the Brilliant*.[131] It is significant that the first nine chapters of this treatise simply summarize the first two books of the *Espousals*, while the following chapters expound with greater precision the doctrine of the third book, devoted to contemplation properly so called. It has been thought that this recasting was prompted by the discussions which arose about 1330–6 in connection with the problem of the immediate face-to-face vision of God by the blessed, a debate which finally led to the intervention of Benedict XII.[132]

With regard to Ruysbroeck's mystical doctrine, properly so called, three essential elements can be distinguished in it: exemplarism, introversion and the life of union.[133] These elements are, of course, entirely traditional, but Ruysbroeck's synthesis of them shows his dependence on the *Wesenmystik* of the spiritual writers of the Rhineland.

The basis of exemplarism is the doctrine of the Trinity. The life of God is a movement of flux and reflux, of expansion and return; it goes forth from the unity of nature from which the three Persons proceed, only to return to unity in mutual delight. In the exemplary ideas, the creature possesses in some sense an eternal life, which makes it share in this flux and reflux.[134] The very structure of the

128 For example, M. d'Asbeck, *La mystique de Ruysbroeck d'Admirable. Un écho du néo-platonisme au XIVe siècle*, Paris, 1930, p. 287.

129 Cf. M. A. Lücker, *op. cit.*, ch. III; S. Axters, O.P., *Geschiedenis . . .*, II, pp. 329–39. This treatise will be found in the Ruusbroec-Genootschap edition, *op. cit.*, IV, pp. 225–308.

130 III, 6; *ed. cit.*, I, pp. 247–9.

131 Ch. XI; *ed. cit.*, III, pp. 33–6.

132 Constitution *Benedictus Deus*, 29 January 1336; Denz., 530. Cf. *Spiritual Espousals*, Wisques translation, vol. III, 2nd ed., 1928, p. 224; L. Reypens, S.J., "Le sommet de la contemplation mystique [in Ruysbroeck]", in *Rev. asc. myst.*, III (1922), pp. 250–72; J. Huijben, O.S.B., "Ruysbroeck et saint Jean de la Croix", in *Études Carmélit.*, XVII, 2 (1932), pp. 232–47; W. H. Beuken, *Ruusbroec en de middeleeuwse mystiek*, Brussels, 1946, pp. 98–100.

133 Cf. L. Reypens, S.J., "Ruusbroec's mystieke leer", in *Jan van Ruusbroec, leven, werken*, Malines, 1931, pp. 151–77; by the same, "Ruusbroec's mystiek als bekroning der inkeeringstheorie", in *Ons geest. Erf*, VI (1932), pp. 257–81.

134 For example, the *Book of the Twelve Béguines*, 28 (*ed. cit.*, IV, pp. 61–3);

soul is modelled on this divine pattern; here Ruysbroeck adopts the well-known Augustinian doctrine. The three higher faculties—memory, understanding and will—derive their natural origin from the unity of the soul. And this unity, like the "unity of essence" which man has in God, and like the "unity of the lower powers", must be possessed supernaturally.[135] That is what a man must do by entering into himself, passing through the three stages described in the *Spiritual Espousals*: active life (*werkend leven*), desire for God (*God-begeerend leven*) and contemplative life (*God-schouwend leven*). He thus discovers the likeness of God in the depths of his soul and is associated with the life of the three divine Persons, until he arrives at the summit of contemplation, that is, at the "union without difference" with God's essence, to "possession". This is the life of union which cannot be lived without "exercising love", and by which the human soul is drawn into the life of the Trinity itself.[136]

For Ruysbroeck, then, as for the mystics of the Rhineland school, contemplation is the culmination of an experience whose description is closely bound up with dogmatic conceptions.[137] It is, certainly, speculative mysticism, but the coherence and balance of Ruysbroeck's thought, both dogmatic and logical, are distinctly superior to what is found in Eckhart. Furthermore—and this is another difference between them—Ruysbroeck had experienced what he speaks of, which gives a reality to his writings, and something personal that brings him close to Suso and the other adherents of the *Brautmystik*.[138] He also differs from his predecessors in the Rhineland, Eckhart and especially Tauler, by not laying so much stress on the "techniques of self-stripping".

Ruysbroeck knew and described the physical phenomena of mysticism. In the second book of the *Spiritual Espousals* (*God-begeerend leven*) he puts them in the first phase of the stage he is describing. These are experiences "in the mind": revelations and

---

Spiritual Espousals, III, 5 (*ed. cit.*, I, pp. 244–7); *Mirror of Eternal Life*, 17 (*ed, cit.*, III, pp. 198–205). On Ruysbroeck's doctrine of the Trinity, see A. Ampe. S.J., *De grondlijnen van Ruusbroec's Driëenheidsleer als onderbouw van de zieleopgang*, Tielt, 1950 (with a Latin résumé).

135 *Spiritual Espousals*, II, 2; *ed. cit.*, I, p. 145.

136 This ascent provides the framework of the best work on Ruysbroeck's mystical doctrine, that of A. Ampe, S.J., *De mystieke leer van R. over zieleopgang*, Tielt, 1957 (with a Latin résumé). A similar descent and ascent, from the Trinity to the Trinity, is found in other contemporary authors, but without Ruysbroeck's genuinely contemplative doctrine; e.g. Henry of Langenstein (†1397) in his *Speculum animae* (French translation by E. Mistiaen, Bruges, 1923).

137 On Ruysbroeck's theology of creation, redemption, and grace, see A. Ampe, S.J., *De geestelijke grondslagen van de zieleopgang naar de leer van R.*, 2 vols, Tielt, 1951–2 (with Latin résumé).

138 Cf. S. Axters, O.P., *De "unio mystica" voor de Brabants-Rijnlandse mystiek van de XIII*[de] *en de XIV*[de] *eeuw*, Brussels, 1949.

intellectual visions. Next, "above oneself and above the mind", although "not absolutely out of oneself", comes rapture. Finally, "above oneself", *boven zichzelf*, come the sudden illuminations which are "works of God himself".[139]

Ruysbroeck knew that in this domain illusion is possible; he had observed it in the case of certain Béguines. The *Spiritual Espousals*, without working out an exact treatise on the discernment of spirits, gives some information useful in this connection. It is difficult to summarize the criteria proposed by Ruysbroeck. The principal one is that false mystics betray themselves by their lack of charity and by their pride.[140] One must also be on one's guard against temptations.[141] Discernment depends upon one of the gifts of the Holy Spirit, that of knowledge.[142] It bestows the knowledge of oneself and the light to guide others.[143] Yet the "soul is thus moved by the Holy Spirit, that is to say, by divine love", only if it is above "the exterior and sensible way", above "the way of natural light", in "the supernatural and divine way". Then the Spirit of God pours forth countless gifts upon man. From him come the three theological virtues and the seven gifts of scholastic tradition. The last and highest of these, that of wisdom, finally fills the reason with light and enables it to contemplate God in intellectual images.[144]

Ruysbroeck exercised a profound influence from his monastery at Groenendael. His disciples, however, in their spiritual treatises, generally proved to be less "speculative" than their master. Gerard Groote, with whom began the *Devotio moderna*, came more than once to renew his fervour at Groenendael, and even declared one day that he esteemed Ruysbroeck's spirit very highly.[145] Many other devout persons, both religious and lay, came to know him and had recourse to his direction.[146] His first biographer, Henry Uten Bogaerde or Pomerius, gives some interesting details on this subject.[147] If "it is true to say that Ruysbroeck's principal master was

[139] II, 24; *ed. cit.*, I, pp. 163–5. Cf. M. Smits van Waesberghe, S.J., *Het verschijnsel van de opheffing des geestes bij Jan van Ruusbroec en Hendrik Herp*, Nijmegen, 1945.

[140] II, 74–7; *ed. cit.*, I, pp. 228–37.

[141] See the book *Of Four Temptations*; *ed. cit.*, III, pp. 45–58.

[142] Cf. *The Kingdom of the Lovers of God*, 18–19; *ed. cit.*, I, p. 36.

[143] Cf. *The Spiritual Tabernacle*, 27; *ed. cit.*, II, p. 122.

[144] This summarizes the doctrine of *The Kingdom of the Lovers of God*; *ed. cit.*, I, pp. 3–100.

[145] S. Axters, *La spiritualité . . .*, p. 100.

[146] Cf. J. Huijben, O.S.B., "Uit Ruusbroec's vriendenkring", in *Jan van Ruusbroec, leven, werken*, Malines, 1931, pp. 101–50.

[147] *De origine monasterii Viridis Vallis et de gestis patrum et fratrum in primordiali fervore ibidem degentium*, edited by the Bollandists, in *Anal. Bollandiana*, IV (1885), pp. 263–322; Wisques translation, vol. VI, pp. 279–315. This biography was the indispensable source for the others, even to the most recent, but its value is still debated.

the Holy Spirit"[148] and that in his works he expressed what his own personal experience had taught him about the journey of the soul towards God, the fact remains that he was not concerned with working out any sort of theory about the art of direction. Even when he speaks of false liberty of spirit, as in the book *Of the Four Temptations*, it never occurs to him to include spiritual direction among the precautions to be taken against it. It is only incidentally that he charges his reader to "have unfeigned respect for superiors".[149]

John Leeuwen (†1374), "the good cook" of Groenendael, was the disciple on whom the speculative aspect of Ruysbroeck's teaching had the most influence. It was he who seems to have clarified his master's thought with all the freedom, simplicity and frankness of a man of humble origin, and sensitive to beauty, to poetry and to the love of God. In his treatise on "what is possessed by the man who is poor in spirit", *Wat dat een armen mensche van geeste toebehoert*, he distinguishes, as Ruysbroeck did, three stages in the spiritual life; the active life, the interior life (*innige*, not *begeerende*) and the contemplative life; but he adds to these a fourth phase, that of *gedochsamheid*, that is, of abandonment, putting oneself completely in the hands of God.[150] A similar pattern can be found in another treatise, "On five kinds of brotherly love", *Van vijf manieren broederliker minnen*.[151] In short, "Leeuwen expresses the highest mystical life more clearly than Ruysbroeck; these heights are true contemplation of God".[152] It does indeed seem that this is immediate contemplation, the primacy being given to love, though there cannot be found in the writers of this period a precision as great as this.

After John Leeuwen, other speculative mystics appeared in the Low Countries and the Rhineland regions, such as Henry Herp (Harphius), who will be discussed later; although those who, like Ruysbroeck's humble disciple, put love before speculation were the more numerous. This tendency is particularly striking in the case of John van Schoonhoven (†1432), who clearly prefers the less lofty regions of asceticism to speculative mysticism. In his view, humble and affective contemplation is to be preferred to the fine

148 Wisques translation, vol. I, 3rd ed., 1937, p. 17.

149 *Ed. cit.*, III, p. 54. Cf. *Spiritual Espousals*, I, pp. 12–14; *ed. cit.*, I, pp. 122–5.

150 Ed. H. Doorestijn, in *Ons geest. Erf*, VIII (1934), pp. 5–38. This division corresponds more or less to that adopted by S. Axters, O.P., in his anthology of Leeuwen's works, which is preceded by a valuable biography: *J. van L. Een bloemlezing uit zijn werken*, Antwerp, 1943; cf. his *Geschiedenis . . .*, II, pp. 291–318.

151 Ed. J. Delteijk, Utrect, 1947; cf. pp. 68–9.

152 L. Reypens, S.J., "Het toppunt der bechouwing naar J. van L.", in *Ons geest. Erf*, IX (1935), p. 59; cf. J. Delteijk, *op. cit.*, p. 77.

intellectual edifice of the Rhineland mystics and of the founder of Groenendael. The influence of the *Devotio moderna is clear.*[153]

Thus the fourteenth century ended with what would seem the boldest attempts ever made to unite theology and mysticism. Probably the spiritual writers of the time felt the danger of theology's becoming an autonomous field of knowledge, cut off from all first-hand experience of its object. Some Dominicans, because they directed souls who were living in the light of love, made an almost desperate effort to keep the two in contact. On the one hand, there was their heritage from the great theologians of the thirteenth century; on the other, the daily reminder of what the life of the soul really is, as it makes its way toward union with God. They did not want the two domains to know nothing of one another, to be divorced from each other: and that was precisely what the theologians of their own order, fervent followers of the Aristotelian method and of scientific systematization in theology, had contributed to make irrevocable.

In point of fact, their efforts were fruitless. Piety was to become an end in itself, and theology also. In the conception which was to be dominant for several centuries, and which our own time has not altogether forgotten, the spiritual man, the pious and fervent Christian, could devote himself to the pursuit of perfection without seeing in dogma anything but a kind of indispensable setting for the play—to its harmony and even to its aesthetic value—but alien to the drama itself. This unbelievable rupture reached its completion in the fifteenth century.

[153] Cf. J. Huijben, O.S.B., "J. van. Sch., leerling van den zaligen Jan van Ruusbroec", in *Ons geest. Erf*, VI (1932), pp. 282–303; W. de Vreese, in *Bibliographie nationale . . . de Belgique*, XXI, col. 883–903; S. Axters, O.P., *Geschiedenis . . .*, II, pp. 350–8.

VII

DISREPUTE

1. The Situation in the Middle of the Fourteenth Century

A CERTAIN weariness of spirit is noticeable during the course of the fourteenth century. The excesses of the Nominalists discredited the processes of reason enlightened by faith; theological argument became more and more a purely verbal exercise, where protagonists lost sight of the fact that the strength of the metaphysical speculation of the great thirteenth-century doctors had lain in its sobriety. Theologians too, possibly unconsciously, played their part in the downfall of speculative mysticism. Neither they nor the masters of the spiritual life were in any doubt as to the reality of contemplative prayer, nor of the demands it makes, but as the Middle Ages drew towards their close, it was its psychological manifestations that more and more occupied their attention. Even in the Rhineland, as early as the beginning of the century people had a liking for visions and revelations; and men's minds as a whole turned in that direction. There is evidence of this everywhere, notably in England with Julian of Norwich († *c.* 1442) and Margery Kempe (†1440), and in Switzerland with St Nicholas of Fluë (†1487). At the same time the speculations on the birth of the Word in the soul, and the latter's return to the divine Nothingness, were looked on with distrust. Men asked themselves whether contemplative prayer was only for an élite, gifted with a particularly subtle mind, and blessed by exceptional spiritual gifts and the advantage of a cloistered life. How true was it to say that man here below can attain to the direct vision of God? Surely contemplation is purely a gift of God? Since the Gospel teaches that love is the one thing necessary, what need is there of a preliminary technique? Were not the old monastic schools and the Franciscan ones right, when they made contemplation consist formally in an act of love, and sought their inspiration in humble meditation on the life of Christ?

There was nothing new in the questions themselves: what was new at this time was the acuteness with which they presented themselves to the spiritually minded. Their answer was to restore love once more to its primordial place in contemplation, basing the spiritual life, its theory as well as its practice, on the data of the Gospel; thus throwing contemplation open to all men. It is specially noticeable how ascetical and moral values are brought to the fore as the concrete expression of the love of God. From another point of view, the humanism, which was coming into being after two centuries when the dialectic of reason had triumphed, was gradually to shift the centre of interest from God to man. There was an increased emphasis on the subjective aspect of contemplation, the objective realities (God, the Trinity, Christ, grace) giving way to moral and psychological notions (love, consolation, virtues and vices). No spiritual writer of course rejected dogma in itself, but some isolated the spiritual life from it, thus bringing about a shifting of perspective which, though it did not end in a synthesis comparable with that of the Spanish sixteenth-century mystics, still tended in that direction. Contemplation then, and everything connected with it, took on a similar aspect, less intellectual and metaphysical, nearer to the gospel of love.

On the whole this anti-speculative reaction took place outside the religious houses. The speculative mysticism of the fourteenth century had developed among the Friars Preachers, and the nuns in contact with them, and in the monastery at Groenendael. Its beginnings may perhaps be traced to the béguinages, but it took so slight a form there that it cannot be considered as originally a lay trend. On the other hand the spirituality discussed in this chapter took shape outside the cloister. Catherine of Siena was a Dominican tertiary, but her personality was of a very different order from that of the Friars Preachers who formed her circle.

The English mystics of the fourteenth century tended towards the eremitical life. The *Devotio moderna* in the Low Countries began with the work of a group of lay preachers whom Gerard Groot gathered round him, and only later developed into communities of regulars. Some spiritual leaders were found among the clergy, but these did not belong to the monastic or mendicant orders: the most famous were d'Ailly and Gerson, and with them the secular clergy once more take a prominent place in the history of spirituality.

At the end of the twelfth century some of the best men had found the traditional monastic life inadequate for their own needs, and for those of the Church: hence arose the Mendicant Orders. Now, at the end of the fourteenth century, the same phenomenon is seen, and those of the faithful who aimed at a fervent spiritual life have the same experience as their forefathers; none of the existing Orders, including the Friars, quite fulfil the needs of the times. The religious moved in a world intellectually and spiritually inaccessible to the more devout among the laity, and in any case their lives were only too often far from exemplary. The Franciscans alone had kept the common touch, and the gospel of love which their founder had bequeathed them was a link between the old Augustinian tradition and the new currents of spirituality. Yet it seemed to many that the Order had betrayed its own ideals, and that the times either called for a new pattern of spirituality or for a new mode of religious life.

2. *Catherine of Siena*

Catherine attracts us with a charm comparable with that of the Poor Man of Assisi,[1] and this makes the historian's task more difficult. Her life, like that of Francis Bernadone, is encompassed by a halo of legends, and there is some difficulty in identifying historical fact in the lovely stories that surrounded her. Even the best of her biographers have not always realized this—very far from it.[2] They had not studied the sources critically, and their statements are not always based on incontestable documents. Historians are indebted to Monsieur Fawtier[3] for having undertaken this work, and having encouraged a scientific publication of sources.[4]

The chief source for Catherine's life is the *Leggenda Maiora* by her confessor Raymond of Capua[5] (†1399); then the *Leggende Minore* by Thomas Cafferini,[6] Massimino of Salerno and others;

[1] There are innumerable works on Catherine of Siena. For 1901–50 see the 1044 titles brought together by L. Zanini in *Miscellanea del centro di Studi Medievali*, I, Milan, 1956, pp. 325–74; II (1958), pp. 265–366; III (in preparation). Bibliographies, sources, studies on sources and the works, biographies.

[2] J. Joergensen, Eng. trans., London, 1938; J. Leclercq, 2nd ed., Tournai, 1947; A. Levasti, Turin, 1947; S. Undset, Eng. trans., London, 1954.

[3] R. Fawtier, *Sainte Catherine de Sienne: Essai de critique des Sources*, 2 vols, Paris, 1927–30. This essay resulted in the biography by R. Fawtier and L. Canet, *La double expérience de Catherine Benincasa*, Paris, 1948.

[4] *Fontes vitae Sanctae Catherinae Senensis historici*, cura et studio M-H Laurent, O.P., and F. Vath, Florence (from 1936 onwards).

[5] Ed. A.A. S.S. Aprilis, III, Paris, 1886, pp. 862–967. Ed. of the *Opuscula et litterae* of Raymund of Capua by H.M. Cormier, Rome, 1895; see the "Registrum litterarum Fr. R. de Vineis Capuani", in the *Monum. Ord. Praed. Hist.*, XIX, Rome, 1937.

[6] Ed. E. Franceschini, Milan, 1942; for the *Supplementum* of Tommaso, see the translation by G. Tinagli, Siena, 1938. The *Miracoli* by the "anonymous of Florence" have been published by F. Valli, Florence, 1938.

and also the authentic writings of the saint: the *Dialogue* which sums up her spiritual teaching,[7] and some *Letters*[8] and *Prayers*.[9]

Some modern historians suspect Catherine's disciples of having embellished the facts in the *Leggende*, and Monsieur Fawtier has no hesitation in drawing a comparison between her portrait in the *Leggende* and that seen in her own writings; on the other hand, to many the two pictures are the same. There is no doubt that to accept as historical fact an opinion no one has ever contradicted is a mistake; but it sometimes happens that one comes across an undoubted fact only through information of debateable value—a possibility which must be borne in mind, and not denied *a priori*. In addition to this, side by side with the human experience of a saint goes a spiritual experience, transcending likelihood and sometimes even purely human possibilities or assumptions.

In writing the life of St Catherine modern critics are faced with serious difficulties. Even the date of her birth is uncertain. According to the tradition of her hagiographers, she was born on the feast of the Annunciation 1347, and died on 29 April 1380 at the age of thirty-three. Other similar resemblances to the life of Christ are a little suspicious, and there is some reason for holding that the true date of her birth was earlier, but it is still an open question.

During her childhood she received exceptional graces: she always spoke of them with discretion, and the hagiographical additions may be discarded. Though the date is disputed, she seems to have been very young when she entered an *ordo de pœnitentia*, becoming a Dominican tertiary. Catherine wished neither to marry, nor to enter religion: she was to say "My cell will not be one of stone nor wood, but that of self-knowledge".[10]

According to tradition, her life as a tertiary was extraordinary: penances, fastings, visions, violent opposition were her daily bread. Catherine had the soul of an apostle, and there soon gathered round her a number of fervent disciples, all devoted to their "dearest mother". Among them were her future biographer, Raymund of Capua, who was both her director and her disciple; there were other Dominicans, clerics, politicians, writers, and devout

[7] Ed. I. Taurisano, O.P., Rome, 1947; E. M. di Rovasenda, O.P., Turin, 1948. French translation by J. Hurtant, O.P., 2 vols, Paris, 1913. (Eng. Trans. by A. Thorold, London, 1925). [This, the only English translation, has no index, and does not correspond with the French version of Père Hurtaud used in this chapter. It therefore seemed best to refer only to the Hurtaud edition.—Trans.]

[8] Ed. N. Tommaseo, 6 vols, Florence, 1939–40 (1st ed., 1860); ed. crit. E. Dupré-Théseider, I, Rome, 1940.

[9] Ed. I. Taurisano, Rome, 1932.

[10] Fawtier-Canet, *op. cit.*, p. 60.

women.[11] Her correspondents[12] range from public sinners to much-tried souls and saints. Soon her zeal grew bolder, and reached out beyond her own city: in 1373 she suggested to Gregory XI in Avignon the preaching of a new crusade, but an unfortunate war between Florence and the Papacy brought the project to nothing. The Pope, however, had welcomed her, and she dared to suggest a return to Rome, which indeed took place on 13 September 1376. But it was not long before the Great Schism in the West took place, and some historians have thought that Catherine's action was partly responsible for it.

Her most famous writing, the *Dialogue*, was not dictated during a five days' ecstasy as is sometimes said,[13] but between December 1377 and October 1378[14]; not that her state of mind or the time she took over it has any particular importance. No one has seriously contested the value or authenticity of the *Dialogue*, in spite of slight variations in the manuscripts, the individual touches of those who put it together, or even of a certain cast of thought and vocabulary which was probably not so much hers as that of her Dominican guides.

Catherine, in the *Dialogue* and especially in her *Letters* which are more spontaneous, records a very complete spiritual experience. She was by nature "touchy and unsociable, stubborn and imperious, yet always ready to go off at a canter"[15]; and it may well be that some of her correspondents did not relish the *voglio*—"I desire"—of her letters, nor her habit of commanding or admonishing them "in the name of Christ" or "in the precious Blood of Christ". She maintained with remarkable assurance that she spoke in the name of the Holy Spirit. What the Spirit gave her to utter was certainly not the scholasticism of Aristotle and St Thomas, on which her Dominican confessor and the other Friars Preachers she met had been nourished; nor was it the speculative mysticism of their brethren of the Rhineland. Catherine's whole cast of mind was that of a mystic and an apostle; she had no interest in theoretical questions. Her teaching does not reflect theological specula-

[11] On the group of Catherine's disciples see J. Wilbois, *Sainte Catherine de Sienne et l'actualité de son message*, Tournai, 1948, pp. 171–88. See also M. Maurice Denis-Boulet, *La carrière politique de Sainte Catherine de Sienne*, Paris, 1939, and M. S. Gillet, *La Mission de Sainte Catherine de Sienne*, Paris, 1946. On Catherine's confessors see H. C. Scheeben, "Katharina von Siena und ihre 'Seelenführer'", in *Geist und Leben*, XXX (1957), pp. 281–93, 369–79.

[12] Analysis by J. Wilbois, *op. cit.*, pp. 189–217. Cf. *Dict. de spirit.*, II, pp. 335–7.

[13] J. Hurtaud, *trad. cit.*, I, p. XLIX.

[14] See E. Dupré-Théseider, "Sulla Composizione del 'Dialogo' di Santa Catatina da Siena", in *Giorn. stor. lettere ital*, CXVII (1941), pp. 161–202; Fawtier-Canet, *op. cit.*, pp. 185–6.

[15] Fawtier-Canet, *op. cit.*, p. 247.

tion: it is in the authentic tradition of Christian mysticism, from the Gospel, St Paul and St John, through St Augustine and St Bernard, to St Francis of Assisi. The soul of her religion was an interior Master, not "a system of concepts, an arrangement of formulas, a solemn din of words".[16] Her whole expression of Christian dogma when she speaks of the creature, of sin, of redemption in the blood of the Crucified, or of the Church, is intuitive, not theological. The images and forms of speech she uses are her own, even if at times reminiscent of her Dominican disciples.[17]

The interior Master gave himself to Catherine, and she responded by a total gift of herself, and this mutual giving is the essence of her spiritual experience.

Granted this, Catherine's teaching appears very simple. It does not fit into a ready-made framework, nor can it be systematized, and it has nothing of the theses of the Schools about it.[18] The *Dialogue* in particular is better read without preconceived notions: its theme is set forth in the prologue, and repeated in the penultimate chapter—the 166th: Catherine, "raising up her desires, addressed four requests to the Sovereign and eternal Father". The first concerned herself, and the *Treatise on Discretion* or spiritual discernment is its answer. The first printed editions referred to Chapters 9–64 by this title; but it may well be that it applies only to chaps. 2–16—those of the first answer which Père Hurtant has summarized under the title of "mercy to Catherine".[19] Whichever hypothesis be true, the most explicit treatment of discretion is found in Chapters 9–11. Discretion is "nothing other than the true knowledge the soul must have of herself and me".[20] Knowing that of herself she is nothing, it is in this self-knowledge that the soul finds true humility.

This feeling of her own nothingness was one of Catherine's principal themes: "Know, daughter, that I am he who is, and thou art that which is not." The whole of spiritual life flows from this view of faith, and it leads to greater self-knowledge, and so to humility and true love of God and of one's neighbour and oneself.[21] By this means, too, exterior practices (in particular of pen-

[16] *Ibid.*, p. 276. M. H. Laurent, O.P., art. "Catharine de Sienne", in *Dict. hist. géogr. ecclés.*, XI, col. 1521, admits that the *Dialogue* was "considerably reshaped after her death".

[17] An exposition of the Theology of Catherine's teaching in the first part of A. Grion, O.P., *Santa Catarina da Siena. Dottrina e fonti*, Brescia, 1953.

[18] On Catherine's extra-Dominican sources see Fawtier-Canet, *op. cit.*, pp. 252–271.

[19] Cf. *trad. cit.*, I, p. LX.

[20] Ch. IX.

[21] Cf. R. Garrigou-Lagrange, "La foi selon Sainte Catherine de Sienne", in *La Vie spirituelle*, XLV (1935), pp. 236–49; T. Deman, "Pour une théologie de

ance), which are only means, are given their right place. So also is the exercise of humility, and charity towards one's neighbour, which is the test of the reality of everything else. "I wish you to know that there is no virtue, nor any fault, which is not manifested by means of one's neighbour."[22]

A little further on are found "Explanations of discernment"[23]: our Lord's reply to Catherine when she asked him what counsel to give those who came to her for advice. Then "When thou, O eternal God, dost honour a soul by visiting her, by what sign shall she recognize that it is truly thou?"[24] This second question refers particularly to prayer, and is answered in Chap. 106. The sign of God's presence is "the joy that I leave in the soul after I have visited her, and a desire for virtue; especially the virtue of true humility, joined with the ardour of divine charity." The devil may also visit the soul, and "first of all make his presence known by joy"; but this is followed by sadness, remorse of conscience, and no desire for virtue . . . giving forth an odour of humility". To joy therefore must be joined a desire for virtue, and above all for humility.[25]

Catherine's second demand concerned "the reformation of Holy Church"; the third "the whole world, and especially peace among those Christians who with so great irreverence and injustice have rebelled against Holy Church". The replies are not in the same order as the requests, but transposed; and have been entitled "mercy for the world",[26] and "mercy for Holy Church".[27] Our Lord explains to Catherine that "mercy for the world" was first shown by the gift of the Word incarnate, the "bridge" which joins this world to heaven; then comes the gift of "conformity to Christ", the means by which this bridge is crossed both by those who till now have missed salvation, and by the soul itself. After passing from servile fear to a self-interested love, the soul rises to perfect love "pure and free", and finally to a divine union, of which she is always sensible.[28] At the term of this ascent lies the gift of tears.

The third answer, "mercy to Holy Church", is not concerned with the whole Church, but with the hierarchy, for it is there that reformation is needed. This part treats of the dignity of the priest-

l'amour d'après l'Epistolario (especially letter 29, ed. Tommaseo)", in *Studi Cateriniani*, XI (1935), pp. 90–9.

[22] Ch. VI. [23] Ch. XCVIII–CIX. [24] Ch. XCVII.

[25] Ch. CVI; cf. ch. LXXI—some passages from Catherine's writings on discretion in *Prudence chrétienne*, Coll. "Cahiers de la Vie Spirituelle", Paris, 1948, pp. 113–120.

[26] Ch. XVII–CXVII. [27] Ch. CX–CXXXIV.

[28] Cf. R. Garrigou-Lagrange, *L'Unione mistica in Santa Catarina da Siena*, Florence, 1938.

hood, what should be the virtues of God's ministers, and which the vices they must avoid. "They are my anointed ones, and I call them my Christs."[29] Finally, the fourth request concerns the needs of the world, and a particular case which had come to her notice.[30] This is answered by the treatise of the "Providence of Mercy", dealing at the same time with the particular case and the general salvation of souls to be drawn out of sin and led to the life of grace and perfect charity. This is followed by a treatise on obedience, and the special Providence of the obedient. The chief teachings of the *Dialogue* are summed up in a short conclusion.[31]

Significantly, for Catherine, the love of God cannot be separated from love for the Church and for one's neighbour,[32] and this love unites itself with our redemption in the blood of Christ, making satisfaction and expiation. "I tell thee truly, the more tribulation abounds in the mystical body of the Church, the more shall it (love) abound in mildness and consolation. With this mildness shall good and holy pastors reform.... Thou shalt suffer, but afterwards I will mingle consolation with thy bitter trials, by the reforming of Holy Church."[33] Love of the Church shines through the whole of the *Dialogue*: "Let there rise up to me unceasingly the sweet-smelling incense of prayers for the salvation of souls; for I will show mercy to the world. It is with these prayers, this sweat, these tears, that I will to cleanse the face of the Spouse, Holy Church."[34]

Nothing can bring sinners back to a state of grace and charity like prayers and holiness of life: and contrariwise the vices of shepherds mean that "the poor are defrauded of what is due to them."[35] Catherine's burning zeal bursts forth up to the last letter she wrote, to Raymund of Capua. "O eternal Father, accept the sacrifice of my life for the mystical body of Holy Church."[36]

Looking at the saint's spirituality as a whole, her attitude on this point is something quite new. St Francis indeed had understood the whole redemptive bearing of Union with Christ crucified, but his thought found little echo. St Gertrude, as will be seen later, is practically alone in speaking in a similar sense, while the great theologians of the thirteenth century, though they treated of the reversibility of merits, paid no special attention to this aspect of the spiritual life. The chief preoccupation until the end of the fourteenth century was rather with the ascent of the soul to God. More

[29] Ch. CXIII.
[30] Chs CXXXV–CLXV.
[31] Chs CLXVI–CLXVII.
[32] Cf. *Dialogue*, ch. VII and XXIV, for example.
[33] Cf. XII; cf. chs IV, V, LXXVI, LXXVIII, etc.
[34] Ch. LXXXVIII.
[35] Ch. CXXIII.
[36] Letter 371 (15–16 Feb. 1380) ed. Tommaseo.

thought was given to the necessary conditions for contemplation than to its redemptive effects, or its place in the life of the Church. Not that this point of view was either narrow or selfish: but Catherine shows herself more obsessed with the needs of the Church. Her concern was with what she herself, the *mantellata* of Siena, could do. But, though she never hesitated to act—and living in the world she enjoyed greater freedom than she would have had in a monastery—yet she always knew that her prayer, her penance, her personal holiness would do even more for the Church than any intervention among men; and in this she revealed herself a true religious.

Another side of Catherine's character is the importance she attaches to knowledge: the knowledge of God and of oneself; and this gives to the *Dialogue* what may be called its intellectual tendency. She follows closely in the footsteps of her Dominican teachers, but goes further than they do. It is not so much her emphasis on the love of God and one's neighbour (no one had dreamed of giving that second place) but her zeal for souls and the stress she lays on the redemptive value of prayer and sanctity united to the satisfaction of Christ crucified.

One feature of her teaching is reminiscent of a particular aspect of the speculative mysticism of the fourteenth century: "Know that I am he who is, and thou art she who is not". She is "nothingness". Before God, the source of all being, all creatures are nothingness of themselves. From this knowledge springs true humility, by which the soul craves to be overwhelmed by him who alone is. One is inevitably reminded of the Rhineland Dominicans, though there are notable differences between their teaching and hers. She never speaks, like Suso, of the Nothingness of God. Unlike him, her language is not ambiguous and does not need to be explained in an orthodox sense. Moreover Catherine knows nothing of the central theme of speculative mysticism—the generation of the Word in the depths of the soul which has stripped itself of all things. Catherine too demands detachment and humility, the knowledge of one's nothingness before God; but the notion that after this self-stripping the Word will come to birth in the soul is altogether foreign to her thought. It would be a mistake, however, to see "anti-intellectualism" in this: it is simply a different cast of mind. For Catherine all was summed up in love and union with Christ crucified. She was more preoccupied with the Church's cause than with the mechanism of contemplation. As she saw it, a love which unites us to the redemptive love of Christ takes precedence over the knowledge of God and of a man's own self; a knowledge which is the starting-point, important of course, but only a beginning. Not that Catherine did not hold the received opinion that eternal happiness consists in the vision of God[37]: but on earth at least the immediate aim is something else. As long as there is still one soul to be bought back, there can be no rest for those who have understood the redeeming Christ and his cross.

It is here that Catherine's chief originality lies. Because of her, spirituality takes a new flight. Both monks and mendicants had had their own special characteristics, valid for their own times. Catherine reminded her contemporaries of what it is that makes a soul capable of acting upon the Church, and upon other souls in need of redemption. It is its ardent love, its deep union with the mystery of the Cross, whence flows upon the world the Blood which redeems it; and not necessarily sanctity in almost complete isolation from the world, or the life of a friar or theologian in an "Order" whose mission and methods are precisely laid down.

Catherine is therefore unintentionally a very representative witness to the dawning disrepute of conventual life and speculative mysticism. She did not live in community, and she preached love with all the spontaneity and ardour of her soul, without trying to analyse its manifestations or its effects.

3. The English Mystics

The English spiritual writers of the fourteenth century are not an altogether homogeneous group. The chief characteristic that they have in common is their distrust of abstract speculation and of conventual life. Probably this trait is simply the result of the English temperament, which tends to be pragmatist and particularist; though one needs to be cautious in characterizing the Anglo-Saxon spirituality of that period, because there are whole strata of the population about which there is no documentary evidence. In particular, we know almost nothing about the spirituality of the monasteries, although these were numerous and often fervent.[38]

The *Ancrene Riwle*, the earliest document in medieval English to set forth rules for any form of religious life, was not, as has been seen, intended for religious living in community, but for lay recluses. It exhibits the trait mentioned above, being a quest for sanctity in solitude, emphasizing the ascetical and practical aspects of the spiritual life to the detriment of the doctrinal and theological

[37] Ch. LXII, for example.

[38] See, for example, the *De substancialibus regule monachalis* and the *De perfectione vivendi*, by the Benedictine Uthred of Boldon (†1397), described and analysed by W. A. Pantin, "Two Treatises of Uthred of Boldon on the Monastic Life", in *Studies in Medieval History Presented to F. M. Powicke*, Oxford, 1948, pp. 363–85. On the religious situation as a whole, see W. A. Pantin, *The English Church in the Fourteenth Century*, Cambridge, 1955.

ones. Prayer, in the *Ancrene Riwle*, is neither liturgical nor even, properly speaking, contemplative. It consists chiefly in practices, formulas, in "devotions", in which the interior sentiment of piety and fervour appears to be an end in itself.[39]

The rule is not an isolated example, except that it was written in medieval English. Other similar documents have come down to us from the thirteenth and fourteenth centuries. Some spiritual *opuscula* are characterized by an individual tendency, which is not only extra-conventual but even extra-hierarchical,[40] such as the *Regula reclusorum Angliae*, primarily practical in tone, and intended for laymen. It goes back to about 1280 and seems to have been the work of a hermit named Walter, formerly an Augustinian canon.[41] A *Speculum inclusorum*, dating from about the middle of the fourteenth century, is fairly systematic in its arrangement. It enumerates the motives for the vocation of a recluse: the possibility of living *iuxta libitum* without danger; the desire for penance; the avoidance of occasions of sin, despite the dangers inherent in the life; and the facilitating of contemplation. The contemplative aspect of the recluse's life is brought out more distinctly than in the *Ancrene Riwle*; thus spiritual reading, devout meditation, and fervent prayer are its very object.

The same eremitical character and the same desire to apply oneself without impediment to contemplation are found in Richard Rolle (†1349), the first great writer of the English school of the fourteenth century.[42] Little is known of his youth. According to the lessons of an office, which are given in an English translation in the York Breviary, Rolle would seem to have become a hermit when very young. It is possible that he may have studied at the Sorbonne, beginning in 1318, and that he there became a doctor of theology. In that case, it would only be on his return to England, after 1326 (when he was more than thirty years old), that he

[39] See p. 275, *supra*.

[40] For example, the six little works intended for devout women and written largely by a feminine author, *The Wohunge of Ure Lauerd*, ed. by W. M. Thompson, Oxford, 1958.

[41] Ed. L. Oliger, O.F.M., "Regula reclusorum Angliae et quaestiones tres de vita solitaria saec. XIII–XIV", in *Antonianum*, IX (1934), pp. 37–84, 243–68. On the English recluses and hermits, see *ibid.*, III (1928), pp. 151–90, 299–320. See also I. Foster, "The Book of the Anchorite", in *Proc. Brit. Academy*, XXXVI (1950), pp. 197–226.

[42] See the anthology of texts, published and unpublished, assembled by C. Kirchberger, *The Coasts of the Country. An Anthology of Prayer Drawn from the Early English Spiritual Writers*, London, 1952. There are studies by R. M. Wilson, *Three Middle English Mystics*, in *Essays and Studies*, IX (1956), pp. 87–112; P. Renaudin, *Quatre mystiques anglais*, Paris, 1945; E. McKinnon, *Studies in Fourteenth Century English Mysticism*, Urbana, Ill., 1934; M. D. Knowles, *The English Mystical Tradition*, London, 1961.

became a hermit. This, however, has been seriously contested.[43] His noviciate consisted of three years of penance and prayer, after which he received graces that may be properly called mystical. Chief among his works[44] are the *Incendium amoris*, translated into English under the name of *The Fire of Love* by Richard Mysin in 1434–5,[45] and the *Form of Perfect Living*.[46] To these must be added the recently edited *Melos amoris*,[47] which is very valuable as an autobiography and apologia for Rolle's personal life. That it was fairly widely read is proved by a manuscript compilation, also published recently.[48] There was also his *Emendatio vitae*, or *The Mending of Life*, which is more moralistic[49]; the *Canticum amoris de Beata Virgine*[50] and finally a commentary on the first verses of the Canticle of Canticles.[51]

One has only to look through the *Fire of Love* and the *Form of Perfect Living* to note the absence of scholastic theory and even of any abstract ideas,[52] which, as a matter of fact, would be easier to explain if their author had not been a student at the Sorbonne. Rolle does not deny that contemplation is an act of the intellect,[53] but he says that it leads the soul to union with God, to love. Its object is the Trinity, the processions and the divine Persons.[54] As this object is unknowable in itself, contemplation always remains obscure, and Rolle emphasizes the essential role played in it by love.[55] For him, this love is directed, in the concrete, to Christ[56];

43 By E. Arnould, *The Melos Amoris of R. R. of Hampole*, Oxford, 1957, app. II, pp. 210–38.

44 *English Writings of R.R.*, ed. H. E. Allen, Oxford, 1931; *R.R. of Hampole, an English Father of the Church, and His Followers*, ed. C. Horstman, 2 vols, London, 1895–6.

45 *English Prose Treatises*, ed. R. Harvey, Orchard Series 106, London, 1896; *Incendium Amoris*, ed. M. Deanesly, Manchester, 1915; *The Officium and Miracula of R.R. of Hampole*, ed. R. M. Woolley, London, 1919; *Selected Works*, by G. C. Heseltine, London, 1930. Cf. E. Schnell, *Die Traktate des R.R. von Hampole "Incendium amoris" und "Emendatio vitae" und deren Uebersetzung durch Richard Mysin*, Leipzig, 1932.

46 There is a French translation of these last two treatises by M. Noetinger, Tours, 1929. For an anthology in French, see *Du péché à l'amour divin*, translated by L. Denis, S.J., Paris, 1926.

47 By E. Arnould; see note 43.

48 Ed. G. M. Liegey, "R. Rolle's Carmen Prosaicum", in *Med. Studies*, XIX (1957), pp. 15–36.

49 Ed. D. Hartford, London, 1913.

50 Ed. G. M. Liegey, "The 'Canticum amoris' of R.R.", in *Traditio*, XII (1956), pp. 369–91.

51 Ed. Y. Madon, in *Mél. Sc. Relig.*, VII (1950), pp. 311–25.

52 Cf. A. Olmes, *Sprache und Stil der englische Mystik des Mittelalters unter besondere Berücksichtigung des R.R. von H.*, Halle, 1933.

53 *Form of Perfect Living*, ch. XII.

54 *Fire of Love*, I, chs VI–VII

55 This idea continually recurs in the *Melos amoris*, as do those of the character of love and its effects; cf. E. Arnould, *op. cit.*, pp. xl–lvi.

56 *Fire of Love*, II, ch. VIII.

it often takes the form of affective devotion, in which the Passion has a prominent place.[57] His devotion to Mary is also worthy of mention.[58]

Rolle accentuates the primacy of the love of God to the point of seeking to deter contemplatives from works of fraternal charity which might distract them from it.[59] The opposition between two occupations of loving God and loving one's brother is one of his frequent themes. He justifies his exclusion of fraternal charity by the extraordinary efficacy of the contemplative's love[60]—an argument which seems to be directed against the Mendicant Orders. Rolle admits that he experienced this pure love[61]; he calls it a fire, *calor*,[62] a spiritual song, *canor*, equal to that of the angels, a rapture, *raptus*, and a sweetness, *dulcor*.[63] He distinguishes two kinds of "ravishing" or rapture, one with loss of the bodily senses and the other without it. The second is more perfect than the first, because it is more meritorious; it consists in "the elevation of the spirit into God by contemplation".[64] This does not seem to lend support to Professor Knowles' view that Rolle's mystical experience can be reduced to phenomena of the natural order,[65] or that of P. Renaudin, who sees *calor, canor*, and *dulcor* as three phases, though often mingled together, of the contemplative life.[66]

Since Rolle lived an independent life, he seldom speaks of the necessity of spiritual direction. He knew, however, that great temptations lie in wait for the solitary, especially for the beginner; the *Melos amoris* emphasizes the snares of the flesh.[67] Prudence, then, is very necessary, but the guide is to be an interior one. He it is who will confer the gift of wisdom and, by this gift, invite the contemplative to "forget earthly things, to think of heaven, and to observe discretion in all his actions".[68] The interior action of the Holy Spirit is therefore of primary importance for Rolle,[69] the more so since the Spirit comes to the aid of the contemplative with his gifts. He supports both the ordinary life of virtue and the life of prayer properly so called; his gifts "are given to those who are called to the joys of heaven, and who live a virtuous life".[70] Rolle

[57] See the meditation on the passion, "De passione secundum Ricardum" (*Possibly a New Work by Richard Rolle*), ed. F. Wormald, in *Laudate*, XIII (1935), pp. 37–48. Cf. M. M. Morgan, "Versions of the Meditations on the Passion Ascribed to R.R.", in *Medium Aevum*, XXII (1953), pp. 93–103.

[58] For example, in his *Canticum amoris de Beata Virgine*, ed. Liegey, *op. cit.*

[59] *Fire of Love*, I, ch. III.

[60] *Ibid.*, I, ch. XXI and *passim.*

[61] *Ibid.*, I, ch. XV.

[62] *Ibid.*, I.

[63] *Ibid.*, II.

[64] *Ibid.*, II, ch. VII.

[65] *English Mystics*, pp. 78–80; see also *The English Mystical Tradition.*

[66] *Quatre mystiques anglais*, p. 41; *Mystiques anglais*, Paris, 1957, pp. 20–5.

[67] Chs II, XVII, XXXIII, etc.

[68] *Form of Perfect Living*, ch. XI.

[69] For example, *Fire of Love*, II, ch. II.

[70] *Form of Perfect Living*, ch. XI.

treats of the gifts in reverse order to the usual one, beginning with wisdom and ending with fear of the Lord, and his attention is chiefly directed to their psychological aspect. This independence with regard to accepted ideas is found again in his *Explanation of the Pater*,[71] which connects certain petitions of the prayer—not very systematically—with the gifts of the Holy Spirit. The first petition is associated with the gifts of wisdom, the second with that of understanding, the third with that of counsel, the fourth with that of fortitude, and the fifth that of knowledge. But he fails to connect the sixth and seventh petitions, as one would expect, with piety and fear of the Lord.

Another spiritual writer, who probably wrote between 1350 and 1370, was even more untouched by the vanities of the schools than Richard Rolle, and even more independent of conventual patterns. This was the anonymous author of the *Cloud of Unknowing*[72] and of various small treatises related to it: the *Epistle of Privy Counsel*, the *Epistle of Prayer*,[73] the *Epistle of Discretion*, and the treatise *Of Discerning of Spirits*.[74]

The *Cloud of Unknowing* is perhaps one of the finest spiritual treatises of the whole fourteenth century, and it has given rise to much debate. There has been, first of all, the question of its authorship. It was probably written by a priest. The name of Walter Hilton, who will be discussed below, has been suggested more than once,[75] but there are solid reasons against attributing it to him; but even the doctrine itself has been the subject of controversy. The work is Dionysian even to its title, which was borrowed from the *Mystical Theology*,[76] and its dominant note is "apophatic". Certain modern philosophers have gone so far as to find in its author, as they have in Eckhart, a precursor of the idealism which was later to "depersonalize" God.[77] This is, however, sheer anach-

[71] In the Noetinger translation, pp. 351–60.

[72] Critical edition by P. Hodgson, London, 1944. There are translations into modern English by J. McCann, O.S.B., London, 1936; and E. Underhill, London, 1934. French translations by M. Noetinger, Tours, 1925; and A. Guerne, Paris, 1953.

[73] Critical edition by P. Hodgson following that of the *Cloud*, *op. cit*.

[74] Critical edition by P. Hodgson, London, 1955. The title *Deonise Hid Divinite* given to this edition is that of a translation (sometimes free, and supplemented by texts from Thomas Gallus) of a Latin version of the *Mystica theologia* of the Pseudo-Dionysius. Also included is a summary of the *Benjamin minor* of Richard of St Victor. The works mentioned above give translations of the epistles also.

[75] For example, by H. L. Gardner, in *Medium Aevum*, XVI (1947), 36–42. But cf. P. Hodgson, "Walter Hilton and 'The Cloud of Unknowing'. A Problem of Authorship Reconsidered", in *Modern Lang. Rev.*, I (1955), pp. 395–406. Miss Hodgson maintains that Hilton's identity with the author of the *Cloud* is more difficult to establish than their distinction.

[76] *Cloud*, ch. III; p. 12, McCann edition.

[77] Cf. G. Hort, *Sense and Thought. A Study in Mysticism*, London, 1936.

ronism. Such a denial of a personal God can hardly be supposed in an author whose Christian faith is above suspicion. It is true that the *Cloud*, by the way in which it speaks negatively of God, is reminiscent of certain trends in fourteenth-century mysticism; but it shows no further trace of a pantheistic tendency. Its sources reveal the author's very definite concern for orthodoxy; while the authority of the Pseudo-Dionysius is invoked for certain apparently adventurous theories, the fact remains that the author of the *Cloud* was acquainted with St Augustine, Richard of St Victor, and the *De adhaerendo Deo*. He never quotes St Thomas Aquinas, but points of contact have been detected between his doctrine and that of the great doctor: for example in the matter of the life of grace,[78] and even in that of the relation between love and knowledge.[79] In many places his vocabulary foreshadows that of St John of the Cross on the divine darkness.[80]

Here the roots are clearly Dionysian. For the author of the *Cloud*, however, when it is a question of going to God, it is love that counts. God may be reached in this life by love, but not by knowledge.[81] The contemplative life is ordered to love, and in this connection the author attacks those who disparage that life. But he has a sounder judgment than Rolle: he recognizes that the active life is "full good and full holy", and that a man in it can attain to perfect charity. The lower form of the active life, indeed, consists "in good and honest bodily works of mercy and charity"; the higher form, in "good ghostly meditations, and busy beholdings unto a man's own wretchedness, with sorrow and contrition, unto the passion of Christ and of his servants with pity and compassion, and unto the wonderful gifts, kindness and works of God." These boundaries define the domain in which active livers dwell, except in the rare moments when they attain to the contemplative life. This latter is described as consisting in love, and in order to pierce the "cloud of unknowing" (of God) one must accept the "cloud of forgetting" (of creatures). These clouds are pierced only by blind "stirrings" or impulses of naked love, which shoot up like sharp darts. This "work", this obscure general contemplation, is not concerned with other objects, but with God alone. To this end the author of the *Cloud* recommends the repetition of a simple word *God, sin, love*. This technique bears a certain analogy to the "aspirations" recommended in the preceding century by Hugh of Balma (who will be discussed shortly), or even to certain aspects

[78] *Cloud*, ch. XXXIV, pp. 83–6. [79] *Ibid.*, ch. LXVII, pp. 156–8; and *passim*.
[80] Cf. D. Knowles, O.S.B., "The Excellence of the Cloud", in *Downside Rev.*, LII (1934), pp. 71–92.
[81] *Cloud*, ch. VIII, p. 33.

of Orthodox hesychasm of the eleventh to fourteenth centuries, and Ignatius of Loyola, following Henry Herp and many others, did not despise such methods.[82]

The whole exposition of the work of contemplation in the *Cloud* is simple and clear, yet at first disconcerting. The author is much more a psychologist than a theologian. On occasions he shows a sense of humour, and does not hesitate to break away from the usual formulas concerning the interior life. Only after repeatedly reading these closely written pages does one find the key to them: then a new landscape appears, and one's experience is correspondingly enriched.

It has already been said, in connection with the active life, that the author of the *Cloud* shows a more balanced judgment than Rolle. This can be seen when he comes to speak of spiritual direction: the *Epistle of Discretion* was intended to help the reader to discern the good and evil movements of the soul. To obtain this discretion and "ghostly wisdom", he must go to "the school of God",[83] and of Christ, "the angel of great counsel".[84] The soul must "say sharply that it will not follow such stirrings, seem they never so liking and pleasant, so high nor so holy, but if it have thereto the witness and the consent of some ghostly teachers—I mean such as have been of long time expert in singular living of extraordinary ways".[85] The author goes on to show that he takes his role as a director seriously, for he is not sparing in his advice to anyone who wishes to progress in virtue and prayer.[86] The director himself, however, must be in contact with God; then his direction will be the art of "teaching and counselling his brethren". As for the disciple, he must rely on obedience and must "meek him to counsel".[87] It is the only way to avoid the illusions[88] and snares of the devil, whose activity is at the bottom of false or suspect mysticism. He acts upon the imagination of those who are inexperienced in spiritual things, and of those who "travail their imagination so indiscreetly that at the last they turn their brain in their heads;

[82] See M. Olphe-Galliard, S.J., "De l'usage et de l'utilité des méthodes contemplatives dans le catholicisme", in *Technique et contemplation* (*Etudes carmélitaines*, 1949), pp. 67–76; on hesychasm, see A. Bloom, *ibid.*, pp. 49–67.

[83] *Epistle of Discretion*, chs. II and IX.

[84] *Ibid.*, ch. VI.

[85] *Ibid.*, ch. IV.

[86] *The Epistle of Privy Counsel* is a long letter of direction intended to help the recipient to practise the "work" of which the *Cloud* speaks.

[87] This can be seen in the *Treatise of Discerning of Spirits*, n. 3 and 4. In this treatise, the author of the *Cloud* reproduces extracts from two of St Bernard's sermons *De diversis*, Nos 23 and 24, with which he mingles his own explanations. The passages in question form part of this personal material. See also *The Epistle of Privy Counsel*, chs IX, X and XII; *Cloud*, chs II, X, XV, XVI, XXXVI, XLVIII, LI, LXXIV, LXXV.

[88] Described in the *Cloud*, ch. XLV; pp. 108–10.

and then as fast at once the devil hath power to feign some false light or sounds, sweet smells in their noses, wonderful tastes in their mouths, and many quaint heats and burnings in their bodily breasts or in their bowels, in their backs and in their reins and in their members."[89] The remedy is always in true contemplative prayer, in the "work" of which the *Cloud* speaks continually: one which enrages the devil.[90] But there is no authentic "work" without humble submission.

Another slightly later writer, Walter Hilton (†1396), shows little of their unconforming outlook. His *Scala perfectionis*, or *Scale of Perfection*,[91] a didactic treatise on the spiritual life, and on the means adapted to lead men to perfection, is more representative of his thought than *The Goad of Love*, his interpolated translation of the *Stimulus amoris*, a Latin work long attributed to St Bonaventure, but probably written by James of Milan, a Franciscan of the thirteenth century.[92]

The *Scale of Perfection* consists of two books, if indeed it was not originally two distinct treatises.[93] In it, Hilton echoes many of Rolle's ideas and especially those of the author of the *Cloud*[94]: so much so that he has been held to be its author. Like his predecessors, he sees union with God to consist chiefly in love. For some, the active life and the works of mercy; for others, the contemplative life. This latter "is the life which belongs to those who for the love of God have left worldly riches, honours, and external activity, and devoted themselves body and soul to the service of God in the interior life."[95] The essential work of that life is contemplation, and perfection is the consummation of perfection in perfect contemplation. Hilton, however, avoids comparing this, like Rolle, with bodily sensations.[96]

In the *Scale* we find that division, common at the time, of contemplation into ascending degrees. The first degree consists "in the knowledge of God and spiritual matters which can be attained by reason. We get this through the teaching of other men and our own

89 *Cloud*, ch. LII; p. 124; cf. chs XLV, XLVI, XVLIII, LI, LVII.
90 *Ibid.*, chs III, pp. 11–12; also ch. XXXIV.
91 Ed. E. Underhill, 2nd ed., London, 1950. There are translations into modern English by G. Sitwell, O.S.B., London, 1953; and L. Sherley-Price, London, 1957. [But cf. an article by D. Noetinger, "The Modern Editions of . . . The Scala Perfectionis", in *Downside Rev.*, CXVIII (1923), pp. 149–57.—Trans.]
92 Ed. C. Kirchberger, London, 1951.
93 Cf. H.L. Gardner, "The Text of the Scale of Perfection", in *Medium Aevum*, V (1936), pp. 11–30. Book I is known in several different versions.
94 Cf. H. L. Gardner, "W. H. and the Mystical Tradition in England", in *Essays and Studies*, XXII (1937), pp. 103–27.
95 *Scale*, I, 3.
96 See G. Sitwell, O.S.B., "Contemplation in 'The Scale of Perfection'", in *Downside Rev.*, LXVII (1949), pp. 276–90; LXVIII (1950), pp. 21–34, 271–89.

study of the Scriptures."[97] The second degree "consists principally in the act of love". It includes a lower stage and a higher one. The lower stage is accessible to all Christians "when the grace of God visits them" and is the normal effect of living a good Christian life.[98] The higher stage is that of "great tranquillity of body and soul . . . peace of heart and a good conscience". Those who have arrived at this stage are "continually praying, keeping their minds on our Lord. And they like to think of the Holy Name of Jesus, for they find it comforting. The remembrance of it feeds their love."[99] Finally, the third degree, that of perfect contemplation, enlightens the soul by the grace of the Holy Spirit and causes it to taste the first-fruits of the heavenly life, "a soft, sweet, burning love". "So powerfully does this come about that by an ecstasy of love the soul for the time being becomes one with God and is conformed to the image of the Trinity." True to the psychological tendency of his school, Hilton compares this union with that of marriage.[100] The grace is "a special gift and not a common one"; "the plenitude of it is reserved for the contemplative and the solitary."[101] It must not be confused with visions and apparitions.[102]

The rest of the treatise aims at preparing the contemplative for this grace. It will be noted that in Book II[103] the image of the "night" is developed at length. "But this night is good and the darkness luminous, for it . . . brings nearer the true day."[104] Painful and purifying as it is, this night is "nothing else than a desire through grace to have the love of Jesus"—a foreshadowing of St Teresa, and especially St John of the Cross.

Hilton does not fail to give the recluse he is writing to some useful advice: she must have discretion and discernment of spirits, and she should have recourse to a spiritual director,[105] especially at the beginning.[106] It is evident that the distrust of conventual spirituality felt at this time had the result of emphasizing the indispensability of spiritual direction, going back to the kind of direction used by the desert hermits of the East.

The English school of spirituality was to produce no more works comparable with the *Cloud of Unknowing*, the *Fire of Love*, or the *Scale of Perfection*. Towards the middle of the fourteenth century, an anonymous solitary on the island of Farne wrote some Latin meditations, addressed to Christ crucified, to Mary, to the angels, to Abraham, David, St John the Evangelist, and St Cuth-

97 *Scale*, I, 4–5. 98 *Ibid.*, I, 6. 99 *Ibid.*, I, 7.
100 *Ibid.*, I, 8. 101 *Ibid.*, I, 9. 102 *Ibid.*, I, 10–11.
103 *Ibid.*, II, 23–8. 104 *Ibid.*, II, 24.
105 Cf. *ibid.*, I, 83; and *Goad of Love*, chs XXX and XXXI.
106 *Scale*, I, 38.

bert. Both in form and in substance, they seem to be derived from St Anselm and St Bernard.[107] Not long afterwards there appeared the treatise *The Chastising of God's Children*,[108] but this again is not on the same level as the works discussed above. It appears to be a series of conferences given to nuns with a view of leading them to a life of personal prayer. The anonymous author warns them against certain doctrines of a quietist nature and against tendencies to "enthusiasm". This leads him to subordinate private prayer to liturgical prayer, running counter in this to the general tendency of previous English spiritual writers. He was influenced by Ruysbroeck, and quotes long extracts from his works, especially from the *Spiritual Espousals*. He was also acquainted with Suso's *Horologium sapientiae*, but he cannot be classed among the disciples of the speculative school of the Rhineland. In reality, he was—like the other English spiritual writers—simply an eclectic, prejudiced against a speculative attitude in spiritual matters. On the other hand, he has a predilection for the ancient monastic writings; in this he is more in the traditional line. It is significant that he thought it necessary to react against excessive speculation, a tendency more dangerous on the Continent than in England: it must therefore not have been unknown in England; possibly it had found a home in certain women's monasteries.

Fairly characteristic of English spirituality in the fifteenth century are two visionaries. With them, even more than with the writers of the fourteenth century, the accent is on the psychological aspects of their experiences, with no great stress laid on theological foundations or moral presuppositions.

Julian of Norwich (†1442) in her *Revelations of Divine Love*[109] gives an account of a long ecstatic vision, or series of "shewings", which was granted her in 1373, when she was thirty years of age. Her book betrays some uncertainty over the problem of sin, but it shows so much faith, humility, devotion to Catholic truth, love, and finally optimism and joy, that the reader feels inclined to accept the truth of her vision.

[107] *The Monk of Farne: the Meditations of a Fourteenth Century Monk*, trans. by a Benedictine of Stanbrook, ed. and intro. by H. Farmer, O.S.B., Baltimore, Md, 1961. Cf. W. A. Pantin, "The Monk-Solitary of Farne: a Fourteenth-Century Mystic", in *Engl. Hist. Review*, LIX (1944), pp. 162–86; by the same author, *The English Church in the Fourteenth Century*, Cambridge, 1955, pp. 245–52.

[108] Critical edition by J. Bazire and E. Colledge, Oxford, 1957. This volume also includes a translation, made in the fifteenth century by Jordaens, of the Latin version of Ruysbroeck's treatise *Van den blinckenden steen*, as this treatise bears a certain relation to the other.

[109] There is a critical edition of the long text by R. Hudleston, O.S.B., 2nd ed., London, 1952; and a translation of the short text into modern English by A. M. Reynolds, London, 1958.

This grace that Julian received showed her, as it were, the whole body of the truths of faith. She sums it up in the revelation of Love: "Wouldst thou witten thy Lord's meaning in this thing? Wit it well: Love was his meaning. Who shewed it thee? Love. What shewed he thee? Love. Wherefore shewed it he? For love. Hold thee therein and thou shalt witten and know more in the same. But thou shalt never know nor witten therein other thing without end."[110]

Margery Kempe (†1440) inspires less confidence. Between 1436 and 1438, she dictated an account of her life, but until 1934, when her manuscript was discovered, the autobiography in its entirety remained unknown.[111] Margery gives evidence of unquestionable good faith, and the emotional strain in which she writes can be explained by remorse for a grave sin committed in her youth. But her excited tone awakens distrust and makes the reader wonder whether she is not a case for a psychiatrist rather than a theologian. Her instability seems to throw doubt on the value of what she says, which in any case has still less of a theological basis than has Julian—so much so, in fact, that she has even been considered a precursor of the unconforming outlook that was to lead to the Reformation.[112]

Many examples of this kind of religious literature, primarily psychological or practical in tendency, can be found in England of the fourteenth and fifteenth centuries. In addition to the authors already mentioned, there are some collections of sermons, such as those in a manuscript in the British Museum,[113] which were probably intended for a lay audience. The content is simple: narratives, lively details and the elements of theology. At the same time, a whole literature of books of devotion developed, which were often simple translations of works that had already appeared on the Continent, or at least taken from them. Sometimes they were in-

110 *Revelations of Divine Love*, ch. 86, Hudleston edition. For an analysis of the spiritual teaching in the *Revelations*, see P. Renaudin, *Mystiques anglais*, pp. 71–82; and especially P. Molinari, S.J., *Julian of Norwich. The Teaching of a 14th-Century English Mystic*, London, 1958.

111 *The Book of Margery Kempe*, critical edition by S. B. Meech and H. E. Allen, London, 1940; version in modern English by W. Butler-Bowdon, London, 1936 (cf. *La Vie spirit., Suppl.*, LV (1938), pp. 60–3). There is a study by K. Cholmeley, *M.K., Genius and Mystic*, London, 1947. Biographical information is given by H. S. Bennett in *Six Medieval Men and Women*, Cambridge, 1955.

112 On Margery's disconcerting devotion to the Eucharist, see "M.K. and the Holy Eucharist", by a Benedictine of Stanbrook, in *Downside Rev.*, LVI (1938), pp. 468–82.

113 MS *Brit. Museum, Royal 18 B. 23*; ed. *Middle English Sermons*, by W. O. Ross, London, 1940. There is much to be found in the anthology by C. Kirchberger previously cited, *The Coasts of the Country*, London, 1952.

tended for princesses, like Margaret of York,[114] sometimes for simple monks[115] or for laymen. Side by side with translations of famous works, like Suso's *Horologium sapientiae*[116]—or, later, the *Imitation*[117]—we find original works like the *Abbey of the Holy Ghost*[118] and the *Remorse of Conscience*, both possibly by Richard Rolle,[119] as well as a poem on the gifts of the Holy Spirit. Another poem, *The Pearl*, is not simply an elegy; its central theme is deeply religious. Baptismal innocence, symbolized by virginity, is represented as a pledge of the happiness of heaven, and into this theme is woven devotion to Christ and the Blessed Virgin.[120] Some of Chaucer's (†1400) verse, too, is in Mary's honour.[121] More prosaically, many of these meditations, sermons and poems deal with deadly sins.[122]

Other writings are only simple handbooks of religious instruction for the laity, like the *Pore Caitif*[123] or the *Instructio pie vivendi et superna meditandi*.[124] This is especially the case with the *Livre des Seynts Medicines* by Henry, Duke of Lancaster (†1361), which is both autobiographical and moralistic. It describes the seven plagues (corresponding to the deadly sins) that have ravaged the author's life and the appropriate remedies for them. Throughout, humour is mingled with humility, and the whole book reveals the writer's penetrating observation of life and his wide experience of contemporary medicine, and of hunting, and the art of soldiering.[125]

114 K. Chesner, "Note on Some Treatises of Devotion Intended for Margaret of York (MS Douce 365)", in *Medium Aevum*, XX (1951), pp. 11–39.

115 For example, the meditations in *The Monk of Farne*, which bear witness to the existence of Benedictine hermits and to the quality of their spirituality. Cf. W. A. Pantin, *The Monk-Solitary of Farne*, *op. cit.*; and H. Farmer in *Anal. monastica*, IV, Rome (*Studia Anselmiana*, 41), 1957, pp. 141–247.

116 Cf. D. Rogers, "Some Early English Devotional Books from Cambray", in *Downside Rev.*, LVII (1939), pp. 458–63 (MS *Cambrai, Ville, 255*).

117 Cf. H. C. White, "Some Continuing Traditions in English Devotional Literature", in *Publications Mod. Lang. Assoc. America*, LVII (1942), pp. 966–80.

118 Cf. A. J. Collins, "Middle-English Devotional Pieces", in *British Museum Quarterly*, XIV (1939–40), pp. 87–8 (in connection with MS *Brit. Mus. Egerton 3245*).

119 Ed. R. H. Bowers, in *Modern Lang. Notes*, LXX (1955), pp. 249–52 (based on MS *Cambridge Univ. Ii. IV. q.*).

120 Ed. E. V. Gordon, *Pearl*, Oxford, 1953. Cf. L. Le Grelle, "La 'Perle'. Essai d'interprétation nouvelle", in *Etudes anglaises*, VI (1953), pp. 315–31. Summary of the various interpretations by B. McAndrew, "The Pearl, A Catholic Paradise Lost", in *American Bened. Rev.*, VIII (1957–8), pp. 243–51.

121 Cf. G. M. Corr, "Chaucer's Praise of Mary", in *Marianum*, XIV (1952), pp. 305–20.

122 Cf. M. W. Bloomfield, *The Seven Deadly Sins. An Introduction to the History of a Religious Concept*, East Lansing, Mich., 1952.

123 Cf. M. T. Brady, "The Pore Caitif. An Introductory Study", in *Traditio*, X (1954), pp. 529–48.

124 Ed. and trans. into English by J. McKechnie, vol. I, London, 1933.

125 Ed. E. J. Arnould, Oxford, 1940. Cf. his *Etude sur le Livre des saintes médecines du duc Henri de Lancastre*, Paris, 1948 (including extracts from the text).

In these writings one can see a characteristic trait of national psychology: it was deliberately pragmatic and particularist in its approach, little drawn to abstract theories. It differs in this from the preoccupations with speculation and the attachment to a conventual framework still to be found on the Continent in the fourteenth century.

This trend in England ran parallel to others of the same nature abroad, such as the *Devotio moderna*. At the end of the fourteenth century and in the fifteenth, spirituality in England takes the same forms as in Holland, possibly as a reaction against the abuse of speculation, but more probably as a result of the national temperament.

4. The "Devotio Moderna"

The full force of the wave of moralism and psychology in the spiritual life was felt on the Continent. The new movement, almost contemporary with the great English spiritual writers, which began in Holland, was later to be christened by John Busch "*the Devotio moderna.*" "The word *devotio* here seems to have kept the general sense of service of God which it had in both Christian and monastic language. But now this service of God is understood differently."[126] What it now meant and what it was in this new movement which was to have a far greater influence on later spirituality than did the English mystics, will presently be seen.[127]

It originated unquestionably with Gerard Groot. Born of a well-to-do family in Deventer, he studied the humanities at Paris, and might have aspired to the highest ecclesiastical offices. In 1374, however, he was "converted". By way of noviceship, he made a short stay at the Charterhouse of Munnikhuizen. He declined the priesthood, out of humility, and only consented to receive the diaconate in 1377 in order to be able to preach. The last years of his life were spent effectively as a preacher and a missionary. His violent language was little to the taste of the ecclesiastical authorities, who regarded him as simply one more of the heretics and other

[126] J. Châtillon, art. "Devotio", in *Dict. de spirit.*, III, col. 714.

[127] For a bibliography, see J. M. E. Dols, *Bibliographie der Moderne Devotie*, Nijmegen, 1941 (incomplete). The history is given in S. Axters, *Geschiedenis van de vroomheid in de Nederlanden*, vol. III, *De M. D.* (*1380–1550*), Antwerp, 1956; R. Post, *De M. D. Geert Groote en zijn stichtingen*, 2nd ed., Amsterdam, 1950; P. Debongnie, art. "Devotion moderne", in *Dict. de spirit.*, III, 727–47. There is an edition of the *Consuetudines fratrum vitae communis* (based on manuscripts of the early sixteenth century) by W. Jappe Alberts, Groningen, 1959. For anthologies of texts, see R. van Reest, *Dichterschap en prophetie. I. Literatuur in de Middeleeuwen*, Goes, 1953; S. Axters, O.P., *Mystiek Brevier*, vols I and III, Antwerp, 1944–6; C. C. de Bruin, *Middelnederlands geestelijk proza*, Zutphen, 1940. See also E. F. Jacob, *Essays in the Conciliar Epoch*, Manchester, 1943, pp. 121–53.

hotheads of the period. In 1383 he was finally forbidden to preach. He died the next year at the age of only forty-four.[128]

Even during his short life, Gerard had trained a band of fervent disciples; his many letters show that his influence was both extensive and deep.[129] He also left a considerable number of autobiographical writings, sermons, and ascetical treatises. They reveal a headstrong personality, practical, little concerned with theory. He was little inclined to admire either the existing forms of the religious life or the married state,[130] a pessimism due to the spectacle presented by the Christianity of the time: monks and other religious were frequently unfaithful to their vocation; the clergy were greedy[131] and incontinent, if not debauched[132]; on every side were to be seen false mystics, more or less tinged with pantheism. All this led Groot to a very realistic conception of the spiritual life: what matters, in the last resort, is conversion of heart, virtue, the endurance of trials, the apostolate and, above all, eternal salvation.

Against this background, and with his temperament, he had nothing in common with speculative mysticism.[133] It is true that he had met Ruysbroeck and even translated some of his writings. And he, just as much as his disciples, read what the Rhineland mystics had written, especially Suso's *Horologium*.[134] Yet both he and his followers looked with suspicion on these mystics, for whom "all that God is by nature, we become by grace".[135] The fundamental orthodoxy of the *Devotio moderna* seems to be absolutely unquestionable, despite the hostile attitude of the hierarchy towards Groot. He has been regarded by some, quite mistakenly, as a forerunner of Protestantism.[136] Obviously his move-

128 On Gerard Groot, see the works mentioned above; in addition, J. van Ginneken, S.J., *Geert Grote's levenbeeld naar de oudste gegevens bewerkt*, Amsterdam, 1942; K. de Beer, *Studie over de spiritualiteit van G.G.*, Brussels-Nijmegen, 1938.

129 Ed. W. Mulder, S.J., *Gerardi Magni Epistolae*, Antwerp, 1933. Cf. J. Tiecke, O. Carm., *De werken van G.G.*, Utrecht, 1941, which gives Groot's works, published and unpublished.

130 In his *De matrimonio*, it appears that he believed it hardly possible for married life to be virtuous.

131 Hence Groot's treatise *De simonia ad beguttas*; ed. W. de Vreese, The Hague, 1940.

132 Hence the famous sermon *Contra focaristas*, "Against fornicators," which probably dates from 1381.

133 A. Lücker, in his *Meister Eckhart und die D.M.*, Leyden, 1950, seems to take too optimistic a view regarding Eckhart's influence on the *Devotio moderna*; cf. L. Reypens, S.J., in *Ons Geest. Erf*, XXV (1951), pp. 215–20.

134 Cf. D. de Man, "M.D. en duitse mystiek", in *Bijdragen v. Nederl. geschied. en oudheidkunde*, VIII, 2 (1940), pp. 100–5.

135 "Quidquid Deus est per naturam, hoc nos efficimur per gratiam", *Epist.* 31. Cf. de Beer, *op. cit.*, pp. 185–7.

136 For example, C. Ullmann, *Reformatoren vor der Reformation*, Gotha, 1866; G. Bonet-Maury, *G. de G., un précurseur de la Réforme au XIVe siècle*, Paris, 1878.

ment was a "reformation"; he was attacking abuses and vices, and the very ones against which the sixteenth-century Reformers were to protest. But the spiritual writers of the Netherlands in the fourteenth and fifteenth centuries revered the Church and her pastors.

By contemplation Groot understood something much simpler than did the Rhineland mystics or the men of Groenendael. For him it no longer bore an intellectual aspect, but was identified in practice with the perfection of charity: *contemplacio seu perfeccio caritatis*. Gerard knew, of course, that all are not bound to this perfection and said so: *non omnes tenentur esse perfectae caritatis seu contemplativi*.[137] Any further definition seemed to him superfluous; he never describes contemplation in itself. The one thing he insists on—and in this he a little resembles the Rhineland mystics—is the necessity of preliminary detachment, of *spiritualis paupertas*,[138] and of effective practice of the virtues. In the concrete, there is no other way than that of "the imitation of the manhood of Christ", *imitacio humanitatis Christi*. By that way, a man is led "to his divinity by contemplation", *ingrediendo ad divinitatem per contemplationem*.[139] As well as contemplation, however, there is a parallel road—the active life. It is a striking fact that the fourteenth century ended by admitting that the two modes of life, contemplative and active, were equivalent. Richard Rolle had risen up against precisely this point of view.

Only once does Groot seem to allude to the necessity of progress in contemplation, when he says that "images of sensible things", *sensibilium phantasmata*, must be transcended in order to attain "a certain spiritual harmony", *spiritualium quamdam armoniam*.[140] As for visions, the true can be distinguished from the false only by their spiritual fruit: enlightenment of the mind and especially increase of charity.[141]

All this did not mean that Groot and his disciples were rejecting what was good in their predecessors' writings. The devout *Meditations* on the life of Jesus or other religious subjects were simply a popularization of a type of literature which had already been known in the previous century, and which was said, mistakenly, to stem from St Bonaventure. In fact, the sources of their affective piety and of their devotion to Christ go even further back; they owe a lot to Cassian, to St John Climacus, to St Bernard, to the

[137] *Epist.*, 45.

[138] *Epist.*, 71. In this connection, see his *Conclusa et proposita*.

[139] *Epist.*, 9. Cf. H. Gall, "De Christus-gedachte bij G.G.", in *Ons geest. Leven*, XX (1940–1), pp. 229–40.

[140] "De quatuor generibus meditationum seu contemplationum", ed. Hyma, in *Archief v. Geschiedenis Aartsbisdom Utrecht*, XLIX (1924), p. 325.

[141] *Ibid.*, p. 304.

early Franciscans, to St Bonaventure's *De triplici via*, and to David of Augsburg.[142] The protagonists of the *Devotio moderna* were not innovators: they differ from their predecessors, however, in the simple, popular character of their piety and in the small part given to intellectual considerations in their preaching and their writings.[143]

Gerard Groot had succeeded in surrounding himself with a circle of friends, of whom he was the director.[144] It may be asked whether he was also their superior, in the conventual sense of the word. He certainly looked askance at monastic obedience, knowing very well what it too often was, both in superiors and in their subjects.[145] His letters, however, bear witness both to his influence as a director and to his concern with obedience. He lays it down as a principle that "the new monk must be humbly obedient to his superiors",[146] whatever their defects may be.[147]

Inevitably Gerard, as he gathered disciples round him, could not help going back to the principles that underlie all religious life. When all is said and done, his effort to reform the religious life of his time resulted simply in the creation of a new form of it. What is more, this new creation was not very different from what was already to be found among the Mendicants or the Canons Regular. One cannot therefore ascribe to him the merit, if it is one, of having created a wholly new and lay movement.[148]

Gerard's first disciple, and his chief one, was Florent Radewijns (1350–1400). He was ordained priest by Gerard's order and after his master's death he took over the direction of the first houses of the "Brothers and Sisters of the Common Life". These houses, which had been established at Deventer and elsewhere from 1383, were the target of the opposition to Groot and his work that continued to rage among the clergy. His death had been hailed on every hand with such delight! But Radewijns and his companions persevered, and the opposition finally died down; the foundation, in 1387, of a house of Canons Regular at Windesheim near Zwolle, gave stability to the work. This house soon became the head of a

142 Cf. E. Mikkers, "S. Bernardus en de M.D.", in *Cîteaux in de Nederlanden*, IV (1953), pp. 149–86; H. Gleumes, "G.G. und die Windesheimer als Verehrer des hl. Bernhard von Cl.", in *Zeitschr. Asz. Myst.*, X (1935), pp. 90–112 (cf. *ibid.*, 35–51); J. Mak, "Christus bij de moderne devoten", in *Ons geest. Erf*, IX (1935), pp. 105–66.

143 Cf. R. Post, *op. cit.*, pp. 132–47.

144 Cf. de Beer, *op. cit.*, pp. 15–34; R. Post, *op. cit.*

145 Cf. de Beer, *op. cit.*, pp. 165–9.

146 *Epist.*, 16; cf. de Beer, pp. 166 *et seq.*

147 *Epist.*, 72; cf. *Epist.*, 57.

148 Cf. M. van Woerkum, S.J., "M.D. en lekenvroomheid", in *Streven*, X (1956–7), pp. 119–26.

huge congregation, which ultimately absorbed the Groenendael monastery itself and a number of monasteries affiliated with it, and which had daughter houses in Germany and France.[149] Its influence was considerable, as is shown by innumerable documents from the most varied quarters. Among those who were led by it to an intense spiritual life were Benedictine and Cistercian monks, Dominican and Franciscan friars, Canons Regular, secular priests and laymen; in many monasteries a reform in observance was brought about by the canons of Windesheim[150]: which shows to what an extent the little movement which rose out of Groot's preaching, and survived only thanks to his friends Radewijns, answered to men's needs.

This success could not have been achieved if the movement had not succeeded in attracting recruits of the highest calibre. Among the disciples of the early years one name stands out: that of Gerard Zerbolt, of Zutphen. Since he was only thirty-one when he died in 1398, he can barely have known Groot,[151] yet, his spiritual teaching, concentrated in his treatise *The Spiritual Ascent*,[152] bears a close resemblance to that of the originator of the *Devotio moderna*. It is a call to conversion, meditation, imitation of the life and death of Christ, death to the world, charity, and humility. The practice of confession, too, is warmly recommended. One should always, so far as possible, go to the same confessor, in order to receive effective direction.[153] Meditation takes on, for Zerbolt, a more systematic aspect than for Groot. He specifies the subject, the time, and the length of the exercise. As for mystical prayer, one can prepare oneself for it, but its reception depends upon God's grace. It is never, moreover, anything but an approximation to the beatific vision or *visio per essentiam*. This *intuitus divinae speculationis*, as Zerbolt calls it, represents the "state of perfection", which is that of "true charity".[154]

149 On Florent Radewijns, his life and works, see M. van Woerkum, *Fl. R.*, Tielt, 1950; also *Ons geest. Erf*, XXIV (1950) and XXV (1951). On the origins of the Brothers of the Common Life and of the congregation of Windesheim, see C. van der Wansem, *Het ontstaan en de Geschiedenis der Broederschap van het Gemene Leven tot 1400*, Louvain, 1958; cf. A. Hyma, *The Brethren of the Common Life*, Grand Rapids, Mich., 1950. On the influence of this congregation in France, see C. L. Salley, "The Ideals of the D.M. as Reflected in the Life and Writings of Jacques Lefèvre d'Etaples", in *Dissert. Abstracts*, XIII (1953), pp. 376–7. For Germany, see W. M. Landeen, "The Beginnings of the D.M. in Germany", in *Research Studies of the State Coll. of Washington*, XIX (1951), pp. 162–202; XX (1952), pp. 221–53; XXI (1953), pp. 275–309; XXII (1954), pp. 55–75.

150 This was chiefly the work of John Busch; cf. S. van der Woude, *Joh. Busch, Windesheimer Klooster-reformator en Kroniekschrijver*, Edam, 1947.

151 Cf. J. van Rooy, *G.Z. van Z. I. Leven en Geschriften*, Nijmegen, 1936.

152 *De spiritualibus ascensionibus*; ed. and trans. into Dutch by J. Mahieu, *G.Z. van Z., Van geestelijke opklimmingen*, Bruges, 1941.

153 See *De spiritualibus ascensionibus*, ch. XIII; pp. 62–6 in the Mahieu edition.

154 *Ibid.*, chs II and XXVI; pp. 14 and 130.

Another disciple of Groot, Gerlach Peters, also follows the main lines of the *Devotio moderna*. His *Soliloquium* is characterized by affective piety, of a practical and psychological nature, and by a Christocentric mysticism. As for his teaching, "the central thought of the *Soliloquium*[155] is liberty of spirit through intuition of the Truth".[156] The road of this liberation is the imitation of the cross of Christ, and its end is union with God, conformity with him, and contemplation. In the measure that this programme is fulfilled, it gives man, here below, a foretaste of heaven.

More important for the subsequent history of the *Devotio moderna* was the influence exercised by Henry Eger of Kalcar, who had been prior of the Charterhouse of Munnikhuizen (†1408). His relations with Gerard Groot are not clear,[157] but what is certain is that he carried on the systematic spirit of Gerard Zerbolt, especially as regards meditation.[158] As yet he lays down no definite psychological rules; its methodical character comes chiefly from the nature of the object meditated upon[159]: *Lectio, meditatio, affectio, oratio, examinatio, compunctio cordis, contemplatio*—all are various aspects as well as the conditions and the subject matter of the exercise.[160]

It would be a mistake, however, to regard methodical meditation as an invention of the *dévots* of Deventer; it was to be found also among the Franciscans. Their spiritual teachers set up the ideal of affective, Christocentric, and mystical piety and sketched out its method; superiors codified its obligation.[161] Unquestionably there was a genuine affinity between the underlying tendencies of the *Devotio moderna* and those of the Seraphic order.[162] Among the names that stand out are those of John Brugman (†1473),[163] Henry

[155] Cf. J. J. Mak, *De Dietse Vertaling van G.P., Soliloquium*, Asten, 1936; E. Assemaine, O.S.B., "G.P.", in *La Vie spirit.*, V (1921), pp. 117–23. There is a French translation, *Le soliloque enflammé*, Juvisy, 1936.

[156] J. J. Mak, *op. cit.*, p. 87; cf. *Soliloquium*, ch. XXXIII.

[157] Cf. R. Post, "H.E. von Kalkar en Geert Groote", in *Studia Catholica*, XXI (1946), pp. 88–92.

[158] Cf. H. Lindeman, "Een tractaat over de overweging van's Heeren lijden aan Hendrik van Calcar toegeschreven", in *Ons geest. Erf*, VII (1933), pp. 62–88.

[159] Cf. M. van Woerkum, "Enige opmerkingen aangaande de methodische meditatie bij de Moderne Devoten", in *Ons geest. Erf*, XXIX (1955), pp. 222–7.

[160] Cf. L. A. M. Goossens, O.F.M., *De meditatie in de eerste tijd van de Moderne Devotie*, Haarlem, 1952 (includes an edition of Florent Radewijns' *Tractatulus devotus*).

[161] Cf. P. Optatus, O.M.Cap., "De Oefening van het inwendig gebed in de minderbroedersorde gedurende de XVe en de XVIe eeuw", in *Ons geest. Erf*, XXI (1947), pp. 113–60.

[162] Cf. W. Schmitz, O.F.M., *Het aandeel der Minderbroeders in onze middeleeuwse literatuur*, Nijmegen, 1937 (not very methodical); W. Lampen, O.F.M., "Geert Grote en de Minderbroeders", in *Bijdragen voor de Geschiedenis van de Prov. der Minderbroeders in de Nederlanden*, No. 24 (1957), pp. 425–32.

[163] See *infra*, ch. VIII, p. 469.

Herp (†1477),[164] and Dietrich Kolde of Munster (†1515).[165] They were all influenced by Ruysbroeck, whose writings they had read and reflected upon.[166]

At this period there also appeared a number of minor works, many of them anonymous, which attempted to systematize devout meditation, or at least to extend its practice. A good many of them were devoted to the contemplation of Christ's passion.[167] There were others on Mary, her joys and sorrows[168]; on the *Pater* or the *Ave Maria*[169]; and on the Canticle of Canticles[170]; others dealt with the virtues, like the collection of meditations known as the "Spiritual Orchard," *Spirituale pomerium*—the name of the author, Henry Uten Bogaerde (of the Orchard), or Pomerius.[171] There were also new *Expositions* of the Mass, such as those of Simon of Venlo[172] and Gherit van der Goude[173]; another and earlier one, which is anonymous, is derived from the commentaries of William Durand and Berthold of Ratisbon.[174] There were, too, collections of various *opuscula*, frequently anonymous: one of these, the *Hortulus devotionis*, was fairly widely read, both in French and in Dutch, at the end of the fifteenth century.[175] At the very end of the Middle Ages there appeared a little mystical treatise, called "The Pearl of the Gospel", *De Evangelische Peerle*. Written in Dutch, by someone devout born about 1463, it markedly influenced the piety of the

164 See *infra*, ch. VIII, pp. 469 *et seq.* 165 See infra, ch. VIII, p. 496.

166 Cf. G. Peeters, "De verhanding Ruusbroec-Herp-Vervoort", in *Handelingen van het 21de Vlaams Filologencongres*, Louvain, 1955, pp. 235–9 (summary of a thesis on Frans Vervoort).

167 For editions or descriptions, see L. M. F. Daniëls, O.P., in *Ons geest. Erf*, XVI (1942), pp. 186–235; P. de Keyser, *Salighe Meditacies des lijdens ons liefs Heeren*, Antwerp, 1942; D. A. Stracke, S.J., in *Ons geest. Erf*, XII (1938), pp. 187–208; C. C. de Bruin, in *Nederl. Arch. Kerkgesch.*, XXXIV (1943), pp. 1–23.

168 For example, *Die sevenste bliscap van onser wrouwen*, ed. W. Smulders, Bois-le-Duc, 1913; D. A. Stracke, S.J., "Bijdrage tot de middelnederlandse devotie: de vreugden en de weeën van Maria", in *Ons geest. Erf*, XXVI (1952), pp. 7–22, 121–44.

169 Ed. D. A. Stracke, S.J., in *Ons geest. Erf*, IX (1935), pp. 268–301, 388–401.

170 For example, the text edited by B. Spaapen, in *Ons geest. Erf*, XIX (1945), vol. II, pp. 83–172.

171 Critical study, with the complete text, by L. Lebeer, *Spirituale Pomerium*, Brussels, 1938.

172 About 1450. Ed. M. Smits van Waesberghe, "Die misverklaring van Meester Simon van Venlo", in *Ons geest. Erf*, XV (1941), pp. 228–61, 285–327; XVI (1942), pp. 85–129.

173 Cf. L. Mees, O.F.M., "Het 'Boexken van der Missen' van G. v. d. G.", in *Franciscana*, X (1955), pp. 93–100.

174 Cf. L. Daniëls, O.P., in *Studia Catholica*, XVIII (1942), pp. 257–91. On devotion to the Eucharist in the fifteenth and sixteenth centuries, see I. Meertens, "De sacramentsdevotie in de middelnederlandsche getijden- en gebedenboeken", in *Studia eucharistica*, Antwerp, 1946, pp. 304–25; cf. *Ons geest. Erf*, XXVII (1953) pp. 113–27.

175 Cf. A. Ampe, S.J., "Het 'Hoefken van Devocien'", in *Ons geest. Erf*, XXX (1956), pp. 43–82.

times, and this influence extended even to the French school of the seventeenth century, as a result of the Latin translation by Lawrence Surius (1545), the Carthusian of Cologne. The doctrine of the *Pearl* has been characterized as a mysticism of assimilation with Christ, by introversion. From this point of view the work shows a continuity with the fourteenth-century mystics of the Rhineland and Brabant. Whole sections of it are taken from Ruysbroeck, while its ideas owe much to Henry Herp.[176]

The zeal for reform which marked the new movement brought forth a whole constellation of preachers. Among these were John Cele (†1415)[177] and the Franciscan John Brugman, who has already been mentioned. Collections of their sermons circulated in manuscript form.[178] One of these, indeed, is really a treatise on mystical theology; it is a pity that its author, who lived at the end of the fifteenth century, is not known.[179]

A similar anonymity in the writings that sprang from the *Devotio moderna*, or within its sphere of influence, shows that the founders' teaching on humility and obscurity has been taken literally. Yet in spite of this, a great many names have come down to us—not only those of the founders and leading masters of the *Devotio moderna*, but also those of a number of lesser writers.[180] A few of them, at least, must be mentioned. One such was John of Schoonhoven (†1432),[181] a disciple of Ruysbroeck, who was remarkable for his indifference towards his master's spiritual speculations. Later on, another master of the *Devotio moderna*, John Veghe (†1504),[182] was more receptive to the influence of the

[176] Ed. Cologne, 1535; Latin translation, Cologne, 1545. See L. Reypens, S.J., "Nog een vergeten mystieke grootheid", in *Ons geest. Erf*, II (1928), pp. 52–76, 189–213, 304–41. This was followed by J. Huijben, O.S.B., in *Ons geest. Erf*, II (1928), pp. 361–92; III (1929), pp. 60–70, 144–64. On the date of composition of the *Pearl* (between 1518 and 1525), see A. Stracke, S.J., "Wanneer werd de Groote evangelische Peerle voltooid?", in *Ons geest. Erf*, X (1936), pp. 85–96. A valuable study of the *Pearl* is in preparation by Fr. van Schoote, S.J. The influence of the *Pearl* will be discussed in greater detail in Vol. III of this *History of Christian Spirituality*.

[177] Sermons, ed. T. J. de Vries, Zwolle, 1949.

[178] Such as the one described by B. Delfgaauw in "Een preeken-cyclus der Moderne Devoten", in *Ons geest. Erf*, XIV (1940), pp. 173–80. On the whole body of literature produced by the *Devotio moderna*, see S. Axters, *Geschiedenis van de vroomheid . . .*, vol. III, especially chs VIII, XI and XII. For the last thirty years, the periodical *Ons geestlijke Erf* has made a point of examining this literature.

[179] Ed. D. A. Stracke, S.J., "Korte handleiding tot de Theologia mystica", in *Bloemen van Ons geest. Erf*, vols VII–VIII, Antwerp, 1932.

[180] See Axters, *loc. cit.*; and P. Debongnie, art. "Dévotion moderne", in *Dict. de spirit.*, III, 729–41. To the names mentioned there, many others might be added.

[181] Cf. J. Huijben, "Jan van Sch., leerling van den zaligen Jan van Ruusbroec", in *Ons geest. Erf*, VI (1932), pp. 282–303.

[182] H. Rademacher has edited his *Lectulus noster floridus* (Hiltrup, 1938) and his *Wijngaerden der Sele* (Hiltrup, 1940) and has also published a study of his life

great Rhineland mystics and also to the rising humanism. Finally, there was the mystical poet known under the name of Sister Bertha (†1514).[183] She too had been influenced by the great Rhineland and Flemish mystics, like Hadewijch and Ruysbroeck, and also by St Bridget of Sweden and her *Visions*.

The last great work of the *Devotio moderna* was the "Rosery" or *Rosetum* of John Mombaer, or Mauburnus (†1501), a writer who took great care to specify the degrees of meditation and prayer.[184] For him, prayer represents the supreme ambition of the religious, and its primary objective is intensity of love. "Among all the occupations of a religious, the highest in excellence is that which is most deeply rooted in charity; in other words, where the heart is inflamed with the most ardent affection."[185] In this work one can discern the tendency which ended in the rigidity of the sixteenth-century methods of prayer.

These various writings show the vitality of the *Devotio moderna* at the end of the Middle Ages, and its influence. Their authors did not confine themselves strictly to a preoccupation with asceticism and reform. Several of them, like Mauburnus, left mystical works, but the majority of these more or less remote disciples of Gerard Groot kept to the modest regions of asceticism and humble affective prayer. Originality was hardly their distinguishing feature.

This was particularly true in the case of the most famous writer of the school, who has purposely not been mentioned till now: Thomas Hemerken a Kempis (1379 or 1380–1471). At the age of twenty he entered the monastery of Mount St Agnes at Zwolle, where he was for a long time master of novices. His delight was to copy, to recast, and to translate the works of his contemporaries and of the great authors of earlier times like St Bernard and St Bonaventure.[186] His own writings, however, were not inconsider-

---

and doctrine, *Mystik und Humanismus der Devotio Moderna in den Predigten und Traktaten des Johannes Veghe*, Hiltrup, 1935; see also H. Kunich, "J.V. und die oberdeutsche Mystik des 14. Jahr.", in *Zeitschr. deutsch. Altertum u. deutsch. Liter.*, LXXV (1938), pp. 141–71; cf. *ibid.*, pp. 105–9.

183 *Suster Bertken*. Her works have been edited by C. C. van de Graft, Zwolle, 1955; cf. M. Smits van Waesberghe, S.J., *Het mystieke dicht- en prozawerk van S.B.*, Roeping, 1944; A. Ampe, S.J., "De geschriften van S.B.", in *Ons geest. Erf*, XXX (1956), pp. 281–320; M. J. G. de Jong, "De compositie van Zuster Bertkens Kerstverhaal", in *Tijdschr. Nederl. Taal- en Letterkunde*, LXXIV (1956), pp. 117–139.

184 Cf. P. Debongnie, *J.M. de Bruxelles*, Louvain, 1928. See the *Rosetum*, Douai, 1620.

185 Quoted in Debongnie, *op. cit.*, p. 248.

186 Cf. J. van Ginneken, S.J., "Was Th. Hemerken een scheppende geest?", in *Ons taaltuin*, X (1941–2), pp. 161–5; "Hoe Th. a K. Pater Brugmans beschouwingen over het lijden van Christus in het latijn bewerkte", *ibid.*, VIII (1939–40), pp. 161–79; "Th. H. en Pater Brugmans 'Leven van Jezus'", *ibid.*, pp. 229–50;

able.[187] Their chief purpose was to guide the young religious in their training for the life of the cloister. Thomas tried hard to awaken in them an attraction for a genuine interior life; to remind them of the examples and the ideal of the founders; and to offer, as food for their meditation, the life and passion of Christ. These writings, though not very original, are among those most representative of the *Devotio moderna*.

The most widely known is *The Imitation of Christ*.[188] Following the tradition of modesty characteristic of his school of spirituality, its author chose to remain anonymous. Hence the well-known debates over the authorship of these four little books. The first three deal with the interior life, the last with the Eucharist. Modern criticism attributes them to Thomas a Kempis,[189] firmly rejecting the brilliant thesis fashionable about thirty years ago according to which Thomas merely completed the compilation of some *opuscula* dating from the beginnings of the *Devotio moderna* and even from Gerard Groot himself.[190] The original language was certainly Latin, but Thomas may have drawn upon sources written in Dutch.[191] The *Imitation* shows the same basic tendencies as works that can certainly be attributed to Thomas a Kempis: an affective devotion and contemplation of Christ's humanity, as a means of attaining to that of his divinity and to union with God by the liberation of the soul. This is most noticeable in Book II.[192] One must not be misled by the title of the book; it is taken from the first words of Book I and is not intended to express the theme of the whole work, which is the interior life and the Eucharist. In the spiritual teaching of these little books, the imitation of Christ is only a secondary theme,[193] and one that appears relatively seldom.

H. Gleumes, "Der geistige Einfluss des hl. Bernhard von Cl. auf Th. a K.", in *Zeitschr. Asz. Myst.*, XIII (1938), pp. 109–20.

[187] *Opera*, ed. M. J. Pohl, 7 vols, Freiburg, 1910–22. There is a recent anthology of passages dealing with the Blessed Virgin, assembled by A. Triclot: *Textes marials de Th. a K.*, Paris, 1958.

[188] Countless editions and translations into every language.

[189] The arguments that have been put forward in favour of Thomas a Kempis, John Gerson, Abbot Gersen of Verceil, Gerard Groot, and others will not be discussed here in detail. The two works which definitely attribute the authorship to Thomas are those of L. M. J. Delaissé, *Le manuscrit autographe de Th. a K. et l'"Imitation de Jésus-Christ." Examen archéologique et édition diplomatique du Bruxellensis 5855–61*, 2 vols, Antwerp, 1956; and of J. Huijben, O.S.B., and P. Debongnie C.SS.R., *L'auteur ou les auteurs de l'Imitation*, Louvain, 1957.

[190] This was the thesis of J. van Ginneken, S.J., set forth in various works and articles published chiefly between 1929 and 1946.

[191] This has been proved by examining the various Dutch versions; see C. C. de Bruin, *De middelnederlanse vertaling van De Imitatione Christi* . . ., Leyden, 1954.

[192] Cf. P. Debongnie, "Henri Suso et l'Imitation de J.-C.", in *Rev. asc. myst.*, XXI (1940), pp. 242–68.

[193] P. Debongnie, "Les thèmes de l'Imitation", in *Rev. hist. eccl.*, XXXVI (1940), pp. 289–344.

Another point to be noted is that Thomas does not seem to admit, either in the *Imitation* or in his other works, the possibility of seeing God's essence in this life, even in transitory fashion. The contemplation that is enjoyed by certain privileged souls is a vision of a lower order, differing from the beatific vision not merely in its duration but also in its nature; it takes place only "by a sideways look, to a small degree, and obscurely".[194]

One feels that Thomas is anxious to make the spiritual life accessible to everyone. He identifies contemplation, in practice, with charity. He recognizes, and even describes, a mystical vision of the divine Truth, but says that this takes place only through a special intervention of grace.[195]

The *Imitation* is really one of the best spiritual directories that the Middle Ages produced. Thomas asks of the spiritual man distrust of himself and of men, a readiness to obey rather than to impose one's own will, and humble obedience to a "wise and conscientious"[196] director, together with confession to him. This attitude is the safest guarantee against the insinuations of the "old enemy".[197]

In the *Imitation* we find summed up the principal tendencies of spirituality in the first half of the fifteenth century.[198] Throughout that century and for many a later generation, this and all Thomas's other works were to remain the simplest and clearest expression of the new ideal. It is true that in the time of Gerard Groot this ideal had been suspect, because of certain connections that it seemed to have with the heterodox mysticism of the fourteenth century. Later, suspicion was aroused anew by the fact that the schools conducted by the canons of Windesheim had some influence upon the rise of humanism, and the Reformation. Luther's esteem for him is well known, to say nothing of Wessel Gansfort's and Erasmus'. It must be recognized, however, that the Church was in need of new blood, and the Christian world urgently needed

[194] *Ex latere, modice, obscure.* Cf. G. Clamens, *La dévotion à l'humanité du Christ dans la spiritualité de Th. a K.*, Lyons, 1931.

[195] See the *De elevatione mentis*, Pohl edition, vol. II, pp. 399 *et seq.* Cf. W. Scherer, "Der ehrwürdige Th. von K. und die mystische Beschauung", in *Zeitschr. Asz. Myst.*, VIII (1933), pp. 242–52.

[196] *Imitation*, Book I, ch. IV. Cf. Book III, ch. LIV, "De diversis motibus naturae et gratiae"; ch. XLII, "Quod pax non est ponenda in hominibus"; ch. XXIII, 'De quatuor magnam importantibus pacem"; Book I, ch. IX, "De obedientia et subjectione". This outlook is found elsewhere in the works of Thomas a Kempis; for example, in *De fideli dispensatione*, 1 (Pohl ed., vol. I, pp. 152, 153); *Vallis liliorum*, 24 (vol. IV, pp. 102–4); *Sermones ad novicios*, 3 (vol. VI, pp. 21–32).

[197] Cf. *Imitation*, Book III, ch. VI

[198] Cf. F. W. Wentzlaff-Eggebert, *Deutsche Mystik zwischen Mittelalter und Neuzeit*, Tübingen, 1947, pp. 139–40.

spiritual renewal. After the extremes of speculation, it was a healthy and beneficial reaction to return to the absolute primacy of charity, to a simple conformity to Christ, to the practice of humility and detachment, to less word-juggling and subtlety, to a more realistic view of the demands of Christian life. It was as if the Church, under the guidance of the Holy Spirit, had instinctively sensed the danger of too extreme an intellectualism in the domain of the interior life and the ascent to God.

Still, one cannot help counting the cost of this very wholesome reaction. The gulf between decadent scholasticism and the new spirituality had the effect of isolating the science of theology from the life of the soul. This constantly widening gulf was to characterize Western spirituality down to our own times. Its effects are most noticeable when we come to the time at which the principal works of the *Devotio moderna*—particularly the *Imitation* and the writings of Henry Herp and Mauburnus—were translated into Spanish. As will be seen, these translations had, through the great Spanish masters, a decisive influence on the subsequent evolution of spirituality.

5. *The Secular Masters*

It has been noted how, during the last decades of the fourteenth century, there emerged such diverse leaders as Catherine of Siena, Gerard Groot, and the first great English spiritual writers. They appeared at the same time and quite independently, having had no contact with each other. They were linked, however, by one common characteristic: the distrust they showed for abstract speculation, and for religious life of the traditional type. France and Germany did not remain untouched by this movement, but it was only some years later that the signs of a similar reaction appeared there. The men who embodied it were neither members of the regular clergy nor laymen; they were the "secular masters" of the spiritual life.

What these new men had in common with the *Devotio moderna* was their rejection of the intellectualism of their time, with its decadence or extravagance. But they were not, for all that, enemies of the intellect. They knew how much Christian doctrine owed to the Fathers, the monastic writers, and the great scholastics, and they turned to all these in their quest for light. In them is seen a concern for authentic sources, and at the same time a drawing apart from a certain type of scholastic thought which could no longer find an answer to the questions—eternal and yet ever new—that are asked by the Christian who is determined to go to God.

From this aspect, the Renaissance had already dawned.[199] It was also the beginning of a danger, unknown to previous centuries and which still threatens us today: that of going back into the past when what is needed is to live and create.

The influence of the secular masters was felt most strongly in France. The first of them in date was Peter d'Ailly (1350–1420). He was chancellor of the University of Paris in 1389, became bishop of Puy in 1395 and of Cambrai in 1397, and was created cardinal in 1411.[200] The sources upon which he drew were chiefly St Bernard, Richard of St Victor and St Bonaventure; they were also to be the chief sources, soon afterward, of Jean Gerson and Robert Ciboule. Like Gerson, Peter d'Ailly distrusted the recent trends in spirituality. He particularly distrusted Ruysbroeck, against whose orthodoxy he is said to have assembled a whole dossier.[201] He had in common with the *Devotio moderna* a wish to make the spiritual life accessible to everyone, and to make meditation more systematic. To that end, he deals with the progress of the soul in the practice of the virtues, with prayer and meditation, rather than with the end to which all these lead: contemplation properly so called. He does not seem to have had any personal experience of contemplation, but he describes it in terms of the doctrine of the five spiritual senses.[202]

The best-known of the French secular masters was Peter d'Ailly's successor as chancellor of the University of Paris, John Gerson (1363–1429).[203] He too showed little enthusiasm for the new tendencies. He clearly expressed his distrust of the Rhineland mystics and of John Ruysbroeck.[204] He belongs rather to the old patristic tradition and especially to that of the Pseudo-Dionysius; there are extant some reflections or *Notulae*, which he made on

199 This is especially true of Gerson. Cf. A. Combes, "Gerson et la naissance de l'humanisme. Note sur les rapports de l'histoire doctrinale et de l'histoire littéraire", in *Rev. moyen âge latin*, I (1945), pp. 259–84.

200 Cf. E. Vansteenberghe, art. "Ailly (Pierre d')", in *Dict. de spirit.*, I, 256–60; and L. Salembier, art. "Ailly (Pierre d')", in *Dict. théol. cath.*, I, 642–54.

201 Cf. R. Guanieri, "Per la fortuna di Ruusbroec in Italia. Le sorprese di un codice Vaticano", in *Rivista Storia Chiesa Italia*, VI (1952), pp. 333–64.

202 His works were published in the volume of *Tractatus et sermones*, Strasbourg, 1490. The French works were published by L. Salembier in the *Revue de Lille*, 1907. Among his Latin works, see the *De exercitio proficientium* (ed. E. Vansteenberghe, in *Beiträge z. Geschichte der Philos. und Theologie Mittelalters.*, *Suppl.*, vol. III (1935), pp. 1231–46).

203 For biographical sketches, see P. Glorieux, "La vie et les œuvres de G. Essai chronologique", in *Arch. hist. litt. doctr. moyen âge*, XVIII (1950–1), pp. 149–92; and the works cited below, especially those of A. Combes. In addition, see H. Dacremont, *G.*, Paris, 1929; and M. J. Pinet, *La vie ardente de G.*, Paris, 1929.

204 In this connection, see A. Combes, *Essai sur la critique de Ruysbroeck par Gerson*, 3 vols published, Paris, 1945–59.

certain passages of the *Celestial Hierarchy*.[205] This commentary shows, however, that the influence of the Areopagite operated upon Gerson "by suggestion rather than by extensive documentation", after the example of the great scholastics, chiefly St Albert.[206] After Dionysius, Gerson's masters were first St Augustine, and then, among medieval writers, St Bernard, the Victorines, St Bonaventure, St Thomas, and the Carthusian Hugh of Balma.[207] It has also been held that Gerson has combined nominalism, and its theory of abstraction, with his own mystical experience to form an original system, a forerunner of Luther's.[208] This is, however, an exaggeration and has been seriously contested.[209]

Gerson's teaching on contemplation is set forth principally in his chief work, *On Mystical Theology, Speculative and Practical*.[210] It is also to be found in various minor works, such as *The Mount of Contemplation* and *Spiritual Beggary*,[211] and another, not very original, on the gifts of the Holy Spirit, cast in the form of a letter. These three *opuscula*, which Gerson addressed to his sisters, were written at Bruges about 1400.[212] The thesis of *On Mystical Theology* is the connection between speculative theology and mysticism. The former depends on the powers of reason, which attain to truth; the latter, on the affective powers, the object of which is goodness. Just as all knowledge is mingled with love, so in mysticism practice should always be united with theory. This outline allows Gerson to set forth a doctrine that is on the whole in agreement with the common fund of medieval tradition, especially of the monastic Middle Ages, and therefore antecedent to the speculations of the fourteenth century.

It has been held that he favoured the view that all are called to mystical contemplation,[213] but it is a suggestion difficult to defend.[214]

[205] *Notulae super quaedam verba Dionysii de Coelesti Hierarchia.* Ed. A. Combes, *Jean Gerson, commentateur dionysien*, Paris, 1940. The old edition of Gerson's Latin works is that of E. du Pin, 5 vols, Antwerp, 1706. It is somewhat rare, but except for a few treatises and sermons of which later editions have been published, one must have recourse to it.

[206] Cf. A. Combes, *J.G., commentateur dionysien*, pp. 427–47.

[207] Cf. J. Stelzenberger, *Die Mystik des J. G.*, Breslau, 1928.

[208] This was the opinion of W. Dress, *Die Theologie G.*, Gütersloh, 1931.

[209] B. J. Stelzengerger, *op. cit.*; and by J. B. Monnoyeur, O.S.B., "La doctrine de G. augustinienne et bonaventurienne", in *Études francisc.*, XLVI (1934), pp. 690–7.

[210] Critical edition by A. Combes, *Ioannis Carlerii de Gerson de mystica theologia*, Lugano, 1958.

[211] These two treatises have been translated into French by P. Pascal under the title of *Initiation à la vie mystique*, Paris, 1943.

[212] Ed. E. Vansteenberghe, "Quelques écrits de J.G. Textes inédits et études", in *Rev. Sc. Relig.*, XIV (1934), pp. 370–86.

[213] Cf. J. L. Connolly, *John G., Reformer and Mystic*, Louvain, 1958; also J. B. Monnoyeur, O.S.B., "G. et l'appel général à la contemplation ou théologie mystique", in *La Vie spirit.*, XXIII (1930), *Suppl.*, [49–68].

Although every Christian should aspire to it, the state of union remains, for Gerson, a gift of God. It presupposes, of course, certain conditions of life and certain dispositions which depend upon the temperament of the individual. Like Thomas a Kempis, Gerson goes as far as denying the possibility of contemplating the divine nature in this life.

In his lifetime he exercised a great influence, especially as a preacher and spiritual director.[215] Many of his sermons, both in Latin and in French, have been preserved. His most remarkable sermons were in the vernacular. "Beginning in 1395, he adopted a homiletic style derived from the Fathers, in which a concise commentary on the day's gospel leads up to a lesson in piety, or in which recur like a *leitmotif* two imperatives: do penance, and believe."[216] The themes of his preaching[217] are drawn from the Word of God,[218] but doctrinal and moral subjects predominate; he uses these to lead souls to the summits of the spiritual life. Scripture provides him with quotations and *exempla*,[219] and the epistles and gospels of the days supply the theme, but he never deals *ex professo* with the message of the Bible as a whole, considered in itself.

As a spiritual director, Gerson summed up his experience in various *opuscula* on the discernment of spirits.[220] In these he shows a prudence inspired by the extremes to which the Rhineland mystics and Ruysbroeck had gone; and also by the case of St Bridget of Sweden, whose revelations had recently been discussed at the

[214] Cf. P. Pourrat, "J.G. et l'appel à la contemplation mystique", in *Rev. apolog.*, XLIX (1929), pp. 427–38.

[215] His teaching at the university should not be forgotten; cf. P. Glorieux "L'enseignement universitaire de G.", in *Rech. théol. anc. méd.*, XXIII (1956), pp. 88–113.

[216] M. de Gandillac, in *Histoire de l'Église* (Fliche–Martin), vol. XIII, *Le mouvement doctrinal du IXe au XIVe siècle*, Paris, 1951, p. 471. Cf. A. Combes, "Sur la date des sermons universitaires de Gerson pour la fête du jeudi saint", in *Arch. hist. litt. doctr. moyen âge*, XV (1946), pp. 338–41.

[217] Fifty-six French sermons have been studied by L. Mourin in *J.G., prédicateur français*, Bruges, 1952, and he has published a certain number of them in various periodicals and in *Six sermons français inédits de J.G. Etude doctrinale et littéraire, suivie de l'édition critique et de remarques linguistiques*, Paris, 1946. To these may be added the sermon on the passion edited by G. Frénaud, O.S.B., *La passion de Notre-Seigneur*, Paris, 1947.

[218] Cf. L. Mourin, *J.G., prédicateur français*, ch. II, pp. 218–86.

[219] *Ibid.*, pp. 346–8 and 388–94.

[220] These were the *De examinatione doctrinarum*, the *De probatione spirituum*, and the *De distinctione verarum visionum a falsis* (*Opera*, vol. I, col. 7–19, 37–59). Cf. A. Chollet, in *Dict. théol. cathol.*, IV, col. 1390–1. There is a study of the *De probatione spirituum* by A. Wittmann in *De discretione spirituum apud Dionysium Carthusianum*, Debrecen, 1939, pp. 42–4. See also P. Boland, O.S.B., *The Concept of Discretio spirituum in John Gerson's "De probatione spirituum" and "De distinctione verarum visionum a falsis"*, Washington, 1959 (a dissertation, with English translations of both treatises and a commentary).

Council of Constance.[221] He brings together all the criteria accepted in the Church, and emphasizes the role of the hierarchy. The discernment of spirits can also be effected by means of natural prudence, common sense, and learning; it can therefore be done "by the method of general art and doctrine," *per modum artis et doctrinae generalis*. But this art must be accomplished by a sort of intimate experience, *per inspirationem intimam, seu internam saporem, sive per experimentalem dulcedinem quamdam*. Finally, it may happen that a charisma comes into play—a gift properly so called. The director himself needs the direction of another. As for the rules of discernment, especially when it is a matter of evaluating extraordinary states, they must take into account, above all, the subject's humility, prudence, patience, "truth" or sincerity, and charity.[222] With a similar pastoral aim, Gerson wrote a considerable number of *opuscula* on "the art of hearing confessions".[223] In little treatises, letters, and sermons, he tried to solve particular problems of moral and spiritual life.[224]

Another French secular master was Robert Ciboule (1403–58). He was a professor of theology in Paris from 1430, and rector of the University in 1437. From 1438 to 1441, he was the ambassador of Charles VII at the Council of Basle, and to the Holy See. In 1451 he was named chancellor of Notre Dame and applied himself to reforming the university. The following year found him preparing a memorandum intended to rehabilitate Joan of Arc. Among all his works, a good many of which are still unpublished,[225] one must be mentioned: the *Livre de Saincte meditacion en congnoissance de soy*. This theological treatise in French puts forward first a general conception of the Christian life, then a technique of meditation, and finally a theory of contemplation. In it, Ciboule is particularly concerned with the meditation whose essential object is self-knowledge, not only on the grounds that it is an important element in any Christian life, but even more because the soul is the image of God, the mirror of the Trinity. This "Christian Socrat-

[221] It was her revelations that occasioned the *De probatione spirituum*. Gerson alludes to the guidance required in cases of extraordinary states in his *Epistola II ad fratrem Bartholomaeum* against Ruysbroeck (*Opera*, vol. I, pp. 80–2); critical edition by A. Combes in *Essai sur la critique de Ruysbroeck par Gerson*, I, pp. 790–804.

[222] This is the subject of *De distinctione verarum visionum a falsis*.

[223] The *De arte audiendi confessiones*, the *De modo inquirendi peccata in confessione*, the *De correptione proximi*, and the *De officio pastorum* (*Opera*, II pp. 446–56, 480–1, 542–58).

[224] For example, in the *De vita spirituali animae* (*Opera*, III, pp. 5–72) and the *Regulae morales* (*ibid.*, pp. 77–106).

[225] For a biographical sketch and bibliographical information, see A. Combes, "Un témoin du socratisme chrétien au XVe siècle, R.C. (1403–1458)", in *Arch. hist. doctr. litt. moyen âge*, VIII (1933), pp. 93–259.

ism", as it has been called, is based on St Thomas Aquinas, St Bernard, and especially Hugh of St Victor and Richard's *Benjamin major*. He follows this last work closely: "Sometimes contemplation is by dilatation of mind, sometimes by elevation, and sometimes by alienation". Whatever may have been his exact position regarding the immediate and intuitive vision of God, he distinctly states that at the highest level of contemplation (that which is "by alienation") "these are special graces of God, which he distributes according to his pleasure and according to his admirable providence to those who render themselves apt for such perfections."[226]

About the same time, Nicholas of Cusa (1401–64) lived in Germany. He was involved in the humanist movement then taking shape in Italy and France, and in the theological controversies connected with the councils of Basle and Florence. After having first opposed the view that the pope is above a council, he became a determined partisan of it. He was in the confidence of Eugene IV and was sent by him to Constantinople, with a view to bringing about a rapprochement of separated Christians. On his return, he wrote his chief work, "On Learned Ignorance," *De docta ignorantia*. Created cardinal in 1450, he was entrusted by Pope Nicholas V with various apostolic missions to the Low Countries, Bohemia, and Germany. In 1452 he became bishop of Brixen, which enabled him to be in constant touch with the Benedictines of Tegernsee, but he came into conflict with Sigmund, Count of Tyrol. Finally he fled to Rome where he became vicar to Pius II.[227]

[226] See *ibid.*, pp. 183–92.

[227] There is a very complete biographical study of Nicholas of Cusa by E. Vansteenberghe, *Le Cardinal N. de C. L'action, la pensée*, Paris, 1920. This may be supplemented by E. Methuen, *Die letzten Jahre des N. von K. Biographische Untersuchungen nach neuen Quellen*, Cologne, 1958. See also P. Rotta, *N.C.*, Milan, 1942 (with a good bibliography); P. Mennicken, *N. von K.*, Trèves, 1950; M. de Gandillac, *La philosophie de N. de C.*, Paris, 1941 (translated into German, with revisions, as *N. von C. Studien zu seiner philosophie und philosophischen Weltanschauung*, Düsseldorf, 1953). There are many studies on his philosophy and various points of his theology.

His works were published by Jacques Lefèvre d'Etaples, Paris, 1514. Critical edition, Leipzig, 14 vols (of which five have been published), 1932 and following years. For the sermons, ed. E. Hoffmann and R. Klibansky, see *Cusanus-Texte*, I, *Predigten*, Heidelberg, 1929; for the treatises, ed. G. Kallen, see *ibid.*, II, Heidelberg, 1935; for the letters, ed. J. Koch, F. Hausmann, G. von Bredow, and E. Maschke, see *ibid.*, IV, Heidelberg, 1944–56. For the *De pace fidei*, ed. R. Klibansky and H. Bascour, London, 1956. See also E. Vansteenberghe, "Autour de la docte ignorance. Une controverse sur la théologie mystique au XVe siècle", in *Beiträge z. Gesch. des Philos. Mittelalters*, XIV, 2–4, Münster, 1915.

For translations into German, see *Schriften des N. von C. in deutscher Uebersetzung*, 13 vols, Leipzig, 1936–47, and Hamburg, 1949–52; also *Schriften des N. von C.*, 3 vols published, Heidelberg, 1949–55. For translations into French, see *De la docte ignorance*, trans. by L. Moulinier, Paris, 1930; *La Vision de Dieu*, trans. by E. Vansteenberghe, Bruges, 1925; and *Œuvres choisis*, trans. by M. de Gandillac, Paris, 1942.

This is not the place for a study of his theology and political doctrine, or the part he played in the rise of humanism. His spiritual teaching is of the general tendency of the fifteenth century. He cannot, however, be ranked without qualification among the anti-speculative spiritual writers of the *Devotio moderna*. On occasion he gave himself up to the loftiest speculation, and recognised no divorce between theology and mysticism. He was an heir of the Rhineland mystics—he owned Eckhart's treatises—and also knew the works of Raymond Lull and St Albert's commentary on the pseudo-Dionysius. He also read widely in every field.

He parted company with the Rhineland mystics, however, and accepted the anti-speculative tendency, in his definition of contemplation by its affective and gratuitous character. He did not admit the possibility of man's attaining, in this life, to the vision of God; this is plainly shown in his well-known sermon *Signum magnum* for the feast of the Assumption, 1439.[228] Here one can detect the influence of the Victorines (although on several points he differs from Richard of St Victor) and of the Carthusian Hugh of Balma. The *De docta ignorantia* even has a distinctly Dionysian flavour: man's highest wisdom consists in realizing his powerlessness fully to grasp reality. The cause of this powerlessness lies in the impassable distance which separates the absolute and the particular, given the relativity and complexity of our knowledge. For a man who wishes to approach the truth there remain not concepts and reasoning, but intuition, which may go so far as to become mystical intuition.

In saying this, Nicholas took a very definite stand, for at that time theologians were divided on the question whether mystical contemplation necessarily presupposes an antecedent or concomitant knowledge. The scholastics in general had replied in the affirmative. Gerson, however, and a few Franciscans had held that this knowledge might be absent in certain cases—though these were the exceptions. In the fifteenth century, certain theologians (such as Vincent of Aggsbach) replied in the negative even more strongly than Nicholas had done; so much so, in fact, that he was sometimes obliged to defend the intellect in spite of his attraction to the traditional Dionysian "darkness". In his eyes, only the beatific vision puts an end to "learned ignorance".[229]

Here is the limit of the anti-intellectual reaction: the rejection of all intellectual element in the contemplative life. An exaggera-

[228] Discussed by E. Vansteenberghe in *Rev. Sc. Relig.*, IX (1929), pp. 376–90.
[229] See E. Vansteenberghe, *Autour de la docte ignorance.*

tion to which Nicholas of Cusa did not commit himself as it stood, though the extremists who surrounded him defended it bitterly.

Nicholas was undoubtedly somewhat eclectic. Thus his *De docta ignorantia* shows traits characteristic of the speculative mysticism of the Rhineland; for example, the doctrine of our birth in the Son. This teaching is also found in the sermon *Dies sanctificatus* for Christmas 1439, intended for "contemplatives", *pro contemplativis.*[230] In this way the Christian comes to transcend himself as a knowing subject and to identify his personality with the object of his contemplation. This conception is curiously akin to one of the basic intuitions of Eckhart.[231]

With this picture of the anti-conventual and anti-intellectual reaction, the description of medieval spirituality may be considered complete. The fifteenth century added no new elements to it. The premises had been laid down, and the years that followed simply revealed the consequences: on the one hand the Reformation, on the other the Catholic revival. The breach between theology and mysticism was, however, to widen. The beginning of the fifteenth century was the seed-time of all this future development.

Henceforward men would live on the capital of the past: the course was set.

[230] Ed. E. Hoffmann and R. Klibansky, *Cusanus-Texte*, I, Heidelberg, 1929.

[231] Cf. E. Hoffmann, "Gotteschau bei Meister Eckhart und Nikolaus von Cues", in *Zangger-Festschrift*, Zürich, 1934, 1033–45. See also H. Wolter, "Funken vom Feuer Gottes. Die Lehre des N. von K. vom geistlichen Leben", in *Geist und Leben*, XXXI (1958), pp. 264–75.

VIII

THE HEIRS OF THE MIDDLE AGES

WITH the originators of the *Devotio moderna*, the spiritual history of the Middle Ages comes to an end—in the sense that at least for some time there is no great new movement or foundation only heirs of the past. Even during the period when speculative mysticism was in the limelight, as well as that in which there was a general reaction against it and the traditional forms of religious life, the old current of spirituality still found followers, both among the monastic orders and among the Mendicants and, it need hardly be said, among the laity as well.

This chapter is concerned with those who followed on in the frame-work of religious life. The two following chapters will consider those who perpetuated the spirit of the lay movements that have already been discussed.[1]

1. Benedictines and Cistercians up to the Fourteenth Century

From the thirteenth century onwards, the new Mendicant Orders, without combating or neutralizing the influence of the old monastic Orders, attracted to themselves the best in European spirituality. This explains why there is so little to be said about the representatives of Benedictine and Cistercian spirituality at the end of the Middle Ages.[2] There is nothing striking, nothing that stands out clearly.

The Benedictines continued to read the Fathers, to copy them, and to live by them, though some forgot their own tradition. One was William of Afflighem (†1297), the abbot of St Trond, who wrote or translated the visions of Beatrice of Tirlemont, the life of St Lutgarde, and the life of Jesus. There was nothing distinctively

[1] Chs II and V. In connection with this chapter and the following one, see M. D. Knowles, *The Religious Orders in England*, II, Cambridge, 1957, ch. XVI, "The Spiritual Life of the Fifteenth Century".

[2] For a survey, see P. Schmitz, *Histoire de l'Ordre de Saint-Benoît*, VI, Maredsous, 1949, pp. 250–8.

monastic about these mediocre examples of the affective *dévot* style which was beginning to spread in the Low Countries.[3]

Individualism, the appeal of a life wholly given to prayer, and perhaps also a certain disillusion with the religious life in decadent communities, is shown by the attraction of the eremitical life still felt by certain minds. Peter Morone (1215–96), before he became pope in 1294 as Celestine V, had founded several hermitages which soon became partly cenobitical. These houses formed the Celestine Order, which spread rapidly, chiefly in Italy and in France.[4] St Sylvester Gozzolini (*c.* 1177–1267) also sought the solitary life and ended by creating a new branch of Benedictines, that of the Sylvestrines. Meanwhile the other Orders that had previously sprung from that trunk—the Camaldolese, the Vallombrosans, the Grandimontains and the Williamites, Fontévrault, Monte Vergine, and Pulsano[5]—continued to recruit members. A little later, Blessed Bernard Tolomei (†1348), like Sylvester in his quest for solitude, became the founder of another branch, the Olivetans, so called from their mother house on Monte Oliveto, near Siena. Like some of the preceding, they still exist today.[6]

Some of these were originally directly eremitical in tendency. The founder, or founders, withdrew into solitude, but soon disciples flocked to them. Then an organization began to take shape, and a real common life reappeared, though sometimes only to a very limited extent.

In the Benedictine monasteries, however decadent they may have been, there were still from time to time men worthy of notice. Such was the abbot of Monte Cassino, Bernard Ayglier (*c.* 1200–1282). He was abbot of Lérins (1256), and was raised to the abbacy of Monte Cassino in 1263 by Urban IV; he then decided to return to the authentic traditions of the Order. To this end he wrote a *Mirror for Monks* (*c.* 1274), which was markedly influenced by the treatise *On Monastic Profession* of the Dominican William Perault.[7]

[3] See J. Franck, "Ein literarische Persönlichkeit des XIII. Jahrhunderts in de Niederlanden", in *Neue Jahrbücher für des Klass. Altertum*, XIII (1904), pp. 424–442; J. van Mierlo, S.J., *W. v. A. en het leven van Jezus en het leven van Sinte Lutgardis*, Antwerp, 1936; by the same author, "Kan W. v. A. ook de bewerker zijn van het leven van Jesus", in *Koninkl. Vlaams. Academie v Taal- en Letterkunde, Verslagen en Mededelingen* (1950), pp. 5–29.

[4] See especially "Saint Pierre Célestin et ses premiers biographes", in *Anal. Bolland.*, XVI (1897), pp. 365–487; F. X. Seppelt, *Monumenta Coelestina*, Paderborn, 1921; F. Baethgen, *Beiträge zur Geschichte Cölestins V*, Halle, 1934; P. Barbaini, *C. V anacoreta e papa*, Milan, 1936.

[5] See P. Schmitz, *op. cit.*, III, pp. 12–27; cf. *supra*, Part I, ch. VI, pp. 127 *et seq.*

[6] For bibliographical information, see Schmitz, *op. cit.*, III, pp. 21–3.

[7] Ed. H. Walter, *Bernardi I Abbatis Casinensis Speculum monachorum*, Freiburg-im-Breisgau, 1901.

He also wrote a long commentary on the Rule of St Benedict.[8] The first of these two works treats of the monastic vows and the obligations they involve; its final part describes the duties of the abbatial office. In this treatise can be seen developments of great precision on the subject of stability[9] and on the obligation of the Rule.[10] In his commentary on the latter, Bernard's exposition emphasizes both these points with much force. He is severe as regards poverty, denying that the abbot has the power of dispensing a subject from it. No monk is to have money at his disposal except for the business of the monastery or for conducting some school. Even then, he is to be only the administrator of property which does not belong to him. To Bernard, monk "proprietors" inevitably sin mortally: *non dubito quin proprietarii sint in peccato mortali.*[11] It is clear what abuses had crept into the Benedictine monasteries.

Later a former monk and abbot of Aniane, who had become bishop of Orvieto, Peter Bohier († before 1389), withdrew to Subiaco and there wrote two commentaries on the Rule, inspired by that of Bernard Ayglier. In his first commentary, which was never published, he makes use of juridical sources as well. The second, which is longer, draws upon the old monastic authors, particularly St Jerome.[12] In addition, he too wrote a *Mirror for Monks* which has not, as yet, been published. These works are not isolated examples: other commentaries appeared in the fourteenth and fifteenth centuries, chiefly in Germany and Austria[13]; as well as "exhortations" intended to encourage the monks in the spiritual duties of their daily life.[14]

The most remarkable flowering of the old Benedictine trunk was at the Saxon monastery of Helfta at the end of the thirteenth century. Among the nuns there was a Béguine from Magdeburg, Mechtilde (1207–82 or 1298). We have already seen the characteristics of her spirituality,[15] and it will be enough to recall here how her *Flowing Light of the Godhead* reflects the whole spirit of the *Brautmystik*, and how also at times her way of expressing herself foreshadows the *Wesenmystik* soon to flourish among the spiritual

[8] Ed. A. M. Caplet, O.S.B., Monte Cassino, 1894.

[9] *Speculum monachorum*, Part I, chs II and V; in the Walter edition, pp. 11–17 and 40.

[10] *Ibid.*, ch. X; Walter, p. 111.

[11] *In Reg. S. Ben.*, cap. 33; in the Caplet edition, pp. 253, 256.

[12] Ed. L. Allodi, Subiaco, 1908.

[13] Cf. P. Schmitz, *op. cit.*, II, 2nd ed., p. 400.

[14] Such as the *Exhortatio de quotidiana exercitatione monachi* by Conrad von Rodenberg, abbot of Johannisberg (†1486). There is a study by P. Volk, O.S.B., "C. von R.", in *Stud. Mitteilungen z. Gesch. Benediktinerordens*, LV (1937), pp. 48–62.

[15] Cf. Part II, ch. VI, §1, pp. 375 *et seq.*

writers of the Rhineland. Mechtilde of Magdeburg had a powerful influence on the nuns of Helfta. One of them was St Mechtilde of Hackeborn (*c.* 1241–99) whose *Book of Special Grace* is the fruit of a contemplation nourished by the liturgy.[16] Her own sister, Gertrude of Hackeborn, who became abbess of Helfta, was also a spiritual daughter of Mechtilde of Magdeburg, as was St Gertrude the Great, the most famous of the Helfta nuns.

St Gertrude was "offered" to the monastery at the age of five, about 1261. Not having chosen monastic life of her own free will, she began by living it half-heartedly. From 1285, however, she took her vocation seriously and from that time until her death, in 1301 or 1302, her life was one uninterrupted ascent towards God. She left the record of her experiences in the *Legate of Divine Love* and in her *Exercises*.[17] The *Legate* was not written wholly by Gertrude herself; Book I is a panegyric of her, and Books III to V seem to have been written by other nuns.[18]

The influence, as far as contemplation is concerned, of Mechtilde of Magdeburg on St Gertrude and Mechtilde of Hackeborn can be seen in the accents of passionate devotion which mark their writings. The *Brautmystik* was common to both of them in spite of the probability of Dominican influence on their doctrine and on their mysticism.[19] For Gertrude, no one can obtain the grace of contemplation except by a special gift of God's goodness,[20] a gift which is not necessarily extraordinary. Miraculous phenomena such as levitation and ecstasies were only rarely to be found among the nuns of Helfta. Gertrude did indeed receive the "impression of the stigmata" in her youth, but they were not visible externally.[21] If contemplation brings to her mind the memory of countless

[16] *Liber specialis gratiae*, edited by the monks of Solesmes, *Revelationes Gertrudianae ac Mechtildianae*, II, Paris, 1877, pp. 1–422; French translation, Paris, 1922. Analysed by Dom Besse in *Les mystiques bénédictins des origines au XIIIe siècle*, Maredsous, 1922, ch. XI.

[17] *Legatus divinae pietatis*, edited by the monks of Solesmes, *Revelationes Gertrudianae ac Mechtildianae*, I, Paris, 1875; *Exercitia Spiritualia, ibid.*

[18] There are French translations by the Benedictines of Solesmes, 2 vols, Paris, 1906; and by P. Doyère, O.S.B., *Le mémorial spirituel* [Book II of the *Legatus*], Paris, 1954. There are also German translations by W. Verkade, O.S.B., *Das neue Gertrudenbuch* (partial), 2nd ed., Beuron, 1955; and by J. Weissbrodt (complete), 12th ed., Freiburg-im-Breisgau, 1954. Dutch translation by M. Molenaar, 2 vols, Bussum, 1951–2.

The *Exercises* have been translated into French by Dom Emmanuel, Paris, 1929 and A. Schmidt, Paris, 1943; and into Italian (anonymously), Praglia, 1936. There is an English translation by a Benedictine Nun of Regina Laudis, Westminster, Md, 1956.

[19] Cf. G. Ledos, *Sainte Gertrude*, Paris, 1904, pp. 116–17. On her interior life, see Dom G. Dolan, *S.G., sa vie intérieure*, Maredsous, 1923; and J. M. Besse, O.S.B., *op. cit.*, chs IX–XI (St Gertrude and St Mechtilde).

[20] *Legatus*, III, 44; Solesmes ed., p. 210.

[21] *Ibid.*, II, 4; Solesmes ed., p. 66.

imaginative "visions" seen and "words" heard—accounts of these are scattered all through her works and their supernatural origin seemed much less doubtful to her than it seems to us, who are tempted to look on them as a mere literary device[22]—yet, she attached more importance to the favour of "feeling the Beloved in herself"—*cum dilectum praecordiis suis immissum se continere sentiret.*[23] This explains the fact that she spontaneously expressed her mystical life in language borrowed from the Canticle of Canticles or from certain verses of St John, speaking in terms of delights, of sweet embraces, and of raptures. This love was not simply a psychological state; it was inseparable from its object, Christ, and its summit is access "into a place that is wonderful beyond aught that can be said, that is, the Heart of Jesus Christ".[24] It has been thought that this is what St Teresa of Avila called transforming union.[25]

This raises the question of the part played by Gertrude in the development of devotion to the Sacred Heart. In answering it, one must first emphasize the importance of the liturgy in her spiritual life,[26] as in that of Mechtilde of Hackeborn. For both of them it was the source of asceticism and its support. It initiated them into the Christian mysteries, and its rhythm marked the succession of their mystical graces. The temporal and sanctoral cycles of the liturgical year,[27] the weekly cycle of the psalter and the daily one of the hours, the celebration of the Eucharist—these constituted the normal framework of their spiritual experiences. This setting, in which every Christian hears the word of God and unites himself with the praise and sacrifice of Christ and the Church, they succeed in putting to a marvellous use: for the liturgy revealed to Gertrude what Christian piety had already taken to itself and delighted to make the object of its meditation—the humanity of Christ. St Bernard had spoken, once or twice, of the Heart of Jesus, but without, by that, envisaging any formal cultus of it[28]; he was thinking

[22] In this connection, see C. Vagaggini, O.S.B., *Il senso teologico della liturgia*, Rome, 1957, pp. 592–7. The imagery in Gertrude's language has been studied by Sr Mary Jeremy, "'Similitudes' in the Writing of St Gertrude of Helfta", in *Medieval Studies*, XIX (1957), pp. 48–54.

[23] *Legatus*, II, 6; Solesmes ed., p. 72.

[24] *Ibid.*, IV, 58; Solesmes ed., p. 476.

[25] G. Ledos, *op. cit.*, p. 157.

[26] On this subject, see the excellent study by C. Vagaggini, *op. cit.*, pp. 591–642; also his *La dévotion au Sacré-Cœur chez sainte Mechtilde et sainte Gertrude*, in *Cor Jesu. Commentationes in litteras encyclicas "Haurietis Aquas"*, II, Rome, 1959, pp. 29–48.

[27] In this connection see the extracts translated under the title of *L'année liturgique d'après sainte Gertrude et sainte Mechtilde*, 2 vols, Maredsous, 1927–8.

[28] Thus *Sermo 61 in Cantica* (P.L., 183, 1072): *Patet arcanum cordis per foramina corporis; patet illud magnum pietatis sacramentum. . . .* On the history of

simply of the person of Christ.[29] William of St Thierry had spoken more explicitly of this Heart, "sure seat of mercy", in which the "secrets of the Son" are seen, and which is the source of all the sacraments of salvation.[30] A little later, Guerric of Igny († *c.* 1160) put still more stress on our Lord's heart of flesh, recalling the wound in his side.[31] These authors made use of scriptural symbols, like that of the ark in which only a small part of mankind was saved, or again certain expressions from St John and St Paul.[32] Richard of St Victor was still more explicit: "If we consider the Heart of Christ, there is nothing sweeter, nothing more merciful. No creature was ever sweeter than this Heart, or ever will be."[33] The tenderness of these words is reminiscent of the hymn *Dulcis Jesu memoria*, but the writer is a long way from thinking of the Heart of Christ apart from his whole being as God made man. From these texts, taken together, it cannot be concluded that an explicit devotion to the Sacred Heart was really widespread as early as the twelfth century.

A more definite move in that direction was made by the Cistercian nun Lutgarde of Aywières (†1246). Before she entered religion, when she was still quite young and was finishing her education at the Benedictine monastery of St Trond, she was torn from a budding romance by a revelation of the Heart of Christ: "Contemplate henceforth what you should love and why you should love it".[34] Soon afterwards she had a vision of the crucified and bleeding Christ.[35] She was elected abbess of St Trond, but fled to Cistercian nuns at Aywières. There, says her biographer, it befell

---

devotion to the Sacred Heart, the best recent study seems to be that of P. Debongnie, C.SS.R., "Commencement et recommencement de la dévotion au Cœur de Jésus", in *Le Cœur* (*Études carmélitaines*, 29, Paris, 1950), pp. 147–92. To this may be added the useful contributions of U. Berlière, O.S.B., *La dévotion au Sacré-Cœur dans l'ordre de Saint-Benoît*, Maredsous, 1923; and of J. Leclercq, O.S.B., "Le Sacré-Cœur dans la tradition bénédictine au moyen âge", in *Cor Jesu*, II, pp. 1–28.

[29] Cf. A. Hamon, article "Cœur (Sacré)", in *Dict. de spirit.*, II, 1027.

[30] *Meditativae orationes*, 6; P.L., 180, 225–6; cf. *De contemplando Deo*, I, 43; P.L., 184, 368.

[31] Sermon IV, *In Dominica palmarum*, 5; P.L., 185, 140. On devotion to Christ's wounds in the Middle Ages, see L. Gougaud, O.S.B., *Dévotions et pratiques ascétiques du moyen âge*, Maredsous, 1925, ch. v.

[32] For example, John 7. 38: *Flumina de ventre eius fluent aquae vivae.* On the interpretation of this text in terms of the Heart of Christ, see H. Rahner, S.J., "Grundzuge einer Geschichte der Herz-Jesu-Verehrung", in *Zeitschr. Asz. Myst.*, XVIII (1943), pp. 61–83, cf. *Biblica*, XXII (1941), pp. 269–302, 367–403.

[33] *De Emmanuele*, I, 21; P.L., 196, 655.

[34] *Vita* by Thomas of Cantimpré; cf. *AA.SS.*, June, vol. IV, p. 192. On Lutgarde, see S. Roisin, "Sainte L. d'A. dans son ordre et son temps", in *Collect. Ord. Cist. reform.*, VIII (1946), pp. 161–72; L. Reypens, S.J., "Sint Lutgarts mystieke opgang", in *Ons geest. Erf*, XX (1946), pp. 7–49.

[35] *Vita*, p. 193.

one day that "a vein burst in her side, at the level of her heart. So much blood came forth that her tunic and her mantle were abundantly bedewed with it. . . . At the same moment, Christ appeared to her. . . . 'Because of the ardour with which you long for martyrdom and which you feel in shedding this blood, your merit in heaven shall be that of martyrdom equal to that which was given to the Blessed Agnes when she was beheaded for her faith in me'."[36]

It would be an exaggeration to make this new devotion a prerogative of the Cistercian Order; it had taken possession of Lutgarde before she entered Aywières, when she was still at St Trond. In any case Hadewijch, too, soon afterwards spoke of it,[37] and also Mechtilde of Magdeburg.[38] If, then, Bernard and others after him sometimes mentioned the Heart of the Lord in their writings, the milieu in which the devotion, properly speaking, grew in favour was chiefly that of the convents of women of the Low Countries and Germany.

The evidence that has been preserved on this form of piety at Helfta does not seem sufficient to indicate that the monastery was a Cistercian house.[39] Mechtilde of Hackeborn, and especially Gertrude the Great, glorified that Heart which Christ had given them as a pledge of his love, as a "refuge", as the place of their rest.[40] Gertrude had, like Lutgarde, been wounded in the heart by a ray darting from the side of Christ:

> When, after receiving the life-giving sacrament, I had come back to my place of prayer, it seemed to me as though there came forth from the crucifix depicted in my book (that is, from the wound in the side) something like a ray of sunshine, in the likeness of a sharpened arrow. It appeared first to stretch forth, then to contract itself and then to stretch forth again, and continuing thus for a time, it sweetly drew my affection to itself.[41]

With Gertrude, this intense union with Christ and his Heart was not yet veiled with the sadness that clothed it four centuries later.

[36] *Ibid.*, p. 200. [37] Letter 22.

[38] *Flowing Light of the Godhead*, Part I, ch. VIII; Part VI, ch. XXIV. [These chapters are omitted in the English translation by L. Menzies cited in ch. VI, *supra*, note 6.—Trans.]

[39] Opinion is still divided on this point. Those who consider that Helfta was Benedictine cite the fact that this monastery does not appear on the lists of Cistercian houses. The others base their argument on the *Liber specialis gratiae* by Mechtilde of Hackeborn, Part I, ch. 28, "De sancto Bernardo abbate". It should be noted, however, that tributes such as she pays to Bernard, whose "Order is imitated by all the others", are frequently paid to other saints; for example, St Benedict (*Legatus*, IV, 11).

[40] See, for example, for Mechtilde, *Liber specialis gratiae*, Part I, ch. 22; II, 19; and *Legatus*, V, 4 (account of her death). For Gertrude, *Legatus*, II, 1, 23; III, 45, 67; etc.

[41] *Legatus*, II, 5; Solesmes ed., p. 69. Cf. *ibid.*, V, 27.

For St Margaret Mary Alacoque, the Heart of Jesus is above all a bleeding heart, suffering from the ingratitude of men and from their sins. The atmosphere that surrounds Gertrude is more serene in the sense that she is united not so much to the sorrow of Christ, "saturated with opprobrium", as to the mystery of his advent which is ever coming to pass. She is fired with the "apostolic zeal" that is re-called in the office for her feast, in the antiphon to the *Benedictus* at Lauds. When she wrote the *Legate of Divine Love*, she declared expressly that she was doing so in the hope that her readers too would glorify the graciousness of the Lord, that they would have compassion on her own unworthiness and would obtain the compunction that would assist their own progress. "May so sweet a fragrance arise to thee from the golden censers of their hearts full of charity, as to make amends abundantly for all the defects of my ingratitude and negligence."[42]

Throughout the *Legate* we find considerations on personal merit, on the fruits of grace and glory produced by a holy life, and on its effects by way of satisfaction. Gertrude also emphasizes its efficacy for the salvation of others. Like Catherine of Siena later, she had the spirit of the Church. She was conscious of what her life as a nun, united to Christ by holiness and prayer, could accomplish for his mystical body. Thus Book III of the *Legate* tells how the communion of saints was revealed to her. She saw the Church under the form of Christ's physical body. One side was clothed in royal garments and represented the faithful souls who distinguish themselves by their merits. The other side, covered with wounds, was naked: this represented the imperfect souls who suffer from vices and many faults. The Lord's attention was first drawn to the charity of the elect, but with his splendid vesture (that is, with their merits) he wiped away the defilement of the others. In other words, Christ communicates his life to the imperfect by means of the merits of the souls who are in charity, and thus is created the mystical union of all the faithful.[43]

But, according to Gertrude, merits have another dimension besides this universal one; they can also be applied by a soul for other specific souls: "Although the Church shares in each of the favours granted to each of the faithful, yet he who receives it has a greater benefit from it, and consequently anyone to whom he desires with a special affection to communicate it will also receive from it greater fruit and benefit.[44]

[42] *Ibid.*, II, 24; Solesmes ed., p. 114. On this point, as on all the rest of this discussion, a great many texts might be cited. The references mentioned give only a few good examples.

[43] *Ibid.*, III, 75.

[44] *Ibid.*, 76; Solesmes ed., p. 269.

Of course, beneath this communication of merit there lie in reality the superabundant merits of Christ's passion. All that the soul that suffers in union with him does is to determine in some way the destination to which his merits are to be applied. Ultimately Gertrude's emphasis is not on our co-redemptive power; it is, above all, on that redemptive love which makes up superabundantly for the deficiencies of men: "Whoever . . . will fortify himself by the example of my Passion, seeking to imitate it . . . , to him I will give, by a special affection, for the increase of his merits, all that I merited by my patience and my other virtues."[45]

Until Gertrude's works were printed in 1536 by John Justus Lanspergius, they remained little known. A few echoes of them can, however, be found in the Franciscans, in Suso, and in Catherine of Siena.[46] With the destruction of the monastery of Helfta by the intruded bishop, Albert of Brunswick, in the middle of the fourteenth century, this centre of intense liturgical and apostolic piety disappeared, and not until the fifteenth century did there appear in the Benedictine Order any movement comparable in depth to that of Helfta, though a few spiritual writings marked the remainder of the fourteenth century.[47]

In the Cistercian Order, also, the writings on spiritual matters varied in quality. The *Lives* written in the thirteenth century reflect fairly well the spiritual activity of the monasteries. Many of the monks were still men of real holiness. Poverty, humility, obedience, austerity, and fidelity to the Rule went hand in hand with devotion—often very affective in character—to the man Christ in his infancy or his passion, to the Eucharist, and to the Blessed Virgin. There is some mention of extraordinary graces. Among the nuns a tinge of speculative mysticism sometimes appears, which reveals or foreshadows their spiritual affinity with the Béguines and the Rhineland mystics.[48]

Some of the Cistercian works of spirituality show either that St Bernard's affective piety persisted among them, or that they were not untouched by the *dévot* atmosphere of their period. Indeed Cîteaux was very much open to the new currents which were more and more affecting Christian piety towards the thirteenth century. Ogier, abbot of Locedio in Piedmont (1205–14), wrote a treatise *Of the Praises of the Holy Mother of God*. It was from this work, which was probably composed before 1205, that there was extracted the much-debated *On the Sorrow of Mary*, attributed at

45 *Ibid.*, 42; Solesmes ed., p. 207.
46 Cf. Debongnie, *loc. cit.*, pp. 173–92.
47 See Schmitz, *op. cit.*, VI, pp. 254–7; and VII, pp. 302–3.
48 Cf. S. Roisin, *L'hagiographie cistercienne dans le diocèse de Liège au XIIIe siècle*, Louvain, 1947.

one time to St Augustine, at another to St Anselm or St Bernard.[49] Its vicissitudes confirm that it is simply an extract. Another Cistercian of the thirteenth century, John of Limoges, was the author, among other works, of some *opuscula* on monastic ascesis, on religious silence, *An Explanation of the Religious Life*, *On Visitations* and *On Elections*.[50] The same tendency is found in the writing of Gerard of Liège, author of a treatise *On the Seven Words of Our Lord on the Cross*.[51] Another work, *On the Seven Remedies against Unlawful Love and the Five Reasons for ardently loving God*,[52] recommends various practices suited to the struggle against carnal love and stimulates the soul to the love of God. Yet another, *On the Doctrine of the Heart*, is a sort of summary of asceticism and mysticism, describing the heart's ascent in highly coloured and allegorical language.[53] The Cistercian abbot Stephen of Salley (†1252) wrote some *Meditations on the Joys of the Virgin Mary*[54] and also a *Triple Exercise*.[55] These meditations do seem to represent "at the very beginning of the thirteenth century, the first stirrings of methodical prayer".[56] His *Mirror for Novices*[57] provides good evidence of the daily life in an abbey of the Order. It reveals the same tendency towards pious meditation on the mysteries of Christ's life; reading and the Divine Office preparing the soul for recollection and prayer. All this is in addition to what has already been said about devotion to the Sacred Heart. In certain monasteries, especially some of the women's, this is explained by the influence of the Béguines, but of course a tender piety towards Christ's humanity and its mysteries had become, by that time, the common property of all Christendom.

2. *The Carthusians*

Like the Cistercians, the Carthusians of the thirteenth and fourteenth centuries made an obvious effort to assimilate the new

[49] Cf. H. Barré, "Le 'Planctus Mariae' attribué à saint Bernard", in *Rev. ascét. myst.*, XXVIII (1952), pp. 243–66.

[50] *Johannis Lemovicensis Opera Omnia*, ed. C. Horvath, O.Cist., 3 vols, Veszprém, 1932. Cf. J. Leclercq, *Anal. S. Ord. Cist.* (1947), pp. 147–54.

[51] Ed. E. Mikkers, O.C.S.O., in *Coll. Ord. Cist. Ref.*, XII (1950), pp. 176–94; XIII (1951), pp. 18–29.

[52] Ed. A. Wilmart, O.S.B., "Les traités de G. de L. sur l'amour illicite et sur l'amour de Dieu", in *Analecta Reginensia* (series *Studi e Testi*, No. 59), Vatican City, 1933, pp. 181–247.

[53] A few old editions of the *De doctrina cordis* are still in existence; for example, that of Naples, 1605, which is very rare. (A copy is to be found in the Vatican Library, *Stamp. Chigi V 110*.)

[54] Ed. A. Wilmart, O.S.B., in *Rev. ascét., myst.*, X (1929), pp. 368–415.

[55] Ed. A. Wilmart, O.S.B., in *ibid.*, XI (1930), pp. 355–74.

[56] A. Wilmart in *ibid.*, p. 356.

[57] Ed. E. Mikkers, O.C.S.O., in *Collect. Ord. Cist. Ref.*, VIII (1946), pp. 17–68.

trends in spirituality—methodical and systematic meditation, and affective devotion to Christ in his mysteries. At least, that is what seems characteristic of their principal spiritual writers at this time.

First is Hugh of Balma, or Balmey, prior to Meyriat (Ain) at the end of the thirteenth century. He was the author of a treatise *On Mystical Theology* which was long attributed to St Bonaventure and printed among his works,[58] but was recently restored to Hugh.[59] This *opusculum* first gives a brief description of the three ways of the spiritual life; purgative, illuminative and unitive. Either the theme of St Bonaventure's *De triplici via* was already widely read, or else, as is more probable, both Bonaventure and Hugh were making use of ideas that were generally accepted in their time. When he treats of contemplation, Hugh shows himself a disciple of Thomas Gallus. On its highest plane, it is purely affective, but it gives "a knowledge of God which is greater than any that is procured by the intelligence and the reason".[60] It is a true "knowledge by ignorance", *cognitio per ignorantiam*.[61] It is hardly necessary to point out that in this Hugh is accepting the Dionysian darkness. To that he adds some "practices", concerned with time, place, posture, etc., which enable the soul to arrive at contemplation.[62] One thought is characteristic of the whole treatise; Hugh emphasizes, especially in connection with the illuminative way, that the soul ascends to God by "anagogical movements". He means by this "ascending acts", petitions "which are naught else but burning sighs, anxious aspirations, evidently begging the Beloved to grant, with a greater joy, that act which raises (the soul) above herself".[63] By this "art" one attains to "the union of love". As models for these aspirations, he recommends the petitions of the Pater, on which he comments.

The essentials of this teaching are also found in a work entitled *On Contemplation*, by another Carthusian, almost a contemporary of Hugh, Guigues du Pont (†1297). Its three parts treat of contemplation from different points of view. Guigues considers it now as speculative and intellectual, now as affective and anagogical. He

[58] *Opera*, Lyons ed. (1668), vol. VII, pp. 657–87; Vivès ed. (1866), vol. VIII, pp. 1–53. Quotations are from this last edition.

[59] See S. Autore, art. "H. de B." in *Dict. théol. cath.*, VII, 215–20; P. Dubourg, S.J., "La date de la Theologia mystica", in *Rev. ascét. myst.*, VIII (1927), pp. 156–161; J. Maréchal, S.J., *Études sur la psychologie des mystiques*, II, Brussels, 1937, pp. 269–72.

[60] *Quaestio unica* (which constitutes the whole treatise), p. 51.

[61] Cap. III, part. IV.

[62] Cap. III, part. III.

[63] "Quae petitiones nihil aliud sunt quam ignita suspiria et inquietae affectiones, dilectum ad sui sursum actionem felicius obtinendam ardentius provocantes" (cap. II, part. II). Guigo I already distinguished ejaculatory prayer, "quasi jaculatas" (*Consuet.*, XXIX, 3).

gives the preference to the latter, but as he admits of intellectual contemplation, his point of view is less exclusive than Hugh's.[64] His concern with numbering the ascending stages of the spiritual life is also noteworthy: in his second treatise particularly he enumerates the "twelve consolations" of the soul, which are the steps in the ladder of contemplation. The tendency is clearly affective, and the fifth step is that of "compassionate love for our Lord." This, however, is only a stage before arriving at contemplation properly so called, which he describes in Dionysian terms: *obumbratio caliginis in cubiculo cordis*. The height of contemplation, at least in this life, is the *mentis excessus* in which the soul reaches God in an ineffable union, without preparation or intermediary. There is nothing more to be hoped for except the bliss of heaven.

Closer to us by a century, Ludolph the Carthusian, or the Saxon (†1378), is still known for his *Life of Christ*,[65] a work which certainly influenced St Ignatius of Loyola.[66] It is not a particularly original piece of work: it owes much to Suso's *Horologium Sapientiae*[67] and especially to the *Meditations on the Life of Christ* attributed to St Bonaventure, not to mention a number of other sources, whether or not Ludolph cites them expressly.

The work is not, properly speaking, a life of Christ. It consists rather of meditations which bring together the teachings of the Bible, theology, and the liturgy on the person and life of Jesus. In Ludolph's own words the meditations have a practical object: "to teach agreeably, enabling (the reader) to taste the delights of Christian piety".[68] Its practical and ascetic aim, together with the fact that it was easy and agreeable to read, made it celebrated. It opened to interior souls an easy access to the Gospels. It furnished preachers with a variety of themes. It explained what prayer is, and taught that the imitation of Christ is the source of all perfection. It had an influence on Christian piety comparable with that of the *Imitation of Christ*, whose title it really better deserved.

[64] See J. P. Grausem, S.J., "Le 'De contemplatione' du chartreux Guigues du Pont (†1297)", in *Rev. ascét. myst.*, X (1929), pp. 259–89; a few fragments of this unpublished work are quoted in the article. See also J. Maréchal, S.J., *op. cit.* pp. 275–84.

[65] Ed. L. M. Rigollot, Paris, 1870; there are many other editions and translations. For a study of Ludolph's life, sources, influence, and doctrine, see M. I. Bodenstedt, *The Vita Christi of Ludolphus the Carthusian*, Washington, 1944; and A. Passmann, "Probleme um L. von S.", in *Archives de l'Église d'Alsace*, III (1949–50), pp. 13–34.

[66] Cf. E. Raitz von Frentz, S.J., "Ludolphe le chartreux et les Exercises de saint Ignace de Loyola", in *Rev. ascét. myst.*, XXV (1949), pp. 375–88.

[67] Cf. L. M. F. Daniels, O.P., "L. van S. en Henricus Suso", in *Ons geest. Erf*, XX (1946), pp. 138–50.

[68] Prologue.

In the fifteenth century, the most eminent theologian and spiritual writer of the Order was certainly Denys of Ryckel (†1471). He came originally from Limburg, and spent almost all his life in the Charterhouse of Roermond. Prodigiously learned, and with rare powers of work and an equally rare gift of contemplation, he left an enormous body of work, in which was put together all the substance of theological and spiritual doctrine accumulated by earlier ages.[69] This makes him, in spite of an eclecticism which prevents his ever being truly original, an excellent witness to all that had been said and written before his time: nothing of any importance escaped him. His sound learning was fed chiefly on the Bible, the Fathers, and the theologians who wrote before the fourteenth century; he mistrusted the new nominalist and Scotist tendencies as well as the speculative forms of mysticism. He stands apart from his own time by uniting theology and mysticism, as the Fathers had done, and as had been done in the twelfth and sometimes in the thirteenth centuries.

He wrote a complete commentary, page by page, on the Bible, which he had read and meditated on assiduously.[70] The overwhelming size of these tomes, which make up one-third of his work, rather discourages the present-day reader, the more so, because in them there is no synthesis such as is commonly found in modern introductions to the study of the Bible. Denys never tires of recommending his readers to study Scripture and meditate on it. He asks of them humility and prudence, purity of heart, compunction, fervour, and respect for the normative authority of the Church. He boldly bids them rise to the level of the inspired books and open their minds to the light from on high, that of the Spirit, without which the Bible will remain a sealed book for them. If, on the other hand, they succeed in putting themselves in the right dispositions, it will become the "threefold table", *triplex mensa*. At this table the Christian is fed sometimes with history—such as events in the life of Christ; sometimes with allegory, which teaches us what we are to believe; and sometimes with anagogy, which furnishes the contemplative with his food, his delight, and his development: "anagogy is a simple elevation of the soul in the contemplation of divine realities."[71] This suggests the influence of

[69] *Opera omnia*, ed. Montreuil (vols I–XIV and XVII–XVIII), Tournai (vols XIVb, XV–XVI, XIX–XLII), and Parkminster (vol. XXVb), 1896–1935; 44 vols in all. Some of the minor works have been translated into French. There is an excellent recent survey by A. Stoelen, O.Cart., art. "Denys le Chartreux", in *Dict. de spirit.*, III, cols 430–49.

[70] See A. Stoelen, *op. cit.*, col. 432; on the old editions of these commentaries, see *Dict. de la Bible*, II (1899), cols 1385–6.

[71] On this subject, see his *De donis Spiritus Sancti*, tr. 3, a. 31; *Opera*, XXXV, pp. 231–2. Other passages are cited in *Dict. de spirit.*, IV, cols 201–3.

Hugh of St Victor, which Denys, moreover, acknowledges. But he knows that, according to ancient tradition, a fourth table is provided—that of "tropology", which is concerned with moral conduct. Scripture is, in fact, a rule of life, the first of all rules. It makes both action and prayer fruitful: "Oh, how good it is to gaze into that mirror!"[72] The reading of the Bible leads to the love of God, to joy, and to spiritual sweetness, as well as to a horror of sin and to the calming of the passions.

These huge commentaries, and indeed all Denys' writings, give the impression that he drew from Scripture definite doctrines of theology and contemplation, although his works contain nothing that cannot be found elsewhere, nothing that cannot be connected ultimately with monastic and patristic tradition.

After the Bible, another source, the *Mystical Theology* of his namesake Dionysius the Pseudo-Areopagite, influenced certain of his ideas on spirituality. These he developed chiefly in his commentary on that work of Dionysius[73] and in his own treatise *On Contemplation*.[74] He divides contemplation into the "speculative affirmative" and the "loving and mystical",[75] a division which foreshadows the modern distinction between acquired and infused contemplation. But for both the starting-point is the same: "The great secret of contemplating well is to love much".[76] He develops his thought more precisely in his *Solutions of Difficulties*[77] and in the four treatises *On the Gifts of the Holy Spirit*.[78] As a good disciple of St Thomas, however, he gives the primacy in contemplation to the intellect, while recognizing that it is aided by love in an activity which in its highest mode is intuitive and immediate. It seems that his position is fairly far removed from that of Hugh of Balma with his anagogical aspirations, while at the same time the whole movement of affective piety dear to the Franciscan tradition and to the *Devotio moderna* is alien to him.

His reading of the Pseudo-Dionysius saved him from giving too large a place to intellectual clarity in contemplation, the object of which indeed remains the "divine darkness": *tenebrae divinae, divina caligo*. These expressions have not only a subjective sense, in that they signify how incapable man is of grasping God, but also

[72] *O quam salubre est hoc speculum intueri!* (*Proemium* of the *Commentary on the Sentences*, XIX, 39).

[73] *Opera*, vols XV–XVI. Cf. G.E.M. Vos de Wael, *De mystica theologia van Dionysius Mysticus in de werken van Dionysius Carthusianus*; Nijmegen, 1942.

[74] *Opera*, XLI. [75] *Ibid.*, cols 739–42. [76] *Ibid.*, col 744.

[77] *Opera*, XVI, pp. 481–95; cf. K. Swenden, "De 'mystica theologia' bij Dionysius van Rijkel", in *Ons geest. Erf*, XXII (1948), pp. 56–80.

[78] *Opera*, vol. XXXV. The second of the four treatises deals with the gifts of wisdom and understanding; see especially pp. 175–93 on the gift of wisdom. See also *Dict. de spirit.*, III, cols 1599–601.

an objective one: God is, in himself, something other than all that we say of him. Hence the importance for Denys of the negative way, *via negationis*, when he seeks to translate mystical experience into human language. His spirituality thus becomes less Christocentric and "less Trinitarian than theistic"[79]—or even Neo-Platonist. At the same time, he does not ignore the *Brautmystik* or the role of the Eucharist in the mystical life.

Denys demands a great deal of the beginner in the way of humility, submission, and even obedience of judgment towards superiors and spiritual guides.[80] If discernment of spirits is called for, the criteria for Denys are those of common sense: humility, charity, and the effective practice of the Christian virtues on the one hand; and on the other pride, obstinacy, presumption, torpor, and hatred.

After Denys, the Order did not produce any comparable genius firmly uniting doctrine and experience. He appears in the middle of the fifteenth century as one of the most prolific writers in the Church. His work still has value, because he succeeded in remaining independent of the currents of his time and drawing upon the true sources of all Christian thought: the Bible, the Fathers, and the great scholastics. He was, of course, an eclectic, but what is a weakness in others enabled him to keep aloof from the partisan controversies of the schools. Although he is not representative of the theological and spiritual thought of his century, he is still today an author whom it is very useful to consult, because he had read and assimilated all that had been said before his time, and his judgments were to the point. His life as a Carthusian gave him the serenity of an almost timeless judgment, while by the openness of his mind and his wide reading he comes out of the enclosure of his monastery.

Among the Carthusian writers of the late Middle Ages,[81] several have left latin translations of various spiritual writings.[82] The best known among them were the Carthusians of St Barbara at Cologne, and it is to them that we owe diffusion of works by the spiritual writers of the Rhineland and Flanders, as well as of those connected with the *Devotio moderna*. Peter Bloomeven (†1536) translated Henry Herp's *Mirror of Perfection*; John Justus Lanspergius

[79] K. Swenden, *op. cit.*, p. 77.

[80] Especially in his *Commentary on Cassian* (*Opera*, XXVII) and in his *De discretione et examinatione spirituum* (*Opera*, XL, pp. 267–305). Cf. A. Wittmann, *De discretione spirituum apud Dionysium Carthusianum*, Debrecen, 1939; cf. *Dict. de spirit.*, III, cols 1097–8, 1264–6.

[81] See, for example, for the Netherlands, the bibliography by H. J. J. Scholtens, "De litteraire nalatenschap van de Kartuizers in de Nederlanden", in *Ons geest Erf*, XXV (1951), pp. 9–43; cf. *Dict. de spirit.*, II, cols 761–6.

[82] Cf. *Dict. de spirit.*, II, cols 756–60.

(†1539), in addition to translating St Gertrude, wrote works largely monastic in character, though one was a *Manual for the Christian Militia* (1538), intended to give laymen a clearer notion of their duties as Christians, and thus to bring about the effective reform of the Church[83]; Dietrich Loher (†1554) edited Denys the Carthusian; and finally Lawrence Surius (†1538), who is known for his numerous translations and editions, including those of the *Meditations on the Life of Christ*, of *the Pearl of the Gospel*, of the works of Suso, and some of the works of Tauler and Ruysbroeck. The Counter-Reformation and the movement of spirituality in the sixteenth and seventeenth centuries owed much of their vitality to this literary activity of the Cologne Charterhouse.[84]

Only one Carthusian, however, seems to have written a really original spiritual treatise; its subject was, however, only Carthusian life itself. This was Pierre Cousturier (†1537) of the Charterhouse of Vauvert near Paris.[85] St Ignatius of Loyola was on terms of spiritual friendship with him and his monastery. That fact, among others, is evidence that in the fifteenth and sixteenth centuries the Charterhouses were genuine foci of spiritual and even intellectual life.[86] A work by a Carthusian of Gemnitz, Nicholas Kempf (†1497), *Of the Right End and Order of Studies,*[87] is a dialogue between the *magistra*, i.e. the Bible, the *sacra pagina*, and the disciple, the theologian. The latter cannot be simply learned: he must "ruminate tirelessly what theology has led him to understand, so as to translate it into affection of the heart and into practical execution."[88]

3. Monastic Figures of the Fifteenth and Sixteenth Centuries

After being to some extent eclipsed in the fourteenth century, the Benedictines regained some of their vigour at the end of the Middle Ages. The *Devotio moderna* was not unconnected with this revival, and the Benedictine monasteries were no different from the other orders in their frequent copies of the *Imitation*, their

[83] A partial edition of his works was published at Cologne in 1554–5; a complete one, in 1630. A modern edition in 5 vols, Tournai, 1890.

[84] See J. Greven, *Die Kölner Kartause und die Anfänge der Katholischen Reform in Deutschland*, Münster, 1935. This influence will be discussed in greater detail in vol. III of this *History of Christian Spirituality.*

[85] Ed. Paris, 1522. For a study of this work, with extensive extracts from Book I, cap. x, see H. Bernard-Maître, S.J., "Un théoricien de la contemplation à la Chartreuse parisienne de Vauvert, Pierre Cousturier dit Sutor (*c.* 1480—18 juin 1537)", in *Rev. ascét. myst.*, XXXII (1956), pp. 174–95.

[86] Cf. J. de Ghellinck, S.J., "Les catalogues des bibliothèques médiévales chez les Chartreux et un guide de lectures spirituelles", in *Rev. ascét. myst.*, XXV (1949), pp. 284–98.

[87] "Dialogus de recto studiorum fine ac ordine", ed. B. Pez, *Bibliotheca ascetica*, IV, Ratisbon, 1724, pp. 257–492.

[88] *Ibid.*, Part II, ch. VI; Pez ed., p. 307.

"exercises", "alphabets", anthologies, collections of prayers, little treatises in spirituality, and methods of prayer. Among the authors who have been edited and studied recently, one may mention Nicholas of Clamanges (*c.* 1368–1437). His *Prayers,*[89] to be said before the canonical hours, are of considerable literary merit, but their spirit is that of the times. Nicholas connects each hour of the Office with a gift of the Holy Spirit. The English poet John Lydgate (†1449 or 1450), a monk of Bury St Edmunds, published "legends of the saints," moral poems, and other writings explaining or paraphrasing the Mass, the hymns of the Breviary, the story of the passion, and the mysteries of the Blessed Virgin.[90]

In central Europe, Jerome of Mondsee (†1475) also reflects the general tendency of the period, defending the affective nature of mystical experience. He was, however, a compiler more than an original mind, as is shown by his treatises *On Contemplation* and on the *Progress of Religious.*[91] Similar ideas are found in the works of his friend and fellow monk Bernard of Waging, prior of Tegernsee (†1472). Both of them were in touch with Nicholas of Cusa, and "learned ignorance" formed the background of their spirituality.[92]

Both monks and nuns continued to copy, and to meditate upon, spiritual texts that went back much further than the new schools. To take a single example, they continued to read and translate the *Mirror for Virgins.*[93] This anonymous treatise, which originated in the Rhineland and is a dialogue between a priest named Peregrinus and a nun named Theodora, dated from the first years of the twelfth century. But on the whole the old Benedictine Order, wherever it regained any of its vitality, allowed itself to be greatly influenced by the new conception of the spiritual life.

The fifteenth century, in spite of the often lamentable situation

[89] Cf. J. Leclercq, O.S.B., "Les prières inédites de N. de Cl.", in *Rev. ascét. myst.*, XXIII (1947), pp. 171–83.

[90] Cf. W. F. Schirmer, *John Lydgate. Ein Kulturbild aus dem 15. Jahrhundert*, Tübingen, 1952. Other poems are described by R. A. Kinefelter, "A Newly Discovered Fifteenth-century English Manuscript", in *Modern Language Quart.*, XIV (1953), pp. 3–6.

[91] For a biography and a list of his writings, see J. Glueckert, O.S.B., "Hieronymus von Mondsee (Magister Johannes de Werdea)", in *Stud. Mitteil Geschichte Benediktiner-Ordens*, XLVIII (1930), pp. 99–201. The sources of the *De profectu religiosorum* have been studied by M. Villier, S.J., "Lectures spirituelles de Jérome de Mondsee (†1475)", in *Rev. ascét. myst.*, XIII (1932), pp. 374–88.

[92] See E. Vansteenberghe, "Autour de la Docte Ignorance. Une controverse sur la théologie mystique au XVe siècle", in *Beiträge z. Gesch. der Philos. Mittelalters*, XIV, 2–4, Münster, 1915, ch. VI. Cf. P. Schmitz, *op. cit.*, VI, pp. 265–6 (for a discussion of other ascetical authors, see pp. 260–75).

[93] It has been analysed by M. Bernards, *Speculum virginum. Geistigkeit und Seelenleben der Frau im Hochmittelalter*, Cologne, 1955; cf. J. B. Valvekens, O. Praem., "Speculum virginum", in *Analecta Praemonstratensia*, XXXV (1959), pp. 166–71.

which is described in the following chapters, gave birth to a series of monastic reforms. Their most striking feature consisted in attempts at federation, the autonomy of the monasteries having been not the least among the causes of decadence. Through the efforts of Ludovico Barbo (1381–1443), the abbey of St Justina at Padua became the head of a group of Italian monasteries.[94] This example is paralleled by that of other "unions", like those of Bursfeld and Valladolid. It meant sacrificing a greater or lesser part of the monastic autonomy envisaged by the Benedictine rule itself. There was, however, no turning back; even today, the Benedictine Order has the aspect of a federation of "congregations", several of which are connected, directly or indirectly, with these "unions" formed in the fifteenth century.

The reforms were not simply administrative ones. An abbot like Barbo, who understood the trends of his time and frankly adapted himself to them, was at the same time a spiritual writer of great influence. He is still known by the *Method of Prayer and Meditation*,[95] in which he affirms as a principle the necessity of methodical prayer, and this the more vigorously because the monks of the fifteenth century no longer lived in isolation from the world as they had done in the early days of monasticism. The time set aside each day for mental prayer had therefore to be used with the maximum efficiency and its subject of meditation carefully defined, though the way was always left open to the soul to a more purely contemplative prayer. There was nothing new in all this: it has already been stated how much the practice of methodical meditation owes to the Franciscans and to the *Devotio moderna*.[96]

In Germany, similar revivals centred around the abbey of Melk, and even more around that of Bursfeld. The latter became, after the Council of Basle, the centre of a "union" to which many monasteries in northern Germany and the Low Countries were affiliated.[97] The most illustrious representative of this federation was John Trithemius, abbot of Spannheim (†1516).[98] He carried on

[94] Cf. I. Tassi, O.S.B., *Ludovico Barbo, 1381–1443*, Rome, 1952.

[95] *Forma* (or *Formula*) *orationis et meditationis*. There have been many editions. It is reproduced by H. Watrigant, *Quelques promoteurs de la méditation méthodique au XVe siècle*, Paris, 1919, pp. 15–28.

[96] In particular, the monastery of St Justina at Padua contributed to the spread of the *Imitation* in Italy. See R. Pitigliani, C.SS.R., *Il Ven. L. Barbo e la Diffusione dell' Imitazione di Cristo per opera della Congregazione di S. Giustina*, Padua, 1943.

[97] Cf. P. Schmitz, *op. cit.*, III, pp. 189–95. The history of the Bursfeld Union has been studied especially by Dom P. Volk; see particularly his work *Fünfhundert Jahre Bursfelder Kongregation*, Münster, 1950; and the article "Bursfeld" in *Dict. hist., géogr. ecclés.*, X, 1389–93.

[98] See especially U. Berlière, O.S.B., "Un écrivain ascétique de la fin du XVe siècle, J.T.", in *Rev. liturgique et monastique*, XIII (1927–8), pp. 21–32, 64–78.

the old spirit of Benedictine monasticism and was untiring in his insistence on flight from the world and love of the cloister. By accepting these two conditions essential to his state of life, the monk can apply himself to prayer and study, which Trithemius considered indispensable to monastic life.[99] He was determined that the Benedictine monasteries should follow the lines traced out by the great teachers of the Order. But when he speaks of prayer, his teaching sometimes reflects more modern tendencies. Thus, for him the contemplation of the crucifix is the great school in which a monk acquires the spirit of prayer.[100]

In Spain, the practice of methodical prayer invaded the new congregation of Valladolid. It spread notably from the abbey of Montserrat, one of whose abbots, Garcia de Cisneros (1455–1510), owed much both to Barbo and to the *Devotio moderna.* He has a considerable importance in the history of Spanish spirituality; a measure of which is his influence on St Ignatius of Loyola. It will be considered more in detail in connection with Spanish spirituality at the dawn of modern times, as it is against that background that Cisneros has a historical significance.[101]

Another illustrious figure of the order at the beginning of the sixteenth century was that of Louis de Blois (Blosius), abbot of Liessies in Hainault (1506–66).[102] Among his many works, *The Mirror of the Soul, Comfort for the Faint-hearted*, and the *Spiritual Instruction* are the most representative of his thought.[103] His spiritual doctrine[104] rests on a solid foundation of humanistic and theological learning. He emphasizes discretion and humility, purity

[99] Cf. L. Cromwell, *Beziehungen zwischen Mystik und Frühhumanismus beim Abt J. Tr.*, Heisenberg, 1925.

[100] This is seen particularly in his *Exhortationes ad monachos* and his *De triplici regione claustralium. Opera*, ed. Maintz, 1604, etc. Cf. P. Schmitz, *op. cit.*, VI, pp. 271–2.

[101] See ch. x, §4, pp. 539 *et seq.*, and vol. III of this *History of Christian Spirituality.*

[102] "Vita", in *AA.SS.*, January, vol. I, pp. 430–56. Cf. J. Peter, *L'Abbaye de Liessies en Hainaut, depuis ses origines jusqu'à la réforme de L. de Bl., 764–1566*, Lille, 1912; F. Baix, art. "Blois (Louis de)", in *Dict. hist. géogr. eccl.*, IX, cols 228–42.

[103] First edition of the *Opera*, Louvain, 1568. There have been many translations into various languages, which are significant as evidence of how widely the influence of the Rhineland and Flemish mystics spread. Some *opuscula* have been published under the title of *Manuale vitae spiritualis*, Fribourg, 1907. There is a biography, with a French translation of the three treatises mentioned here, by the Benedictines of Wisques, *Louis de Blois. Sa vie et ses traités ascétiques*, 2 vols, Maredsous, 1927–32; they also published his *Œuvres spirituelles*, 3 vols, Paris–Poitiers–Tours, 1911–22. An English translation was made by B. A. Wilberforce, O.P., and R. Hudleston, O.S.B., *The Spiritual Works of L. of Bl.*, London, 1925–1926.

[104] There is a sketch of his doctrine in vol. III of the *Œuvres spirituelles* (trans. by the Benedictines of Wisques, Tours, 1922), pp. 1–92.

of heart and the interior life. At the same time, he is fond of quoting Ruysbroeck, Suso, and especially Tauler. Blosius too wanted to restore his abbey to its past fervour. His *Mirror for Monks*[105] and his *Monastic Statutes*[106] were a kind of programme of reform, whence their markedly ascetic character. The abbot of Liessies was not prepared to accept collective mediocrity; he meant to open to all the road to holiness and to Christ.[107] His Christocentric outlook made him adopt the *dévot* language of his time; he expresses ardent devotion to the Passion, to the Heart of Jesus, and to the Five Wounds.[108]

Another humanist monk, though not belonging to what is usually called the Benedictine Order, lights up the early years of the sixteenth century. This was Blessed Paul Giustiniani (1476–1528), a Camaldolese.[109] He founded the Congregation of Monte Corona, not far from Ancona, in order to return to a more perfect practice of the eremitical life. The Order of Camaldoli had, indeed, been drawn towards the active life and had taken on a distinctly cenobitical form. Giustiniani's writings fill twelve volumes, preserved in the archives of the Congregation. Of these endless pages of manuscript, which reveal an extraordinary literary activity and a humane culture astonishing in a hermit, nothing has been published except a treatise *On the love of God*.[110] All his work is marked by a very firm teaching on the monastic life. It was his aim to give the eremitical life a sound doctrinal foundation. The hermit has a vocation that is his alone: he proclaims, in his own way, the kingdom of God, and his life is a source of graces which spring up to fall back upon the Church. He is a "martyr", a witness to Christ. Such a conception was certainly quite alien to most of the religious of the time! But Giustiniani's culture had given him the habit of reflecting attentively on the fundamental problems inevitably raised by the monastic revival, and he had also read the ancient writings of the monks and of the Fathers, as well as St Bernard and St Albert the Great. He thought very highly of the spirit of the early Franciscans.[111] On the other hand, he had been

105 English translation in vol. III of *The Spiritual Works*. This is an old anonymous translation, Paris, 1676, revised and edited by R. Hudleston, O.S.B. The introduction includes a biographical sketch.

106 *Statuta monastica*, ed. U. Berlière, O.S.B., Padua, 1929.

107 For a sketch of his monastic spirituality, see J. Delaygue, "L. de Bl., un réformateur bénédictin", in *Rev. monastique*, No. 148 (1957), pp. 97–111.

108 See U. Berlière, *La dévotion au Sacré-Cœur* . . ., pp. 94–8.

109 Cf. J. Leclercq, O.S.B., *Un humaniste ermite, le bienheureux Paul Giustiniani (1476–1528)*, Rome, 1951; by the same, *Seul avec Dieu. La vie érémitique d'après la doctrine du bienheureux P.G.*, Paris, 1955.

110 *Secretum meum mihi o Dell'amor di Dio*, pref. by A. Stolz, O.S.B., Frascati (Rome), 1941.

111 Cf. J. Leclercq, *Seul avec Dieu* . . ., pp. 163–7.

very little influenced by the *Devotio moderna.* All this explains why Giustiniani, with his return to the origins of Camaldoli and thence to the origins of all monastic institutions, appears an anomaly to the historian of monastic reform in the fifteenth and sixteenth centuries. In reality, he must be considered a providential link in the tradition of the pure monastic ideal.

The three preceding sections have primarily concerned themselves at length with the changes in the monastic Orders properly so called, from the end of the twelfth century to the Reformation. To view, at close range, how those who inherited the old monastic spirit reacted in the face of the new currents which were to end in the foundation of the Mendicant Orders, to the *Devotio Moderna,* and finally to the humanist Renaissance. It will have been noticed that, with a few exceptions like Denys the Carthusian and Paul Giustiniani, the writers of these Orders were strongly influenced by the spirituality of their time. In particular, they accepted the new methods of prayer. Ought one to blame them for it? They were simply men of their time, and it may well be that the influence of the *Devotio moderna* saved the monastic Orders from irreparable ruin. This it did, at least indirectly, by reviving their fervour and so allowing them to survive, to prepare descendants who would one day discover again the monastic gospel in its original purity.

4. *Preachers and Mystics in the Mendicant Orders*

Any discussion of the Mendicant Orders at the end of the Middle Ages amounts more or less to giving a list of their most illustrious members. These men were not creators. They followed the lines laid down by their founders, only departing from them in adopting, as the heirs of the monastic orders had done, the spirit of the *Devotio moderna.*

The Franciscan Order produced, in the fourteenth century, one striking theologian, William of Ockham (*c.* 1290–1349). The real significance of his work, however, can only be seen from the point of view of theology and politics, so that this is not the place to discuss the *venerabilis inceptor* in detail, or to judge his sometimes bold theories.

There arose in the Order, as in earlier times, men who were deeply attached to the spirit of St Francis. This was notably the case with St Francis of Paula, founder of the Minims (*c.* 1436–

1507).[112] But above all the Order produced preachers, among whom one of the most celebrated was St Bernardino of Siena (†1444).[113]

His *Latin Sermons*[114] are a valuable source for reconstructing his teaching. They were not, in fact, delivered in the form given in the texts, which resemble treatises rather than sermons, but because of this the ideas are more exactly and profoundly expressed. The *Italian Sermons* are more spontaneous, and contain picturesque descriptions of the life of the time.[115] In dogmatic theology Bernardino was much influenced by Duns Scotus, whereas in moral, ascetical, and mystical theology he turned rather to other great doctors like Thomas Aquinas, Bonaventure, and Alexander of Hales.[116]

In his spiritual teaching, he emphasized humility and was reserved over visions, revelations, ecstasies, and similar phenomena. He combined discretion in ascetics with an ardent devotion to Christ and a repeated affirmation of the primacy of love.[117] These were the fundamental themes of traditional Franciscan spirituality and of the new currents that had become popular since the end of the fourteenth century.

His readiness to accept the new trends is evident, especially in his devotion to the Holy Name of Jesus. The beginnings of the cultus in the Middle Ages have already been discussed,[118] and it will

112 Cf. R. Aubenas, in *Histoire de l'Église* (Fliche–Martin), vol. XV, pp. xxvii and 171–3; G. Roberti, *Storia della vita di s.F.d.P.*, Rome, 1916, pp. 287 and 356–7; A. Renaudet, *Préréforme et humanisme*, Paris, 1916. For the efforts at reform made by the Spanish Franciscans, see "Las reformas [franciscanas españoles] en los siglos XIV e XV", in *Archivo ibero-americano*, XVII (1957). See also "Introducción a los origines de la Observancia en España. Las reformes de los sigles XIV y XV", in *Archivo Ibero-Americano*, II, 17, Madrid, 1958.

113 There are biographies by P. Thureau-Dangin, *Un prédicateur populaire dans l'Italie de la Renaissance, S.B. de S.* (*1380–1444*), Paris, 1926; and O. Mund, O.F.M., *B. von S. Ein Rufer in der Not*, Münster, 1949 (with a good bibliography). Cf. *S.B. da S. Saggi e ricerche pubblicati nel quinto Centenario della morte* (*1444–1944*), Milan, 1945. See also the articles published in the *Bollettino di studi bernardiniani* from 1935 to 1950.

114 *Opera omnia*, 5 vols, Venice, 1745; modern critical edition, 7 vols, Quaracchi, 1950–9. There are editions of the *Sermoni latini* by D. Pacetti, O.F.M., 3 vols, Siena, 1929–32 (two of these volumes are the edition of the *De inspirationibus*), of the *Prediche volgari* by P. Cannarozzi, 5 vols, Pistoia–Florence, 1934–40; and of the *Operette volgari* by D. Pacetti, O.F.M., Florence, 1938.

115 Cf. Arsenio da Casorate, O.M.Cap., *La donna nelle prediche volgari di S.B. da S.*, Rome, 1955 (on women and their manner of life at that period in Tuscany).

116 Cf. D. Scaramuzzi, O.F.M., *La dottrina del B. G. Duns Scot nella predicazione di S.B. da S.*, Florence, 1930. On his moral teaching regarding the family, see B. Nardini, O.F.M., "La famiglia cristiana nel pensiero di S.B.", in *Bollettino di Studi bernardiniani*, X (1944–50), pp. 22–54; regarding the economic sphere, A. E. Trugenberger, *S.B. da S., Considerazioni sullo sviluppo dell'etica economica cristiana nel primo Rinascimento*, Berne, 1951.

117 Cf. A. Blasucci, O.M.Conv., "La spiritualità di San B. da S. O. Min. (1380–1444)", in *Miscell. Francescana*, XLIV (1944), pp. 3–67.

118 See Part II, cap. II, §1, p. 244.

be recalled that the feast was celebrated in England in the thirteenth century, with a Mass and Office. Bernardino formulated its object more precisely and became the apostle of the *written* name of Jesus in the form of the monogram IHS. His work reached its most successful point in 1432 when a bull of Pope Eugenius IV confirmed the orthodoxy of the devotion against its detractors, and in 1451 when, at the battle of Belgrade, the invocation of the Name of Jesus gave victory to Christians against the Moslems. The Franciscan Order wanted to show its approval of Bernardino's teaching and adopted a special Mass, from which was derived the one later inserted in the Roman missal. At the same time, confraternities of the Holy Name increased in number, and a votive Mass was composed which was widely used. But it was not until 1721, under Innocent XIII, that the office and Mass became part of the Roman liturgy, and only under St Pius X was the feast given its present date.[119]

Another Franciscan, a Dutchman, adopted even more wholeheartedly the new ways of thinking. John Brugman (†1473) belonged to the tradition of the *Meditations on the Life of Christ* attributed to St Bonaventure. His *Devout Exercises* ("Devote Oefeninghen") draws a picture of the life of Jesus; with his *Meditations on the Passion* in Dutch (as yet unpublished) they were drawn upon by later compilers of similar volumes, such as Thomas a Kempis.[120]

But the most notable spiritual writer in the Franciscan Order, at about the same period, was Henry Herp (or Harphius, i.e. native of Erp) of Brabant (†1477). He too was much influenced by the new trends. He seems to have read Hugh of Balma; but the influence of John Ruysbroeck was even more decisive, so much so that he has been called his herald.[121] Herp had a very wide influence

[119] See P. R. Basiotto, O.F.M., *History of the Development of Devotion to the Holy Name*, St Bonaventure, N.Y., 1943.

[120] See L. Verschueren, O.F.M., art. "Brugman (Jean)", in *Dict. de spirit.*, I, cols 1967–8; T. Brandsma, O. Carm., "Pater Brugman's 'Considerationes de passione Domini' gevonden", in *Tijdschrift v. Taal en letteren*, XXVII (1939), pp. 71–85; by the same, various articles in *De Gelderlander*, XCI (1939) and in *Annalen . . . der Wetenschap onder de Katholieken in Nederland*, XXXIII (1941), pp. 163–91. On Brugman's sources, see F. A. H. van den Hombergh, "Vijf eeuwen Verering en verguizing van J.B. Bijdrage tot het bronnenkritiek", in *Bijdragen voor de Geschiedenis van de Prov. der Minderbroeders in de Nederlanden*, No. 24 (1957), pp. 329–41. His sermons have been edited by P. Grootens, S.J., *Onuitgegeven sermoenen*, Tielt, 1948; and A. van Dijk, O.F.M., *Verspreide sermoenen*, Antwerp, 1948. His *Life of Jesus* has been translated into modern Dutch by M. Goossens, O.F.M., *J.B. Leven van Jesus*, Ruremonde–Maaseik, 1947.

[121] A number of studies have been published by L. Verschueren, O.F.M., in *Ons geest. Erf* from 1929 to 1932; in *Etudes franciscaines*, 1933 and 1934; in *Collectanea franciscana neerlandica*, II (1931), 345–93; and in the collection *Jan van Ruusbroec, leven, werken*, Malines, 1931, pp. 230–62. The most complete work is

himself, especially in Spanish mysticism of the sixteenth century, and in his own Order until the end of the seventeenth.[122] His teaching is expressed chiefly in the *Mirror of Perfection*, recently republished[123]; in a compilation of *opuscula* under the title of *Mystical Theology*, which was widely read in the sixteenth and seventeenth centuries[124]; in his *Sermons*[125]; and in a treatise *On the Precepts of the Divine Law*.[126] His aim was to translate Ruysbroeck's speculative doctrine into affective language. His conception of the relations between God and man was, like Ruysbroeck's, theocentric. God is first; man attains to him by knowledge and especially by love—a Franciscan trait. Hence the necessity of the accomplishment of God's will, the sign of its accomplishment being progress in renunciation, virtue and prayer. Following Hugh of Balma, Herp gives an important place in prayer to "aspirations" (*toegheesten*).[127] With this preference there goes a certain mistrust of spiritual consolations, which are neither a sure index of perfection nor a guarantee of divine action. Above the active interior life, and above the contemplative life, there is a third life, the life of "superessential contemplation" (*ouerweselic*) characterized by its gratuity and passivity. There is a Franciscan primacy of love and imitation of Christ—those *exercitia Christiformia*—in this ascent of the soul, whose setting is not unlike that of Ruysbroeck; but, unlike him, Herp holds that at the summit of the mystical life there is a direct contemplation of God's essence. That was probably one of the themes that later brought Herp into favour with the Spanish *Alumbrados*. In 1586 as a result of controversy on the point, the Index allowed a corrected edition of Herp's works in which the word *superessentialis* (the Latin equivalent of *ouerweselic*) was nearly always replaced by *supereminens*. Herp's close kinship with the leaders of his time is also apparent in his definite acceptance of methodical meditation. The Franciscan Order had laid the

---

that of D. Kalverkamp, O.F.M., *Die Vollkommenheitslehre der Franziskaners Heinrich Herp* (†*1477*), Werl in Westphalia, 1940. On the place of his birth, see A. Meuwese, "De Mysticus H.H. De kwestie van zijn geboorteplaats", in *Brabantia* (*Tilburg*), II (1953), pp. 79–83.

122 Cf. P. Groult, *Les mystiques des Pays-Bas et la littérature espagnole du XVIe siècle*, Louvain, 1927; Fidèle de Ros, O.M.Cap., *François d'Osuna*, Paris, 1936; and especially, by the same, *Un inspirateur de sainte Thérèse, le frère Bernardin de Laredo*, Paris, 1948.

123 *Spieghel der Volcomenheit*, ed. L. Verschueren, O.F.M., 2 vols, Antwerp, 1931. The Latin versions (Cologne, 1513, and Venice, 1524) are significant as showing the spread of his thought and its interpretation in modern times.

124 *Theologica mystica*, Cologne, 1556; etc. Translated into French by J. B Machault, S.J., Paris, 1617. Bérulle possessed a copy.

125 Nuremberg, 1484; etc. 126 Maintz, 1474; etc.

127 Cf. C. Janssen, O.Carm., "L'oraison aspirative chez Herp et ses prédécesseurs", in *Carmelus*, III (1956), pp. 19–48.

foundations of the method, and its spiritual writers had built up the ideal which was at once affective, Christocentric, and mystical. Legislation on this point was derived from the prescription in the Franciscan Rule according to which the friar's whole life should be ordered to piety and prayer. Herp was only a link, though an important one, in a tendency which his Order had set in motion. Later are found Franciscan adaptations of the method perfected by Cisneros and St Ignatius of Loyola.[128]

In the fifteenth century, decadent and troubled as it was, the Franciscans still gave to the Church defenders of faith and morals. Among these were St John Capistran (†1456),[129] St John della Marca (†1476),[130] Blessed Bernardino of Feltre (†1494)[131] and Bernardino de' Busti (†513).[132] There were some among them who did not hide their sympathy for the Spirituals' branch of their Order. One such was Bartholomew Cordoni (†1535),[133] known chiefly for his little treatise *On the Union of the Soul with the Supereminent Light*, published posthumously in two editions.[134] The Index condemned it in 1584 on account of a certain temerity of language, which assimilated mystical union to the hypostatic union, put forward a theory of the "perpetual Mass" sung by the soul in the bosom of the Godhead, spoke of a "spiration" between God and the soul, and exalted faith at the expense of works. Other

[128] Cf. P. Optatus, O.M.Cap., "De oefening van het inwendig gebed in de minderbroedersorde gedurende de vijftiende en de zestiende eeuw", in *Ons geest. Erf*, XXI (1947), pp. 113–60; Remigius ab Alosto, O.M.Cap., "De oratione mentali in Ordine Fratrum Minorum Capuccinorum", in *Collect. frances.*, IX (1939), pp. 164–92.

[129] There is a biography by J. Hofer, *Johannes von Capestrano*, Innsbruck, 1936; an Italian version was brought out at Aquila, 1955. The works are described by A. Chiappini in *Reliquie letterarie capestranesi*, Aquila, 1927, and *Produzione letteraria di S. Giov. da C.*, Gubbio, 1927. A series of studies appeared in *Studi francescani*, LIII (1956), pp. 203–394. The treatise on women's adornments has been edited by A. Chiappini, *S. Giov. da C., Degli ornamenti specie delle donne*, Siena, 1956.

[130] Cf. D. Pacetti, "Le prediche autografe di S. Giov. della Marca", in *Arch. francisc. hist.*, XXXV (1942), pp. 296–326; XXXVI (1943), pp. 75–97. His other writings are, in general, unpublished. There are biographies by G. Caselli, *Studi su S. G. della M.*, 2 vols, Ascoli Piceno and Offida, 1926; and M. Sgattoni, *La vita di S. G. della M.*, Zara, 1940. On his action at Terni, cf. A. Ghinato, in *Arch. francisc. hist.*, XLIX (1956), pp. 106–42, 352–90.

[131] The *Sermoni* have been edited by Carlo da Milano, Milan, 1940. The other treatises (*De modo confessionis, De perfectione christiana*, etc.) exist only in the sixteenth-century edition. There are biographies by Ludovic de Besse, *Le bienheureux B. de F. et son œuvre*, Tours, 1902; A. Pellin, *Beato B. da F.*, Lecco, 1938; and F. Casolini, *B. da F., il martello degli usurai*, Milan, 1939.

[132] His works on the Blessed Virgin, or *Mariale*, exist only in old editions. Cf. especially G. Galli, "Due ignote edizioni quattrocentine della 'Corona della Beatissima Vergine Maria' di fra' Bernardino de' Busti", in *Miscellanea bibliografica in memoria di Don Tommaso Accurti*, Rome, 1947, pp. 103–24.

[133] Cf. N. Santinelli, *Il beato B.C. e le fonti della sua mistica*, Città di Castello, 1930.

[134] By Pichi in 1538 and by Malfetta in 1539.

ascetical writers were incontestably orthodox, such as Anthony de Guevara (†1545)[135]; the Blessed Camilla Baptista Varani (†1524)[136]; St Catherine of Bologna (†1463), whose most notable work was *On the Arms Necessary for the Spiritual Combat*[137] and finally Frans Vervoort (†1555) who was "the greatest disciple of Ruysbroeck in the sixteenth century".[138]

The Dominican Order, at the end of the Middle Ages, lost the *éclat* that it had until the fourteenth century. Like the Franciscans, however, it still gave great preachers and apostles to the Church. Particularly in the preaching of St Vincent Ferrer (†1419) there shone forth devotion to the Church and zeal for its reform, concern with preserving the faithful from false spiritual influences of every kind, and zeal for leading the decadent religious Orders back to the right ways by giving those responsible a sense of their duties. He was known especially for his *Sermons* and for a *Treatise on the Spiritual Life*[139]; St Antonius of Florence (†1459) was a moralist of great repute.[140] The doctrine of both these preachers was simple. They gave ascetical advice and did not dwell much upon contemplation properly so called; probably that explains the success

[135] Cf. Fidèle de Ros, O.M.Cap., "Guevara, auteur ascétique", in *Archivo ibero-americano*, II, 6 (1946), pp. 338–99.

[136] Cf. G. Boccanera, "Biografia e scritti della B. C.-B. da V., clarissa di Camerino (1458–1524)", in *Miscell. francisc.*, LVII (1957), pp. 64–94, 231–94, 333–65; published in book form as *Le opere spirituali*, Jesi, 1958. For a biography and some texts in translation, see "I dolori mentali di Gesù nella sua Passion secondo le rivelazioni della B. Battista Varani (1458–1524)", in *Rev. Ascet. e Mistica*, IV (1959), pp. 150–8.

[137] *Le armi necessarie alla battaglia spirituale.* First editions, Bologna, 1470 and 1474; frequently republished and translated. There are many biographies; see especially J. Heerinckx, art. "C. de B.", in *Dict. de spirit.*, II, cols 288–90; J. Stiénon du Pré, *Sainte C. de B.*, Paris, 1949.

[138] Cf. A. Ampe, S.J., and A. Deblaere, S.J., "Nieuw werk van Frans Vevoort", in *Ons geest. Erf*, I (1945), pp. 211–26. Among other studies of his life and works, there may be mentioned that of E. Rombouts, "Studie over de 16e eeuwse prozaschrijver F.V. en zijn afhankelijkheid van de middeleeuwse mystieke passieliteratur", in *Koninkl. Vlaams. Academie v. Taal- en Letterkunde, Verslagen en Mededelingen* (1955), pp. 422–39.

[139] There is a biography by M. M. Gorce, O.P., *St. V.F.*, Paris, 1935. See especially *Biografía y escritos*, ed. J. M. de Garganta, O.P., and V. Forcada, O.P., Madrid, 1956. The *De vita spirituali* will be found in the *Opuscula ascetica*, ed. M. J. Rousset, Paris, 1899. Selected sermons on the life of Christ have been published in English translation by S.M.C., *A Christology from the Sermons of St Vincent Ferrer*, London, 1954. French translations include *Traités de la vie et perfection spirituelle de S.V.F. et du bienheureux Albert le Grand*, by M. J. Rousset, 2 vols, Paris, 1924; *Œuvres de S.V.F.*, by H. Fages, 2 vols, Paris, 1909; and *La Vie spirituelle* (texts) by M. V. Bernadot, Saint-Maximin.

[140] His *Opera a ben vivere* is a programme of life for a person living in the world (cf. *Dict. de spirit.*, I, cols 725–6); ed. L. Ferretti, Florence, 1923; and C. Angelini, Milan, 1936. There is a French translation by Thiérard-Baudrillart, *Une règle de vie au XVe siècle*, Paris, 1921. His *Summa Theologica* has been recently republished (Graz, 1959). There are biographies by A. Masseron, Paris, 1926; and P. Bargellini, Brescia, 1947.

of their preaching.[141] As for Jerome Savonarola, he played the role of a reformer, if not indeed of a prophet. Certain of his works are quite remarkable, such as the *Triumph of the Cross* and *The Simplicity of the Christian Life*. But in the end his extremism and the political course he adopted cost him his life; he was burnt at the stake in Florence on 24 May 1498.[142] Other Dominicans, such as the Blessed John Dominici (†1419),[143] devoted themselves to guiding souls in the highest spiritual paths.

Moreover, in a century in which compromises were preparing the way for the Reformation, the Dominican Order maintained itself at a theological and spiritual level that commands respect. The Friars Preachers were still concerned with the solid training of novices, as we know from an anonymous work.[144] More than one of them deplored the state of religion and sought to remedy it.[145] This was particularly the case with Baptist of Crema (†1534), whose influence on St Gaetano of Thiene and St Anthony Maria Zaccaria is important, since they were the first, in the sixteenth century, to attempt the reform of the clergy.[146] In another field, a Dominican of the same period became illustrious as a commentator on St Thomas and as an exegete: Thomas de Vio, or Cajetan (†1534). This is not the place to examine his theological doctrines: his work suffices to show that the Order had not lost its strong intellectual tradition. In spiritual matters, his notable contribution was to clarify the time-honoured but inexact statement that religious profession is equivalent to a second baptism. Profession is only a

141 See, for example, a summary of a sermon by St Vincent Ferrer published by C. Brunel, "Le sermon en langue vulgaire prononcé à Toulouse par S.V.F. le vendredi saint 1416", in *Bibl. Ecole Chartres*, CXI (1953), pp. 5–53.

142 Cf. *Studi Savonaroliani*, 3 vols, Ferrara, 1952–3. There are biographies by G. Dore, *S.*, Turin, 1928; R. Roeder, *S.*, Paris, 1933; M. Brion, *S., le héraut de Dieu*, Paris, 1948; V. Magni, *S. ou l'agonie de Florence*, Paris, 1946; R. Ridolfi, *S.*, Paris, 1957. The Italian original of this last biography, 2 vols, Rome, 1952, includes notes which were omitted in the French translation. There is an edition of the *Prediche e scritti* by M. Ferrara, 2 vols, Florence, 1952; of the *Lettere* by R. Ridolfi, Florence, 1933. Some new *Edizione Nazionale delle opere di G.S.* began to appear in 1955, under the direction of R. Ridolfi (Rome). For a bibliography see M. Ferrara, *Bibliografia savonaroliana*, Florence, 1958; cf. *Edizioni Savonaroliane della biblioteca communale Ariostea*, Ferrara, 1952.

143 See his letters of direction addressed to the Dominican nuns of Venice, ed. A. Biscioni, Milan, 1839; cf. P. Mandonnet, O.P., in *Histor. Jahrbuch*, XXI (1900), pp. 388–402. Some of these letters have been translated into French by A. M. F. [Festugière], O.P., in *La Vie spirit.*, XXVI (1931), pp. 292–304; XXVII (1931), pp. 58–65.

144 Ed. R. Creytens, O.P., "L'instruction des novices dominicains à la fin du XVe siècle", in *Arch. Fratrum Praedic.*, XXII (1952), pp. 201–25.

145 See, for example, R. M. Martin, O.P., "Le 'Planctus religionis' de Jean de Bomal, O.P., deuxième professeur dominicain de l'ancienne université de Louvain (†1477)", in *Miscellanea J. Gessler*, Antwerp, 1948, pp. 835–44.

146 Cf. L. Boglioglio, *Battista da Crema. Nuovi studi sopra la sua vita, i suoi scritti, la sua dottrina*, Turin, 1952.

sacramental, and there can be no question of the remission of original sin (if by chance the professed had not been baptized) or that of mortal sins (if he had not been absolved from them previously). Like every other work that proceeds from grace, profession remits venial sins; it is only as a work of satisfaction that it has an effect on mortal sins. and then only as regards the penalty for them, not as regards the guilt.[147]

The traditionally Dominican theses were sometimes watered down, even among the theologians of the Order. A typical case is that of the Dutchman Thierry of Delft († after 1404), author of a *Summa theologica* which was one of the first to be written in the vernacular, the *Table of the Christian Faith*.[148] Thierry is not concerned with describing mystical experience in speculative terms, as his brethren of the Rhineland had done. He simply uses the data of experience, even when he is treating of extraordinary psychological states. In all this, he shows a certain independence of his Order's traditions.

5. *The other Religious Orders*

The creation of new religious Orders was a phenomenon characteristic of the end of the Middle Ages. The example of Bernard, Norbert, and Bruno—and, later, of Francis and Dominic—resulted in a flowering whose beneficial effects cannot be denied. These new Orders are significant: they bear witness not only to the fervour of their founders but also to their keen sense of the needs of the Church. She was indeed menaced by serious dangers, and the old Orders too often gave the impression, if not the certitude, of being impotent to ward them off.

The multiplication of the new Orders, however, raised a problem. What was the organic function, in the body of the Church, of these Orders—leaving aside the monastic bodies—whose apostolic aims were so alike? Some emphasized preaching, others missionary work in heathen lands, but they were not really distinguished one from another by any difference in precise objective. Some honoured one mystery and some another (for example, the Servites, the Gesuati, and the Croziers) and they owed their origin in great measure to

147 The Carmelite Thomas of Walden (†1431) had already done some work along these lines. For Cajetan, see *In Sum. Theol.*, II^{a}–II^{ae}, q. 189, a. 3, ad 3; cf. F. Vandenbroucke, O.S.B., "La profession, second baptême", in *La Vie spirit.*, LXXVI (1947), pp. 250–63; by the same, *Le moine dans l'Eglise du Christ*, Louvain, 1947, pp. 80–1. Since Cajetan belongs chiefly to the history of theology, only one reference will be cited here: M. J. Congar, O.P., "Bio-bibliographie de C.", in *Rev. Thomiste*, 1935.

148 In Middle Dutch, *Tafel van den Kersten Ghelove*, ed. L. M. F. Daniels, O.P., 4 vols, Antwerp, 1937–9. On Thierry of Delft, see L. M. F. Daniels, *Meester Dirc van Delf, zijn persoon en zijn werk*, Nijmegen, 1932.

local circumstances. These contingencies might make it possible to identify them, but they were not enough to explain the proper role of each in the Church. To understand their function one should perhaps remember the difference between them and the monastic Orders. The latter represent the Christian life tending to its eschatological end; and to some extent they already realize that end. They are the living image, in the Church, of that final goal towards which it is moving. From that point of view, monastic life really should take one single form, as is the case even today in the East. If, in the West, a number of "Orders" developed within that manner of life—bodies organized independently of, and parallel to, one another—this came about as a result of contingent circumstances: local needs for reform, the personal aspirations of their founders, not to mention the favour of princes and political events. But the non-monastic Orders, by taking on specialized tasks, none of which belongs exclusively to any one of them, have at least this significance for the Church: they show that, before arriving at her eschatological goal, as yet she is wholly a militant body.

Another difficulty arose from the fact that ordination to the priesthood soon became general in the non-monastic Orders. They thus laid themselves open to the accusation that was made against them in the thirteenth and fourteenth centuries, that of duplicating the functions of the secular clergy, without having any organic connection with the diocesan structure of the Church. This objection would have been much less pertinent if it had been simply a question of lay associations, like the one that Francis of Assisi had originally wanted to form. The only aim of that kind of organization was to help the simple faithful to live the Gospel to the full; they could not give umbrage to the clergy. The difficulty was considerably increased when the new Orders began to spread more or less everywhere throughout Christendom. From that time, their objectives being practically the same, they came into competition with the secular clergy. In the same city, the same diocese, the same region, almost all over the Church, there arose several distinct hierarchies and communities, parallel to the secular hierarchy, and all pursuing similar ends.

The problem became still more acute in the sixteenth century, when the Orders of clerks regular were founded. Yet their very appearance made it abundantly clear that the secular clergy were unequal to their task. It is this that accounts for the establishment, at first local and temporary, of the Orders which had been founded in earlier centuries and their subsequent spread and stabilization.

The reason for their multiplication lay in the deep deficiencies of the secular clergy everywhere, and for this reason their foundation must be seen as providential.

One last difficulty remains, and that is the fact that these religious Orders persisted, even when the objectives of their founders had been attained, even when they had proved impossible of realization, even when another objective had been substituted for the one intended. The answer seems to lie in the last occurrence: that no founder meant to link his work with apostolic tasks no longer needed, and it was surely better to turn to other work. Many of the old Orders, for lack of this adaptation, had condemned themselves to vegetate or die, and they were to be the first victims of great social or religious upheavals such as the Reformation, the French Revolution, and the progress of atheism and Marxism.

In the twelfth and thirteenth centuries, several religious institutes took the name of Croziers, and still later various communities and confraternities were founded under the title of the Cross. The Crozier Order, which still exists today, was founded about 1210, it would appear, by a canon of Liège, Theodore de Celles. It was not approved or really organized until 1248. It was connected both with the crusades and with the reform of the canons regular, and was influenced by the trend of popular piety. Theodore probably had an opportunity in 1209, at the time of the Albigensian crusade, to meet St Dominic, and this event may well have been a determining factor in his undertaking. The rule of the new canons was indeed based on the Dominican constitutions. The Order expanded considerably, up to the time of the Reformation, in the Low Countries and neighbouring regions. It readily accepted the spirit of the *Devotio moderna*, as its ideal was similar to that of the canons of Windesheim. The "Brothers of the Holy Cross", who were canons, emphasized the contemplative side of their institute. Only the first generation seems to have been concerned with the preaching of the Crusade and the care of pilgrims and crusaders. After the promulgation of the Statutes of 1248, the scope of the apostolate was relatively reduced, and it is only in modern times that the order has turned to missionary work. No doubt it thus returned in a modern form to the original aim of its founder, but in so doing it became what is now called a "mixed Order". Its spirituality is centred on cultus of the Cross, of the Blessed Virgin, and of its own patron saints. The case of the Croziers is a good illustration of an Order which very soon abandoned the exact aim for which it had originally been instituted and adopted apostolic tasks identical with those of other religious groups, except for honouring the mystery of the Cross in a more special way.[149]

The Order of Our Lady of Mount Carmel was organized at about the same time, under the influence of the movement which was drawing the attention of all Western Christendom to the situation of the Holy Places. At the beginning of the thirteenth century some Latin hermits had settled on the famous mountain where the memory and example of Elias were still alive. Other hermitages soon became connected with those of Carmel. They increased in number, spreading into Syria and even into Europe, and finally became associated to form a distinct Order. St Simon Stock governed it until 1265, but he transformed it into a semi-active Order. The apparition of our Lady, in which she bestowed on him the privilege of the scapular, is well known. The Order ceased to exist in Palestine in 1291, when its last members there were massacred, and from then onwards it definitely lost its eremitical character. During the Middle Ages it had a lively intellectual and spiritual influence in the West,[150] but it did not escape the general decadence that marked the end of the period. There were, therefore, various attempts at reform. The best known of these was that of the "discalced" in Spain, undertaken by St Teresa of Avila and St John of the Cross. It took a purely contemplative form for the Carmelite nuns, with a mixed life for the friars.[151] Fervent devotion to our Lady dates from the beginning of the order,[152] as does apostolic zeal; St Teresa of Avila, and later her disciple of Lisieux, strongly asserted that aspect of their contemplative vocation.

There was a similar evolution from the eremitical form of religious life towards a mixed form, in the case of the Hermits of

[149] Cf. M. Vinken, art. "Croisiers", in *Dict. hist. géogr. eccl.*, XIII, 1042–62; by the same, *De spiritualiteit der Kruisheren*, Antwerp, 1953 (an excellent historical and spiritual study, in which several old texts were published). A valuable *Devotus libellus de perfectione fratrum sancte crucis* has been edited by A. van de Parsch, O.S.C., "Een tractaatje over volmaakheid. Uit een Keuls Kruisheren-handscrift van de XVe eeuw", in *Clair-Lieu*, XI (1953), pp. 49–84. Another spiritual work (fourteenth century) has been studied by C. van Dal: "Rond 'Vestis nuptialis'", in *Clair-Lieu*, XI (1953), pp. 3–29.

[150] See, for example, I. Rosier, O.Carm., *Biographisch en bibliographisch overzicht van de vroomheid in de nederlandse Carmel van 1235 tot het midden der achttiende eeuw*, Tielt, 1950.

[151] On the history of the Carmelites, see Melchior de Sainte-Marie, art. "Carmel", in *Dict. hist. géogr. eccl.*, XI, 1070–104; Jean Le Solitaire, *Aux sources de la tradition du Carmel*, Paris, 1953; H. Peltier, *Histoire du Carmel*, Paris, 1958 (a popular treatment).

[152] Cf. Elisée de la Nativité, O.C.D., "La vie mariale au Carmel", in *Maria*, II, Paris, 1952, pp. 833–61; C. Catena, O.Carm., "Il culto dell' Immacolata Concezione nel Carmelo", in *Carmelus*, I (1954), pp. 290–321 (especially the fourteenth century); V. Hoppenbrouweres, O.Carm., "Virgo purissima et vita spiritualis Carmeli", in *Carmelus*, I (1954), pp. 255–77 (fourteenth century).

St Augustine. The origin of their Order is to be found in some hermitages, chiefly Italian, which grouped together and adopted the rule of St Augustine, until in 1256 they were approved and organized by Alexander IV.[153] A few names stand out, such as that of Henry of Friemar (†1340), an historian and theologian, whose treatise *On the Four Instincts* has been preserved. It is a sort of summary of the discernment of spirits; the "four instincts" come from God, from the angels, from the demons, or from the world. They can be distinguished from one another by means of signs which Henry enumerates. Denys the Carthusian, however, either disputes the value of these signs or restates them with some modification.[154] Another Hermit of St Augustine, Simon Fidati (†1348) wrote a work *On the Deeds of the Saviour*, which belongs to the tradition of the *Lives of Christ*.[155] Jordan of Saxony (†1380)—to be distinguished from his Dominican namesake—composed, among other things, a directory for the use of the Hermits. It includes a treatise on the religious and spiritual life, a history of the Order from 1250 to 1350,[156] and some meditations on the life of Christ.[157]

Among the Canons Regular of St Augustine, one has become well known since his identification with the *Idiota*, the unknown author of *Contemplations on Divine Love*, who deliberately concealed his identity under that pseudonym. He was Raymond Jourdain, abbot of Selles-sur-Cher, near Bourges († before 1400). While his doctrine followed the various currents of his time, it seems to belong to that of the *Brautmystik* more than to any other.[158] Another Augustinian hermit, St Laurence Justinian (†1455), who became Patriarch of Venice, wrote various *opuscula* on the ascetical life and a few on mysticism: *The Chaste and Spiritual Marriage of the Word and the Soul, The Bouquet of Love, The Fire of Divine Love*. The titles of these works show clearly enough their tendency: the emphasis is placed on the love

[153] For a history of the order see U. Mariani, art. "Eremitani di S. Agostino", in *Encicl. Cattol.*, V, 485–7. Cf. *Augustiniana*, VI (1956).

[154] *De quatuor instinctibus*; ed. Venice, 1498, etc. Extracts have been published by A. Wittmann, *De discretione spirituum apud Dionysium Cartusianum*, Debrecen, 1939, pp. 52–66. On Henry of Friemar, see W. Hümpfner, in *Zeitschr. des Vereins fur Thüringische Geschichte und Altertumskunde*, XXII (1914), pp. 49–64.

[155] Basle, 1517, etc. Cf. M. G. McNeil, *Simone Fidati and His "De Gestis Domini Salvatoris"*, Washington, 1950. See also M. Mattioli, *Il beato Simone Fidati de Cascia e i suoi scritti editi ed inediti*, Rome, 1898.

[156] *Jordani de Saxonia O.E.S.A. Liber Vitas fratrum, ad fidem codicum recensuerunt* . . . R. Arbesmann and W. Hümpfner, New York, 1943.

[157] Antwerp, 1940, etc. John of Salerno (†1388) may also be mentioned; his *Opere volgari inedite* have been edited by N. Mattioli, Rome, 1901.

[158] Latin edition by T. Raynaud, S.J., Lyons, 1632, etc. French translation by Boissieu, Saint-Maximin, 1923; Italian translation by E. Piovesan, Florence, 1954.

of God in contemplation.[159] The treatise entitled *The Tree of life* contains a section *On prayer*; one of its chapters lays down a division of contemplation into six degrees modelled on that of the *Benjamin major* of Richard of St Victor.[160]

Some reference must be made here to other Orders that arose at this time. The Servites of Mary were instituted at the beginning of the twelfth century[161]; the Gesuati, founded by the Blessed John Colombini (†1367), devoted themselves to penance and to works of mercy, especially towards the sick.[162] The Theatines, founded at Rome in the sixteenth century by St Gaetano of Thiene (†1547), constituted the first congregation to be called clerks regular. The goal that they set themselves was the reform of the clergy and the Christian people; and, for the members of the congregation, an exemplary priestly life and the apostolate.[163] The Barnabites, or "Congregation of St Paul", were founded with the same intent and about the same time, at Milan, by St Anthony Maria Zaccaria (†1539).[164] It has been said above how much St Gaetano and St Anthony Maria owed to the Dominican Baptist of Crema.[165]

So, at the end of the fifteenth century and the beginning of the sixteenth, the best and most fervent among the members of the clergy felt the urgency of the need of reform in the Church. They saw that what was necessary above all was to convert their fellow priests—to make them aspire to that indispensable holiness of life without which their action is fruitless, and to take up in earnest the apostolic work. The situation of the Church at that period amounted to a paradox. The hierarchy, from the Sovereign Pon-

[159] Cf. E. Amann, art. "Laurent Justinien", in *Dict. théol. cath.*, IX, cols 9–10.

[160] Ch. x; ed. Venice, 1721, pp. 62–3; cf. p. 182. Serafino de Fermo, a Canon Regular of the Lateran, may also be mentioned here. He was the author of some spiritual *opuscula*, and an ardent apostle along the lines of Anthony Maria Zaccaria. Cf. G. Feyles, *S. da F., canonico regolare lateranense (1496–1540). La vita, le opere, la dottrina spirituale*, Turin, 1942.

[161] Cf. A. M. Lepicier, *L'Ordre des Servites de Marie*, Paris, 1929; G. Berti, *La sanctificazione dell'anima e il merito secondo Maestro Lorenzo da Bologna* [† *c.* 1392] *dell'Ordine dei Servi di Maria*, Gembloux, 1939.

[162] Cf. G. Pardi, "Il beato Giovanni C. da Siena", in *Nuova rivista storica*, XI (1927), pp. 286–336; *Letters*, ed. A. Bartoli, Lucca, 1856. A new edition has been prepared by G. Petrocchi; in this connection see his "Le lettere del beato C.", in *Convivium* (1950), pp. 57–72, and his *Ascesi e mistica trecentesca*, Florence, 1957, pp. 148–75.

[163] Cf. G. Chiminelli, *S.G.T. cuore della Riforma cattolica*, Vicenza, 1946; *Letters*, ed. F. Andreu, Rome, 1946. Various studies in *Regnum Dei, Collectanea Theatina*, Rome, since 1945; especially F. Andreu, "La spiritualità di San Gaetano", in *Regnum Dei*, IV (1948), pp. 40–66.

[164] Cf. O. Premoli, *Storia dei Barnabiti*, 3 vols, Rome, 1913–25; the collection *I Barnabiti al IV centenario della fondazione*, Genoa, 1933; G. Chastel, *S.A.M. Zaccaria*, Paris, 1930.

[165] See §4, p. 473.

tiff down to the most insignificant curate, had to receive new strength from bodies which, by definition, were outside the framework of hierarchical organization, and which sometimes were exempt from diocesan authority. So true then was it that the secular clergy could not avoid the clutches of "the world" and its concupiscences, unless they accepted obligations, and adopted a discipline exemplified in the religious life.

IX

LAY SPIRITUALITY FROM THE FOURTEENTH TO THE SIXTEENTH CENTURY

1. Pessimism

CERTAIN aspects of spirituality during the fifteenth century and the beginning of the sixteenth have already been noticed; in particular, the extent to which the spirit of the *Devotio moderna* had affected the great majority of the spiritual writers of that period.[1] Among the clergy, consecrated by their state to the service of Christ and the Church, it governed their ideas and religious practices, and even the laity were far from being unaffected by it.

Men's minds, even among the most religious, were profoundly disturbed. Europe had been shaken by a series of crises which had destroyed, for many, all pleasure in life and even all confidence in Providence. There had been the ravages of the Black Death of 1348,[2] and the Hundred Years' War was exhausting the resources and the energies of both camps.[3] The condemnation of Joan of Arc, and her execution at the stake at Rouen, 30 May 1431, left one side with a bad conscience (especially after the rehabilitation of 6 June 1456) and the other with a sense of disillusionment: the Maid had not "thrown the English out of France", as she had promised to do. Many English, as well as French, saw the conflict

[1] See *supra*, chs VII and VIII. In connection with this chapter, see M. D. Knowles, *The Religious Orders in England*, II, Cambridge, 1957, ch. XVI, "The Spiritual Life of the Fifteenth Century".

[2] Cf. Card. F. A. Gasquet, *The Black Death of 1348*, 2nd ed., Oxford, 1908; J. Nohl, *The Black Death*, London, 1926; H. van Werveke, "De zwartte dood in de Zuidelijke Nederlanden, 1349–1351", in *Meded. v. de Kon. Vl. Acad. Wetensch., Lett., en Sch. Kunsten v. België, Kl. d. letteren*, XII, 3, Brussels, 1950.

[3] On this war, see particularly H. Pirenne, A. Renaudet, E. Perroy, M. Handelsman, and L. Halphen, *La fin du moyen âge*, I, *La désagrégation du monde médiéval (1285–1453)*, Book I, ch. V, and Book II, ch. VI; H. Pirenne, *Histoire de l'Europe, des invasions au XVIe siècle*, Paris, 1936, Book VIII, ch. II; E. Perroy, *La guerre de Cent ans*, Paris, 1945.

as insoluble, and realized their common guilt over the trial.[4] The Great Schism of the West followed: two-thirds of a century passed by the popes at Avignon in an "exile" which was often viewed as a new "Babylonian captivity". From 1378, for forty years, there were two popes, one at Rome and the other at Avignon. It is not difficult to see why many theologians and lawyers (among them Pierre d'Ailly and Jean Gerson), while realizing more fully the oneness of the Church, yet faced as they were with a deadlock between the two parties, should have ended by holding that a Council was above the Pope. An attempted solution failed at the synod of Pisa in 1409, and finally, the Council of Constance succeeded, on 11 November 1417, in electing Martin V who was recognized by everyone. It need hardly be said that the prestige of the papacy was very low, and only through the efforts of Eugene IV, in the middle of the century, did it once more prevail over the Council and conciliar theories.[5] But the papacy was not to remain on the heights for long: at the end of the fifteenth century and the beginning of the sixteenth, the chair of Peter was occupied by popes who were, of course, the Vicars of Christ, but even more statesmen, warriors, or resplendent sovereigns and patrons of art. The clergy, at every level, gave way to the lures of pleasure and money-making, forgetting even the most elementary pastoral duties. The gloomy picture that John Burchard, master of ceremonies at the Vatican, draws of the pontificates of Sixtus IV, Innocent VIII, Alexander VI, Pius III and Julius II, makes this only too clear.[6] He may have exaggerated here and there, but the picture as a whole is still dark enough to explain the scandal given to Christendom and the resulting discouragement and pessimism.

Voices were raised in protest against the abuses in the Church and among her leaders. Nicholas de Clamanges wrote, in 1400 or 1401, what was really a pamphlet *On the ruin and reform of the Church*, in which the lives of the clergy were mercilessly described against the background of the Great Schism. His was at first a lone voice; only in the next century, when the Church's hold over men's minds was growing still weaker, did it have any success.[7] A similar

[4] See *infra*, §4, pp. 504–5.

[5] On the Avignon popes, see G. Mollat, *Les Papes d'Avignon*, 9th ed., Paris, 1950. On the Great Schism of the West, a work is in preparation by F. Delaruelle, P. Ourliac and E. R. Labande which will be vol. XIV of Fliche–Martin, *Histoire de l'Église*. In the meantime, see N. Valois, *La France et le Grand Schisme d'Occident*, 4 vols, Paris, 1896–1902; W. Ullmann, *The Origins of the Great Schism. A Study in Fourteenth-Century Ecclesiastical History*, London, 1948.

[6] See Burchard's diary, the *Liber notarum*, ed. E. Celani, 2 vols, 1907–13; or L. Thuasne, 3 vols, Paris, 1883–5. Extracts have been translated into French by J. Turmel, Paris, 1932.

[7] *De ruina et reparatione Ecclesiae*, which was already in print in 1483 (in the

note had already been struck at a slightly earlier date, in a versified *Lament of the Church over Germany* by Conrad of Megenberg († 1374).[8] It will be seen further on how, at the end of the fifteenth century, there were more and more of these cries of alarm.

At the same time, civil society was more and more forgetting its wholly religious foundations, described by the *summas* of the thirteenth century and respected by princes like St Louis. The struggle between Boniface VIII and Philip the Fair had only been a prelude. Now the lay spirit, of which there are glimpses in the thirteenth and fourteenth centuries, was becoming more mature. Theology was losing its hold over social and political philosophy, while nationalism was asserting itself ever more strongly.[9] The old Christendom was crumbling away, the medieval theocracy had decayed,[10] and a new humanism was beginning to appear.

Even more depressing are some of the literary productions of that period; they are of a kind previously unknown. The literature of courtly love, even in its least admirable passages, was of a different order from works like Boccaccio's *Decameron* or the licentious *Treatise on Perfect Love*, of the late fourteenth century[11]; though it must not be forgotten that there were also works like *The Praise of Purity* by the priest John Rothe († 1434),[12] and various writings on the vocation of women, their education, their studies, their place in the home, or their virtues—love, beauty, the courteous life.[13] Henry, Duke of Lancaster († 1361), wrote the *Livre des Seynts Medicines*, a spiritual treatise on the deadly sins and the means of overcoming them.[14] That the soul that has succumbed to temptation and is in a state of sin is still capable of receiving grace and being converted is the teaching of *Wisdom, Who is*

---

first edition of Gerson's works, at Cologne). Cf. A. Coville, *Le Traité de la Ruine de l'Église de Nicolas de Clamanges et la traduction française de 1564*, Paris, 1936.

8 *Planctus ecclesie in Germaniam*; ed. H. Kusch, *Klagelied der Kirche über Deutschland*, Berlin–Darmstadt, 1957; extracts translated into German are included in H. Kusch, *Einführung in das lateinische Mittelalter*, I, *Dichtung*, Berlin, 1957, pp. 664–81.

9 For a survey of this critical period in social and political history, see J. Chevalier, *Histoire de la pensée*, II, *La pensée chrétienne*, Paris, 1956, pp. 538–55; Pirenne, Renaudet, *et al.*, *op. cit.*, Book I, ch. IX; H. Pirenne, *Histoire de l'Europe . . .*, Book VIII; G. de Lagarde, *La naissance de l'esprit laïque au moyen âge*, 6 vols, Paris, 1934–46, vol. I.

10 Cf. M. Pacaut, *La théocratie. L'Église et le pouvoir au moyen âge*, Paris, 1957, pp. 217–24.

11 *Tractatus de perfecto amore*, ed. G. Bruni, Rome, 1954.

12 Johannes Rothe, *Das Lob der Keuschheit*, ed. C. A. Schmid and H. Neumann, Berlin, 1934.

13 Cf. R. Kelso, *Doctrine for the Lady of the Renaissance*, Urbana, Ill., 1956.

14 Ed. E. J. Arnould, Oxford, 1940. See *supra*, p. 427.

Christ,[15] a moral poem written about 1460. The same spirit runs through the *Manuel des péchés*, a manual for confession intended for laymen, and its English translation *Handlyng Synne* by the Gilbertine canon Robert Mannyng.[16] The laity rarely went to communion despite the encouragement of the hierarchy and the teaching of theologians.[17]

By now the breakdown was becoming worse. It was no longer simply a question of the divorce between theology and mysticism; the phenomenon was bigger and more general. There was the opposition between the Church and a civil society becoming conscious of its autonomy; the cleavage between the faithful and their ecclesiastical superiors, often incapable and unworthy; and between the old spiritual and intellectual tradition and the new spirituality, which laid stress on the subjective and psychological aspects of the Christian life. The ideals, the confident hope, still put before the people by their pastors and by spiritual writers, were shaken by such horrors as the Black Death, the Hundred Years' War, the Great Schism, the debauchery and greed of the clergy, and the baseness and violence of men's own lives.

Many considered that Christendom was in a state of sin. That is probably what explains the extraordinary success at Rome of the great Jubilees of 1450 and even of 1500—the date at which the papacy was at its lowest level. Countless multitudes flocked to Rome in 1450, eager to obtain pardon for their sins. Earlier jubilees had for their chief object the veneration of the tombs of the Apostles and of their relics, whereas "now they came primarily to obtain a grace from the pope".[18] The papacy had recovered the prestige it had lost at the time of the Great Schism, and throughout Christendom there was a sudden upspringing of faith in the supreme authority: the indulgence proclaimed by the pope could give salvation to the pilgrims who went to Rome, the *roumieux*.[19] But the abuses connected with indulgences led the mass of Christians to

[15] Cf. J. J. Molloy, O.P., *A Theological Interpretation of the Moral Play "Wisdom, who is Christ"*, Washington, 1952.

[16] See *supra*, p. 345.

[17] For example, those of the University of Prague, in connection with Mathias of Janov; cf. A. M. Petru, O.P., "Universitas et Archiepiscopus Pragensis saec. XIV de frequenti communione laicorum", in *XXV Congreso eucaristico internacional* (1952), vol. II, Barcelona, 1953, pp. 569–72.

[18] E. Delaruelle, "La piété populaire à la fin du moyen âge", in *Relazioni . . . X Congresso Internaz. Scienze Storiche*, Rome, 1955, vol. III, Florence, 1955, pp. 515–37; see esp. p. 521. A bibliography is given for the jubilee and for the contemporary trends in popular devotion.

[19] On the place held by the Pope in the life of the faithful, see M. Maccarone, *Vicarius Christi*, Rome, 1952; or his "Il Papa 'Vicarius Christi'. Testi e dottrina dal sec. XII al principio del XIV", in *Miscell. P. Paschini*, I, Rome, 1948, pp. 427–500.

see this salvation as the result of a kind of magic; as something that can be bought from God. Luther's attacks on works which do not make man just, and his claims that only faith saves, can easily be foreseen.

The pessimism of men's minds is shown, and at its gloomiest, in the macabre sensibility of the fifteenth century. The plague that had depopulated the West certainly had something to do with it. It was not enough to practise the art of living a good life; that of dying well was more important; life is fragile and eternity to be dreaded. A treatise on *The Art of Dying* or *Ars moriendi* was circulated in various forms, a fact that proves how widely it was disseminated. It was derived from an *opusculum* of that title which had been brought to the notice of the Council of Constance by Gerson. Its anonymous author would seem to have been the Viennese theologian Nicholas of Dinkelsbühl (†1433).[20] The treatise praises death and advises the reader to meet the decisive moment well. The author enumerates the trials that await a dying man: the demon of despair, and especially his attacks on the faith. At the hour when he must leave all things, a wretched human being still clings to earthly goods, and his thirst for life is intensified. But prayer and meditation are still the weapons with which to overcome the Evil One.

The treatise had a great influence. Erasmus also wrote an *Art of Dying*, but in the meantime other similar works appeared, such as that of Thomas Peuntner. In this, more than in the first *Ars moriendi*, the pastoral point of view is brought to the fore. Thomas offers much advice to the priest called to a deathbed.[21]

At the same time, there appeared a number of treatises encouraging men to endure trials with fortitude[22] and attempting to give them "consolation", sometimes of a rather stoical nature, as in *On the Consolation of Theology*, inspired by Boethius' *Consolation of Philosophy*.[23] This type of literature abounded. Luther him-

[20] Cf. R. Rudolf, *Ars moriendi. Von der Kunst des heilsamen Lebens und Sterbens*, Cologne, 1957; M. C. O'Connor, *The Art of Dying Well. The Development of the Ars moriendi*, New York, 1942; R. Rudolf, "Der Verfasser des 'Speculum artis bene moriendi'", in *Oesterreich. Akad. Wiss., Philos.-hist. Kl. Anzeiger*, LXXXVIII (1951), pp. 387–98; A. Tenenti, *Il senso della morte e l'amore della vita nel Rinascimento. Francia e Italia*, Turin, 1957; by the same, *La vie et la mort à travers l'art du XVe siècle*, Paris, 1952. On the artistic value of the woodcuts with which editions of the *Ars moriendi* very soon began to be illustrated, see E. Mâle, *L'art religieux de la fin du moyen âge en France*, Paris, 1908, pp. 412–21.

[21] Cf. R. Rudolf, "Thomas Peuntners Sterbebüchlein", in *Festschrift für W. Stammler*, Berlin, 1953, pp. 172–8; ed. by the same, Bielefeld, 1956.

[22] For example, those described by A. Auer, O.S.B., *Leidenstheologie im Spätmittelalter*, St Ottilien, 1952.

[23] Cf. A. Auer, O.S.B., "Johannes von Dambach [†1372] und die Trostbücher vom 11. bis zum 16. Jahrhundert", in *Beiträge z. Gesch. Phil. Theol. Mittelalt.*, XXVII, 1–2, Münster, 1928.

self, amid the upheavals of the sixteenth century, read and echoed the theme in some of his own works.[24]

This obsession with death is also shown in the literature of the *Danses macabres*. There were a good many writings of this kind (the name possibly being taken from the Maccabees), or with the similar title of Jean Le Fèvre's *Dans macabre* (fourteenth century).[25] But the idea of the Dance of Death was not only taken up by poets; it also seized upon the imagination of artists. Throughout western Europe there appeared frescoes, drawings, woodcuts, windows, and carvings depicting a procession in which skeletons mingled with the living in a funereal gaiety. The earliest example seems to have been the "danse macabre" in the cemetery of the Innocents in Paris; it was still to be seen there in the seventeenth century and probably dated from 1424 or 1425. It had clearly been inspired by earlier writings.[26]

2. *Satanic Fever*

It would be going rather far to say that the religion of the fifteenth century was a morbid one. It is true that the aspect of Christendom was one calculated to strengthen the naturally pessimistic. Men's nerves were on edge; and it is not impossible that in their taste for the horrible, the sadistic, and the appalling they sought some collective outlet for their disquiet. But there were many other factors too, and not all of them unhealthy.

The same reasons account for the attention given, from the fourteenth century onwards, to manifestation of diabolical marvels. The extent to which "Satanism" had evolved can be realized by remembering the measured terms in which St Thomas Aquinas had dealt with the subject of diabolical temptations. In certain passages he even shows a prudent scepticism towards marvels that were all too readily attributed to the devil.[27]

A superstitious fear of Satanism, in various form, was nothing new, far from it.[28] But from about 1400 on, it rose to fever-pitch in Christendom. It is a fact that, from then on until the seventeenth century, it was endemic in western Europe: there was no truce in

24 Cf. H. Appel, *Anfechtung und Trost im Spätmittelalter und bei Luther*, Leipzig, 1938.

25 Cf. G. Huet, "La Danse Macabre", in *Moyen Age*, Series II, XX (1917–18), pp. 148–67.

26 Cf. J. M. Clark, *The Dance of Death in the Middle Ages and the Renaissance*, Glasgow, 1950; E. Mâle, *L'art religieux de la fin du moyen âge en France*, Paris, 1908, Part II, ch. II, pp. 388–412; A Tenenti, *La vie et la mort à travers l'art du XVᵉ siècle*. The literature on the subject is extensive; see R. Bossuat, *Manuel bibliographique de la littérature française du moyen âge*, Paris, 1951, pp. 522–4; *Supplement*, Paris, 1955, pp. 108–9.

27 See *supra*, p. 336.

28 See *supra*, pp. 256–7.

the warfare. Later, when Europe expanded overseas, the mission countries became the scene of diabolical marvels. They were a proof to apologists, just as much as to the masses, of the falsity of pagan superstititions, therefore of the truth of the Christian faith. There is apparently well-founded evidence of such happenings, especially in Japan and Angola.

Soon one of the tasks of the Inquisition was to be the repression of all the "impieties" that were springing up: witchcraft, worship of the devil, and a traffic with him, often suspected of morbid sexuality. One of the principal acts in this severe programme of suppression, which was in accordance with the habits of the period, was the bull *Summis desiderantes* of Innocent VIII (5 December 1484). By it both ecclesiastics and laymen were ordered to allow the inquisitors full freedom of action; which shows that the danger seemed grave. Other popes, down to Paul V in 1623, were to renew the order.[29] The wise counsel of Alexander IV was forgotten; in 1257 he had advised inquisitors not to concern themselves too much with matters of witchcraft.

After the bull came the notorious treatise "The Hammer of Witches", *Malleus maleficarum*. Its authors were two Dominicans, who had been behind the bull, Henry Institoris, or Kramer, and James Sprenger. Their treatise was "the most influential of all works of this kind"[30] and went into twenty-nine editions before 1669. It gives rules to be followed in witchcraft trials, and, as may easily be imagined, the procedures recommended for extracting confessions are not always humane: torture has a prominent place. Even Joan of Arc was tortured when she was accused of witchcraft, and men really believed that there was an actual "Church" of Satan.[31] It was not until the seventeenth century that the injustice of many of the trials was realized. The repression unleashed by Innocent VIII had given birth to a kind of contagion, a collective psychosis. A Jesuit, Friedrich von Spee (1591–1635), realized

[29] For the history of the witchcraft trials, see K. Bihlmeyer and H. Tuchi, *Kirchengeschichte*, vol. II, 12th ed., Paderborn, 1948, pp. 502–4; E. de Moreau, S.J., *Histoire de l'Eglise en Belgique*, V, Brussels, 1952, pp. 363–70 (pp. 363–6 summarize the history of witchcraft from the fifteenth to the seventeenth century for the whole of Europe); R. Aubenas, "L'Eglise et la Renaissance", in Fliche–Martin, *Histoire de l'Église*, XV, Paris, 1951, pp. 376–83 (excellent). The last two works give useful bibliographical information. See also the following dictionary articles: "Hexen", in *Lex. Theol. Kirch.*, V, 1–6; "Sorcellerie", in *Dict. théol. cath.*, XIV, 2394–417; "Satanismo", in *Encicl. Cattol.*, X, 1956–7.

[30] Strasburg, 1486. There have been many editions and translations. Cf. E. Moreau, *loc. cit.*, p. 364. This document is discussed in A. Huxley, *The Devils of Loudun*, ch. v.

[31] Cf., for example, J. Ruiz de Larrinaga, O.F.M., "Fr Martin de Castañega y su obra sobre las supersticiones", in *Archivo ibero-americano*, XII (1952), pp. 97–108.

that the rigorous measures employed had been, to all intents, ineffective,[32] but his remonstrances came too late. The peaks of violence were in fact from about 1530–50, and in Spee's own day, about 1580–1620. At last Urban VIII (1623–44) was to counsel greater moderation.

It was in the sixteenth century that art shows most traces of "Satanism". One has only to recall the paintings of Hieronymus Bosch (†1516), Albrecht Dürer (†1528), and Brueghel the Younger, known as "Brueghel of Hell" (†1637 or 1638).[33] Even natural science was not unaffected: as early as the thirteenth century, Roger Bacon had called for the scientific study of magical practices, so as better to penetrate the secrets of nature.[34] His wish was fulfilled at the time of the Renaissance, when study of the natural sciences rose to a new height. Even genuinely learned men had recourse to magic. The fashion also influenced social conceptions, with the widespread idea that woman, the daughter of Eve, could serve as Satan's intermediary in order the more easily to tempt man, and draw him to evil.

It must be realized that after the Reformation witch-hunting did not remain the monopoly of Catholics; Protestants had their share in the general terror. This explains why everywhere public authority took a hand in the matter. Spain, with the *Nemesis Carolina* of Charles V in 1532 and later the ordinances of Philip II, quite certainly took the prize. In France it was not until 1682, with a decree of Louis XIV, that the tribunals obeyed the advice of Urban VIII, and witches and sorcerers were no longer hunted down. By that time, in any case, the excitement was dying down everywhere.[35]

How did the theologians react to this curious business? Whereas the masters of the thirteenth century had shown such reserve, those of this period seem to have been infected by the general contagion; at least, they took no steps to oppose it. The diabolic marvels that

[32] This is the thesis of his *Cautio criminalis* (1631). Cf. H. Zwetsloot, *Friedrich Spee und die Hexenprozesse*, Trèves, 1954.

[33] On the demoniacal in art, see *Cristianesimo e ragione di stato*, in *Atti del II Congresso Internazionale di Studi Umanistici*, edited by E. Castelli, Rome, 1953, pp. 167–308 and the illustrations.

[34] Cf. A. G. Little, *Roger Bacon*, London, 1929; F. Alessio, *Mito e scienza in Ruggero Bacone*, Milan, 1957.

[35] On this whole subject, see the well-documented study by E. Brouette, "The Sixteenth Century and Satanism", in the anthology *Satan*, London, 1951; M. J Pratt, *The Attitude of the Catholic Church towards Witchcraft and the Allied Practices of Sorcery and Magic*, Washington, 1915. The literature on this period is vast. See the bibliography in the French edition of *Satan* (*Études carmélitaines*, Paris, 1948), pp. 648–58 and 661–2, which is not included in the English translation mentioned above; also that in the article "Satanismo", in *Encicl. Cattol.*, X, 1957–8.

astounded the masses made the inquisitors feel that they were at grips with supernatural forces. When they questioned their theological colleagues on this point, they were confirmed in their opinion; their experiences, they were told, were in accord with Christian dogma. This pernicious trend could not have been resisted by any of those concerned without better equipment than the slender weapon of discourses on the *impugnatio* of the demons in various *summas*. "Deviltries" drew them into the field of human psychology. That psychology, even when distorted, or perverted by the Prince of this world, is still the psychology of a human being, body and soul. And, to understand this, the inquisitors and theologians had only an abstract metaphysical doctrine of the soul, quite incapable of giving them dependable guidance as to the safe line of conduct to follow in concrete cases. The most elementary modern textbook on depth psychology would have taught them more. The repressive measures therefore were found to fail, the fever and anguish to continue unabated. It would have been better to leave it alone, as Urban VIII and Louis XIV understood too late.

3. *Popular Piety*

At the end of the Middle Ages, popular piety was not by any means wholly dominated by pessimism and satanism. Although the faithful were affected by the contagion of collective terror, the Christian pulse beat strongly. Faith was not extinct, nor the hope of better times—nor, among the more spiritually minded, the hope of the kingdom of God. Apostles of evangelical charity were still to be found, and popular preachers often drew immense crowds. The characteristic of the fifteenth century is a particular manner of conceiving religion and of practising its fundamental virtues.

The traditional sources of piety were unchanged. The Bible still held as important a place in popular piety as it had done up to the fourteenth century.[36] This is shown by the increase in the number of translations into the vernacular. Luther, in asserting that under the papal régime the Bible had been unknown to the people, was obviously wrong[37]; he shows the passion of a theologian and reformer who was never more than a second-rate historian.[38] By the time of the invention of printing there were numbers of these

[36] See *supra*, pp. 243–50 and 344–8.
[37] See H. Rost, *Die Bibel im Mittelalter. Beiträge z. Geschichte und Bibliographie der Bibel*, Augsburg, 1939, pp. 309–420.
[38] Cf. H. Grisar, *Martin Luther*, Paris, 1931, pp. 275–6.

translations in many European countries, and the new art further increased their circulation.[39]

The Bible still had a real influence on art. Up to the end of the Middle Ages, the work of the artist still expressed a deep religious experience, a kind of contemplation. But different subjects had come into favour: the "mysteries" and the "meditations on the life of Christ" had given artists a more tender sensibility, and to this was added a more acute consciousness of man and his destiny.[40] Liturgical life did not disappear as the Middle Ages decayed. It should not be judged from evidence such as the journal of John Burchard, which has already been mentioned. His diary (he was master of ceremonies at the Vatican under Alexander VI) is not an edifying work, though the writer acknowledges the worthy manner in which that pope celebrated Mass. Then there was Paride Grassi (†1528), who left a similar journal covering the years 1504 to 1521, as well as a treatise *On the Ceremonies of Cardinals and Bishops*.[41] Like Burchard, he records a great many deplorable if picturesque details, such as the abuse of indulgences granted on every occasion by the popes, lamentable celebrations of the liturgy, and a way of life for which there could be no excuse.

It was among the people and such of their usual guides as were most fervent—the monks and friars—that there was a real liturgical practice. Their spirit was often that of the *Devotio moderna,* and of the fourth book of the *Imitation,* but frequently it degenerated into superstition. When, later on, Luther attacked the "idolatrous" deviations in the Eucharistic cult he was right when he was attacking genuine abuses. On the other hand, some good *Explanations of the Mass* appeared, such as those of Simon of Venlo and William of Gouda.[42]

There was, however, one new liturgical development, a natural result of the great invention of the times. In 1474 there appeared the first printed edition of the *Missale Romanum,*[43] and this event was to have far-reaching consequences. It prepared the way for a movement towards uniformity of rite and a precision in rubrics

[39] A good survey of this subject is given by G. Ricciotti in the article "Biblia, versione moderne", in *Encicl. Cattol.,* II, col. 1556–78.

[40] Cf. E. Mâle, *L'art religieux de la fin du moyen âge*, Paris, 1908.

[41] *Diarium curiae romanae*, ed. C. G. Hoffmann, *Nova Script. ac Monum. Collect.*, I, Leipzig, 1731; *De caerem.*, Venice, 1582.

[42] Cf. M. Smits van Waesberghe, S.J., "De misverklaring van Meester Simon van Venlo", in *Ons geest. Erf*, XV (1941), pp. 228–61, 285–327; XVI (1942), pp. 85–129.

[43] Ed. R. Lippe, *Missale Romanum Mediolani 1474*, 2 vols (Henry Bradshaw Society, 17 and 33), London, 1899–1907. The second volume points out the variants represented by the later printed missals down to that of St Pius V (1570). These variants, as regards the ordinary of the Mass, were concerned chiefly with the rubrics; cf. vol. I, pp. 198–212, and the corresponding section of vol. II.

which inevitably raised the dignity of celebrations; and, it was to lead, less than a century later, to the missal prepared by order of the Council of Trent and printed under Pius V in 1570.

It is abundantly clear from the history of the Reformation that superstitions in liturgical practice existed in the fifteenth century. The Reformers said, over and over again, that the Roman Mass was only a human institution and that it was a tissue of impieties impossible to accept, particularly as a "work" by which the papists looked for salvation, or again as encouraging an improper veneration of the saints.[44] In point of fact, there was no more in the sanctoral of the missal than there is now, but the people as a whole were only too inclined to divert even the holiest actions to strictly utilitarian ends. An extremist like Luther paid little attention to the traditional theology of the Mass, which sees in it the sacrifice of Christ, sacramentally renewed in the liturgical assembly: he confounded in one common reprobation its sacrificial character and the popular counterfeit in which the meaning of the rite was falsified, and the rite itself changed into a magical formula. The ordinary of the Mass was not overloaded with "human inventions"; it was the one that was adopted by the missal of Pius V—the same, in fact, that we have today. The text of the Roman canon was not riddled with superstitions. In its essential parts, it went back to a period which was recognized by the Reformers themselves as authentically Christian: to the fourth century (*De Sacramentis*, St Ambrose); to the third (*Traditio apostolica*, St Hippolytus of Rome); and even, for the words of institution, to the very origins of Christianity. The Roman canon, as Luther knew it, had been fixed for almost a thousand years, and during all that time neither the Church nor her adversaries had found any fault with it. This venerable text had been taken over, just as it stood, by the first printed missals; and it was to appear, unchanged, in that of 1570.

It must be admitted, however, that popular superstition often went beyond the limits of the tolerable. The Council of Trent set up a commission of inquiry whose report is most valuable for the history of the religious mentality of the sixteenth century *On the abuses of the Mass*.[45] Its report was laid before the Council on 8 August 1562. It confirms the fact that certain of Luther's accusations were well founded. Doctrine properly so called, however,

[44] See, for example, Luther's *Articles of Smalkald*; there is a French translation in L. Cristiani, *Luther tel qu'il fut*, Paris, 1955, pp. 186–93.

[45] *De abusibus missae*. The text is in *Concilium Tridentium*, ed. *Görresgesellschaft*, VIII, pp. 916–21. A *Compendium abusuum* follows, pp. 921–4. On the *cultus* of the Eucharist at the end of the Middle Ages, and on the work of the Council of Trent, see A. Duval, O.P., "Le concile de Trente et le culte eucharistique", in *Studia eucharistica*, Antwerp, 1946, pp. 379–414.

does not seem to have been compromised by these abuses, except by the clergy's lack of learning or by certain oddities, like the Marian interpolations in the *Gloria in excelsis* that were found here and there.[46] What the commission deplored was chiefly negligence and incomprehension in matters of discipline: excessively frequent votive Masses, often superstitious in character; too many Masses celebrated in the same place and at the same time; expressions of questionable value in certain Masses of the saints, an endless variety in the rites, especially at the beginning and end of Mass; negligence and dirt in the care of the liturgical vestments and places of worship; celebrations lacking in dignity; the greed of the clergy; traffic in Mass stipends, unworthy ministers, unsuitable places of worship, profane music, and so forth.

The Council thought it well to react against the diversity of liturgical practice—hence the publication of an official Roman missal and breviary[47]—and against vagaries in the celebration of Mass—hence precision in the rubrics. At the same time it took measures of a much wider nature to restore holiness of life among the clergy.

This was a great deal, and in the course of time dignity of worship was really re-established. But it is permissible to think that the persistence of liturgical Latin, during the whole of the Middle Ages and down to modern times, contributed to widen the gulf that already separated the people and the clergy from one another. The Reformers had seen this danger: as early as 1525, Luther was celebrating the Lord's Supper in German. The Fathers of Trent were not so radical. As Latin was still the common language of the well-educated, the Council went no further than to say that it was not expedient (*non expedire*) to use the vernacular in the liturgy, though the clergy were admonished to explain the Mass frequently to the people.[48]

One of the characteristics of popular spirituality, divorced as it had become from the Divine Office (which had formerly been the real prayer of all the faithful, but was now reserved to canons and the regular clergy and ordinarily recited in common), was the increased number of prayer-books. There were collections of prayers, or *preces devotae*, of which the earliest examples are found in the

[46] For example, in the missal printed at Venice in 1505; cf. Lippe, *op. cit.*, II, p. 99.

[47] Decree *De reformatione*, session XXV (*Conc. Trid.*, IX, p. 1106).

[48] Session XXII, ch. VIII and Can. 9. On the liturgical work of the Council of Trent, see J. A. Jungmann, S.J., "Das Konzil von Trient und die Erneuerung der Liturgie", in *Das Weltkonzil von Trient*, Freiburg-im-Breisgau, 1951, vol. I, pp. 325–36; H. Schmidt, S.J., *Liturgie et langue vulgaire. Le problème de la langue liturgique chez les premiers Réformateurs et au concile de Trente*, Rome, 1950.

Carolingian period. There were also a multitude of *Books of Hours*. At first these were combined with the psalter and were made up of various supplements to it; later they consisted of these supplements only. They make up a considerable part of the medieval works of devotion still found in libraries today.[49] They almost always contain the calendar, some fragments from the Gospels, prayers to our Lady and her Little Office, the Hours of the Cross and of the Holy Spirit, the Penitential psalms, the Office of the Dead, suffrages (those that were then increasing in number at Lauds and Vespers) and the Litany of the Saints. Finally, there were countless prayers for all the circumstances of life, prayers to sanctify its various stages, prayers with which to assist more devoutly at Mass. Perhaps what most distinguishes these Books of Hours from the Divine Office is their directly practical aim of sanctifying various circumstances. The Office too marks the divisions of the day and sanctifies it, but it is more disinterestedly dedicated to the praise of God in the contemplation of the mysteries of salvation in yearly, weekly and daily cycles.

In these books, which the laity preferred, superstitious formulas were sometimes to be found, like the prayer in honour of the 6,666 wounds of Christ, to which was attached an indulgence of 6,666 days. In general, however, the level was high, and hundreds of these prayers are noteworthy for their accents of sincerity and confidence.[50]

Meditation and devotion were still directed principally to the mysteries of our Saviour's birth and passion, and those of Mary. There was a special predilection for these in the Low Countries[51] and the Rhineland.[52] In Spain, also, the Dominican John Torque-

[49] For example, in that of Rotterdam; see D. van Heel, O.F.M., *Middeleeuwse handschriften op godstienstig gebied in het bezit van de Bibliotheek der Gemeente Rotterdam*, Rotterdam, 1948. See also F. X. Haimerl, *Mittelalterlich Frömmigkeit im Spiegel der Gebetbuch literatur Süddeutschlands*, Munich, 1952 (from 850 to the Reformation). For Paris, see V. Leroquais, *Les livres d'heures manuscrits de la Bibliothèque Nationale*, 3 vols, Paris, 1927; *Suppléments*, Paris, 1943 (there is an excellent introduction in vol. I). There are numerous monographs, including H. Leclercq, art. "Livre d'heures", in *Dict. arch. chrét. lit.*, IX, 1836–82; H. Bohatta, *Bibliographie des livres d'heures*, 2nd ed., Vienna, 1924. There seems to be no general work from the artistic point of view; but see G. Ronci, art. "Libro d'ore", in *Encicl. Cattol.*, VII, 1320–3; and Leroquais, *op. cit.*, I, Introduction.

[50] Leroquais, *op. cit.*, I, p. xxxi.

[51] Many of the texts have been studied or edited in *Ons geest. Erf.* In particular see D. A. Stracke, S.J., *Een devote week-oefening tot het H. Hart van Jesus*, XII (1938), pp. 187–208; L. M. F. Daniëls, O.P., *Van den seven ghetijden der passien onses Heren*, XVI (1942), pp. 186–235. See also *Indica mihi. . . . Très pieuses méditations sur la vie et la passion du Christ, d'après un manuscrit du XV*[e] *siècle par un auteur franciscain inconnu*, translated from Old Flemish by M. M. Saeyeys, Paris, 1926.

[52] As an example, the treatise on the passion by Henry of St Gall may be cited; ed. K. Ruh, Thayngen-Schaffhausen, 1940; cf. his "Studien über Heinrich von St

mada (†1468) left some *Meditations or contemplations on the life of Christ*,[53] and a considerable number of "prayers and moralities" are found in French manuscripts.[54] All these writings clearly drew their inspiration from Scripture and from the medieval authors, St Anselm, St Bernard, St Bonaventure, the author of the *Meditations on the life of Christ*, and Ludolph the Saxon. Their aim above all was to give a realistic and historical account of the mysteries. The devotion of the "Way of the Cross", which spread at that time, belongs to the same class. There was a great increase in the number of "stations", calvaries, pietas, and representations of the Annunciation or the entombment, and these were of a kind calculated to appeal to the sensibilities.[55]

Meditation on the life of Christ naturally led the soul to Mary's mysteries. Hymns were still written about her in which her privileges were extolled with tender affection.[56] It is, in fact, in a fifteenth-century hymn from Salzburg that we find the first use of the title "co-redemptrix".[57] On a more popular level, the rosary—150 Aves, with meditations on the joyful, sorrowful, and glorious mysteries—was a psalter accessible to everyone. Its spread was in part the work of a Dominican from Brittany, Alain de la Roche (†1475) (not remarkable, as a matter of fact, for common sense).[58] Another devotion that was becoming popular was the *Angelus*, which had developed from the ringing of bells for the curfew.[59] Preachers, too, praised the glories of the Blessed Virgin. For example, a certain French Dominican named Guillaume Pépin

---

Gallen und den 'Extendit manum'—Passionstraktat", in *Zeitschr. schweizer. Kirchengeschichte*, XLVII (1953), pp. 210–30, 241–78. Other such works include the *Passio* of Klaus Schulmeister (MS *Engelberg 339*) and the pseudo-Bonaventurian *Stimulus amoris.*

[53] Cf. P. Rodríguez Arias, "Un incunable", in *Revista de Bibliografía nacional*, I (1940), pp. 45–7.

[54] See, for example, H. M. Rochais, O.S.B., "Prières et moralités en ancien français. Manuscrit 18 de l'abbaye de Ligugé", in *Mél. Sc. Relig.*, XIV (1957), pp. 150–66. On poems dealing with the passion of Christ, see *Hist. litt. France*, XXXIII (1906), pp. 355–69; bibliography in R. Bossuat, *op. cit.*, pp. 286–8.

[55] Cf. H. Thurston, S.J., *The Stations of the Cross: An Account of their History and Devotional Purpose*, London, 1906. Antoninus a Sant'Elia a Pianisi, O.F.M. Cap., *De pio viae crucis exercitio disquisitio historica, iuridica, ritualis*, Rome, 1950. For the Annunciation, see W. Messerer, "Verkündigungsdarstellungen des 15. und 16. Jahrhunderts als Zeugnisse des Frömmigkeitswandels", in *Archiv. f. Liturgiewissensch.*, V, 2 (1958), pp. 362–9.

[56] Examples are given in G. Meersseman, O.P., *Der Hymnos Akathistos im Abendland*, I, Fribourg (Switzerland), 1958.

[57] Cf. R. Laurentin, "Le titre de corédemptrice", in *Marianum*, XIII (1951), pp. 396–452.

[58] Cf. A. Walz, O.P., *De Rosario Mariae a Sixto IV ad S. Pium V*, Rome, 1959; J. Huizinga, *Le déclin du moyen âge*, Paris, 1948, pp. 244–5; art. "Alain de la Roche", in *Dict. arch. chrét. lit.*, I, 1306–12.

[59] Cf. art. "Angelus", in *Dict. théol. cath.* (U. Berlière), and in *Dict. arch. chrét. lit.* (W. Henry).

(†1533) left a collection of 55 sermons, *Rosarium aureum*, corresponding in number to the beads of the Rosary.[60]

There were also an immense number of works on the Immaculate Conception, now more and more widely accepted throughout the Christian world.[61] Other writings dealt with our Lady's joys, sorrows, her marriage, her sufferings, her death, and her assumption. Many writers, such as Jean Miélot, who followed in the steps of Gautier de Coincy, perpetuated the memory of her miracles,[62] and religious art delighted in representing her as the Mother of mercy.

Mystery plays took up the themes of the Passion of Christ, the mysteries of our Lady, and the lives of the saints.[63] In France particularly, the Palatine *Passion*[64] of the fourteenth century had a great influence. This genre was developed in the fifteenth century, particularly by Eustache Marcadé,[65] Arnoul Gréban,[66] and Jean Michel[67] in long poetical compositions. Arnoul Gréban especially is well known for his beautiful *Mystère de la Passion*.

Among the plays about Mary may be mentioned the forty *Miracles de Notre-Dame* preserved in the Bibliothèque Nationale in Paris.[68] This was probably the repertory of a Parisian confraternity dedicated to the veneration of our Lady. In the Low Countries, a play called *The Seventh Joy of Our Lady* seems to date from the middle of the fifteenth century.[69]

[60] Cf. G. Polestra, O.P., *Il Salutate Mariam di Guglielmo Pépin, O.P.*, Florence, 1950. This *Salutate Mariam* is composed of seven sermons from the *Rosarium*, published for the first time in 1513.

[61] In this connection, see the summary in R. Aubenas, "L'Église et la Renaissance", in Fliche–Martin, *Histoire de l'Église*, XV, pp. 339–41.

[62] We may mention at least H. P. Ahsmann, *Le culte de la Sainte Vierge et la littérature française du moyen âge*, Utrecht–Paris, 1930. A bibliography is given in R. Bossuat, *op. cit.*, pp. 288–97. For the miracles, see L. Delisle, "Les miracles de Notre-Dame, par Jean Miélot, secrétaire de Philippe le Bon", in *Bull. Comité des travaux histor.*, 1886, p. 32.

[63] A very complete inventory is given for France by L. Petit de Julleville, *Les mystères*, 2 vols, Paris, 1880. There is a bibliography in R. Bossuat, *op. cit.*, pp. 550–66; *Suppl.*, pp. 115–16.

[64] Ed. G. Frank, *La Passion du Palatinus, mystère du XIVe siècle*, Paris, 1922. (The *Palatinus* is a manuscript of the Palatine fonds of the Vatican.)

[65] His *Mystère de la Passion* has been edited by J. M. Richard, Paris, 1893.

[66] His *Mystère de la Passion* has been edited by G. Paris and G. Raynaud, Paris, 1878 (modern adaptation by C. Gailly de Taurines and L. de la Tourasse, Paris, 1901); the *Mistère de la Nativité de Nostre Saulveur Jhesu Christ*, by M. Martel, Paris, 1938; A. Pauphilet, *Jeux et sapiences du moyen âge*, Paris, 1941, pp. 1–372.

[67] Only one printed edition of his *Passion de Jhesu Crist* is known: *Paris, Bibl. Nat. Rés. Yf. 69*, or *Rés. Yk. 35, 0.* Cf. K. Kruse, *J. Michel*, Greifswald, 1907; O. Jodogne, *Trois vies romancées dans la Passion de J. Michel*, Brussels, 1945.

[68] Cangé MS, *Bibl. Nat. fr. 819–820.* Ed. G. Paris and U. Robert, 8 vols, Paris, 1876–93.

[69] Edited and translated into Modern Dutch by W. Smulders, *Die Sevenste Bliscap van Onser Vrouwen*, Bois-le-Duc, 1913; modern adaptation by V. Delille, Maldeghem, 1909.

The ideas of the period also had an influence upon preaching. Books on the art of preaching appeared in increasing numbers, especially in England and Germany.[70] At the same time, the scholastic way of thinking was on the wane. This can be seen, for example, in the treatise on preaching written by Maurice of Leyden.[71] A certain change had taken place: preaching was now on the people's own level, but the theory of it amounted to no more than agreeing with and approving the successes of the great vernacular preachers—Gerson, St Vincent Ferrer, St John Capistran, St Bernardino of Siena, St Antoninus of Florence, John Dominici and Jerome Savonarola. These men succeeded in adapting their preaching to the mentality of their congregations. People crowded to listen to Vincent Ferrer preaching for five or six hours on end, and would come back after lunch to hear the rest.

Other efforts were made to simplify the presentation of religion, adapting it to pastoral needs. They helped to dam the rising tide of laicism and humanism, whose aim was a reaction against the decadence of the clergy; and though the tide was too strong, the efforts must not be underestimated. To take only one example: a German Franciscan, Dietrich Kolde of Münster (†1515), was a popular preacher, but he saw that it was not enough to stir up the crowds in a passing movement of fervour and enthusiasm. They, and especially their often wretched and barbarous pastors, must be left with something more than emotional memories. So, to provide something durable, Dietrich wrote. Among his various spiritual writings of a more or less popular character was a sort of directory for laymen, a sort of catechism—the oldest one in German. This was something new, a type of literature which finally was to be recognized by the publication of the Catechism of the Council of Trent. Dietrich revised and improved his work several times: it is preserved in three forms—a "little" catechism (1470); another "intermediate" one; and finally the "big" catechism, which may have been composed as early as 1468, but was printed only about 1480.[72]

[70] See T. M. Charland, O.P., *Artes Praedicandi. Contribution à l'histoire de la rhétorique au moyen âge*, Paris, 1936, cf. p. 110.

[71] See D. Roth, *Die mittelalterliche Predigttheorie und das Manuale Curatorum des Johann Ulrich Surgant*, Basle–Stuttgart, 1956, Part I, chs VI and VII. Cf. Charland, *op. cit.*, p. 70.

[72] There is a biography of Dietrich by A. Groeteken, Kevelaer, 1935. A critical edition has been published by C. Drees, *Der Christenspiegel des D.K. von M.*, Werl in Westphalia, 1954. There are studies by C. Drees, "Der älteste gedruckte deutsche Katechismus und die niederdeutschen Volksbücher des seligen D.K. von M.", in *Franzisk. Studien*, XXXVII (1955), pp. 53–74, 189–217, 388–410; and by P. J. Goyens, *Un héros du Vieux-Bruxelles, le B^x Thiérri Coelde (†1515)*, Malines, 1929. There may also be mentioned, as evidence of a distinctly pastoral

The same spirit as in the previous centuries animated the cultus of the saints at the end of the Middle Ages—pilgrimages to their tombs or their shrines, veneration of their relics, confraternities in their honour[73]; but it had now a greater emotional content, a certain anguish about salvation, and a good deal of superstition. Louis XI of France is a famous example of this spirit, a figure in which the most contradictory aspects can be seen. As a politician he was quite unscrupulous; at the same time a *dévot* drawn to saints and pilgrimages, covered with medals and relics as though they were amulets; he built churches, he founded pious works or processions; he was the king who managed to bring back the Holy Oil in 1483.[74]

From what has been said thus far there begin to emerge certain "lines of force" of lay spirituality at the end of the Middle Ages. First of all, faith was still lively, mingled, however, with a great deal of superstition over relics, indulgenced prayer, famous places of pilgrimage, and large alms to monasteries. Most of the faithful believed that these would effectively preserve them from all kinds of misfortunes in this world, and from damnation in the next. The conviction was only too general, and the clergy did nothing to shake it. In vain did the great preachers and the theologians react against it and call for conversion of heart; their efforts were of no avail against a superstition which had become part of the pattern of living.

Another characteristic of this popular piety is the progressive weakening of the traditional bonds that united the Christian community. Men were anguished and pessimistic in the face of the spectacle presented at that time by the world, by Christendom, and by the hierarchy. They were haunted by the fear of Satan, and superstitious in their faith in "works" and in certain practices which they considered sovereignly efficacious for salvation. Because of all this, they tended more and more to forget the traditional forms of common worship. The *Books of Hours* are only one example among a hundred of this individualistic tendency. Even at Mass—the act which is, above all others, that of the Christian community—these books offered pious formulas of a purely personal nature. Each one isolates himself from the rest of

---

approach, the *Treatise on the Love of God* by a disciple of Nikolaus von Dinkesbühl, *c.* 1430; ed. J. Ancelet-Hustache, Paris, 1926.

[73] See R. Aubenas, *op. cit.*, pp. 344–57. Useful information on the confraternities will be found in L. Spätling, O.F.M., *De apostolicis, pseudoapostolis, apostolinis*, Munich, 1947, chs XIII and XIV.

[74] There are many biographies of Louis XI; attention should be called to J. Calmette, *Le grand règne de Louis XI*, Paris, 1938. On Louis' religious life, see R. Aubenas, *op. cit.*, pp. 354–6.

the congregation to recite them to himself and to derive all their spiritual fruit. The priest said or sang the Mass, "his" Mass; the members of the congregation, for their part, tried to elicit the appropriate sentiments, paying no attention to the chants, prayers and readings of the fore-Mass which are designed to inspire precisely such sentiments. One cannot blame them: the clergy gave little thought to making the most of the liturgical texts! The religion of the laity, in short, came to consist more and more in their personal relations with God. A private prayer which seemed more effectively to bring the individual into conscious contact with God was more esteemed than communal prayer, whose psychological efficacy was less obvious. The faithful no longer understood that liturgical prayer comes first, as the prayer of the whole body of the Church united to Christ, nor did they see that the Church's intentions, in which every Christian should share, are there expressed. This led logically to a progressive depreciation of sacramental practice. What was sought in Holy Communion, which was still rare in any case, was chiefly a stimulant of interior religion. A paradoxical truth emerges from all this: on the one hand, the fifteenth century was excessively attached to those "works" which Luther was soon to denounce as inefficacious for salvation; on the other, it was preparing the way for Protestantism, in the sense that salvation was thought of as a personal affair to be treated between God and the soul, without any attention being paid to the Church, its tradition, its hierarchy and its sacraments.

Individualism was linked with a third characteristic, namely a pietistic conception of the soul's relationship with God. The dominant note in fifteenth-century piety is an affective one; it was tender and even pathetic. It had an ear for the psychological overtones of the Christian mysteries, and what it sought in them was a source of lively emotions. Here again there is a shift which, paradoxically, foreshadows the Reformation. The Reformers rejected Catholic sentimentality and reacted in the direction of Puritanism; but the fact remains that the anticipated "Pietism" of the fifteenth century prepared the way for "the faith which saves without works". It led to that "fiduciary" faith in which theological adhesion to the word of God shifts to the psychological plane, and which attaches more importance to the impact of that word heard in the course of reading than to the hidden action of sacramental life.

The Reformation, in several of its distinctive characteristics, was the term of a spiritual movement that had already taken shape in the fifteenth century. Its originators were strong characters who sought to give it a substratum of dogma, but before their time the current of popular piety was already driving the thinking members of the laity, in a reaction against the superstitions of the masses, to accept, among the ideas then in vogue, too individualistic a conception of the relation of the soul with God. It was this very conception which entered, to a greater or lesser degree, into the ideas of Luther, Calvin and their disciples, and did so without the slightest difficulty.[75]

4. Mystics among the Laity

Any picture of lay piety in the fifteenth century must take into account people living in the world and seeking to practise Christianity to perfection. It has already been seen that, amidst the general chaos, illustrious representatives of the secular clergy and of the religious Orders had inherited the traditions of the past.[76] Among the laity also there were to be found men whose spirituality was very pure, whose religion was often enlightened and free from all superstition. Their merit was all the greater in that circumstances were so unfavourable. These holy layfolk came to swell the ranks of the saints with the clergy and regulars who were afterwards canonized in great numbers. They show clearly that in the fifteenth century there was a very real spiritual vitality in spite of dark shadows.[77] They were often to be found, like St Catherine of Siena, in the ambit of religious Orders.

Some of them were remarkable for their love for the poor and the sick. Often they had been prevented from carrying out some secret plan of entering religious life, and so gave themselves to works of charity. This was nothing new. Hospitals, lazar-houses and hotels-Dieu had existed for a long time, and many spent themselves there with wonderful devotion, at the bedside of the sick, serving Christ in their persons. The wretched received the benefit of all sorts of foundations, and despite the new lay spirit, the giving of alms was still considered a work that would assist the salvation of the benefactor as well as the plight of the recipient. Public assistance had not yet taken the place of that charity which, in the spirit of the Gospel, transmits from man to man, not administratively, the love that God pours forth upon the world. To form an idea of what holiness was, at that time, among laymen, one must take into account these myriad institutions, confraternities and instances of anonymous zeal. In comparison with the few names that have become famous, how many have been forgotten!

[75] On the origins of the Reformation, see the remarks of L. Febvre, "Les Origines de la Réforme française et le problème des causes de la Réforme", in *Au cœur religieux du XVIe siècle*, Paris, 1957, pp. 3–70.

[76] See *supra*, ch. VIII.

[77] See G. J. MacGillivray, "Sanctity in the Fifteenth Century", in *Clergy Review*, XXVI (1946), pp. 113–22.

Two holy women deserve a mention here, St Frances of Rome (1384–1440) and St Catherine of Genoa (1447–1510). Frances, the wife of Laurence Ponziani and the mother of a family, had her attention drawn to the misery that existed round her palace, in the district of Trastevere (today it is still among the poorest in Rome). There, little by little, she formed a group of oblates or tertiaries affiliated spiritually to the monastery of Monte Oliveto. In 1433 she installed them in Rome in the convent of the Tor de' Specchi. Although she was favoured with signal graces—an account has been preserved of 97 visions that she is said to have had—she never sacrificed active charity to contemplation. And so that the action of the oblates might be more effective, they had neither monastic vows nor enclosure. Thus she concentrated all her energies on something useful and holy, a course in striking contrast with the monastic customs of the time.[78]

St Catherine of Genoa, a Franciscan tertiary, was equally characterized by love of the poor and the sick. Her life, unlike that of Frances Ponziani, had a tragic side. Her brother, John Fieschi, a Ghibelline patrician, wished to ally himself with the political enemies of his family, and so married Catherine, at sixteen, against her will, to the violent and sensual Julian Adorno, one of the plebeian leaders of a powerful Guelph family of Genoa. Catherine's own desire was for the religious life, and it may well be imagined that, in spite of her desire to keep the peace, the marriage was not a happy one. Finally Julian, having himself no scruples about seeking compensation elsewhere, thought it best to give Catherine her freedom. Catherine took advantage of the separation to give herself to a life of extraordinary penance and continual prayer.

Contemplation did not prevent her, any more than it had Frances of Rome, from devoting herself to the service of the poor and the sick. There had been in Genoa since 1403 a "Council of Mercy" whose four members administered the property of the hospitals. Some ladies assisted them, and these called upon Catherine for aid. Without hesitation, she gave herself completely to this new vocation. Soon Julian, whose almost incredible prodigality had been brought to an end by financial ruin, was himself won over by the heroism of his wife. This was in 1477, and thenceforth they both lived only for the great hospital of Genoa. Their life of charity lasted for twenty years, until Julian died in 1497. At this juncture, Catherine broke off her penances and took as her director the priest

[78] Her life and visions are recounted in *AA. SS.*, March 9; cf. P. T. Lugano, *I processi inediti per Francesca Bussa dei Ponziani, 1440–1453*, Vatican City, 1945; Mme Berthem-Bontoux, *Vie de sainte Fr. R.*, Paris, 1933; *Vies des saints* (Benedictines of Paris), vol. III, March, pp. 197–211.

Cattaneo Marabotto. Suffering had given her, once so independent, a sense of her own weakness. During the last ten years of her life, surrounded by a group of fervent disciples, she underwent a real purgatory, in which interior details of crucifying intensity were mingled with a sort of increasing *inedia* and with nervous and organic disorders.[79]

Marabotto gathered all that Catherine told him and used this material in composing her *Life*, as well as two treatises, the *Purgatory* and the *Dialogue*.[80] This *Opus catherinianum* has given rise to much controversy, bearing chiefly on the autobiographical character of the *Life* and on the question whether the other two works are authentic—if not word for word, at least as a whole. Baron von Hügel was severe on these writings. He considered them the product of a long process of elaboration by Catherine's disciples, and held that Battista Vernazza, one of the fervent members of the group, had given them a final touch after the death of Marabotto.[81] But this very radical position has been qualified; an examination of the existing manuscripts seems to show that they go back further than Battista. Some evidence, in fact, points to Cattaneo Marabotto as the true author of the *Life* and the *Treatise on Purgatory*, with the collaboration of other disciples. There is no doubt, however, that the *Purgatory* was Catherine's own work, but this seems to be true of the first part of the *Dialogue* only.[82]

Her own life best illustrates her teaching. The twofold purgatory, bodily and interior, through which she passed was really her fundamental experience.[83] It would be foolish, however, to see in her

[79] Biographies include L. de Lapérouse, *La vie de S.C. de G.*, Tournai–Paris, 1948; L. Sertorius, *Katharina von G.*, Munich, 1939; E. Lucatello, *La patrona degli ospedali e la patrona delle infirmiere*, Rome, 1944; O. Norero, *S.C.*, Genoa, 1947. See also *AA. SS.*, Sept., vol. V, 15 Sept., pp. 123–95. Useful articles will be found in *Dict. de spirit.*, II, 290–325; *Vies des Saints* (Benedictines of Paris), vol. IX, Sept., pp. 308–12; *Dict. hist. géogr. eccl.*, XI, 1506–15 (P. Debongnie, C.SS.R.).

[80] Editio princeps, Genoa, 1551. There is a critical edition of the *Trattato del Purgatorio* by Valeriano da Finalmarina, O.M.Cap., Genoa, 1929. The first translation into French appeared at Paris in 1598 and was important on account of its wide distribution. There are modern French translations of the principal works by P. Debongnie, C.SS.R., *La grande dame du pur amour, S.C. de G., 1447–1510. Vie et doctrine et Traité du purgatoire* (Etudes carmélaiitnes), Paris, 1960. For a translation into modern Italian, see *Opere di S.C. de G.*, Modena, 1956. There is a translation of almost all the *Purgatorio* into German in L. Sertorius, *op. cit.*

[81] *The Mystical Element of Religion as Studied in Saint Catherine of Genoa and Her Friends*, London, 1908; 2nd ed., 1923.

[82] On this whole subject, see U. Bonzi da Genova, O.M.Cap., "L'opus catherinianum et ses auteurs. Etude critique sur la biographie et les écrits de saint C. de. G.", in *Rec. ascét. myst.*, XVI (1935), pp. 351–80.

[83] Cf. P. Debongnie, C.SS.R., "Le 'purgatoire' de C. de G.", in *Études carmélitaines*, XXIII, II (1938), pp. 92–101. On Catherine's teaching, see *Dict. de spirit.*, II, 290–325; Tito da Ottone, O.M.Cap., "Fede e pietà nel 'Trattato del purga-

teaching only a theorizing about the purification of the soul, even granted that it was based on personal experience: she lived, above all, for love—love of God, of Christ, and of men. This divine love was undeniably accompanied in her case by mystical phenomena, and even by extraordinary states, though it may well be that the memory of the disciples who recounted them was not altogether trustworthy. Did they give a faithful picture of their "spiritual mother"? One would not like to be quite certain. In addition there is the question of Catherine's physical and psychological constitution, weakened by a life of frightful penances. But one thing is certain, and it is enough to vouch for her sanctity: her burning charity. God was not its only object; Catherine understood that her love would not be genuine unless it were also directed to the outcasts of this world.

That her influence was very great is clearly shown by the group of spiritual disciples surrounding her during her last years. It was not lessened by her unhappy life, from the forced marriage in her youth to the purgatory of her last years. In addition to her confessor Marabotto, her disciples included a kinswoman Tommasina Fieschi (1448–1534), who, after having been married, retired to a convent and wrote several little works of Spirituality.[84] Battista Vernazza (†1587) has already been mentioned[85]; her father, Ettore Vernazza (†1524), was also a disciple of Catherine's. Others were the priest Giacomo Carenzio (†1513) and a Friar Minor of the Observance, Angelo Carletti da Chivasso, who founded the *monte di pietà* of Genoa, and may have written the second part of the *Dialogue*.[86] A later *Abridgement of Perfection*, probably the work of Isabella Bellinzaga (1552–1624), shows the posthumous influence of Catherine.[87]

There were others, among the mystics of this period, who were irresistibly drawn to live for God alone with no thought of turning towards the needy. This was the case of Blessed Osanna Andreasi (1449–1505), a Dominican tertiary of Mantua. She greatly resembled St Catherine of Siena, not only because, like her, she was a lay-

---

torio' di santa Caterina de Genova, terziaria francescana", in *Collect. francisc.*, IX (1939), pp. 5–33, 153–63; and M. Petrocchi, *L'estasi nelle mistiche italiane della riforma cattolica*, Naples, 1958, pp. 29–41.

[84] Cf. U. Bonzi da Genova, O.M.Cap., "Le traité des sept degrés de l'amour de Dieu de T.F.", in *Rev. ascét. myst.*, XVI (1935), pp. 29–86.

[85] On Battista, see U. Bonzi da Genova, O.M.Cap., "La Vénérable B.V.", in *Rev. ascét. myst.*, XVI (1935), pp. 147–79.

[86] Cf. M. Bessone, *Il beato Angelo Carletti da Chivasso*, Genoa, 1950.

[87] Cf. M. Viller, S.J. and G. Joppin, S.J., "Les sources italiennes de l'Abrégé de la perfection. La vie de sainte Catherine de G. et les œuvres de la M. Battista Vernazza", in *Rev. ascét. myst.*, XV (1934), pp. 381–402; J. Dagens, *Bérulle et les origines de la restauration catholique*, Bruges, 1952, pp. 133–7.

woman living in the world, but also by the nature of her interior life and by her apostolic zeal for the interests of the Church.[88]

St Nicholas of Flüe (1417–87) is even more remarkable. There is one feature in his life which sets it apart, at the outset, from those of the other lay mystics. He alone, among them all, never thought of associating himself with any religious order. In the fifteenth century, despite the general decadence of religious houses, fervent laymen scarcely conceived that one could respond fully to the call of interior grace except in the cloister. The advice given by the *Imitation*, in the middle of the century, is a good illustration. Thomas a Kempis advised the spiritual man to renounce all things, and the whole book is conceived in terms of the religious life. Even when relaxed, the monastery was the normal place for the interior life. If for some reason or another a man could not realize his dream of entering it, he affiliated himself to a third order or a confraternity.

There was nothing like this in the life of Nicholas of Flüe. In obedience to his parents, he had married; he was a good husband and had ten children. He took part in the political life of his country and in Switzerland's struggle against the tyranny of Austria. He became renowned for the visions with which he had been favoured from early childhood. He himself declared that he had had them from infancy, and affirmed that he could distinctly remember his birth and his baptism! One would be inclined to reject such an affirmation without examination, but in fact Nicholas was a well-balanced man, active and enterprising. It can at least be gathered that he was called to the contemplative life at an early age. It was not, however, until 1468, when he was more than fifty years old, that he was able to carry out his desire for a life entirely consecrated to God. He then left his wife and children and became a hermit. For almost twenty years, he lived on the Eucharist alone.[89]

It does not seem to have been simply his marriage that kept Nicholas from entering any of the existing religious Orders. His life was marked from the start with such a force of divine grace—and with so personal a one—that one may well wonder whether, if he had been free sooner, he would have chosen anything but solitude. Did his life show that the conventual life of the period no longer

[88] There are biographies by G. Bagolini and L. Ferretti, Florence, 1905, and by A. Magnaguti, Padua, 1949. A sketch of her spirituality is given by M. Pettrochi, *op. cit.*, pp. 43–51.

[89] There is a historical commentary on the life of Nicholas in *AA.SS.*, March 21. See also *Vies des Saints* (Benedictines of Paris), vol. III, March, pp. 498–500. Biographies and studies of his spirituality include B. Lavaud, O.P., *Vie profonde de N. de F.*, Fribourg (Switzerland), 1942; A. von Segesser, *Bruder Klaus von Flüe*, Fribourg (Switzerland), 1936; A. Andrey, *Bruder Klaus, S.N. de F.*, Vatican City, 1945; R. Durrer, *Bruder Klaus*, 4 vols, Sarnen, 1914–21.

attracted those who really wanted to consecrate themselves wholly to the interior life? Not necessarily. The call of grace escapes, and will always escape, in certain cases, from the common norms. It comes to some, as it did to Nicholas, when they are very young. No one can say why, except by appealing, as does St Paul, to the designs of divine mercy. Nicholas of Flüe, then, stands out as a prophet in an age when the traditional structures were worm-eaten—a sort of John the Baptist, charged with reminding men, by his very vocation, of God's absolute transcendence and of the sovereign power and gratuitousness of his call.

With Nicholas, however, we do not find that dilemma which gnawed at the consciences of so many others, probably less overflowing with the grace of God than he was: whether to obey God or man. Nicholas never saw his call from God as one that set him apart from the Church and its hierarchy. On the contrary, when crowds flocked to his hermitage, he warned them against the innovations that were soon to arise under the name of Reformation. Nicholas lived in God. All the rest—the future, all the distress of men and of the Church—he left to the care of Providence.

This absolute confidence in Providence also characterized the most extraordinary saint of the century, the Maid of Orleans. Her story is too well known to be retold here. Countless biographers, not all of them remarkable for a critical sense, have turned and still turn to the touching figure of the young girl from Greux-Domrémy (*c.* 1412–31).[90]

Her story has a charm even for those who are strangers to the Christian faith. There is something fascinating about her vocation. Her "voices"—St Michael, St Catherine and St Margaret—became more and more peremptory: "Go to the aid of the King of France! You must go to France! Daughter of God, go to Robert d'Audricourt, in the town of Vaucouleurs, that he may give you men to accompany you!" Then came her departure dressed as a man; her ride to Chinon, where she met the Dauphin, then to Orleans, which she entered on 29 April 1429; the raising of the siege by the English on 8 May; the liberation of the towns along

[90] The bibliography on Joan of Arc is enormous. First to be mentioned are J. Quicherat, *Le procès de condamnation et de réhabilitation de J. d'A., dite la Pucelle*, 5 vols, Paris, 1841–9; P. Champion, *Le procès de condamnation de J. d'A.*, 2 vols, Paris, 1920–1; P. Doncoeur, S.J., *Là minute française des interrogatoires de Jeanne la Pucelle*, Paris, 1952. There are biographies, of varying degrees of merit, by G. Hanotaux, Paris, 1911; P. Champion, Paris, 1934; R. Pernoud, *Vie et mort de Jeanne d'Arc*, Paris, 1954; O. Englebert, *Vie de J. d'A. par elle-même*, Paris, 1940; D. T. Enklaar and R. R. Post, *La fille au grand cœur. Études sur J. d'A.*, Groningen, 1955. The biographies published by Anatole France and Jacques Cordier have at least the advantage of recommending caution to the Catholic historian in dealing with Joan of Arc.

the Loire, of Auxerre, and of Troyes; the coronation of Charles VII at Rheims on 17 July; and the entrance into St Denis on 26 August. Finally, at Compiègne on 23 May 1430, Joan was wounded and captured by the enemy. Then began the long calvary of her imprisonment. At Rouen, a Frenchman, Cauchon, bishop of Beauvais (Joan had been taken in his territory) presided at the infamous trial that was to give a moral victory to the English. The methods used were indefensible; torture and intimidation. At last they had what they wanted: Joan was found guilty of witchcraft and of being a relapsed heretic. She was condemned to death, and the sentence was carried out at Rouen on 30 May 1431. Before she died at the stake she was heard to cry out six times: "Jesus!"

This iniquity haunted the memory of later generations. Proceedings for her rehabilitation were opened in 1454. On 7 July 1456 the tribunal reversed the judgment of 1431. It further ordered expiatory ceremonies in the course of which the original document was torn up and a cross was erected in the Vieux-Marché.

In certain of its aspects, Joan's vocation resembles that of Nicholas of Flüe. Like him, she responded to an irresistible call, and she behaved like a true prophet, speaking "in God's name". Her mission, even more than that of Nicholas, ruled out the possibility of conventual life. "God hath chosen the things that are not, that he might bring to nought things that are"; and what are the weakest instruments, humanly speaking, can become powerful in his hands.

But Joan's sanctity must not be confused with her mission, or even with her martyrdom. When the Church beatified her on 18 April 1909, and canonized her on 16 May 1920, it was not because she was a martyr, or the liberator of France. It was not even because of the "voices" that constantly guided her. The Church never vouches for such phenomena, known as "private revelations". What entitled Joan to the honours reserved to the saints was her love, a love wholly obedient to God and respectful to the Church. The name that her voices gave her, "Daughter of God", was more true than might appear at first sight. It was because she lived as a true daughter of God that Joan was holy. She believed, with a faith that cleaved to God once and for all. She hoped, with a hope that was not dismayed either by the delays of Providence or by the incredible hesitations of men. She loved with a love that never failed. Her message, her mission and her martyrdom were, in her own eyes, nothing but the means or the consequence of giving herself to God without reserve.

X

TOWARDS THE REFORMATION AND COUNTER-REFORMATION

1. The Humanist Renaissance

THE general evolution of Christian ideas and life in the fourteenth and fifteenth centuries foreshadows the religious crisis of the sixteenth.

Monks and religious fell lower and lower in the estimation of the faithful. The laity, and a good many of the secular clergy, felt that the cloister was not the only place where salvation was to be found, nor even a life of fervour. They felt the same distrust of theologians, and of their efforts to fit the facts of spiritual experience into scholastic theory. The result was that many a layman and clerk turned back to the simplicity of the pure Gospel. They can hardly be blamed for this, but the result was to widen the gulf between dogma and mysticism. Spirituality was henceforth a psychological experience, which in itself could dispense with revelation and dogma, and, even more, with theology, scholastic or otherwise.

This bent of mind took concrete form in the movement that came to be known as the *Devotio moderna*. Its influence, as has been seen, was tremendous, so much so that it touched even those who were the heirs of the old religious Orders, monastic or mendicant. A fortiori, the piety of the laity was thoroughly imbued with it. It may well be questioned, however, whether this influence was all in one direction. The *Devotio moderna* may have owed its success to the fact that it was able to express, to authenticate and in some sense to absorb, the new tendencies that were appearing in the religious life of Western Christendom.

This new "devotion" and, more precisely, its subjective and individualistic piety provided fertile soil for the growth of an idea that was to be one of the central ones of the Lutheran reformation: justification by faith alone. The mediation of the Word made flesh; the Incarnation, prolonged into the present by the Church; the hierarchy of the Church and its sacraments—all these great realities of Christianity could remain outside the field of vision of a devout

Christian formed by the new piety. They also attached considerable importance to what are now called "devotions" and, in so doing, were already laying themselves open to the criticisms made by the Reformers denouncing a superstitious and idolatrous attachment to practices, rites and indulgences which had no value other than that of the embryonic faith which inspired them.

While the laity remained more or less alienated from the hierarchical and sacramental organization of the Church, engaged as they were in denouncing its abuses, they were at the same time experiencing what might be called today a collective "end of a world" complex. They were thus fully prepared to give a favourable reception to the new world that was coming into being: the world of the humanist Renaissance and of the Reformation.

The humanist movement took shape in Italy as early as the fourteenth century.[1] It flowered in the course of the fifteenth, but it was only in the second half of that century and especially in the sixteenth that it extended to the whole of Europe. It affected most of the domains of civilization: literature, philosophy and the arts. The new style of thought, and of artistic and literary expression, was based on a return to classical antiquity, on a rediscovery of it; hence the name Renaissance. It began in a society which was still wholly permeated with the Christian way of life and with Christian dogma: in going back to pagan antiquity, it ended, if not in questioning the truth of Christianity itself—for that, men have waited till the modern world—at least in ignoring all that was most essential in its doctrine. In the fifteenth century and at the beginning of the sixteenth, the inhabitants of a certain world of letters were living on a hollow Christianity, from which the core had been removed. They fed upon the illusion that pagan wisdom in its highest forms—and it had assumed sublime forms—is one with Christian wisdom, provided that the latter silences the demands of dogma and of the Gospel. Ultimately, such a wisdom has no use

[1] The bibliography relating to the humanist Renaissance is very extensive. The reader who seeks to inform himself on the subject must have recourse to other works than this *History of Christian Spirituality*. He will find a good introduction to it in the following: R. Aubenas, "L'Église et la Renaissance (1449–1517)", in *Histoire de l'Église* (Fliche and Martin), vol. XV, Paris, 1951, especially Book II, chs I to III (pp. 201–74); H. Pirenne, A. Renaudet, *et al.*, "La fin du moyen âge", in *ibid.*, II, ch. XI (pp. 499–563); H. Pirenne, "Histoire de l'Europe des invasions au XVIe siècle", in *ibid.*, Book IX (pp. 396–487); L. Génicot, *Les lignes de faîte du moyen âge*, Tournai–Paris, 1952, ch. XII (pp. 370–95); J. Chevalier, *Histoire de la pensée*, II, Paris, 1956, ch. VIII (pp. 565–722; valuable bibliography); F. Hermans, *Histoire doctrinale de l'humanisme chrétien*, I, *L'aube*, Tournai–Paris, 1948. Among recent works may be mentioned two collections of studies: *Medioevo e Rinascimento. Studi in onore di Bruno Nardi*, 2 vols, Florence, 1955; *Courants religieux et humanisme à la fin du XVe siècle et au début du XVIe siècle*, Strasbourg Colloquium, May 9–11, 1957, Paris, 1959; and L. Febvre, *Au cœur religieux du XVIe siècle*, Paris, 1957.

for God or for Christ. Only man remains—whence the term "humanist" that has come to be attached to that Renaissance. It was much more than a simple enthusiasm for certain literary and artistic forms, or a purely formal imitation of antiquity, as the historians of the nineteenth century believed. It was a new conception of the world and of man. And man, as a result of a sort of Copernican revolution, now tended to take the place of God.

The veneration that the humanists professed for classical antiquity seems to us today naïve. It has even been characterized as "a completely romantic devotion".[2] It is understandable that it should have arisen in Italy, where so many traces of that antiquity are to be met with. Another factor was the social evolution which, in Italy more than anywhere else, was lessening the difference between nobles and commoners. The nobles were abandoning their traditional profession of arms and leaving it to the *condottieri*; commoners were climbing in the social scale, with the aid of the fortunes they had made in manufactures or commerce, or even in politics. A striking example of this was the Florentine family of the Medici.

Florence, the city in which Dante was born, was the city in which the Renaissance shone with the greatest brilliance. It was marked by a certain paganism which even today strikes the modern tourist as he goes about the city and visits the Palazzo Vecchio, the Pitti palace and the Uffiizi gallery. Little by little, a real intellectual aristocracy was coming into being.[3] Its language was still, with few exceptions, Latin—no longer the debased Latin of the schools and universities, but that of Cicero and Virgil. This unity of language contributed much to the international character that the humanist movement soon developed. It was not until later that there appeared frontiers within the republic of letters, when intellectuals everywhere began to follow Dante's example and write in their national languages—not to mention the divisions produced in Christian Europe by the Reformation and by the first appearances of unbelief.

In this republic of letters, the first names that stand out in history belong to the fourteenth century: those of Petrarch (†1374) and Boccaccio (†1375). Petrarch was born in 1304 at Arezzo, of a Florentine family in exile, and received his literary training in Provence. He perfected it in the course of various journeys which

[2] H. Pirenne, A. Renaudet, *et al.*, *op. cit.*, p. 508.

[3] On the Italian Renaissance, see especially A. Chastel, *L'humanisme italien* (Bibl. d'Humanisme et de Renaissance, No. 16), Paris, 1954; F. Bérence, *La renaissance italienne*, Paris, 1955; E. Cassirer, P. O. Kristeller and J. H. Randall, *The Renaissance Philosophy of Man*, Chicago, 1948; E. Garin, *Il pensiero pedagogico della Umanesimo*, Florence, 1958.

took him successively to Paris, to the Low Countries, to Germany, and finally in 1337 to Rome.[4] His renown as a poet and man of letters was established when he was crowned with laurel on the Capitol on 8 April 1341.[5]

Despite a religious crisis through which he passed after birth of an illegitimate daughter and the entrance of his brother Gerard with the Carthusians, Petrarch's career continued as it had begun. The love of glory was always one of his strongest motives, as well as his aspiration towards the ideal world that antiquity painted for him. Cicero and Virgil, in his eyes, were something more than perfect literary forms. He did not despise these, but he was more interested in the men than in their style. Cicero especially he valued as a *magister vitae*. The goal of knowledge is the good life, and eloquence is only a useful means of persuasion, to lead its hearers to virtue. Francesco Petrarch was, indeed, chiefly concerned with ethics. They took the place that had still been occupied, a few decades earlier, in works such as Dante's, by metaphysics and theology.[6] Petrarch went still further; he was among the first to pursue a social idea of virtue and to concentrate his efforts on forming good citizens. His aim was to bring about peace in society, and thereby to procure it for himself and his disciples. For *otium* is necessary for anyone who wishes to attain to truth.[7]

There are many indications, scattered through Petrarch's work, that testify to the depth of his religious life. He was certainly neither a philosopher nor a theologian; he was satisfied with being a poet and moralist. But that poet and moralist witnessed with

[4] There are bibliographies by U. Bosco, *Petrarca*, Turin, 1946; L. Bernero, Avignon, 1948; H. Enjoubert, Paris, 1948; etc. Various items of biographical information will be found in E. H. Wilkins, *Studies in the Life and Works of Petrarch*, Cambridge, 1955.

[5] On Petrarch's literary activity, see G. Billanovich, *Petrarca litterato*, I, *Lo Scrittoio del Petrarca*, Rome, 1947. On his connection with Cicero, see the same author's "Petrarca e Cicerone", in *Miscellanea G. Mercati*, IV, Vatican City, 1946, pp. 88–106.

For Petrarch's works, see the following: *Opera*, 4 vols, Basle, 1556. There is a new Italian "national edition", of which six volumes have appeared: *Africa*, ed. N. Festa, vol. I, Florence, 1926; *Rerum memorandarum libri*, ed. G. Billanovich, vol. XIV, 1954; and *familiarium libri*, ed. V. Rossi and U. Bosco, vols X–XIII, 1933–42. The following works may also be mentioned: *De vita solitaria*, ed. A. Altamura, Naples, 1943; *De otio religiosorum*, Italian translation by L. Volpicelli, Rome, 1928; *Psalmi penitentiales*, French trans. by H. Cochin, Paris, 1929; *Rerum servilium libri*, trans. by G. Fracassetti, 2 vols, Florence, 1869–70; *Lettere*, ed. and trans. E. Carrara, Milan, 1928; *De sui ipsius et multorum aliorum ignorantia*, ed. L. M. Capelli, Paris, 1906 (French translation by J. Bertrand, Paris, 1929); *Lettres sur son ascension au mont Ventoux*, ed. H. Sebert, Haumont, 1944.

[6] On all this, see particularly J. H. Whitfield, *Petrarch and the Renascence*, Oxford, 1943.

[7] On this aspect of Petrarch's thought, see especially L. Russo, *Ritratti e disegni storici. Seria terza. Studi sul Due- e Trecento*, Bari, 1951, ch. IX.

sorrow the conflict between the human and the divine. He lived in hope of a complete interior liberation. He was fundamentally a Christian—too much of a Christian to doubt that the true solution to the conflict from which he suffered was to be found in the traditional faith.[8]

Nevertheless, a whole world lies between Petrarch and the other great Christian authors who, scarcely a century earlier, had drawn their inspiration from antiquity. Thomas Aquinas had been a passionate reader of Aristotle and had used him as an instrument for developing a whole dogmatic system. Petrarch too read the ancients, but on the whole he accepted the postulate which puts man in the centre of the vista, though he recognized its limitations and felt within himself the tragedy of man's bonds. Dante, who was only slightly his elder, had also realized the inhumanity of the human comedy, but in the fullness of his genius had been able to transform it into a divine one by conjuring up the solutions of Christian dogma. Petrarch himself was aware of those solutions, but once the question had arisen in that form, his disciples would arrive at a humanism that was cut off from its Christian foundations and therefore incapable of giving any meaning to man himself; whose end term is an atheistic existentialism, powerless to resolve the absurdity of man's condition. The preliminary symptoms of the whole evolution can be detected as early as the *Trecento*. This century, in which the break between theology and mysticism became complete, prepared the way for another break—that between man and God.

A Florentine contemporary of Petrarch, Boccaccio, was his fervent disciple. Boccaccio's love of antiquity was even stronger than his master's. He had the first copies of the *Iliad* and the *Odyssey* brought from Greece at his own expense. A great part of his fortune was devoted to disinterring the masterpieces of Greek and Latin literature and to disseminating them. His wide knowledge of mythology enabled him to write a treatise *On the Genealogies of the Gods*. In other works he sets forth, as examples, illustrious men and celebrated women, chiefly chosen from among those whose memory had come down from antiquity. His best-known work is *The Decameron*, a collection of tales. Divided into ten days (whence the title) it consists of imaginary narratives, supposed to have been told at the rate of ten a day by some noble young men and women who had taken refuge in a villa in the neigh-

[8] On Petrarch's religious thought, see E. Piggioli, *Il pensiero religioso di Francesco Petrarca*, Alba, 1952. Some aspects of the conflict have been described by K. Heitmann, *Fortuna und virtus. Eine Studie zu Petrarcas Lebensweisheit*, Cologne, 1958.

bourhood of Florence to escape the plague of 1348.[9] The spirit that animates the tales is not on the same level as their literary quality; Christian morality is flouted and contempt for religion is complacently displayed. Boccaccio was the first humanist to parade his paganism.

Stimulated by Petrarch and Boccaccio, Florence became the stronghold of literature and the arts. The humanists of the fifteenth century, led on by Coluccio Salutati (†1406), set out enthusiastically on the new path. The studies of antiquity became common and soon penetrated to the *studium* of the city. Among the great names were Leonardo Bruni, Angelo Poliziano, Pier Paolo Vergerio; and there were many more. Their example was followed in other cities as well. At Pavia, for example, Lorenzo Valla (1405–57) tried, like Petrarch, to integrate Ciceronian anthropocentrism with Christianity. In justifying Epicurus, he did not hesitate to defend a morality based on pleasure.[10] Leone Battista Alberti (1404–72), although he was closer to Stoicism, belongs to the same tradition. In him can be seen how marked was the effect of humanism on the practical outlook of the merchant aristocracy of Florence.[11]

At the same time, that city was becoming the seat of a Platonic academy. The Byzantine George Gemistos, known as Pletho († *c.* 1452), has often been considered, but wrongly, as its founder.[12] One of its most illustrious masters was Marsilio Ficino (†1499). He translated Plato and Plotinus into Latin, and sought to effect a synthesis of Platonism and Aristotelianism. His religious position has been much debated. There can be no doubt that he was a Christian—more precisely, an Augustinian and even a Thomist. On the other hand, his philosophy of religion, which was strongly anthropocentric, was imbued with the Dionysian *via negationis*,[13]

[9] Biographies and studies: H. Hauvette, *Boccace, Etude biographique et littéraire*, Paris, 1914; C. Grabher, *B.*, Turin, 1941; G. Billanovich, *Restauri boccacceschi*, Rome, 1945; U. Bosco, Rieti, 1929; L. Russo, *Ritratti e disegni storici . . .*, chs XI–XIII. Some works of Boccacio are included in the series *Scrittori d'Italia* (Bari). The *De casibus virorum illustrium*, the *De claris mulieribus*, and the *De montibus*, however, are available only in editions of the fifteenth and sixteenth centuries. There have been many editions and translations of the *Decameron*.

[10] The philosophical and religious writings of Valla have been edited by S. Radetti, Florence, 1953; on his religion, see the same author's study in *Medioevo e Rinascimento*, II, pp. 595–620. See also S. Mancini, *Vita di L. V.*, Florence, 1891; and Franco Gaeta, *Lorenzo Valla*, Naples, 1955.

[11] On all this, see J. H. Whitfield, *Petrarch and the Renascence*, Oxford, 1943.

[12] His works are in P.G., Vol. 160; they were edited by C. Alexandre and translated into French by A. Pellisier, Paris, 1858. See J. W. Taylor, *Pletho's Criticism of Plato and Aristotle*, Menasha, Wis., 1921; F. Masai, *Pléthon et le platonisme de Mistra*, Paris, 1956; A. Chastel, *Art et humanisme à Florence*, Paris, 1958.

[13] Ed. Basle, 1561; 2 vols, Paris, 1641; etc. See, in addition, the *Supplementum Ficinianum*, 2 vols, ed. O. Kristeller, Florence, 1937. Studies by W. Dress, *Die Mystik des M. F.*, Berlin, 1929; H. Jedin, "Die Mystik des M. F.", in *Römische Quartalschrift*, XXXIX (1931), pp. 281–7; J. Festugière, *La philosophie de l'amour*

and he was convinced of the basic continuity of all religions. His rather esoteric Christianity showed a certain leaning towards hermetic lore and led him to take an interest in the more extraordinary phenomena of the contemplative life.[14]

One of the most brilliant stars in the firmament of the Italian Renaissance was the young Giovanni Pico, prince of Mirandola, who died in 1494 at the age of thirty-one.[15] His immense learning is well known. He drew up 900 theses *in omni genere scientiarum*, by which he intended to attempt the synthesis of the whole of human knowledge—pagan, Jewish and Christian. When thirteen of these theses were condemned, and then the work as a whole, he at first rebelled. But under the influence of Savonarola he finally died in the dispositions of a monk, having, it would appear, expressed a wish to enter the Friars Preachers.

As the sixteenth century dawned, the movement of men of letters away from the Christian faith becomes even clearer. The artist and thinker Leonardo da Vinci (1452–1519) is an enigmatic figure; we do not know whether he really held the faith of his ancestors.[16] Machiavelli (1469–1527), in his *Prince*, built up a theory of statecraft by which the most unscrupulous proceedings of modern politics can be justified.[17] Pomponazzi (†1525) worked out a purely natural theology.[18] Paracelsus (†1541) and Copernicus (†1543) already sensed that science and faith are two different approaches to the truth, but their contemporaries were not yet prepared to follow their lead. Whenever men of the new learning put forward scientific theories that contradicted what were then considered truths forming an integral part of Christian doctrine, the faithful almost unanimously approved their condemnation by the Church.

The influence of Italy was tremendous. To describe it, one would have to describe a whole Europe modelled after its pattern, with

---

de M. F. et son influence sur la littérature française du XVIe siècle, Paris, 1941; G. Saitta, *M. F. e la filosofia dell'umanesimo*, Bologna, 1954; and particularly R. Marcel, *Marsile Ficin*, Paris, 1958, especially ch. x.

[14] Cf. E. Garin, "Ritratto di M. F.", in *Belfagor*, VI (1951), pp. 289–301.

[15] Editions of the *De hominis dignitate*, of the *Heptaplus*, of the *De ente et uno*, and of the *Disputationes adversus astrologiam divinatricum* by E. Garin, Florence, 1942. Biographies by L. Gautier-Vignal, Paris, 1937; P. J. Cordier, Paris, 1957; E. Garin, Florence, 1937. Pico is studied by L. Bouyer in *Autour d'Erasme*, Paris, 1955, pp. 77–84.

[16] Cf. A. Valensin, S.J., *Regards*, II, Paris, 1955; E. Troilo, Venice, 1954; *L. de V. et l'expérience scientifique au XVIe siècle*, Colloquium of the C.N.R.S., July, 1952, Paris, 1952. His treatise *On Painting* has been translated into French by Peladan, Paris, 1910.

[17] Among recent works, see G. Sasso, *Niccolo Machiavelli. Storia del suo pensiero politico*, Naples, 1958. *Opere maggiori*, ed. P. Carli, Florence, 1934. There is a study by A. Renaudet, *M.*, Paris, 1956.

[18] There is an edition of his *Tractatus de immortalitate animae* by G. Morra, Bologna, 1954.

active groups in all the centres of intellectual life everywhere, even as far away as Hungary and Poland. In Germany, the figure of Nicholas of Cusa overshadows all the rest; he has already been discussed in a previous chapter.[19] Before long England was to have a chancellor who was a saint as well as a humanist: Thomas More. He was acutely aware of the problems raised by the Reformation, but his fidelity to the Church cost him his life. His tragic fate, like that of the bishop of Rochester, John Fisher, belongs to the history of the Reformation itself more than to that of its preliminary symptoms at the end of the Middle Ages. More, with his famous *Utopia,* belongs to the earlier humanism. In it he draws a picture of an ideal society, combining the most varied notions of antiquity and certain new aspects which had been brought out by the Renaissance.[20]

The Dutchman, Erasmus (†1536) dominated the whole of Europe with his learning. His many travels and his relations with the religious and political circles of every country show how much his contemporaries valued his knowledge of antiquity, of the Bible, and of the Fathers. But his story, too, belongs more to the Reformation than to its antecedents. It would be going too far, however, to represent him as a precursor of modern irreligion, or even as a Reformer (in the sense that the word has come to have for the modern Catholic). He should rather be seen as carrying on the tradition of patristic thought, while earnestly desiring the reform of the Church.[21]

In France, Christine of Pisano (1364–1430), has been called "the *doyenne* of professional literary women".[22] A Venetian, she nevertheless spent most of her life in France, having married a man who was notary to Charles V and Charles VI. Her fervent humanism did not prevent her being a good Christian or from spending the

19 See *supra*, pp. 444 *et seq.*

20 See vol. III of this *History of Christian Spirituality.* Recent work on More and on the interpretation of his *Utopia* has been summarized and brought up to date by P. Mesnard, "Vers un nouveau portrait de saint Thomas More", in *Intériorité et vie spirituelle* (*Recherches et débats*, No. 7), Paris, 1954, pp. 221–34. On the *Utopia*, see the edition by M. Delcourt, Paris, 1936; cf. F. Battaglia, *Saggi sull' "Utopia" di T. M.*, Bologna, 1949; E. L. Surtz, S.J., *The Praise of Pleasure*, Cambridge, Mass., 1957; and, by the same, *The Praise of Wisdom*, Chicago, 1957. For an English biography, see R. W. Chambers, *Thomas More*, London, 1935.

21 See vol. III. A. Renaudet, in his *Etudes érasmiennes*, Paris, 1939, ascribed to Erasmus a sort of anticipated "modernism". This point of view has been contested, or qualified in various ways, by L. Bouyer in *Autour d'Erasme*; A. Auer, *Die volkhommene Frömmigkeit des Christen nach dem Enchiridion militis christiani des Erasmus von Rotterdam*, Düsseldorf, 1954. For the influence of Erasmus on Spain, see M. Bataillon, *Erasme et l'Espagne*, Paris, 1937. In English, see D. Knowles, *The Religious Orders in England*, III, Cambridge, 1959, ch. XI, "Erasmus".

22 R. Gout, *Le miroir des dames chrétiennes*, Paris, 1935, p. 305.

last eleven years of her life in a convent at Poissy. Her last work was a poem in praise of Joan of Arc, which was finished on 31 July 1429 while the saint was still alive. Her *Cité des Dames*, her *Livre des trois vertus*, and her *Livre de la Paix* reveal her as a woman unrivalled in her time—so much so, that modern historians and writers have seen in her a precursor of modern feminism. She shows that in the Middle Ages a woman of culture could make her mark, on her own merits, in the young republic of letters. She had read not only the Bible, but Aristotle and Seneca, Cicero and Boethius, and countless other writers of antiquity. Among the more recent writers, she had read Dante and Boccaccio; the latter's treatise *De claris mulieribus* was one of the principal sources of her *Cité des Dames.*[23]

French humanism too, in the time of Charles VI, began to include some who, without attaining the level of their Florentine and Italian rivals, still should not pass unnoticed. The presence of the pontifical court at Avignon, and the frequent commercial and political relations with Italy, had something to do with this literary flowering. Among the French humanists were the two brothers Gontier and Pierre Col (†1418 and † after 1417).[24] Jean de Montreuil (*c.* 1354–1418), secretary to Charles VI and provost of Lille, was in touch with the chancellor of Notre-Dame de Paris, Jean Gerson, and admired his work for the unity of the Church. It appears, however, that his supposed letters to Gerson, on which the latter's reputation as a humanist was based, were not after all addressed to him[25]; several of them were intended for a Hermit of St Augustine named Jacques Legrand, who was himself a warm lover of classical literature.

Jacques wrote a *Sophilogium* which enjoyed great popularity for two centuries and has only recently been rescued from oblivion.

[23] *Œuvres poétiques*, ed. M. Roy, 3 vols, Paris, 1886–96; *Le livre des fais et bonnes meurs du sage roy Charles V*, ed. S. Solente, 2 vols, Paris, 1939–40; *La vision Christine*, ed. M. L. Towner, Washington, 1932: "Dittie sur Jeanne d'Arc", in J. Quicherat, *Procès de condamnation et de réhabilitation de J. d'A.*, V, Paris, 1841; *Le livre de la Paix*, ed. C. C. Willard, La Haye, 1958 (excellent bibliography, pp. 215–19); *Le livre de la mutation de fortune*, ed. S. Solente, 2 vols, Paris, 1959. There is a study by W. L. Boldingh-Goemans, *Chr. de P., 1364–1430*, Rotterdam, 1948 (bibliography, pp. 296–8). Extracts have been published in R. Gout, *op. cit.*, pp. 305–12. There are still other editions of various less important writings.

[24] See A. Colville, *Gontier et Pierre Col et l'humanisme en France au temps de Charles VI*, Paris, 1934. There is a valuable study on the influence of Italian humanism in France, by F. Simone, "Note sulla fortuna del Petrarca in Francia", in *Giornale stor. Letter. ital.*, CXXVII (1950), pp. 1–59; CXXVIII (1951), pp. 1–40, 145–75.

[25] On this question, see A. Combes, *Jean de Montreuil et le chancelier Gerson. Contribution à l'histoire des rapports de l'humanisme et de la théologie en France au début du XVe siècle*, Paris, 1942; cf. A. Coville, *Gontier et Pierre Col . . .*; and A. Thomas, *De Ioannis de Montserolio vita et operibus*, Paris, 1883.

His aim was to instil in his readers a love for wisdom and for the virtues, to instruct them regarding the various "states of life" (ecclesiastic, noble and plebeian), and finally to prepare them for death. To this end he had collected a number of quotations from ancient writers. His intention was remarkable: not, as one might suppose, to put classical culture at the service of the Church. "Precisely the contrary. It was, in point of fact, a matter of the Church going out to meet the new culture and providing living souls, in danger of being wounded or killed by this pagan Renaissance, with the only vaccine that could immunize them against all that was harmful in it, and so ensure that it would be beneficial to them; the light of the Gospel and the grace of our Saviour Jesus."[26]

The first humanists had not the slighest intention of separating either from the Church or from the Gospel. To be convinced of this fact, one has only to compare them with the writers who appeared a century later, and whose Christianity is much more debatable.[27] There is still a considerable difference of opinion about some of the latter, who lived at so crucial a period in the Church's history. One is Jacques Lefèvre d'Etaples (*c.* 1450–1536).[28] According to one view,[29] he finally arrived, amidst the passionate quarrels of the Reformation, at "a mysticism indifferent to all dogmatic considerations." Others hold him to have remained "wholly Catholic" and "wholly Roman".[30] Wherever the truth lies, we are indebted to him for an edition of the Pseudo-Dionysius and for a Latin version of Ruysbroeck's *Splendour of the Spiritual Espousals.* The least that can be said is that, like Erasmus, he longed for the reform of the Church. There was also Guillaume Budé (1468–1540) whose activity was not confined to the domain of letters. He plunged into the sciences and into Christian philosophy and became involved in the movement for reform. "Despite his humanism, and even because of it, Budé meant to be, and to remain, a representative of a reformed aristocratic Catholicism."[31] But this "aristocratic Catho-

[26] Cf. A. Combes, "Jacques Legrand, Alfred Coville et le 'Sophilogium'", in *Augustiniana*, VII (1957), pp. 327–48, 493–514; VIII (1958), pp. 129–63 (including letters addressed by Jean de Montreuil to Jacques Legrand, and extracts from the *Sophilogium*); cf. p. 163. See A. Coville, *De Jacobi Magni vita et operibus*, Paris, 1889.

[27] On humanism in France about 1500, see A. Renaudet, *Préréforme et humanisme à Paris pendant les premières guerres d'Italie* (*1494–1517*), 2nd ed. revised, Paris, 1953.

[28] See *ibid.*; also, among recent works, Renaudet's "Un problème historique: la pensée religieuse de Jacques Lefèvre d'Etaples", in *Medioevo e Rinascimento*, II, pp. 621–50.

[29] A. Renaudet, *Un problème historique . . .*, p. 650.

[30] F. Hermans, *op. cit.*, I, ch. IV.

[31] J. Bohatec, *Budé und Calvin*, Graz, 1950, p. 103. Cf. J. Plattard, *G. B. et les*

licism" is precisely the problem: is there a religion of the élite, distinct from that of the masses?

Certainly all the humanists of that time thought of themselves as an élite. The refinement of their culture isolated them from the masses: Horace's *Odi profanum vulgus* might have been their motto. The ideas that they represented, those which they spread and defended, were in no way those of Christians in general, at least not until the Reformation. The faithful, or the great majority of them, continued to live on another plane. Their *Credo* was intact, despite the errors and superstitions to which they were inclined. The republic of letters, of course, did not question the Christian faith as such. Most of its citizens were sincerely convinced, even then, that there was no real opposition between the traditional heritage of Christianity and the best teaching of pre-Christian antiquity. They acknowledged that truth is necessarily one, and that the humane learning could not really contradict dogma.[32]

These humanists had, in fact, as St Thomas Aquinas had, a profound faith in the unity of truth. Those who were now enthusiastically reading Plato, Virgil and Cicero were in line with the most illustrious doctors of the Church. The difference lay in the fact that they were so infatuated with the wisdom, philosophy and arts of antiquity, that inevitably those who came after them would question revelation itself. The effects of this attitude of mind were clearly felt when the day came for humanism to emerge from the closed world of men of letters and touch the masses. Then it would become apparent how much there was in the "religion of humanism", as it has sometimes been called, that was actually harmful to Christianity.

2. *Reformers and Sects*

The Reformation did not come into being of itself. It had been preceded by movements that were closely akin to it in spirit and even in dogmatic position. It must be remembered that in the twelfth and thirteenth centuries the Church had already been troubled by a ferment of heresy, especially in northern Italy and southern France. The movements had been characterized, generally speaking, by a violent anti-hierarchical and anti-sacramental reac-

---

origines de l'humanisme français, Paris, 1923. On the subsequent influence of Lefèvre d'Etaples and Budé, see vol. III of this *History of Christian Spirituality*.

[32] To chart the curve of the Church's reactions to the humanist Renaissance, see the survey by L. Bouyer in *Autour d'Erasme*. There may also be mentioned, as a general reference, J. Dagens, *Bibliographie chronologique de la littérature de spiritualité et de ses sources (1501–1610)*, Paris, 1952.

tion, which inevitably quarrelled with certain aspects of Christian dogma. The Waldensians, among other groups of this kind, certainly meant to remain Christians, but during the fifteenth century they were periodically in trouble with the Inquisition. In these survivors from the anti-Roman reactions of the Middle Ages the Reformers recognized their own precursors.[33] The Catharists constituted a much more radical movement; the dualistic doctrine that they professed was so opposed to fundamental dogmas like the unity and goodness of God that they cannot be considered Christians.

Similar tendencies produced the more or less heterodox bodies that appeared in Germany in the fourteenth to sixteenth centuries, for example the groups of "Friends of God", certain of which survived until the end of the Middle Ages.[34] A considerable number of little sects sprang up, more or less everywhere, showing the same indignation at the abuses in the Church: its wealth, and the vices of its ministers. Among them may be mentioned the "Brethren who have chosen poverty", *Fratres voluntarie pauperes*, and those Fraticelli who called themselves "Poor Apostles", *Pauperes apostoli*.[35] Often they truly aimed at a life of penance, austere and genuinely evangelical. It is sometimes difficult to distinguish them from confraternities, for example, in the case of a sect of Flagellants which arose in Germany and the Low Countries at the time of the Black Death (1347 to 1350), and which even adopted a rule.[36]

Other groups were plainly fantastic. A sect of Hussites, the Adamites, were said to imitate the garb of our first parents and to hold that all women should be in common; they were described by Aeneas Sylvius Piccolomini in his *History of Bohemia*.[37] Some "Barefooted Poor Men", who had risen up against the hierarchy and sacraments of the Church, attracted attention to themselves in the middle of the fifteenth century, in the neighbourhood of Heilbronn in the Rhineland. In Spain, in Flanders, and in Russia the same thing happened. France was not spared, either: at the beginning of the fifteenth century the priest Jean Langlois, the

[33] See the summary by R. Aubenas in *L'Église et la Renaissance*, XV, pp. 369–372.

[34] See, for example, R. Frauenfelder, "Ein Kreis von Gottesfreunden im spätmittelalterlichen Schaffhausen", in *Beiträge zur vaterländischen Geschichte . . . des Kantons Schaffhausen*, XIII (1936), pp. 77–85.

[35] Cf. L. Spätling, O.F.M., *De Apostolicis, pseudo-apostolis, apostolinis*, Munich, 1947, pp. 186–9.

[36] Cf. A. Coville, "Documents sur les Flagellants", in *Histoire littér. France*, XXXVII, 2 (1938), pp. 390–411.

[37] See E. Werner's contribution in T. Büttner and E. Werner, *Circumcellionen und Adamiten. Zwei Formen Mittelalterlicher Haeresie*, Berlin, 1959.

friar Jean Vitrier, and the "scholar" of the College de Bourgogne at Paris, Hémon de la Fosse, scandalized their contemporaries by their theories, which often attacked the doctrine of the Eucharist. Their cases were referred to the Sorbonne, and Langlois and Hémon ended their careers at the stake.

Some historians have accumulated numberless points of contact between the doctrines propagated by Meister Eckhart and those of the Reformers. Caution is required, however, before seeing Martin Luther (on the basis of resemblances that are often superficial) as a disciple of the Rhineland mystics.[38] The same may be said of the *Theologia Deutsch*, which may have influenced the Reformer; as has been seen, he published a version of it arranged according to his own ideas. But the work itself, in its original text, is certainly in the tradition of the Church.[39]

The *Devotio moderna* is a more likely precursor. This movement, a lay one in its beginnings, was anxious to reform the Church but without any intention of separating from it. Its originators and its great spiritual writers were unquestionably orthodox. Nevertheless, by the middle of the fifteenth century, there are signs among some of its theorists of a tendency that was soon to take so many upright men out of the Church. This was particularly true of Erasmus, who had been educated by the Brothers of the Common Life. Before him, another of their pupils, Wessel Gansfort (†1489), who was at the university of Heidelberg between 1456 and 1458 and took sides with the realists against the nominalists, emphasized the value of spiritual communion or *manducatio spiritualis*, though he did not deny the Real Presence. Besides this, his errors regarding the Church, the papacy, purgatory and indulgences won him the approval of the Reformers. He also left a small spiritual work, the *Ladder of Meditation*, "Scala meditationis", conceived according to the formal method of prayer, which at this time was being more and more elaborated.[40]

All these different phenomena—humanism, the sects, the *Devotio moderna*—together with what has been said in the preceding chapter about popular piety in the fifteenth century, help to explain, at least in part, the coming of the Reformation. It is abundantly clear, however, in spite of the views of certain historians, that the

[38] In this connection may be mentioned, among other works, H. Bornkamm, *Eckhart und Luther*, Stuttgart, 1936.

[39] Cf. W. Thimme, "Die 'Deutsche Theologie' und Luthers 'Freiheit eines Christenmenschen'", in *Zeitschr. Theol. Kirche*, XIII (1932), pp. 193–222.

[40] Ed. A. Hardenburg, Groningen, 1614; the *Farrago rerum theologicarum* had been published as early as 1522. Cf. M. van Rhijn, *Studien over Wessel Gansfort en zijn tijd*, Utrecht, 1933.

Reformation was not the necessary consequence of these phenomena.[41]

Among the premonitory signs of the Reformation there were some that came still closer to it than the movements which have just been discussed. First of all must be mentioned the agitation that arose in England in connection with Lollardy. The movement is explained, in large part, by the political and social situation in that country. Increasing unrest had ended in a revolt of the peasants in 1381; a year later, it produced a sect which the people called "Lollards" (probably meaning "hymn-singers"). But causes of a religious character also lay behind its origin. One has only to remember the corruption among bishops and in ecclesiastical courts; the simony of the benefice-hunting clergy; the non-residence of pastors; the legitimate grievances of the lower clergy; the superstitions; the abuse and exploitation of pilgrimages; the traffic in indulgences; the payments made for confession.[42] To these were added the antagonism between the secular clergy and the Mendicants, the isolation of countless monasteries that no longer had any appreciable influence over the lives of the people, and the political and judicial functions that were too often committed to the clergy. This dark picture was not confined to England, but a review of its various aspects helps to explain Wycliffe's reaction and certain demands of Lollardy.[43]

According to English historians, Wycliffe and Lollardy prepared the way for the emancipation of the Anglican Church, for the schism which was to take place a century and a half later.[44] Perhaps

[41] This was the view of J. Mackinnon, *The Origins of the Reformation*, London, 1939; cf. p. 431. The article by L. Febvre, "Une question mal posée. Les origines de la Réforme française et le problème général des causes de la Réforme", in *Rev. historique*, CLXI (1929), pp. 1–73, although it favours the Protestant point of view, is nevertheless worth reading; it was reprinted in *Au cœur religieux du XVI*[e] *siècle*, Paris, 1957.

[42] This practice had been very widespread for a long time, although at reasonable prices. Cf. G. Schreiber, "Liturgie und Abgabe. Busspraxis und Beichtgeld, an französischen Nieder-Kirchen des Hochmittelalters", in *Histor. Jahrbuch*, LXXVI (1957), pp. 1–14. On the survival of Lollardy at the beginning of the fifteenth century, and on the *Treatise on the Jubilee* (of St Thomas Becket, celebrated in 1420) as an "affirmation of orthodoxy against the Lollards, who disparaged the veneration of the saints and despised the power of the keys", see R. Foreville, *Le jubilé de saint Thomas Becket, du XIII*[e] *au XV*[e] *siècle (1220–1470). Etude et documents*, Paris, 1958; cf. p. 58.

[43] In this connection, see G. M. Trevelyan, *England in the Age of Wycliffe*, 4th ed., London, 1946, especially pp. 104–82. W. A. Pantin, *The English Church in the Fourteenth Century*, Cambridge, 1955, gives a picture that is not so exclusively confined to the negative aspects. Interesting details can be gleaned from F. A. Gasquet, O.S.B., *The Eve of the Reformation*, London, 1900.

[44] This is the view presented in K. B. McFarlane's popular work *John Wycliffe and the Beginnings of English Nonconformity*, London, 1952; also in H. M. Smith, *Pre-Reformation England*, London, 1938; and L. Sergeant, *J. W., Last of the Schoolmen and First of the English Reformers*, New York, 1893.

these authors tend to exaggerate the religious significance of the social ferment that was taking place at that period. The first revolts—that of the peasants, for example—demanded a greater measure of social and political justice, increased material well-being, the removal of the collectors of pontifical taxes, as much as and more than the reform of the Church.[45] Logically, it seems that John Wycliffe himself should have had troubles with secular authority, rather than that of the Church, but the contrary happened. From the time of his sojourn at Oxford in 1378, Wycliffe took a stand primarily against the Church.[46] As early as 1375, he was already writing in defence of the rights of the state against the papacy,[47] which brought him the favour of the king and prosecutions from the bishops. Finally Gregory X summoned him before his tribunal and condemned him. Wycliffe protested; still he was not excommunicated. His doctrines were censured by a synod held at Canterbury in 1382 and at the Council of Rome in 1412. They were categorically condemned at the Council of Constance on 4 May 1415, and then in the bulls *Inter cunctas* and *In eminentis* of 22 February 1418.[48] By order of the Council, his remains—he had died in 1384—were to be exhumed, burned and thrown into the river; this sentence was not carried out until 1428.

There was certainly enough in his doctrines to cause anxiety to the hierarchy. Among his boldest and most radical opinions are to be noted his denial of transubstantiation in the Eucharist; his rejection of the traditional notion of it as sacrament and sacrifice, of the sacerdotal character as distinct from that of the baptized, and finally of the power of order, the *opus operatum*; errors over absolution (it was better to confess to a devout layman than to a bad priest); his rejection of the Roman primacy, of the episcopate, and of indulgences. Such heresies were tantamount to an elimination of the sacral element from Christianity and a denial that the Church was composed of anyone besides devout members of the faithful —good Christians. Virtue, holiness and a state of grace became the only true criteria of belonging to the Church. This was the

[45] Without enlarging on this subject, R. R. Betts calls attention to it in *Correnti religiose nazionali ed ereticali della fine del secolo XIV alla meta del XV*, in *Relazioni . . . X Congresso Intern. Scienze Storiche*, III, pp. 485–513 (in English).

[46] For biographies of Wycliffe, see the works cited in the preceding notes. To these may be added H. B. Workmann, *J. W., a Study of the English Medieval Church*, 2 vols, Oxford, 1926, taking into consideration the corrections contributed by J. H. Dahmus in *The Prosecution of J. W.*, New Haven, 1952.

[47] *Opera omnia*, 36 vols, London, 1883 and following years; *Select English Works*, ed. T. Arnold, 3 vols, Oxford, 1870–1; *Summa de ente*, ed. S. H. Thomson, Oxford, 1930. On his translation of the Bible, see S. L. Fristedt, *The Wycliffe Bible*, I, Stockholm, 1953.

[48] The text of the 45 theses that were condemned is given in Denz., 581–625.

meaning of the thesis on the "Church of the predestinate". The juridical and sacral were replaced by the fervour of piety.

In putting forward such theses, Wycliffe was not arguing as a speculative theologian, but as a reformer. From them he drew some extreme conclusions regarding the "synagogue of Satan", as he called the Roman Church, and the "four sects" (he wrote a treatise entitled *De quatuor sectis novellis*), which were those of prelates, monks, canons and the other religious orders. These were distinct from the "sect of Christ", which was the true Church of charity; they were ruining its unity and playing Satan's game.

Wycliffe also attacked ecclesiastical ownership. God alone had *dominium* over material goods, and under him the temporal sovereign, if he was in God's grace.[49] The divine authority in the Church belonged to the Bible as read and interpreted in the Church, under the guidance of the Fathers, the early councils and theologians worthy of the name. Scriptural truth was warranted not by the Church as a juridical and sacramental body, but by living Christian experience, solidly anchored in tradition. It must be noted that Wycliffe's theology of Scripture read by the Church is not so indefensible as his conception of the Church itself.[50]

In defence of Wycliffe, it must be said that he came on the scene at a crucial period of social unrest in England, and his theories coincided, in many of their aspects, with the bitter laments over the Church and its leaders that were being raised at the same period by mystics who were entirely orthodox: one has only to think of St Catherine of Siena. Moreover, the reformer always led an austere life, and continually proclaimed the superiority of virginity over marriage; he may even be regarded as a sort of "ancestor of puritanism".[51] All this explains the personal enthusiasm of his fervent disciples.

Out of this movement there soon emerged a sort of confraternity, the Poor Priests. To the sacral and juridical priesthood of the Church they opposed their priesthood of the word. Their preaching, and the anticlerical tracts which they distributed among the people, encouraged the agitation which still goes by the name of Lollardy. Wycliffe's disciples, by force of circumstances, offered a religious justification—a label of uprightness—to men who sought, above all, greater social justice and a less corrupt political régime;

[49] Wycliffe's first two treatises, written in 1375, were *De dominio divino* and *De civili dominio*.

[50] Cf. his *De veritate sacrae scripturae*. The same might be said of John Huss's doctrine on scripture, in the *Inceptio* of his commentary on the Sentences. See P. de Vooght, O.S.B., *Les sources de la doctrine chrétienne d'après les théologiens du XIVe siècle et du début du XVe*, Bruges, 1954, pp. 168–200, 218–33.

[51] L. Cristiani, art. "Wyclif", in *Dict. théol. cath.*, XV, col. 3606.

and the result was that the movement to which Wycliffe had given his support moved, in some sense, beyond him.[52]

Despite the severe repression organized in 1388, Lollardy increased and soon took on the aspect of a genuine schism. The crisis was resolved, however, in 1407, when Convocation adopted thirteen rigorous "constitutions" aimed against the writings, doctrines and disciples of Wycliffe. By the time of the Protestant Reformation, Lollardy had been practically forgotten. It had, however, predisposed certain minds in England to reject the authority of the Roman see, to stigmatize the temporal power of the Church, and to exalt the authority of the king and Parliament even in religious matters. Furthermore, England had become accustomed to tolerating various little sects, which survived throughout the whole of the fifteenth century, professing doctrines similar to those of Lollardy.[53] But the country as a whole, about 1500, was Catholic and intended to remain subject to the Holy See.

A few weeks after the Council of Constance had condemned Wycliffe's forty-five propositions, it took the same action with regard to thirty others from the works of the Czech John Hus (*c.* 1370–1415).[54] In this connection the relations existing between Bohemia and England at the end of the fourteenth century must certainly not be overlooked. The two countries were united by a common stream of ideas, and this bond seems to have arisen out of the marriage of Richard II of England with Anne of Bohemia, sister of King Wenceslas IV, in 1382. There are references to Wycliffe's first writings being read in Bohemia in the very year of the wedding, and Czechs were studying at Oxford. Hus did not, however, derive his inspiration from Wycliffe alone; a strong movement for reform existed in Bohemia even before the Englishman's work was known there. But Hus, as he read Wycliffe's writings, found in them the same theses that were being put forward by the Czech reformers.[55] He was, however, on his guard against those statements of the English reformer that were definitely heretical. Unquestionably he intended to remain orthodox, but in the suppression of heresy there was no distinction made between him and Wycliffe. After the condemnation of 1415, in fact, Martin V drew up in 1418 a list of 39 articles on which accused persons should be interrogated if they were suspected of holding the doctrines of Wycliffe or Hus[56]; thus the two names

[52] Cf. H. M. Smith, "Lollardy", in *Church Quarterly Rev.*, CXIX (1935), pp. 30–60.

[53] See P. Janelle, *L'Angleterre catholique à la veille du schisme*, Paris, 1935, pp. 40–8.

[54] Denz., 627–56.

[55] Cf. J. Loserth, *Huss und Wiclif. Zur Genesis der Hussitischen Lehre*, 2nd ed., Munich–Berlin, 1925 (a superficial treatment).

[56] The bull *Inter cunctas* of 22 February, 1418; Denz., 657–89.

appear closely coupled. Hus, however, by then had already been condemned at Constance, in default of Wycliffe, and the Czech reformer died at the stake on the very day that the sentence was pronounced, 6 July 1415, without having abjured his doctrines.[57] An account of his death, both moving and horrifying, is given in some letters which purport to be by the Florentine Poggio, and in a report by Mladenowic. Another letter of Poggio's (an authentic one) describes the death of Hus's friend Jerome of Prague, who, after having escaped death a first time, was re-arrested and executed on 30 May 1416.[58]

Through the fiery preaching of Hus, Wycliffe's reforming doctrines reached the masses. The Czech and Russian historians (since 1948 particularly) have been right, in one sense, in seeing the Hussite crisis as an interesting chapter in the history of class warfare. But in stressing that aspect of the matter they fail to consider the limited part played by social factors in Hus's life and writings. His express intention, which he still declared at the stake, had been to "wrest men away from sin", priests and monks above all. That intention was, without question, pure and sincere, but no service was done to it by certain doctrinal errors and especially by psychological mistakes such as denouncing the vices of the clergy from the pulpit.[59]

His doctrines were closely akin to those of Wycliffe, but he put forward a milder and on the whole orthodox version of all of them except those concerning the Church of the predestinate and the primacy of the Pope—for example, those concerned with the Real Presence, absolution and the power of order. When he dealt with the Church, he taught, as Wycliffe did, that it was the assembly

[57] The sources were collected by F. Palacky, *Documenta Mag. Joh. Hussii vitam, doctrinam, causam illustrantia*, Prague, 1869; this includes Mladenowic's account of the trial and death of Huss. There are biographies by M. Vischer, *J. H. Sein Leben und seine Zeit*, 2 vols, Frankfurt, 1940 (reissued as *J. H. Aufruhr wider Papst und Reich*, Frankfurt, 1955); K. Roubiczek, *Warrior of God. The Life and Death of J. H.*, London, 1947 (written for the edification of Protestants); C. H. Kurz, *J. H. Ein Vorkämpfer der Reformation*, Giessen, 1956; P. de Vooght, O.S.B., *L'hérésie de J. H.*, Louvain, 1960.

[58] Cf. *Todesgeschichte des J. H. und des Hieronymus von Prag, geschildert in Sendbriefen des Poggius Florentinus*, Constance, 1957. It is safer to rely on Mladenowic's account (see note 57). For the case against the authenticity of the Poggio letters, see R. G. Salomon, "Poggio Bracciolini and Johannes Hus", in *Journal of the Warburg and Courtauld Institutes*, XIX (1956), pp. 174–7.

[59] For a recent bibliography on the Hussite movement, and an opinion on the interpretation of it, see R. R. Betts, *loc. cit.* See also P. de Vooght, O.S.B., "Actualité de Jean Huss", in *Istina* (1959), pp. 83–92. The works of Hus were edited by V. Flajšhans, 3 vols, Prague, 1903–8. A new edition in 25 volumes has been announced by the Academy of Sciences of Prague. There are many partial editions, especially since 1947. The *De Ecclesia*, particularly, has been re-edited by S. H. Thomson, Cambridge, 1956.

of the predestinate alone—which is true provided one considers only its eschatological end. It does seem that Hus, unlike Wycliffe, realized this: he does not deny the visible terrestrial Church; he even tries in an obscure sort of way to reconcile the fact with Wycliffe's thesis.

As for authority in the Church, according to Hus it was, above all, a question of fact; moreover, it was bound up with grace. A bishop who habitually lives an evil life is not a true bishop.[60] Probably Hus was prepared for him to retain his status as a bishop and all his power, and for the faithful to obey him provided he commanded nothing intrinsically wrong. But the "true" pastor was to be recognized by his manner of life as much as by his canonical credentials. The ambiguity was clear, and as may be supposed it called into question a good many sordid interests.[61] Christ, he went on to assert, is the one supreme head of the Church; what is meant by a pope whose tiara is contested by one or two antipopes?

In the body of doctrine represented by the thirty articles condemned at Constance, one thesis at least certainly deserves to be called heretical and is not susceptible of any orthodox interpretation. This was the ninth: "The papal dignity comes from the emperor, and its termination, like its institution, is in the emperor's power." This was to lay down as a principle that the emperor was superior to the pope; it was to call in question the pope's supremacy. But in defence of Hus, it is permissible to wonder what his judges—the fathers of the Council assembled at Constance by the antipope John XXIII—thought about this point. The matter was not as clear at that time as it is for Catholics today. Wycliffe's errors on transubstantiation, on which Hus had also been questioned, do not appear in the thirty articles. In one sense it is true to say that Hus was condemned for the errors of many other agitators, and especially for those of Wycliffe.[62]

The execution of Hus did not put an end to the admiration in which he was held. The "Bohemian Brethren" survived throughout the whole fifteenth century and down to modern times.[63] Among

[60] Proposition 30; Denz., 656. Cf. P. de Vooght, O.S.B., "La notion wyclifienne de l'épiscopat dans l'interprétation de Jean Huss", in *Irénikon*, XXVIII (1955), pp. 290–300.

[61] Cf. P. de Vooght, O.S.B., "Quel est le sens de la 30e proposition de Huss: 'Nullus est episcopus dum est in peccato mortali' condamnée par le concile de Constance?", in *L'Eglise et les Eglises*, II, Chevetogne, 1955, pp. 241–61.

[62] See P. de Vooght, O.S.B., *L'hérésie de J. H.*, Louvain, 1960, ch. XII.

[63] Cf. J. Macek, *Die Hussitische revolutionäre Bewegung*, Berlin, 1958; P. Brock, *The Political and Social Doctrines of the Unity of Czech Brethren in the Fifteenth and Early Sixteenth Centuries*, La Haye, 1957; J. T. Müller, *Geschichte der Böhmischen Brüder*, 32 vols, Herrnhut, 1922–31; V.-L. Tapié, *Une Eglise tchèque au XVe siècle: l'unité des frères*, Paris, 1934 (a popular treatment).

the influences that affected them can be distinguished those of the Waldensians, the Picards,[64] the Taborites, and the Utraquists whose practice it was to communicate under both kinds. A leader came forward for them in the person of Peter Chelčicky.[65] As time went on, they were more and more isolated by persecutions, by wars, by intestine divisions and by their own doctrinal development. In 1467, they broke completely with the Church and set up an autonomous clergy.

For them, as for Chelčicky himself, scripture was the basis of social teaching. All men had a right to justice and equality. Society must take its law from the gospels, and all the institutions of the state must be progressively replaced by Christian charity. Social dignities and functions must be left to pagans; Christians must reject them, for their exercise is necessarily bound up with violence. The just society was composed of Christians living in accordance with the precepts of the Gospel, as did those of the primitive Church. Unhappily this ideal had been ruined by the *Donatio* of Constantine and the official recognition of the Church by the state. But the Bohemian Brethren had every intention of reviving it.

Chelčicky, an intransigent spirit, did not hesitate to oppose his masters Wycliffe and Hus when, in his view, they deviated from the Gospel. They, especially Wycliffe, had confidence in the providential role of the civil power—providential, because the civil authorities could constrain the Church to reform itself. The Bohemian Brethren on the contrary, showed the greatest distrust of the civil power. It could hardly have been otherwise, considering how they had been persecuted and had been the victims of fratricidal wars.[66]

It has been pointed out[67] that this movement was identified with the national consciouness of Bohemia in opposition to the Empire. None of the earlier heretical movements had that aspect. But the illogicality of the Bohemian Brethren is obvious: on the one hand, their only programme consisted in a return to the Gospel; on the other they were yielding to the pressure of a premature nationalism which, though it may be healthy enough if kept within proper limits, becomes quite opposed to the Gospel when it is carried to extremes. They were right in denouncing those of their opponents who were moved, as champions of orthodoxy, not so much by zeal

[64] Cf. F. M. Bartos, "Picards et 'Pikarti'", in *Bull. Soc. Hist. Protest. franç.*, LXXX (1931), pp. 465–85; LXXXI (1932), pp. 8–28.

[65] In connection with Chelčicky, see especially P. Brock, *op. cit.* For a bibliography, see E. Petru, *Soupis dila Petra Chelčického a literatury e něm*, Prague, 1957.

[66] Cf. R. R. Betts, "Some Political Ideas of the Early Czech Reformers", in *Slavonic and East European Review*, XXXI (1952–3), pp. 21–35.

[67] R. R. Betts, *Correnti religiosi* . . ., p. 497.

for doctrinal and moral purity or for the peace of society as by a wish to further their own interests, power and positions. In the Bohemian crisis, many leaders of the Church, as well as emperors and kings, were only too vulnerable to such charges.

This political aspect of the problem had changed very little at the beginning of the sixteenth century. The only difference was that in the events of that century it took on a much wider significance. The whole of Germany was involved, and its princes saw in the Reformation a convenient way to free themselves from the sovereignty of the emperor and enrich themselves from the spoils of the Church. At the same time, England gradually became convinced that the Pope and the Spanish Hapsburgs were plotting her ruin. In France the obsession with encirclement by the Hapsburgs came near to being a real psychosis. The Reformation successfully exploited these national sensibilities.

Another point brought out by the Bohemian crisis is a new disruption of Christendom. It has been seen what divisive elements were introduced into the Church by the doctrinal and spiritual crises of the fourteenth century and by humanism in the fifteenth. All that was lacking to complete this gloomy picture was political divisions. Henceforward Christian unity was threatened both in the doctrinal sphere and in that of the political unity of western Europe. The first war of religion had taken place. Others were to follow, in which differences of creed would be mixed up with the claims of nationalism.

A return to the past seems to be a peril to Christendom and its unity: the humanists went back to antiquity, and their "religion" bore the seeds of a paganism which was no less real for being unavowed. The *Devotio moderna* also turned to the past, to the Gospel, and to the simplicity of love. It was as distrustful of speculative mysticism as of sterile theology. But its spirituality isolated men's faith from their spiritual experience. The reformers of the fifteenth century wanted to re-establish the evangelical purity of the early Church, and there they were right. But their proceedings were so provocative that the Church, with the help of the civil authorities, persecuted or extinguished them; or else, as in Bohemia, their evangelical teaching, their criticism of the Church and of the authorities, came just at the right time to support social and political demands that could not be extinguished.

3. Catholic Efforts for Reform

In the fifteenth century, then, Christendom was threatened on three fronts: thought, spirituality, and social and national life.

This threefold danger was the more grave in that most of the faithful were poorly equipped to meet the new situation, and before long to confront heresy. Their spirituality was pessimistic, superstitious, and "devotional"; their lives only too often at variance with the Gospel, and even openly immoral; their theology decadent. All these factors were to weaken and hold back the work of the Counter-Reformation.

It may be doubted whether the stake was any more efficacious. The execution of Hus at Constance was only one episode in a crisis which recurs throughout the fifteenth century. That of Savonarola at Florence, at the end of the century, did not prevent the papacy from sinking into decadence even more shameful than the scandalous one that had been so harshly denounced by the Dominican. Moreover, the significance of such executions may well be questioned when one recalls that, between that of Constance and that of Florence, there was one at Rouen: Joan too had gone to the stake for the crime of heresy. Yet she had not, like Hus and Savonarola, stirred up the masses against the hierarchy of the Church. She had only one idea, and that a political one. It was the real reason for her execution, and the process of rehabilitation did at least this much good, that it cleared her memory of any suspicion of heresy. It was otherwise with John Hus. He had aroused the whole of Bohemia with his preaching, demanding the reform of the Church. His mistake lay in accepting too undiscerningly the suspect doctrines of Wycliffe. Such contrasts come readily to mind. They show, first, that the death penalty, exacted ostensibly for the crime of heresy, could serve as an instrument for grievances of quite another order; secondly, they make it clear that neither the stake at Constance nor that at Florence succeeded in stifling voices that were demanding the reform of the Church, any more than they succeeded in arresting its decadence.[68]

It would be a mistake, however, to suppose that the Church had no other remedy to apply to this progressive erosion of its unity and its power. It has already been seen that Christian piety, from the fourteenth century to the sixteenth, contained many hopeful tokens of what was to come. One of the most efficacious movements toward Catholic reform was the *Devotio moderna*. One may deplore the fact that it opened the way to a piety that was deliberately undogmatic, but those who took it up had not the slightest intention of rejecting the traditional Christian dogmas, of choosing between them, or of substituting others for them. Certain

[68] Cf. R. Aubenas, "L'Eglise et la Renaissance", in *Histoire de l'Eglise*, XV (Fliche–Martin), Paris, 1951, pp. 280–91, 300–1, 306–11.

historians have seen in it, not without reason, a preparation for the work of the Council of Trent.[69]

There was also the activity of the great councils of the fifteenth century—Constance, Basle and Florence. There is no need to sketch their history here; the point to remember is simply that the principle of reform was put forward in trenchant terms. Then, the great preachers of penance did much to purify the practice of religion and Christian morality. Among them were St Bernardino of Siena, St John Capistran, St Vincent Ferrer and St Antoninus of Florence. In addition there were several popes whose sincere desire to reform the Church must be recognized: Eugene IV; Nicholas V who was assisted by Nicholas of Cusa; later, the humanist Pius II, with Dominic de' Domenici; and finally Paul II.[70]

New religious Orders were created, sometimes with the express aim of reforming the clergy; for example, the Orders of regular clerks founded by St Gaetano of Thiene (†1547) and St Antony Mary Zaccaria (†1539). Their influence was far from negligible: the Theatines gave the Church more than two hundred bishops. It was also at this period that the Franciscan trunk put forth a new branch—the Capuchins, founded by Matthew of Bascio in 1528.[71] The old Orders took measures to reform themselves and adopted the new forms of spirituality. The Benedictines, for example, united among themselves and adopted more sharply defined forms of organization in order to react against a spiritual decadence. One result was the creation of the first Benedictine congregations (in the modern sense of the word)—those of St Justina of Padua, of Valladolid and of Bursfeld.

At the same time, a clearer and purer conception of the pastoral role of a bishop was developing. In the Middle Ages the bishop was only too frequently a feudal lord. Now it became clear to many that he would have to become once again a father and shepherd of his people. A great forerunner of this development was Claude de Seyssel (1450–1520), who was bishop of Marseilles and later archbishop of Turin. He wrote a *Treatise on the Threefold State of the Wayfarer*[72] which was truly a "monument of the pastoral tradition". It proclaims the duties of the bishop and denounces the

[69] See, for example, C. Gutiérrez, S.J., "Sentido y valoración del Concilio tridentino", in *El Concilio de Trento*, Madrid, 1945, pp. 363–95.

[70] Cf. B. Llorca, S.J., "Antecedentes de la reforma tridentina. Conatos de reforma de la Iglesia anteriores a Trento", in *Estudios eclesiasticos*, XX (1946), pp. 9–32.

[71] Cf., among others, Melchiorre da Pobladura, *Historia generalis Ord. Fr. Min. Capucc.*, 4 vols, Rome, 1947–50.

[72] *Tractatus de triplici statu viatoris*, Paris–Turin, 1520. On Claude de Seyssel, see P. Broutin, S.J., *L'évêque dans la tradition pastorale du XVIe siècle*, Brussels, 1953, ch. II (includes complete bibliographical information).

abuses that can creep into the exercise of his charge. "Bishops are the leaders of the people; they are the vicars of the true leader, Christ." As such, they must preach, by word and by example, and even bear the cross. Later, in 1536, Gasparo Contarini, who was to prepare the way for the work of the Council of Trent, wrote a treatise *On the Duty of the Bishop*.[73] In it (it was written when he was still a layman) he called upon prelates to cultivate theological rather than humane learning. Matteo Giberti (†1543), bishop of Verona and a model pastor, renounced all the benefices he held in Rome and after his appointment betook himself as soon as possible to his episcopal city.[74] Still others—and those not the least important—by their actions prepared the way for the Tridentine decrees on residence (session VI) and the choice of bishops (sessions XXII and XXIV). Before long, the pastoral ideal was to be incarnate in the lives of Charles Borromeo and Robert Bellarmine. Manuals for bishops, too, would appear, such as the "mirrors for bishops"[75] and the *Stimulus pastorum* by Bartholomew of the Martyrs.[76]

Finally, more and more efforts were made to give the secular clergy a better theological training. Universities like those of Cologne and Louvain contributed a great deal to this movement, as did the schools conducted by the canons of Windesheim.[77] In France, Spain and Portugal, steps in the direction of reform were undertaken by synods, by legations and publications.[78] The role played by the Charterhouse of St Barbara at Cologne has already been described; it was very far from negligible.[79] Its prior Gerard Kalckbrenner (†1566) encouraged, by every possible means, the activity of the Jesuits at Cologne and in the whole of Germany.[80]

On the whole, "reformation met with very strong resistance, which was sometimes encouraged by public opinion".[81] This is not surprising, when one remembers the factors that frustrated even the best efforts. To these may be added the clumsiness of some of the Reformers. Hus and Savonarola were extreme cases of this; their intemperate language and their lack of psychological acumen could only end by inspiring distrust, even in the most faithful servants of

[73] *De officio episcopi*, in his *Opera*, pp. 401–31, Paris, 1571, or Venice, 1589. Cf. Broutin, *op. cit.*, ch. III.

[74] Cf. Broutin, *op. cit.*, ch. IV. [75] *Ibid.*, chs V–XI.

[76] Rome, 1564; Paris, 1596. Cf. Broutin, *op. cit.*, ch. VII.

[77] See, for example, P. Polman, O.F.M., "De wetenschappelijke opleiding van den noord-nederlandschen clerus secularis in de XVIe eeuw", in *Ons geest. Erf*, VIII (1934), pp. 398–417.

[78] R. Aubenas, *loc. cit.*, pp. 291–311.

[79] See *supra*, pp. 461 *et seq.*

[80] See J. B. Kettenmeyer, S.J., "Aufzeichnungen der Kölner Kartänserpriors Kalckbrenner über den sel. Peter Faber", in *Arch. histor. Soc. Jesu*, VII (1939), pp. 86–102.

[81] R. Aubenas, *loc. cit.*, pp. 298–9.

the Church. If such men did not succeed in avoiding blunders, it was very probable that others, less known or anonymous, would for similar reasons be ineffective in their action upon souls.

In this context, the crucial problem was that of the real Church. Where was it? And in the Church, where lay the legitimate and supreme authority? Certain of the theses of John Hus's treatise *On the Church* had been censured, but as other authors developed the subject on sounder lines, its importance became increasingly clear. As early as the beginning of the fourteenth century (1302) the Augustinian James of Viterbo had written a treatise *On Christian Government*.[82] Much later, there appeared a *Treatise on the Church* by the Dominican John of Ragusa (†1443)[83]; then, a *Summa on the Church* by the Dominican Cardinal Torquemada (†1468).[84] John of Ragusa was moved to write his treatise by the wish to answer the false ecclesiology of the Hussites and of the separated Eastern Christians. He sought chiefly to determine the marks of the true Church, and ended with those that had been laid down by St Augustine: purity of doctrine, universal agreement, miracles, charity, stability in time, continuity in the succession of bishops and popes, and catholicity. Torquemada was more detached from the preoccupations of his time. His ecclesiology is in the tradition of the ancient theologians, who did not hesitate to include in the economy of the Church the whole of dogma, the whole Christian view of the world and of life.[85]

Despite his preoccupation with apologetics, John of Ragusa was not concerned with defending the faith as such. That was not in danger in Christendom, in spite of the growing ascendancy of humanism. It was more a matter of convincing men who were disturbed and bewildered by visible scandals, that this Church which appeared only too human was in truth the *congregatio fidelium*. It was the mystical body of Christ; the Holy Spirit was its soul, but it was governed by men. It was not made up of the elect only: cockle was mingled with the good grain.

[82] *De regimine christiano*, ed. H. X. Arquillière, *Le plus ancien traité de l'Église*, Paris, 1926.

[83] Unpublished. Cf. G. Thils, "Le 'Tractatus de Ecclesia' de J. de R.", in *Angelicum*, XVII (1940), pp. 219–44.

[84] Cologne, 1480; Rome, 1489; etc. Cf. J. S. Stockmann, *J. de T., O.P., vita eiusque doctrina de corpore Christi mystico*, Haarlem, 1951; K. Binder, *Wesen und Eigenschaften der Kirche bei Kardinal J. de T., O.P.*, Innsbruck, 1955; P. Theeuws, "Jean de Terrecremata. Les relations entre l'Eglise et le pouvoir civil d'après un théologien du XVe siècle", in *L'organisation corporative du moyen âge à la fin de l'Ancien Régime*, Louvain, 1943, pp. 135–78; P. Massi, *Magisterio infallibile del papa nella teologia di G. d. T.*, Turin, 1957.

[85] On definitions of the Church from the thirteenth century to the present day, see J. C. Fenton, "Scholastic Definitions of the Catholic Church", in *American Eccles. Rev.*, CXI (1944), pp. 59–69, 131–45, 212–28.

One of the principal grievances expressed against the Mendicants was precisely that they were too much immersed in the things of this world. In the fourteenth and fifteenth centuries, for example, there were violent controversies over the poverty of religious. The seculars accused the regulars of keeping up a mere façade of poverty, and the old sarcasms of William of St Amour were revived.

The Friars Minor put up a defence and published a number of treatises on the absolute poverty of Christ and his apostles.[86] They did this with some caution; the thesis seemed to them to be simply more probable than the opposite one. The master-general of the Dominicans, Hervé Nedellec (†1323), on his side, replied to a pontifical consultation in 1322 or 1333 by a treatise *On the Poverty of Christ and the Apostles*. In this work he set forth the Thomist thesis that poverty is only a means to perfection. Use and possession are inseparable, especially as regards perishable goods. In any case, Jesus and the apostles did possess goods, exactly like other men, and not only for "use".[87] Later there was the famous quarrel between the archbishop of Armagh, Richard FitzRalph (†1360), and the Friars Minor.[88] FitzRalph went so far as to deliver a discourse against the ideal of poverty in the consistory of 8 November 1357. But in the same consistory a Dominican, Bartholomew of Bolsenheim, defended the Mendicants against FitzRalph's accusations.[89] This however did not put an end to the prejudices against them: Chaucer, a little before 1400, was still sharply critical of the regulars of his time,[90] and brought up again the Lollards' grievances against them.[91]

[86] For example, the *De paupertate Christi* by the Franciscan cardinal Bertrand de la Tour; cf. P. Gauchat, O.M.Conv., *Cardinal Bertrand de Turre, Ord. Min. His Participation in the theorical Controversy concerning the Poverty of Christ and the Apostles under Pope John XXII*, Rome, 1930.

[87] Ed. J. G. Sikes, "Hervaeus Natalis: De paupertate Christi et apostolorum", in *Arch. hist. doctr. litt. moyen âge*, XI (1937–8), pp. 209–97.

[88] Cf. L. L. Hammerich, *The Beginning of the Strife between R. F. and the Mendicants. With an Edition of his Autobiographical Prayer and his Proposition "Unusquisque"*, Copenhagen, 1938. Several studies on this same subject by A. Gwynn, S.J., have appeared in *Studies* from vol. XXIII (1933) to vol. XXVI (1937).

[89] Cf. G. Meersseman, O.P., "La défense des Ordres mendiants contre Richard FitzRalph par Barthélémy de Bolsenheim (1357)", in *Arch. Fratr. Praedic.*, V (1935), pp. 124–73. See J. Leclercq, O.S.B., *L'idée de la royauté du Christ au moyen âge*, Paris, 1959, ch. VI.

[90] See A. Williams, "Chaucer and the Friars", in *Speculum*, XXVIII (1953), pp. 499–513; by the same, "Two notes on Chaucer's Friars", in *Modern Philology*, LIV (1956–7), pp. 117–20.

[91] Cf. J. L. Copeland, "The Relations between the Secular Clergy and the Mendicant Friars in England during the Century after the Issue of the Bull 'Super cathedram' (1300)", in *Bull. Institute of Historical Research*, XVI (1938–9), pp. 34–5 (abstract of a doctoral dissertation). Useful information is given in A. Gwynn, S.J., *The English Friars in the Time of Wyclif*, Oxford, 1940.

The source of the conflict was not merely the avarice of the secular clergy and the greed or vanity of the Mendicants; the latter were also criticized for the exaggerated spiritual privileges which they had extorted from the Holy See[92] and from the Council of Basle.[93] The rivalry was so bitter that in 1414 the rector of the University of Vienna, Nicholas of Dinkelsbühl, denounced proprietorship on the part of religious, basing himself on the Bible and the Fathers.[94] And in 1464, the Carmelite Henry Parker had only to deliver a sermon on poverty in London to arouse passionate controversy.[95]

The significance of this dispute, which had then been going on for two centuries, is clear enough. The Mendicants, even when their observance was mitigated, were a living reproach to many seculars, despite the bitter dissensions by which they were divided. Their principal grievance against the secular hierarchy at all levels—which was also the grievance of the mass of the faithful—was not so much their loose living as their greed. The great temptation was money. It was wresting from Christ souls which had been consecrated to him. The reform of the Church needed to begin by a reform of the clergy with regard to money.

4. The Beginnings of the Spain of the Mystics and the Apostles

In the sixteenth century, at the dawn of the modern age, European spirituality looked towards Spain, where Ignatius of Loyola, Teresa of Avila and John of the Cross shone with unparalleled brilliance. Their influence in the Church has lasted down to our own times. That golden age, as Spanish historians like to call it, did not burst unheralded upon Christendom; in the spiritual domain there had been a preparation for it.

The political and material prosperity of the Iberian Peninsula may be judged by certain facts on which it is hardly necessary to dwell. The "reconquest" of the country from the Moors and the

[92] Cf. H. Lippens, O.F.M., "Le droit nouveau des Mendiants en conflit avec le droit coutumier du clergé séculier du concile de Vienne à celui de Trente", in *Arch. francisc. histor.*, XLVII (1954), pp. 241–92; L. Hödl, "Zum Streit um die Bussprivilegien der Medikantenorden in Wien im 14. und beginnenden 15. Jahrhundert", in *Zeitschr. Kath. Theol.*, LXXIX (1957), pp. 170–89.

[93] The documents have been assembled, and a historical survey given, by G. Meerssseman, O.P., in *Giovanni di Montenero, O.P., difensore dei Mendicanti. Studi e documenti sui concili di Basilea e di Firenze*, Rome, 1938.

[94] Cf. H. Menhardt, "Nikolaus von Dinkelsbühls deutsche Predigt vom Eigentum im Kloster", in *Zeitschr. f. deutsche Philologie*, LXXIII (1954), pp. 1–39, 268–91, LXXIV (1955), pp. 36–41.

[95] Cf. F. R. H. du Boulay, "The Quarrel between the Carmelite Friars and the Secular Clergy of London, 1464–1468", in *Journal Eccles. History*, VI (1955), pp. 156–74.

fall of Granada in 1492 greatly promoted peace and material prosperity. The marriage of Ferdinand and Isabella in 1469 united the whole of Spain under one rule, and before long a dynastic alliance connected it with the Low Countries, Italy, the Empire and Bohemia. Maritime expeditions, from 1492 onwards, led to the discovery and conquest of the New World, which was to be the source of incalculable riches.

In the rapid development of its intellectual life, Spain could rival France and Italy. The universities could boast of celebrated masters. That of Salamanca, which had existed since 1242, had 8,000 students in the sixteenth century, divided into twenty-five colleges and fifty religious communities. New universities were being founded. That of Alcala was established between 1498 and 1510 by Cardinal Ximenez de Cisneros; that of Coimbra, in the wake of Lisbon, in 1537. As early as the fifteenth century, humane studies were introduced into the intellectual centres. The religious Orders did not hold aloof from this movement: Franciscans, Dominicans and Carmelites vied with one another in theological and humane learning. Among the Dominican theologians, the greatest was Francisco de Vitoria (1492 or 1493–1546), who taught at the University of Salamanca.[96] Other illustrious members of the Order were Dominic de Soto (1494–1560) and Melchior Cano (1509–60).

In their religious life, the people of Spain presented violent contrasts. On the one hand, much during the last centuries of the Middle Ages exemplified its reality and even its vigour. Apart from the celebrated pilgrimage to St James of Compostela and the frequent and touching manifestations of popular devotion to the Blessed Virgin, it may be remembered that Spain was the native land of St Dominic; moreover, all the religious Orders, including the contemplatives like the Cistercians and Carthusians, had numerous monasteries there. The foundation of the military Orders is explained by the proximity of the Moors. The ransoming of captives was the special mission of the Mercedarians[97] and Trinitarians.[98] The Mendicants, too, were firmly established in the peninsula; one of the most illustrious of their tertiaries was Ramon Lull, who is still the pride of Spain and especially of Catalonia.

[96] Among the works on Francisco de Vitoria, there may be mentioned R. Gonzalez, *F. de V. Estudio bibliografico*, Buenos Aires, 1946; a summary of this theological and juridical ideas by J. Chevalier, in *Histoire de la pensée*, II, *La pensée chrétienne*, Paris, 1956, pp. 655–65; V. Beltrán de Heredia, O.P., *F. da V.*, Barcelona, 1939.

[97] In connection with them, see José-Maria de la Cruz Moliner, O.C.D., "Escuelas españoles de espiritualidad", in *El monte Carmelo*, LXV (1957), pp. 28–41.

[98] Cf. Antonlno Deil'Assunta, *Les origines de l'Ordre de la S. T.*, Rome, 1925.

Finally, it should be added that the Bible was translated into Spanish as early as 1252, by order of Alfonso X.

There was also a dark side to the picture. In Spain, as elsewhere, many of the faithful were discouraged by the spectacle of the papacy at Avignon and of the Great Schism. The general mediocrity of the clergy, there as elsewhere, was not calculated to raise their spirits. The Franciscan Alvara Pelayo (*c.* 1350) was already denouncing this situation in the fourteenth century, his *Lament upon the Church*[99] echoing similar writings north of the Pyrenees. Later, another Franciscan, who became archbishop of Toledo and primate of Spain, Ximenez de Cisneros (1436–1517), undertook a work of reform first within his own Order and then in his own ecclesiastical domains.[100] The tribunals of the Inquisition were established in Spain by a bull of 1 November 1478 in the reign of Ferdinand and Isabella, as a permanent institution endowed with extensive powers in everything concerning the faith. A Dominican of lamentable fame, Thomas de Torquemada (†1498), was named Grand Inquisitor.

The justification for this measure was the exasperation provoked among the Christians by the Jews. Unscrupulous Jewish usurers and bankers often feigned conversion. But even converted Jews or "*maranos*" were compelled to leave Spain in 1492, the same year in which the Moors of Granada were finally overcome. The tribunals of the Inquisition, however, continued to prosecute offences against the faith; they turned against the Moors who had remained in Spain after the conquest feigning conversion to Christianity—the "Moriscos", as they were called. After that, they attacked the *Alumbrados*, or "*illuminati*", who had appeared in Toledo by 1512 and soon spread throughout all Spain. They showed marked resemblance to the Flemish and Rhineland mystics, and readily accepted the new ideas of Erasmus (whose writings were translated into Spanish at an early date) and of the Reformers.[101] Finally the

[99] There have been many editions: Lyons, 1517, etc. Cf. N. Jung, *Un franciscain théologien du pouvoir pontifical au XIVe siècle*, Paris, 1931.

[100] Cf. L. Fernandez de Retana, *Fray X. de C.*, Madrid, 1952; K. Hefele, *Der Kardinal X. und die Kirchlichen Zustände Spaniens am Ende des 15. und Aufang des 16. Jahrhunderts*, 2nd ed., Tübingen, 1851.

[101] Cf. B. Llorca, S.J., *Die Spanische Inquisition und die "Alumbrados"*, Berlin–Bonn, 1934. On all the heterodox movements in Spain, see the monumental work of M. Menendez Pelayo, *Historia de los heterodoxos españoles*, 8 vols, Santander, 1946–8; especially vol. II, epilogue (on the Jews and Moslems); vol. III (Erasmians and Protestants); and vol. IV, Book V (Alumbrados, and converted Jews and Moors). There is a newer edition (Bibliot. Autores Cristianos), two volumes of which appeared in 1956 (Madrid). To these may be added the book to which one must so often refer for the history of religion in Spain in the sixteenth century: M. Bataillon, *Erasme et l'Espagne. Recherches sur l'histoire spirituelle du XVIe siècle*, Paris, 1937; cf. ch. IV. There is a Spanish translation, revised by the author, in two volumes (Mexico–Buenos Aires, 1950).

Inquisition assailed the avowed "Erasmians". One of the best-known of these was Jean de Valdes (†1541), author of a *Dialogue of Christian Doctrine*, published in 1529, and of another dialogue entitled *The Christian Alphabet*; he was condemned by the Inquisition in 1559.[102] Its tribunals were not finally abolished until the beginning of the nineteenth century.[103]

It is difficult for men of the twentieth century to understand this fierce and intolerant aspect of Spanish religion. The tortures and *autos-da-fé* of the Inquisition can be explained in part by the mentality of the time; any division within Christendom endangered collective security. One must also remember the state of almost constant tension of spirit in which Spaniards had lived during the eight centuries of the Moorish occupation. The Spanish character also played its part. It is idealistic in the extreme, and in the sixteenth century Spaniards were convinced of the superiority of their own country and of its mission in the Church and in the world. It also includes common sense, which balances the extravagances of idealism; Sancho Panza complements Don Quixote in reality as well as in Cervantes' immortal work. But this aspect of the Spanish character was eclipsed at that time, in every domain, by the ambitions of political expansion. The whole country, hungry for domination and intoxicated with the gold of the New World, gave too many examples of intolerance, debauchery and cupidity for one to praise its Christianity unreservedly.

At the head of the movement for Catholic reform in Spain[104] were the great religious Orders. Some of them, in the fifteenth century and at the beginning of the sixteenth, experienced a new fervour. This was the case with the Dominicans. The reformed congregation which Alvaro of Cordova (1423–34) had attempted to form had been supported by Cardinal Torquemada at Valladolid, then by the Benedictine priors Garcia de Frias (1436–51) and Juan de Gumiel (1451–62), by the Italian Dominicans, by the masters-general of the Order, and by the Catholic kings. Not until 1504 was the whole province of Castile united to it. Soon afterwards

[102] Cf. Domingo de Sta. Teresa, O.C.D., *Juan de Valdes. 1498(?)–1541. Su pensamiento religioso y las corrientes espirituales de su tiempo*, Rome, 1957. There is an edition of the *Alfabeto cristiano* by B. Croce, Bari, 1938; and of the *Dialogo de doctrina cristiana* by M. Bataillon, Coimbra, 1925.

[103] Cf. H. C. Lea, *A History of the Inquisition of Spain*, 4 vols, New York, 1906–7; B. Llorca, S.J., "La Inquisicion española", in *Comillas*, Santander, 1953. A survey and bibliography are given in *Encicl. Cattol.*, VII (1951), col. 48–9.

[104] For a description of the spiritual situation in Spain at the end of the Middle Ages, see M. Bataillon, *op. cit.*, ch. I; and J. Brouwer, *De achetergrond der Spaansche Mystiek*, Zutphen, 1935, ch. II. See also *Mediaeval Mystical Tradition and Saint John of the Cross*, by a Benedictine of Stanbrook Abbey, London, 1954, chs I and VI; and especially E. Allison Peers, *The Mystics of Spain*, new ed., London, 1952 (includes a good anthology).

the reform spread to the provinces of Aragon and Portugal. The Dominican Order in Spain at that time, as has been seen, possessed some great theologians. It is worthy of notice that this reform owed much, through the intermediary of the congregations of Lombardy and Florence, to St Catherine of Siena and Girolamo Savonarola.[105]

Among the Franciscans, the spiritual awakening was chiefly due to the influence of the Low Countries. While the Dominicans of the sixteenth century were distinguished for their theological learning, the Franciscans were renowned for a galaxy of masters of the spiritual life. They were not men of real creative ability, but some of them had the good fortune to be read, and attentively meditated upon, by a reader of such genius as St Teresa of Avila.

The greatest of them was Francisco de Osuna (*c.* 1492–1540).[106] To understand his writings one must bear in mind his sojourn in the Low Countries, at Antwerp about 1535, and his sympathy with, if not his open adhesion to, the *Alumbrados*, who were then beginning to increase in number. He was clearly influenced by the group of them known as the *Recogidos*, who specially emphasized the importance of "recollection" in the mystical life.[107] Nevertheless, as may be seen from his writings,[108] he never swerved an inch from the path of orthodoxy. He might, in fact, be charged with being too impersonal. *The Gracious Banquet*, or *Gracioso Combite*, a treatise on the Eucharist which appeared in 1530, is derived from the *Rosetum* of the Brabantine writer John Mombaer[109] and from other sources including Gerson. Even more impersonal are his six celebrated *Alphabets*,[110] so called from the alphabetical scheme of the different sections. The first and sixth of these treatises are de-

105 See V. Beltrán de Heredia, O.P., *Historia de la reforma en la Provincia de España (1450–1550)*, Rome, 1939; by the same, *Las corrientes de espiritualidad entre los Dominicos de Castilla durante la primera mitad del siglo XVI*, Salamanca, 1941.

106 See Fidèle de Ros, O.M.Cap., *Un maître de sainte Thérèse, le P. François d'Osuna. Sa vie, son œuvre, sa doctrine spirituelle*, Paris, 1936.

107 As opposed to the *Dejados*, whose spirituality was built around the idea of abandonment. Cf. M. Bataillon, *op. cit.*, pp. 179–90. The influence of the *Alumbrados* in the modern period, especially in connection with St Teresa of Avila, will be studied in vol. III of this *History of Christian Spirituality*.

108 Analysed by Fidèle de Ros, *op. cit.*, Part II, with a list of the editions (which are, with a few exceptions, from the sixteenth century) and the translations. Besides the works to be mentioned below, he wrote a curious treatise on betrothal, marriage and widowhood entitled "Compass of the States", *Norte de los estados*; also sermons and scriptural treatises in Latin, of little interest.

109 Cf. Fidèle de Ros, *op. cit.*, pp. 204–19.

110 Only the third of these has appeared in a modern edition (Madrid, 1911), which reproduces that of Burgos, 1544. The *Alphabets* have been translated, since the sixteenth century, into Latin and other languages. There is a French translation, published in nine parts by the Abbey of Lérins, 1899–1908; an English one, *The Third Spiritual Alphabet*, trans. by a Benedictine of Stanbrook Abbey, London, 1931; Westminster, 1948.

voted to the passion of Christ; the second and fifth to the ascetical life; and the third and fourth to the mystical life. It is the *Third Alphabet* that Teresa of Avila seems to have meditated upon, perhaps as early as 1537.[111] In it, Francisco derives a great deal from St Bernard, from Richard of St Victor, and from Gerson. Without being a plagiarist, he was a popularizer who purloined without a qualm what he read in the works of others, and presented it to his readers in his own style. In fact, he did not stop at stating their doctrinal positions as his own; sometimes he even copied their writings without telling his readers so.

In what respect, exactly, was he influenced by the spiritual writers of the Netherlands? The *Third Spiritual Alphabet* and the *Fourth* had already been published at the time of his visit to the Low Countries, and "the explicit quotations in them from our mystics are rare, to say the least. There is only one, and that is from Mauburnus (John Mombaer)".[112] There are also some passages reminiscent of Harphius and Ruysbroeck.[113] Taken together, these are certainly not enough to establish a close literary dependence. From the doctrinal point of view, however, the relationship emerges more clearly. The points of contact have been described as follows:

> The idea of seeking God in the depths of the heart, by detachment from sensible things and by recollection; of possessing him by a simple act of the intellectual powers, denuded of all images; of giving a principal place, in the contemplative life, to Christ, God and man; and finally, of not restricting the mystical life to a few privileged souls. It may be added that Osuna was not unacquainted with the theory of God's image imprinted on our souls, and that, without the slightest doubt, he was influenced by our authors of the (Low Countries) in his affirmation of the excellence of mental prayer.[114]

But here one must be cautious: the fact that these doctrines are found in certain spiritual writers of the Netherlands and also in the writings of Francisco de Osuna does not necessarily prove that he was influenced by them. He quotes, or copies, from many other spiritual writers, among whom the points just mentioned were common property. In the case of the *Rosetum* the dependence is more marked. It was known in Spain from the end of the fifteenth

111 Cf. Fidèle de Ros, *op. cit.*, pp. 617, 625.
112 Cf. P. Groult, *Les mystiques des Pays-Bas et la littérature espagnole du XVIe siècle*, Louvain, 1927, p. 122.
113 *Ibid.*, pp. 130–41. On Ruysbroeck's influence on the Spanish mystics, see H. Hatzfeld, *Estudios literarios sobre mistica española*, Madrid, 1956, ch. II.
114 Groult, *op. cit.*, p. 142.

century, and was probably translated into the vernacular.[115] In this case, we may even speak of literal borrowing, and that in connection with a somewhat bold doctrine condemning vocal prayer as an obstacle to contemplation.

This brings us close to Francisco's sympathy with the *Alumbrados*, as well as to the bonds that attached him to the *Recognidos*. Through all his work there runs a wholesome and beneficial reaction against certain "anti-illuminists", who disparaged the life of prayer, having become quite rightly suspicious of it because of the imprudence of the "illuminated". Francisco's aim was to keep to the golden mean. He strongly emphasizes the spiritual importance of *recogimiento* or "recollection", which leads to an exclusive contemplation of God. He describes its degrees, which are those of beginners, of those making progress, and of the perfect. He works out a whole theology of the call to recollection, its conditions, and its essentially gratuitous character—*gratia gratis data*.[116] In a word, he gave a positive meaning to the apparently anti-intellectual adage that was used to sum up the action of man in recollection: "to think nothing", *no pensar nada*. This "nothingness" of thought, according to Francisco, is merely a simplification of the soul so that it can tend towards God alone: *atento a solo Dios y contento*. There is something in Francisco of the great German mystics: the idea of attaining to God by a recollection that presupposes absolute self-stripping of all created things.[117] At the same time, it also foreshadows Teresa of Avila and particularly John of the Cross.[118]

Among the disciples of Francisco de Osuna[119] there was a Franciscan lay brother who had a fairly wide influence. This was Bernadino de Laredo, who died in the same year as his master, 1540. In 1535 he published at Seville a treatise on contemplative prayer entitled *The Ascent of Mount Sion*, "Subida del Monte Sion". A second edition, much revised, appeared in 1538. The method advocated in this *Ascent* is intellectual, and belongs to the Victorine tradition. In the third part of the work (the part that was the most

[115] Treatise XIII, ch. III of the *Third Alphabet*, referring to the Rosetum (Douai edition, 1620), ch. 8, p. 11; ch. 10, p. 14. On the extent to which spiritual works from the Netherlands were read in Spain, see P. Groult, *op. cit.*, Part I, chs IV–VI.

[116] On this point, see Fidèle de Ros, *op. cit.*, Part III, chs III–VII.

[117] J. Brouwer, *op. cit.*, pp. 180–90, emphasizes this relationship.

[118] Cf. Fidèle de Ros, *op. cit.*, pp. 617–30. The influence of Francisco de Osuna in the modern period will be studied in more detail in vol. III of this *History of Christian Spirituality*.

[119] Two of them, at least, may be mentioned here: Antonio de Guevara (†1545) and Alonso de Madrid († *c.* 1550). Cf. Fidèle de Ros, "Antoine de Guevara, auteur ascétique", in *Etudes francisc.*, L (1939), pp. 306–32, 609–36; J. Christiaens, "Alonso de Madrid, Contribution à sa biographie et à l'histoire de ses écrits", in *Lettres romanes*, IX (1955), pp. 251–68, 439–62.

thoroughly revised in 1538), Bernadino studies the contemplation of the "perfect". He describes it as attaining, after a consideration of our lowliness and after imitating Christ in his sufferings, to the godhead "either in the mirror of creatures or in itself". The Dionysian influence is evident, but the author also draws in characteristic fashion upon Hugh of Balma and upon Harphius, whose *Mirror of Perfection* he knew. Thus, to arrive at union with God, the best road to take is that of affective aspirations and of love rising above all knowledge.[120] Bernadino prefers these aspirations to the sweetness of spiritual consolations. He displays a piety that is deliberately devotional in the sense that it centres on secondary objects, with the danger that the primary place of God and Christ may be forgotten. With his *Josephina*, for example, he became one of the promoters of devotion to St Joseph.

Teresa of Avila declared that she had read the *Subida del Monte Sion*[121] with great profit. In fact, she esteemed it more highly than the *Third Alphabet*.[122] The *Subida* does in fact present an outline of the stages in the interior life that were to be described by the great Carmelite in her autobiography. In it, contemplation is viewed under its psychological aspect rather than in terms of its object. Already in the fourteenth century this tendency was beginning to appear, in the works of many spiritual writers: it now attained a high degree of perfection. While she recognized the importance of dogma, St Teresa's aim was to describe what she felt. She was influenced in this approach by reading the *Third Alphabet* and *The Ascent of Mount Sion*. In adopting their psychological orientation, Teresa was indirectly influenced by the conception of contemplation that was simple and affective, devoid of any intellectual claims.

There was yet another respect in which Spanish spirituality of the fifteenth and sixteenth centuries was indebted to the Low Countries. Its course was certainly influenced by a Benedictine abbot of Montserrat, Garcia Jimenez de Cisneros (1455–1510). Seeking to reform his monastery, he took measures like those already adopted by the congregation of St Justina at Padua. Thus his reform included, first the centralization of the monasteries (this was the origin of the Congregation of Valladolid), and then, as regarded the interior life of the monks, the assiduous practice of methodical prayer. Cisneros owed much to the spiritual writers of the *Devotio moderna*, like John Mombaer[123] and Gerard of Zutphen, as well

[120] See Fidèle de Ros, O.M.Cap., *Un inspirateur de sainte Thérèse, le Frère Bernardin de Laredo*, Paris, 1948. There is a modern English translation of the Subida by E. Allison Peers, *The Ascent of Mount Sion*, London, 1953.

[121] *Vida*, ch. XXIII.

[122] Cf. Fidèle de Ros, *Un maître de sainte Thérèse . . .*, pp. 324–35.

[123] Cf. P. Debongnie, *Jean Mombaer de Bruxelles, Abbé de Livry. Ses écrits et*

as to the Fathers, and to such universally known authors as St Bonaventure, Hugh Balma, Thomas a Kempis, Gerson, and Ludolph the Carthusian. His reform at Montserrat led him to compose some spiritual directories,[124] among which must be mentioned the well-known *Exercises for the Spiritual Life,*[125] which were published simultaneously in Castilian and Latin and were soon being read all over Europe. The book was not, however, an original work; it is only a compilation, in which Cisneros' touch can rarely be discerned. This spiritual anthology describes the three "ways": purgative, illuminative and unitive. Through these the disciple passes by three series of "exercises", thus to arrive at a fourth stage, which is contemplation. By this means Cisneros aimed to bring his monks back to the practice of prayer.

The continued fame of the treatise is due to the fact that it had a certain influence on the *Exercises of St Ignatius of Loyola.* As he visited Montserrat in 1522, and afterwards kept in touch with one of the monks, he may have practised the *Exercitatorio* of Cisneros. But Ignatius was too much himself to repeat or reproduce anyone else's formula just as it stood, even though he had derived benefit from it. His *Exercises* are no piece of plagiarism, as a superficial criticism may too readily suggest. Such a criticism might much more justly be made of Cisneros.[126] It is interesting to note, however, that it was through the Benedictines that Ignatius first came in touch with the *Devotio moderna* and adopted its methods. Thus the old monastic Order played a part in a development of a work that was to leave its mark on the entire Church in modern times.

Outside the religious Orders, the only noteworthy spiritual writer in Spain at this period was Master John of Avila (1500–69).

---

ses réformes, Louvain, 1928, pp. 290–4; P. Groult, *Les mystiques des Pays-Bas . . .*, pp. 92–100.

124 They are to be found in the manuscript *Montserrat No. 39*, and are described by M. Alamo, art. "Cisneros (Garcia ou Garzias de)", in *Dict. de spirit.*, II, col. 919–20. A better biography of Cisneros is that by G. M. Columbás, O.S.B., *Un reformador benedictino en tiempo de los reyes católicos, G. J. de C., Abad de Montserrat* (*Scripta et documenta*, 5), Montserrat, 1955.

125 *Exercitatorio de la vida spiritual.* There have been many editions and translations, which are cited in A. Albareda, *Bibliografia dels Monjos de Montserrat* (*segle XVI*), Montserrat, 1928, pp. 43–142. A new Castilian edition was brought out by F. Curiel in 1912 (Barcelona). There is a French translation by J. Rousseau, *Exercises spirituels et directoire des heures canoniales*, Paris, 1902; and an English one by E. Allison Peers, *The Book of Exercises for the Spiritual Life*, Montserrat, 1929.

126 On this question, see A. Albareda, O.S.B., "Intorno allo scuola de orazione metodica stabilita a Monserrato dall'Abate Garsias Jimenez de Cisneros (1493–1510)", in *Arch. Hist. Soc. Jesu*, XXV (1956), pp. 254–316. On the connections between the two works, see the summary in *Dict. de spirit.*, II, col. 917–19.

Among other works, several of which have recently come to light,[127] he wrote a commentary on a verse of Psalm 44, *Audi, filia*.[128] This spiritual treatise, which was published in 1556, came under suspicion and was condemned by the Inquisition. It is therefore very rare today, and when it was re-issued in 1574, after the author's death, its text was revised. The reason for the condemnation was not so much that the work contained doctrinal errors as that John of Avila was of Jewish descent. His teaching is, in fact, distinctly Christological and to a great extent derived from St Paul. Its principal themes are Christ, the mysteries of his passion, his mystical body, and the love of God and one's neighbour—a love that is disinterested and heroic. John of Avila was influenced by Francisco de Osuna, whose doctrine concerning recollection he adopted, but he put more emphasis on the role of grace than did Osuna, and especially on the central place of Christ in the spiritual life. He does not at all follow Osuna and Laredo in their psychological descriptions of the interior life; his spirit is still that of the patristic age, and of the Middle Ages up to the thirteenth century. St Teresa read his work, but she seems to have been less influenced by him than by Laredo.

Thus it is clear that the great spiritual writers of the Catholic Counter-Reformation in Spain were the heirs of the *Devotio moderna*. It is paradoxical that it should also have influenced the heterodox Reformers of the sixteenth century in some of their most characteristic lines of thought.

The elements in sixteenth-century Spanish spirituality that were derived from the *Devotio moderna* can be characterized in a few words. First of all, there was the primacy of the psychological aspect—of the subjective side of the interior life, even of the contemplative life. More attention is paid to mental and emotional reactions than to the object, or rather the objective content of contemplation. Prayer, by a shift that is only natural when it is seen from this new angle, becomes in a sense a matter of psychological technique. Without thereby admitting the existence of an "acquired contemplation" (which is a contradiction in terms), it systematized the necessary preliminary dispositions, the progressive development

127 There is a critical edition, not yet complete, of the *Obras completas* of Juan d'Avila, by L. Sala Balust, of which two volumes have appeared (Madrid, 1952–1953), including letters, minor writings, sermons, and spiritual conferences. It also includes a biography of Juan d'Avila and the bibliography. The *Sermones del Espiritu Santo* have been edited by J. C. Simancas, Madrid, 1957.

128 While awaiting the completion of the edition by L. Sala Balust, we must use the older editions of the works of Juan d'Avila published at Madrid in 1927 and republished in 1941. There is a French translation by J. Cherprenet with a good introduction (Paris, 1954); this translation was made from the original text of 1556.

of meditation leading to conversion and interior prayer, and finally the stages of contemplation properly so called. Here Ignatius Loyola and Teresa of Avila were to play a leading role, though the way had been prepared for him by Cisneros, for her by Laredo and Osuna.

As interest became concentrated on this way of praying, there was a general depreciation of the liturgy. Without debating here the merits of the motives that led the Society of Jesus to abandon the choral office, it can simply be stated that there came into being in the sixteenth century a mentality according to which that office was reserved for contemplatives. The active Orders had something better to do for the greater glory of God.

To put it precisely, the spiritual evolution of the Middle Ages had ended by producing an acute consciousness of the apostolic responsibility of the Christian, whatever his state of life, but especially if he was committed and dedicated to the service of God. If he was engaged in the active life, he would be active up to the hilt, but his action must be nourished by a prayer which, to be fruitful, must be as concentrated as possible. If he was a contemplative, he would have, as Teresa of Avila did, a keen sense of the responsibility he had assumed with regard to the Church. He would be brought to an interior death in union with the redemptive death of Christ, by the choral office indeed, but above all by mental prayer. At the same time, mental prayer was the best means at his disposal to make him useful to the Church as well as to the souls of sinners or those separated from Catholic unity.

In short, the contribution of sixteenth-century Spain was to remind the Church that it is a collective undertaking for the redemption of the world, and that to that end it is interior prayer that gives strength to the apostle, just as it gives the contemplative an apostolic aim and range. Apostolic aim, and interior prayer—these were the two poles of the new conception of spirituality which was then taking definite shape in Spain. The same basic characteristics were to remain stamped upon modern spirituality up to our own day.

The spiritual crisis of which the end of the Middle Ages saw the solution may be summed up thus: What had been the greatness of St Paul's and St John's teaching on the spiritual life was extrinsic to the *Devotio moderna*. The monastic Middle Ages, before the advent of scholasticism, had, at its deepest level, lived on this New Testament mysticism. From now onwards, though the scriptural outlook was not wholly forgotten, mystical experience was thought of not so much in terms of an experience of the data of

Revelation in themselves, as of an experience in the framework of, and guaranteed by, these data.

The point at which this gradual falling away began was at the end of the fourteenth century, at the time when the weariness brought about by a speculative mysticism, nominalism and a growing disgust with the idea of a religion reserved for an élite, brought about a reaction against speculation, and even against the monastic life itself. This reaction took concrete form in the *Devotio moderna,* the appearance of which coincided fairly closely with the breach between theology and mysticism that has been pointed out earlier. This was the exact point at which the spiritual life became a fact of experience, valid as such—no longer the experience of a fact valid in itself.

If another conclusion can be drawn from what has been said, it is that in the sixteenth century, when the Church was confronted by the Reformation, the only solid school of spirituality was the Spanish one, which was itself derived in part from that of the Low Countries and the *Devotio moderna.* As the Reformation spread, the *Devotio moderna* came to an end as an organized group, but its spirit persisted. The spiritual predominance of Spain over the rest of Europe in the sixteenth century runs parallel with a hegemony of which only the political aspects are usually noticed. The councils, the religious Orders founded in the preceding century, the various attempts at reform in the monastic Orders, the efforts to reform the episcopate—none of these was an effective rampart against the Reformation. The great Mendicant Orders could still produce some illustrious names in the fifteenth century, but in the sixteenth they had only theologians who were out of touch with pastoral problems. In any case their remedies were usually too late.

To sum up, it cannot be too often pointed out that *the Catholic reformation began in the fourteenth century with the Devotio moderna.* The latter bore within itself the seeds of a movement which could become, in the hands of extremists, the Reformation properly so called. But of itself it also led to the Catholic reform of the Counter-Reformation. Although this *Devotio moderna* became too institutionalized in the course of the fifteenth century, and so lost the spirit of its beginnings, it is still true that Spain carried on its light; and its influence on modern spirituality was prodigious.

APPENDIX

Byzantine Spirituality

by

LOUIS BOUYER

of the Oratory

BYZANTINE SPIRITUALITY

THE knowledge and appreciation of Byzantine spirituality has in a few years passed through strange vicissitudes. Unknown or little known, was not Byzantium the very symbol of a rigidity which, if not already that of a corpse, bore within itself the seeds of death? Later, its vitality was rediscovered, only to be caricatured. Then those who realized the injustice of the caricature, instead of bringing serious criticism to bear upon it, thought it simpler to make the picture even blacker in order to assert the excellence of what had been previously stigmatized. Neither side took the trouble to understand: each was in such a hurry to condemn or justify the same things that they had not time to make sure that these really existed. It is the eternal story of the golden tooth that Fontenelle told so well.

However, at last we seem to be starting on the only fruitful method—an unprejudiced study of the texts, of the whole corpus of writings, seen in their historical and literary setting. A book on Gregory Palamas[1] like that of Jean Meyendorff is one of the first signs of the new era.

At this stage it is clear that the history alone of Byzantine spirituality would need a volume to itself, and it is equally clear that such a book would be premature.[2] Not only is there need for a series of scientific monographs written in a spirit of eirenical sympathy—Meyerdorff's work is a splendid example—but if these are to become feasible much work in editing texts has to be done, and above all in finding manuscripts; and this has only just begun

[1] Jean Meyendorff, *Introduction à l'étude de Grégoire Palamas* (vol. III of the series "Patristica sorbonensia"), Paris, 1959. See also the little popular work by the same author, *Saint Grégoire Palamas et la mystique orthodoxe*, Paris, 1959. The only serious criticism that could be made of these excellent books is that their author, in emphasizing the Macarian elements in Palamite thought, has perhaps a slight tendency to minimize what it has derived from the Evagrian tradition.

[2] In the absence of any general work on Byzantine spirituality as a whole, reference must be made to the valuable bibliographical information and excellent analyses to be found in Basile Tatakis' book *La philosophie byzantine*, Paris, 1949 (the second supplementary volume of E. Bréhier's *Histoire de la philosophie*). This book is, in fact, an over-all study of the development of Byzantine religious thought. This bibliography can be supplemented by the more recent one provided in G. H. Beck, *Kirche und theologische Literatur im byzantinischen Reich*, Munich, 1959.

to take shape. This sketch therefore has as its object merely to give an idea of the riches that are only now being caught sight of, and which, as they are laid bare, make the problems much more complex than they appeared in those too hasty efforts in which interpretation, whether polemical or apologetic, ranked before discovery.

Byzantium and its Spirituality

Far from having congealed as though by a miracle, whether in 1054—the date usually considered decisive for the schism—or earlier, we now know that Byzantium, as much as or even more than our Latin Middle Ages, has never ceased to live and change.[3] What remained constant, what she inherited indeed from Christian antiquity, was something that in the West first Charlemagne, and then the Othonian emperors, then the kingdoms which broke up the Empire in an attempt to renew it, were over and over again to try to imitate and make their own: the persisting ideal of a sacral Christianity in which the whole of human life, whether individual or collective, not only bears the imprint of the Gospel, but takes it for its law. One can of course cavil endlessly at the paradox, indeed at the contradiction, latent in a society—and that an earthly one—which takes as its law that which St Paul shows as transcending all law. The fact remains that the greatness of Byzantium is her determination to put into practice with perseverance, and indeed to realize with an unexampled continuity, this ideal in her culture and in all her civilization. Her spirituality is clearly marked with this ideal: particularly the two great institutions or cultural creations which, while they were the most impressive product of that spirituality, quickly became, if not its very sources, at least its most lasting stimulant. The two—the liturgy, and iconography[4]—are obviously connected, and reflect together the hierarchical and symbolic view of the universe, and the life of man which unfolds itself within it, into which Byzantium projected her Christian ideal.

A work which had a great influence, the *Mystagogia* of St Maximus the Confessor, illustrates better than any other, as early as the seventh and eighth centuries, a liturgy in the full process of development, which was to determine once and for all the shape of

[3] See the works of C. Diehl, especially those on Byzantine art, and also the three volumes by Louis Bréhier, *Le monde byzantin*, Paris, 1948–50.

[4] On the liturgy, see Mercenier, Paris and Bainbridge, *La Prière des Églises de rite byzantin*, 3 vols, Chevetogne (no date); and Archdale King, *The Rites of Eastern Christendom*, 2 vols, London, 1950. On iconography, see especially André Grabar, *La peinture byzantine*, Paris, 1957.

the iconography and was to materialize in its definitive organization. We know that this iconography was so completely applied to the whole of a church that it became, as it were, both its spiritual and its visible structure.

At the same time there was another no less essential element in Byzantine spirituality: while it did not contradict the former, there remained always an unresolved tension between them. It was a "Christ factor" drawing its inspiration from the Gospel, its sovereign liberty perpetually in contrast with the hieratic structures. It quickened them, but no more destroyed them than it allowed itself to be absorbed by them.

Thence came a series of pairs which, if not entirely derived from the first two, are at least related to them. It was the opposition between the Evagrian or Dionysian inspiration and that which flowed from Macarius, between an (apparently) hellenized intellectual mysticism and one rooted in the Bible—and to that extent hostile to that intellectualism which tended to identify "spirit" and "pure intelligence". Then there is the opposition between the monasticism of Studios and that which during this period increasingly, had its centre on Mount Sinai: that is, between a cenobitic life, in its essence liturgical and social, part of the life of the Empire which it made every effort to spiritualize, and the monasticism of the desert, of silence and interior solitude. Lastly is found the opposition of a humanism (the direct ancestor of our Renaissance) to an eschatological mysticism, through which, in spite of herself, Byzantium was in her latter days to find Athos the holy mountain imposing itself upon her. It must, however, never be forgotten that these conflicting points of view were not so much an opposition of party to party, or individual to individual, though in a crisis they sometimes take this form, as tensions bearing fruit in each school of thought, almost in each individual. To take only the last of the great names of Byzantine spirituality: the theologian Nicholas Cabasilas, a layman, did not hesitate to say that "holy men" (by which he meant "holy monks", these being the only "holy ones" known to him or Byzantium) are incomplete men; which did not prevent him in the end taking the side of Gregory Palamas: that is of eschatological mysticism against humanism.[5] There were in addition two further conflicts—one against an enemy within the gates: iconoclastic radicalism, which was to have such far-reaching consequences and to contribute to the triumph of Islam, the foe without *par excellence*; the other against a foreigner rather than an enemy—the Latin Catholic, whose folly in the Crusades had the mischievous result of making him only too real an enemy and one

[5] Letter from Cabasilas to Synadinos, quoted in Tatakis, *op. cit.*, p. 279.

whose belated and clumsy, though real, friendship hastened on the catastrophe of Byzantium. The pure intellectualism to which the hellenism of Byzantium tended took shape as iconoclasm in its opposition to the historical realism of her Christianity. "Latinism" was to some extent a bogy which Byzantium conjured up, for the Westerners were more barbarians than Latins, though their stupidity, even when their intentions were good, still more when they were not, was such as to make the bogy seem only too real. Byzantium had already been dangerously turned in on herself by the Nestorian and Monophysite quarrels, and she was finally to shut herself up in the unreal dream in which Islam imprisoned her. It can be said that the survival at the end of the Byzantine Middle Ages of orthodox Christianity, in an almost exclusively monastic and liturgical form bears the mark of this irrealism; but in saying this it must be borne in mind that we have no greater cause for satisfaction when we consider the collapse of monastic and liturgical tradition that was taking place in the West at the same time. The West probably bears at least as much responsibility for the defeat of Byzantium as she does herself.

The Legacy of St Maximus

There were two writers at the end of the patristic period the importance of whose part in transmitting patristic spirituality and transforming it into the spirituality of Byzantium cannot be denied: St Maximus the Confessor and St John Climacus. They have been studied in the previous volume[6] as the term of patristic tradition, but we are concerned with them here as the sources of the veritable Byzantine tradition.

It is in his *Mystagogia*[7] that St Maximus is seen most clearly as the father of Byzantine spirituality. There is no doubt that this small treatise did more than anything else to give a standing to the areopagitical writings, to which however it gave a very personal interpretation. In it he achieves, by going back to their common source in St Gregory of Nyssa, a synthesis of his own between the mysticisms of the Pseudo-Dionysius and Evagrius. As an example one may take this passage on the progressive degrees of knowledge in religion.

> He used to say (the old man of whom Maximus pretends only to be the interpreter) that in the soul there are five couples which are related to the one couple in which God expresses himself to us. By couples I mean intelligence (*nous*) and its expression

[6] *The Spirituality of the New Testament and the Fathers*, London, 1963, pp. 433 and 426 respectively.

[7] P.G., 91, 657 *et seq.*

(*logos*), wisdom and prudence, contemplation (*theoria*) and practice, knowledge and virtue, unceasing knowledge (*aleston*) and faith. God expresses himself to us in a unique couple, truth and goodness (*agathon*) in which the soul is united to the God of all things as she passes through the other couples. She imitates the unchangingness and beneficence of the divine nature and its work (*energeia*) by a firm and unshakable and freely chosen adherence (*hexis*) to the beautiful (*en toi kaloi*)—

What he said was that the intelligence, impelled by wisdom, attains to contemplation and by contemplation to knowledge, by knowledge to the unceasing knowledge, by this unceasing knowledge to truth, which is the term of this impulse of the mind, where its nature, power, application and act find completion. He used to say that indeed wisdom is the power of the intellect; contemplation, its application; knowledge, its operation; incessant knowledge, the perpetual and constant (*hektiken*) motion of that wisdom, that contemplation, and that knowledge, as of its power, its application, and its operation [directed] to the object of the knowledge that transcends all knowledge—a motion whose term is truth, as the object of a knowledge that can never end. What a wonderful thing, that incessant knowledge should attain its fulfilment, which can only be attained by finding its term in the truth that is God! For God is the truth towards which the intellect moves endlessly and incessantly [*alestos*]. There is no end to its movement, as there can be no term where there is no distinction. For the wonderful greatness of God's infinity knows no quantity, no division, and absolutely no distinction, and we cannot attain to any knowledge that would make us comprehend it according to its essence. That which, indeed, cannot be the object of any distinction or comprehension can be for no one a term.

Similarly, the *logos*, moved by prudence, arrives at action; by action, at virtue; and by virtue, at faith, that is, at the firm and unavoidable conviction (*plerophoria*) of divine things, a conviction which the *logos* has at first in potentiality by prudence, and which it afterwards displays in its operation by the showing forth of works. For according as it it written, "faith without works is dead" [James 2. 20], and nothing that is dead and inefficacious would be numbered among beautiful things (*tois kalois*) by anyone who is of sound mind. But by faith one comes to the good, in which the *logos* finds its term, its own workings ceasing, and its power, application, and operation being consummated therein.[8]

What is most personal about this passage is also what is most biblical in its inspiration, even though it is expressed in more or less platonizing terms. It is the idea that God is inseparably truth and goodness, so that one cannot truly know him without at the

[8] *Mystagogia*, ch. I; P.G., 91, 664 *et seq.*

same time conforming one's life to that goodness. Notice that this is what Maximus calls faith, making it, when brought to its fullness by charity, the summit of the spiritual edifice, whereas Evagrius, following Origen, considered it rather as its base.

Maximus vigorously affirms the necessary unity of the spiritual intelligence (the *nous*) with the whole of life, in man—as in God. The development of the *nous*, then, takes place conjointly with that of life itself, by the blossoming out of nature into a power which by its application is brought into act (operation: *energeia*). The power of the intellect is wisdom, which is applied by contemplation and achieves its full actualization in knowledge.

Nevertheless, just as the intellect is inseparable from its living expression (its *logos*), so on the plane of life, wisdom is translated into prudence, contemplation into action, knowledge into virtue. But knowledge itself is transcended in the "incessant knowledge" which attains to the very truth of God, while that which is faith *par excellence* (the faith that finds its fulfilment in works of charity) makes his goodness ours.

In this plan, the fundamental place given by Evagrius to the *nous*, to pure intellect, is retained and at the same time is corrected, by the necessary joining together of the *nous* and the *logos* in which it expresses itself, and which is the corporeal manifestation of the soul's being. Thus, wisdom and prudence, theoretical and practical knowledge, will develop *pari passu*, in a contemplation not divorced from action, which ends in a knowledge inseparable from virtue. But this knowledge itself transcends itself in a higher knowledge which plunges us in God; while our virtue in the same way culminates in a faith which inundates us, so to speak, with God's own goodness. (It must not be forgotten that *pistis* means not only our faith but also God's own fidelity to his promises.)

Thus the *praktike* and the *theoria* of Evagrius, the purgative and illuminative way of the Pseudo-Dionysius, become rather concomitant aspects of one single initial progress, tending towards knowledge-virtue, which finally flowers into "unceasing knowledge". This, like Evagrius's "knowledge of the Trinity", goes beyond all distinct knowledge; and as in the unitive way of the Pseudo-Dionysius, his union and divinization, we lose ourselves beyond self in God. Then, especially as in St Gregory of Nyssa, God appears as the bottomless abyss, in which the soul's perfection and rest lies in its attainment of overflowing and unfathomable life. This, however, is but faith in its fullness, which opens us at last unreservedly to God's truly divine action in us: to his essential goodness which is one with his truth, and which we contemplate at first shining forth as beauty, but which in the end is communicated to us as very goodness, dispossessing us of ourself, so that God may be all in all.

In this spiritual world of Maximus, there are three things that particularly merit our attention. The first is that platonizing intellectualism, while it is accepted, is definitely corrected by a vitality and realism that are thoroughly biblical and Christian. The second is that the divine transcendence is conceived as the bottomless abyss of an infinite creative spontaneity and, by that very fact, as eminently mysterious. The third is that the communication of God (the divinization and union by faith of which Dionysius spoke) takes place on the level of a divine operation (*energeia*) which, while it brings the human operation to fulfilment, does not destroy it—quite the contrary. This is precisely what faith means for Maximus: the complete surrender of man at his highest point of expression to God manifesting himself fully: the *logos* of the whole man being lit up by the divine *logos* made flesh.

There is no doubt that Maximus' liturgical symbolism is connected with this profound vision, so fully in accord with his Christology, of the two natures, each remaining completely itself at the summit of union. On the one hand, the Church in which the sacred liturgy is to unfold is an image of God and at the same time of the whole world, including spirit and matter inseparably united, and of the material world itself. On the other hand, the Church and man are reciprocally images of one another, while man's soul, by itself, is also an image of the Church. Thus man, celebrating the liturgy corporeally and with his whole soul, is identified with the Church, which enables him to attain, through the sensible world, to the intelligible world, and beyond that even to God.

All this, however, would have no real content, no effective possibility, were it not that in the liturgical action Christ himself is present, uniting in himself the creator and his creation, God and man, and filling the action with his own mystery.

> Jesus, my God and Saviour, fulfilling himself in my salvation (*sumplerothenta di emou sozomenou*) returns to himself in his perfect fullness, from which he can never again fall; he gives me, man, back to myself—or rather to God, from whom I received being and towards whom I tend; there to find at last that good being (*to eu einai*) so long desired. He who has been able to learn these things by the experience that he has had of what is told him, will know fully (for he has already had the luminous proof of it) what gives him his own dignity: how the image is restored to the dignity of being made according to the Image, how its archetype is honoured, what is the mystery and the power of our salvation, and that for which Christ died; how we can dwell anew in him,

and he in us, as he has said, and how "the word of God is right, and all his works are done with faithfulness [Psalm 32.4]."[9]

Thus for Maximus, liturgical symbolism—a replica of the cosmic and ontological symbolism of the universe as he, influenced by Dionysius, conceives it—is charged in Christ with a dynamism that is fundamentally historical, which makes fruitful the dynamism inherent in our nature. That nature is indeed conceived by Maximus as being inseparably both "intellect" and the living expression of intellect in actions (that is, in the whole of corporeal life) which are, as it were, its *logos*.

Here indeed we find the soul of Byzantine spirituality inasmuch as it is a liturgical spirituality, governed more and more explicitly by the symbolism of the image, of a creation that recognizes in itself its kinship with its Creator by tending wholly towards him, while he on his side draws it to himself in the grace of the Incarnation.

The Legacy of St John Climacus

The writings of St John Climacus provide the ascetical counterpart of this mystique. The character of the *Ladder* as a veritable encyclopedia of asceticism has already been emphasized. There was indeed no monastic author of the patristic period whom the abbot of Sinai had not read, and from whom he had not taken over some expression word for word—including Latin authors like Cassian, and even St Gregory the Great. He adopted the framework of Evagrius, making *apatheia* the end and goal of ascesis. According to his own teaching, ascesis tends to be perfected and transcended in contemplative prayer, but he is much briefer and more reserved on this matter, and particularly on the content of contemplative prayer, than he is on ascesis itself.

He gives a remarkable definition of the latter, completely Evagrian in its terminology: it is "a death of the soul and a death of the intellect before the death of the body".[10] The contemplative life is like an anticipated resurrection, which follows this anticipated death.[11] The means *par excellence* of ascetical mortification is, for him, obedience, and is accompanied by unceasing meditation upon death.[12]

Not that the ascetic is enamoured of death as such; on the contrary, he dreads it more than anyone, but he dreads it in so far as it entails a separation from God.[13] The voluntary death of asceticism,

[9] *Ibid.*, ch. v; 676 B–C.
[10] P.G., 88, 667.
[11] *Ibid.*
[12] *Ibid.*
[13] *Ibid.*, col. 756.

however, is for him the means of overcoming that ineluctable death which is the result of sin. Dead to the world and the flesh through *apatheia*, he can rise again to God through prayer. And perfect prayer will finally lead him to God.

> The fear of death is an emotion that is natural to man and an effect of his disobedience. But the fact that the horror of death makes us tremble is a proof that we have not expiated our sins by repentance. Jesus Christ feared death, but he did not tremble at it, showing clearly, by each of these two effects, the two different qualities that belonged to the two natures which he had united in his person.
>
> Just as bread is the most necessary of all foods, so meditation on death is the most useful of all our spiritual practices. It leads those religious who live in community to embrace the works and exercises of penance, and to find the greatest pleasure in humiliations and contempt. As for solitaries, who are removed from all the tumult and all the turmoil of the world, it produces in them a complete abandonment of all earthly cares, a continual prayer, and a strict guard over their thoughts. And all these virtues are both the daughters of this mediation and also at the same time its mothers. As tin can be taken for silver when seen by itself, but never fails to look different when the two are seen next to one another, so the fear of death that is according to nature appears manifestly different from that which is above nature, when it is exposed to the discernment of those who know how to judge spiritual things. . . .
>
> As the Fathers declare that perfect love is not subject to any fall, in the same way I can affirm that perfect meditation on death is not subject to any fear.[14]

This ascetical doctrine, undeniably austere, was to be at the back of the whole Byzantine spiritual tradition. The liturgical and iconographical splendours of Byzantium presuppose it, for the divine world which they suggest is explicitly another world than that of the senses, the world that lies beyond death. This world of the resurrection in which it moves is indeed—and this has sometimes been too much forgotten in the recent rediscoveries of the Christian East—a radically eschatological world. The only access to it open to us at present is that of monastic asceticism, and that is formally recognized as being a voluntary death to this world.

Sinaitic and Studite Monasticism

Monasticism retained to the end, despite the most violent reactions against it, a central place not only in Byzantine spirituality

[14] Sixth degree of the *Ladder*; P.G., 88, 793–7 (from the French translation by Arnaud d'Andilly).

but in the whole of Byzantine civilization. It was, however, to develop somewhat different tendencies: two of these took shape very early, around two main centres.

The first of these centres was the monastery of St Catherine (formerly St Mary) on Mount Sinai,[15] where St John Climacus pursued his whole career.

At an early date, so it would seem, some hermits withdrew to the mountain. They were probably attracted there by the associations of the Exodus and of the revelation of the divine Name to Moses as a prelude to the Decalogue of the Covenant. It is possible that the earliest of them fled there, at the end of the third century, to escape the persecutions raging against Christians in Egypt. In any case, a century later, when Etheria came to Sinai as a pilgrim, there were already a number of them there to welcome her and guide her devotion. Their solitude was not, however, very secure. The desert nomads made inroads upon them from time to time, and a few days after Christmas 373 there was a veritable hecatomb of solitaries. A monastery was therefore built, under Justinian, in the years 527 to 535, which took on the aspect of a fortress. In this monastery the religious, hitherto scattered, were gathered together.

The monastery always kept as a legacy from its origins a distinctly eremitical spirit and, more or less as a result of the influence of the place itself and of the associations attached to it, a definitely mystical one. The mosaic of the apse (one of the most ancient that have come down to us), which is devoted to the mystery of the Transfiguration, witnesses to this.

It was, therefore, Sinai in particular that preserved the wholly interior ideal of prayer absorbed in God, that of the old anchorites in the deserts of Egypt. Abbot John's *Ladder* shows this, despite the preponderant place that it gives to asceticism. His ideal of prayer, however soberly he sets it forth, banishes a variety of thoughts, as does that of Evagrius. He concentrates on the prayer of a single word, thus taking up again a practice that may go back as far as Macarius the Egyptian; and one that Diadochus of Photike, Barsanuphius and John the Prophet bear witness to as early as the end of the fifth century and the beginning of the sixth. It is characterized more precisely by what he calls "the memory of Jesus."

Hesychia [he says] is an incessant act of worship and a con-

[15] On the monastery of St Catherine, see Dom Patrice Cousin, *Précis d'histoire monastique*, Paris, 1956, pp. 91 *et seq.* For a general survey of the history and geography of Orthodox monasticism, see the article by Fr Boris Bobrinsky in volume No. 30 of *Contacts* on *Athos et le monachisme orthodoxe*, Nice, 2nd trimester, 1960.

tinual presence before God. Unite the memory of Jesus with your breathing; then will you understand the usefulness of *hesychia*.[16]

Although this text is the only one of its kind in the work of St John Climacus,[17] its historical importance has been justly pointed out. It is in fact the first text to connect "the memory of Jesus" with breathing itself, which certainly already seems to mean that one should aim at making the invocation of the Saviour's Name coincide with the rhythm of breathing. In point of fact, it was precisely in the setting of Mount Sinai that Byzantine hesychasm, which crystallized in that practice, was to arise.

At a slightly later date probably, some *Centuries* were composed (falsely attributed to Hesychius of Jerusalem) in which that sentence of St John Climacus became the starting-point for the first systematic development of the "Jesus prayer", as they were the first to call it. This most significant text seems to have originated from another monastery of Sinai, that of the Burning Bush. There will be occasion to speak of it again further on.

At Constantinople, monasticism had appeared by the end of the fourth century; it was, little by little, to take a very different direction from that of Sinai.[18] The monastery of Alexander, on the Asiatic bank of the Bosphorus, had first been suspected of Messalianism because it aimed at perpetual prayer. The monks, called Acemetae (those who never go to bed), kept up uninterrupted praise in the oratory by means of alternating choirs. Yet this community was to become the centre for the spread of a neo-Basilian type of monasticism that was not only rigorously cenobitic but active, and even social, in its orientation as well as in its organization. About 463 the Acemetae were magnificently installed in the city itself by the consul Studios, from whom they received the new name of Studites. Absolved of all suspicion of heresy by their opposition to Eutyches and by their good relations with Rome, they became the most powerful monastic body in Constantinople, and one of the most active in their manifold works of charity. Finally, in the ninth century, their hegumenos St Theodore gave them a *typikon* (a rule) which was very Basilian in spirit. It was, during the following centuries, to become the model rule for the great cenobitic monasteries of the East, throughout the Byzantine empire and even, as we shall see later, in the Slav lands.

16 P.G., 88, 1112C.

17 See *La Prière de Jésus*, by A Monk of the Eastern Church, 3rd ed., Chevetogne, 1959, p. 28. See also the brief but very important communication by Mgr Basil Krivocheine to the Patristic Congress in Oxford, 1951.

18 On monasticism at Constantinople, see Dom Patrice Cousin, *op. cit.*, pp. 88 *et seq.*

The monastery of Studios was to be linked with the last struggle against iconoclasm, as well as with the reform of the Church and of society—all spheres in which St Theodore the Studite was no less distinguished than he was for his *typikon*. Indeed, it may well be said that the Studite type of monastery was the home of that Byzantine Christianity in which society, become hierarchical in the most exact sense of the word—that is, organized as a collectivity that is not only Christian but wholly sacral—ultimately becomes one vast *panegyris*. In it, everything was centred on the liturgy, and this in turn extended to the whole of existence (as we see in the *Book of Ceremonies* by Constantine Porphyrogenitus). The array of icons, which at this period came to occupy the whole surface of churches, was disposed in such a way as to fill the whole earthly horizon with a spiritual cosmos expressed in symbols. It was probably at this point that the spiritual ideal of Byzantium—an ideal that was essentially monastic—attained the height of its grandeur. Yet there is something equivocal about this universal transfiguration that a monastic Christianity wished to impose on the whole world, by itself expanding to the dimensions of earthly society.

The spirit of Sinai, one of separation from the world and spiritual liberty, characterized by the absolute transcendence of God as well as by the personal spontaneity of the monk, who was there considered not as a cell in a huge institution but as a "charismatic" figure, was perpetually to batter against the Studite spirit. From this irreducible tension between Sinai and Studios there would develop what was probably best in Byzantine spirituality.

Elias Ekdikos

Nothing is known of Elias Ekdikos[19] except his name. He is usually thought to have lived in the eighth century, but even that is uncertain, and some would put him in the eleventh or even the twelfth century. His writings are closely akin to those of Maximus, especially to the *Mystagogia*, from which he took over, word for word, the speculations on the symbolism of the Church. In fact, Elias's *Anthologion* has been attributed by some manuscripts to Maximus himself.[20]

The two men differ, however, on one important point. Like Maximus, Elias believes in a close connection between practice and contemplation. But unlike Maximus, he does not admit that one is

[19] See B. Tatakis, *op. cit.*, pp. 58–62; also Jean Gouillard, *Petite Philocalie de la Prière du Cœur*, Paris, 1953, pp. 161 *et seq.*

[20] This explains why his works are to be found in two separate places in Migne: P.G., 90, 1401 *et seq.*, and 127, 1128 *et seq.*

simply parallel to the other. He agrees that practice does indeed accompany contemplation, but contemplation goes beyond it. Moreover, the contemplation that enables us to see things in their eternal reasons is, as for Evagrius, only a first stage. The true gnostic goes beyond this, to attain a higher contemplation in which, Elias tells us, the Logos in person makes himself known directly to the soul. It is true that practice and contemplation are like two lamps, which must both be kept alight during the whole of life. For practice has no solidity without contemplation, and contemplation is not authentic if practice is wanting. But while action predominates in beginners, for those who are progressing contemplation becomes dominant.

More precisely:

> The man of active life has, as it were, a veil upon his heart when he prays, for the knowledge of sensible things cannot be revealed as long as one is attached to them; whereas the contemplative alone, by virtue of his detachment, can see the glory of God, in part, with uncovered face.
>
> The prayer that accompanies spiritual (*pneumatikes*) contemplation, in which flows, like milk and honey, the gnosis of providence and of God's judgment, is the promised land; while that which accompanied physical gnosis is Egypt, in which the memory of the grossest desires comes back to those who pray. But prayer that is simple (*haple*) is the manna of the desert, which, by its uniformity (*dia to monoeides*), conceals from the impatient the good things of the promise which they desire, while to those who resign themselves to this "very light food" it procures a better nourishment, and one that is permanent.[21]

This brings us back very near to Evagrius (who was, it must be remembered, the chief source for Maximus himself). But here the thought of Evagrius has been recast. The contemplation of creatures, for Elias as for Evagrius, leads to that of providence and of the judgments of God. Above all that, however, the higher gnosis abolishes all separate ideas. At first sight, therefore, it is an impoverishment, as Elias recognizes; it seems like a return to the desert and to the "very light food" of the manna. But for him who perseveres, he says, this manna, at first sight so pale and tasteless, will become like a foretaste of heavenly knowledge.

Later Elias comes back, though in a way no less characteristically his own, to Maximus' parallelism between action and contemplation. But in doing so, he connects it with the idea—which goes back to the origins of monasticism—that he who approaches nearest to God by asceticism must come back to the world, but in pure charity.

[21] P.G., 90, 1437.

> The active man, because of his painful efforts, desires to be freed in order to be with Christ (cf. Philippians 1.23), but the contemplative prefers to remain in the flesh, both because of the joy he receives in prayer and also for the benefit of his neighbour here below.[22]

Thus the connection between action and contemplation is not so much a parallelism as a dialectical progress. Action makes no progress except in so far as it opens itself to contemplation, which will itself flourish only on the basis of renewed action. But it comes to full flower, here below, only in a higher mode of activity, in which charity alone definitely has the ascendancy.

St Simeon the New Theologian

Elias Ekdikos is generally held to have been a monk of Sinai, even though he was clearly the disciple of Maximus, who was of Constantinople. At the beginning of the eleventh century, the monasticism of the new Rome was invaded by the spirituality of Sinai; but, here again, the foreign influence did not exclude what was original—far from it. In fact, St Simeon was to implant in the heart of Studite monasticism a spirituality that was wholly "pneumatic" and "Christic", one which the monks of Sinai had scarcely more than sketched out.[23]

Simeon, who may well have taken the name of his spiritual father, his name in the world being George, must have been born about 950, in the town of Galatai, in Paphlagonia. He was sent to Constantinople at an early age, to live with a relative who was a functionary at court, and there he prepared for an official career. The sudden death of his protector turned him towards the monastery of Studios, where Simeon the Devout became his "spiritual father". He deliberately guided him in the direction of mysticism, long before the younger man had made up his mind to become a monk himself.

There is no doubt that the master he had found exerted a considerable influence on him—the thorough cultus with which he

[22] *Ibid.*

[23] On St Simeon the New Theologian, see the article by J. Gouillard in the *Dict. Théol. cath.*, XIV, cols 2941 *et seq.* Also see especially the two articles by Mgr Basil Krivocheine, "The Brother-loving Poor Man", in *Christian East*, II (1953–4), pp. 216–27; and "The Most Enthusiastic Zealot", in *Ostkirchliche Studien*, vol. 4, No. 2, Wurzburg, 1955, pp. 108–28. The edition of Simeon's works in Migne (P.G., 120, 287 *et seq.*) is very defective. Mgr Krivocheine is preparing a critical edition, particularly of the *Catecheses*; see his article, "The Writings of Saint Symeon the New Theologian", in *Orientalia Christiana Periodica*, XX (1954), pp. 298–328. The series *Sources chrétiennes* has published a critical edition, with a French translation of the *Chapitres théologiques et pratiques*, by J. Darrouzès, A.A., No. 51, Paris, 1957.

never ceased to honour him shows this. The elder Simeon (who was favoured with spiritual experiences, particularly the gift of tears) was already bringing an ardent mystical aspiration into the monasticism of Studios, which till then had been limited to asceticism and the active life. At the same time he was leading this monasticism, fairly rigidly set in its institutional framework, back to the old ideal of an essentially charismatic spiritual fatherhood.

However, what made the deepest impression on the young man (he tells us himself that he was barely twenty) at this time was the writings of Mark the Hermit, which the monk gave him to read. In the event, the spirituality of this author was to be the seed of the "new theologian's" deepest personal convictions. Mark emphasizes that the forgetting of God is the source of sin; he insists on the restoration in us of "memory" (that is, conscious attention) directed to him whose grace alone is our life, and finally the constant exultation with which that "memory" should fill us.

Simeon himself has taken care to tell us precisely which were the three "chapters" in Mark's work that he made his own above the rest:

> If you seek to be healed, take care of your conscience, and do what it tells you: this will profit you.
>
> He who seeks active grace of the Holy Spirit before practising the commandments is like a slave bought for money who, the moment he is bought, demands his freedom.
>
> He who prays physically, without having yet acquired spiritual knowledge, is like the blind man who cried, "Son of David, have mercy on me", but, when his eyes were opened and he saw the Lord, no longer called him "son of David" but "Son of God", and worshipped him as he ought.[24]

From the first of these he deduced a generous obedience to inspirations that urged him to greater fervour, and especially to a systematic cultivation of prayer. But while the second persuaded him that no one can draw near to God without an energetic ascesis, the third assured him that Christ does not refuse his grace to him who seeks it thus.

> From that day, he never went to bed with his conscience reproaching him: why did you not do this or that? Thus he always listened to his conscience, never leaving undone whatever

[24] From the sermon *On Faith*, the Greek text of which has been edited by I. Hausherr in *Orientalia Christiana*, No. 45, pp. LVII–LXX. The English translation given above is from *Writings from the Philokalia*, translated from the Russian *Dobrotolubiye* by E. Kadloubovsky and G. E. H. Palmer, London, 1951, p. 144. [In all passages quoted here from that translation, the words in parentheses (which appear in the Dobrotolubiye) have been omitted.—Trans.]

On Mark, see *The Spirituality of the New Testament and the Fathers*, pp. 425–6.

it suggested to him. And every day his conscience added more and more to his usual rule, and in a few days his evening prayers swelled to great proportions. During the day, he had charge of the house of a notable patrician; he went daily to the palace and busied himself with material affairs in such a way that no one realized what had happened to him. During his prayers, addressing himself to our Lord Jesus Christ, he fell at his pure feet as if he had been there in the flesh, and implored him to have mercy on him, as once he had on the blind man, and to open the eyes of his soul.[25]

One evening, an overwhelming experience befell him, which prepared him for the transformation of his whole life:

> One evening, when he was praying, and saying in spirit: "God, have mercy on me, a sinner", a divine light suddenly (*aiphnes*) shone on him from above and filled the room. The young man no longer knew whether he was in the house or under a roof, for on all sides he saw nothing but light: he was not even aware of being on earth . . . He was one with this divine light and it seemed to him that he himself had become light and left the world altogether. He was filled with tears and unspeakable joy.[26]

In this experience we find the two most characteristic traits of Simeon's mysticism: the vision of light, and the tears that accompany it.

After this experience he began to feel more and more drawn toward the monastery, but he hesitated long before he decided to enter it. At last, in 976, when he was already a senator, he made up his mind; and so after a farewell journey to his native country, he entered Studios the following year. He was entrusted to Simeon the Devout to be trained, but the rest of the Community viewed with little favour the ardour with which he had at once abounded in his master's sense. He was refused profession at Studios itself, but, at the instance of his "spiritual father", was accepted by Anthony, *hegumenos* of the daughter monastery of St Mammas at Xirokerke. A few years later, he was ordained priest, and soon afterward he became *hegumenos*. At the time of his entrance, the monastery had been in a rather decadent spiritual condition, and in addition its material situation had been far from flourishing. During the twenty-five years that Simeon was in office, he transformed it into a fervent and prosperous community.

The "catechesis" (that is, the abbatial allocution) which he gave on his entering upon his office shows very well what his spiritual ambition was: to urge his monks to a life that would be not merely

[25] *On Faith*; *Writings from the Philokalia*, p. 145 (slightly modified).
[26] *Ibid.*; *Writings from the Philokalia*, pp. 145–6.

fervent but also contemplative in its bent, even truly mystical. At the same time, it reveals at once his characteristic mixture of sincere humility and irrepressible *élan*. It was this latter that impelled him to recount his own experience that he might call others to share it. At the very beginning of his discourse, he says:

> Brethren and Fathers, I wish to speak to you about that which contributes to the progress of the soul, but I am ashamed of your love—as Christ, who is the Truth, is my witness—for I know my unworthiness. I should therefore prefer to remain in silence, and never to raise my head or look a man in the face, because I feel that my conscience condemns me for having been designated, in my unworthiness, to guide you all, as though I were someone who knew the road—I who, in reality, do not know what lies under my feet, and have not yet found the road that leads to God....

From this, however, he passes to the idea that it is the commandments of God which lead us to him, and that their only end is love. But when he comes to that point he is as though rapt out of himself by this thought:

> Permit me to speak to him [to love, *Agape*] for a moment, by way of introduction.... For, having made mention of that Love without stain, O my beloved Fathers and Brethren, his light suddenly shone in my heart; I was ravished by his sweetness and lost all sense of outward things ... O most desirable *Agape*, blessed is he who has embraced thee, for he will never again desire to embrace with passion any beauty that is born of earth ... Praiseworthy is he who pursues thee, more praiseworthy he who has found thee; more happy is he who has been loved by thee, who has been received by thee, taught by thee, who has dwelt in thee, who has been nourished by thee with an immortal food, with Christ our God....
>
> ... O divine Love, where is Christ in thee? Where hast thou hidden him? Why, having taken the Saviour of the world, hast thou withdrawn from us? Open thy door a moment for us, unworthy though we be, so that we may see Christ who suffered for us, and may believe in his mercy; so that, having seen him, we may no more die. Open to us, thou who didst become for him the door to his appearing in the flesh; thou who didst constrain the heart of our Master, rich and free as he was, to bear the sins and weaknesses of all men. Do not reject us, saying "I know you not!" ... O Love, thou art that which encircles me, burns me, and sets my heart painfully afire with an infinite desire for God and for my Brethren and Fathers. Thou art the teacher of the prophets, the companion of the apostles, the strength of the martyrs, the inspiration of the fathers and teachers, the

perfection of all the saints. And now it is thou who dost establish me in my present ministry.

He concludes with these words:

> You are the children of God, whom God has given to me as my children, my heart, my very eyes. To use the words of the apostle, you are my glory and the seal of my teaching. Let us then strive, by every means, my beloved brethren in Christ, loving one another, to accomplish the service which is that of God as well as of myself, whom you have chosen to be your model and your spiritual father (though I am far from being such), so that God may rejoice in your concord and in your success; and I, in my humility, will also rejoice to see your lives progressing in accord with God... in the contrition and tears by which the interior man is purified and filled with divine light and belongs entirely to the Holy Spirit....[27]

Archbishop Basil Krivocheine was certainly right in emphasizing the importance of this allocution. It sums up the whole of Simeon's programme as a master of the spiritual life. It was his application of it that won him enthusiastic disciples, but also increasing opposition which went so far as a first revolt, on the part of a group of his monks, against his mystical tendencies and (they said) against his tendency to set himself up as a model. At first he was upheld by ecclesiastical authority, but later that was to turn against him, chiefly in the person of the *syncellus* Stephen of Nicomedia. The pretext was his public cult of Simeon the Devout, who had died by 986 or 987; but the underlying reason was probably his exaltation of the spiritual authority of accomplished mystics, as opposed to that of priests or hierarchs who were not "spirituals."

More or less driven to resign in 1005, Simeon was sent into exile in 1009, to Palonkiton on the other side of the Bosphorus. There he settled down in the ruined oratory of St Marina, which he soon turned into a new spiritual centre and another monastery. Although an attempt was made to reinstate him in office very soon after his forced departure, he preferred to renounce it for ever rather than to weaken his teaching. It was therefore at St Marina that he died in 1022, and only his remains returned to Constantinople, thirty years later.

Simeon's Teaching

Many of the Western authors who have studied Simeon's work and thought, either in his own writings or in those of his disciple

27 There is an English translation of the text (as yet unpublished) in B. Krivocheine, "The Most Enthusiastic Zealot", pp. 110 *et seq.*

and biographer, the Studite monk Nicetas Stethatos,[28] see in his mysticism a dangerous illuminism which would open the door to a doctrine of "spiritual fatherhood" subversive of all ecclesiastical authority. Certain Eastern Orthodox writers have simply turned these commentaries round and made Simeon the first champion of an anti-Western mysticism, going hand in hand with the rejection of the typically Roman conception of the Church. This is to put an imaginary construction on Simeon's teaching, and to give a biased interpretation of it, which the work of an author already mentioned—Archbishop Basil Krivocheine, a monk of Athos who is both a man of learning and also a direct heir to the Eastern monastic tradition—has helped to dissipate.

Simeon is connected with the tradition of the Pseudo-Macarius by his emphasis on the conscious character of the life of the Spirit in us and on mystical experience as a normal factor in an authentic Christian life, as well as by his translation of this experience into terms of light. In this connection, Archbishop Krivocheine has pointed out the obvious dependence of Simeon's *Catechesis* 34 upon the second part of the *Great Letter* of "Macarius" edited by Werner Jaeger. This is the context in which the strong expressions of the New Theologian are to be understood. Hausherr has brought out a hitherto unpublished *Catechesis*, the title of which speaks for itself: "on those who think that they have the Holy Spirit, without any feeling of his virtue." Simeon speaks in this way throughout all his writings. He is particularly categorical in the twentieth of his *Gnostic and Theological Chapters*:

> As for him who has not merited to attain to such a degree of perfection, and to obtain possession of such benefits, let him blame no one but himself, and let him not excuse himself by saying that the thing is impossible, or else that, if perfection does come to us, we are unconscious of it! On the contrary, let him learn with certitude from the divine Scriptures that the thing is possible, and true, realized in act, and in conscious action! Each man deprives himself of its benefits in proportion to his transgressions and his neglect of the commandments.[29]

As Vladimir Lossky[30] very justly pointed out, this doctrine must be seen in relation to the idea, fundamental in ancient monastic

28 See Mlle Marie Chalendard's introduction to her edition and translation of the *Spiritual Paradise* of Nicetas Stethatos (No. 8 in the series *Sources chrétiennes*, Paris, 1943); also I. Hausherr, *Un grand mystique byzantin. Vie de Syméon le Nouveau Théologien (949–1022) par Nicétas Stéthatos*, with a French translation of the unpublished Greek text, Rome, 1928 (in *Orientalia Christiana*, XII).

29 From the French translation by Darrouzès, *op. cit.*, p. 85.

30 V. Lossky, *Essai sur la théologie mystique de l'Église d'Orient*, Paris, 1944, pp. 215–16.

spirituality, that a life of sin is immersion in the "forgetting of God", which is the same as torpor of the true consciousness, slumber of the soul. Monastic life, on the other hand, as wakefulness, as a perpetual "vigil", tends of itself to restore true consciousness. This consciousness is identified with the "knowledge of God", with that "gnosis of the Trinity" which Evagrius opposed to *agnoia*—and *agnoia*, ultimately, represents hell. In this sense the whole point of monastic asceticism is to tend towards mysticism. Simeon takes up again the idea of St John Climacus that asceticism is a voluntary death, justified only by the anticipated resurrection to which it leads, a resurrection identified with the higher form of prayer to which the monk can and should attain.

> The resurrection of all men is brought about by the Holy Spirit. And I do not mean the resurrection of the body at the end of time . . . , but the spiritual regeneration and resurrection of dead souls, which takes place spiritually every day. By means of the Holy Spirit, this resurrection is given by Christ, who died once and rose again, and who is risen and rises up in all those who live worthily. With him, there rise those souls which died with him, in intention, by faith; and he bestows on them the kingdom of God, even now, and forever.[31]

For Simeon, however, this experience must necessarily be based on a life ruled by the commandments of God, and the commandments (he emphasizes once again) all converge in love. The practices of asceticism, for him as for Cassian and the whole great monastic tradition, have no other immediate aim than the perfect realization in use of God's will.

> Make no mistake about it: without works, faith alone will profit us nothing. In that case, indeed, faith is dead, and the dead do not obtain life unless they begin by seeking it in the accomplishment of the commandments. In that accomplishment, charity brings forth in you its fruits, with interest: almsgiving, compassion towards our neighbour, gentleness, humility, tears, patience in adversity, chastity, and purity of heart, by which we are made worthy to see God. In charity the Holy Spirit comes to us and enlightens us; he regenerates us, makes us sons of God, clothes us in Christ, lights the lamp of the soul, makes us sons of light, dispels the darkness in our souls, and makes us know that henceforth we participate in eternal life. That is why I tell you not to trust in any other action, as in fasting alone, or vigils, or other corporal mortifications, so as to despise this obedience to the commandments of God—as though we could

[31] *Sixth Catechesis.* The text is translated in B. Krivocheine, "The Most Enthusiastic Zealot", p. 115.

be saved by observances, without these commandments, which cannot be....[32]

But, for all that, Simeon (faithfully echoing Mark the Hermit) lays no less stress on the fact that this whole Christian life, and its perfection above all, is only a gift of grace, and that it cannot be lived except in and by the faith that recognizes that grace.

> All those who have been perfected in holiness and virtue have not been saved by the works of justice, but quite gratuitously. ... But in that case, someone will perhaps say, what remains of his own to one who has obtained salvation? If indeed his own will stands in need of a higher power, what is still his own? What remains to him is simply to hear salvation proclaimed, to burn with desire for it, and to know him who can save him....[33]

And he goes on at once to add that these very things are themselves a gift of God, so that:

> Our whole salvation has been established in our Lord Jesus Christ. That is why he is called King and Lord: because he reigns, by the Holy Spirit, over all those who believe in him, and as King and Lord of his faithful, he himself works through them that which pleases him.[34]

This being so, it is not surprising that the experience of the Spirit, however normal it may be said to be in the Christian life, should break in upon us suddenly and inexplicably, always taking us as it were unawares when it comes.

> A man who, instead of avoiding and running away from the suffering of the heart produced by the fear of eternal punishment, willingly accepts it in his heart, will be determined, as he progresses, to tighten this bond ever more and more, and will thus advance more quickly. It will lead him to the presence of the King of Kings. When this comes to pass, then, as soon as he sees, however dimly, the glory of God, his bonds of fear will at once fall off, his executioner will hasten away, and his heart's grief will turn into joy which will become in him a fountain of life or a spring for ever gushing forth: physically, rivers of tears; spiritually, peace (*galenen*), meekness and unspeakable delight, together with courage and free and unhindered readiness to strive towards every fulfilment of God's commandments. This is not possible for beginners, but only for those who are well on

[32] From the Latin translation by Pontanus in P.G., 120, 428 CD.
[33] The first part of this passage is given in K. Holl, *Enthusiasmus und Bussgewalt*, Leipzig, 1898, p. 76; the remainder, in the Latin translation by Pontanus, P.G., 120, 376 D. The two are cited together by Gouillard in his article in *Dict. théol. cath.*
[34] P.G., 120, 377 CD.

the way; the spring itself becomes the light of the perfect suddenly (*aiphnes*) changing and transforming their heart.[35]

Simeon's habitual emphasis on the suddenness of the transforming experience, together with his constant use of the adverb *aiphnes* (suddenly), have suggested to some (particularly to Fr. Cyprian Kern) a Platonic influence. But Archbishop Basil Krivocheine has pertinently stressed that the character of Simeon's mystical experience rules this out.[36] It was not for him in any way an experience of absorption and fusion—his autobiographical descriptions show this plainly—but rather one of personal relationship: a dialogue with Christ, and his indwelling in us by the Spirit.

An account of his first experience of this kind (complementary to the one already quoted) is altogether characteristic. In it he tells us, in so many words, that, to him who has this experience of light, sweetness and tears, "someone appears before him." The dialogue then opens: "Art thou God?" "Yes, I am he who became man for thee."[37] There is, in fact, no mysticism that is more expressly "pneumatological" and "Christological" than Simeon's. The preface to his *Hymns of Divine Love* is one passionate invocation of the Spirit:

> Come, true light. Come, eternal life. Come, hidden mystery. Come, nameless treasure. Come, inexpressible reality. Come, person who flies from human comprehension. Come, abiding gladness. Come, light that knows no dusk. Come, true hope of all the saved. Come, resurrection of the dead.... Come, thou for whom my wretched soul has longed, and still longs. Come, alone, to the alone; for I am alone, as thou dost see. Come, thou who hast set me apart and caused me to be alone upon the earth. Come, thou who hast made thyself the object of my desire, and who hast caused me to desire thee—thou to whom none can aspire. Come, my breath and my life. Come, consolation of my contemptible soul. Come, my joy, my glory, and my delight forever. I thank thee that thou hast made thyself one Spirit with me, without confusion, movement, or change; and that though thou art God above all, thou hast become all in all for me.[38]

The very heart of these *Hymns* is that meditation on Christ which makes us live in him that he may live in us:

[35] *Practical and Theological Precepts*, No. 69, in *Writings from the Philokalia*, pp. 112–13.

[36] "The Most Enthusiastic Zealot", p. 117, note 41.

[37] Quoted in *La Prière de Jésus*, p. 38. The text of this discourse, with a French translation, is given in I. Hausherr, "La Méthode d'oraison hésychaste", in *Orientalia Christiana*, IX, Rome, 1927, pp. 174–207.

[38] From the Latin translation by Pontanus, P.G., 120, 507–9.

> We are the members of Christ, and our members are Christ... You also, if such is your desire, will become one of his members. And so all the members of each one of us will become the members of Christ, and Christ our member, and he will make all in us that is ugly and ill-shapen beautiful and noble, adorning it with the splendour and beauty of his Godhead. And we shall all become gods and intimately united with God: and our bodies will seem to us without stain, and since we have all partaken of the likeness of the whole body of Christ, each one of us shall possess all of Christ. For the One who has become many remains the One undivided, but each part is all of Christ.[39]

Simeon never tires of drawing from this doctrine its effects on fraternal charity:

> How can some men confine Christ our Lord to one poor man when he is indivisibly divided and exists totally in every poor man? Let us suppose that a hundred beggars are as one Christ, for Christ remains perfectly indivisible. Then if a man gives a coin to ninety-nine poor men, but reviles, chastises and sends away one other empty-handed, to whom do you think he has done this? Of course to Christ himself who has said, says and will always say: "Inasmuch as ye have done it unto one of the least of these my brethren, ye have done it unto me."[40]

After reading these passages, one can understand in what sense Simeon could say that only in mystical experience, and in the outpouring of love that accompanies it, is the reality of the sacraments of baptism and the Eucharist accomplished in us. It is no less clear that the luminous experience he speaks of constantly, as "Macarius" did, has nothing in common with any pantheistic ecstasy. The proof is that Simeon connects it constantly with the gift of tears, which is the sensible manifestation of *katanwxis*, compunction. This compunction is the same as Jeremias's "circumcision of the heart", or Ezechiel's "change of heart". In exactly the same way, the luminous (or, more precisely, fiery) vision of God's presence and life is a purely Biblical legacy. One has only to read these two passages:

> Whosoever seeks compunction with all his soul will find it. Or rather, it comes of itself and finds him who seeks it laboriously. And even if he has a heart harder than copper, iron, or diamond, as soon as compunction reaches it, it becomes more malleable

39 *Ibid.*, col. 532 BC. (The English translation cited here is from H. A. Reinhold's anthology *The Spear of Gold*, London, 1947, pp. 283–4.—Trans.)

40 (*Practical and Theological Precepts*, No. 129, in *Writings from the Philokalia*, p. 128.—Trans.) In the French edition, XLII of the *Chapitres théologiques et pratiques*, Darrouzès, p. 110.

than wax. For compunction is the divine fire that melts mountains, sweetens all things, transforms them into a paradise, and changes the souls that receive it . . . All this the divine fire of compunction brings about with tears, or rather, by means of tears.[41]

And again:

Metanoia causes tears to spring from the depths of the soul. And tears purify the soul and completely destroy great sins. After tears have effaced them, the soul is consoled by the divine Spirit and watered by the sweet rivers of compunction. Enriched by compunction from day to day, it produces the fruits of the Spirit . . . And when the soul has achieved this by a happy zeal, it becomes a member of the family of God—a house and dwelling-place of the divine Trinity, clearly contemplating its Father and its God, and conversing with him daily.[42]

In the same way, in the twenty-five *Gnostic and Theological Chapters*, the abstract expressions (which he takes from Evagrius and not from "Dionysius", whom he seems to ignore deliberately) are not to be understood in the sense of any intellectualist mysticism. The same is true of the assertion, in this same text, that we must make our way back to the One. It is not a question of a process of purification by progressive abstraction. Simeon is simply emphasizing the completely ineffable character of this experience in which Christ visits man and inundates him with his Spirit—an experience which is irreducible to anything sensible or intellectual that is in the power of man.

This experience of life in Christ, vivified by the Spirit, is of the greatest importance for Simeon. It accounts for the expressions he used which clashed with the ideal of the Studites (essentially a disciplined one) even before disquieting the ecclesiastical authorities of Byzantium. They have made modern writers frown, or no less unwisely rejoice, in their hurry to explain what they misinterpret.

Simeon did not hesitate to say that priests and bishops had no authority to teach spiritual truths if they did not first live the life which they were to foster in others, and that the same was true *a fortiori* of monastic superiors whose authority was purely institutional. Echoing a monastic tradition that goes back much further, he did not hesitate to prefer the spiritual direction of a lay monk to the absolution of a priest, if the former was a genuine mystic and the latter was not. Although, when Simeon himself lived in the world, the mystical impulse that moved him carried him quite

[41] *Fourth Catechesis*. Translated in B. Krivocheine, "The Most Enthusiastic Zealot", p. 125.

[42] *Ninth Catechesis, ibid.*

naturally toward the cloister, yet he recognized that true monasticism is of the "Spirit" and not of the "letter", and was the first to admit that in some cases the monastic ideal may well be better realized by men of the world than by those who are monks by profession. Here again, there is nothing that cannot be found in the oldest *Apophthegms*, but the familiar themes are given a new and vigorous expression:

> Some canonize life in the desert, others life in common in monasteries, others authority over men, to instruct and teach them and administer churches, all works which give to many food for body and soul. For myself, I would not wish to single out any of these states of life nor to exalt one and depreciate another. In any case, no matter what a man's works are, or his practice, full of blessedness is the life lived for God and according to God . . .
>
> As men living in the world and purifying their senses and hearts from every sinful lust are worthy of praise and approbation, so men living in mountains and caves and yearning for the the praise and blessings and glory of men are deserving of blame and contempt. . . .[43]

There is no reason to see in all this, as some have been only too quick to do, any disdain for the Church as an institution. The meaning is rather that only in the Spirit does the institution find its end, and therefore it should be in the hands of men who live completely by and for the one reality of the Spirit.

It would be ludicrous to see in Nicetas Stethatos's participation in anti-Latin polemics a consequence of his master Simeon's position, as though opposition to Rome went as a matter of course with a fundamentally spiritual conception of the Church. It was the authorities of Byzantium, not those of Rome, who, as the schism approached, tried to pick a quarrel with Simeon and his disciples. Nicetas' anti-Latin grievances had absolutely nothing to do with this question of authority. What is more, far from opposing the current of neo-Georgian reform which in the west inspired Leo IX, and even his clumsy emissary, Cardinal Humbert, Simeon, in his emphasis on the "spiritual" way in which authority, and all ecclesiastical functions, should be exercised in the Church, represents the echo, or the typically Eastern parallel, of the same aspirations and the same ideals.

[43] (*Practical and Theological Precepts*, Nos. 100 and 104, in *Writings from the Philokalia*, pp. 120–1—Trans.) French edition, Darrouzès, *op. cit.*, pp. 100, 101.

The Byzantine Liturgy and Iconography

It was, however, about this time (towards the beginning of the second millennium) that what may be called institutional Christianity attained, in Byzantium itself, its unsurpassed perfection. As the fruit *par excellence* of the strictly Studite tradition, the ideal that it embodied was not unruffled by the charismatic Christianity of the two Simeons and their disciples. It would be a mistake, however, to think that the two were purely and simply opposed to one another. In point of fact, Simeon's monasticism—wholly interior though it was, and therefore with an undertone of individualism—had been nourished by the Studite tradition. He, in return, left more than one indelible mark of the "evangelical" spirit upon the main products of that essentially ecclesiastical and hierarchical tradition: the Byzantine liturgy, as we know it today, and the inconography which was closely connected with its development.

Just as the monasticism of Studios was a transposition of Basilian monasticism, so the Byzantine liturgy, which it elaborated, probably owes to foreign influences what appears to us most striking in it.

To get an idea of the ancient liturgy of Constantinople, one must go not so much to the Byzantine liturgy of today as to the Armenian, which was influenced by the Great Church before the monophysite schism.[44] The Byzantine liturgy on the other hand, at least as the Studites reshaped it, is in many respects the child of Syria, and more precisely of the Syrian monks of the laura of St Sabbas, which, it will be remembered, had been founded at the end of the fifth century in the valley of the Cedron.

The most ancient Byzantine hymns, the *Kontakia*, came from Syria. Romanus Melodus, who was born at Emesa (the present Homs) at the beginning of the sixth century, was a deacon first at Beirut and later at Constantinople. He brought there the ancient hymnology of eastern Syria, that of St Ephrem and his disciples, and hellenized it. It seems to have been, in form as well as in substance, simply a Christian variant of the *piyutim*, the liturgical poems of the synagogue in which the *haggadah's* lyrico-mystical commentary on the Scriptures was laid down.[45] The *Kontakion* was made up of isosyllabic lines, grouped into acrostic stanzas. Two centuries later, St Andrew of Crete, who came originally from Damascus and was for a time a monk at St Sabbas (as were his compatriots and imitators, St John Damascene and Cosmas, the

[44] On this whole subject, see the works cited in note 4. For a good summing up of the question, see I. H. Dalmais, *Les liturgies d'Orient*, Paris, 1959, pp. 39–40 and 108.

[45] On this point, see Jefim Schirmann, "Hebrew Liturgical Poetry and Christian Hymnology", in *The Jewish Quarterly*, XLIV (1953), pp. 123 *et seq.*

future bishop of Maiouma), added to the *Kontakion*, or substituted for it the *Canon*. This was a series of tropes interpolated between scriptural hymns of the vigil, and probably derived from the series of antiphons used at Antioch. The final flowering of this hymnody took place among the monks of Studios, who brought the liturgical books of St Sabbas to the New Rome.

It seems that it was monks of the great monastery of Constantinople—Theodore, Theophanes, and Joseph the Hymnographer—who finally perfected the books of the Byzantine liturgy whose basis is their *Typikon* (the ordinary of the office), their *Oktoekhos* and *Parakletike*, for the Sunday and week-day office, their *Triodion* for Lent and their *Pentecostarion*, for Paschal time. These established the pattern for later texts which (even up to modern times in Slav countries) were invariably modelled upon them. After the victory of orthodoxy over iconoclasm in the spring of 842—which was, in many ways, the victory of Studios—its liturgy was in fact adopted by all the churches, first of the city, and then of the empire. The eucharistic liturgy of Antioch (which is known as the liturgy of St John Chrysostom but is certainly much older) then displaced, except during Lent, the ancient anaphora to which the name of St Basil is given. This liturgy of St Basil may have been of Egyptian origin, but Basil may have given it its final from.

At the same time, the icons (again following the example of Syria) not only came systematically to cover the entire inner surface of the church, but were erected as well like a mystical screen between the sanctuary and the people. Thereupon, the principal prayers of the priest having become inaudible, the deacon began to lead the faithful in a parallel prayer in the form of *ektenai* (litanies). All that remained was to replace the ancient procession of the faithful at the offertory by the office of the *proskomide* (a symbolic preparation of the elements), and the liturgy took on the aspect which we know today.

Nothing left a deeper mark upon it than the iconoclast controversy and the manner in which it was overcome. Germanus of Constantinople, then St John Damascene, and later the patriarch Nicephorus and Theodore the Studite,[46] drew from it a theology of the visible creation as a symbol of the invisible, and of the Incarnation as a manifestation of the divinity in humanity, which was to become the very soul of Byzantine liturgical celebration. It is found above all in Germanus's treatise on the liturgy, *Ecclesiastical History and Mystical Contemplation*,[47] which is a development of the *Ecclesiastical Hierarchy* of the Pseudo-Dionysius and still more of

[46] On all these writings, see B. Tatakis, *op. cit.*, pp. 102 *et seq.*
[47] P.G., 98, 384 *et seq.*

the *Mystagogia* of St Maximus. The disciples and successors of Germanus reflected and meditated so thoroughly on this treatise that its Greek text has survived only in a form crowded with interpolations, which were added in great numbers even up to the twelfth century.[48] We can thus follow the development of the way in which the Byzantine liturgy was interpreted by the very men who completed its structure.

The principle, however, is certainly St Germanus's own.

> The Church is the heaven on earth in which God, who is above the heavens, dwells and moves. It represents the crucifixion, burial, and resurrection of Christ. More glorified than the tabernacle of the testimony of Moses, it was prefigured in the patriarchs and founded upon the apostles. In it is the propitiatory and the holy of holies, since it was foretold by the prophets, adorned by the hierarchs, perfected in the martyrs, and enthroned upon their holy relics.[49]

Thence comes a whole interpretation of the liturgy as veiling under visible symbols the reality of heavenly worship; and at the same time iconography unfolds to our eyes (as Nicephorus says) the interpretation of Scripture and of the sacred rites that is given us by oral tradition.[50]

The cupola, with the *Christos Pantokrator* surrounded by the incorporeal powers, represents the heavenly Church. At the curve of the apse, the Virgin praying, surrounded by the apostles, leads the earthly Church to meet him, a meeting presaged by the symbol of the *hetoimasia* (the preparation): an empty throne, prepared for the Judgment, surmounted by a cross or the book of the Gospels. Lower down, the "divine liturgy" is depicted, in which the angels hold the instruments of the passion; this balances the representation of the Last Supper which dominates the iconostasis, beneath the crucifix. A procession of saints advances toward the altar, the doctors appearing like the very pillars of the Church. On the iconostasis, at the right of the royal door, Christ is again depicted; on the left, the Virgin. Next to Christ is John the Baptist; next to the Virgin, the patron saint of the church, and the archangels Michael and Gabriel are shown at the ends.[51]

The twelve great feasts are also represented: those of the Virgin—her Nativity, her entry into the Temple, the Presentation, the Annun-

[48] See the article on St Germanus by F. Cayré in vol. VI of the *Dictionnaire de Théologie catholique*, cols 1307–8.

[49] *Ecclesiastical History*, P.G., 98, 384 B–385 A.

[50] Nicephorus of Constantinople, *Antirrhetici*, III, P.G., 100, 381 C.

[51] On this whole subject, besides the book by A. Grabar cited in note 4, see the two works by J. D. Stefanescu, *L'Illustration des liturgies dans l'art de Byzance et de l'Orient* (Brussels, 1936) and *Iconographie de la Bible* (Paris, 1938).

ciation, the Dormition; those of the Saviour—the Exaltation of the Cross, Christmas, Epiphany, the Transfiguration, Easter, Ascension, and Pentecost.[52] As these feasts succeed each other through the year, as also in every celebration of the liturgy, we live again the history of the Redemption. It is the road by which we ascend from earth to heaven, whence the Son came down that he might lead us back after him. So we take our place, as part of the hierarchy of the Church, in the great choir of the heavenly hierarchy, that is of the incorporeal powers who endlessly praise him who dwells in light inaccessible. Sin had shut us out, but the celebration of the holy mysteries makes us once more part of this choir.

This celebration, which would otherwise be overwhelming in its grandeur, is all shot through with heartfelt appeals to the Virgin and to Christ. This is particularly true of those hymns, typically Syrian in their humanity, which were bequeathed to Byzantium. They are prayers full of filial or fraternal tenderness, in which the sacred majesty of the divine mystery is, so to speak, incarnate in all that is most human. They give the mystical drama a historical dimension and at the same time make it more personal. Thus the soul meets its God made man in that endless marriage-feast in which the Church is born from the Cross, by wedding the risen Christ.

There are, for example, the tragic lamentations of Good Friday:

> On this day he is suspended on the gibbet who suspended the earth upon the waters. The king of angels is crowned with thorns; purple is flung over him in derision, who cast the sky over the clouds. He is buffeted who, at the Jordan, set Adam free. The Spouse of the Church is fastened with nails; the Son of the Virgin is pierced with a lance. We adore your sufferings, O Christ; show us also your glorious resurrection![53]

Then again, the exultation of Easter:

> Christ is risen from the dead! By his death he has conquered death, giving life to those who are in the grave![54]

Above all, there is the invitatory for the Transfiguration:

> Come let us go up to the mountain of the Lord, to the house of our God, and let us contemplate the glory of his transfiguration, a glory such as an only Son holds from his Father. In his light,

[52] See the introductions to the liturgy of these feasts in vol. II, Part I, and vol. II, Part II, of the work by Mercenier cited in note 4.

[53] From the French of Mercenier, *ibid.*, vol. II, Part II, p. 189.

[54] *Ibid.*, p. 268 (modified translation).

> let us see light; and carried away by the Spirit, let us sing forever the praises of the consubstantial Trinity.[55]

But there is also the wonderful confidence of the Dormition of the Virgin:

> As she departed, the All-Pure raised her hands on high, her hands that had truly embraced God in his body, and as a Mother she said to her Child: "Protect forever those whom you have made your own, and who cry out to you, 'Let us, the redeemed, praise the Creator alone, and exalt Him forever'."[56]

The Origins of Hesychasm and the "Jesus Prayer"

There is no doubt that Orthodox piety in the following centuries was chiefly nourished by this liturgy; yet it was not in a liturgical Christianity, a mysticism above all ecclesiastical and hierarchical, that the spirituality of Byzantium was to realize itself in its deepest and most intimate form. This other path, a wholly interior one, was that of hesychasm. Its ultimate expression was a prayer as far removed as possible from the magnificent formulas of the Studites, even from the outbursts of personal lyricism that they succeeded in incorporating into the heart of their most hieratic mysteries. The "Jesus Prayer", in which all hesychasm is concentrated, is in fact simply the unwearying repetition of the invocation, "Lord Jesus Christ, Son of God, have mercy on me." It may even consist in the name alone: "Jesus!"

The Fathers of the desert had already recommended the *monologistos* prayer, while the emphasis on *hesychia* (the rest in God which is the aim and end of *apatheia* itself) was certainly one of their major themes. In the preceding volume are quoted two apophthegms attributed to Macarius the Egyptian by a Coptic collection.[57] If they are authentic, Macarius must be recognized as the originator of the Jesus Prayer and of its whole spiritual context. Otherwise, as has been said, the first distinct formulas of this prayer are found in Diadochus of Photike.[58] After him, its use was taught by Barsanuphius and John the Prophet. Barsanuphius did not hesitate to put it on a level with psalmody. He did not draw the conclusion, as was done later, that it could with advantage replace the psalmody, but only said that the two should be practised equally. John advised using it in time of temptation, opposing it to the "antirrhetic" method advocated by Evagrius, which consisted

[55] *Ibid.*, vol. II, Part I, p. 266.
[56] *Ibid.*, p. 305.
[57] *The Spirituality of the New Testament and the Fathers*, pp. 376–7.
[58] *Ibid.*, pp. 430–2.

in confronting the temptations and criticising the sophisms they imply. "Nothing remains for us to do, weak as we are," he said, "but to take refuge in the name of Jesus."[59]

Not until St John Climacus, however, does one find the "remembrance of Jesus" made into the *monologistos* prayer to banish the multiple thoughts (*logismoi*) that Evagrius excludes from pure prayer. Evagrius certainly never foresaw this interpretation of his thought! But, as has been said, it is chiefly in a text from the *Ladder* that for the first time, so far as we know, these three terms are directly connected: the remembrance of Jesus, the control of the respiration, and *hesychia*: "Let the remembrance of Jesus combine with your breathing; then you will understand the use of *hesychia*."[60]

It has also been pointed out with truth that we find in John the theme of "the eye of the heart", which is able to see the divine "Sun of the intelligence" in a vision in which he who contemplates sees himself filled with light.[61] But in the *Ladder* these two lines of thought are not yet formally associated. Yet the first spiritual treatise which, though not actually one on the Jesus prayer, still begins to concentrate the whole of spirituality on it, also came from Mount Sinai. This was the centuries ascribed to Hesychius of Jerusalem, though there is general agreement that it is to be attributed to an author, or group of authors, belonging to the monastery of Batos (the Burning Bush) on the slopes of the mountain of the theophany. They derive from St John Climacus, from whom they cite the text quoted above, but after "your breathing" interpolate the phrase "and your whole life". This addition is very characteristic of the all-embracing character which the "remembrance of Jesus" was beginning to take on.[62]

It should be noted that it was in these centuries that the term "Jesus prayer"[62a] was first used, or alternatively *epiklesis Iesou* (invocation of Jesus), and in them its effects were described for the first time. By it the mind is purified and unified, with the result that our thoughts "play within it as fishes play and dolphins leap

[59] *Ibid.*, p. 426. Cf. the anonymous work previously cited, *La Prière de Jésus*, pp. 26–7.

[60] Cf. *supra*, p. 557. [61] Cf. *La Prière de Jésus*, p. 28.

[62] *Ibid.*, p. 29. The quotation is from the *First Century* of the Pseudo-Hesychius, No. 99. The Greek text is in Migne, P.G., 93, 1479–544. There is an English translation of the *Centuries* in *Writings from the Philokalia*, pp. 277–321. It will be noticed that in this translation the texts are sometimes numbered differently from those in Migne.

[62a] There is indeed, before that, a text in St John Climacus (fifteenth degree of the *Ladder*, P.G., 88, 889 D), but it is not absolutely certain that his expression used in it refers to this practice.

in a calm sea".[63] This effect comes about little by little. At first the name of Jesus is the lamp that lightens our darkness; later it becomes a full moon in the sky of our heart; finally, it is the rising sun.[64] Then a dialogue with Christ begins, in which he, having become the master of our heart, makes his will known to it.[65] Here it is expressly presupposed that the prayer has become constant: we are to be "ceaselessly breathing" it.[66] Then the holy name, which has become the sun of our mind, creates in it thoughts which are wholly luminous.[67] "Truly blessed is he who cleaves with his thought to the Jesus prayer, constantly calling to him in his heart, just as air cleaves to our bodies or the flame to the candle."[68]

The invocation of the Holy Name, in fact, gives us a share in it.[69] Here the formulation is more and more explicit, but there were other writings, no less important for the history of hesychasm, which, though they did not mention the Jesus prayer, yet created the spiritual atmosphere which crystallized round it.

The primary importance, in this connection, of the body of writings attributed to Macarius the Egyptian has already been pointed out. The fifty spiritual *Homilies* and the *Great Letter*, recently brought to light by Werner Jaeger, teach that the whole spiritual life is to be concentrated on a continual prayer, itself closely bound up with the guarding of the heart, and all this tending, by "attention to the Lord" in *nepsis* (sobriety of thoughts) and *hesychia*, toward a consciousness (*aisthesis*) and full conviction (*plerophoria*) of Christ's living presence in us, through a transforming experience of light. The combination of these elements (the synthesis of which is so typically "Macarian") is what gives the Jesus prayer its characteristically hesychast atmosphere, even though the writings of the Pseudo-Macarius never mention the prayer itself.[70]

The same must be said of the work of St Simeon the New Theologian, not only because of his search for mystical experience, but also for the wholly "Christic" and "spiritual" character which that search assumes, as distinct from a piety that is simply exterior or chiefly social. Simeon himself may have practised the Jesus Prayer; it seems quite possible, considering the manner in which his biographer, Nicetas Stethatos, recounts Simeon's first experience.

63 *Second Century*, No. 54; *Writings from the Philokalia*, p. 311, No. 156.
64 *Ibid.*, No. 64; *Writings . . .*, p. 313, No. 166.
65 *Ibid.*, No. 84; *Writings from the Philokalia*, p. 317, No. 186.
66 *Ibid.*, No. 87; *Writings . . .*, p. 317, No. 187.
67 *Ibid.*, No. 94; *Writings . . .*, p. 319, No. 196.
68 *Ibid.*
69 *First Century*, No. 96; *Writings . . .*, p. 298, No. 97. [In the *Dobrotolubiye* this expression is explained by the parenthetical clause "so that we may have it embedded in our heart"—Trans.]
70 Cf. *The Spirituality of the New Testament and the Fathers*, p. 378.

His own description of it has already been quoted. What Nicetas tells us is:

> Then, as he was praying, he was filled with a great joy and inundated with burning tears. . . . Not being yet initiated into such revelations, in his amazement he kept crying aloud untiringly, "Lord, have mercy on me!" In this light, therefore, he was given the strength to see; and behold, there appeared in the high heavens a sort of luminous cloud, without form or shape, and full of the ineffable glory of God. . . .[71]

The whole question, obviously, is whether or not Simeon's *Kyrie eleison* is addressed to Christ. It seems quite probable that it is, when one remembers the dialogue related by Simeon himself in connection with this experience.[72]

However that may be, the "Jesus Prayer" is never mentioned otherwise, either by Simeon or by his disciple Nicetas. But it is understandable that his eager readers should have had no difficulty, during the Byzantine Middle Ages, in attributing to Simeon the composition of the important *opusculum* entitled *"The Method of Attention and Prayer."*[73] This treatise, however, brings us to a new summit of Byzantine spirituality: the holy mountain of Athos.

Athonite Hesychasm

The beginnings of monasticism on Athos go back to the ninth century.[74] At that period, hermits began to settle in the mountain solitudes of the peninsula. The great rise of monasticism there, however, started with the foundation of Lavra by St Athanasius (who had come from Mount Olympus in Bithynia), on the advice of his friend the *basileus* Nicephorus Phocas, in 962 or 963. A few years later (975), three noblemen from Andrinopolis founded Vatopedi. Then the Georgians built Iviron (980). After that the number of monasteries, many of them foreign, went on increasing. Xiropotamos also was founded in the tenth century; in the twelfth, the monastery of St Panteleimon, which was first Greek and later Russian (the Rossikon); and again, in the twelfth, the Serbian

[71] This text is quoted more completely, and commented upon, in *La Prière de Jésus*, pp. 37–8.

[72] *Ibid.*

[73] Only a modern Greek version of this text is given in Migne, P.G., 120, 702–710. The first critical edition (with a French translation) was undertaken by I. Hausherr, *La méthode d'oraison hésychaste*, pp. 174–207. (See *Writings from the Philokalia*, pp. 152–61.—Trans.) See also Gouillard, *Petite Philocalie . . .*, pp. 206 *et seq.*

[74] See Amand de Mendietta, *La presqu'île des Caloyers: le Mont-Athos*, Paris, 1955. Also Dom P. Cousin, *op. cit.*, pp. 94 *et seq.*; and the whole volume of *Contacts* cited in n. 15, *supra.*

monastery of Chilandar; and there were others. Thenceforth, Athos became the centre *par excellence* of Byzantine spirituality. In particular, the Jesus prayer was there given a new systematization; and hesychasm, which later spread into all the Orthodox lands, took on its definitive form.

Nicephorus, whom hagiorite tradition represents as living about the middle of the fourteenth century and being of Latin origin, seems to be the most ancient witness to hesychasm on Mount Athos. Some think that in fact he belongs not to the fourteenth century but to the thirteenth or perhaps even to the twelfth.[75] In any case, his treatise *On the Guard of the Heart* marks a decisive step in the technique of the Jesus Prayer.[76] Here is found, apparently for the first time, the idea that the control of the breathing "makes the mind return to the heart". The guard of the heart itself is then connected with the unceasing repetition of the sacred formula, accompanying each breath.

> Thus, having banished all discursive thought from the mind (for you can do this if you want to), cause it to cry out: "Lord Jesus, Son of God, have mercy upon me!"—and force it, instead of all other thought, and try, in place of any other thought, to have only this one constant cry within.[77]

All this would agree with Fr Hausherr's supposition that the *Method* attributed to St Simeon is really the work of Nicephorus himself. The treatise is summarized as follows in the best modern work on the history of the Jesus Prayer, the author of which is a "monk of the Eastern Church" who has chosen to remain anonymous:

> In order to pray, one must close the door of one's cell, put oneself in a state of tranquillity, sit down, bow one's head upon one's breast, look at the middle of the body, hold one's breath, and make a mental effort to find the "place of the heart" (that is, to picture that organ to oneself), while repeating the "epiclesis of Jesus Christ". At the beginning, one experiences only distress and darkness, but soon one perceives a sort of light. Thenceforth, as soon as an evil thought arises, and even before it has finished taking shape, it is thrust out and annihilated. "By the invocation of the Lord Jesus, the winds of the passions melt and vanish like wax." This result, of course, is not obtained in a day. One must pass through the successive stages of the conquest of

[75] See I. Hausherr, "La méthode d'oraison hésychaste", and "Note sur l'inventeur de la méthode hésychaste", in *Orientalia Christiana*, XX (1930), No. 66. Also *La Prière de Jésus*, pp. 32 *et seq.*, and 41 *et seq.*

[76] P.G., 147, 945 *et seq.* Cf. *Writings from the Philokalia*, pp. 21–34, and Gouillard, *Petite Philocalie . . ., op. cit.*, pp. 185 *et seq.*

[77] P.G., 147, 956; *Writings . . .*, pp. 33–4.

the passions, the sweetness of psalmody, and the substitution of the Jesus Prayer for psalmody, and then at last one attains to *theoria*—fixed and undeviating contemplation. Thus is built the spiritual house into which Christ will come. All this is not out of our reach. The rest you will learn, with God's help, by practising the guard of the mind and by holding Jesus in your heart. For it has been said, "Sit in your cell, and your cell will teach you all things." Exquisite words, which might have been written by the author of the *Imitation*.[78]

It may be said that this is precisely the point at which the Jesus Prayer turns into a spiritual technique. Yet it must be noticed that, at this stage, no definite importance is attached to the details of the formula used. The modern Greek version of the *Method*, more or less a paraphrase, twice mentions the ancient formula "Lord Jesus Christ, have mercy on me." The treatise *On the Guard of the Heart*, adds "Son of God". But the old text of the *Method* speaks simply of "the invocation of Jesus".[79]

What is very characteristic of both treatises, as well as the idea of "making the mind descend into the heart", is the use of a certain psycho-physiological technique to effect this. One must first sit down and establish calm within oneself—physically to begin with. Then comes psychological concentration, which is bound up with a certain attitude, gazing on the centre of the body and holding one's breath deliberately. It is in this new context that the invocation of the Holy Name is linked with the breathing.

Behind all this, two elements can be distinguished which are closely connected but still remain distinct from one another. The first is an implicit, but quite definite, protest, if not against Evagrius, at least against a certain Evagrian (and, in a measure, Dionysian) line of spirituality which is predominantly intellectualist. The *nous* is to descend into the heart; which means simply that the struggle against particular thoughts, a distraction from transcendent contemplation, has now become a struggle against inordinate desires. At the same time the struggle itself is dominated by the idea of a total subjection to Christ, not only of our thoughts but also of our feelings and our wishes. This is therefore a return to a biblical anthropology which makes the "heart" (seen as the source of all our deep decisions) and no longer the *nous* (pure intelligence) the centre and summit of our personality. And this return is part of a wider movement of a spirituality that, decisively rejecting the search for an abstract deity by an unduly spiritualized man, substitutes for it the search for the incarnate God by the whole man.

[78] *La Prière de Jésus*, pp. 39–40.
[79] *Ibid.*, p. 40.

Nevertheless, this approach tends to be expressed with a realism (itself thoroughly biblical in origin) that undeniably has its strange aspects. The "heart" tends to be identified with the physical organ, and the "spirit" with breathing: for that reason the concentration of physical attention on the centre of the body, combined with holding the breath, comes to play so definite a part.

One must not, however, lay too great a stress on these terms. It must be recognized that there is an element of symbolism in them—a symbolism that lies somewhere between a brutal realism and a fading into a pure mental sign. It goes together with an instinctive sense of the subtle relationship that connects the physical behaviour of a human being with his most intimate psychological processes. But the entire context shows that the resulting technique, at this stage, certainly is not, and cannot be, isolated from a synthetic view of spiritual progress that is very traditional.

With St Gregory of Sinai, who died in 1346,[80] a further step seems to have been taken. He himself learned the Jesus Prayer, in what might be called its primitive form, from the monk Arsenius. But when he settled on the new Holy Mountain, he proceeded to systematize it in terms of the *Method*, adopting the whole content of that work, and also pushing its formulas and ideas somewhat further.

His treatise *On the Contemplative Life and Prayer* appears to be in the direct line from St Simeon. He makes, however, two contributions which are in many ways rectifications. The first of them is undeniably an improvement; the second may be more debatable. Simeon had stated that the gifts which are conferred in principle at baptism do not come to their full realization except in one in whom the gift of the Spirit has become conscious. Gregory explains this by saying that the mystical life is simply *energeia*—the operation, fully actualized, of the Spirit conferred at baptism. Then again, Simeon had emphasized that the experience of this gift is to be found in the path of the commandments of God. Gregory, referring to this, proposes as a parallel road, and one that is shorter and easier, the continual invocation of the Lord Jesus. It was to this point that every possible distortion of hesychasm was to attach itself, as well as the wild misunderstandings of which it was to be the object. Gregory himself, of course, makes it very clear that he does not mean this distinction in the sense that the Jesus Prayer could dispense one from keeping the commandments. On the contrary, he says explicitly that its efficacy depends on humility and

[80] See *ibid.*, pp. 44 *et seq.* The works of St Gregory of Sinai are in Migne, P.G., 150, 1239 *et seq.* For English translations, see *Writings from the Philokalia*, pp. 35–94.

contrition, both of them virtues which it is better suited to develop than any other practice. All this did not prevent his formula from opening the way to unfortunate ambiguities.

His second treatise, *On the Contemplative Life and the Two Modes of Prayer*, set forth more precisely what he meant by the practice of prayer. Once again, it cannot be better summarized than in the words of the contemporary author cited before:

> One should apply oneself to the Jesus prayer in the morning. One should remain seated and deeply bowed. One must pronounce the formula "Lord Jesus Christ, have mercy on me" perseveringly, with all one's soul and mind. The *nous* will force the intellect to descend into the heart. As one pronounces the name of Jesus, one will be nourished by this divine name as by a food. (This gives us a glimpse of a sort of eucharistic use of the name of Jesus—the Jesus prayer regarded as a spiritual communion.) One should apply oneself to giving its full meaning to each word of the invocation "Son of God, have mercy on me." (Here the formula is not stereotyped.) The formula of invocation, moreover, must not be changed too often, for plants do not take root if transplanted too frequently. The Jesus prayer enables us to attain the state described by St Paul the Apostle: "I live, now not I, but Christ lives in me." Psalmody and reading are also allowed.[81]

Gregory's third treatise is of particular interest in connection with the question of the actual words used in the Jesus Prayer. The work is entitled *How a Hesychast Should Sit Down to Pray and Not Arise Too Soon*. In it we learn that, among the author's contemporaries, some said simply, "Jesus, have mercy on me." Gregory quotes St Paul's statement that no one can say "the Lord Jesus" except in the Spirit (1 Cor. 12.3) and concedes that this shortened formula is more easily assimilated "because of the weakness of our spirit". No one, indeed, can say "Lord Jesus" purely and perfectly until he has arrived at the higher experience of the Spirit. Again, it matters little whether the words are actually uttered by the lips or only said mentally; the best practice is to alternate the two. These remarks are interesting because they prove that the hesychasts of the fourteenth century, in their use of the "method", were very far from the crass materialism that has sometimes been lightly attributed to them.

The immediate sources of St Gregory of Sinai present an extremely delicate problem. At the end of the eighteenth century, Nicodemus the Hagiorite, once again, represented him as being a contemporary of Nicephorus, which is at least doubtful. Further-

[81] *La Prière de Jésus*, pp. 45–6.

more, we are told that on his arrival at Mount Athos, he found only three monks who were really proficient in the contemplative life: Isaias, Cornelius and Macarius. We are also told, however, of his admiration for an anchorite of the Holy Mountain who was his contemporary. This was St Maximus Kapsokalivitos, so called because he burned down his hermitage to escape the crowds who came to consult him. He was a friend of the emperors John Cantacuzenus and John Paleologus, and we know that in his prayer he joined together "the remembrance of Jesus and that of the Theotokos".[82] This may be an allusion to a formula, of which the words have not been preserved, which included the names of both Jesus and Mary; or it may simply refer to his harmonious fusion of piety towards Mary with what he himself seems to have called "the spiritual prayer". We do not know.

Another author of this period should be mentioned, one who is too little studied—St Theoleptus, archbishop of Philadelphia. He too has come down to us as one of the masters of St Gregory Palamas (he seems to have died between 1310 and 1320). It has been justly said that his contribution to hesychasm is summarized in the following passage from his *Model breviary of ascetic life*:

> Pure prayer unites in itself mind (*nous*), word (*logos*) and spirit (*pneuma*), invokes the name of God in word (*logos*), looks up at God, whom it is invoking, with a mind (*nous*) free from wandering; and shows contrition, humility and love in spirit (*pneuma*). Thus it inclines towards itself the eternal Trinity, the Father, the Son and the Holy Spirit—the One God.[83]

Not the least of the surprises to be found in the history of hesychasm is this formula that seems to be (whether by influence or by mere coincidence) a direct echo of medieval Augustinianism.

St Gregory Palamas and the Hesychast Controversy

At about this time there broke out, in connection with hesychasm, a philosophico-theological controversy whose complexity was equalled only by its violence. It led to the thoroughly theological synthesis, by St Gregory Palamas (1296?–1359), who was first a monk of Athos and later bishop of Thessalonia. Unfortunately, the manner in which this controversy has been prolonged or unhappily revived down to our own times hardly tends to shed light on the exact significance of Gregory's spiritual theology. Not until quite recently has there been a scholarly study, patient and serene in tone.

[82] *Ibid.*, pp. 47–8.
[83] P.G., 143, 393. Cf. *La Prière de Jésus*, pp. 49–50; also *Writings from the Philokalia*, p. 391, No. 20; and Gouillard, *Petite Philocalie . . .*, pp. 221 *et seq.*

Fr Jean Meyendorff's work at last enables us to see the true origins of the Palamite controversy, and consequently to appreciate objectively the merits of this man who was the last great spiritual writer of medieval Athos, and certainly its most powerful theologian.[84]

It is impossible to enter here into the details of the polemic stirred up by the Calabrian monk Barlaam who called the hesychasts Messalians and *omphalopsuchoi* (that is, people for whom the soul is situated in the navel). The directly spiritual motives involved were mingled with a concern, at least equally strong, for a humanistic philosophy. In addition, sociological problems—even economic ones—played their part in the background. It is enough to say that the first modern scholar in the West who applied himself to the study of these disputes, Fr Martin Jugie, A.A., contributed not a little to obscure their exact import by supposing that Barlaam was in fact an intrepid defender, in the East, of Aristotelian and Thomistic thought.[85] The most obvious result of this simplification was not only to make Gregory Palamas appear, quite gratuitously, a heretic in the eyes of modern Catholics, but also to give the Eastern Christians the most fantastic misconceptions of what authentic Thomism really is.

Indeed, the greatest merit of Jean Meyendorff's study is to have made it clear that Barlaam, though he was a latinizer, was for all that not in the least a Thomist, but rather a Platonizing humanist, radically nominalist and anti-mystical. By comparison, Gregory Palamas appears as a strong realist and, like most of the later Byzantine theologians (despite the cliché reiterated in the West), much more of an Aristotelian than a Platonist. But what strikes us most about him is his defence—very well informed, and at the same time very conscious of the spiritual values at stake—of a spiritual tradition that was not only Byzantine but patristic. Even if his theological system bristles with difficulties for us, we can at last understand the real import, for the Greeks, of the decisions by which the controversy was closed. Barlaam was condemned at the imperial council of Sancta Sophia in 1341. In 1355, the Palamite doctrine was proclaimed as the official doctrine of the Byzantine Church. Furthermore, in 1351, the council of the Blachernae had incorporated, in the *Synodikon* for the Feast of Orthodoxy,

[84] J. Meyendorff, *Introduction à l'étude de Grégoire Palamas* and *Saint Grégoire Palamas et la mystique byzantine* (see note 1). See also his edition (with a French translation) of the *Défense des saints hésychastes*, Louvain, 1959. Previously, Mgr Basil Krivocheine had published a most illuminating study in *The Eastern Churches Quarterly*, 1938, No. 4.

[85] See his articles "Palamas" and "Palamite (controverse)" in the *Dictionnaire de Théologie catholique*, XI.

anathemas against Gregory's other adversaries, including the archaizer Akindynos and the humanist philosopher Nicephorus Gregoras. In these circumstances, it becomes difficult to see, in the canonization of Gregory Palamas in 1368 by the patriarch Philotheus, a mere anti-Latin manifestation, schismatical and more or less heretical. The Byzantine church itself certainly saw it as a fresh proclamation and more precise definition of a spiritual tradition whose substance comes from the great Greek Fathers, through the intermediary of what was best in Byzantine spirituality.

In the *Tomus hagioreticus*, which was also signed by all the *hegumenoi* of the Holy Mountain in 1340–1, Palamas sums up as follows against Barlaam's anti-hesychast accusations the arguments that he had already developed in his *Triads in Defence of the Holy Hesychasts*:

> The doctrines which today are a common heritage, known by all and openly proclaimed, were, under the Mosaic law, but mysteries, accessible in advance only in visions to the prophets. On the other hand, the good things of the world to come, which are prophesied by the saints, constitute the mysteries of the evangelical community, for the Spirit makes the saints worthy of this vision. They receive these good things and behold them in advance, as first-fruits.
>
> Some of them, indeed, have been initiated by actual experience: all those who have abandoned the enjoyment of material goods, human glory, and the sinful pleasures of the body, and have preferred the life of the Gospel, and who have furthermore confirmed that abandonment of the world by embracing obedience to those who have attained maturity in Christ. With no other care than themselves, by rigorous attention and pure prayer, having attained to God by a mystical and supra-intellectual union with him, they have been initiated into that which surpasses understanding. . . . This deifying grace of God is said by the divine Maximus, speaking of Melchisedech, to be uncreated and eternal, proceeding from the eternal God.[86]

The doctrine that was more and more firmly adopted by the Byzantine Church, in the course of the conciliar and patriarchal decisions noted above, was, properly speaking, that of this Tomus. It is important therefore clearly to see its significance. The first point to be emphasized is its general affirmation of the orthodoxy of hesychast spirituality, without going into the details of the tech-

[86] The text of the *Volume* is given in Migne, P.G., 150, 1225 *et seq.* (taken from the edition of the *Philokalia* published at Venice in 1782). The translation here is from that of Meyendorff in *Saint Grégoire . . .*, pp. 96 *et seq.* The works of Palamas are incompletely and inaccurately given in Migne (P.G., vols 150 and 151). For a study of the manuscript tradition and of the various editions, see Meyendorff, *Introduction . . .*, pp. 331 *et seq.*

nique which had developed, little by little on Mount Athos. The second is the noteworthy statement that mystical experience is the normal counterpart of a properly oriented ascetical life. The third is the very strong consciousness of the continuity of this experience, in monastic tradition, with prophetic experience, and of its character of a foretaste of that experience of heaven which is promised in the gospels. Finally must be mentioned the emphasis placed by the Tomus on the fact that mystical experience, however mysterious it may be, is (as the Fathers and notably St Maximus bear witness) a direct experience of God in himself, and not merely of his created effects.

As for the theology developed by Palamas to defend and illustrate this doctrine, especially in his homilies on the Transfiguration, only such aspects of it as bear directly upon spirituality will be discussed here.

In the first place, it is interesting to note that, unlike his contemporary St Gregory of Sinai, Gregory is not concerned with the details of the psycho-physiological technique of Athonite hesychasm. He adopts one element of it, and one alone: the possibility of a vision of God, a vision in which the body is in some way involved. This is what led him systematically to connect the luminous vision of "Macarius", Simeon and the hesychasts with the light of Thabor (that is, with the vision of the transfigured Christ) and, more generally, with all the scriptural visions of God that are expressed in terms of light and fire.[87]

It also led him to re-appraise the expressions used in the Macarian tradition, as opposed to the Evagrian, by which religious anthropology was again centred on the "heart" in the biblical sense of the word, rather than on the *nous*, that is, pure intelligence.[88] What is more, he drew from it not only a very prudent justification of the idea that a method of spirituality in which the body has a share is entirely scriptural and Christian, but he also developed the more precise notion that, in the mystical vision, our whole being, body and soul, is associated, in a manner mysterious but real, with those first-fruits of the resurrection which are constituted by that experience. This idea, it will be remembered, is already found in more than embryonic form in Diadochus of Photike.[89]

At this point, to reply to Barlaam's accusation that the hesychasts claimed to see the essence of God with their bodily eyes, Palamas put forward the famous distinction between the divine essence and the divine energies. He certainly did not invent this distinction, but

[87] See his Homilies 34 and 35, on the Transfiguration.
[88] On this, see Meyendorff, *Introduction . . .*, pp. 195 *et seq.*
[89] Cf. *The Spirituality of the New Testament and the Fathers*, p. 431.

he developed it and probably gave it a new precision. According to him, no creature can participate in the essence of God, which is invisible not only to the eyes of the body but also to those of the soul itself—indeed, to any created spirit whatever. On the other hand, the energies of God, although they are uncreated and are inseparable from his essence, can be participated in by the whole man. Thus the light of Thabor can be called "uncreated", even though the apostles saw it shining from the very face of the transfigured Christ, as the first-fruits of his resurrection and their own.[90]

What are we to think of this distinction? It must be admitted it is foreshadowed, at least, by the Cappadocians, particularly St Gregory Nazianzen, in a text which is quoted in the preceding volume and there commented upon. What is more, it seems to be in direct line with the Jewish conception of God's transcendence and immanence. In that conception, God in himself is distinguished (though never separated) from his Face, his Angel, his Presence, or his Word, through which he enters into contact with his creatures.

This is not to say that such a distinction does not raise the thorniest metaphysical problems. We shall not, however, discuss them here, but it seems difficult to deny, after the work of Jean Meyendorff, that Gregory Palamas himself never emphasized the philosophical aspect of his thought. Still less did the Church of Byzantium when it approved his doctrine and canonized him. Like the Cappadocians, or the rabbis before them, all that he sought to affirm was the possibility of a real and immediate contact between man and God in divine grace, while rejecting any sort of pantheism or "divinization" which would make us "gods" in the pagan hellenistic sense.

The Centuries of Callistus and Ignatius of Xanthopoulos

There can be no better verification of what Palamas sought to defend, and what the Eastern Church canonized in his work, than to examine the last great spiritual work produced by medieval hesychasm: the *Centuries* of Callistus and Ignatius of Xanthopoulous.[91] The two authors (the first of whom was patriarch of Constantinople for a very short time in 1397) were both monks of an Athonite monastery, a dependency of the monastery of the Pantocrator, in the second half of the fourteenth century. Their work does not contain a single echo of the controversies just

[90] See Meyendorff, *Introduction . . .*, pp. 279 *et seq.* For a discussion of the problem from the Thomist point of view, see E. Mascall, *Existence and Analogy*, London, 1949. That of Père Jugie is considerably more simplified.

[91] These *Centuries* are in Migne, P.G., 147, 685–812. English translations will be found in *Writings from the Philokalia*, pp. 162–270.

described, although it followed closely upon them. An examination of it shows the beneficial effect of the work of St Gregory Palamas, and especially of his deliberate effort to restore hesychasm to its place at the heart of the ecclesiastical, biblical, and liturgical tradition. Once again the anonymous author (to whom so much is owed) of the contemporary work on the Jesus Prayer may be quoted:

> The *Centuries* are a complete rule of life for a hesychast. The centre of this life is the Jesus prayer. As for technique, the *Centuries* recommend the formula: "Lord Jesus Christ, Son of God, have mercy on me." They distinguish two movements: an upward one towards Jesus Christ in the first part of the prayer, "Lord Jesus Christ, Son of God . . . ," and a return upon oneself in ". . . have mercy on me." The rhythm of breathing is to be associated with this double movement. This practice produces a certain warmth in the heart. What is of greater significance, the *Centuries* put the Jesus prayer into a whole ascetic context. They take the hesychast and lead him through the day from dawn to dusk. They lay the foundation for *hesychia*, saying that it cannot exist without orthodox faith and good works; thus the danger of quietism is eliminated. Then come precise practical direction: the exhortation to silence, to reading of the Scriptures, to nocturnal vigils, to prostrations (three hundred per day), to fasting (a diet of dry vegetables, bread and water; wine is sometimes permitted), to communion "with a pure heart," and to psalmody for those who are not yet capable of concentrating on the Jesus prayer. Through the detail of these observances, the spiritual goal is always kept in view. It is to attain a state in which the soul, given up to the Jesus prayer, can say with the Canticle of Canticles, "I have been wounded by love."[92]

Nicholas Cabasilas

One last name must be mentioned in this sketch of a history of Byzantine spirituality: that of the lay theologian Nicholas Cabasilas. A friend of the emperor John Cantacuzenus (1347–54), he was a humanist and diplomat, but above all a man of real spirituality, eager to live to the full the tradition of his Church and to give it full expression.[93] After some hesitation, and without ever

92 *La Prière de Jésus*, pp. 55–6.

93 On this author, there is the enthusiastic book by Mme Lot-Borodine, *Un maître de la spiritualité byzantine au XIVe siècle: Nicolas Cabasilas*, Paris, 1958. It is a pity that this stimulating study is not more restrained. A similar reservation should be made about articles by the same author on the doctrine of deification in the Greek Church, published as early as 1932 and 1933 in the *Revue de l'histoire des religions*. These articles helped greatly to draw attention to the value of Byzantine spirituality, but they contributed little to the critical study of the development of its themes.

taking part in the Palamite controversy, Cabasilas definitely parted company with the crowd of Byzantine humanists who, with Demetrius Cydones, were, by rejecting Palamas, to sharpen the already radical opposition between the two tendencies, monastic and humanist, in Byzantine spirituality.

His two treatises, *Life in Jesus Christ*[94] and the *Commentary on the Divine Liturgy*,[95] constitute a sort of final synthesis of the two great streams of Byzantine spirituality. The first of these books is an explanation of Christian initiation (baptism, confirmation, and the Eucharist) and the second is a detailed commentary on the eucharistic liturgy. As such, they are in line with the *Mystagogia* of St Maximus and the *Ecclesiastical History* of St Germanus and the whole tradition of Studite spirituality, with its ecclesiastical and hierarchical character. Nevertheless, in their underlying spirit—evangelical, christocentric, interior—they owe a tremendous amount to hesychasm. It is nowhere more clearly expressed than in the idea, so dear to Cabasilas, that Christ is not only the head of his body, of which we are the members, but also its heart.

> By the bread of life it is given us to become members of Christ much more perfectly than by any other sacred rite. For, just as the members of a body live by the head and the heart, so "he that eateth me, the same shall live by me," says the Saviour. . . . In accordance with the normal part played by the heart and the head, we are moved and we live as he lives himself. . . . He communicates life to us as the heart or the head communicates it to the members. . . .
>
> Whoever has made up his mind to live in Christ must necessarily keep himself dependent on that heart and that head, for life comes to us from nowhere else. . . . Our members must remain pure, because they are the members of Christ, dependent upon the heart which is Christ; we must have the same feeling and will as his.[96]

[94] This treatise is given in Migne, P.G., 150, 493–725. It was translated into French by S. Broussaleux in *Irenikon*, and was published separately by the priory of Amay in Belgium, 1932.

[95] This treatise is also in Migne, P.G., 150, 368–492, and was translated into French by S. Salaville, A.A., in the fourth number of "Sources chrétiennes". An English translation by J. M. Hussey and P. A. McNulty has been published by the S.P.C.K. in 1960.

[96] These texts from the *Commentary on the Divine Liturgy* (P.G., 150, 596 D–597 D, 453, and 648 D) were cited together in this order by S. Salaville, A.A., in his article "Cabasilas" in the *Dictionnaire de spiritualité*.

INDEX OF NAMES

I. Persons

II. Places